ENCYCLOPEDIA OF WOMEN'S FOLKLORE AND FOLKLIFE

ENCYCLOPEDIA OF WOMEN'S FOLKLORE AND FOLKLIFE

Volume 1: A–L

Edited by
Liz Locke
Theresa A. Vaughan
Pauline Greenhill

GREENWOOD PRESS
Westport, Connecticut • London

GR
470
.E63
2009
VOL. 1

Library of Congress Cataloging-in-Publication Data

Encyclopedia of women's folklore and folklife / edited by Liz Locke,
Theresa A. Vaughan, and Pauline Greenhill.
    p. cm.
    Includes bibliographical references and index.
    ISBN 978-0-313-34050-5 ((set) : alk. paper) — ISBN 978-0-313-34051-2 ((vol. 1) :
alk. paper) — ISBN 978-0-313-34052-9 ((vol. 2) : alk. paper)
    1. Women—Folklore—Encyclopedias. I. Locke, Liz. II. Vaughan, Theresa A., 1966–
III. Greenhill, Pauline, 1955–
    GR470.E63 2009
    398′.352—dc22   2008032981

British Library Cataloguing in Publication Data is available.

Library of Congress Catalog Card Number: 2008032981
ISBN: 978-0-313-34050-5 (set)
        978-0-313-34051-2 (vol. 1)
        978-0-313-34052-9 (vol. 2)

First published in 2009

Greenwood Press, 88 Post Road West, Westport, CT 06881
An imprint of Greenwood Publishing Group, Inc.
www.greenwood.com

Printed in the United States of America

The paper used in this book complies with the
Permanent Paper Standard issued by the National
Information Standards Organization (Z39.48–1984).

10 9 8 7 6 5 4 3 2 1

To All Women Folklorists and their Allies—Past,
Present, and Future

CONTENTS

List of Entries ix

Guide to Related Topics xiii

Preface xvii

Acknowledgments xxi

Overview Essays xxiii

    Women's Folklore xxiii

    Folklore About Women xxxv

    Folklore of Subversion xlvii

    Women Folklorists lix

The Encyclopedia **1**

Selected Bibliography/Web Sites 731

Index 733

About the Editors and Contributors 761

LIST OF ENTRIES

Abortion
Activism
Adoption
Aesthetics
Aging
Altar, Home
American Folklore Society—
    Women's Section
Androgyny
Aphrodisiac
Assault, Supernatural
Autograph Book

Babysitting
Ballad
Banshee
Barbie Doll
Barker, Ma
Basketmaking
Bat Mitzvah
Beadwork
Beauty
Beauty Contest
Beauty Queen
Belly Dance
Best Friend
Birth Chair
Birthdays
Blind Folklore
Bloody Mary
Body Modification and
    Adornment
Borden, Lizzie
Breastfeeding
Brideprice

Calamity Jane
Camplore
Charivari/Shivaree
Chastity
Cheerleading
Childbirth and Childrearing
Cinderella
Class
Clique
Coding
Consciousness Raising
Cosmetics
Courtship
Couvade
Cowgirl
Crafting
Crime-Victim Stories
Croning
Cross-Dressing
Curandera
Cursing
Cyberculture

Daughter
Deaf Folklore
Death
Diet Culture
Divination Practices
Divorce
Dolls
Doula
Dowry

Elder Care
Embroidery
Engagement

Erotic Folklore
Ethnicity
Eve
Evil Eye

Family Folklore
Fans, Language of
Farm Women's Folklore
Fashion
Female Genital Cutting
Feminisms
Festival
Fieldwork
Film
First Nations of North America
Flowers, Language of
Folk Art
Folk Belief
Folk Costume
Folk Custom
Folk Dance
Folk Drama
Folk Group
Folk Medicine
Folk Music and Folksong
Folk Photography
Folk Poetry
Folklife
Folklore Feminists
    Communication
Folklore Studies Association of
    Canada
Folktale
Foodways
Fortune-Teller

Gardens
Gender
Girl Scouts/Girl Guides
Girls' Folklore
Girls' Games
Glass Ceiling
Goddess Worship
Gossip
Graffiti
Grandmother
Graves and Gravemarkers
Gullah Women's Folklore

Hair
Handclapping Games
Helpmate
Henna Art/*Mehndi*
Herbs
Hip-Hop Culture/Rap
Home Birth
Homeless Women
Housekeeping
Humor

Immigration
Indian Maiden
Infertility
Initiation

Jewish Women's Folklore
Jingle Dress
Joke
Jump-Rope Rhymes

Knitting

La Llorona
Lacemaking
Lament
Laundry
Legend, Local
Legend, Religious
Legend, Supernatural
Legend, Urban/Contemporary
Lesbian and Queer Studies
Lesbian Folklore
Lilith
Lilith Fair
Local Characters
Lullaby

Magazines, Women's and Girls'
Magic
Maiden, Mother, Crone
Marriage
Mass Media
Material Culture
Matriarchy
Memorate
Menarche Stories
Menopause
Menstruation
Midwifery
Military Women's Folklore
Miscarriage
Mother Earth
Mother Goose
Mother-in-law
Mother's Day
Mothers' Folklore
Muslim Women's Folklore
Myth Studies

Naming Practices
Nature/Culture
Needlework
Nursing

Occupational Folklore
Old Wives' Tales
Oral History

Paperfolding and Papercutting
Personal-Experience Narrative
Photocopylore
Piecework
Politics
Popular Culture
Pottery
Pregnancy
Princess
Processional Performance
Prostitution/Sex Work
Proverb
Public Folklore
Purdah

Quiltmaking
Quinceañera

Race
Rape
Recipe Books
Recitation
Red Riding Hood
Region: Australia and New
  Zealand
Region: Canada
Region: Caribbean
Region: Central America
Region: Central Asia
Region: East Asia
Region: Eastern Europe
Region: Mexico
Region: Middle East
Region: Pacific Islands
Region: South America
Region: Southeast Asia
Region: Sub-Saharan Africa
Region: United States
Region: Western Europe
Rhymes
Riddle
Rites of Passage
Ritual
Roadside Crosses
Rugmaking
Rumor

Saints
Sampler
Scandal
Scrapbooks
Self-Help
Sewing
Sex Determination
Sexism
Sexuality
Sister
Sleeping Beauty
Sorority Folklore
Spa Culture
Spinning
Spirituals
Stepmother
Storytelling
Suffrage Movement
Sunbonnet Sue
Superstition

Text
Tradition
Tradition-Bearer
Transgender Folklore

Vagina Dentata
Vaginal Serpent
Valentine's Day
Vampire
Veiling
Violence

Virgin, Cult of the
Virgin of Guadalupe
Virginity

Wage Work
Walled-Up Wife
Weaving
Wedding
Wedding, Mock
Wicca and Neo-Paganism
Wife Sales

Witchcraft, Historical
Women Religious
Women Warriors
Women's Clubs
Women's Friendship Groups
Women's Movement
Women's Music Festivals
Women's Work

Yellow Woman/*Irriaku*
   Stories

GUIDE TO RELATED TOPICS

Domestic Life

Altar, Home
Babysitting
Childbirth and
    Childrearing
Crafting
Embroidery
Family Folklore
Farm Women's
    Folklore
Folk Custom
Folk Medicine
Folklife
Foodways
Gardens
Helpmate
Herbs
Home Birth
Housekeeping
Knitting
Laundry
Lullaby
Material Culture
Mothers' Folklore
Needlework
Old Wives' Tales
Quiltmaking
Recipe Books
Rugmaking
Sampler
Scrapbooks
Sewing
Women's Folklore
Women's Work

Feminism

Abortion
Activism
Class
Coding
Consciousness Raising
Croning
Feminisms
Folklore About Women
*Folklore Feminists
    Communication*
Glass Ceiling
Humor
Lesbian and Queer
    Studies
Lesbian Folklore
Lilith Fair
Matriarchy
Nature/Culture
Politics
Race
Rape
Sexism
Suffrage Movement
Sunbonnet Sue
Women Folklorists
Women's Folklore
Women's Movement
Women's Music Festivals

Folklore as a Profession

American Folklore Society—
    Women's Section

Fieldwork
Folklore About Women
*Folklore Feminists
    Communication*
Folklore Studies Association of
    Canada
Lesbian and Queer Studies
Myth Studies
Public Folklore
Women Folklorists
Women's Folklore

Life Cycle

Adoption
Aging
Bat Mitzvah
Birth Chair
Birthdays
Breastfeeding
Brideprice
Charivari/Shivaree
Childbirth and
    Childrearing
Courtship
Couvade
Croning
Daughter
Death
Divorce
Doula
Dowry
Elder Care
Engagement
Family Folklore

Female Genital Cutting
Girls' Folklore
Girls' Games
Grandmother
Graves and Gravemarkers
Henna Art/*Mehndi*
Home Birth
Initiation
Maiden, Mother, and Crone
Marriage
Menarche Stories
Menopause
Menstruation
Midwifery
Mother's Day
Mothers' Folklore
Naming Practices
Pregnancy
Quinceañera
Rites of Passage
Sexuality
Sister
Sorority Folklore
Stepmother
Tradition
Veiling
Virginity
Wedding
Wedding, Mock
Wife Sales

Material Culture

Aesthetics
Altar, Home
Barbie Doll
Basketmaking
Beadwork
Birth Chair
Body Modification and
   Adornment
Crafting
Dolls
Dowry
Embroidery
Fans, Language of
Fashion
Flowers, Language of
Folk Art
Folk Costume
Folk Photography
Folklife

Gardens
Graffiti
Graves and Gravemarkers
Hair
Henna Art/*Mehndi*
Jingle Dress
Knitting
Lacemaking
Material Culture
Needlework
Paperfolding and Papercutting
Piecework
Pottery
Quiltmaking
Recipe Books
Roadside Crosses
Sampler
Scrapbooks
Sewing
Spinning
Sunbonnet Sue
Weaving
Women's Work

Regions of the World

Region: Australia and New
   Zealand
Region: Canada
Region: Caribbean
Region: Central America
Region: Central Asia
Region: East Asia
Region: Eastern Europe
Region: Mexico
Region: Middle East
Region: Pacific Islands
Region: South America
Region: Southeast Asia
Region: Sub-Saharan Africa
Region: United States
Region: Western Europe

Religion/Ethnicity

Altar, Home
Bat Mitzvah
Belly Dance
Curandera
Ethnicity
Eve
Evil Eye
Female Genital Cutting

First Nations of North America
Folk Belief
Goddess Worship
Gullah Women's Folklore
Henna Art/*Mehndi*
Hip-Hop Culture/Rap
Immigration
Indian Maiden
Jewish Women's Folklore
Jingle Dress
La Llorona
Legend, Religious
Legend, Supernatural
Lilith
Muslim Women's Folklore
Naming Practices
Purdah
Quinceañera
Race
Saints
Spirituals
Superstition
Veiling
Virgin, Cult of the
Virgin of Guadalupe
Wicca and Neopaganism
Women Religious
Yellow Woman/*Irriaku* Stories

Sexuality

Abortion
Androgyny
Aphrodisiac
Assault, Supernatural
Beauty
Beauty Contest
Beauty Queen
Body Modification and
   Adornment
Chastity
Cosmetics
Cross-Dressing
Diet Culture
Erotic Folklore
Fashion
Gender
Hair
Humor
Infertility
Lesbian and Queer Studies
Lesbian Folklore

Menarche Stories
Menopause
Menstruation
Miscarriage
Prostitution/Sex Work
Purdah
Rape
Rites of Passage
Scandal
Sex Determination
Sexuality
Transgender Folklore
Vagina Dentata
Vaginal Serpent
Veiling
Virginity

Verbal Lore

Ballad
Barker, Ma

Bloody Mary
Borden, Lizzie
Calamity Jane
Cinderella
Cursing
Family Folklore
Folk Music and Folksong
Folk Poetry
Folktale
Girls' Folklore
Gossip
Joke
Jump-Rope Rhymes
La Llorona
Lament
Legend, Local
Legend, Religious
Legend, Supernatural
Legend, Urban/Contemporary
Lilith

Local Characters
Lullaby
Memorate
Menarche Stories
Mother Goose
Mothers' Folklore
Myth Studies
Old Wives' Tales
Oral History
Proverb
Recitation
Red Riding Hood
Rhymes
Riddle
Rumor
Sleeping Beauty
Spirituals
Storytelling
Yellow Woman/*Irriaku*
    Stories

PREFACE

The *Encyclopedia of Women's Folklore and Folklife* is, in many ways, a pioneering work of scholarship. Our foremothers helped to set us on the path when they turned their attention to women's folklore in the 1970s and 1980s. Claire Farrer's edited work, *Women and Folklore: Images and Genres*, published in 1975, was an early effort to collect in an accessible volume folklore scholarship about women's informal cultures. Other important articles and compilations followed, including a special issue in 1987 of the *Journal of American Folklore*, the American flagship journal of Folklore Studies, devoted to scholarship about women entitled *Folklore and Feminism*. These and other especially significant works are listed in the "Selected Bibliography" section of this book.

Despite more than 150 years of work by academics, ethnographers, public sector folklorists, artists, archivists, and others, on the many genres of folklore included here, and due to the groundbreaking work mentioned above, these volumes represent the discipline of Folklore's first concerted attempt to bring its attention fully to bear on those collective folkways, engagements, attitudes, and preoccupations specific to the lives of women and girls, and on the contributions by women folklorists to the scholarship thereof. It is our hope that it will make a significant contribution towards achieving the field's founding and long-avowed goal of providing ways to better understand the deep—if often trivialized, marginalized, or unexplored—ways and means by which we all enact the creative art of being human. We have been exceedingly fortunate to have attracted the participation of some of the originating scholars in the field of Women's Folklore as contributors to the *Encyclopedia of Women's Folklore and Folklife* and as members of its advisory board.

The *Encyclopedia* is organized so that it can be used in a variety of ways. The four leading overview essays—"Women's Folklore," "Folklore About Women," "Folklore of Subversion," and "Women Folklorists"—represent a broad survey of folklore scholarship about, and largely by, women. More specifically focused subject entries follow in alphabetical order. Some grapple with large topics: ballads, folktales, material culture, race, and politics, to name just a few. Others cover smaller, more specific topics of interest to both professional and general readers: autograph books, the language of fans, Mother's Day, needlework, and Yellow Woman/*Irriaku* stories, for example. Each article is written from the perspective of a folklore scholar, and relies upon the highest academic standards of scholarship and analysis.

At the end of each topic entry, we have provided a list under the heading "See Also" of related entries in the *Encyclopedia* that will lead the interested reader to more information on that topic. We also have assembled a suggested reading list for each entry. These references serve as valuable resources for those seeking to expand their acquaintance with scholarship on women's folklore, and, taken together, provide a nearly comprehensive survey of the literature on women's folklore to date. A thematic grouping of all of the entries, listed in the front matter under "Guide to Related Topics," is designed to aid readers who seek to understand the general scope of the *Encyclopedia* in terms of the umbrella genres of women's folklore.

The *Encyclopedia* also contains fifteen articles listed under the heading "Region," ranging from Australia, New Zealand, and the Pacific Islands to Southeast and Central Asia to sub-Saharan Africa, Europe, and South America. Each region entry highlights the most salient women's folklore genres enacted in that part of the world. However, the *Encyclopedia* cannot and does not make any claims to being comprehensive of all women's, and girls' folkways and their expressions in context. Given that women and girls comprise at least half the population of the planet, it was decided early on that the *Encyclopedia's* scope and size must be limited in some way so as to make possible its eventual appearance in print. Its primary focus, therefore, is on the contexts and traditions of women residing in North America, the home of most of its contributors. During the years in which the headword list was brainstormed, compiled, and amended, we solicited manuscripts from authors whose expertise could collectively encompass as many of North America's heterogeneous cultures and traditions as possible. Our efforts were rewarded with a variety of articles on genres and practices specific to its African, Latino, and Asian diasporas, as well as to its First Nations peoples; however, ultimately, and perhaps inevitably, the present work contains lacunae that beg to be filled in subsequent editions. These volumes attempt to respond to an urgent need in folklore scholarship, but they are also a call for more workers in the field to bring their considerable skills and training to bear on the lifeways, concerns, and traditions of the world's women and girls.

The folklore told and used by women is not necessarily the same as folklore *about* women. In fact, it is seldom if ever the same. Folklore about women is frequently disparaging, as is especially clear in reference to female sexuality itself. Folklorists, especially North American folklorists, have long avoided any discussion of sex as unseemly, or beneath the notice of serious scholars. This attitude arose in part from the deeply felt puritanical traditions that North Americans inherited along with the rest of our history; and in part, from an overly romantic sensibility about just who "the folk" are. Starting in the 1920s, Vance Randolph (1892–1980) collected a huge number of jokes told by Ozark mountain people, and discovered that "the folk" were very fond of what we call "dirty jokes." He was vilified for decades by other folklorists who thought his work prurient, voyeuristic, destructive, and unhealthy. But dirty jokes are part of the folk's repertoire, and today, folklorists have him to thank for bringing to light their many rich cultural expressions about human sexuality.

Today, we have a different sense of who the folk are. For the most part, they are us. And responsible folklore scholars no longer shy away from the more brutal realities of the world we inhabit—its racism, sexism, homophobia, religious intolerance, war, and the other cruelties of everyday life—as they are reflected in the expressions of the folk. The coverage of female sexuality in this volume may occasionally make the reader feel uncomfortable; however, the duty of folkloristics is to observe and report what the folk actually think and do and say, not what we might wish they would think and do and say. Since the beginning of recorded history, female sexuality has been the butt of many a dirty joke; unfortunately, this remains the case today. We regard it as our responsibility to shed as much light as possible on this aspect of North American folklife.

The reader will also note that the overall tone of the *Encyclopedia* is unabashedly feminist in its perspective. Feminist scholarship has enriched the entire field of Folklore, not only in those areas pertaining to women, and it was feminist scholars who first made a concerted effort to turn the field's attention to women's concerns. Without the feminist impetus, much of the work included in these volumes would never have been undertaken, and so we make no apologies for this orientation. Feminist scholarship has also helped us understand that we must be attentive to our differences in order to truly understand our common humanity; therefore, the reader will find attention given to ethnicity, class, sexual orientation, and politics throughout the *Encyclopedia*.

ACKNOWLEDGMENTS

The editors wish to thank the senior folklore scholars who comprised our advisory board—Norma Cantú, Rosan Jordan, Jo Radner, Cathy Preston, Riki Saltzman, and Marilyn White—without whose generosity with their time, talents, encouragement, and endurance this encyclopedia would never have materialized. They are the true mothers of this pioneering publication.

Each writer whose work is included here responded to our call, did the research, wrote articles, and hung in there with us as the work progressed. Please accept our heartfelt thanks for your dedication to the project.

One of these days, he'll get those roses we promised, but for now we wish to express our appreciation to Thomas A. Green, who sent us to George Butler at Greenwood Press, whose enthusiasm for the project encouraged us to go forward and whose style made the heavy lifting easier. Thanks also to Nancy Stair for her fine copyediting, Vicki Swope for her meticulous indexing, and our project managers, Colleen Simeral at Cadmus Communications Corp. and Bridget Austiguy-Preschel at Greenwood Press.

We wish to extend our thanks for the support of the American Folklore Society's Women's Section, whose members first articulated the pressing need for an encyclopedia of women's folklore and folklife, and to Todd Hallman for recognizing that need.

Liz extends her thanks to Theresa—not only for inviting me to participate in the project, but for making my new life in Oklahoma possible; to Pauline, without whose extraordinary assistance during the final stages of the editorial process the project might never have reached completion; to David Long, whose direction and friendship has made my life as an expository writing teacher at Oklahoma University so improbably satisfying; to Bridget Love for the loan of her laptop when my own computer died of exhaustion; to my Indiana University Folklore teachers, especially Greg Schrempp, William Hansen, Henry Glassie, and Dick Bauman, for nurturing my intellect and respecting my ambitions; and, finally, to Joss Whedon, Terry Pratchett, and Lucy Lawless for keeping my heart alive in this new American millennium.

Theresa thanks Liz and Pauline for coming on board once she realized just how much work a project of this magnitude actually involves, and for being editorial goddesses. I also would like to acknowledge my professors at the University of Michigan and Indiana University, especially those who made me consider the concerns of women. Students Tamara Robbins-Anderson, Mark Reimer, and Candace Carollo were helpful at various times during the project. Finally, my gratitude goes to my children Cian and Sarah, who frankly were not much help in getting work done—both having been born while the encyclopedia was in progress—but who certainly have made life immeasurably richer; and to my husband Kieran, who is unfailingly supportive, brings me flowers, and never balks at changing dirty diapers.

Pauline thanks Juliette Loewen and Kendra Magnusson for helping in the work on last-minute editorial matters. I thank Theresa for being willing to take this project on in the beginning, and for seeing it through to the end with the kind of friendship and patience we could all emulate. And I thank Liz for recognizing the funny side of it all (most of the time!) and for being a constant reminder that it would, truly, get done.

OVERVIEW ESSAYS

Women's Folklore

Women's folklore—discourse that women create about ourselves but also about others—is too often presumed to be identical to women's culture as it is understood in Euro North America. But women's folklore does not relate exclusively to domestic life—motherhood, children, and food—the conventional domain of women. Only sexist thinking sees male culture as "human" and women's culture as specific only to women and girls. The discourses women create, communicate, and negotiate extend over the entire range of human experience; traditional and popular culture reveals the diversity of modes and forms by which we manage our lives and experiences. Women's folklore also demonstrates women's power and resistance. In fact, explicit or implicit resistance to the strictures of patriarchy characterizes the majority of women's folklore and is one of the few generalizations that can be accurately made about it.

Despite often negative evaluations of women's cultures by academics and in the social mainstream, the centrality of women is evident in folklore. Women's traditional and popular culture is found in, and pertains to, both public and private spheres of society, and is as diverse as the women who create and maintain it. Women's folklore is characterized by multiplicity of meaning, as evidenced in feminist coding, as well as ambivalence about and resistance to patriarchy. Some distinctive aspects of women's folklore include collaboration, assemblage from diverse elements, and recycling. Much feminist or women-centered scholarly research also has the latter qualities.

The category "woman" commonly designates an inferior place to which some people are assigned and through which they must negotiate. Because of the near-universal subordination of women and girls to at least some men, but more saliently to White capitalist heteropatriarchy—a structural system in which some men and male values, based in race, class, and sexuality as well as gender, dominate almost all women and children politically, socially, and domestically—most women speak from the social, cultural, and economic margins. But our location outside hegemony (power expressed not only via direct political and economic control, but more pervasively in terms of social relationships, experience, and consciousness) often gives women a genuinely comprehensive understanding of the structures of power. Like other marginalized groups, many women have come to understand power both with regard to the structures we must negotiate on a daily basis and also in terms how we might imagine alternatives to them. In the process, many have come to agree that "the personal is political."

Women have been the source of much of what has been collected and published about traditional folklore genres. For example, "Beginning folklore students learn that the brothers Grimm collected primarily from women servants and relatives in the early 1800s" (Farrer 1975: xi). Women also have been the unacknowledged source of much of what we know about ballads and other folksongs; female singers figure prominently in North American collections, and fieldwork with the Scottish traditional singer Anna Brown (1747–1810) laid crucial groundwork for later theorizing concerning ballad and song traditions. Because such women's folklore was not explicitly connected to traditional female roles, and/or because the content was not exclusively female-centered, much traditional and popular culture collected from women was received as part of a common—either non-gendered or presumptively male—heritage.

Additionally, there is no way of telling how much of the cultural materials anthropologists, linguists, sociologists, and folklorists have purportedly collected from men—almost always the presumed experts—were actually gathered from women. Linguist Jennifer Coates gives an example from a Polish dialect atlas, in which the principal informant was "seventy-five years old ... rather deaf and slow. He was interviewed in the presence of his daughter-in-law, who is described as an energetic, intelligent woman, a good informant.... [and] who replied to most of the questions" (Coates 1993: 53). One wonders why she was not acknowledged as the principal informant. Coates concludes wryly, "How often a female relative gave the responses which are credited to a man, we cannot tell" (ibid.).

Often women's influences are difficult, if not impossible, to separate from the texts and performances of male singers. For example, when collecting from a noted community folksinger in rural Newfoundland, Gerald Pocius discovered that the man's wife was actually the more accomplished singer, but that after her marriage she had assumed a more secondary, supportive role. Many folksong collectors have commented on the importance of female support for male singers in their provision of prompting for both text and tune memory.

Most Euro North American societies explicitly admonish women to be silent, and abhor, ridicule, and sometimes even violently quiet those who are not. Proverbs about women's incessant talk can be found from England— "Foxes are all tail and women are all tongue"—to France—"Where there is a woman, there is never silence"—to Jutland—"The North Sea will sooner be found wanting in water than a woman at a loss for a word" (quoted in Coates 1993: 16)—and beyond. But there are also presumptions about the qualities and forms of women's talk. Women are enjoined against swearing and taboo language—"A whistling sailor, a crowing hen, and a swearing woman ought all three to go to hell together" (ibid.: 20). Whatever form women's language takes, it is viewed negatively. Where innovation is culturally valued, women are stereotyped as conservative speakers; where privileged forms of pronunciation and vocabulary are seen as affected and self-conscious, women are perceived as using higher status-associated forms. Even the genre divisions within folkloristics (the academic study of folklore) reflect negative attitudes toward women's narratives. Men tell stories; women gossip.

Conversely, viewing traditions in women-centered terms, rather than comparing them—usually unfavorably—with androcentric (centered on men) interpretations, often illuminates the position of women; for example, it reveals that women and girls are not confined exclusively to the home and domestic sphere. Although men are often associated with the public sphere and women with the private, the actual confinement of women to the field of the domestic is much less common than is a symbolic confinement of women in the home:

> The private sphere of women's personal experience ... does not depend on physical location, sexual exclusivity, type of material, or the number of participants. It is a mode of social interaction, a space where none need fear ridicule or embarrassment, where handwork often accompanies talk, where participants feel that they all share several bonds, where narratives emphasize those bonds, and where each participant is seen as equally capable of and willing to contribute personal information (Yocom in Jordan and Kalčik 1985: 52).

While the private sphere of family and friends may offer women respite from the demands of patriarchy, and even transformative alternatives to hegemony, this is not the case for all. For every woman of Color who finds her home a haven from a racist society, there is a woman whose home is a locus of abuse and terror. With very few exceptions, however, women in all cultures and throughout history have worked, provisioned our families, and socialized beyond the confines of our own homes. Women are participants in the public sphere, just as men are part of the private domain; however, our presence in public is generally perceived as a problem that must be strictly regulated. Traditional cultures have played significant roles in keeping women "in our place."

As the examples about language above attest, some of the most difficult challenges to women's status are those put forward as humor. For example, Pepito or Jaimito jokes in Mexican and Spanish tradition invariably portray women in unfavorable ways, and blonde jokes (never told about blonde men) serve to demean and silence not only blondes, but all women. Control over women does not require explicit admonitions, rules, walls, or veils. Women firefighters, for example, face constant challenges from their fellows, their clients, their community, and sometimes even their friends and family who fear that their sex renders them inadequate for the physical and psychological tasks involved. Women in responsible positions are the subjects of rumors that undermine their authority and power by asserting that they were promoted over more qualified men, presumably by granting sexual favors or otherwise manipulating their way to the top. Women who are seen as outside their proper role-sphere are criticized by men and women alike for their dress, speech styles, and physical appearance; they are subjected to sexual harassment and sometimes even sexual assault. Mass-media reportage (newspapers and periodicals) consistently refers to women politicians, CEOs, and other major figures by their given names, instead of using the (male) standard surname. And traditional forms of narrative, song, poetry, and even yard art (for example, the bending-over fat-bottomed female figure which adorns so many suburban flower beds) are vehicles by which to demean and undermine women in our own homes and communities.

Public (men) versus private (women) discursive dichotomies remain insidiously pervasive, in part because of the supports for them in traditional cultures. For example, contemporary legends graphically describe the dangers women face when we enter public spaces, particularly if we venture there alone. In these texts, women are raped and killed, particularly in cars, shopping malls, and parking lots—locations particularly difficult for women to avoid even if our primary work is based in our domestic spaces. Legends of women who discover killers in the backseats of their cars, or who are kidnapped from the mall bathroom overlook the fact that statistically in North America, women are in much greater danger of being attacked in our own homes than anywhere else. Even with the consistent underreporting of domestic and family violence, it, rather than violence from strangers, presents the greater danger to women.

The binary opposition of public/private maintains great explanatory power in resolving a multitude of sociocultural paradoxes. It shows how women's experiences are confined and restricted in patriarchy, but it also demonstrates the need to move beyond such limitations. Women's folklore reflects the social, cultural, and economic diversity of the women and girls who make and use it, as well as the diversity of people who define ourselves or are defined by others as female or feminine. The categories "woman" and "feminine" embrace a wide range of ethnicities, races, religions, sexual orientations, sex/gender identities, classes, ages, nationalities, and locations. Each of these loci affects the types of folklore women rely on to communicate with and express ourselves.

Feminist writers have stressed multiplicity of meanings within women's folkloric texts. For example, one explicitly feminist perspective on women's culture that highlights multiple understandings is Joan N. Radner and Susan S. Lanser's ideas about strategic coding. They argue that "acts of coding— covert expressions of disturbing or subversive ideas—are a common phenomenon in the lives of women, who have so often been dominated, silenced, and marginalized" (Radner 1993: vii). Women, like members of other marginalized groups, use multiple, interpretable messages to protect ourselves from the negative consequences of being perceived as subversive.

Yet the multiplicity of possible interpretations raises questions about intended meanings. Feminist analyses that crack these codes may be exposing interpretations that are deliberately coded. Indeed, in several cases in which feminist folklorists have engaged in interpretive decoding, the texts' creators have denied that they intended any such significance. However, the presence of oppressive conditions, marginalization, and risk, as well as multiple communities of listeners (some sympathetic, some not) increase the likelihood that women's messages will be coded, deliberately or otherwise.

Feminist coding is pervasive. For example, males-only clubs in Saint John, New Brunswick, Canada, traditionally invited the city's mayor to their annual events. When the first female mayor, Elsie Wayne, was elected in 1983, the St. Andrew's Society told her that she was "the wrong gender" to attend and asked her to "send a male." Over his protests that he was the wrong religion, she dispatched a Jewish colleague. "'I went to Samuel Davis and I said Samuel you have to go representing me at the St. Andrew's Society and he said Els, what's a Jewish gentleman going to do there? I said you're the right gender darlin'" (Hersey 1998: 172). Upon receiving the next invitation, this time from the St. Patrick's Society, she decided to go in disguise. She obtained a waitress outfit and served the head table, to the great amusement of workers and members alike. Mayor Wayne annually contrived to attend so called "male-only" parties: sometimes she went cross-dressed; perhaps most notably, one year she jumped out of a cake.

While Wayne's symbolic statements could be interpreted as merely humorous, or even as buying into traditional female roles, her interventions pointed out that it was not women per se who were excluded from these clubs. Women did, in fact, enter them as workers—to clean, cook, serve, play music, and/or (presumably, perhaps covertly) to perform sexual or sexualized services. Wayne's coded modes of party-crashing showed that the presence of women performing labor, especially in its domestic forms, would be tolerated, even encouraged. Instead, the exclusion was to women members, women guests, and, above all, a woman mayor.

Another example of feminist coding is the bachelorette party, a women-only pre-marriage ritual found across North America. It appropriates the rites of the male bachelor party but derives its power from juxtaposition with traditional, domestically located and focused bridal showers. A bachelorette party, or "girls' night out," celebrates female sexuality in what some participants see as just a bit of fun—drinking, dancing, and watching male strippers. But it can also be experienced as a perpetuation of female stereotyping of women as heterosexuals whose primary connections are with males. The bachelorette party's meanings, simultaneously conservative and liberating, present a complex, if ambivalent, symbolic reading of the contradictory constructions of North American female sexuality.

As these examples demonstrate, women may perform the same actions as men, using the same traditional genres as men, but we often do so differently—sometimes by choice, sometimes not. Religious holiday observances, seen from a female vantage point, offer particularly good examples of such contradictions. Leslie Bella analyses the Christian tradition of Christmas as more than just a period of happy celebration with family and friends and the observation of a holy day. Christmas dinner, for example, while presented by popular culture as a relaxing break from the mundane, creates a huge task for many women. Managing a family Christmas extends far beyond one meal; it involves cooking and baking, shopping and entertaining, cleaning and decorating, sometimes extending weeks or even months before the actual date.

Women's beliefs, narratives, songs, and material culture may reflect conventional Euro North American ideas of women as cooperative rather than competitive, passive rather than active, nurturing rather than aggressive, and so on. Carol Mitchell notes that women tell jokes that have content as well as narration styles that are "less openly hostile and aggressive" than men's, and that women prefer same-sex audiences, whereas men are willing to tell off-color jokes to same-sex, opposite-sex, and mixed-sex audiences (Jordan and Kalčik 1985: 185). Linda A. Hughes and Marjorie Harness Goodwin nuance the "conventional wisdom concerning girls and their games" (Hughes in Hollis et al. 1993: 143), showing how their play can mediate between cooperative and competitive poles, and involve both individual and group aspects.

Sometimes, women's folklore is transmitted via media so different from those conventionally used by men that male folklorists had difficulty recognizing it as traditional. For example, few middle- and upper-class men in Euro North America require telephones for transmitting narratives—because their mobility isn't limited socially or economically, they can simply go to a venue where storytelling takes place on a face-to-face level. However, for many women, "the telephone plays the predominant role in transmitting folklore, as well as in keeping . . . in touch with the outside world and passing on news" (Dégh in Jordan and Kalčik 1985: 9). Linda Dégh discusses the case of two women who might otherwise be isolated in their Gary, Indiana, homes by lack of mobility and lack of English, who regularly telephone each other to tell stories. She comments, "The telephone is almost the exclusive communication link between members of the [Hungarian] immigrant generation" (ibid.). Men in the same community are likely to have contacts beyond it because they tend to work with non-immigrants or non-Hungarians; most have learned English and have become adept at negotiating public or private transportation.

Vera Mark examines the traditional genre of the tall tale—a genre perceived as quintessentially masculine—at the Moncrabeau Liars' Festival in the terms of the texts and participation of female performers. Mark's work exemplifies a research strategy often associated with feminist methodology—the active participation and conscious reflection of the fieldworker herself. Mark performed at the festival, and she eloquently describes the difficult tightrope she and other women performers walked in choosing an uncontroversial topic, then creating "an amusing story without resorting to licentiousness" (Hollis et al. 1993: 250).

Resistance, both passive and active, is often manifest in women's folklore. "The (male) picture of the ideal woman . . . usually omits the role of revolutionary activist" and folklore offers "glimpses of women's resentment of the repressive role given them" (Jordan in Jordan and Kalčik 1985: 42–43). Karen Baldwin's family storytellers include women who are by no means passive, don't defer to male storytellers, and often win by "getting the last word in" (1985: 161).

Without women's participation in religion, as adherents, supporters, and infrastructural functionaries, religious institutions could not operate. M. Jane Young looks at household and community, underlining the balanced relationship between women and men in Western Puebloan society, and that culture's focus on the sacredness of both reproduction and life. Margaret K. Brady shows how Mormon women use visionary narratives to mediate the personal, social, and spiritual dimensions of pregnancy and birth. Elaine J. Lawless describes how female Pentecostal preachers must balance their positions as women and as preachers, their domestic and sacred powers. Cynthia Vidaurri demonstrates how women's participation in the annual Niño Fidencio celebration and as "*materias*" (vehicles) for this work throughout the year stabilizes and insures the persistence of the tradition.

A traditional genre that has often been associated with women is the life story or autobiography. Though some cultures, including some Inuit groups, discourage women from talking about themselves, Robin McGrath shows how Inuit women circumvent this taboo by talking only about their youth and old age (relatively less restricted periods) or by fictionalizing their accounts to make their apparent subject an animal or object. Elaine Jahner, working with a Sioux woman, noted how her life story emphasizes the positive. Julie Cruikshank collaborated with Yukon First Nations women to publish a range of their narrative repertoire—including myths and personal-experience narratives—available in English so these elders' grandchildren and great-grandchildren will continue to have access to them.

At (Asian Indian) Gujarati weddings, the singers are women, but their songs express three distinctly different emotions and intentions. Corresponding to the three stages of rites of passage—separation, transition, and reincorporation—singers present songs of solidarity, of insult, and of conciliation. Solidarity songs draw family members together, including those who have been in conflict, so that the ceremony offers a united front to those in attendance:

> Place some roses in a vase,
> Sprinkle *kum kum* and print the invitations,
> Send them to all four corners of the world (quoted in Edwards and Katbamna 1988: 165).

Insult songs, *fatana*, are abusive but not obscene. However, "the insults contained in *fatana* are ritual and not real. Any song which includes a blatant element of truth in relation to the other part is likely to cause great offense" (ibid.: 167). Finally, conciliation songs, *valave*, assert the social order, reminding the bride especially of her new family. Their expression is very positive:

> You have given us your daughter
> We shall keep as well as you did
> We shall not break our trust
> When she asks for water, we shall give her milk ...
> The bride is still only young
> We shall take good care of her (ibid.: 168).

There have also been searches for genres specifically, or even definitionally, female. While opinions differ on how ubiquitous any one such genre may be, women's expressions do tend to highlight particular qualities, including collaboration, reciprocity, assemblage, reuse/recycling, and an ephemeral character.

One of the first attempts to identify a female traditional genre came from the research of Susan Kalčik, and related to the collaborative personal-experience narrative storytelling forms developed in women's consciousness-raising groups. Kalčik explores the strategies women use in these groups: ensuring everyone has an opportunity to contribute, alternating competition and support, and always incorporating humor (for example, "My doctor thinks my vaginal infection is all in my head; he has a strange picture of my anatomy") (1975: 5). Kalčik found that consistent with the purpose of these groups—the concern for recognizing commonality in experience and the political in the personal—"It was not necessary . . . to be explicit when an experience was shared by everyone, for a few words were enough to trace the outline of a story" (ibid.: 6). These kernel stories could be developed into more elaborated narratives, often collaboratively; they frequently came to comprise a shared repertoire. Jennifer Coates' research in Britain on all female groups similarly suggests "that women . . . build progressively on each others' contributions, that topics are developed jointly, and that shifts between topics are gradual rather than abrupt" (1988: 105). Sandra Dolby Stahl's work contributed to making the genre better known among academic folklorists who did not necessarily read feminist theory.

Altar-making is another candidate for a woman's genre, especially in Euro North America. Women create, arrange, and produce altars to a multitude of religious and secular figures—from family members, to celebrities, to saints and other religious figures. Kay Turner and Suzanne Seriff examined a St. Joseph's Day feast in rural central Texas "not as a symbolic or material expression of women's subordination to men . . . but rather as a . . . community-wide expression of the power of women's work" (Hollis et al. 1993: 93). This event involves a wide variety of expressions—food and decoration as well as more traditional prayer and praise. A prayer explicitly connects the domestic and the sacred:

> There is room for Jesus, Joseph, and Mary
> This is no longer my house,
> It is that of Jesus, Joseph and Mary (ibid.: 109).

In like manner, it is women who are in charge of the construction of and care for ephemeral public altars set up for religious processions and for *matachines* celebrations in the southwest, especially in New Mexico and Texas.

Needlework arts are also female-dominated. Linda Pershing considers piecework as peacework, including a women's anti-war project in which women all across the United States made panels for a ribbon that literally encircled the Pentagon on August 4, 1985, to commemorate the tragedy of the atomic bombing of Hiroshima and Nagasaki. The women's imagery included concerns for "wholeness and relatedness" (Hollis et al. 1993: 340). Pershing uses artist Miriam Shapiro's term "femmage"—the use of traditionally women-associated techniques in collages that are personal and intentional, yet make political connection to the world beyond the maker's individual experience. Pershing calls the Ribbon Around the Pentagon "an exercise in femmage, a material tribute to the diversity and distinctive nature of women's values and aesthetics, particularly when juxtaposed with the Pentagon, a quintessentially male symbol of military might" (ibid.: 342).

Quilting is also considered a quintessentially feminine art. Quilting has a paradoxical quality: it can be hugely creative or a mundane reproduction of patterns; it can involve solo or group work, or both; it has variable literal and figurative layers—sometimes no more than a decorative cover, sometimes a tremendously warming object; it is at once aesthetic and functional; and it recycles materials but may also be wholly new. Joyce Ice's research indicates concern for both process and product; quilters' and others' preferences for handmade over machine-produced is both aesthetically and socially based. And although quilting is usually thought of as a female genre, men are not entirely excluded. Research by Susan Roach in Texas and Susan Shantz in Saskatchewan shows how men (sometimes shamefacedly or secretly) also participate in, and often greatly enjoy, the process of quilting.

Piecework, patchwork, and femmage demonstrate the importance of recycling and thrift in women's culture. These processes have strongly practical associations with women's position in society. In North America as of 2004, women in paid labor earned about 75 percent of the wages paid to men; many have little or no access to independent sources of income and are fully dependent upon their partners for money. In these circumstances, provisioning the home cheaply is economically necessary—but it can also be a source of creativity and sociability. Garage/yard/tag/car-trunk sales, for instance, offer women opportunities not only to acquire items at low prices, but also to make and maintain social connections in our neighborhoods and communities. Recycling and reusing material is ecologically sound, reducing unnecessary waste and rampant consumerism, and allows women a creative outlet as well as a source of income.

Recycling as a principle of women's culture and communication includes the recycling of words. Feminist theorists such as Mary Daly and Dale Spender have pointed out the importance of returning to the older meanings of words like "spinster" and "hag" to remove their pejorative connotations against aging in women and against women who choose not to marry. They point out that women can take words that are used against us, like "bitch," and reappropriate them as markers of female power, as did the publishers of *Bitch* magazine. Many feminists point out that more women (and men) need to use the term "feminist" to describe ourselves in order to correct the narrow and inaccurate stereotypes in the mainstream media about feminism and its ideals/ideas.

If there is a uniquely female biological process, it is surely conception and birth. Historically, women have supported each other through birthing and mothering. Until the early years of the twentieth century, and longer in some locations, most North American women relied heavily on informal information shared by female friends and family members to guide them through pregnancy, childbirth, and many aspects of childrearing. Most communities had one or more female experts who took on the roles of midwife and doula to assist pregnant and birthing women. In many communities in the American Southwest, *parteras* or *comadronas* (midwives) still practice, although now they must be licensed and be registered practitioners.

Not all women experience—or want to experience—giving birth, but so far, birth is a procedure confined to biological females. Nevertheless, this restriction has not prevented males throughout time from trying to appropriate birth, literally or figuratively. Marta Weigle discusses how male cultural analysts have understood creation myths in limited, male-defined terms; creation myths may be "*ex nihilo* ['out of nothing'] . . . accomplished through spittle, verbal command, laughter, sneezing, 'calling down,' thought, wind, and forming and pronouncing certain written Foundation Letters" (1987: 428). Weigle points out that many Aboriginal and First Nations creation myths include female elements of parturition and midwifery, but were excluded in cosmogonic narrative categories by patriarchal definitions. Robbie E. Davis-Floyd critiques allopathic medicine's notion of the birth process and advocates for a consideration of how the "cultural treatment of birth" might lead to an understanding of "the disappearance of old options and the opening of new ones" (Hollis et al. 1993: 321). Popular culture, too, has imagined female men, parturient men, including but not limited to Arnold Schwarzenegger's portrayal of a pregnant man in *Junior* (1994). Even the Easter Bunny is usually a male figure who has appropriated female fertility in his annual distribution of chocolate eggs (except in Mexican tradition, where she is *La Coneja* ("a female rabbit").

Women and feminist fieldworkers often access women's traditional and popular cultures differently than do their male and anti-feminist counterparts, uncovering traditions of which other researchers may be unaware. For example, ethnographer Stephanie Kane, researching Embera (Choco) mythography in Panama, discovered that stories about a heroic transgressor named Jeropoto that she collected from women included a crucial aspect missing from the published versions collected by male fieldworkers and missionaries—his request to drink menstrual blood. The strong cultural taboo in Euro North American society against discussing menstruation (sometimes even among women) has led to what ethnologist Suzanne Lussier has called a secret tradition.

In Canada, the best known collectors of traditional culture in the twentieth century were female. Edith Fowke (1913–1996) and Helen Creighton (1899–1990) paid at least equal attention to women and their traditions—something their male contemporaries often failed to do. They especially included women performers in their studies. Creighton, an upper-middle-class Nova Scotian, collected farmers' and fishers' culture, working most extensively within easy driving distance of her home in Dartmouth. She fit fieldwork into her other responsibilities, including caring for her elderly parents for much of her adult life. She was motivated by an interest in writing and a concern for celebrating Canadian Maritime culture. As an unmarried woman visiting strangers alone, she had to be circumspect about both her methods and the material she gathered. Creighton was notoriously negative about bawdy songs and stories, though she was otherwise very catholic in what she collected (if not always in her publications). She wrote:

> At Little Harbour on the eastern shore I was once recording Ned MacKay in a fishing shack with some half dozen of his friends sitting around listening. A young Lunenburgher came in and contributed a number that not only had no merit as a song, but was definitely vulgar. I let the machine run and when it was over the young man went out laughing while the local fishermen fidgeted in embarrassment. I put the machine in reverse and remarked that I had erased it from the tape. You wouldn't believe how those few words eased the situation (Creighton 1975: 162).

In contrast, Edith Fowke, a lifelong socialist born in rural Saskatchewan, did most of her fieldwork in Ontario and was well known for her interest in bawdy materials. Fowke, who was married, apparently did not have the same difficulties as a fieldworker in needing to censor her collection in order to retain the respect of male informants. But she also published works focusing on women. One of her last books was a collection and analysis of the repertoire of Ontario singer LaRena Clark. In it, Fowke notes

> Folksinging is one art in which women have always excelled. Here they have been able to hold their own with men because this is an art that can be learned and practiced in the home. It does not require any special education or training, the lack of which has so consistently handicapped women in other fields.... Simply put, men tend to sing outside the home and women sing within it. However, the great women singers transcend that boundary. Originally, most of them learned and sang their songs in the home but many went on to sing them in public as well (Fowke and Rahn 1994: 1).

In the southwestern United States, several women folklorists collected and wrote books, creative or documentary, that chronicled the folkways of women in their communities. The most recognized are Fabiola Cabeza de Baca, Cleofas Jaramillo, Aurora Lucero White, and Jovita González Mireles. While Zora Neale Hurston remains one of the most well-known African American folklorists, others have followed in her footsteps, collecting and analyzing the music and traditions of African American communities. A fictionalized narrative by Ella Cara Deloria called *Waterlily* presents a detailed depiction of Sioux life, and Cabeza de Baca's *They Fed Them Cactus* chronicles a historical period and cultural reality of the people of New Mexico.

Women also participated in collecting traditional culture by helping their husbands with fieldwork. Like much other women's work, such collaborations often go unrecognized. But those who collected as anthropologists and folklorists are by no means alone as women fieldworkers and presenters of traditional culture. Many who write community columns in local weekly newspapers are writing the ethnography of their town. For example, Canadian Jean Heffernan, who produced the Springhill column for the *Amherst Daily News*, described local events—weddings, anniversaries, and town council meetings—but also documented politics, sports, tourism, professional and commercial life, education, religion, child and adult pastimes, and local customs. Much of her writing demonstrates feminist coding, subtly alluding to women's knowledge and local understandings. More research on local weekly newspaper columnists would certainly illuminate both historical and current folklore by and about women. Although women collectors have consistently been ignored and underrated in Euro North American folkloristics, our approaches that prioritize the lives and experiences of those with whom we work, study, and publish, and our frequent blurring of subject and self both prefigure and exemplify contemporary fieldwork practice. *See also:* Altar, Home; Childbirth and Childrearing; Coding; Consciousness Raising; Doula; Folklore of Subversion; Fieldwork; Feminisms; Festival; Folk Music and Folksong; Folktale; Folklore About Women; Girls' Games; Girls' Folklore; Joke; Mass Media; Menstruation; Midwifery; Myth Studies; Personal-Experience Narrative; Piecework; Quiltmaking; Rites of Passage; Sexism; Storytelling; Wage Work; Wedding; Women's Work.

References

Bella, Leslie. *The Christmas Imperative: Leisure, Family and Women's Work*. Halifax: Fernwood, 1992.

Buchan, David. *The Ballad and the Folk*. Boston: Routledge and Kegan Paul, 1972.

Cabeza de Baca, Fabiola. *We Fed Them Cactus* (Paso por aqui series on Nuevomejicano Literatuare). Albuquerque: University of New Mexico Press, 1994.

Cantú, Norma E., and Olga Najera-Ramirez, eds. *Chicana Traditions: Continuity and Change*. Urbana: University of Illinois Press, 2002.

Coates, Jennifer. "Gossip Revisited: Language in All-Female Groups." In *Women in Their Speech Communities*, eds. Jennifer Coates and Deborah Cameron, 94–121. London: Longman, 1988.

Coates, Jennifer. *Women, Men and Language*. Second edition. London: Longman, 1993.

Creighton, Helen. *A Life in Folklore*. Toronto: McGraw-Hill Ryerson, 1975.

Cruikshank, Julie. *Life Lived Like a Story: Life Stories of Three Yukon Native Elders*. Vancouver: University of British Columbia Press, 1990.

Deloria, Ella Cara. *Waterlily*. Lincoln: University of Nebraska Press, 1988.

Dolby Stahl, Sandra. *Literary Folkloristics and the Personal Narrative*. Bloomington: Indiana University Press, 1989.

Edwards, Viv, and Savita Katbamna. "The Wedding Songs of British Gujarati Women." In *Women in Their Speech Communities*, eds. Jennifer Coates and Deborah Cameron, 158–174. London: Longman, 1988.

Farrer, Claire R., ed. *Women and Folklore: Images and Genres*. Prospect Heights, IL: Waveland Press, 1975.

Fowke, Edith, and Jay Rahn. *A Family Heritage: The Story and Songs of LaRena Clark*. Calgary: University of Calgary Press, 1994.

Greenhill, Pauline. "Radical? Feminist? Nationalist? The Canadian Paradox of Edith Fowke." *The Folklore Historian* 20 (2003): 22–33.

——— and Diane Tye, eds. *Undisciplined Women: Tradition and Culture in Canada*. Montreal: McGill-Queen's University Press, 1997.

Hersey, Linda. *Elsie!–An Authorized Biography of Elsie Wayne*. Saint John, NB: Neptune Publishing, 1998.

Hollis, Susan Tower, Linda Pershing, and M. Jane Young, eds. *Feminist Theory and the Study of Folklore*. Urbana: University of Illinois Press, 1993.

hooks, bell. *Outlaw Culture: Resisting Representations*. New York: Routledge, 1994.

Hurston, Zora Neale. *Folklore and Autobiography*. New York: Library of America, 1995.

Jackson, Bruce, ed. "Folklore and Feminism." Special issue of *Journal of American Folklore*, vol. 100, no. 398 (1987).

Jordan, Rosan A., and Susan J. Kalčik, eds. *Women's Folklore, Women's Culture*. Philadelphia: University of Pennsylvania Press, 1985.

Lawless, Elaine J. *Women Escaping Violence: Empowerment through Narrative*. Columbia: University of Missouri Press, 2001.

Mathieu, Jocelyne, ed. "Femmes et Traditions/Women and Tradition." Special issue of *Canadian Folklore canadien*, vol. 15, no. 2 (1993).

Pocius, Gerald. "'The First Day That I Thought Of It Since I Was Wed': Role Expectations and Singer Status in a Newfoundland Outport." *Western Folklore* 35 (1976): 109–122.

Radner, Joan Newlon., ed. *Feminist Messages: Coding in Women's Folk Culture*. Urbana: University of Illinois Press, 1993.

Seelhorst, Mary. "'The Assailant in Disguise': Old and New Functions of Urban Legends About Women Alone in Danger." *North Carolina Folklore Journal*, vol. 34, no. 1 (1987): 29–37.

Stoeltje, Beverly J., ed. "Feminist Revisions in Folklore Studies." Special issue of *Journal of Folklore Research* 23, no. 3 (1988).

Turner, Kay. *Beautiful Necessity: The Art and Meaning of Women's Altars*. New York: Thames & Hudson, 1999.

Tye, Diane, and Anne Marie Powers. "Gender, Resistance and Play: Bachelorette Parties in Atlantic Canada." *Women's Studies International Forum*, vol. 21, no. 5 (1998): 551–561.

Vidaurri, Cynthia. "Las Que Menos Queria el Nico: Women of the Fidencista Movement." In *Chicana Traditions: Continuity and Change*, eds. Norma E. Cantú and Olga Najera-Ramirez, 133–142. Urbana: University of Illinois Press, 2002.

Pauline Greenhill, Diane Tye, and Norma E. Cantú

Folklore About Women

Women are the subject of a great many traditional and popular ideas, beliefs, and practices. Folklore contributes greatly to the process of turning biologically sexed beings into symbolically and culturally gendered ones—both female and male—hence, much folklore about women serves to create, recreate, and reinforce ideas about the differences between women and men.

In Euro North American societies, such processes begin at least at the moment of birth, when the inevitable question, "Is it a boy or a girl?" is first posed. There are only two options—and the answer must be unequivocal. One of the strongest folkloric notions about women is that they exist in a biological and cultural unity: that sex always goes along with gender; whoever is sexed female must be gendered female, and vice versa. This binary dividing of women from men problematically excludes all other genders and all other sexes. Yet the fiction that women are a unity (even if they are, as Simone de Beauvoir famously suggested in 1953, one defined primarily as "the Other") persists cross-culturally.

In the folklore of Euro North America, girls wear pink and are made of "sugar and spice and everything nice." Boys wear blue and are made of "snips (or snakes) and snails and puppy dog tails." As the pink girls age into pink ladies, they increasingly derive their worth—and are judged by their peers and others—in terms of their physical appearance. If sexually adventurous, they are "sluts" or "whores." If modest, they are virgins until they marry. Upon marriage, they remain faithful to their husbands; indeed, they are sexually active only for the purposes of procreation. These madonnas, once they have outlasted their reproductive capacity, become "old wives" who gossip with others of their kind but are no longer useful to society in any fundamental way. Patriarchy imposes these limitations on women, but feminism critiques such notions, not only because they are discriminatory, but also because they unreasonably limit the human potential of women.

"Men have not only excluded, ignored, and otherwise rendered women invisible, they have, for centuries, appropriated women as a semiotic object and made her female form highly visible both to represent their established order and to redress it" (Babcock 1987: 398). In fact, however, even in Euro North American cultures, folklore about women also includes material that is much more subtle and multivocal. Women and men alike create folklore about women that accurately and significantly interprets women's experiences, knowledge, and understanding about the world. Yet women and men also create folklore about women that demeans, misrepresents, and pathologizes women and their lives. Folklore about women, then, remains almost as complex as its subjects.

One of the earliest works explicitly linking women and folklore is T. F. Thiselton-Dyer's 1906 *Folk-Lore of Women*. Though billed as women's folklore—the traditional and popular culture created by women and mainly for women—the book instead describes folklore about women, as its chapter heads indicate: Woman's Characteristics; Woman's Beauty; Woman's Dress; Woman's Eyes; Woman's Tongue; Woman's Goodness; Bad Women; Woman's Love; Woman's Hate; Love Tests; Woman's Secrets; Red-haired Girls; Woman's Fickleness; Local Allusions to Women; Woman's Will; Women and Marriage; Women as Wives; Young and Old Maids; Widows; Woman's Curiosity; Sister Legends; Brides and their Maids; Superstitions about Women; Woman's Tears; Woman's Blushes; Daughters; and My Lady's Walk. This list is a remarkable inventory of women's otherness: women are indivisible—almost all are the singular "woman," except when they are bad, local, or heterosexually attached; women are metonymous (the part stands for the whole) in dress, eyes, tongue, tears, and blushes; women are characterized by appearance and relationship; and their qualities are simple and often binary: love/hate, fickleness, curiosity, and willfulness.

The outlier in this series, "My Lady's Walk" refers to places named after women. It marks the incongruity of feminine-named or even feminine-associated spaces and the need for explanation thereof, such as: "a tradition told in connection with the Spindleston Hills, which are commonly said to be haunted by a lady nicknamed 'The Wandering Shepherdess.' The story goes that a certain lady, after the death of her lover, abandoned rank and wealth, and spent her remaining days following sheep on the hills, and even now the peasants affirm she may at times be seen doing the same walk, reminding us of the lady with her lantern, who in stormy weather walks up and down the beach at St. Ives on the Cornish coast" (Thiselton-Dyer 1906: 246–247).

A later work purporting to discuss *The Female Hero in Folklore and Legend* by Tristram Potter Coffin first considers Cleopatra, Helen of Troy, and Guinevere. It continues with a thematic look at women associated with roses (including "grotesque" ones); traditions concerning murdered women; folklore about witches; a consideration of Mother Goose; descriptions of theatrical and film stars; and finally texts about women who were successful in hitherto male roles.

The first feminist consideration of folklore about women was Marta Weigle's *Spiders and Spinsters*. Although its main focus is on women and mythology, the work was groundbreaking not only in its variety of perspectives on myth, including symbol, cultural avatar, mystery, ritual, model, and charter, but for its generally cross-cultural perspective. The chapter on heroines, for example, considers Joan of Arc, classical figures, and folktale heroines, including a number from North American First Nations peoples.

Only seven years separated the publication of Coffin's book in 1975 and the release of Weigle's in 1982, yet they are worlds apart in terms of their perspectives on women. The differences cannot only be attributed to the sexes of the authors, but to the fact that feminism began to infiltrate folklore scholarship in the mid-1970s. Scholars trained before that period could get away with writing about women in distancing and othering ways; afterward, it became essential for folklorists to recognize gender as a significant element to be reckoned with in their analyses of traditional and popular culture.

Materials describing traditional and popular culture relating to women have become more commonplace with the development of feminist analysis and theory, and with the international proliferation of feminist movements. A bold cross-cultural generalization that women tend to be associated with nature and men with culture has proved remarkably consistent, though the manifestations of the tendency vary considerably. Ideas about women tend to cluster around aspects of their bodies, their biology, and their reproductive capacity—but there is, of course, a great proliferation and variety of cultural discourses related to these facets of women's lives.

Though symbolic division of the sexes seems a cross-cultural concern, the extent to which cultures physically separate women and men varies. Anthropologist Lila Abu-Lughod characterizes the Islamic Middle East as practicing mutual avoidance between the sexes. In parts of Melanesia, active aggression and antagonism between the sexes leads to fear of one another, but also to symbolic statements which express those fears, as when men incise their penises so they bleed in imitation of menstruation. But such cultures fall short of the economic Northern Hemisphere's stereotype of grinding, continuous oppression of Southern-Hemisphere women. Unlike so many of their Euro North American sisters, these women experience active female solidarity, encouraged and supported through rituals and stories.

Male social scientists of the past too often interpreted the traditional culture expressed, created, and performed by women among women as private, and the culture expressed, created, and performed by women for male or mixed groups as public. Their definitions often became something of a self-fulfilling prophecy—women's practices were per se private and men's per se public, regardless of their actual contents or circumstances of presentation and performance. Sometimes these kinds of distinctions characterize relations within particular societies. Folklorist John Szwed noted that information communicated between men at the local store was called "news." The identical information, passed among women in their homes, was called "gossip." Feminists criticize such dichotomies—whatever their sources—as tending to reinforce sexist binary oppositions. However, it is invariably worth paying attention to traditional cultural contexts, that is, by whom and for whom a text is presented and represented, as well as its contents. Folklore about women is communicated by women and men, in private and in public, and can correspond to or differ from conventional notions of women and their roles.

Many stories about actual women tend to reinforce the idea that adult females who act outside the domestic sphere are remarkable and noteworthy. Ella Lauchner Smith, who taught history at Mount Allison University during World War II, became the subject of a cycle of narratives which survive to this day in the small university town of Sackville, New Brunswick, Canada, where she lived and worked. Folklorist Diane Tye explains the ambivalence of these kinds of stories. On the one hand, they mark Smith as a local character who violates social codes by treating public space as her own:

> Dr. George J. [Trueman, then university president] used to have a lot of visitors to Sackville during the summer and this was when they had a chapel in the old Centennial ... Hall. And it was on the third floor and it was a lovely little chapel. It really was.... And he had a visitor this particular day and of course they used to go on a visitation of the campus and Dr. George J. told this man, he said, "Now," he said, "This is our Centennial building here, our administration offices, but," he said, "There's something on the third floor that we're really quite proud of. Mount Allison never had it before." And he took him up to show the chapel and he went through the door and into the chapel, here was these ladies' clothes and undies and everything all hung on a line drying. And Dr. George J. Trueman knew who they belonged to because there was no one else on the campus that would do a thing like this, you know.... Just like army banners, you know, they were all drying. And of course he spoke to her about it and he said how embarrassing it was because he had this friend from Toronto or Montreal who was being conducted on this visitation of the Mount A. campus and she said, "Well," she said, "I don't think God would mind me trying to be clean and having my clothes in the chapel drying" (Tye in Mathieu 1993: 31).

Tye's analysis suggests that Smith's frugal behavior probably resulted from the fact that her social position as a faculty member was not matched, especially in those days before equal pay legislation and policies, with a sufficient income and pension. The university's and the people of Sackville's judgments of Smith as an eccentric—both compared with other women and compared with other academics—failed to recognize the reasons behind her actions. On the other hand, both town and gown seem to revel in Smith's flaunting of convention. Whether in the tellingly sacrilegious yet critical image of her "undies ... like army banners" displayed in the church, or in stories about her apparently equal unconcern for the time and privacy of everyone from the local children and her neighbors to the university president and the town doctor, the narratives mark her as a rebellious woman.

Many of those who told Smith stories were her male former students, concerned to mark her location outside women's traditional space. But the students also seem to have envied her manifest ability to turn her own relative powerlessness into a tactic to control the world around her. In the accounts, Smith is never at a loss for words; nor is she cowed by her apparent superiors. Her students of the day, seeking to maintain or even improve their own social position through post-secondary education, would have been unwilling to disturb the status quo, however much they might wish to do so.

In contemporary politics, women who, like Smith, invade traditionally male territory, invariably receive attention from the mainstream media that marks the inappropriateness of their location. Elaine K. Miller suggests that the general themes of cartoons that depicted U.S. vice-presidential candidate Geraldine Ferraro were:

> 1. There are "special interest" groups trying to get into the action or even take over.... 2. Women, constituting one of these "special interest" groups, are especially pushy or even threatening.... 3. As a group, women are interchangeable.... 4. Gender roles and power are reversed.... 5. Ferraro appears in domestic or explicitly sexual contexts (Jordan and Kalčik 1985: 362).

Although female politicians are generally seen as acting outside their traditional roles as women, some actual women are near-incomprehensible in sociocultural terms. The idea that women are invariably nurturant precludes certain kinds of female killers. Women who kill their children and female serial killers are particularly unimaginable. Belle Gunness, "The Lady Bluebeard," an American female serial killer preceding Aileen Wuornos, "apparently murdered at least one husband, several women and children, and numerous would-be suitors who had answered her matrimonial advertisements placed in Norwegian-language immigrant newspapers" (Langlois in Jordan and Kalčik 1985: 109). In the Indiana community where these murders took place, she and her "murder farm" are celebrated in stories. Her roles include monster, trickster, and (beyond the oral tradition) victimized heroine.

All these women, from Smith to Gunness, were remarkable, and remarked upon, precisely because they did not fit a preexisting stereotype of women's behavior or character. However, many women who similarly stand partially outside the conventional expectations for their appearance, role, status, and/or activities label themselves, and/or receive their community's label, as witches. The character of the witch, like the traditional roles of women generally, manifests a profound ambivalence. Witches are alternately (and sometimes even simultaneously) powerful and weak.

Folktale witches often take the villain's role. As old, ugly women, they contrast with the young, beautiful heroine. However, folklorist Kay Stone's "Things Walt Disney Never Told Us" suggests that this polarization is more marked in the popular culture interpretations of traditional narratives. In her examination of folktale collections from Germany, France, England, and the United States, Stone found that tale collections include stories in which women who are not "unusually patient, obedient, industrious, and quiet," as are Disneyfied heroines, but instead "slovenly, unattractive, and lazy," can nevertheless be quite successful. Stone also interviewed women and girls, many of whom refigured the stories they knew to turn passive heroines into active ones (Farrer 1975: 44).

Indeed, many storytellers turn erstwhile evil witches into veritable feminist icons. Feminist revisions point out that fairytales and their characters are not simply taken literally and uncritically by their female (and male) readers and listeners. Reconfigured tales also critically reverse or play with conventional Euro North American expectations for women's lives:

> Once upon a time, in a land far away,
> a beautiful, independent, self-assured princess
> happened upon a frog as she sat,
> contemplating ecological issues
> on the shores of an unpolluted pond
> in a verdant meadow near her castle.
>
> The frog hopped into the princess' lap
> and said: Elegant Lady,
> I was once a handsome prince,
> until an evil witch cast a spell upon me.
>
> One kiss from you, however,
> and I will turn back
> into the dapper, young prince that I am
> and then, my sweet, we can marry
> and set up housekeeping in your castle
> with my mother,
> where you can prepare my meals,
> clean my clothes, bear my children,
> and forever feel grateful and happy doing so.
>
> That night, as the princess dined sumptuously
> on lightly sautéed frog legs
> seasoned in a white wine
> and onion cream sauce,
> she chuckled and thought to herself:
>
> I don't fucking think so (e-mail communication).

But witches are not confined to fairy tales. In Atlantic Canada, women who lived alone, belonged to an ethnic or racialized minority, or were otherwise marginalized were often identified as witches. Rumored to have evil powers, these women were further isolated by stories about their actions. Alienating as the experience of being called a witch certainly was, many women nevertheless used their witch identity, capitalizing on community beliefs that witches would punish those who crossed them to ensure that they received enough food and supplies to live. Few community members would dare to refuse a witch's request, and fear of her retribution encouraged many to ensure that her needs were met.

Yet witchcraft accusations, which notoriously led to trials and executions in seventeenth-century America, could also lead to community sanctions. Folklorist Natalie Kononenko's study of witchcraft in Ukraine shows that suspicion against witches sometimes led to verbal and physical attacks, and even to murder, although she argues that most of their activity was "utterly mundane" (in Magliocco 1998: 81). Newfoundland witches could also be subject to violent reprisals, many of which had magical elements: shooting an image or token of the witch, or bottling one's own urine to block the witch's power.

More recently, the term "witch" has acquired positive connotations for those who seek a women-centered spirituality. Revival Witches or Wiccans, in a form of Neo-Paganism, seek to connect with nature and worship a goddess associated with the moon. Feminist Witches have reclaimed the term "witch" and reversed her negative polarity in Euro North American thinking, celebrating her supernatural power, sexuality, and environmentalism. Scholars bitterly dispute the authenticity of the rituals contemporary Wiccans practice, but many practitioners argue that their activities have historical as well as spiritual validity.

Chicana writers redefine and resistantly interpret traditional feminine figures. The Virgin of Guadalupe, venerated since the 1530s, exemplifies ideal womanhood, combining virtue and motherhood. Pat Mora rewrites her as violently avenging the protagonist's actions:

> .... I stopped the bribes
> hoarded soft petals
> didn't lay them at your feet
> didn't speak to you at all.
> If some day in a dark church
> I wait for a nod, smile, wink,
> will you just smash your foot
> into my mouth? (1986: 77).

Poet Carmen Tafolla (2004: 18–20) reconceptualizes La Malinche, mistress of Hernan Cortez who conquered the Aztecs, not as a second Eve who lost the Mexican paradise, but as the founder of a new people. The Mexican version of *La Llorona* involves a beautiful mestizo woman who has borne children out of wedlock to a Spaniard, and on hearing of his impending wedding, kills them all, then roams the streets and waterways, weeping. In the Aztec version, she is a pre-Conquest seer who predicts the fall of the empire, and similarly screams in anguish. Writer Sandra Cisneros (1992: 43–56) transforms her into a self-aware, feminist figure, whose cry is instead a laugh.

Similar ambivalence characterizes the traditional and popular culture surrounding wholly invented characters such as Barbie. For many feminists, the Mattel doll represents the literal impossibility of Euro North American iconic femininity: no one is simultaneously that tall, blonde, wasp-waisted, long-necked, long-legged, and conical-breasted. Actual women's and girls' emulation of Barbie, and of other unachievable or unhealthy images, such as the anorexic, barely post-pubescent "heroin chic" models whose airbrushed photographs filled the women's magazines of the late twentieth century, do nothing to advance women's equality in Euro North American culture. However, children and adults who play with Barbie dolls are not constrained by the scripts offered to them by her manufacturers and promoters. Despite—or perhaps because of—what sociologist Mary F. Rogers calls Barbie's "emphatic femininity," her plastic body now accommodates queer sexualities, anti-bourgeoisie sensibilities, and other alternative possibilities.

Art historian and lesbian activist Erica Rand argues that Barbie play—and work—by both adults and children can alternate between straight and queer readings. Like the actual humans who sustain an interest in her, Barbie is never wholly reducible to a simple, unified sexuality. Contemporary artists have conceptualized and developed Lesbian Barbie, who is invisible; Totally Out Barbie, who "wears a leather jacket, freedom rings, pink triangle, and a woman-symbol earring, highly visible given her short hair"; and preoperative transsexual Kendra, "a dyke trapped in the body of a dreamboat" (1995: 159). Rand argues that such "Barbie subversion" is begged by the manufacturers' and marketers' silences about who/what the doll really is, making her an excellent vehicle for social criticism.

Mattel's strategy of naming of Barbies after their clothes, accessories, and lifestyles has spawned numerous items of sardonic Internet-circulated humor. One widely distributed example promises, "At long last here are some NEW Barbie dolls to coincide with her and OUR aging gracefully" and includes:

> Bifocals Barbie. Comes with her own set of blended-lens fashion frames in six wild colors (half-frames too!), neck chain, and large-print editions of *Vogue* and *Martha Stewart Living*.
>
> Hot Flash Barbie. Press Barbie's bellybutton and watch her face turn beet red while tiny drops of perspiration appear on her forehead. Comes with hand-held fan and tiny tissues.
>
> Bunion Barbie. Years of disco dancing in stiletto heels have definitely taken their toll on Barbie's dainty arched feet. Soothe her sores with the pumice stone and plasters, then slip on soft terry mules.
>
> No-More-Wrinkles Barbie. Erase those pesky crow's feet and lip lines with a tube of Skin Sparkle-Spackle from Barbie's own line of exclusive age-blasting cosmetics.
>
> Mid-Life Crisis Barbie. It's time to ditch Ken. Barbie needs a change, and Alonzo (her personal trainer) is just what the doctor ordered, along with Prozac. They're hopping in her new red Miata and heading up to the Napa Valley to open a B and B [bed-and-breakfast inn]. Includes a real tape of "Breaking Up is Hard To Do."
>
> Postmenopausal Barbie. This Barbie wets her pants when she sneezes, forgets where she puts things, and cries a lot. She is sick and tired of Ken sitting on the couch watching the tube, clicking through the channels. Comes with Depends [a brand of adult diapers] and Kleenex. As a bonus this year, the book *Getting In Touch With Your Inner Self* is included (e-mail communication).

Despite second-wave feminist assertions that women could not see themselves in Barbie, but could only try to be like her, women of the feminist third wave are recreating her in their own images. Their ambivalence about Barbie and, crucially, about their own lives finds expression in this popular culture, as it does in other folklore about women.

For lesbian, bisexual, and queer women, finding themselves in traditional and popular culture can be difficult and problematic. Films, for example, too often make lesbianism entirely invisible or represent lesbian women as "killer dykes" or hypersexualized predators. Many, then, create their own traditions to develop and claim community. Even before the recent legalization in Massachusetts, California, and Canada of same-sex marriage, commitment ceremonies have been popular in North America. Drawing upon various religious customs, but rewriting them or inventing new traditions, these ceremonies can alternately claim equivalence with heterosexual marriage rites and queer them entirely. Either way, they disrupt the conventional folklore about women.

Women find other ways to express their presence and to contest patriarchal views. Many speak directly about their own experiences in oral histories. Sometimes the discussion and presentation of oral history is part of community culture and knowledge. Canadian First Nations elders frequently use stories about their own lives and experiences as part of the teaching of culture and history to younger people. Angela Sidney, Kitty Smith, and Annie Ned, three Yukon Native elders, collaborated with anthropologist Julie Cruikshank to publish *Life Lived Like a Story*. They included stories from the past as well as mythical tales, peopled by many women: Good Luck Lady, Game Mother, The Stolen Woman, The Woman Who Was Thrown Away, the women's female relatives—mothers, grandmothers, "Mrs. Dickson's Aunt"—as well as themselves. Angela Sidney remembered a story from her childhood about "The Old Woman under the World":

> There are two old ladies down below who look after the world.
> One is supposed to be sleeping.
> The other holds up the Earth with a pole.
> When she shakes it, that's when there's supposed to be an earthquake.
> That old lady there with the pole is supposed to be Death.
> She always argues—she's the one who always says,
> "Let people sleep for good when they go to sleep,
> Let them die."
>
> That Death Woman wants to kill people before their time.
>
> But Sleep Woman says,
> "No!
> Can't you see how my boss put a good pillow for me to sleep on?
> And you want me to let her go to sleep for good?
> No. No—I won't do that."
> Those two old ladies.
> One is Sleep Woman, the other is Death Woman (Cruikshank 1990: 74).

The women in these First Nations stories are not secondary characters, and they are certainly not the limited creatures Thiselton-Dyer implies. They demonstrate and exemplify (as do the other characters in the stories) both proper and improper behavior. Cree women's reminiscences and personal stories about their daily lives are recorded in Freda Ahenakew and H. C. Wolfart's *Our Grandmothers' Lives as Told in Their Own Words*. They discuss in great detail everything from encounters with bears to household chores.

Clearly, not all folklore about women is untrue. Nevertheless, misogynist traditions—true, false, or somewhere in between—abound. For example, Francis Colbert of Job's Cove, Conception Bay, Newfoundland, often recited "St. Peter at the Gate" at local weddings. This text, about a wife and husband requesting admission to heaven, exemplifies the idea that folklore about women serves to accentuate gender differences:

> Now, the woman was long, she was lank, she was thin, and she had a scraggly beard growed on her chin.
> But the man was short and plump and stout and his features were built so he was rounded out (Wareham 1976: 208–211).

The male talkers (the husband and St. Peter) always think before they speak; the sole female speaker, the wife, who takes the majority of the recitation's lines, has a single, almost uninterrupted monologue. Ultimately, good and bad, first and last, heaven and hell are reversed to the husband's benefit and the wife's detriment. He gets into heaven. St. Peter says:

> "Thirty years with that woman there, no wonder the man hasn't got any hair.
> Smoking is bad, cursing is not good, well, he smoked and he cursed, I should say he would.
> Thirty years with a tongue so sharp. Say, Angel Gabriel, give him a harp,
> Give him a harp with golden strings and pass in, good sir, where the angels sing.
> See that on the finest of foods he feeds, he's had about all the hell that he needs,
> Doesn't seem the right thing to do to roast him on Earth and hereafter, too." (ibid.).

In contrast, the wife goes "down below"; St. Peter sends her to hell not only because she usurped the position of control in the marriage but also because she dared to criticize the saint himself. It cannot be entirely coincidental that this is a wedding recitation; it presents some clear indications as to wives' ideal behaviors: submissive, husband-pleasing cooks who should be uncritical, and, above all, silent.

Not all traditional culture that implicates women is as retrogressive as the previous example. Though transgenderism may seem a relatively new phenomenon to Euro North Americans, historians have discovered that for several centuries individuals have crossed sex/gender boundaries. Women often dressed as men in order to have access to male work. Histories and traditions alike have celebrated (and sometimes ridiculed) such women. Perhaps the most famous cross-dressing historic military figure to Euro North Americans was Joan of Arc, who led French troops to victory over the English and was eventually burned at the stake. But she was certainly not the first, nor the last, such woman. Historian Lauren Cook Burgess estimates that 400 women served in the U.S. Civil War, dressing and being treated as men.

Women who dressed as men in search of adventure, work, or love also became the subjects of broadside ballads, disseminated originally in print in

Britain and later transmitted through oral tradition in many parts of Anglo North America. The song "The Soldier Maid" is a good example:

> Oh what a pretty maid in my time I have been,
> They forced me from my parents, a soldier I became,
> They forced me from my parents and certainly I'm undone....
>
> ... My officer he taught me a stately man to be,
> The soldiers all admired me, my fingers were so small,
> And they learned me to beat upon the drum the best of all.
>
> Oh when I went to my quarters the night time for to spend
> I was not ashamed for to lie among the men,
> And hauling off my small clothes to myself I ofttimes smiled,
> A-lying with the soldiers a maid all the while.
>
> Oh many were the battles that I fought upon the field,
> And many a brave fellow was forced from me to yield,
> I was guarded by my general for fear I would be slain....
> Then they sent me over to London to take charge of the tower,
> I never was discovered until that day and hour,
> When a lady fell in love with me I told her I was a maid,
> And straight unto my regiment my secrets were betrayed.
>
> Then up steps the officer, he made no more to-do,
> He asked me the questions, I answered him quite true.
> He laughed at the joke and he smiled as he said:
> 'It's a pity we should lose such a drummer as a maid.'
>
> .... And if our King does want more men those Frenchmen to be slain,
> I will boldly stand with sword in hand and fight for him again (quoted in Greenhill and Tye 1997: 114–115).

This song, and most others featuring cross-dressed women, shows the protagonist as being particularly skilled at the male labor she performs. The best drummer, admired by all the soldiers, she is so valuable that the general guards her, not the reverse. The text also plays extensively with the sexual possibilities of the woman's role: "undone"—and thus, perhaps, fundamentally transformed—by her new experiences, she's a maid though she sleeps with men every night, and is discovered only when another woman falls in love with her. These songs about adventurous women are particularly popular with female singers, both now and in the past.

The only text from this genre that involves a man dressing as a woman, "The Shirt and the Apron," has no such positive implications for the protagonist. A sailor is forced to wear a woman's "shirt and apron" because they are the only ones available after he has been seduced and robbed of all his belongings, including his clothes, by a sex worker. He endures humiliation from his peers—unlike the cross-dressed women, he is not disguised by his apparel, but is perfectly recognizable:

> The sailors saw me come on board those words to me did say,
> "Ah you poor old chap, you've lost your cap, since you've been gone that way."
> "Is this the new spring fashion, Jack, the ladies got on shore,

Where is the shop that's selling it, or is there any more?"
"O Jack, my boy," the captain cry, "I thought you for Wigginstown!
I know you could buy a better suit than that for fifty pounds" (Greenleaf and
Mansfield 1933: 223)

However, he must also go back to sea because he can't afford to return
home without the money he had saved.

Folklorist Margaret Mills has shown that Afghan folktales—even when told
in conservative Muslim communities—involve sexual role-switching and even
sex changes. "Men act like women in order to penetrate the private sphere to
gain access to women, or involuntarily as victims of male aggression in the
form of actual or threatened homosexual rape. By contrast, women most often
act like men to gain mobility in the outside world, both to avoid sexual contact
and to rescue family members (mostly male) who are confined or incapaci-
tated" (in Jordan and Kalčik 1985: 195). Tales in which sex changes occur are
much more ambivalent. Men's stories about women who undergo sex change
see it as her reward; women's stories make the sex change instead a stigma.

Presumptions about women form much of the folklore about women.
Recent feminist critiques have noted the ways in which even feminist movements have presumed whiteness, ability, heterosexuality, middle class, and a
host of other characteristics in the women they describe. Yet increasingly, even
within the Euro North American context, considerations of African American
and African Canadian women, Chicanas, Aboriginal and First Nations women,
women with disabilities, older women, girls, women whose first language is
not English, and a host of other marginalized groups are gaining attention.

Time and time again, folklore about women returns to the obsession with
distinguishing them from men. The qualities associated with women and men,
particularly in Euro North American societies, tend to be polarized into binary
oppositions. It is sometimes difficult to remember that women and men have
much more in common than in differentiation, and that the biological and cultural possibilities of each are by no means exhausted by the two categories.
The scientist mythology of recent trends in sociobiology, for example, built
around purportedly cross-species differences between male and female animals, produces a multitude of nonsensical constructions from duck rape and
cockroach rape to the cross-cultural presumption of male supremacy even in
species where females choose their reproductive partners, rear their young
separately, hunt, and show other forms of control. As always, traditional and
popular culture—folklore—is not limited to any particular group of people,
but crosses cultures, classes, and sexes/genders. *See also:* Ballad; Barbie Doll;
Cross-Dressing; Feminisms; First Nations of North America; Folktale; Gossip;
Housekeeping; *La Llorona*; Lesbian Folklore; Lesbian and Queer Studies; Na-
ture/Culture; Old Wives' Tales; Oral History; Personal-Experience Narrative;
Transgender Folklore; Virgin of Guadalupe; Veiling; Witchcraft, Historical;
Wicca and Neo-Paganism; Women's Folklore; Women's Movement.

References

Abu-Lughod, Lila. "A Community of Secrets: The Separate World of Bedouin Women." *Signs* 10
(1985): 637–657.
Ahenakew, Freda, and H. C. Wolfart. *Our Grandmothers' Lives as Told in Their Own Words.*
Saskatoon: Fifth House Publishers, 1992.

Babcock, Barbara. "Taking Liberties, Writing from the Margins, and Doing It with a Difference." *Journal of American Folklore* 100 (1987): 390–411.

Burgess, Lauren Cook, ed. *An Uncommon Soldier: The Civil War Letters of Sarah Rosetta Wakeman alias Pvt. Lyons Wakeman*. Pasadena, MD: Minerva Center, 1994.

Cisneros, Sandra. "Woman Hollering Creek." In *Woman Hollering Creek and Other Stories*. New York: Vintage, 1992.

Coffin, Tristram Potter. *The Female Hero in Folklore and Legend*. New York: Seabury Press, 1975.

Cruikshank, Julie. *Life Lived Like a Story: Life Stories of Three Yukon Native Elders*. Vancouver: University of British Columbia Press, 1990.

de Beauvoir, Simone. *The Second Sex*. Reissue edition. New York: Vintage Books, 1989 [1953].

Farrer, Claire R., ed. *Women and Folklore: Images and Genres*. Prospect Heights, IL: Waveland Press, 1975.

Greenhill, Pauline, and Diane Tye, eds. *Undisciplined Women: Tradition and Culture in Canada*. Montreal: McGill-Queen's University Press, 1997.

Greenleaf, Elisabeth Bristol, and Grace Yarrow Mansfield. *Ballads and Sea Songs of Newfoundland*. Cambridge, MA: Harvard University Press, 1933.

Herrera-Sobek, Maria. "Social Protest, Folklore, and Feminist Ideology in Chicana Prose and Poetry." In *Folklore, Literature, and Cultural Theory: Collected Essays*, ed. Cathy Lynn Preston, 102–166. New York: Garland Publishing, 1995.

Hollis, Susan Tower, Linda Pershing, and M. Jane Young, eds. *Feminist Theory and the Study of Folklore*. Urbana: University of Illinois Press, 1993.

Jordan, Rosan, and Susan J. Kalčik, eds. *Women's Folklore, Women's Culture*. Philadelphia: University of Pennsylvania Press, 1985.

Langlois, Janet L. "Mothers' Double Talk." In *Feminist Messages: Coding in Women's Folk Culture*, ed. Joan Newlon Radner, 80–97. Urbana: University of Chicago Press, 1993.

Magliocco, Sabina, ed. "Special issue: Wicca." *Ethnologies*, vol. 20, no. 1 (1998).

Mathieu, Jocelyne, ed. "Special issue: Femmes et Traditions/Women and Tradition." *Canadian Folklore canadien* 15, no. 2 (1993).

Mora, Pat. "To Big Mary From an Ex-Catholic." *Borders*. Houston: Arte Público, 1986.

Rand, Erica. *Barbie's Queer Accessories*. Durham, NC: Duke University Press, 1995.

Rogers, Mary F. *Barbie Culture*. London: SAGE Publications, 1999.

Szwed, John. "Gossip, Drinking, and Social Control: Consensus and Communication in a Newfoundland Parish." *Ethnology* 5 (1966): 34–41.

Tafolla, Carmen. "La Malinche." In *Sonnets and Salsa*. San Antonio: Wings Press, 2004.

Thiselton-Dyer, T. F. *Folk-Lore of Women*. Chicago: A. C. McClurg & Co., 1906.

Thomas, Jeannie Banks. *Naked Barbies, Warrior Joes, and Other Forms of Visible Gender*. Urbana and Chicago: University of Illinois Press, 2003.

Tye, Diane. "Narrative, Gender, and Marginality: The Case Study of Ella Lauchner Smith." *Canadian Folklore canadien*, vol. 13, no. 2 (1991): 25–36.

Wareham, Wilfred. "The Monologue in Newfoundland." In *The Blasty Bough*, ed. Clyde Rose. Portugal Cove, St. Philip's, NL: Breakwater Books, 1976.

Weigle, Marta. *Spiders and Spinsters: Women and Mythology*. Albuquerque: University of New Mexico Press, 1982.

Pauline Greenhill

Folklore of Subversion

Folklore is an accessible tool of subversion because the vernacular—common knowledge—belongs to the people. Folk art forms do not require special training or certification from outside the community. They do not require special equipment and expense. Profoundly accessible, folk arts and folklore are critical tools for disrupting, challenging, and resisting powerful social systems and social injustice.

The performance of folktales, proverbs, jokes, songs, and life stories embodies and transmits cultural traditions and values. These traditions represent a body of shared understandings to which people are intellectually and emotionally committed. However, because folk genres are accessible, fluid, and used contextually, individuals and groups can use them to reformulate cultural notions to comment critically and persuasively on social life. This freedom is significant for both social theory and social change because folk-expressive traditions—drawing on societal knowledge and used spontaneously and creatively by individuals—provide sites at the intersection of culture and human agency.

For women, folk arts have been especially important because women traditionally have had far fewer avenues than men for expression and participation in the public sphere. In many cultures, women and girls have less access to education than do men and boys and may not be able to read and write, but they still produce material culture, oral cultural, dance, and ritual. Through their cultural expressive traditions, women define alternative social ideas and knowledge, articulate opposition to social injustice, and give voice to their creativity and aesthetic values. Even when done from a relatively disempowered position, this resistance is an exercise of power in the social construction of meaning. Culture is not a fixed, unified, or clearly bounded whole, but rather is part of an ongoing process of revision and negotiation. Through their expressive culture, and despite various constraints, women actively participate in this process to produce culture and social knowledge.

Thus, culture often involves subversion, which can be understood in several ways. First, women have used their folk genres to define an alternative cultural space and to critique and subvert patriarchal gender relations. Second, women have used their traditions to subvert oppression against other identity groups to which they belong. Third, women's subversive use of folk practices is sometimes a coded or individual struggle for recognition or change in the face of oppressive gender relations. Finally, some theoretical issues are especially relevant: How do we know to what degree subversive intent lies within a text or in a particular performance in context? To what degree is subversion unconscious or conscious on the part of the performer? Are these subversions of dominant ideology an effective exercise of power?

Here, gender is understood as the social construction of sex. That is, "woman" does not refer to an essential or universal experience, but rather to the cultural ideas and roles that are ascribed to female persons. Therefore, women's culture refers to the body of ideas and social practices within women's spheres of social life. Almost always, within a particular culture the position of women is not only different that that of men, but is characterized by a subordinate position within a male-dominated social order. Through their expressive culture, women challenge and subvert these oppressive power relations; they give voice to their experience, knowledge, and personhood.

For women, sharing stories and personal-experience narratives may be a means of mutual affirmation and mutual recognition that reflects the experience of being gendered—that is, being situated as female within a particular society. For example, in North America in the 1960s, women's consciousness-raising groups created a space for women to share their stories in order to collectively examine their experiences and identify how they were constrained and defined by the gender system. The personal became political.

When women meet and present a worldview that they know is contradictory to men's, it can be seen as an act of rebellion and subversion. In many cultures, women have their own expressive genres through which they comment on their lives in all-women settings. In Turkmenistan, a vast repertoire of women's genres—girls' songs, wedding songs, fortune-telling songs, lullabies, and lamentations—are a means through which women voice their experiences, pain, and dreams. In many societies, including some in Ireland, Greece, New Guinea, and India, women perform distinct genres of oral lament poetry that are often critical of male domination and vent anger at the person who died as well as people in power and the lamenter's relatives. In Jiangyong County, Hunan Province, China, women produced a body of literature in their own written language that is illegible to men although this language is increasingly disused and may die out with the current generation. Women in the Adirondack region of New York State, left out of many of the rituals of hunting culture, organize together, and engage in humorous, subversive discourse that critiques men.

These forms of women's expression may serve to channel anger, sorrow, and trauma in ways that offer a strategy for dealing with life's hardships. For example, Paxtun women in the Northwest Frontier Province of Pakistan share lament narratives with a distinct aesthetic in all-women gatherings. In these tales, women relate personal experiences of suffering and loss, as well as injustice and angry protest. They evaluate the narratives by their degree of pathos: a good story "makes you cry until you don't want to hear more." While they may not like their situation, these women are able to create a realm where they validate and value each other.

The folktales of South Indian women—especially rural, non-literate women—often express women's experiences, and they are often stories of hardship. Several of these South Indian folktales are about stories themselves and affirm the need for stories to be told, suggesting women's consciousness of this process. In Afghan and Persian folklore, the trope of woman as trickster is ambiguous. The image of women as deceptive and untrustworthy is highly negative and draws from the Qu'ranic story of Havá's (Eve in the Judeo-Christian Bible) role in offering the Devil's apple to Adam. However, particular narrators can use women's trickster tales to portray female characters using their trickery as a form of power for the weak toward worthy outcomes and to support justice.

Women's subculture in the Rajasthan province of India encompasses women's own oral genres performed in all-women contexts. Women discuss and joke about sex and tell elaborate stories that mock men. Stories, humor, and songs are important not only for their content, but also for the pleasure, comfort, and bonds resulting from communal laughter at shared experiences and perceptions.

Women may discuss otherwise-taboo topics such as sexuality and being the subjects (not objects) of desire. In Iran, women's genres of humorous games and stories, *baziha*, are shared at all-women gatherings on festive occasions and give expression to women's sexuality and desire. In Morocco, the *shikha* is a woman artist who performs publicly at weddings and other festivities to audiences of both men and women. At these performances, norms about women, gender, and voice are transgressed as the female shikha focuses on sexual themes, affirms the sexual agency of women, and embraces a style characterized by sexually enticing body movements. While this transgression is valued as entertainment in certain settings, shikhas themselves are culturally constructed and socially marginalized as "loose women" because of this type of performance. Meanwhile, shikhas, typically from the poor economic class, gain financially from their performances.

Shikha cultural expression indicates the agency of women and, further, that women do not joyfully and naturally acquiesce to the roles and constraints imposed on them by society. Women, in fact, critically analyze their social situations and engage, even from an often extremely disempowered position, in defining their identities, negotiating power relations, and shaping their societies.

Gender relations are always complex. While women may critique men through their expressive traditions, they may simultaneously strive to preserve the honor of their households and the same men they criticize. Further, while men might be culturally defined as superior to women within a particular group, they might hold an oppressed position relative to other men within wider society.

Also, it is necessary to recognize that women's culture is not always subversive. Folkways may communicate messages regarding how women should conform to their social roles and sometimes warn about the repercussions of violating cultural norms. However, clearly, throughout the world, women articulate their resistance to male dominance, present alternative social interpretations, and offer practical knowledge through folkways and cultural expressive traditions that are specific to various collectivities of women. While folklorists have increasingly examined these traditions over the past thirty years, they have remained largely ignored or unrecognized by laypersons and scholars alike.

Identity is complex. Women's gendered identities intersect and overlap with other socially constructed identities of race, ethnicity, religion, class, sexuality, and politics, all of which encode power relations. That is, some racial, ethnic, religious, or other identities are privileged in relation to others, and cultural knowledge includes awareness of these power differences. Through their expressive culture, women—often in alliance with men—may challenge cultural domination and political violence, or interrogate the constraints of class and changes in the dominant mode of production.

Women in subordinate groups can be multiply marginalized and may use folklore to resist violence against their cultural group and/or sexual violence perpetrated in the context of racism and political violence. Maintaining cultural identity in the face of slavery, colonization, and assimilation is in itself subversive. Women's cultural knowledge and practice is often critical to a group's survival.

Enslaved Africans brought to the Americas, while stripped of all material possessions, retained their systems of knowledge in their minds. While some of their knowledge—for example, regarding rice cultivation and black-smithing—was valued and exploited by slave owners, most African knowledge was feared, dismissed, or actively quelled. To maintain an African-based identity and culture under the conditions of slavery and the prohibition of education was an act of subversion. African knowledge, beliefs, practices, and aesthetics that were retained formed a valuable resource for expressing identity, comfort, and coded communication—all of which can be seen as forms of resistance—during more than four centuries of violent dislocations, slavery, and subsequent oppression. Much of this knowledge was expressed or adapted through African American women's folkways, including oral history and storytelling, religious traditions, quilting, needlepoint, basketweaving, herbalism, healing practices, and cooking. Thus, African American women's folk arts are a critical part of the struggle for freedom and an affirmation of the existence and persistence of a valuable cultural heritage even in the diaspora of the aftermath of slavery.

African American women's expressive traditions were an intellectual resource that could be put to certain specific uses. For example, enslaved women's quilts contained African symbolism, continuing the tradition in many African cultures where women encode secret symbols in textile design. Quilts were used by both enslaved and free women as coded communication during the abolition movement to stamp out the practice of slavery. Quilts intentionally draped over a porch railing might signify through their coded designs, legible only to insiders, that a particular home was a safe haven on the Underground Railroad, a social network that facilitated emigration from slave to free states. Based in large part on interviews with a Gullah quilter who was the descendent of slaves, Tobin and Dobard (1994) argue that some of this symbolism gave reference to a set of survival skills for enslaved people escaping to the North. For example, the pattern "Flying Geese" may have referred to geese whose conspicuous northern flight in the spring serves as a directional guide to those escaping. The pattern "Drunkard's Path" may have indicated that it was important to travel in a non-linear and non-predictable pattern in order to elude capture by trackers.

Cooking practices involved strategies for making do with scarce provisions. The less desirable parts of an animal, typically considered waste products, left for slaves—such as the intestines—were made more appealing with herbs from a small garden in the form of chitlins. To find a way in the face of slavery and social injustice is subversion. To make this way appealing is a folk art.

In Chile in the 1970s and 1980s, lower middle-class, middle-aged women sewed appliqué tapestries, *arpilleras*, which depicted the loss of loved ones due to the political violence that killed tens of thousands under the leadership of Augusto Pinochet. The arpilleras were smuggled out of the country and sold to generate international awareness and raise money as part of these women's "strategies to challenge fear, feed their children, engage in a new form of political activism, and of struggle against authoritarianism" (Agosin 1994: 12). This women-led movement relied on a women's folkloric tradition to voice protest when men's political protest was silenced by murder. Ironically, the lack of significance attributed to women and their sewing traditions allowed their political activism to develop with fewer political reprisals. Meanwhile, many found the practice of telling the story of the violation of their human rights, their loss, and their suffering through this artistic form in the community of other women affirming and comforting.

In South Africa during the 1960s and 1970s, Xhosa oral historians and storytellers—typically male and telling in the courtyards—articulated resistance that was significant for motivating the anti-apartheid struggle. When the government's National Party policies removed men by force from communities to migrant barracks, the absence of the courtyard dramatically constrained this form. Women, however, whose storytelling was associated with the kitchen and hearth, took up this role. Many women storytellers and oral historians performed narratives in order to comment critically on and call for resistance against social injustice.

Resisting Poverty and Commercialization

It is often hard to untangle the issues of class oppression from those of gender or cultural oppression. Often women have less economic power due to gender relations in the family and the occupational spheres that relegate them primarily to the home and out of public contexts. There is an ongoing debate regarding whether class oppression is enforced through racism or racism is simply class oppression in disguise. Clearly, however, women are able to comment critically on economic conditions and contravene economic constraints through their expressive traditions. Also, women's folkways provide strategies for meeting needs and desires despite economic hardship. Further, the significance of women's unpaid domestic work and family leadership for the economic well-being of the household may be the subject of folklore.

In India, as in many parts of the world, power relations are inscribed in food and eating rituals, for example, where members of a household eat in order of their status. The idealized woman controls her appetite so there is more for others, and this ideal is portrayed throughout Indian folklore. This rationalizes the dismissal of women's desire. In the low potter caste near Banaras in Eastern Uttar Pradesh, where they are often denied food for days by mothers and mother-in-laws, women tell folktales in which women satisfy their appetites in ways that fly in the face of convention—and are rewarded by the gods. As potter women have more freedom of movement than women in other castes, they also gather secretly to find ways to secure food for themselves.

In Rangely, Maine, women developed a tradition of cloth doll-making through which they asserted a value system centered on the nurturance of children (Yocom 1993). This tradition, among other community activities, was passed on to daughters, and was the basis of the town's annual children's doll parade over a nearly twenty-year period.

In the face of increasing commercialism, the women maintained their preference for cloth dolls and rejected the expense of commercial dolls that they also saw as inconsistent with their value of children's well-being. They characterized Barbie as the kind of self-centered woman who would abuse her children, and the Cabbage Patch doll with its blank stare as similar to an abused child.

Lower-middle-class and poor women decorate and embellish their homes through folk arts. During the 1960s and 1970s, one Polish-American woman engaged in a number of crafts, making crocheted bedspreads and braided wool rugs for the many members of her family. When shorts skirts were in style, she obtained wool for making braided rugs from 1940s calf-length wool skirts she bought at thrift shops for pennies. She crocheted inexpensive durable acrylic yarn to create colorful washable bedspreads. She crafted bedspreads by sewing together circles of scrap fabric which were gathered in the center to create a flower-like form, and then attached to a solid backing. Shortly before she died, she explained to her granddaughter that she would look in catalogues and desire products that she could not afford: "I made these things so that I could have beautiful things, too" (Satlowski, J., 1996).

Some women's stories comment on women's folklore and folkways. These tales may be seen as reinforcing a gendered division of labor or constraints on women's sexuality, such as the glorification of chastity. But they also speak to the significance of women's labor, roles, and skills in the face of poverty and political violence against the family. A low-caste Indian woman tells a story about a king who asks the queen about the difference between himself and a peasant man. The queen answers his question by trading places with the peasant's wife. Through her thrift and the skillful execution of her household tasks, such as meal preparation, the peasant thrives, and eventually becomes the king. Meanwhile, the king begins to lose everything through the slovenliness of the wife, until he becomes a peasant. This suggests that the identity of the king—including his greatness—is inextricably bound with that of his female partner. This story makes the invisible labor of a woman visible and demonstrates how her unpaid labor has material consequences for her family.

At the beginning of the twenty-first century, women using their folkways as a means to achieve group and economic empowerment may be an intentional transnational process. For example, in southern Uganda, a not-for-profit program, Beads for Life, facilitates the sale of colorful beads handcrafted from paper by women. They are struggling with illness and loss of family members due to AIDS in the context of a long-standing civil war during which thousands of children have been kidnapped by militia and forced to become child soldiers. Through its Web site, http://www.beadsforlife.com, women in North America hold parties where the issues these women face are discussed and their beads are sold. Connie Regan-Blake, one of the leading storytellers of the storytelling renaissance that emerged in the United States in the 1970s, visited Uganda in 2007 to collaborate on projects and performances. Women's folk traditions provide a means for them to connect across boundaries of region, race, class, and language, and to talk about their experience as women within their particular social context and a larger international political economy.

Individuals may also encode feminist messages in their folk arts. The technical skills and aesthetics with which a particular woman executes her craft or performance may resist the drudgery, monotony, and objectification of repetitive utilitarian gendered work and give expression to the intelligence, creativity, and spirit of the individual. Conversely, women may resist domestic labor in a disguised form by professing their incompetence. Or, women may critique women's work through their folktales.

In the field of Cultural Studies, there has been a continuing trend away from seeing meaning as placed in the expressive work through the conscious intentions of its creator, an idea widely critiqued as the "intentionalist fallacy." It is argued, for example, that authors—or performers—may unconsciously encode cultural meaning of which they are unaware into their texts. This theoretical trend has involved questioning the authority of the author who is seen as shaped by the cultural and ideological context within which she is situated, and the recognition of the power of the reader to take oppositional stances to dominant texts, such as classical literature or Hollywood films, and to use those texts in creative and diverse ways.

Meanwhile, in Folklore Studies, there has been an opposite trend toward the recognition of the power of the folk artist to define meaning through the communicative act. Rather than cultural artifacts being classified and dissected in isolation from their context, the folk performer is brought more toward the center of, or even as a partner to, the analysis of discourse. The folk performer's agency in and interpretation of what they do is emphasized.

These different disciplinary trends reflect a common attempt to (1) interrogate the power relations differently encoded in the two disciplines traditionally, and (2) to see aesthetic expression as integrated within its economic, political, and social context. Meaning is seen less as a unitary object to be identified, but rather as a product of social interaction and negotiation among the creative producers, the cultural context, the performance or text, and its recipients. Because folklore encodes culture and because folklore can be used contextually in performance, the analysis of folklore gets at the intersection between culture and human agency. Studies of individual folk artists suggest that these artists bring their own aesthetics to bear in subverting cultural norms that idealize a unitary and essentialized ideal of women in their culture and subverting the monotony of domestic chores—while crafting their own identities and distinctive niches within their cultural group or even within the wider society.

Pueblo potter Helen Cordero invented the Storyteller, which is the clay figure of a male storyteller surrounded by children who are sitting on his legs, climbing his body, or otherwise attached to him. This image represents the male role of telling the sacred stories that regenerate the culture. At the same time, however, Cordero spoke through her pottery, widely celebrated for its artistry, and taught Pueblo pottery to non-Pueblo society. That is, she represented her culture and generated culture in a way usually reserved for men. In fact, the permissibility of her work was much discussed and deliberated among the male elders of her community. Meanwhile, Cordero impacted Pueblo expressive traditions in lasting ways while gaining economic prosperity.

In the early 1990s, an administrator at a major U.S. university participated in an art competition for the staff. At a time that the new chancellor introduced the concept of total quality management, she appropriated the university's organizational chart, a familiar icon to the staff, and substituted male/female icons from the 1950s for the typical boxes used to represent people in the organizational charts. She identified who was male and female in those positions and the distribution portrayed nearly everyone at the lower end of the chart as female and those at the top as male. She also juxtaposed "public" quotes over "private" anonymous quotes she collected from various sources. The overall effect was to expose the difference between corporate rhetoric and practice, implying hypocrisy and casting doubt upon the university's proclaimed altruistic intentions. She was permitted to make public statements that would not normally be tolerated from a university employee. She won the competition's Most Popular and Best in the Show, two honors which the chancellor had to hand to her personally in a public ceremony. One of the few higher ranking female administrators at the university bought the piece for $250 and hung it in her office (Komar 1993).

Women may subvert the pressures of and supposed insignificance of domesticity through coded resistance or, conversely, by honoring skillful domestic work and through competition. Women may claim incompetence at women's chores in order to relieve themselves of them rather than directly refusing to do them. Some folktales describe women rewarded despite their incompetence at a particular chore, such as spinning. Other folktales describe women performing tasks disguised as males for their incompetent husbands and bringing prosperity to their families. These different expressive strategies all disrupt cultural notions of gendered work.

Other folktales describe women performing their traditional tasks skillfully or maintaining chastity through their cleverness with the result that their previously peasant husbands trade places with kings. While such stories embrace and promote notions of gendered work, they ironically elevate women by making the making women's otherwise invisible labor enormously visible and critical to the characters in the story. In North America, at a time when almost all middle-class women were homemakers, women coordinated their domestic chores, and also coordinated leisure time and compared skills. For example, in a Polish American community in Detroit during the 1950s, women did chores such as laundry on the same day of the week. In rural prairie towns in western Canada, women competed to see who would get their chores done first; the first one in the backyard to hang up the laundry was seen as the best housekeeper. These expressive strategies embrace cultural notions of gendered work, but provide ways for women to both work together to support each other and find camaraderie as well as to express and gain recognition for individual skill, adding elements of pleasure to what might otherwise be experienced as drudgery.

Research on women's subversive use of folk expressive traditions raises several theoretical tensions: the question regarding whether subversion can be unconscious, how subversive meaning may be relayed through the text or context of a particular performance, and to what degree subversive expression is in fact empowering or leads to social change. These involve larger issues regarding culture, meaning, and power. More research is required for a better understanding of these significant concepts. Feminist folklore scholarship is significant for social theory in that the research methodologies developed and the insights obtained from these issues can provide knowledge regarding gender, the social construction of meaning, and the negotiation of power relations.

Intentionality Versus Unconscious Subversion

Resistance can be constructed in many ways. Often the subversive content of folklore is coded—that is, not completely overt—allowing its creator plausible deniability because risk is always associated with challenging power. Sometimes this is a life and death risk, and other times the risk is more subtle and complex.

For example, while institutionalized slavery was practiced in the United States, slave songs, quilts, and the rhythm of blacksmith hammering encoded information on safety and escaping to the North. During the 1970s, in a rural town in North Carolina, three women friends conducted elaborate pranks to bring general public embarrassment in two different instances where a man had abused one of their friends, in one case physically and in the second psychologically. The fact that they were the perpetrators of these pranks was never revealed to anyone, including their spouses or the friends who were abused, other than the researcher.

Some have argued that coded resistance may even be unconscious on the part of the performer. For example, Linda Pershing (1993) describes a small quilting group that created a quilt as a surprise for one of its members who was not included in this particular project. The quilt with several panels depicted the popular Sunbonnet Sue, typically a figure of girl-child sweetness, doing actions that compromised the innocent image—for example, smoking, showering with Overall Bill, burning her bra, and pregnant in her wedding dress. While Pershing saw feminist subversion in this quilt, the quiltmakers protested that the quilt simply reflected an innocent prank directed at the quilter who was the recipient of the gift.

Content Versus Context

Increasingly, meaning is recognized to lie neither entirely within a story's text nor within the intentionality of the performer. The tensions regarding where meaning lies and how it is negotiated are central to understanding how women use folklore in subversive ways. Professional feminist storytellers have reflected on how they have appropriated patriarchal stories for feminist purposes. Kay Stone (1993) and Susan Gordon (1993) describe their interpretations of and artistic choices in performing stories from the Grimm brothers' *Kinder- und Hausmärchen.* Gordon describes different settings in which she has told "The Handless Maiden," how some listeners have responded, and how those responses have shaped her own insights about the tale. Both storytellers found and sought to share messages of strength, transformation, and healing in what have often been characterized as patriarchal stories of brutally victimized and punished heroines. Elizabeth Fine (1999) argues that Kentucky storyteller Beverly Carter-Sexton encoded resistance to male dominance and social commentary on Appalachian social relations in her telling of the "Lazy Jack" tale from the body of classic Jack Tales.

How Effective is Subversion?

Arguably, women's subversive discourses actually preserve the status quo by providing a safety valve to release tensions that might otherwise get out of control, ultimately forcing a change in social relations. If subversion remains largely unconscious or unacknowledged, it may not exert much moral pressure. It is also often unclear whether the expression of protest or alternative perspectives leads to a change in power relations or social norms.

Meaning is fluid, and it is not always clear if the meaning of a particular text or performance is, in fact, subversive. Texts typically have inherent ambiguities, opening them to alternative interpretations and uses by diverse audiences. Texts are multivocal. Even a performer's own discussion of her work can be disputed as reflecting historical and cultural ideology in ways in which the creator is unaware. Culture is a dynamic negotiation of meaning in which the participants may not have equal power. Women are active in this process, which often requires subverting domination based on gender and heterosexism, and other times subverting domination toward both men and women in their cultural or economic groups.

When women share their stories and experience, they are affirmed. While they may not like their situation, there is a realm where women recognize, validate, and value each other. While such a space might be seen only as a safety valve, these moments may help provide comfort in a way that promotes mental and even physical health during various personal or household challenges, hardship, or crises. Critical information that helps others survive may be exchanged in these settings. Even when they do not directly call for change, such performances do provide a place where women's experience and perspective are privileged. This can be seen as a site of resistance and incipient protest. It speaks to the fact that people can remain free to interpret and define their experiences.

Women have often been the preservers of culture and physical survival in the face of severe oppression or genocide. Women are more likely to physically survive political violence and genocide, as for example in Rwanda after the 1994 genocide there. The dismissal of women's culture works to the advantage of their group when women are less scrutinized by authorities and therefore more able to carry on cultural traditions without punishment or death. In the south Siberian provinces of Khakassia and Tuva, during political and religious persecution, women shamans became increasingly prominent as they were less likely to be perceived as a threat to the authorities, which allowed for the preservation of some culture. Similarly, the home is more inscrutable than other arenas of social life. For African Americans, the home functioned as a critical site of resistance—characterized by safety, dignity, and an integrity of being—where women created a sanctuary from the harsh and life-threatening economic and political realities of racist oppression, "where all that truly matters in life took place" (hooks 1990).

Individual women draw on this body of women's culture in different ways, making daily choices regarding how to negotiate power and meaning in their lives. This may have some impact on their lives and be a resource for women to survive or even thrive. Thus, Raheja and Gold (1994) argue that women's expressive traditions have "narrative potency"—that is, they operate in the world and get results. *See also:* Class; Coding; Consciousness Raising; Dolls; Eve; Folk Art; Folk Music and Folksong; Folktale; Foodways; Gardens; Gender; Gullah Women's Folklore; Joke; Lament; Lullaby; Personal-Experience Narrative; Politics; Pottery; Proverb; Quiltmaking; Race; Rugmaking; Sexuality; Sunbonnet Sue; Storytelling; Tradition; Violence; Wage Work; Women's Work.

Jessica Senehi

References

Agosin, Marjorie. *Tapestries of Hope, Threads of Love.* Albuquerque: University of New Mexico Press, 1996.

Babcock, Barbara A. "'At Home, No Womens are Storytellers': Potteries, Stories, and Politics in Cochiti Pueblo." In *Feminist Messages: Coding in Women's Folk Culture,* ed. Joan Newlon Radner, 221–248. Urbana: University of Illinois Press, 1993.

Blackwell, Carol. *Tradition and Society in Turkmenistan: Gender, Oral Culture and Song.* Richmond: Curzon Press, 2001.

Bourke, Angela. "More in Anger than in Sorrow: Irish Women's Lament Poetry." In *Feminist Messages: Coding in Women's Folk Culture,* ed. Joan Newlon Radner, 160–182. Urbana: University of Illinois Press, 1993.

Coughran, Neema. "Fasts, Feasts, and the Slovenly Women: Strategies among North Indian Potter Women." *Asian Folklore Studies,* vol. 57, no. 12 (1999): 257–274.

Fine, Elizabeth. "'Lazy Jack': Coding and Contextualizing Resistance in Appalachian Women's Narratives." *National Women's Studies Association (NWSA) Journal,* vol. 11, no. 3 (1999): 112–137.

Fox-Genovese, Elizabeth. *Within the Plantation Household: Black and White Women of the Old South.* Chapel Hill: University of North Carolina Press, 1988.

Fuchs, Denise. Personal communication, 2005.

Gordon, Susan. "The Powers of the Handless Maiden." In *Feminist Messages: Coding in Women's Folk Culture,* ed. Joan Newlon Radner, 252–288. Urbana: University of Illinois Press, 1993.

Grima, Benedicte. *The Performance of Emotion among Paxtun Women: "The Misfortunes Which Have Befallen Me."* Austin: University of Texas Press, 1992.

Hofmeyr, Isabel. "Not the Magic Talisman: Rethinking Oral Literature in South Africa." *World Literature Today,* vol. 70, no. 1 (1996): 88–93.

hooks, bell. *Yearning: Race, Gender, and Cultural Politics.* Boston, MA: South End Press, 1990.

Kapchan, Deborah A. "Moroccan Female Performers Defining the Social Body." *Journal of American Folklore,* vol. 107, no. 423 (1994): 82–105.

Komar, Amy. Personal communication, June 5, 2003.

Jassal, Smita Tewari. "Bhojpuri Songs, Women's Work and Social Control in Northern India." *Journal of Peasant Studies,* vol. 30, no. 2 (2003): 159–206.

Lanser, Susan S. "Burning Dinners: Subversions of Domesticity." In *Feminist Messages: Coding in Women's Folk Culture,* ed. Joan Newlon Radner, 36–53. Urbana: University of Illinois Press, 1993.

Liu, Fei-Wen. *Women Who De-silence Themselves: Male-Illegible Literature (Nushu) and Female-Specific Songs (Nuge) in Jiangyong County, Hunan Province, China.* PhD diss., Department of Anthropology, Syracuse University, 1997.

McMahon, Felicia. "The Worst Piece of 'Tale': Flaunted 'Hidden Transcripts' in Women's Play." *Play Theory & Research*, vol. 1, no. 4 (1992): 251–258.

Mills, Margaret A. "The Gender of the Trick: Female Tricksters and Male Narrators." *Asian Folklore Studies*, vol. 60, no. 2 (2001): 237–258.

Parks, Francis McMillan. Personal communication, November 28, 1994.

Pershing, Linda. "'She Really Wanted to Be Her Own Woman': Scandalous Sunbonnet Sue." In *Feminist Messages: Coding in Women's Folk Culture*, ed. Joan Newlon Radner, 98–125. Urbana: University of Illinois Press, 1993.

Radner, Joan Newlon, ed. *Feminist Messages: Coding in Women's Folk Culture.* Urbana: University of Illinois Press, 1993.

Raheja, Gloria Goodwin, and Ann Grodzins Gold. *Listen to the Heron's Words: Reimagining Gender and Kinship in North India.* Berkeley: University of California Press, 1994.

Ramanujan, A. K. "Toward a Counter-System: Women's Tales." In *Gender, Genre, and Power in South Asian Expressive Traditions,* eds. Arjun Appadurai, Frank J. Korom, and Margaret A. Mills, 33–55. Philadelphia: University of Pennsylvania Press, 1991.

Safa-Isfahani, Kaveh. "Female-Centered World Views in Iranian Culture: Symbolic Respresentations of Sexuality in Dramatic Games." *Signs*, vol. 6, no. 1 (1980): 33–53.

Satlowski, Genevieve. Personal communication, April 16, 1996.

Satlowski, Jane. Personal communication, April 18, 1996.

Senehi, Jessica. Fieldnotes, May 22, 1997.

Stone, Kay F. "Burning Brightly: New Light from an Old Tale." In *Feminist Messages: Coding in Women's Folk Culture,* ed. Joan Newlon Radner, 289–306. Urbana: University of Illinois Press, 1993.

Stone, Kay, with Marvyne Jenoff and Susan Gordon. "Difficult Women in Folktales: Two Women, Two Stories." In *Undisciplined Women: Tradition and Culture in Canada*, eds. Pauline Greenhill and Diane Tye. 250–265. Montreal: McGill-Queen's University Press, 1997.

Tobin, Jacqueline L., and Raymond C. Dobard. *Hidden in Plain View: A Secret Story of Quilts and the Underground Railroad.* New York: Anchor, 1999.

Van Deusen, Kira. *Singing Story, Healing Drum: Shamans and Storytellers of Turkic Siberia.* Montreal: McGill-Queen's University Press, 2004.

Wadley, Susan S. *Struggling with Destiny in Karimpur.* Berkeley: University of California Press, 1994.

Yocom, Margaret R. "'Awful Real': Dolls and Development in Rangely, Maine." In *Feminist Messages: Coding in Women's Folk Culture*, ed. Joan Newlon Radner, 126–154. Urbana: University of Illinois Press, 1993.

Women Folklorists

Women folklorists include all female persons trained in the academic practice of Folklore Studies (folkloristics), and, by some definitions, women who, while not having had formal training, nonetheless collect, analyze, theorize, or valorize traditional and popular culture. Not all women folklorists study women's folklore, and not all those who study women's folklore are women. Further, not all women folklorists are feminists and not all feminist folklorists are women.

As in other academic areas, what many women—feminist or otherwise—bring to the study of folklore is what gender and science feminist scholar Evelyn Fox Keller calls "a feeling for the organism," referring to the theory, methods, and analysis advanced by geneticist Barbara McClintock. Enlisting their "feeling for the organism" is part of how women folklorists—especially but not exclusively feminists—have redefined the field of Folklore and reconfigured its study in terms of personal identification with its subjects (human) and objects (texts of all kinds—material, social, verbal, musical, ritual, and so on). Women folklorists generally want to understand these subjects and objects as much as possible from the subjects' and objects' own perspectives. For example, feminist folklorist and anthropologist Ruth Bunzel, studying Pueblo pottery, did not just talk to potters about their techniques and designs; she apprenticed herself to them and learned how to make the pots herself. This kind of hands-on research technique gives scholars a deep, experiential understanding of creation, construction, and style.

Part of their "feeling for the organism" comes from the fact that many women folklorists have been insiders in the cultures they study. Their perspective is already empathic in interpretation. Such researchers don't want to be, nor do they claim to be, objective—in the sense of being distanced and/or unbiased—in their perspectives. Rather, they acknowledge their personal location and use it as a tool to engage directly with their material. Bias is always present in any work, but acknowledged bias can aid in comprehending why a scholar sees and interprets the world as she does. Understanding researcher subjectivity, then, is generally more important to women folklorists than attempting an objectivity that ultimately cannot be achieved.

The value of many women folklorists' work is in bringing both insider understanding and scholarly rigor to the analysis. As scholars, they exhibit what feminist anthropologist Donna Haraway calls "the privilege of partial perspective" (1988) in two senses. First, as individuals who are involved with and compelled by the people, events, and texts they study, they have special access to insider knowledge about them, and they approach that knowledge in a spirit of critical appreciation. Second, they recognize that their perspective is not and can never be complete; it is only one of many possible understandings of a group or genre. In sum, rather than suspending their own feelings and understandings, women folklorists often enlist them as essential parts of their theory and practice.

Historically, women folklorists of all intellectual and scholarly backgrounds, but particularly those not formally trained in academic folkloristics, have been dismissed and belittled by the mainstream/malestream of the discipline. Women folklorists' experiences in the academy have not always been happy ones; they have been derogated, dismissed, and diminished, often quite openly and directly (see for example Stekert 1987). However, thanks to the rise of feminist folkloristics in the 1970s, their work is now being reevaluated and their contributions recognized. At the American Folklore Society meeting in Austin, Texas, in 1972, women folklorists who recognized the need to turn concerted attention to women's folklore and women's folklife began to organize themselves in a caucus within the Society (the caucus eventually became the Women's Section).

Even before the second wave of feminism brought many women into colleges and universities, many studied, researched, and wrote as academic folklorists. Zora Neale Hurston (1891–1960)—an African American writer and fieldworker trained at Barnard College by anthropologists Franz Boas, Ruth Benedict, and Margaret Mead—was a member of the Harlem Renaissance, a scholar, and social activist. Probably her best known folklore study is *Mules and Men* (1935), but she also worked as a journalist and wrote novels, the most famous being *Their Eyes Were Watching God* (1937). Her work, written clearly from the perspective of an insider, seeks to represent the perspectives and language of African Americans. It breaks the boundary between fiction writing, memoir, and folklore theory.

Elsie Clews Parsons (1875–1941), a privileged White American folklorist, was also "an early feminist sociologist and pacifist who used her wealth, position, and intellect to champion social freedom and women's rights" (Babcock 396). She used her personal wealth to support anthropological and folkloristic research, and was herself a prodigious and well-published researcher. However, it is only recently that folklorists have taken Parsons and her work seriously. Criticized by influential folklorist Richard Dorson for attempting unsuccessfully to emulate male scholarship in a "rigid and colorless" way (quoted in Babcock 397), Parsons was also the subject of revisionist work that inappropriately focused on her "personal life and eccentricities" (Joanne Mulcahy, quoted in ibid. 398) rather than on her scholarship.

Edith Fowke (1913–1996) researched Canadian folklore. From her earliest involvement with traditional and popular culture, she maintained a dialogue with the intellectual and social currents of her time, but felt she never achieved the recognition and status she deserved. She saw her intellectual practice as meriting the status of a "professional" folklorist; in the United States particularly, being a professional was the ideal of the discipline. She was a prodigious collector and publisher of an extraordinary range of folklore materials from folksongs and ballads to children's lore, and she authored a variety of scholarly books and articles. Nevertheless, she was rejected by academic folklorists as a popularizer, abhorred some forms of theorizing in the discipline, and despite her call for tolerance and open-mindedness, held many apparently unshakeable views about the centrality of Anglo culture in Canada and the need for folklorists to concentrate their efforts on textual materials only.

Feminist folklorist Pauline Greenhill has called Fowke a "paradox" for her ambiguous relationship to feminism, nationalism, and radical leftist politics. While Fowke was politically radical—too far left for parts of the socialist New Democratic Party of the 1940s to 1960s—she was academically conservative. Though she published labor songbooks (for example, Fowke and Glazer 1973), her analysis of labor, industrial, and protest song was limited and near-sighted. While she sought to become known as Canada's premiere folklorist, she tried even harder to obtain recognition from folklorists in the United States, whom she regarded as constituting the discipline's intellectual center. Finally, though Fowke described herself as a feminist, she rarely employed a women-focused perspective in her work. Greenhill concludes: "I don't wish to suggest that Fowke was not radical, feminist, nor nationalist; I'm suggesting instead that the radical, feminist, and nationalist qualities that seemed to pervade her other activities do not seem to have made their way into her studies of traditional culture" (2003: 30).

Women not academically trained in folkloristics whose contributions have recently been reevaluated include two Nova Scotian Canadians whose works have been assessed from feminist perspectives by feminist folklorist Diane Tye. Helen Creighton was a self-taught folklore collector whose studies encompassed, for example, First Nations, Gaelic, Scottish, and Acadian traditions; and songs, beliefs, magic, and folktales. Creighton herself was a believer in predestination; for example, she believed that being born with a caul made her lucky. The fact that she came from a historic Nova Scotian family—though her class status was often, but not always, higher than those from whom she collected—made her very much an insider; she was personally a nationalist and Nova Scotia booster. Though mainstream folklorists dismissed her as a little old lady, too prudish to use alcohol to get people to cooperate in her fieldwork, her eclectic collecting and publication and her appreciation for traditional culture are now considered valuable assets for a fieldworker. Tye comments that the "principles that underlie her work are as complex as those that motivate academic folklorists" (Tye 2005).

Jean Heffernan, a local columnist for Springhill, Nova Scotia's *Amherst Daily News* in the 1950s, was not the kind of writer usually perceived as a folklorist or ethnographer. Her work, though it describes a wide range of social and cultural activities in Springhill, is often dismissed as mere reportage. Yet Diane Tye convincingly argues not only that Heffernan's intentions were ethnographic—cultural description—but also that exactly because she was not trained in the folkloristics of her time, she transcended many of its limitations. She recognized her community's ethnic diversity, where other Canadian folklorists of the period might have limited their vision almost exclusively to Anglo materials. She considered industrial and workers' traditions, rather than holding to the anti-modernist view then in academic vogue, which saw rural cultures as the true (and sometimes the only) folk societies. She looked at women's activities well before they were understood as central to understanding cultures. And she understood popular traditions as ongoing parts of community life, not as dying vestiges of outdated notions.

Women folklorists in Latino communities in the United States worked in the twentieth century to document the traditional cultures and customs of Latino communities in New Mexico, Texas, Arizona, and Puerto Rico. Jovita González de Mireles completed her master's degree in Folklore at the University of Texas under the direction of J. Frank Dobie in 1930, published numerous essays in the journal of the Texas Folklore Society, and became president of the society. She wrote numerous articles on the folklore of south Texas and an historical novel, *Caballero* (1996). She lived in Corpus Christi, Texas, where she taught bilingual education. Other Tejana students of traditional culture whose work focused on the traditions of south Texas are Femina Guerra (1941a, 1941b), Soledad Perez (1951), and Rogelia Garcia (1970).

In New Mexico, Cleofás M. Jaramillo was a founding member of the Santa Fe Folklore Society, while Aurora Lucero White Lea was deeply involved in the collection and classification of Latino regional folklore, as evidenced in her best-known books, *The Folklore of New Mexico* (1941) and *Literary*

Folklore of the Hispanic Southwest (1953). Carmen Gertrudis Espinosa (1970) and Mela Sedillo (1935, 1937) also conducted their research in New Mexico. In Arizona, Luisa Espinel (1946) and Patricia Preciado Martin (1992) collected the traditional Spanish-language songs and lore of the region. Maria Herrera Sobek, author of *The Mexican Corrido: A Feminist Analysis* (1993), did her work on the ballad form and on various other folk genres, including *pastorelas* (Christmas plays) and children's folklore. The first anthology of Chicana folklorists, *Chicana Traditions: Continuity and Change* (Cantú and Najera Ramirez 2002), was a significant step, but much remains to be done in the area of U.S. Latina Folklore Studies.

Some Latina folklorists have worked in the public sector; such is the case of Brazilian Maria Carmen Gambliel in Idaho, and Mexican Olivia Cadaval and Chicana Alicia Gonzalez at the Smithsonian Institution. Noted women who value the traditional arts and foster the development of folklore projects in the Latino community include Carmen Febo-San Miguel, who runs the Taller Puertoriqueño Cultural Center in Philadelphia, and Graciela Sánchez, the director of the Esperanza Peace and Justice Center in San Antonio. Aside from the work of ethnomusicologists like Laura Larco, who has studied Peru's folk music, and Brenda Romero, who explores both U.S. and Mexican musical traditions, little has been done to document the role of women in Latino folk music traditions.

Since Zamora O'Shea in the 1930s, creative writers have also chronicled Latino folklore. Among their contemporary works are numerous publications on folklore geared for children by women like Chicana Pat Mora (2000, 2004) and Puerto Riceñas Marisa Montes (2000) and Carmen Bernier-Grand (2002). These women's work, enriched because of their cultural insider's perspective, attests to their commitment to the preservation of traditional cultural practices.

Public Folklore in the United States has been extensively affected by women folklorists, who have been part of that field since its inception. Until recently, however, they were not recognized as folklorists. Most were in unofficial, unpaid, and generally unrecognized positions. Around the turn of the twentieth century and into the 1930s, much of their work was a combination of settlement and missionary work designed to uplift isolated rural communities or poverty-stricken urban areas.

In the early years of the twentieth century, Massachusetts-born Olive Dame Campbell (1882–1954) worked with her husband, John, to document Appalachian culture in western North Carolina. She not only documented cultural traditions but also, most significantly, played an active role in making sure her own and others' work was preserved and passed along via the John C. Campbell Folk School in Brasstown, North Carolina, still a going concern today. Dame Campbell established the school in memory of her husband and was instrumental in establishing its philosophy, based on the Scandinavian folk school model for adult education.

A more academic but still socially motivated group of American women entered the field in the 1920s, including luminaries such as Zora Neale Hurston, whose fieldnotes concerning folksongs, games, tales, and beliefs are part of the archival holdings at the American Folklife Center at the Library of Congress. While Hurston was in Florida, Sidney Robertson Cowell (1903–1995) was documenting folksongs around the United States. Born in San Francisco, Cowell worked as a music educator in California, where she studied with composer Ernest Bloch and composer, theorist, performer, teacher, publisher, and impresario Henry Cowell. The director of the Social Music Program of the Henry Street Settlement on the Lower East Side of New York, she also worked for ethnomusicologist Charles Seeger during the 1930s and collected folk music in Virginia, Arkansas, Tennessee, and North Carolina. At the fourth National Folk Festival in 1938, she recorded Swedish, Lithuanian, Norwegian, and Finnish music performed by Chicagoans and Finnish, Gaelic, and Serbian music performed by Minnesotans. She also worked for the Farm Security Administration (FSA), one of Franklin Roosevelt's New Deal agencies, to assist new immigrants in Wisconsin, Minnesota, and Michigan. Later, in Washington, DC, Cowell crucially developed and sought funding for folksong collecting projects through arts organizations. In the late 1930s, she began to document folk music in California as part of the Works Progress Administration (WPA); she and Eleanora Black published *The Gold Rush Song Book* in 1940.

By the turn of the twenty-first century, women dominated Public Folklore positions in the United States. Significant contributions to public sector discourse and practice have been made by Winnie Lambrecht in Rhode Island, Alexandra Swaney in Montana, Andrea Graham in Nevada and South Dakota, Maida Owens in Louisiana, Tina Bucuvalas in Florida, Riki Saltzman in Iowa, Maria Carmen Gambliel in Idaho, Joyce Ice at the International Museum of Folk Art in Santa Fe, Betsy Peterson at the Fund for Folk Culture in New Mexico, Amy Skillman at the Institute for Cultural Partnerships in Pennsylvania, and Betty Belanus at the Smithsonian Institution in Washington, DC. Their many accomplishments include publications, films, festivals, folk arts in education programs, radio shows, Web sites, and refugee arts initiatives and advocacy programs.

Women folklorists have also long been involved with the establishment of not-for-profit folklife programs. With Bill Ferris, Judy Peiser founded the Center for Southern Folklore in the 1970s. In the 1980s, Jane Beck founded the Vermont Folklife Center; Betsy Peterson, Kay Turner, and Pat Jasper started Texas Folklife Resources; and Debora Kodish established the Philadelphia Folklore Project. In the early part of the twenty-first century, Amy Kitchener founded the Alliance for California Traditional Arts and Gwen Meister launched the Nebraska Folklife Network.

Much of this activity could not have occurred without Bess Lomax Hawes, the first director (1977–1991) of the National Endowment for the Arts' (NEA) Folk Arts Program, now known as the Folk and Traditional Arts Program. Fondly known as "Bess" to her colleagues, she grew up in Texas with her father John Lomax, who with his brother, Alan, was among the first to document American folksongs as distinct from European forms and to regard seriously the folklore of working-class Americans. Hawes collaborated with them on *Our Singing Country: Folk Songs and Ballads* (1941) and on folksong transcriptions with Ruth Crawford Seeger. She later became part of New York City's folksong revival as a member of the Almanac

Singers. With Bessie Jones, she coauthored *Step It Down* (1972), a book about African American children's games. Hawes began working for the Smithsonian in the mid-1970s. In what is probably her most influential role, Hawes worked during her long tenure at the NEA to firmly establish national and state Folklore Programs. When she retired in 1991, she had nearly achieved her goal of having a folk arts coordinator in place in every U.S. state. Hawes was also central, along with Nancy Hanks, in creating the NEA's National Heritage fellowships, awarded annually to deserving folk and traditional artists around the United States.

Nancy Sweezy, recipient of the NEA's 2006 Bess Lomax Hawes National Heritage Advocacy award, began influencing the field by documenting and publicizing a pottery style favored in the South. In the 1950s, Sweezy, a New Englander and a potter herself, worked with Ralph Rinzler to start a craft program as part of the annual Newport Folk Festival. Also with Rinzler, and with weaver and National Heritage Fellow Norman Kennedy, she founded Country Roads, Inc., a not-for-profit organization committed to researching and marketing folk crafts. Sweezy moved to Seagrove, North Carolina, in 1968, where she started an apprenticeship program at Jugtown Pottery, improved its practices, and changed its marketing strategies. She wrote *Raised in Clay: The Southern Folk Pottery Tradition* (1984). In the 1980s, Sweezy, in concert with the International Institute of Boston, secured NEA funding to help large numbers of Southeast Asian refugees document their own traditions as they adjusted to life in the United States. The result was a series of still-ongoing festivals, workshops, exhibitions, apprenticeships, and school programs focusing on Cambodian, Lao, Hmong, and Vietnamese folk artists.

Another woman central to American Public Folklore is Peggy Bulger, director of the American Folklore Center (AFC) at the Library of Congress since 1999. Bulger has been a folksinger, Florida's first State Folk Arts coordinator, administrator at the Bureau of Florida Folklife Programs, and director of folk arts at the Southern Arts Federation. Best known for documenting a variety of folk and traditional Florida artists, she is also coauthor with Tina Bucuvalas and Stetson Kennedy of *South Florida Folklife* (1994), the editor of *Musical Roots of the South* (1992), and the producer of *Deep South Musical Roots Tour* (1992) and *Drop On Down in Florida* (1981). During her time at the Library of Congress, she spearheaded the development and expansion of the Veterans' History Project and created partnerships with state folk arts coordinators to bring traditional artists from across the United States to perform at the Library of Congress and the Kennedy Center in Washington, DC.

Public sector women folklorists demonstrate the ongoing connections that women have maintained in the field between activism and scholarship. Those links are also sustained by a growing number of American women academic folklorists who are gaining accolades and professional respect for their writing and teaching on a wide variety of methods, theories, traditions, and genres. Some women trained in folkloristics have become known beyond the discipline. Among them are Barbara Kirshenblatt-Gimblett, author of *Image Before My Eyes: A Photographic History of Jewish Life in*

Poland, 1864–1939 (1977), now established in Performance Studies and in Hebrew and Judaic Studies, and Rayna Green, editor of *The Encyclopedia of the First Peoples of North America* (2000), celebrated in anthropological circles for her insider knowledge of First Nations cultures as well as for her wry commentary upon White appropriation of it.

A few individuals like Elli Kaija Köngäs Maranda, whose work with her husband, Pierre Maranda, resulted in numerous publications on Finnish and Finnish American folklore and structuralist theory, and Linda Dégh, especially notable for her work on Hungarian and American legends, beliefs, and folktales, honed their feminist analysis in male-dominated Folklore Departments. At a time when far fewer women had academic positions, they were recognized for their theoretical sophistication and depth of cultural understanding. Many women pioneered particular areas of folklore research. For example, Karen Baldwin, author of *Folk Arts and Folklife in and around Pitt County: A Handbook and Resource Guide* (1990) and coeditor of *Herbal and Magical Medicine: Traditional Healing Today* (1992), was among the first to understand and appreciate family folklore and to recognize the family as a cultural group that sustains but also develops its own traditions.

But feminist folkloristics per se found its first official recognition in a special issue of the *Journal of American Folklore* (*JAF* 88, no. 347), published in 1975, edited by Claire R. Farrer, and republished in 1986 as *Women and Folklore: Images and Genres*. Farrer's introduction established research on women as having a history as well as a future. Remarkably diverse—including work on new and old genres, and diverse groups, languages, and locales—the publication made Susan Kalčik, Inez Cardozo-Freeman, Beverly J. Stoeltje, and Kay F. Stone particularly, as well as Farrer herself, some of the official foremothers of feminist folkloristics in North America.

Twelve years later, in 1987, another special issue of *JAF*, more boldly entitled *Folklore and Feminism*, showed how far research by and about women had come and again reflected a wide variety of study areas and genres. Particularly telling were works by Barbara Babcock, Debora Kodish, and Ellen J. Stekert that reflect upon women's experiences conducting folkloristic research. The issue also included Joan N. Radner and Susan S. Lanser's first iteration of their now enormously influential concept of feminist coding, as well as work by Marta Weigle, whose *Spiders and Spinsters* (1982) is arguably the first monograph in American feminist folkloristics.

Other distinguished women who participated in the 1987 issue include Kay Turner, mentioned above, who brought feminist folkloristic perspectives to popular studies of women's altars and later published on lesbian love letters and dream narratives; Margaret K. Brady, who worked with Navajo and Mormon peoples; Elaine J. Lawless, who developed the concept of "reciprocal ethnography," a method by which she and her consultants' interpretations meet in the written text they produce, explored the lives of women preachers in *Holy Women, Wholly Women* (1993), and became an editor of *JAF*; and Rachelle H. (Riki) Saltzman, mentioned above, who became a well-respected public folklorist. A special issue of the *Journal of Folklore Research*, edited by Beverly J. Stoeltje, appeared in 1988 (*JFR* 25, no. 3) and included work by Patricia Sawin on women in the Finnish epic *Kalevala*, as well as Stoeltje's own studies on gender in the American rodeo.

Contributors to the 1987 *JAF* issue, Susan Tower Hollis and M. Jane Young, with Linda Pershing, edited and contributed to a collection entitled *Feminist Theory and the Study of Folklore* (1993), which also includes significant articles by Rayna Green, Debora Kodish, Amy Shuman, Margaret R. Yocom, Elaine Lawless, Robbie E. Davis-Floyd, and Judith Levin, among others. Pershing is also celebrated for her linking of feminist folkloristics with Peace Studies, as in her *The Ribbon Around the Pentagon: Peace by Piecemakers* (1996).

Two other pivotal collections of essays by American women feminist academic folklorists are noteworthy. In 1985, Rosan A. Jordan and Susan J. Kalčik edited *Women's Folklore, Women's Culture,* which includes now-classic works by the editors as well as by Margaret R. Yocom, whose article reflects on women folklorists conducting fieldwork with other women; Susan Roach on quilting; Janet Langlois on serial killer Belle Gunness; Carol Mitchell on joke telling; and Margaret Mills—who had also written extensively on the trajectory of women and feminism in American folklorists—on sex, sexuality, and transgender in Afghan oral tradition. Underlining their importance as women folklorists, Stone and Baldwin also contributed to this special issue.

Joan N. Radner's *Feminist Messages*, published in 1993, includes a study by Polly Stewart on classic ballads, one by Angela Bourke on Irish women's laments, and another by Cheryl L. Keyes on female rappers. Feminist folklorists Pershing, Yocom, Babcock, and Stone also contributed. Women folklorists were the first to directly apply notions of coding to the understanding of women's culture. The concept of feminist coding has since been employed by theorists to examine a wide range of texts and practices, but has also been extended to lesbian, gay, and bisexual culture.

Since the early 1990s, the numbers of women academics doing feminist folkloristics have increased tremendously; mentioning each one would be an impossibly giant task, worthy of a folktale heroine. Indeed, even trying to note the most significant women folklorist foremothers is daunting—and like older sisters in folktales, we have undoubtedly failed. The successful completion of such a task will require the most resourceful, capable, and quick-witted younger sister—not mere humans like ourselves! *See also:* Aesthetics; American Folklore Society—Women's Section; Ballad; Feminisms; Festival; Fieldwork; Film; Folk Art; Folk Drama; Folklife; *Folklore Feminists Communication*; Folk Music and Folksong; Folktale; Immigration; Pottery; Public Folklore; Region: Canada; Region: Mexico; Region: United States; Tradition-Bearer; Women's Folklore.

Norma E. Cantú, Pauline Greenhill, and Rachelle H. Saltzman

References

Abrahamian, Lavon, Nancy Sweezy, and Sam Sweezy, eds. *Armenian Folk Arts, Culture, and Identity*. Bloomington, IN: Indiana University Press, 2001.

Babcock, Barbara A. "Taking Liberties, Writing from the Margins, and Doing It with a Difference." *Journal of American Folklore* 398 (1987): 390–411.

Bernier-Grand. Carmen T. *Shake It, Morena!: And Other Folklore of Puerto Rico*. Brookfield, CT: Millbrook Press, 2002.

Black, Eleanora, and Sidney Robertson Cowell. *The Gold Rush Song Book*. San Francisco: Colt Press, 1940.

Bucuvalas, Tina, Peggy Bulger, and Stetson Kennedy. *South Florida Folklife* (Folklife in the South Series). Oxford, MS: University Press of Mississippi, 1994.

Bulger, Peggy, ed. *Musical Roots of the South*. Atlanta, GA: Southern Arts Federation, 1992.

Bunzel, Ruth Leah. *The Pueblo Potter: A Study of Creative Imagination in Primitive Art*. New York: Dover Publications, 1972 [1929].

———. *Juan Bobo: Four Folktales from Puerto Rico*. New York: Harper Collins, 1994.

Cabeza de Baca Gilbert, Fabiola. *We Fed Them Cactus*. Albuquerque: University of New Mexico Press, 1994 [1954].

Castro, Rafaela G. *A Dictionary of Chicano Folklore: A Guide to the Folktales, Traditions, Rituals and Religious Practices of Mexican Americans*. Santa Barbara, CA: ABC-Clio, Inc., 2000.

Cantú, Norma E., and Olga Najera Ramirez, eds. *Chicana Traditions: Continuity and Change*. Urbana: University of Illinois Press, 2002.

de Caro, F. A. "The Women's Movement in A. F. S.: A Brief Chronology." *The Folklore Historian* 1: 1–4 (1975).

Espinel, Luisa. *Canciones de Mi Padre: Spanish Folksongs from Southern Arizona*. Tucson: University of Arizona, 1946.

Espinosa, Carmen Gertrudis. *Shawls, Crinolines, Filigree: The Dress and Adornment of the Women of New Mexico, 1739–1900*. El Paso: Texas Western Press, 1970.

Farrer, Claire R. *Women and Folklore: Images and Genres*. Prospect Heights, IL: Waveland Press, 1986.

Fowke, Edith. "A Personal Odyssey and Personal Prejudices." In *Undisciplined Women: Tradition and Culture in Canada*, eds. Pauline Greenhill and Diane Tye, 39–48. Montreal: McGill-Queen's University Press, 1997.

——— and Joe Glazer. *Songs of Work and Protest*. New York: Dover Publications, 1973.

Garcia, Rogelia O. *Dolores, Revilla, and Laredo (Three Sister Settlements)*. Waco, TX: Texian Press, 1970.

Greenhill, Pauline. "Radical? Feminist? Nationalist? The Canadian Paradox of Edith Fowke." *The Folklore Historian* 20 (2003): 22–33.

——— and Diane Tye. *Undisciplined Women: Tradition and Culture in Canada*. Montreal: McGill-Queen's University Press, 1997.

Gonzalez de Mireles, Jovita. "Tales and Sons of the Texas–Mexicans." In *Man, Bird, and Beast*, ed. J. Frank Dobie. 86–116. Austin: Texas Folklore Society, 1930a.

———. "Social Life in Cameron, Starr, and Zapata Counties." Master's thesis, University of Texas, 1930b.

———. "Among My People." In *Tone the Bell Easy: Slave Songs, Mexican Tales, Treasure Lore*, ed. J. Frank Dobie, 99–108. Austin: Texas Folklore Society, 1965 [1932].

———. *Dew on the Thorn*, ed. José E. Limón. Houston: Arte Publico Press, 1997.

Guerra, Fermina. "Mexican and Spanish Folklore and Incidents in Southeast Texas." Master's thesis, University of Texas, 1941a.

———. "Rancho Buena Vista: Its Ways of Life and Traditions." In *Texian Stomping Grounds*, eds. J. Frank Dobie, Mody C. Boatright, and Harry H. Ransom, 59–77. Dallas: Southern Methodist University Press, 1967 [1941b].

Haraway, Donna. "Situated Knowledges: The Science Question in Feminism and the Privilege of Partial Perspective." *Feminist Studies*, vol. 14, no. 3 (1988): 575–599.

Herrera-Sobek, María. *The Mexican Corrido: A Feminist Analysis*. Bloomington: Indiana University Press, 1990.

———. *Chicano Folklore: A Handbook*. Westport, CT: Greenwood Press, 2006.

Hewitt, Mark, and Nancy Sweezy. *The Potter's Eye: Art and Tradition in North Carolina Pottery*. Chapel Hill: University of North Carolina Press, 2005.

Hollis, Susan Tower, Linda Pershing, and M. Jane Young. *Feminist Theory and the Study of Folklore*. Urbana: University of Illinois Press, 1993.

Hurston, Zora Neale. *Their Eyes Were Watching God*. Urbana: University of Illinois Press, 1978 [1937].

———. *Mules and Men*. New York: HarperCollins, 1990 [1935].

Jaramillo, Cleofas M. *Cuentos del Hogar/Spanish Fairy Tales*. El Campo, TX: Citizen Press, 1939a.

——. *The Genuine New Mexico Tasty Recipes: Potajes sabrosos*. Santa Fe, NM: Seton Village Press, 1981 [1939b].

——. *Shadows of the Past/Sombras del Pasado*. Santa Fe, NM: Seton Village Press, 1941.

——. *Romance of a Little Village Girl*. San Antonio, TX: Naylor Co., 1945.

Jordan, Rosan A., and Susan J. Kalčik, eds. *Women's Folklore, Women's Culture*. Philadelphia: University of Pennsylvania Press, 1985

Jones, Bessie, and Bess Lomax Hawes. *Step it Down*. New York: Harper & Row, 1972.

Keller, Evelyn Fox. *A Feeling for the Organism: The Life and Work of Barbara McClintock*. New York: W. H. Freeman, 1983.

Lucero-White Lea, Aurora. *The Folklore of New Mexico*. Santa Fe, NM: Seton Village Press, 1941.

——. *Literary Folklore of the Hispanic Southwest*. San Antonio, TX: Naylor Co., 1953.

Martin, Patricia Preciado. *Songs My Mother Sang to Me: An Oral History of Mexican-American Women*. Tucson: University of Arizona Press, 1992.

Montes, Marisa, and Joe Cepeda. *Juan Bobo Goes to Work/Juan Bobo Busca Trabajo*. New York: Harper Collins, 2000.

Mora, Pat. *House of Houses*. Boston: Beacon Press, 1997.

——. *Aunt Carmen's Book of Practical Saints*. Boston: Beacon Press. 1999.

Mora, Pat, and Domi (illustrator). *La noche que se cayó la luna: Mito Maya*. Berkeley, CA: Groundwood Press, 2000.

Mora, Pat, and Domi (illustrator). *La carrera del sapo y el venado*. Berkeley, CA: Groundwood Press, 2004.

Otero-Warren, Nina (Adelina). *Old Spain in Our Southwest*. New York: Harcourt Brace and Co., 1936.

Perez, Soledad. "Mexican Folklore from Austin, Texas." In *The Healer of Los Olmos and Other Mexican Lore*, ed. Wilson Mathis Hudson, 71–127. Dallas: Southern Methodist University Press, 1951.

Pershing, Linda. *The Ribbon around the Pentagon: Peace by Piecemakers*. Knoxville: University of Tennessee Press, 1996.

Radner, Joan Newlon, ed. *Feminist Messages: Coding in Women's Folk Culture*. Urbana: University of Illinois Press, 1993.

Sedillo, Mela. *Mexican and New Mexican Folk Dances*. Albuquerque: University of New Mexico Press, 1935.

Stekert, Ellen. "Autobiography of a Woman Folklorist." *Journal of American Folklore* 398 (1987): 579–585.

Stoeltje, Beverly J., ed. "Special Issue: Feminist Revisions in Folklore Studies." *Journal of Folklore Research*, vol. 25, no. 3 (1988): 141–242.

Sweezy, Nancy. *Raised in Clay: The Southern Folk Pottery Tradition*. Washington, DC: Smithsonian Institution Press, 1984.

Tye, Diane. "'A Very Lone Worker': Women-Centred Thoughts on Helen Creighton's Career as a Folklorist." *Canadian Folklore canadien*, vol. 15, no. 2 (1993): 107–117.

——. "Lessons from 'Undisciplined' Ethnography: The Case of Jean D. Heffernan." In *Undisciplined Women: Tradition and Culture in Canada*, eds. Pauline Greenhill and Diane Tye, 49–64. Montreal: McGill-Queen's University Press, 1997.

Weigle, Marta. *Spiders and Spinsters: Women and Mythology*. Albuquerque: University of New Mexico Press, 1982.

Zamora O'Shea, Elena, Leticia M. Garza Falcon, and Andres Tijerina. *El Mesquite: A Story of the Early Spanish Settlements Between the Nueces and the Rio Grande*. College Station: Texas A&M University Press, 2000 [1935].

A

Abortion

Abortion is the deliberate termination of a pregnancy. Throughout history and throughout the world, folklore and traditions addressing various means to "hasten the menses" have been informally transmitted from mother to daughter and from midwife or herb woman to community women. Abortion induced by herbs—tansy, pennyroyal, rue, and birthwort are well-known abortive agents—or by physical manipulation is well documented in North American folklore, and was fairly common in early America. Techniques included herbal infusions, herbal drinks, bloodletting, and, later, drug formulations and mechanical devices. Today, many herbs used as abortifacients (means of inducing abortion) remain popular in the North American alternative health market, and countless urban/contemporary legends addressing the prevention of conception or the termination of pregnancy, from douching with Coca-Cola, Seven-Up, or an aspirin mixture, to jumping up and down, or taking a hot bath immediately after intercourse, remain in informal circulation.

Until the nineteenth century, the law did not recognize a pregnancy until the stage of "quickening" (the first fetal movement perceived by a pregnant woman during the fourth or fifth month of gestation). Society and common law regarded a pre-quickening pregnancy only as a stoppage of regular menstruation, or "blocked" menses; terminating unwanted pregnancies (typically resulting from illicit and socially unacceptable relationships) was legal, although practiced on the margins of normative acceptability. Terminating a pregnancy after quickening was a common-law offense.

By the mid-nineteenth century, abortion had shifted from a limited last resort to a common practice of U.S. women to regulate their own fertility and limit family size. Abortionists advertised their services in newspapers, and medical manuals commonly contained information about abortifacients. Historians estimate that one of every five pregnancies in mid-nineteenth-century America was aborted.

In the 1820s–1840s, state legislatures began to place restrictions on who could perform abortions, but not necessarily on abortion procedures.

In practice, these measures were a move by the medical profession to co-opt the medical care of women and drive out of business midwives and other alternative practitioners, such as abortionists, herbalists, and midwives.

In the years following the Civil War, the laws regarding abortion changed dramatically. Horatio Robinson Storer and the American Medical Association, in legislatures across the United States, sought to outlaw abortion at any stage of gestation for reasons related to standards of practice rather than to religion, as is commonly assumed. A majority of states prohibited abortions and established criminal penalties for both practitioners and patients. The 1873 Comstock laws (aimed primarily at pornography) prohibited selling or advertising any article or medicine that caused abortions. In 1869, the Roman Catholic Church also prohibited abortion under any circumstances.

Despite the anti-abortion laws and legal decisions of the second half of the nineteenth century, abortion remained a common and available practice, although primarily an underground one. Every girl or woman knew what references to "female regularity" and a "perfect cure" meant; advertisers continued to offer preparations that guaranteed "regular menses"; and doctors who performed abortions discreetly advertised their services.

By the 1930s, anti-abortion laws were being actively enforced, and physicians providing abortion services were prosecuted. As prosecutions increased and contraceptive technologies and access to them improved (due in large part to the efforts of Margaret Sanger), abortion returned to its earlier marginalized social status as a "back alley" (and frequently dangerous) solution to an unwanted, unexpected pregnancy.

In 1973, the U.S. Supreme Court decided *Roe v. Wade*, prohibiting most restrictions on abortion during the first three months of pregnancy. Unlike any other Supreme Court decision in U.S. history, however, the legal right of a woman to choose abortion has been continuously challenged in the United States, usually on religious or moral grounds, for more than thirty years. The availability of abortion services has declined markedly in most regions of the country, primarily due to the fact that fewer medical schools are required to provide instruction. In 1996, 86 percent of all counties in the United States provided no abortion services, and 32 percent of all women aged fifteen to forty-four lived in those counties (http://www.plannedparenthood.org). The Supreme Court of Canada decided that anti-abortion legislation was unconstitutional in 1988 on the grounds that "forcing a woman, by threat of criminal sanction, to carry a fetus to term unless she meets certain criteria unrelated to her own priorities and aspirations, is a profound interference with a woman's body and thus a violation of her security of the person." Since 1991, abortion in Canada has been treated like any other medical procedure (http://www.duhaime.org). *See also:* Folk Medicine; Herbs; Legend, Urban/Contemporary; Midwifery; Politics; Pregnancy.

References: Brodie, Janet Farrell. *Contraception and Abortion in Nineteenth-Century America*. Ithaca, NY: Cornell University Press, 1997; *Duhaime.org*. "Canadian Abortion Law." http://www.duhaime.org/LegalResources/FamilyLaw/tabid/343/articleType/ArticleView/articleId/27/Abortion-Law-in-Canada.aspx (accessed August 8, 2008); Luker, Kristin. *Abortion and the Politics of Motherhood*. Berkeley: University of California Press, 1984; Mohr, James C. *Abortion in America: The Origins and Evolution of*

National Policy, 1800–1900. New York: Oxford University Press, 1984; Planned Parenthood. "Medical Training for Abortion and Contraceptive Services." http://www.plannedparenthood.org/pp2/portal/files/portal/medicalinfo/abortion/fact-abortion-training.xml (accessed March 16, 2005); Riddle, John M. *Eve's Herbs: A History of Contraception and Abortion in the West.* Cambridge: Harvard University Press, 1999.

Amanda Carson Banks

Activism

Activism generally refers to action or advocacy undertaken to effect social change. While activism has an overtly political motive, it frequently contains cultural and expressive components as well. Particularly when enacted in public, activism utilizes tradition and symbolism to promote its message. Tradition has often been seen as an obstacle to social transformation; however, groups and individuals seeking change—the labor, civil rights, antiwar, feminist, and environmental movements, for example—have effectively incorporated traditional and folkloric elements into their political actions. Participants share rituals, street performances, songs, and personal-experience narratives across movements and generations.

The folksong is perhaps the best known of these traditional expressions. Women folk singers like Joan Baez, Judy Collins, and Bernice Johnson Reagon played central roles in both the folk revival and the political movements of the 1960s. Similarly, songs such as "Which Side Are You On?" written by Florence Reese during a coal miners' strike in Harlan County, Kentucky, became standards during demonstrations by a variety of groups, as did spirituals like "We Shall Overcome" and "We Shall Not Be Moved." The folksong enabled social criticism while encouraging group participation.

However, activism, like politics more broadly, is often seen as a masculine realm; many women have pointed to the sexism in social movements that values some aspects of activism, such as public speaking, while denigrating or ignoring others, such as office work—work typically performed by women. Some women have responded with "women only" groups or with political actions that use distinctly feminine forms of expression. In her essay "Peace Work out of Piecework: Feminist Needlework Metaphors and the Ribbon around the Pentagon," Linda Pershing documents a group of women whose protests against nuclear armament utilized needlepoint, a traditional craft of women. In 1985, to mark the fortieth anniversary of the atomic bombing of Hiroshima and Nagasaki, 20,000 people encircled the Pentagon, the Capitol Building, and the Lincoln and Washington memorials with some fifteen miles of hand-sewn ribbons. Pershing argues that the women involved appraised the event less on its effect on military policy than on the satisfaction they gained from the group sewing process, perhaps suggesting a different way to examine and assess women's activism.

In addition to studying its traditional elements, some folklorists are involved in their own forms of activism, whether through scholarship or its application. Public folklorists in particular may find themselves in the political role of cultural preservation. However, there has been some controversy in Folklore Studies about the role of advocacy, with some arguing that folklorists should attempt to maintain an objective distance from their subject matter. Many feminist scholars argue, however, that this is neither possible nor desirable, and that the personal, political, and intellectual are inseparable. As Debora Kodish observes in her essay, "On Coming of Age in the Sixties," the vote at the 1992 American Folklore Society's annual meeting to oppose anti-gay initiative pending in Oregon exemplified the potential connections between social change and the discipline of Folklore. *See also:* Folk Music; Politics; Public Folklore; Tradition.

References: Garland, Anne Witte. *Women Activists: Challenging the Abuse of Power.* New York: Feminist Press, 1988; Kodish, Debora. "On Coming of Age in the Sixties" *Western Folklore* 52 (Spring 1993): 193–207; Pershing, Linda. "Peace Work out of Piecework: Feminist Needlework Metaphors and the Ribbon around the Pentagon." In *Feminist Theory and the Study of Folklore*, eds. Susan Tower Hollis, Linda Pershing, and M. Jane Young, 327–57. Urbana: University of Illinois Press, 1993.

Audrey Vanderford

Adoption

Adoption is an alternative way to become a parent, or, from a baby's, child's, or, more rarely, adult's perspective, to acquire parents other than one's biological progenitors, and, with them, new family and other kin. Whether adoption is formalized by a particular culture's laws or enacted as customary practice, it has long involved traditions and incorporation rites. All cultures have customs to socially create parental ties (normally defined by biology). Adoption tales abound in religion, legend, and folk narrative.

For example, the biblical book of Exodus recounts Moses's adoption by the Egyptian pharoah's daughter after her father decreed that all first-born Hebrew boys be put to death. To save her baby brother's life, Miriam placed Moses in a basket and set it in the Nile among the bulrushes. Pharoah's daughter, who found the baby, raised him in her father's court. Further, text from the book of Ruth is traditionally used in Jewish adoption ceremonies. Ruth, a non-Hebrew who wed Boaz, attached herself to Boaz's mother Naomi after her first husband's death and became the first convert to Judaism, saying, "Your people shall be my people, and your God my God." This adult adoption-conversion story is critical to Jewish adoptions when non-Jewish children need to be incorporated as Jews as well as family members. For both Moses and Ruth, adoption was a choice as well as an obligation for all involved.

In China and Japan, adoption has been a way for childless families—or those with daughters only—to acquire sons to pass on the family name. Poor relatives might allow their sons to be adopted by wealthier families, thus ensuring their children's and extended family's future. Adoptive parents might also acquire a son who could care for them in old age and maintain rituals for the ancestors. A similar, though less formalized, system in medieval Europe had the same purpose. Apprenticeships of young boys to master craftsmen provided occupational security. The masters would effectively become fathers to boys as young as seven or eight, whose apprenticeship lasted at least seven years.

As least as far back as colonial times, First Nations peoples have had ritual adoption ceremonies to incorporate non-Aboriginals or people from other groups. Similarly, families with several children might often offer one to childless kin. No stigma was attached to the birth parents (as is often the attitude in Euro North American cultures); rather than relinquishing or giving up a child, the biological parents' act was seen as generosity in sharing abundance.

In the United States and Canada, from the mid-nineteenth century on, giving up a child for adoption was the preferred alternative for unwed mothers. Adopting made unpaid labor as well as an heir available to childless couples. Despite this economic necessity, orphans, especially those from unmarried mothers, were stigmatized as "bastards"; the women and children, not the illegitimate fathers, were sanctioned for out-of-wedlock relations. Thus, upon adoption, children's origins were usually concealed, even from themselves; only very recently have legal adoption records been opened to biological parents and children.

With the opening of birth records, two motifs have dominated personal-experience narratives about adoption, which often appear in women's magazines and daytime talk shows. One group of stories recounts searches for biological children and "real" parents that result in reunions of adopted children with their biological parents (rarely are failed searches or unhappy reunions reported). Others involve the reunion of adult twins separated at birth (usually with companion accounts of similar tastes, traits, and life choices). These stories serve to underline popular beliefs in biological determinism over cultural development.

In the late twentieth century, the women's movement and women's greater economic freedom has destigmatized pregnancy for single women, particularly in Canada and the United States, making fewer babies available for adoption. These social processes have also fostered a trend toward purposeful single parenthood via adoption among the White middle class. Adoption also provides a route to motherhood for women in their thirties and forties who have focused on their careers rather than on finding partners and bearing children, as well as for gays and lesbians wanting to parent either individually or as committed couples.

A rise in U.S. demand for babies has made international adoption an attractive alternative for both single and partnered middle-class Americans, and has contributed to contemporary traditions and practices. Americans show a marked preference for adopting girls. Though international adoption in the United States dates at least to the Korean War, the orphan airlift upon the 1975 departure of Americans from Vietnam marked the beginning of the institutionalized adoption of Southeast Asian children—especially girls with American fathers. China's one-child policy, aimed at controlling its rapidly growing population, has created a pool of abandoned daughters, who are more frequently relinquished than boys in patriarchal cultures. China's laws required that adoptive parents be over thirty-five; until the early twenty-first century, Chinese law did not prohibit single individuals from adopting children. More recently, Americans have adopted children from Romania, Latin America, the Sudan, and Somalia in large numbers.

Rumors of baby-buying and baby-selling in Cambodia and Guatemala have resulted in the shutdown of those nations' adoption programs. International adoption is also replete with cautionary tales about non-certified social workers who claim to be legal adoption agents; obstacles in dealing with immigration and other authorities; in-country customs and cultural faux pas; medical horrors (malnutrition, unsanitary practices, or lack of medical care and resulting long-lasting health problems); and with narratives about the adoption experience (both positive and negative).

An explosion of Internet Listservs puts adoptive parents—prospective and experienced—in touch with one another. Through electronic communication, rituals related to adoption have become increasingly traditional and cut across cultures. Traditions include "forever family" customs that honor the culture of biological parents (such as Buddhist altars, spirit houses, New Year's celebrations, performing arts, visual arts, and literature) and "gotcha days" celebrating the date upon which the child was adopted. Also known as "airplane day" or "family day," the latter celebration can be marked by longing for absent birth parents. Remembrances can include life books, baby albums that show the child's life history before and after adoption. Culture camps, dance, and culture classes have proliferated, forming the structural underpinnings for emergent forms of modern adoption lore. *See also:* Naming Practices; Ritual.

References: Andrews, Jan, and Simon Ng. "The Pincoya's Child." In *Out of the Everywhere: New Tales for Canada*, 35–42. Toronto: Douglas & McIntyre, 2000; Bierhorst, John, and Mary K. Okheena, eds. *The Dancing Fox: Arctic Folktales*. New York: Harper-Collins Publishers, 1997; Eldridge, Sherrie. *Twenty Things Adopted Kids Wish Their Adoptive Parents Knew*. New York: Dell Publishing, 1999; Estés, Clarissa Pinkola. (Audiotape). *Warming the Stone Child: Myths and Stories about Abandonment and the Unmothered Child*. Boulder, CO: Sounds True Recordings, 1990; Hazelton, Hugh, ed. "Ñucu the Worm." In *Jade and Iron: Latin American Tales from Two Cultures*, retold by Jürgen Riester, trans. Patricia Aldana, 19–20. Toronto: Douglas & McIntyre, 1996; MacLeod, Jean, and Sheena Macrae. *Adoption Parenting: Creating a Toolbox, Building Connections*. Warren, NJ: EMK Press, 2006; O'Malley, Beth. *LifeBooks: Creating a Treasure for the Adopted Child*. Winthrop, MA: Adoption-Works Press, 2000; Saltzman, Rachelle H. "Incorporation Rituals: Naming Ceremonies." *C.A.R.T.S. (Cultural Arts Resources for Teachers and Students) Newsletter*. New York: City Lore, vol. 4 (2000): 8.

Rachelle H. Saltzman

Aesthetics

Aesthetics—defined here as a set of formal criteria that separates art from craft, and art from life experience—was strongly influenced by eighteenth-century European attitudes. Historically, aesthetics has been applied to facilitate the appreciation of the beauty of an art object by understanding the artist's technical skills and artistic intent. During the period known as the Enlightenment, formal principles governing taste, originality, and aesthetic judgment became determinants of artistic excellence and quality. They were exclusively focused on the art object, thus negating the influence of local sociocultural contexts and changing ideologies of beauty. Enlightenment aesthetics spawned a distinctive cultural consciousness that continues to support an elite art world of fine-arts museums, galleries, academic art institutions, dealers, connoisseurs, critics, and scholars. Such consciousness engenders and maintains a number of evaluative concepts that are foreign to the appreciation of the folk arts and perpetuate the marginalization of women's art work: the concepts of artistic genius, the uniqueness of the art object, the primacy of self-expression and innovation, "art for art's sake," art's transcendence, and aesthetic autonomy. By universalizing artistic qualities across space and time, attitudes privileging aesthetic autonomy tend to nullify or ignore cultural and gender differences while supporting exclusionary practices of the art establishment and promoting "great works of art."

The discipline of folkloristics demands that when investigating the arts of folk cultures, all aspects of the art context (including the creative process) are examined in order to understand their symbolic frameworks and integration into other parts of cultural life. The study of individual folk artists also includes their social and biographical circumstances. Thus, the application and understanding of folk aesthetics encompasses an appraisal of individualistic and idiosyncratic elements mediated by standards already recognized within their local communities.

Folk aesthetics (ethnoaesthetics) pertain to a "micro-level" of artistry at the local, community, and regional levels—an "aesthetics of experience" based on local ways of being creative. An internal (insider) understanding of ethnoaesthetics is shared by its producers and audience based on identity, knowledge of technical skills, the intricacy and amount of work involved, shared design concepts, and local judgments about what constitutes interesting themes. A local system of aesthetics dispenses with universals in favor of specific groups' criteria for judging the excellence and value of their own artwork. In Joyce Ice's (1993) study of aesthetics and women's quilting groups, she emphasizes the social considerations of reaching consensus about pattern choice, color, stitching, etc., as part of the process of shared artistic decision-making. Thus, the quilt is both the social and aesthetic product of this creative process. The resultant value judgments become the yardstick by which creativity, symbolic action, and the power inherent in making art are measured. Its dimensions are determined by the traditions embedded in the local aesthetic system, which are collectively validated and refined by the artists themselves. Such locally agreed-upon standards shape artistic decisions by either commanding conformity or by setting boundaries to be transgressed.

Feminist perspectives on aesthetics are critically attentive to forms of women's creative expressiveness (particularly domestic arts like quiltmaking and needlework), which are usually considered peripheral or invisible by the dominant culture. Folklorists M. Jane Young and Kay Turner mention a need "to allow folklore [and feminist aesthetics] to speak for and about the traditions of women's difference as this is manifested in their material life activities and then given voice through a range of expressive means" (20). According to art critic Lucy Lippard, the most effective way to pursue this is through a dialogue which opens up questions about the way social and political issues and ideas are addressed through art practice, artworks, events, and how they relate to the position of women in different contexts.

Central to women's folk aesthetics are ideas about creativity, the meaning or significance of art-making (to both insiders and outsiders), inclusiveness, collaboration, relationship, and reflexivity as a form of meditative feedback flowing between art and life. Reflexivity continuously engages individual artistic expression with social interaction. African American quiltmakers, for example, often improvise on basic patterns such as the "square-in-a-square" motif, which allows artists, mindful of tradition, to follow their own instincts and responses to visual space, color, line, proportion, and shape. While they exercise freedom and spontaneity, they are always aware of the rules they flout as they introduce new variants and innovative solutions. Rules inspiring flexibility and improvisation, that is, traditional practices coexisting with different modes of innovation, are sustained and affirmed by communities of insider African American quiltmakers. But outsider "standard-traditional" quilters, although they might recognize the basic patterns, may find the irregularities and idiosyncrasies of such quilts aesthetically unintelligible.

Folk aesthetics is itself subject to the evaluative judgment of outsiders (collectors and connoisseurs), a situation which echoes the vertical hierarchical standards in place in the mainstream art world. Within that context, different genres or classes of art objects are considered to have more or less artistic value or merit; for example, women's domestic arts are often less valued than sculptures created by male folk artists. And for some scholars, determining authenticity (or an authentic cultural expression)—distinguishing the genuine from the ersatz or the fake—is a primary concern. The agreed-upon standards of the mainstream art world insist that a folk artist must be "untutored" or unexposed to formal art training. In addition, the artist must be "pure," that is, naïve, unsophisticated, or untainted, and in pursuit of a singular (rather than a communal) vision. When these attitudes are examined, they appear to mirror or replicate the art establishment's position vis-à-vis "artistic genius" and uniqueness in the fine arts. Popular Culture Studies scholars have succeeded in tempering some of this inverse purism by introducing notions of "the hybrid" (art forms combining all types of influences) and "the transformative," wherein art changes in response to emergent cultural identities, commercial stimuli, and globalization.

Developing concepts involving exchange, borrowing, fluidity, ingenuity, integration, and resilience demonstrate the dynamics of art-making that occurs despite the existence of evaluative categories that privilege purity and promote exclusion. The challenge of women's aesthetics and the ethnoaesthetic approach is in their demand that we base our appraisals of excellence and beauty on local, collaborative, and inclusive art practices in combination with an understanding of how aesthetic power operates in various sociocultural contexts. *See also:* Beauty; Folk Art; Folk Group; Quiltmaking; Needlework.

References: Armstrong, Robert Plant. *The Affecting Presence: An Essay in Humanistic Anthropology.* Urbana: University of Illinois Press, 1971; Bartra, Eli, ed. *Crafting Gender: Women and Folk Art in Latin America and the Caribbean.* Durham, NC: Duke

University Press, 2003; Becker, Howard S. *Art Worlds*. Berkeley: University of California Press, 1982; Deepwell, Katy, ed. *New Feminist Art Criticism: Critical Strategies*. Manchester and New York: Manchester University Press, 1995; Fine, Gary Alan. *Everyday Genius: Self-Taught Art and the Culture of Authenticity*. Chicago and London: University of Chicago Press, 2004; Hollis, Susan Tower et al. eds. *Feminist Theory and the Study of Folklore*. Urbana: University of Illinois Press, 1993; Ice, Joyce. "Women's Aesthetics and the Quilting Process." In *Feminist Theory and the Study of Folklore*, eds. Susan Tower Hollis, Linda Pershing, and M. Jane Young, 166–177. Urbana: University of Illinois Press, 1993; Korsmeyer, Carolyn. "Feminist Aesthetics." 2004. http://plato.stanford.edu/ entries/feminism-aesthetics/ (accessed July 14, 2005); Whitten, Dorothea S., and Norman E., eds. *Imagery and Creativity: Ethnoaesthetics and Art Worlds in the Americas*. Tucson: University of Arizona Press, 1993; Young, M. Jane, and Kay Turner. "Challenging the Canon: Folklore Theory Reconsidered from Feminist Perspectives." In *Feminist Theory and the Study of Folklore*, eds. Susan Tower Hollis, Linda Pershing, M. Jane Young, 9–28. Urbana: University of Illinois Press, 1993.

Suzanne P. MacAulay

Aging

Aging is the natural process by which living organisms develop biologically and grow older. This process includes a decline in biological functions and ultimately death. In human beings, gender is an important variable in the aging process; biological changes affecting women have profound social, psychological, emotional, medical, and economic consequences. Ageism, whether personal or institutional, is the stereotyping of and discrimination against individuals on the basis of age, and specifically old age. Reflecting societal attitudes toward aging, folkloric images of maturing women range from the nurturing, postmenopausal wise woman endowed with supernatural powers (Germany's Mother Holle and the Oracle in *The Matrix*) to the ugly, hungry hag (Russia's Baba Yaga and Gretel's witch) whose disposition evokes terror.

In the United States and Canada and throughout most of the industrialized world, an unprecedented number of individuals are living well into old age. In 1900 in the United States, life expectancy for men was 48.3 years and for women 51.1 years; the number of individuals who survived to old age was relatively small. However, because of medical innovations and advances in public health education, the number of older people in the U.S. population has tripled since the turn of the century.

In *The Coming of Age* (1972), French philosopher Simone de Beauvoir examines the universally grim plight of older people throughout time. She describes how they suffer from lack of respect from younger people, loss in productivity, and other negative experiences; she provides poignant evidence that most cultures deny the intrinsic worth of older people despite their repertoires of fables that exalt the elderly. It is a modern phenomenon that women live longer than men by approximately seven years. As a result, women outnumber men in the general population, especially at the older end of the age spectrum. Judith Worell characterizes the increasingly long lives of women compared with men in the second half of the twentieth century as an "historic feminization of the world" (2001: 96).

Because of social double standards regarding gender and aging, many women grow old with much greater apprehension than do men. The dread of growing older—and so purportedly less sexually attractive—in patriarchal societies is a long-held attitude illustrated by the saying, "Old age is woman's hell," attributed to Ninon de Lenclos, a seventeenth-century French writer and courtesan. Whereas a man's graying hair may mark him as "distinguished" by age, a same-aged woman suffers social denigration for having lost her youthful physical appearance.

Consider the social significance of feminine beauty and youth reflected in the folktales collected by Wilhelm and Jacob Grimm in the nineteenth century. In many of the original 168 tales, youthful beauty is not only emphasized as the ideal for women, it is associated with goodness, wealth, and social privilege. In contrast, aged women are generally characterized as mean and ugly villains. Although most of these tales are no longer widely recognized by North American audiences, those that have survived in the contemporary imagination—and marketplace—include those in which beautiful young women (such as Cinderella, Snow White, and Sleeping Beauty) in conflict with infamous older women dominate the plot.

The youthful feminine ideal has been perpetuated during the past 150 years through adaptations and retellings of folktales produced by the children's book and film industries, most notably by the Walt Disney Company's films and related product merchandising. Compare, for example, the benevolent Sea Witch of Hans Christian Anderson's tale, "The Little Mermaid," with Ursula, the terrifying virago of the Disney film of the same name. It has long been noted there are few roles for women film actors over forty. When images of women of advanced years do appear in film, popular culture, and narrative folklore, they are often poor and ill or overly ambitious, menacing, or otherwise distasteful: self-absorbed wealthy matrons, witches with gnarled arthritic hands, impoverished peasant ladies laboring in the fields, black-draped widows in mourning, and old hags devouring children for food.

The late twentieth-century boom in the cosmetic industry and an increasing demand for cosmetic plastic surgeries attest to the struggle that some women, especially those from the middle and upper classes, face with self-esteem as they age. Their desire for continued social acceptance, fear of losing the opportunity for sexual intimacy, and anxiety about the potential onset of debilitating medical conditions are among the reasons that they view aging as a psychological challenge. While rural Mexicans and Canadians are more likely to exhibit the traditional respect accorded to the aged than are Americans reared on unrelentingly promoted images of "Generation X," old women are increasingly invisible in these societies as well, and their life experiences dismissed as irrelevant.

While women's medical problems that accompany aging are similar to those of aging men, among whom heart disease and cancer are leading causes of death, older women suffer more frequently than men from gender-linked medical conditions such as osteoporosis, urinary incontinence, insomnia, and depression. And unlike those of previous generations, today's geriatric illnesses are chronic rather short-term. Chronic illnesses have economic consequences that affect women disproportionately, including the likelihood that middle-aged women will provide their unpaid eldercare. Coupled with their own weakening and, in some cases, crippling medical conditions, elderly women commonly find their financial security at risk. In the United States, "women over the age of sixty-five are twice as poor as men in the same age group" (Eisler). And older (unmarried) lesbians, particularly if African American, face the distinct possibility of homelessness upon the death of a property-owning partner (Shavers).

Ironically, older women were historically the first medical practitioners; as such, they enjoyed social reverence. As healers, their curative knowledge and power aligned them with the wisdom of the ancient goddess Sophia. Today, their wisdom is instead scorned as "old wives' tales." Many historians and anthropologists locate the Spanish Inquisition in Europe as the beginning of the demise of the "wise old women" archetype. Threatened by the status of women healers, church authorities declared them agents of the Devil and effectively changed public opinion about them through witch hunts. In addition, traditional myths of Pagan origin were revised to further stigmatize the image of the once-powerful older woman.

To counter some of the stereotypes about women and aging, a proliferation of publications began appearing in last decades of the twentieth century, including *Women of a Certain Age* by Lilia Rubin (1979); *In Full Flower: Aging Women, Power and Sexuality* (1993) by Lois W. Banner; *The Fountain of Age* (1993) by Betty Friedan; and *The New Ourselves, Growing Older: Women Aging with Knowledge and Power* (1987; 1994) by Paula Doress-Worters. In 1989, feminist studies reached a significant milestone with the first issue of the *Journal of Women and Aging*, a scholarly venue for interdisciplinary research.

Public policy in the United States is increasingly reflecting a demographic shift in favor of aging women. While reproductive choice, inequality in the workforce, and childcare were the prominent social issues in the later part of the twentieth century, the concerns of older women are becoming more evident in the new millennium. These include displaced homemakers, widowhood, elder caregiving, social isolation and poverty, and gender-related medical research and health care.

Older women's activism has spawned several influential advocacy organizations. Two, the Gray Panthers and the Red Hat Society, have produced positive new icons to celebrate the aging process; and there has been a renewed interest among scholars about colonial midwives, Mexican *curanderas* (folk healers), Hopi/Navajo Spider Woman stories, to name a few areas of research. For example, today we know that pre-Columbian Aztec elder women participated in the ritual ingestion of *pulque*, a liquid fermented from the maguey plant, along with male priests.

Recognition of the inestimable value of older women is, however, emerging in literature. Ultima, the *curandera* of Rudolfo Anaya's *Bless Me, Ultima*, the most widely read novel by a Mexican American author, is a prime example. Sharply diverging from typical characterizations of elderly women, Ultima represents goodness and wisdom. She also serves as tradition-bearer and a model for keeping cultural traditions alive. *See also:*

Beauty; Class; Cosmetics; Croning; *Curandera*; Elder Care; Grandmother; Old Wives' Tales; Tradition-Bearer; Women's Friendship Groups.

References: Anaya, Rudolfo. *Bless Me, Ultima.* New York: Warner Books, 1999; Baker-Sperry, Lori, and Liz Grauerholz. ."The Pervasiveness and Persistence of the Feminine Beauty Ideal in Children's Fairy Tales." *Gender and Society,* vol. 17, no. 5 (October 2003): 711–726; Banner, Lois W. *In Full Flower: Aging Women, Power and Sexuality: A History.* New York: Vintage, 1993; Beers, Mark H., ed. *The Merck Manual of Health and Aging.* Whitehouse Station, NJ: Merck & Co., Inc., 2004; De Beauvoir, Simone. *The Coming of Age.* New York: G. P. Putman's Sons, 1972; Doress-Worters, Paula. *The New Ourselves, Growing Older: Women Aging with Knowledge and Power.* New York: Simon & Schuster, 1994; Eisler, Riane. "The Feminine Face of Poverty." June 22, 2007. http://www.alternet.org/rights/50727 (accessed June 22, 2007); Friedan, Betty. *The Fountain of Age.* New York: Simon and Schuster, 1993; Perrone, Bobette, H. Henrietta Stockel, and Victoria Krueger. *Medicine Women, Curanderas, and Women Doctors.* Norman: University of Oklahoma Press, 1989; Shavers, Regina, as told to Daisey Hernandez. "Gay, Gray and Black." *Colorlines* (Fall 2005): 23–24; Worrell, Judith, ed. *Encyclopedia of Women and Gender: Sex Similarities and Differences and the Impact of Society on Gender.* San Diego: Academic Press, 2001; Weigle, Marta. *Spiders and Spinsters: Women and Mythology.* Albuquerque: University of New Mexico, 1982.

Gilda Baeza Ortego

Altar, Home

Home altars are image-laden material expressions of personal devotion created to serve as sacred places of communication and mediation between an altar-maker and her chosen deity or deities. The creation and use of personal home altars is an ancient women's religious tradition practiced in cultures worldwide. The tradition engages women from diverse religious backgrounds, including Greek Orthodox, Roman Catholic, Hindu, Buddhist, various sects of the African diaspora such as Brazilian Candomblé, Cuban Santería, and others. The word "altar" generally defines a sacred site set apart for communication between deities and humans, but another sense of the term suggests that an altar forms a threshold or gateway, a meeting place of the sacred and the mundane. In contrast to the formal altars found in churches and temples, a woman's home altar informally expresses her faith and devotion.

Consisting of a special grouping of selected religious images and other symbols, a home altar visually represents its maker's personal relationship with the deities, saints, or ancestors she depends upon for help and comfort in her daily life. Never merely representational, the home altar also serves as an active performance site for the rituals and prayers that are instrumental for engaging relationships with divine resources. In many families, the tradition can be traced back for generations, but it is also evolving in North America as new religious and spiritual options emerge. Within the past forty years, feminist, lesbian, and women's art movements have brought new practitioners to the altar tradition through the emergence of the women's spirituality movement. Neo-Pagan revisionist movements such as Wicca also embrace the practice. Even individuals with no affiliation whatsoever simply adapt personal altar-making to their own beliefs and needs.

Still, for most practitioners, the tradition is maternal in lineage; by observation or instruction, women learn to keep an altar from their mothers and grandmothers. They also learn the power of communicating at the altar—saying prayers, making petitions for help, and giving thanks—as a way of maintaining alliances with favored deities or interlocutors. Traditional home altars often feature a central religious image passed down within the family. A Hindu woman's altar might feature Durga; a Mexican Catholic's might display the Virgin of Guadalupe. Mothers often donate images to their newly married daughters' altars, or leave altar objects and images to them as a legacy after death. Through this image, a woman inherits a relationship with a particular deity who, like a revered family member, is known, honored, and relied upon for help.

The history of women's creation and use of domestic altars continues from ancient times to the present. In the West, the earliest home altars known to have been created by women date from the Neolithic period (4000–6000 BCE) in Old Europe and Anatolia (now Turkey). Reserved primarily as sites for presenting offerings or sacrifices to fecund, earth-based goddesses and their consort gods, ancient altars presumably were used to enhance fertility, to invite protection, and to memorialize ancestors.

These same functions prevail today; women still pray at their home altars for a good birth, for security of home and family, and to honor the dead. In its long history—evident in the archaeological and historical record for Mycenaean, Greek, Roman, Pagan, and early Christian cultures—the domestic altar in Western tradition has changed little in basic construction. To view a contemporary Catholic Mexican American woman's home altar side-by-side with a Transylvanian house cult table from the fifth millennium BCE or to see an altar dedicated to the goddess by a feminist in 1985 next to an altar dedicated to the goddess in Mycenae 4,000 years earlier, immediately confirms their visual similarity. On a simple table or other platform surface, votive statues or pictures of local deities are surrounded by instruments for communicating with them: lamps, candles, incense burners, amulets, and offerings such as shells and flowers. Contemporary altars also feature printed materials such as prayer books and secular items such as family photographs and personal mementos, but the visual aesthetic of the altar is consistent, and its communicative purpose has remained virtually unchanged for millennia.

Though bound by certain conventions, the tradition still invites variation; no altar looks exactly the same, nor is it used exactly the same way. Certain items (the inherited central image, for example) may remain for a lifetime, but home altars are not fixed sites; they change as the women who make them change. Altar-makers affirm the particularity of the tradition to themselves as individuals and as women; for them, personal devotion trumps institutional dogma. At their altars, women remake and reinvent the usefulness of cultural symbols, both sacred and secular, according to their own histories, purposes, needs, desires, and beliefs. Altar-makers take the received aspects of the tradition and wed them to a creative—and often highly imaginative—impulse. For example, amid typical saints' statues and votive candles arranged on a shelf or dresser, folk Catholic home altars may be covered with family photos, display pictures of local political figures, feature unusual personal symbols such as a child's stuffed animal, or make use of homemade decorative effects such as hand-embroidered altar cloths or glittered paper plates. It is not unusual to find modern altar-makers using their home desks and computers as the base around which their altars are composed.

The visual aesthetic of altars is defined by a propensity for layering and accumulation. Objects and symbols are integrated into a coherent visual field that marks their interdependence and connection to each other. Altars exemplify the process that feminist artist Miriam Schapiro aptly named *femmage* (derived from "collage" and "assemblage") referring to women's artistic process of collecting and creatively joining seemingly disparate elements into a functional whole (Meyer and Schapiro: 66–69).

All the objects on the altar are signs of relationship; each one tells a story of attachment to others, whether they are sacred, social, or nature-based relations. An image of the Virgin Mary testifies to the altar-maker's ongoing relationship with her; a son's photo bespeaks his mother's care; a small heap of stones signifies a love of the Earth.

The altar specifies a context for building and sustaining relationships by serving as a site to seek divine help in initiating, repairing, restoring, remembering, and protecting the vitality of human social life. Appeals made there constitute a catalog of situations requiring care and help such as healing the sick, seeking a blessed union in love or marriage, or finding a new home. The intimacy and familiarity of the altar provides an ideal setting for meditation, prayer, and petition. The home altar's longevity is no doubt related to the singular privacy it affords in giving women a place to speak to the divine without restraint. There, a woman meets her deities and speaks to them with assurance in their mutual ability to create change and to heal. Women ascribe great efficacy to the personal prayers and petitions for help made at their altars. What women ask for most—and receive—at their altars is healing. Healing of body, mind, and spirit is the active result of the good relationships between women and their divine allies promoted at the altar site. Asking and receiving fashion a bond of trust, and this bond fortifies a fundamental labor performed at the altar: the movement from problem to solution in the work of living. As Mexican American altar-maker Margarita Guerrero affirms, "Here with my saints and the Virgin I have accomplished many things. I have prayed and they answer me. And always I have made things better for myself and others" (Turner: 47). *See also:* Cult of the Virgin; Virgin of Guadalupe; Wicca and Neo-Paganism.

References: Gargaetas, Patricia. "Altared States: Lesbian Altarmaking and the Transformation of Self." *Women and Therapy* 16/2–3 (1995): 95–105; Gimbutas, Marija. *The Goddesses and Gods of Old Europe.* Berkeley: University of California Press, 1982; Meyer, Melissa, and Miriam Schapiro. "Waste Not/Want Not: Femmage." *Heresies* 4 (1978): 66–69; Raven, Arlene. "The Art of the Altar." *Lady-Unique-Inclination-of-the-Night, Cycle 6:* 29–41. Special Issue on Women's Home Altars, ed. Kay Turner. Austin, TX: Sowing Circle Press, 1983; Turner, Kay. *Beautiful Necessity: The Art and Meaning of Women's Altars.* New York and London: Thames & Hudson, 1999.

Kay Turner

American Folklore Society—Women's Section

The Women's Section of the American Folklore Society is a subsidiary organization of the American Folklore Society devoted to networking women members of the Society and promoting research on women's folklore. The American Folklore Society, founded in 1888, is itself the principal non-governmental organization in the United States for promoting and organizing the scholarly study of folklore. Its individual members are primarily academics, archivists, museum personnel, and persons who work for government and private agencies, such as arts councils, who are engaged in promoting interest in folklore, folklife, and folk art. The Women's Section was officially established in 1976.

The Section had its genesis in the activities of the second-wave U.S. women's movement of the late 1960s and the 1970s that sought "women's liberation," that is, equality for women. The general spirit of this movement ramified within learned societies, such as the Modern Language Association, which were influential in directing developments within academic disciplines. Many women felt that the academic societies to which they belonged were male-dominated and less encouraging of women's endeavors than of men's, and they set out to remedy that situation. At the annual meeting of the American Folklore Society in Austin, Texas, in 1972, informal meetings led to the establishment of a semiofficial women's caucus to address concerns about women's participation in the folklore establishment. At that time, the Society, unlike some similar groups, did not have a structure that established Sections, subgroups devoted to particular interests. When the Society moved toward such a structure, the caucus became an official Section.

The first panel on women's folklore and fieldwork was held at the 1973 American Folklore Society's annual meeting, where women presented their fieldwork findings on the folklore of women, including Inez Cardozo-Freeman on Mexican girls' games; Agnes F. Hostetler on native costumes of Oberwallis, Germany; Susan Kalčik on personal-experience narratives in women's consciousness-raising groups; and Kay Stone on the construction of female heroes in the tales collected by the Grimm brothers. Along with additional papers, this research was published in the groundbreaking January 1975 issue of the *Journal of American Folklore*, edited by Claire Farrer. The Women's Section of the American Folklore Society continues to support this kind of work, offering awards such as the Elli Köngäs Maranda prize for scholarship on women's traditions.

The Women's Section serves primarily to connect women members of the American Folklore Society, though it also promotes women's folklore and other academic areas of particular interest to women. It does so primarily through meetings at the annual conference of the Society and through the publication of the *Folklore Feminists Communication (FFC)*. Claire Farrer, Rosan A. Jordan, and Susan Kalčik started the journal in Austin, Texas, in 1973; it continues to publish news items, bibliographies, and brief research articles. Its name is a play upon the august folklore monograph series published in Finland, the *Folklore Fellows Communications*, in which, of course, "fellows" suggests that the publication is by and for men. It was briefly called *Folklore Women's Communication*, but the newer name was finally established as appropriate to the feminist orientation of the Women's Section, which took it over as its own publication.

In addition to providing a forum for the discussion of women's issues, the Section has also sponsored periodic "cronings" of women members of the Society when they reach the age of fifty, holding croning ceremonies every few years at Section meetings. The structure of these ceremonies varies and has involved elaborate costuming, ritual, joking, and singing. Thus, in addition to its other functions, the Section has provided a playful way of celebrating how women age and celebrating senior women in the Society, while also making the point that folklorists recognize the great importance of coming-of-age rituals. *See also:* Croning; *Folklore Feminists Communication*; Women Folklorists.

References: de Caro, F. A. "The Women's Movement in A. F. S.: A Brief Chronology." *The Folklore Historian* 1: 1–4 (1975); "Women's Section of The American Folklore Society." http://www.artlore.net/ffc.html (accessed August 8, 2008).

Rosan A. Jordan and Margaret R. Yocom

Androgyny

The English word "androgyny" comes from the Greek for "male" (*aner*) and "female" or "wife" (*gyne*). It refers to the simultaneous presence of both male/masculine and female/feminine elements in one entity or symbolic system. The image of the androgyne in the Western world comes to us in an etiological tale by Plato (*Symposium* 189c–193e) that describes our "original human nature" as one in which each person had two halves; but after the gods split apart the androgynes (who combined both male and female natures), human beings have been sexed dichotomously as male and female. "Hermaphrodism" is a related term; "hermaphrodite" is the scientific-medical term for individuals of double, doubtful, or mistaken sex (now more commonly called "intersexed") who usually blend physical female and male features rather than embody both. In *Metamorphoses Book IV*, the Roman poet Ovid tells of Hermaphroditos, the son of the ideal male type (Hermes) and ideal female type (Aphrodite); a perfectly formed male (blend), s/he later joined (doubled) with the perfectly formed female nymph Salmacis as an hermaphrodite, appearing neither male nor female but noticeably containing aspects of both.

The modern idea that the image of the androgyne is an archetypal expression of the union of opposites, an indicator of "psychic wholeness," comes to us from Marie-Louise Von Franz and C. G. Jung's work on medieval and Renaissance alchemical texts. In their analytical psychological formulation of the collective unconscious, sex and gender play highly significant roles, so it is unsurprising that the Androgyne archetype acts as a mediating or uniting psychic principle; its appearance in dreams, for example, may indicate a return to health after a long illness or the need for greater recognition by an individual's conscious mind to consult her unconscious "inner masculine" (Animus) for guidance in achieving psychic balance.

Other students of psychology, biology, medicine, religion, and gender/sex may concern themselves with the androgynous regarding the configuration and balance of masculine and feminine elements, how they come together, and their physical, emotional, social, and metaphysical consequences. However, like Jung's, these approaches usually privilege masculine elements, two-sex/two-gender bipolarities, heterosexuality, and the notion of one sex per body.

Psychologist Sandra Bem began research in the 1970s on androgyny to counter the pervasive gender polarization that occurs in both science and society. She developed the Bem Sex Role Inventory (BSRI) based on cultural definitions of gender-appropriate behaviors, which yields scores for sex-typed, cross-sex-typed, and androgynous individuals. Bem later ascertained that "androgyny" was still too gender-specific a term (favoring the male/masculine and the one-body-per-sex model), and so, while not entirely repudiating the concept of androgyny, turned her attention toward cultural variables in gender identity.

In 1980, History of Religions scholar Wendy Doniger (O'Flaherty) published a cross-cultural process typology of androgyny that includes psychological and mythological androgynes in three categories: splitting, a type in which a female-male combination must divide/be divided in order to mature or procreate; fusing, in which submerged (male or female) elements must become integrated for wholeness to be achieved; and the two-in-one, a type in which female and male persons (or gods) unite in perfect love or in a sacred marriage symbolizing the union of opposites. Among the folkloric pseudo-androgynes she identifies are competitive ones, including those who exchange or alternate between sex roles or sexes. In these and all types, "male androgynes by far outnumber female androgynes and are generally regarded as positive, while female androgynes ... are generally negative" (284).

However notorious it has been for its gender dimorphism, North American popular culture has long been fascinated with "the androgynous look"—from the flapper of the 1920s, whose ultra-slim body was admired for its boyishness, to pop singers like Madonna and Annie Lennox, whose occasional appropriations of masculine gestures and clothing have gained them large followings among both men and women. *See also:* Cross-Dressing; Fashion; Gender; Sexuality; Transgender Folklore.

References: Bem, Sandra Lipsitz. *The Lenses of Gender: Transforming the Debate on Sexual Inequality.* New Haven and London: Yale University Press, 1993; Doniger (O'Flaherty), Wendy. *Women, Androgynes, and Other Mythical Beasts.* Chicago and London: University of Chicago Press, 1980; Jung, C. G. *Mysterium Coniunctionis.* Trans. R. F. C. Hull. *The Collected Works of Jung, Vol. 14.* Princeton, NJ: Princeton University Press, 1970; Von Franz, Marie-Louise. *Alchemy: An Introduction to the Symbolism and the Psychology.* Toronto: Inner City Books, 1981.

Liz Locke

Aphrodisiac

Derived from the name of the Greek goddess of sexual desire, Aphrodite, the term aphrodisiac has traditionally been applied to any substance reputed to induce sexual desire, increase sexual performance, or enhance sexual pleasure. The history of aphrodisiac use stretches back some 3,000 years and encompasses an impressive variety, from plants and herbs, animal parts, perfumes, cosmetics, and love charms to recreational drugs, prescription drugs, and hormone preparations. Indeed, its long and colorful history powerfully illustrates the common ground between folk wisdom and medical science. Many would-be wooers obtained from the village wise woman (a practicing herbalist) aphrodisiacs such as mandrake, wormwood, pego palo, ginseng, and kola nuts, whose chemical properties have been linked with currently researched treatments for sexual dysfunction: hallucinogens, plant estrogens, and caffeine. At the same time, belief (the placebo effect) might easily be identified as the key ingredient in all folk aphrodisiacs, and for this reason, charms figured as heavily as herbal concoctions.

The principle of sympathetic magic ("like produces like") often governed the identification of plants and animal parts as appropriate sexual remedies. Culturally, vigorous sexual performance has been more readily associated with the male than with the female so that phallic shapes have been far more commonly suggestive as aphrodisiacs. Rhinoceros horns, shark's teeth, carrots, John the Conqueror root, bananas, maize, and cucumbers are a few of the items whose aphrodisiac reputation rests on their phallic appearance. The discouragement of female sexual desire made women's solicitation of aphrodisiacs a relatively hushed endeavor. However, some female folk traditions allowed room for interpretation; the preparation of cockle bread involved pressing a lump of kneaded dough against the vulva, baking it into this shape, and then presenting the bread to a desired male. So-called "sex herbs" and charms for women tended to focus more directly on fertility than on sexual pleasure. Reputed conception aids included fecund fruits such as tomatoes, the genitals of female animals associated with prolific reproduction such as rabbits and dogs, and human female fluids crucial to childbearing, particularly breast milk and menstrual blood. The Roma (Gypsy) spell of offering a new bridegroom food or drink mixed with a few drops of the bride's menstrual blood in order to ensure a happy and fruitful marriage derives from this latter tradition.

More liberal attitudes concerning female sexuality, along with expectations of continued sexual performance among today's aging North American population, have more than ensured the continued popularity of aphrodisiacs. Among youths, recreational drugs like MDMA (known as Ecstasy or X) have been considered potent aphrodisiacs, but—like the "date-rape drug," Rohypnol—their effect consists primarily in the loosening of inhibitions and diminishment of memory rather than in a chemical provocation of libido, an effect they share with possibly the most widespread and socially acceptable aphrodisiac, alcohol. Conversely, proven libido enhancers like Stilbestrol and Viagra, essentially hormone replacement therapies (HRTs), suggest that a decrease in sex drive for both older men and older women is a problem in need of "fixing." *See also:* Aging; Cosmetics; Folk Belief; Folk Medicine; Folklore About Women; Foodways; Herbs; Magic; Popular Culture; Rape; Sexuality; Superstition; Witchcraft, Historical; Women's Folklore.

References: Mervis, Cynthia, and Angela Hines Watson. *Love Potions: A Guide to Aphrodisiacs and Sexual Pleasures.* Los Angeles: Jeremy Tarcher, 1993; Taberner, Peter V. *Aphrodisiacs: The Science and the Myth.* Philadelphia: University of Pennsylvania Press, 1985; Wilen, Lydia, Joan Live, and Be Well Wilen. *Folk Remedies That Work.* New York: Perennial, 1996.

Andrea Austin

Assault, Supernatural

The three best known supernatural assault phenomena are known as the old hag, the incubus, and the succubus. While the old hag phenomenon is a nonsexual experience, incubi and succubi attack during sleep to have sex with their victims. A child is sometimes born of this union. There is much confusion and contradiction in the uses of these terms as both victims and researchers use them interchangeably; however, descriptions of the events given by assault victims are always in agreement.

The old hag phenomenon, also known as sleep paralysis, is closely examined by David J. Hufford in *The Terror That Comes in the Night: An Experience-Centered Study of Supernatural Assault Traditions* (1982). While researching night terrors, Hufford discovered that men and women of all ages and backgrounds seemed to experience nocturnal assault of the same kind. All reported "waking" to find "someone" sitting on their chest, suffocating and paralyzing them, until the victim was able to "get rid of the thing." Almost all victims report hearing strange noises—anything from newspapers being torn to high heels on linoleum, and the attacker is frequently female (although most victims don't actually see a "hag"). The phenomenon is experienced by many individuals throughout their lives, sometimes causing them to fear falling asleep.

Hufford describes a female traction patient's disturbing experience of an old hag visit:

> ... [Sharon] was, of course, lying on her back as she had since her admission about a week before. Shortly after she closed her eyes she heard the door to her room open ... She then heard footsteps ... Sharon said that, as odd as it seems, her first thought was that several nurses were coming in with their shoes off ... she found that she could not move. Then she suddenly saw a bearded, male face suspended in mid-air ... it struck her as malevolent (Hufford 88).

Sharon went on to describe feeling as though she were being lifted from the bed and pushed into it at the same time. She was paralyzed and could not scream for help. Her assault ended when a nurse walked into her room, whereupon she woke from sleep. Victims of this phenomenon report being able to suddenly move or scream and this is what makes the attack cease. Some have been known to go so far as to "prepare" their bed before going to sleep in hope of killing the hag when she appears. In his 1850 book, *Sleep Psychologically Considered with Reference to Sensation and Memory*, Blanchard Fosgate (who uses the term "incubus" to describe events that are undeniably old hag occurrences) cites overeating before bedtime as the cause for the feelings of suffocation and paralysis and hypothesizes that a simpler diet will cure the ailment (137).

Hufford also records interviews that include ways to "rat out" the malevolent person thought to be behind the "haggings," who is assumed to be a witch, or a friend who feels mistreated and wants revenge. The old hag is best known as such in the Atlantic Provinces of Canada, where a report of having been "hagged" or "hag-rid" the night before may not be considered especially noteworthy, and is experienced by sleepers of all ages (Hufford: 2–5).

The experience may also haunt a dreamer in the form of a recurring nightmare. The old hag phenomenon is very much alive today; there are support groups, chat rooms, and Web sites devoted to sharing experiences and knowledge about it. An episode of television's *Buffy the Vampire Slayer* entitled "Killed By Death" features a demon called Der Kindestod, who sits on the chests of hospitalized children and drains the life from them.

An incubus is a male demon who has sex with a woman in her sleep; its female counterpart is a demon known as a succubus who ravages sleeping men in a similar fashion. Incubi are thought to be fallen angels in league with the Devil, attacking victims in order to produce children who are his spawn. (The Arthurian magician Merlin is said by some to have been the product of an incubus union.) At least since the publication of Bram Stoker's *Dracula*, highly sexualized vampire figures tend to be placed in the incubi/succubi category because they attack in the night. Folklore's most infamous succubus is Lilith, Adam's first partner, sometimes associated with the Christian Devil, who is said to produce demons as her children.

The medieval text *Malleus Maleficarum* ("The Witch's Hammer") deals with incubi/succubi. In it, we are told that demons are able to sire offspring; however, since their bodies aren't corporeal, they need to obtain sperm from another source. To further their goal, incubi and succubi may work together: the succubus has a sexual encounter with a human male to gather sperm, which she either transforms directly into a male demon or gives to an incubus to impregnate his female victim. The children born of such unions are said to belong to the man who "donated" the sperm, not to the demon; however, these offspring are likely to be inclined toward bad behavior and drawn to Satan. *See also:* Folk Belief; Legend, Supernatural; Lilith; Memorate.

References: Des Hotel, Rob, and Dean Batali. "Killed By Death." *Buffy the Vampire Slayer*, Season Two, Episode 18. Dir. Deran Serafian; Fosgate, Blanchard. *Sleep Psychologically Considered with References to Sensation and Memory.* New York: Da Capo Press, 1982; Guazzo, Fancesco Maria. *Compenduim Maleficarum: The Montague Summers Edition.* New York: Dover Publications, 1988; Hufford, David J. *The Terror That Comes in the Night: An Experience Centered Study of Supernatural Assault Traditions.* Philadelphia: University of Pennsylvania Press, 1982; Summers, Montague, ed. *The Malleus Maleficarum of Heinrich Kramer and James Sprenger.* New York: Dover Publications, 1971.

Tamara Robbins-Anderson

Autograph Book

Autograph books are small bound albums intended for friends' signatures and brief verses. Popular among Euro American women and men in the nineteenth century, they became an amusement for children in the late 1800s. While some autograph books of that period contain only signatures, others record verses, reminiscences, and good wishes for the recipient. Schools, summer camps, and, more recently, instructional weekend workshops are among the most popular settings for autograph-book signings. Folklorists and other scholars have found them to be significant sources of information about girls' and women's cultural traditions.

J. S. Ogilvie published an influential compilation of nineteenth-century autograph rhymes, *Seven Hundred Album Verses*, in 1884; it offered the reading public, among other items, sample verses for use on Valentine's Day and other holidays. Most of the rhymes in Ogilvie's book extol the importance of friendship, asking the recipient to cherish happy memories of time spent together. Genteel British and American women carefully considered which autograph album verses would express the depth of their friendships.

In his study of autograph books in New York in the second half of the nineteenth century, folklorist W. K. McNeil found that clever verses signaling remembrance and friendship were the most popular. "Remember me," has several versions, including "Remember me early / Remember me late / Remember me ever / Your old schoolmate." Another favored form is the letter code, as in "YYUR / YYUB / ICUR YY4me" (Too wise you are / Too wise you be / I see you are too wise for me"), a technique that has come back into use among electronic text-message users at the start of the twenty-first century.

Simon J. Bronner's *American Children's Folklore* (1988) includes a broad range of children's autograph rhymes, many of which are funny and critical rather than complimentary. For example, the "Roses are red" pattern, taken from Valentine's Day verse, has many permutations, including "Roses are red, violets are black, you'd look better with a knife in your back." Such verses give young writers a chance to develop variations on familiar sentimental themes.

Some verses address young women's maturation, emphasizing love, sexual desire, marriage, and childbearing. A typical inscription in a girl's album states that "If all the boys lived across the sea, oh, what a swimmer [girl's name] would be." Another anticipates her future children's needs: "When you get married and have twins, don't call on me for safety pins." Since these rhymes predate modern feminism, it should not be surprising that they focus on romance and childrearing.

Since the early 1990s, children's use of autograph books has declined, although books like Joanna Cole's *Yours Till Banana Splits: 201 Autograph Rhymes* (2004) help to keep verse traditions going. The online encyclopedia Wikipedia offers virtual autograph books for children and adults, with room for a limitless number of e-mail signatures (favorite quotations chosen by e-mail users and appended to e-mail messages), as well as such neutral comments such as "A sig, a sig, I give you a sig" ("A signature, a signature, I give you a signature"). Autograph books retain their social and entertainment functions as they continue to evolve. *See also:* Childbirth and Childrearing; Rhymes; Valentine's Day.

References: Bronner, Simon J. *American Children's Folklore.* Little Rock, AR: August House, 1988; Cole, Joanna. *Yours Till Banana Splits: 201 Autograph Rhymes.* Darby, PA: DIANE Publishing Company, 2004; McNeil, W. K. "From Advice to Laments Once Again: New York Autograph Album Verse, 1850–1900." *New York Folklore Quarterly,* vol. 25, no. 3 (1970): 168–95; Ogilvie, J. S. *Seven Hundred Album Verses.* New York: J. S. Ogilvie and Co., 1884.

Elizabeth Tucker

B

Babysitting

The term "babysitting" refers to the job of supervising children while their parent or parents are away from home. The typical North American babysitter is a young female, eleven to eighteen years of age, who is known to the family and has a good rapport with its youngest member or members. Ideally, she is reliable, trustworthy, and mature enough to know how to behave in an emergency. Babysitting is frequently a girl's entrée to the world of paid work. Grandmothers and other relatives may be enlisted to babysit, but such persons are not usually paid an hourly wage to do so. Increasingly, it is considered acceptable for a babysitter to be a teenage boy trusted by the family.

Babysitting rose in popularity in the United States after World War II. Many working families began to move into newly created suburbs, and while they could not afford professional day care for their children (and after-school care did not yet exist), they could employ a teenager from the neighborhood for a nominal fee to watch younger children for brief periods of time. Today, with the availability of day-care centers for middle- and upper-class families, most parents hire a babysitter only occasionally. It is more likely for working-class parents to do so, as day care may be prohibitively expensive, even when it is available. Babysitting wages are fixed by unofficial community standards, generally varying today in the range of $6 to $15 per hour, depending on how many children and for how long they are to be watched.

Part-time babysitting has largely superseded the full-time roles of governess or nanny, even among the wealthy. These women generally performed the tasks of a surrogate mother—they were paid to feed, bathe, clothe, soothe, discipline, and educate the children in their care. Some elite families still employ a full-time housekeeper, but her job is likely limited to caring for the domestic sphere regardless of the presence of children; care of a child is considered a separate duty, if not as highly skilled a task. Scarr (1984) notes that the "sitter" plays a temporary role as monitor; she watches, but is not expected to educate, and she is not usually responsible for any housekeeping chores.

The benefit of hiring a youthful babysitter versus an older caregiver is in the fact that she is typically considered a source of entertainment for the children, rather than an authority figure. However, a parent cannot observe how the sitter spends her time with the children. While most day-care facilities are accredited by the state, and parents can observe their children interacting with other adults and teenagers, the unobserved babysitter is free to place the children in her care in front of a television and not interact with them at all. The babysitter's young age can also make coping with the demands of difficult children unwieldy. When surveyed, most sitters felt uncomfortable dealing with kids who have behavioral problems. The incidence of child abuse is higher with babysitters than with professional child-care workers.

Many urban legends dealing with the dark side of babysitting have emerged over the years. In one of them, a young woman thinks she is alone after the children have gone to sleep. A series of frightening phone calls, however, reveals that there is a crazed killer in the house. In some versions, the girl gets away, but the children are murdered. The role of the babysitter in these stories is that of the helpless female at the mercy of a randomly murderous male. In another urban legend, it is the parents who are warned about unpredictable teenage behavior. Concerned that their babysitter might be smoking marijuana in their home, they call to check on the baby; the babysitter assures them that the baby is fine and the turkey is in the oven. Puzzled over her remark about the turkey, the parents return home to discover that the babysitter has placed their child in the oven (http://snopes.com). It may be said, however, that such stories are designed more to convey negative gender stereotypes about young females than they are about the perils of babysitting. *See also:* Childbirth and Childrearing; Gender; Girls' Folklore; Legend, Urban/Contemporary; Occupational Folklore; Wage Work; Women's Work.

References: American Red Cross. "Babysitter's Training." http://www.redcross.org/services/hss/resources/provider_bbs.html (accessed August 8, 2008); Scarr, Sandra. *Mother Care, Other Care.* New York: Basic Books, Inc., 1984; Seelhorst, Mary. "'The Assailant in Disguise': Old and New Functions of Urban Legends About Women Alone in Danger." *North Carolina Folklore Journal*, vol. 34, no. 1 (1987): 29–37.Snopes.com, Urban Legends Reference Pages. "Wasted and Basted." http://www.snopes.com/horrors/drugs/babysit.htm (accessed August 8, 2008); Werner, Emmy E. *Child Care: Kith, Kin, and Hired Hands.* Baltimore: University Park Press, 1984.

Claire Dodd

Ballad

The oldest and simplest definition of the ballad is still the best: a song that tells a story. The ballad is usually distinguished from the lyric, a song that, while it may imply or suggest a story, emphasizes emotional response to a person, thing, or situation. English-language ballads are conventionally divided into two main types, the classic or Child ballad and the broadside ballad. Classic ballads are part of a larger European oral repertoire with roots in the Middle Ages, in which the narrative mode is typically impersonal and expresses no overt judgment, however extreme the action. The narrative usually progresses via dialogue and incremental repetition, often depending, in part, on traveling stanzas or commonplaces, lines and phrases adapted and refitted for use in many different ballads. Broadside ballads emerged with the development of the popular press. First circulated in print, either on single sheets called broadsides or, later, in newspapers, many broadside ballads quickly entered oral tradition and took their place alongside classic ballads. Typically, such ballads are composed in response to dramatic happenings, and they typically express a clear judgment and affect. Broadside ballads sung in North America include songs of both British and U.S. origin.

The Hispanic ballad also flourishes in parts of the United States, having reached a height during the Mexican Revolution. Here too there is a division corresponding roughly to that between classic and broadside ballads. *Romances*, like impersonal classic ballads, have links to international ballads, while *corridos* are more emotionally flavored narratives composed in the United States or in Mexico in response to dramatic events. A variant of the form emerged in the late twentieth century; the *narcocorrido*, a form of the outlaw ballad, it extols the exploits of drug traffickers and drug lords.

Believing the classic ballad to be nearly extinct in oral tradition, Francis James Child (1825–1896), a Harvard professor, published a comprehensive collection of them between 1884 and 1898. (His daughter, Helen Child Sargent, in cooperation with George Lyman Kittredge, published a one-volume edition in 1904.) Working mostly from printed sources or manuscript collections, Child gathered all the known English-language ballads from the European repertoire as well as some that may have been created in the British Isles in the mold of international ballads. Scholars still identify versions of classic ballads by the titles and numbers that Child assigned in his collection. Broadside ballads, however, are usually identified by the titles and numbers that G. Malcolm Laws, Jr., assigned them in two surveys first published in the 1950s. (The standard collection of ballad tunes is the four-volume compendium that Bertrand Harris Bronson published between 1959 and 1972.)

A favorite theory of ballad origin in the nineteenth and early twentieth centuries held that they were created communally by group improvisation. In 1921, Louise Pound (1872–1958), then at the University of Nebraska, published *Poetic Origins and the Ballad,* in which she decisively refuted the theory of communal origin, revealing the contradictions inherent in the theory and drawing on her own fieldwork to show how ballads actually function in communities. It took another quarter-century, however, for her view to win general acceptance.

The women's world revealed in the classic or Child ballads is of a piece with the women's world represented in *Märchen*, medieval literature, and classical drama. Characters fall into a limited number of heterosexual female types, including the faithful but hapless beloved, the false beloved, the jealous rival, the seduced maiden, the bereaved mother, the cruel mother, and the wife taken advantage of in the absence of her husband. Parents or a brother may interfere fatally, though the maiden may call upon her beloved and be rescued. The lover himself may prove false and wed another, though that will often lead to the death of all three—the betrayed woman, the false lover, and the hapless wife. Or the young wife may run off with another man. Maria Herrera Sobek (1990) finds the same archetypal representations in corridos.

There are also negatively represented dangerous women: the murderous second love of "Young Hunting," the lady who causes the death of Little Musgrave in "Little Musgrave and Lady Barnard," "Bonnie Barbara Allen" who will not relent from her anger, and the Jewish or Gypsy woman who kills young "Sir Hugh." But as in Märchen, medieval literature, and classical drama, there are also resourceful women who prevail against the odds. Susy Pye rescues "Lord Bateman." The murderess of "Young Hunting" answers to no one but a parrot. "The Bailiff's Daughter of Islington" sets off and finds a surprisingly rich young man. "Lady Isabel" tricks her would-be murderer and succeeds in drowning him. The wife of "Geordie" usually succeeds in rescuing her husband in U.S. versions of that ballad. And even "Mary Hamilton," abandoned to the gallows by her king-lover, achieves an almost enviable dignity.

The humorous ballads, too, present both positive and negative images. The clever maids in "The Baffled Knight" and "The Broomfield Hill" easily trick their would-be seducers or rapists, and the clever adulteress in "Our Goodman" has an answer for every challenge. The ballad of "The Wife Wrapped in Wether's Skin," however, rationalizes wifebeating, and "Get Up and Bar the Door" suggests that women are not satisfied unless they have the last word. Yet in some American versions of "The Farmer's Curst Wife," the misogyny is reversed: the wife's adventures demonstrate that women are better than men—because when they go to hell, they can come back again.

Broadside ballads present a somewhat narrower picture of situations in which women find themselves or figure, and self-sufficient women characters are rare. When soldiers and sailors go off to war, they leave sweethearts behind to moan. Sometimes these women follow and achieve distinction as soldiers or sailors themselves before being found out. Sometimes they remain behind to prove true when their loves return and test them. Some young gentlewomen fall for men of lower station, and either succumb to family pressure and die, overcome the pressure and go off happy, or discover the young man is false and perish. Women with champagne tastes cause their lovers or husbands to turn highwayman to support them in style—seldom successfully. Women are usually less significant characters in outlaw ballads, though the wife of "Brennan on the Moor" rescues her husband from the sheriff, only to have him prove false with a girl who then betrays him. Young men, often soldiers, seduce young women and disappear. Sometimes the girl dies, sometimes she tricks another man into marrying her, and sometimes she names the baby after his father. Frequently, too, the heroine loves a ne'er-do-well who ends up murdering her. (Murder ballads are considered a sub-genre in their own right.) In broadside ballads of

U.S. origin, a young woman may live on a farm or may cross the prairies. One such heroine, in "A Fair Lady of the Plains," fights Natives (or cattle rustlers) alongside her husband. Also in U.S. ballads, wives and mothers figure significantly as gauges of the emotional significance of an event: they kiss their husbands, who go off to die in train wrecks or mine disasters; they kiss their sons as they go off to prison; or they survive to mourn their dead.

Humorous broadside ballads, like their Child counterparts, have something of the fabliau about them. In "The Warranty Deed," a new groom finds that his wife is constituted more by artificial parts (glass eye, wooden leg, false teeth, wig, etc.) than "real woman." In "The Dumb Wife," a man finds a doctor to cure his wife of muteness, but not one to cure her then of scolding. In "The Old Maid and the Burglar," the woman in question wants to marry the burglar hiding under her bed. And "The Old Woman of Slapsadam" tries to drown her blind husband, and herself ends up drowned.

Occasionally, however, the woman gets the upper hand. In "Father Grumble," a man and woman change jobs for a day on a bet, and the woman wins. In the relatively rare "The Dog in the Closet," the wife confounds her husband by substituting the family dog for the lover her husband has locked in the closet. A girl refuses "The Young Man Who Wouldn't Hoe Corn." And "Sweet Betsy from Pike" proves irrepressible in every situation that arises on the Oregon Trail. "La Martina," sung as a dialogue, has the husband inquiring about a horse that is not his, among other belongings that the wife's lover has forgotten in his quick departure.

As is clear, a bourgeois sensibility is characteristic of broadside ballads. In songs of the U.S. South, however, the broadside ballad may incorporate African American elements and a more bicultural sensibility to emerge as a blues ballad. Blues ballads are characterized by an impressionistic, lyrical, less linear narrative, and by personalization, or focus on the individual central character combined with a more ego-centered emotional affect. Typically, too, they feature an expansion of the female presence in the ballad. This "feminization," as it has been called by Renwick (2001), includes expanding the list of female characters while narrowing the list of males, and emphasizing the reactions of female characters while reducing the level of social comment. It does not require, however, that all female characters be treated sympathetically. Outside the South, the broadside ballad retains its older, bourgeois sensibility.

The Southern Appalachian mountains are one of the great repositories of Child (and also broadside) ballads in the United States, as Olive Dame Campbell (1882–1954) of Medford, Massachusetts, discovered in 1908. Her husband, John C. Campbell, had accepted a Russell Sage grant to study social agencies working in the southern mountains. Accompanying him on his survey, she heard Ade B. Smith sing "Barbara Allen" at Hindman Settlement School. Campbell recognized it as one of the ballads that Child had believed to be on the verge of extinction when he published his collection. Campbell asked Smith to sing all the ballads she knew so that she could take them down. As the survey continued elsewhere, Campbell eventually collected more than sixty ballad texts and tunes. With these in hand, she met British folksong scholar Cecil Sharp (1859–1924), who was then visiting the United States. She persuaded Sharp to come to the mountains to gather ballads and folksongs in a more systematic way than had been possible for her and her husband. Sharp and his assistant, Maud Karpeles (1885–1976), in 1916, 1917, and 1918, spent a total of forty-six weeks there, he taking down tunes from the mountaineers while Karpeles recorded the texts.

While Sharp was collecting at the Pine Mountain Settlement School in Kentucky, he met Evelyn Kendrick Wells (1891–1979). Wells had taken a ballad course under Katharine Lee Bates (1859–1929) at Wellesley College, and eventually returned there to revive the ballad course; she published *The Ballad Tree* in 1950, the first handbook to draw extensively upon the U.S. ballad repertoire. Two children who sang for both Sharp and Wells at Pine Mountain belonged to the Ritchie family of Viper, Kentucky. Their younger sister, Jean Ritchie (1922–), became a celebrated performer of ballads, made numerous commercial recordings of ballad performances as well as of other types of songs, and ultimately published the family repertoire in versions she had polished during her years of performance and research.

Another of the singers who sang for Sharp and Karpeles was Jane Hicks Gentry (1863–1925) of Hot Springs, North Carolina. Gentry was a member of the large Hicks-Harmon family of Watauga County, and was considered one of the finest ballad singers Sharp knew, with a repertoire of twenty-three Child ballads in addition to many other songs. Gentry was also a fine story-teller who communicated the first major collection of Hicks family stories to Isabel Gordon Carter in 1924. In 1938, collector Anne Warner (1905–1991) went to Watauga County with her husband Frank to meet a cousin of Jane Hicks Gentry, the dulcimer maker Nathan Hicks of Beech Mountain. The Warners returned many times to Beech Mountain and nearby towns over the next forty years to gather songs from the extended Hicks family, in which women were more likely than men to sing ballads, while the men more often played instruments or told tales. The Warners also collected from singers on the North Carolina Outer Banks and from the Northeast. Lena Bourne Fish, who sang for them and Helen Flanders (see below) in the 1940s, had a particularly large repertoire, probably more than 100 songs, featuring both Child and broadside ballads as well as lyric folksongs. After her husband's death, Anne Warner cataloged their collection and edited *Traditional American Folksongs from the Anne and Frank Warner Collection* (1984). Collectors have continued to gather songs and tales from the Hicks-Harmon clan in the years since Cecil Sharp and the Warners first visited them, resulting in a family repertoire that is probably the best documented in the United States.

Early collectors of romances and corridos such as Arthur Campa, Juan Rael, and Aurelio Espinoza found classic romances, like "La Delgadina," a story of incest, and "El Hijo Desobediente," being sung in California, New Mexico, and other parts of the Southwest. In Texas, Américo Paredes (1976) found these along with corridos about migrating north to work on the railroad or in cattle drives, as in "El Corrido de Kiansis" that dates from the 1860s. Paredes' now-classic discussion of border ballads, *"With His Pistol in His Hand": A Border Ballad and Its Hero* (1958), influenced the founders of the Chicano movement of the 1960s and 1970s.

In the years after World War I, it became clear that New England was a second major repository of classic ballads in the United States. Helen Hartness Flanders (1890–1972) began to collect folk songs for the Vermont Commission on Country Life in 1930. Her work attracted the attention of Phillips Barry (1880–1937), who became her mentor and occasional collaborator. Flanders and her colleague Marguerite Olney collected extensively all over New England, eventually establishing the Helen Hartness Flanders Collection at Middlebury College, in Middlebury, Vermont. Between 1960 and 1965, Flanders published *Ancient Ballads Traditionally Sung in New England* with a commentary by Tristram P. Coffin and tune transcriptions by Bruno Nettl. Other significant female collectors in New England were Mary W. Smyth, Fannie Hardy Eckstorm, Joanna C. Colcord, and Eloise Hubbard Linscott.

Women produced significant ballad collections from other parts of North America as well. Emelyn Elizabeth Gardner published a folklore collection, including ballads, from the Schoharie Hills of New York state, soon followed by a publication jointly edited with Geraldine Jencks Chickering, *Ballads and Songs of Southern Michigan.* Louise Pound published Nebraska songs; Mary O. Eddy published an Ohio collection; Sidney Robertson Cowell collected in Appalachia, the Ozarks, the Midwest, and the West Coast; and Margaret Larkin published an important collection of cowboy songs and ballads. Collecting continued in the southern mountains, with resultant publications such as those of Jean Thomas, Ethel Park Richardson, and Dorothy Scarborough, and the recordings of Mary Elizabeth Barnacle. Important early Canadian collections include those of Helen Creighton, from Nova Scotia, and of Elizabeth B. Greenleaf, Grace Y. Mansfield, and Maud Karpeles from Newfoundland (before it became a part of Canada). The most significant Canadian collector of the twentieth century, however, was surely Edith Fowke (1913–1996), especially notable for her work among lumbermen and her studies of particular family repertoires; her many collections include ballads, folksongs, and children's rhymes. Fowke also oversaw the publication of choral and concert versions of traditional Canadian ballad material.

The tradition of female scholarship in ballad studies exemplified by Bates and Wells at Wellesley and Pound at Nebraska has continued in the innovative teaching, research, and contributions to ballad theory of Thelma James at Wayne State University, Mary Ellen Brown at Indiana University, Linda Morley at Harvard, and Kathleen E. B. Manley at the University of Northern Colorado. Ruth Crawford Seeger edited the music for a number of important ballad collections as well as producing two volumes of American folksongs for children, families, and educators. Eleanor Long published a monograph on "The Maid Freed from the Gallows," as well as numerous articles. Dianne M. Dugaw published overtly feminist ballad scholarship in her studies of cross-dressing in ballads. Anne Cohen has studied the murder of and ballads about Pearl Bryan. Sara Garcia, Maria Herrera-Sebok, and Yolanda Broyles-Gonzalez have done considerable work on Hispanic ballads, corridos, and *cancion ranchera*. Rae Korson headed the Library of Congress Archive of Folk Song from 1956 to 1969.

The list of important North American ballad singers that includes Jane Gentry and her cousins, Jean Ritchie and her sisters, and Lena Bourne Fish, includes others. Emma Dusenbury of Mena, Arkansas, buried in a pauper's grave in 1939, may have been the greatest of the U.S. ballad singers. Her repertoire was vast, encompassing much of the southern mountain repertoire as well as many rare items. Mrs. Frank Pipkin, a migrant worker in California during the dust bowl days, recorded English ballads for Charles L. Todd. Texas Gladden sang for Sara Gertrude Knott at National Folk Festivals. Almeida Riddle, an Arkansas singer who became a professional performer in her later years (corresponding with the folksong revival of the late twentieth century), also had a large ballad repertoire that she added to all her life. She published a book about her singing in cooperation with folklorist Roger Abrahams.

Canadian singer La Rena Clark published a book about her family's singing in cooperation with Edith Fowke. The internationally famous Carter family recorded ballads, and Mother Maybelle Carter sang ballads in performances and recordings with her daughters after the breakup of the original family group. Arhoolie Records' catalogue contains works by female singers in the corrido tradition, including those of the legendary Lydia Mendoza. Recordings issued by the Library of Congress, Folkways, June Appal, and other distributors in the second half of the twentieth century, featuring singers such as Aunt Molly Jackson, Sara Ogan Gunning, and Ruth Crawford Seeger's daughter Peggy, further attest to the richness of the U.S. women's ballad repertoire. *See also:* Courtship; Class; Cross-Dressing; Death; Folk Music and Folksong; Fieldwork; Marriage; Storytelling.

References: Bronson, Bertrand Harris. *The Traditional Tunes of the Child Ballads.* Princeton, NJ: Princeton University Press, 1959–1972; Broyles-Gonzalez, Yolanda. *Lydia Mendoza's Life in Music/La Historia de Lydia Mendoza* (with CD). New York: Oxford University Press, 2003; Campa, Arthur. *The Spanish Folksongs in the Southwest.* University of New Mexico Bulletin. Language Series 5 (1, 2). Albuquerque: University of New Mexico Press, 1933; Child, Francis James. *The English and Scottish Popular Ballads.* Boston: Houghton Mifflin, 1882–1898; Espinoza, Aurelio. "Los Romances Tradicionales en California." In *Homenaje a Menéndez Pidal*, series no. 3: 299–313. Madrid, Spain: Imprenta de los sucesores de Hernando, 1925; Flanders, Helen Hartness. *Ancient Ballads Traditionally Sung in New England* (four volumes). Philadelphia: University of Pennsylvania Press, 1960–1965; Gardner, Emelyn E., and Geraldine J. Chickering. *Ballads and Songs of Southern Michigan.* Ann Arbor: University of Michigan Press, 1939; Herrera-Sobek, Maria. *The Mexican Corrido: A Feminist Analysis.* Bloomington: Indiana University Press, 1990; Laws, G. Malcolm, Jr. *American Balladry from British Broadsides: A Guide for Students and Collectors of Traditional Song.* Philadelphia: American Folklore Society, 1957; ———. *Native American Balladry: A Descriptive Study and a Bibliographical Syllabus.* Revised edition. Philadelphia: American Folklore Society, 1964; Paredes, Américo. *"With His Pistol in His Hand": A Border Ballad and Its Hero.* Austin: University of Texas Press, 1958; ———. *A Texas-Mexican Cancioner: Folksongs of the Lower Border.* Urbana: University of Illinois Press, 1976; Pound, Louise. *Poetic Origins and the Ballad.* New York: Macmillan, 1921; Ramirez, Olga Najera, ed. *Chicana Traditions: Continuity and Change.* Urbana: University of Illinois Press, 2002; Renwick, Roger deV. *Recentering Anglo/American Folksong: Sea Crabs and Wicked Youths.* Jackson: University Press of Mississippi, 2001; Wells, Evelyn K. *The Ballad Tree.* New York: Ronald Press, 1950; Wilgus, D. K., and Eleanor Long. "The Blues Ballad and the Genesis of Style in Traditional Narrative Song." In *Narrative Folksong: New Directions*, eds. Carol L. Edwards and Kathleen E. B. Manley, 435–82. Boulder, CO: Westview Press, 1985.

William Bernard McCarthy

Banshee

Referring to an Irish supernatural death messenger, the word "banshee" comes from the Irish *bean sí*, meaning "woman of the otherworld" or "woman of the fairies." The banshee is also called *badhbh*, or *bean chaointe* (crying woman) in different areas of Ireland. According to Irish folklore, the banshee is a solitary female spirit whose mournful keening foretells the impending death of a family member. Belief in the banshee exists throughout rural and urban Ireland, almost certainly originating in the goddess figures of early Irish mythology. Evidence for this may be found in the name *badhbh*, used mainly in southeast Ireland, which derives from the name of the Irish war goddess Badb, found in early Irish literature.

Today, many Irish believe that banshees warn only families of pure Irish ethnicity and of specific lineage, particularly those whose names begin with "'Mac," "Mc," or "O." Some scholars assert that the belief that banshees protect Irish families of specific lineages emerged during the sixteenth and seventeenth centuries, when many aristocratic family lands were confiscated by the English government. In this context, the banshee figure serves not merely as a defender of Irish nobility, but as a protector of Irish land, reflecting the theme, pervasive in Irish literature and folklore, of the mythic unions between goddesses of the land and its rightful owners.

The banshee's keening wail is usually reported in the vicinity of the home of a person who is about to die, the family dwelling still being the site of most human deaths. However, it is claimed that the banshee's cry has been heard at the family residence even when the doomed person is temporarily or permanently away from home. It is believed that the banshee will follow a person across the ocean to distant lands; she is also believed to attend funerals, her voice blending in with the mourners' cries.

More commonly heard than seen, the banshee is nevertheless thought to be physically present wherever her cries are heard. She is described by some as an old, small, relatively unattractive woman with silver-gray hair streaming to the ground; others depict her as a young woman with long red hair. Her clothing is a long nightdress in green, white, or gray, often covered by a cobweb-like textured gray cloak, all of which cling to her thin body. She is invariably described as having a pale face and thin body, her eyes red from centuries of crying. The banshee often lives near water, such as a lake, river, or well, where she can be seen washing an article of clothing belonging to one who is about to die; however, she is not limited to any one location or landscape.

The banshee figure is also reported in Highland Scotland, where she is called the *bean nighe* or "little washer by the ford." The bean nighe is believed to be the spirit of a woman who died in childbirth; she is small in stature, dressed in green, with webbed feet and long, pendulous breasts. She is most often seen washing the bloodstained clothes of one about to die. However, anyone who sees her before she reaches the water is granted three wishes, and those brave enough to suckle at her breast are adopted as her own and granted special favors. *See also:* Death; Family Folklore; Folk Belief; Legend, Supernatural; Region: Western Europe; Superstition.

References: Guiley, Rosemary, ed. *The Encyclopedia of Ghosts and Spirits*. New York: Facts on File, 2000; Lysaght, Patricia. *The Banshee: The Irish Death Messenger*. Boulder, CO: Roberts Rinehart Publishers, 1986; ———. "Aspects of the Earth-Goddess in the Traditions of the Banshee in Ireland." In *The Concept of the Goddess*, eds. Sandra Billington and Miranda Green, 152–65. London: Routledge, 1996; ó hÓgáin, Dáithí. "Banshee." In *Myth, Legend, and Romance: An Encyclopaedia of Irish Folk Tradition*. New York: Prentice Hall Press, 1991; Wilde, Lady. *Ancient Legends, Mystic Charms, and Superstitions of Ireland: With Sketches of the Irish Past*. London: Chatto & Windus, 1899.

Erin Stapleton-Corcoran

Barbie Doll

An adult doll made in the United States and marketed to children beginning in 1959, Barbie was the brainchild of Ruth Handler, a founding member of Mattel Toy Company. Barbie's plastic body, with its improbable measurements and prominent breasts (modeled after a German sex doll), has generated much controversy and folklore.

Inspired by watching her daughter play with paper dolls and by the idea that an adult doll could help girls deal with the changes that their bodies undergo during puberty, Handler pitched her idea to a male colleague at Mattel. According to Handler, Mattel initially dismissed it, horrified by the thought of a doll with breasts. Handler persisted, creating a doll that has been a remarkable, long-term success for Mattel—so much so that if all Barbies sold by the end of the twentieth century were lined up head to toe, they would circle the Earth at least eleven times. Mattel maintains that, by the end of the twentieth century, two Barbies were sold in the world each second. After creating Barbie and surviving breast cancer, Handler went on to establish a firm that designed mastectomy prostheses. She describes her life as going from breasts to breasts.

From her inception, the Princess of Plastic has been controversial. She began life fully formed with a job as a fashion model; by 1965, she was an astronaut. Some men, disturbed by the mass distribution of a doll with a career, told the media that playing with Barbie dolls would turn little girls into independent, "viperous" women (Thomas 2003: 123). However, discomfort with such dolls was not new. For example, adult dolls were used to display women's fashions in Europe and North America in earlier centuries. Female fashion (often more harshly criticized than men's) was seen as a manifestation of women's vanity, artifice, and pretense, and dolls were guilty by association. Also, dolls had been ascribed a role in witchcraft rituals, and early courts used ownership of them as evidence against those accused of being witches. Add to these pejorative historical associations some of the contemporary concerns about Barbie dolls, and it's a wonder that Barbie's press has not been even more negative. Currently, Barbie's unlikely proportions generate charges that she perpetuates unhealthy body images for women. Barbie easily taps girls' curiosity about their sexuality because of her adult physique and her long, sometimes Godiva-like hair. In 1968, Mattel created Christie, Barbie's Black friend; 1980 saw Black Barbie and Hispanic Barbie. There have been numerous ethnic Barbies since then, but critics charge that these dolls still look far too much like blonde Barbie to make them acceptable as toy role models for non-white, non-blonde, and non-thin girls and women.

Along with Barbie's perfect plastic body, her mane of hair defines her very being. While parents express all sorts of concerns about Barbie, children embrace her, in part because they can play with her hair. When Mattel's research revealed that little girls liked hair play, her tresses were made abnormally long. The children were extending to Barbie the folk customs of hair play—combing, styling, and braiding—that they were doing at home and at slumber parties with their friends. Mattel commodified some of this folkloric behavior; the list of Barbie incarnations that emphasize hair includes Twirly Curls Barbie, Super Hair Barbie, Hollywood Hair Barbie, Troll Hair Barbie, Glitter Hair Barbie, and Hula Hair Barbie, to name but a few.

According to Thomas (2000), Barbie is an excellent example of commodified folklore (folklore and folkloric themes translated into marketable objects). Other folkloric currents employed in the marketing of Barbie dolls include legendry, folktales, mythology, rites of passage, holidays, and folk costumes. Legend-inspired Barbies include numerous angel and mermaid Barbies, some of which come with special effects; for example, bubbles come out of the head of one mermaid Barbie when her buttocks are squeezed. Fairy tales inspired the creation of Rapunzel Barbie and Sleeping Beauty Barbie; classical mythology was the impetus for Greek Goddess Barbie. Weddings are one of the most popular rites of passage for Barbie, but there's also Quinceañera Teresa, celebrating her fifteenth birthday, one of the Barbie Family and Friends dolls. Many Barbies are associated with holidays, such as Mardi Gras, Valentine's Day, and Christmas. The Barbie Dolls of the World Collection relies on folk costumes, depicted with varying degrees of accuracy, to indicate nationality.

Mattel markets a staggering array of Barbies engaged in various occupations, for example, Paleontologist Barbie, and avocations such as Harley-Davidson Barbie. Barbie also appears as famous media figures, for example, Marilyn Monroe Barbie and Addams Family Barbie and Ken. Ken, Barbie's boyfriend, appeared on the market in 1961. Barbie also reportedly inspired the 1964 creation of the G. I. Joe doll, who was rechristened as an action figure for boys.

Despite the accessories and cultural scripts that Mattel markets along with Barbie (see http://Barbie.com), those who play with her often use the doll to reflect their own interests. Folk play with and folklore about Barbie is thus wildly divergent. Gays and lesbians recode Barbie to reflect their experiences and worldviews, and young children often mirror and extend their own family environments and interests in their Barbie play, so Barbie-play stories range widely in both content and style. For example, representative topics of some oral accounts of children's play include Barbie as Godzilla, Barbie dating Ken, baking Barbie heads in the oven, utilizing Barbie to explore anatomy and sexuality, and stealing all of a sibling's Barbie dolls and filling every toilet tank in the household with them.

Barbie play does not end with childhood; playful parodies focusing on Barbie abound on the Internet. This electronic folklore (e-lore) criticizes

Barbie's body, situates her in real-life situations, and demonstrates her usefulness as a vehicle to address key issues in contemporary women's lives. E-lore parodies include descriptions of Hacker Barbie, Bag Lady Barbie, Menopausal Barbie, Lipstick Lesbian Barbie, Birkenstock Barbie, Blue-Collar Barbie, Punk Barbie, and Transgender Barbie (formerly known as G. I. Joe). Interestingly, although G. I. Joe has garnered some criticism as a war toy, Barbie has drawn more cultural fire and critique, as e-lore parodies indicate. In the 1960s, a Nazi G. I. Joe was marketed but few noticed; however, every Barbie hairstyle and hemline receives attention. While parodies that focus on the problematic nature of Barbie's "body beautiful" are abundant, the Internet is largely and disturbingly silent when it comes to similar critiques of G. I. Joe's "body violent." *See also:* Coding; Cyberculture; Dolls; Fashion; Folk Costume; Folk Custom; Folklore of Subversion; Folktale; Girls' Games; Hair; *Quinceañera*; Rites of Passage; Sexism; Valentine's Day; Women's Work.

References: Barbie.com. http://barbie.everythinggirl.com (accessed March 18, 2005); duCille, Ann. "Barbie in Black and White." In *The Barbie Chronicles: A Living Doll Turns Forty*, ed. Yona Zeldis McDonough, 127–142. New York: Touchstone, 1999; Handler, Ruth, with Jacqueline Shannon. *Dream Doll: The Ruth Handler Story*. Stamford, CT: Longmeadow Press, 1994; Lord, M. G. *Forever Barbie*. New York: Avon Books, 1994; Rand, Erica. *Barbie's Queer Accessories*. Durham, NC: Duke University Press, 1995; Rogers, Mary. *Barbie Culture*. London: Sage Publications, Ltd., 1999; Stern, Susan. *Barbie Nation: An Unauthorized Tour*. Distributed on videocassette by New Day Films, 1998; Thomas, Jeannie Banks. "Ride 'Em Barbie Girl: Commodifying Folklore, Place, and the Exotic." In *Worldviews and the American West: The Life of the Place Itself*, eds. Polly Stewart, Steve Siporin, C. W. Sullivan III, and Suzi Jones, 65–86. Logan: Utah State University Press, 2000; ———. *Naked Barbies, Warrior Joes, and Other Forms of Visible Gender*. Urbana and Chicago: University of Illinois Press, 2003.

Jeannie Banks Thomas

Barker, Ma

As the mother of four sons, all of whom committed serious crimes in the 1920s and 1930s, Ma Barker is often considered a criminal figure herself. However, there is no direct evidence, other than her long-standing devotion to her sons and their welfare, that this was the case.

Born as Arizona Donnie Clark on October 8, 1873, in Ash Grove, Missouri, Barker was known as Arrie, and then as Kate, but was dubbed "Ma" in the newspapers following her death by FBI gunfire on January 16, 1935, in Oklawaha, Florida. She married George Barker, a farmer in southwestern Missouri, in 1892, and raised four sons: Herman, a robber of stores, who shot himself in the head when trapped by the police in 1927; Lloyd, who served twenty-five years in federal prison for robbing a mail truck; Arthur (known as "Dock"), a violent gangster who died while attempting to escape from Alcatraz Prison in 1939; and Fred, another violent gangster, who died alongside his mother in 1935. After she and George separated in the mid-1920s, Barker lived with various sons in a series of homes and apartments in Missouri, Oklahoma, Kansas, Minnesota, Illinois, and elsewhere, sometimes under an assumed name to avoid detection.

Although her four sons had long criminal records, Barker herself was never once arrested, photographed, or fingerprinted by law-enforcement officials. Accordingly, it is difficult to believe FBI Director J. Edgar Hoover's claim that she was "the most vicious, dangerous, and resourceful criminal brain of the last decade," who "became a monument to the evils of parental indulgence" (1938: 9). Similar claims were made by Melvin Purvis, one of Hoover's lead agents at the FBI, who wrote that she "could handle a machine gun as well as the next man," and that she ruled over the twenty-five members of her criminal gang "like a queen. Her word was law" (1938: 151–52).

Barker was probably not as innocent as claimed by Alvin Karpis—she probably was the true leader of their criminal gang. "The most ridiculous story in the annals of crime is that Ma Barker was the mastermind behind the Karpis-Barker Gang," he wrote. "It's no insult to Ma's memory that she just didn't have the brains or know-how to direct us on a robbery.... You only had to spend a few hours with Ma to see she wasn't the criminal type. She was just an old-fashioned homebody from the Ozarks" (1971: 80–81).

The fact that Barker was born and raised in the Ozarks region of south-western Missouri may help to explain her contradictory images. One stereotypical view is that Ozark mountaineers are primitive, violent, and deceptive, reinforcing the FBI's view that Barker was one bad mother. The other view stereotypes her as a simple Ozark hillbilly, a woman who loved playing bingo, doing jigsaw puzzles, listening to the radio, and stuffing "herself with cotton candy all night," as Karpis described her (1971: 91). The true story of Ma Barker probably lies somewhere in between. *See also:* Mothers' Folklore.

References: Browder, Laura. *Her Best Shot: Women and Guns in America.* Chapel Hill: University of North Carolina Press, 2006; Burrough, Bryan. *Public Enemies: America's Greatest Crime Wave and the Birth of the FBI, 1933–34.* New York: Penguin Press, 2004; Caras, Mark, writer/producer. *Ma Barker: Crime Family Values.* Biography series. Arts and Entertainment Network, 1997; Hoover, J. Edgar. *Persons in Hiding.* Boston: Little, Brown and Co., 1938; Karpis, Alvin, with Bill Trent. *The Alvin Karpis Story.* New York: Coward, McCann & Geoghegan, 1971; Purvis, Melvin. *American Agent.* New York: Garden City Publishing Co., 1938.

James I. Deutsch

Basketmaking

One of humankind's oldest forms of material culture is weaving and, in North America, archaeological evidence indicates that basketmaking likely arrived with the first people to arrive from the Old World before the close of the last Ice Age. In some cultures, the story of the creation of the world involves a basket. For example, in Hopi culture, the four animal origins of people floated in a basket boat on everlasting water. The Washoe tell of Washoe, Miwok, Maidu, and Northern Paiute emerging from a water basket filled with cattail down, seeds, and grass. The Passamaquoddy people tell of how Glooskap made the first human by shooting a bow and arrow at the basket (ash) tree; the First Nations came out of the ash tree bark.

Across time and cultures, basketweaving overwhelmingly has been considered the domain of women. Indigenous stories place the creation of baskets alongside that of humankind and often link it to women's work. For instance, a Yakima story tells of the creator giving the first woman a little basket which held the skills of art and design that could be imparted to her descendants. Navajo speak of the first Twins who made baskets of reeds and declared that basketmaking should be "women's work."

Regardless of date of origin, basketweaving has been and continues to be a widespread and important part of Indigenous North American cultures. Sites of spiritual, historical, and cultural importance have Indigenous names connected to baskets or basket materials. Tewa-speaking people in the Southwest, for example, tell of the place the Apache settled as Basket Mountain, noting that this is why Apache are such fine weavers. Stories abound in numerous First Nation communities that provide instruction in the skills and knowledge associated with basketmaking, along with other aspects of living.

Knowledge of weaving itself is inextricably tied to knowledge of the natural world: weavers know what materials can be used for weaving, where they grow, and how they should be harvested and prepared. In Native communities, the gathering and preparation of materials often involves prayers, songs, chants, and rituals as the weavers take the resources they require from Mother Earth. Traditional gathering is done with an acute awareness of the need to protect and nurture these natural resources, and weavers are often the first to notice any changes in the environment.

On a practical level, First Nation peoples have relied on basketry for nearly every activity in their daily routines. Baskets have been used as containers for food and water, and carriers for everything from babies to firewood, fish traps, clothing, floor coverings, burial shrouds, hunting decoys, and even boats. They have also been critical to the proper performance of ceremonial practices ranging from naming ceremonies to funerary rituals.

Immigrants to North America, whose weaving traditions also span many generations and cultures, adapted their weaving styles to embrace available materials and the needs of life in a new land. Although Indigenous weavers and immigrant weavers freely borrowed techniques from each other, distinctive traditions remain firmly rooted in specific communities due to commonly available resources, important traditional cultural meanings and purposes, and/or their economic value.

Within the realm of weaving, the term "basketmaking" refers to items covering a wide range of materials, techniques, and functions. Weaving can be done with any material that is pliable enough to be plaited, coiled, twined, braided, linked, and looped. Traditionally, weaving was done with natural materials (black ash, lauhala, sedge, reed, river cane, horsehair, birch bark, grasses, conifer roots, pine needles, etc.), but weavers incorporated manufactured materials as they became available. Natural materials can be dyed with color and woven forms can be embellished with additional materials to create surface effects. Patterns and designs incorporated into the weave are often linked to ethnic and community traditions, and sometimes mark the passing on of knowledge from one artist to another.

Most weavers traditionally make objects for use in their own families or communities, but some weavers also make a living by selling their work.

For instance, in Appalachia, numerous weaving businesses supply their communities with white oak baskets. Native people throughout North America have found a ready market for their work, and continue to sell woven objects to tourists, collectors, and traders.

Technology and international trade have had tremendous impacts on the arts of basketmaking. Today, most of the items that were woven out of necessity are now commercially produced, usually out of industrial-age materials. Baskets of natural fibers made in countries where labor is cheap are imported to the United States from all over the world, supplanting more costly local weaving traditions. Even where weaving activity has persisted, weavers have found their sources of natural materials negatively impacted by urban sprawl, the widespread use of pesticides, and growing restrictions on access to land.

Despite these challenges, weaving continues. In the late twentieth century, a number of basketmakers' associations formed in North America for the purpose of perpetuating the knowledge related to gathering and preparing materials as well as to the crafting of woven objects. For instance, the 2,000-member Association of Michigan Basketmakers hosts annual conferences and workshops, maintains a study collection of more than 300 items at the Michigan State University Museum, and is actively involved in documenting the history of their organization. Organizations of Native weavers hold annual gatherings, honor elders, support apprenticeships, and work actively to engage young women and men in learning the skills and the cultural knowledge associated with weaving. Native organizations have also led efforts to work with government agencies and private developers and landowners to protect endangered plant materials and to increase access to restricted gathering sites.

The criteria of what makes a good woven basket or other object has always been dependent on the intentions of the maker and the aesthetic standards of the community in which and for which it was made. Basketmakers have been consistently inventive in their use of materials, in the forms they create, and how they decorate or adorn their work. Many baskets have been woven for the sheer pleasure of making an idea into a tangible form. Baskets, old and new, are included in museum and private collections as both art and as important exemplars of historical and cultural knowledge. *See also:* Aesthetics; Folk Art; Material Culture; Tradition; Tradition-Bearer; Weaving; Women's Work.

References: Turnbaugh, Sarah Peabody, and William W. Turnbaugh. *Indian Baskets.* Atglen, PA: Schiffer Publishing Ltd, 2004; Wyckoff, Lydia L. *Woven Worlds: Basketry from the Clark Field Collection at the Philbrook Museum of Art.* Tulsa: Philbrook Museum of Art, 2001.

Marsha MacDowell

Bat Mitzvah

This coming-of-age ritual for Jewish girls, which serves to acknowledge them as adult members of their communities, is relatively recent. In the span of over 5,000 years of Jewish history, the first evidence of a *bat mitzvah* rite occurred in the nineteenth century in Baghdad. Rabbi Joseph

Chaim ben Elijah al-Hakam observed that if a twelve-year-old girl received a dress as a gift from her parents and made the appropriate blessing for wearing a new garment, she became a bat mitzvah ("daughter of a commandment"). This is a far cry from the rite as it is practiced today in North America, where it is typically just like a *bar mitzvah*, in which a boy chants in Hebrew from the Torah, the parchment scrolls containing the Five Books of Moses (Genesis, Exodus, Leviticus, Numbers, and Deuteronomy), leads prayers usually during a Shabbat (Saturday) morning service, and delivers a *d'var* Torah, a discourse on some aspect of Judaism related to the particular Torah portion for that week. A generation ago, however, girls in conservative and orthodox Judaism were not permitted to read from the Torah; their *bat mitzvot* or *b'nai mitvah* (two versions of the plural of this term in Hebrew) consisted instead of reading from the *Haftarah* (the books of the prophets, for example, Micah, Ezekiel, etc.). This is still the case for girls in some orthodox Jewish congregations.

Over the last fifty years, however, the bat mitzvah has evolved in two ways. First, it has become a staple of synagogue life for girls in all denominations of Judaism, including orthodoxy, the latest to join in publicly celebrating girls' coming of age. Second and somewhat less commonly, it is viewed by some women as an opportunity to invite their newly menstruating daughters into the circle of adult Jewish women in the context of a revived ritual for women called *Rosh Hodesh* (the monthly New Moon festival), which provides a space for Jewish women to explore their roles, needs, and dreams regarding Jewish tradition.

In 2000, the Lubavitcher Hasidim, an ultraorthodox sect characterized by significant emphasis on outreach to unaffiliated Jews and ecstatic worship in the form of dancing, singing, and praying, started a Bat Mitzvah Club movement, which is a fusion of the North American consciousness-raising groups of the 1960s and 1970s and the Girl Scouts/Girl Guides. Another program, also founded in 2000, is run by an independent institute in Philadelphia called "Rosh Hodesh: It's a Girl Thing!"; it is nondenominational and focuses on making the bat mitzvah a meaningful and supportive rite of passage. A major emphasis of both groups, and in fact, of all b'nai mitzvah preparation, regardless of the branch of Judaism, is on each girl's spiritual preparation during the year preceding the rite of passage into religious adulthood. This time provides an opportunity to learn about puberty, tradition, relationships, God, Israel, self-esteem, and a myriad of other topics important to Jewish girls and women. It is too soon to say, however, what impact, if any, these new movements will have on the evolution of the bat mitzvah rite.

A small minority of girls chooses to adapt the ritual *mikvah* (bath) to their coming-of-age ceremony. While observant Jewish women (and men) have traditionally practiced ritual immersion to create spiritual purity with a physical act before their wedding, observant married women also follow this custom each month after their menstrual periods. Girls who do this immerse themselves in a preliminary mikvah as a way of leaving behind their girlhood and coming out of the water with a new identity.

Related to the ritual recognition of a girl's first period (menarche), which frequently and not coincidentally coincides with the bat mitzvah, some mothers have devised a coda to the public ritual by inviting their daughter's closest friends, female relatives, and teachers (who may bring gifts of blessings, poetry, song, dance, and visual arts and crafts) to recount stories of their own coming-of-age experiences. Because many women who came of age prior to the 1960s never had a bat mitzvah themselves, such events can help to repair past wounds of exclusion from Jewish traditions.

Three ritual objects that have become integrated into the bat mitzvah celebration in the reform, reconstructionist, and conservative movements are the *tallit* (prayer shawls), *kippot* (ritual head coverings), traditionally worn by men, and *Kos Miriam* (Cup of Miriam). Both tallit and kiddish cups (traditionally, silver cups to contain the wine that sanctifies every Jewish holiday and rite of passage) are traditional b'nai mitzvah gifts, as are Shabbat candlestick holders (the beginnings of all Jewish holidays are marked by the lighting of candles). Tallit and kippot making has become a significant cottage industry among female artists and crafts people. Kos Miriam, created in the 1990s by a Rosh Hodesh group in Boston, is a goblet used for many ritual occasions. Water is poured into it to symbolize Miriam's Well, a miraculous and legendary source of water in the desert, named for the prophet Miriam, the sister of Moses. Miriam's Cup has also claimed its place besides the cup of wine set aside for the Prophet Elijah on Passover.

Another innovation in the bat mitzvah ceremony involves references to historical Jewish women. The final benediction and several prayers now invoke ancestral mothers, Sarah, Rebecca, Rachel, and Leah, along with the "fathers," Abraham, Isaac, and Jacob—a practice that has also carried into holiday and weekly Shabbat services. The Jewish Women's Archives (http://www.jwa.org) encourages girls to draw from the wealth of role models to bring meaning to a bat mitzvah ceremony. As the bat mitzvah evolves, it invites girls into the fold as adults who are inspired and mandated to make Jewish tradition their own in ways their female ancestors could never have imagined. *See also:* Consciousness Raising; Girl Scouts/Girl Guides; Jewish Women's Folklore; Legend, Religious; Menarche Stories; Menstruation; Personal-Experience Narrative; Rites of Passage Ritual.

References: Adelman, Penina, Ali Feldman, and Shulamit Reinharz. *The JGirl's Guide: The Young Jewish Woman's Handbook for Coming of Age.* Woodstock, VT: Jewish Lights Publishing, 2005; Milgram, Rabbi Goldie. *Make Your Own Bar/Bat Mitzvah.* San Francisco: Jossey-Bass, 2004; Reclaiming Judaism.org. http://www.ReclaimingJudaism.org (accessed August 11, 2008); RitualWell.org. "Ceremonies for Jewish Living." http://www.ritualwell.org (accessed August 8, 2008).

Penina Adelman

Beadwork

Beadwork is a stitching technique as well as an embellishment that uses multiple round, faceted, or tubular beads to create and enhance surface decoration. Beads are commonly applied to fabric, skins, baskets, and even musical instruments, producing patterns that vary in design, application, and meaning. Frequently, beadwork is a field of densely textured and colored patterns, but it can also be the cumulative effect of single strands of beads or magically potent beads adorning the body or decorating cult stat-ues. No matter how they are used, beads add visually dynamic accents to cloth and embroidery. The relationship of gender to bead production often divides men's work, fashioning hard materials (stone and bone carving or glassblowing), from women's efforts, creating beads from organic sub-stances such as clay or seeds. This division of labor, however, is subject to context. For example, in some Venetian glass workshops, women practice a highly skilled and time-consuming technique that involves making and deco-rating individual glass beads by using a small, concentrated flame. Bead threading and stitching are predominantly done by women.

Working with beads includes the familiar fiber techniques of sewing, weaving, and looping. Beads are either integrated into foundation fabrics or are applied externally, thus amplifying the aesthetic properties of decorative stitchery. They can be embedded in ground fabric through crocheting and knitting by separately inserting single beads between each stitch. Beadweav-ing involves passing a beading needle and thread at right angles across the vertical warp fibers on a bead loom. This method creates individual or "free-standing" beaded strips of geometric motifs derived from the grid pat-tern of warp and weft threads. The most free and creative application of beads is bead embroidery, which adds a vibrant layer of ornamentation to fabric. Embroidery techniques offer greater variety and experimentation than beadweaving. They range from the linear arrangement of beads worked in vertical and horizontal rows to flowing asymmetrical composi-tions of curvilinear elements fabricated from different sizes and types of beads worked in an array of stitches and glowing colors. These stitches are mainly variants of couching stitches, in which one stitch crosses over and anchors strings of beads at regular intervals.

Over the centuries, European glass beads or trade beads gradually replaced traditional, more natural materials such as precious and semiprecious stones, shells, quills, animal teeth, and bone. Usually the province of women, bead-work is a translation process which converts and adapts customary practices to suit new materials and techniques. After European contact, Native American needlework evolved new techniques ranging from the use of quills, bone, and shells within rather abstract rectilinear design fields to the employment of glass beads in a European style of representational floral embroidery. Beads reflect prestige and status, but their luminous, brilliant visual effects and rarity also inspire symbolic associations beyond those of identity and aesthetics. In some cultures, they are believed to have magical properties that ensure fertility and ward off evil, as well as religious significance mediated by different belief systems and ritual observances. The revival of opulent Victorian bead-work during the counterculture era of the 1960s and 1970s in North America stimulated a taste for handcrafted and decorative needlework as well as a fascination with the otherworldly or intangible dimensions of adornment. *See also:* Embroidery; Folk Art; Magic; Material Culture; Needlework; Piecework; Sewing; Weaving.

References: Barnes, Galer Britton. "Finery and Bright Colors." *Piecework* 1, no. 2 (1993): 72–75; Coe, Ralph T. *Sacred Circles: Two Thousand Years of North American Indian Art*. London: Arts Council of Great Britain, 1976; Sciama, Lidia D., and Joanne

B. Eicher, eds. *Beads and Bead Makers: Gender, Material Culture and Meaning*. Oxford and New York: Berg, 1998.

Suzanne P. MacAulay

Beauty

Beauty, like its opposite, ugliness, is determined according to cultural context and relations of power. Definitions of the beautiful and corresponding aesthetic standards in art and philosophy shift subtly with each generation and according to social values specific to the time and place. That which is beautiful, attractive, and pleasing to the eye will be admired and enjoyed, idealized, and offered as a model against which the nonbeautiful is measured. Although it is said that beauty lies in the eye of the beholder, in fact, dominant discourses on beauty prescribe its qualities, and these are represented, iterated, and transmitted to the populace through mass-media cultural productions in both elite and folk-art forms.

For example, in the context of twentieth-century North America, the definition of beauty insofar as it is attached to female and male physical attractiveness is largely aligned with a young, physically fit, able-bodied, and slim physique. This beauty standard is reflected in popular culture, where it is linked with valued characteristics such as affluence, intelligence, good health, success, happiness, vitality, and sexual appeal. Folklorists understand that a cultural study that examines the discourses, artifacts, rituals, and practices of beauty and beautification in a particular place and time will uncover much about the hegemonic ideas and power arrangements characteristic of that location and moment.

Historical and cross-cultural analyses of corporeal beauty rituals also indicate their ethnic specificity. Traditional beauty rituals practiced through generations often include a spiritual component. For example, body painting in some ancient and contemporary Australian and North American Aboriginal cultures and heritages is used for ceremonial ritual, adornment, and decoration, and is highly symbolic of community membership, position, and identity.

Insofar as beauty rituals are part of a cultural heritage, they symbolize the belief system of that community. For example, in ancient and contemporary Asian, Middle and Far Eastern, African, and South American cultures and heritages, beauty secrets form part of the oral tradition of women's wisdom, including recipes combining natural organic ingredients to enhance and improve health and to beautify the body. In many cultures worldwide, adornment of the female body with henna art (*mehndi*) signifies a rite of passage such as marriage; beauty rituals are often part of traditional ceremonies during which older women decorate, encode, and enlighten the next generation about matters of life and love.

In the industrialized cultures of North America, dominant discourses of beauty circulating in the mass media reflect the values of a capitalist economy, on a patriarchal, Eurocentric, normatively heterosexual social order, and on a binary sex-gender system. This is reflected in the mass-production of beauty products and processes marketed to women, which encourage participation in physical and behavioral transformations to emulate an idealized version of female beauty widely regarded as both unachievable by women and a heterosexist male fantasy; much of what makes it "ideal" is that it is docile, submissive, and highly eroticized. Taken together, the icons of female beauty in Western media—the Barbie doll, technologically-altered photographs of professional celebrities and models via the culture industries (television, magazines, film, and video), and beauty-pageant contestants—represent standards of (virtual or phantasmatic) physical perfection unattainable for most women.

As a rule, bodily adornment, decoration, and practices of female beautification are less about spirituality, community, or rites of passage in North American mass culture than they are about power and the commodification of a very limited range of bodily stylizations. The business of beauty culture includes technologies and professions involved in modification and beautification of hair, skin, and fingernails, through fashion, cosmetics, diet, and reconstructive surgeries. In spas, salons, and design houses, largely female cultural domains (with the exception of the plastic surgery field), women practice and purchase the skilled trades of the beauty industries in a quest for physical attractiveness and the sexual and social power that is wielded by those who possess it.

Technologies of beauty are folk artifacts which reveal the historical development of Western culture's pursuit of physical beauty. Examination of the production of cosmetic products, fashion photographs, weight-loss advertisements, and patent drawings for corsets and the like—many of which represent the work of female inventors, artists, and entrepreneurs—reveals its dominant ideologies of the beautiful.

Limited definitions of beauty demarcated by and compatible with the hegemony of heteropatriarchy have inspired women's activism. The historic protest of the Miss America Pageant in 1968 included the spectacle of "freedom trash cans" into which second-wave feminists invited onlookers to toss fashion magazines, girdles, and lipstick. This media-savvy event symbolized a celebration of women's natural beauty over the artificiality of the beauty queen; a similar political ideology was reflected in the slogan "Black is Beautiful," popularized by the civil rights movement of the same period. *See also:* Aesthetics; Barbie Doll; Beauty Contest; Beauty Queen; Cosmetics; Diet Culture; Fashion; Feminisms; Hair; Henna Art/*Mehndi*; Magazines, Women's and Girls'; Marriage; Mass Media; Popular Culture; Race; Rites of Passage; Ritual; Sexism; Sexuality; Spa Culture; Women's Movement; Women's Work.

References: Banks, Ingrid. *Hair Matters: Beauty, Power, and Black Women's Consciousness.* New York: New York University Press, 2000; Black, Paula. *The Beauty Industry: Gender, Culture, Pleasure.* New York and London: Routledge, 2004; Blackwelder, Julia Kirk. *Styling Jim Crow: African American Beauty Training During Segregation.* College Station: Texas A&M University Press, 2003; Etcoff, Nancy. *Survival of the Prettiest: The Science of Beauty.* New York: Anchor, 2000; Gavenas, Mary Lisa. *Color Stories: Behind the Scenes of America's Billion-Dollar Beauty Industry.* New York: Simon & Schuster, 2002; Gimlin, Debra L. *Body Work: Beauty and Self-image in American Culture.* Berkeley: University of California Press, 2001; Peiss, Kathy. *Hope in a Jar: The Making of America's Beauty Culture.* New York: Metropolitan Books, 1998; Riordan, Teresa. *Inventing Beauty: A History of the Inventions that Have Made Us Beautiful.*

New York: Broadway Books, 2004; Scranton, Philip, ed. *Beauty and Business: Commerce, Gender, and Culture in Modern America*. New York: Routledge, 2000; Wolf, Naomi. *The Beauty Myth: How Images of Beauty are used Against Women*. New York: Perennial, 2002 [1991].

Sidney Eve Matrix

Beauty Contest

Like a romantic fairy tale performed on the stage, a beauty contest allegedly creates the opportunity for every young woman to make the fantasy her own. Because beauty contests have proliferated in many locations and have been adapted for a variety of settings, most young women can enter a beauty contest of one kind or another; however, the majority cannot hope to meet the standards set by contemporary beauty pageants. Competing against each other for the fictitious title of "queen," young women are displayed onstage, where they perform a talent such as singing or dancing for an audience, including a small group of judges chosen by the organization sponsoring the event. The woman judged to embody the ideal qualities of the sponsoring organization is crowned and awarded prizes. She then becomes a local, national, or international celebrity known as Miss America, Miss Ghana, Miss Navajo, or a similar title. Their titles point to a strict body of rules governing the contestants regarding marriage and sexuality; they must not be married, nor should they have ever been married or pregnant. These and other qualifications suggest that beauty contests serve as rituals of initiation and social presentation for young women.

Initially proposed in 1854 by P. T. Barnum, an organizer of circuses and variety shows, the first recorded American beauty contest was held at Rehoboth Beach, Delaware, in 1880. In the twenty-first century, these contests are ubiquitous and can be adapted to any public event, institution, or civic entity, even in war zones. In 2006, the Russian republic of Chechnya held its first beauty contest, and the fifteen-year-old winner was named Beauty of Chechnya. In another innovation, the women's prison system in Brazil hosted beauty contests in 2005; 603 inmates from ten prisons competed for the title Miss Penetenciaria.

The two global contests, Miss Universe and Miss World, have stimulated interest in beauty contests worldwide. Moreover, an unanticipated result of globalization has been a resurgence of nationalism, a phenomenon that has imbued beauty contests with added significance, as they bring recognition to the nation state. Often, these events generate reflections of political issues, as occurred in the Miss America contest in 1968, in Mexico at the 2007 Miss Universe pageant, in India at the 1996 Miss World contest, and in Nigeria at the 2002 Miss World contest. In 2001, in the fourth Face of Africa contest, whose rules require hips no larger than thirty-six inches on girls taller than five feet six inches, all 100 of Uganda's entrants were judged "too short and too broad" to be called beautiful by Western standards (Duval Smith); the ruling caused an international controversy because African societies often have beauty standards that are dramatically different from the Western model of the tall, thin female body.

In addition to its intimate relationship to nationalism and local pride, the beauty-contest phenomenon functions as a ritual of gender distinctions, defining the position of women in contemporary societies. The beauty contest, like all initiation rituals, instructs women in the role of womanhood and then presents them to society. However, pageant contestants are also judged and a winner selected. Contestants are instructed with regard to beauty and talent, but they also learn to compete against other women. Equally significant, they learn how to obtain sponsors and how to represent them. Winners of large contests advertise the products of their sponsors as well as speak out about social issues. Though rigid standards govern the contestants, the rewards are empowering: winners receive cash, scholarships, cars, and travel. Especially important, they receive public attention, and with it, a degree of authority.

Feminists of the 1960s and 1970s criticized beauty pageants, especially bathing-suit competitions in which contestants display their nearly nude bodies for the judges' approval. Even the sex-positive feminists of the twenty-first century have used the theme of beauty pageants to mock the patriarchal ideas they enact. For example, CODEPINK Women for Peace has staged parody contests that included prizes for I Miss Liberty, Miss Appropriated Funds, Miss Take, Miss Fire, and Miss Managed.

In response to feminist critiques, contest organizers introduced the awarding of academic scholarships as prizes and now require that contestants identify a social cause with which they wish to be identified. In order to revise traditional pageant vocabulary, today's organizers are urged to remove words like "poise" and "beauty" from beauty-contest discourse. Consequently, many young women have been persuaded to believe that they are participating in scholarship contests, despite the fact that they are displayed onstage and judged on their performance. Also significant is the fact that the bathing-suit competition has returned to many pageants. However configured, beauty contests remain ritual events in which young women learn a female role that conforms to patriarchal expectations. *See also:* Activism; Beauty; Feminisms; Initiation; Race; Ritual.

References: Banet-Weiser, Sarah. *The Most Beautiful Girl in the World.* Berkeley: University of California Press, 1999; Cohen, Colleen B., Richard Wilk, and Beverly Stoeltje, eds. *Beauty Queens on the Global Stage.* New York: Routledge, 1996; Craig, Maxine Leeds. *Ain't I a Beauty Queen?* New York: Oxford University Press, 2002; Duval Smith, Alex. "Ugandans 'too big' to enter beauty contest." *The Independent* (UK). May 26, 2001. http://news.independent.co.uk/world/africa/article246025.ece (accessed December 19, 2007); Osborne, Angela Saulino. *Miss America: The Dream Lives On.* Dallas: Taylor Publishing Company, 1995; Watson, Elwood, and Darcy Martin, eds. *There She Is, Miss America.* New York: Palgrave Macmillan, 2004.

Beverly J. Stoeltje

Beauty Queen

A beauty queen is a person (typically a woman) chosen to serve as a symbolic representation of a collective identity by a group of people to represent them (or some of them) to a larger, often national, audience. As such, beauty queens are chosen through beauty pageants or contests, which can vary in reference to social context, setting, and judging criteria. During her reign, a beauty queen often makes appearances at public functions wearing a tiara (crown) and sash (often emblazoned with the title she holds and/or her sponsors' names).

Recently, analyses of beauty queens have spanned the globe as they are increasingly seen to represent socially defined collective identities such as nations, ethnic/racial groups, or organizations. From the local Miss Snake Charmer Queen of Texas to the internationally broadcast Miss Universe contest, beauty queens remain a popular symbolic vehicle for the assertion and definition of collective identities over time.

Criticism of beauty queens has been fairly consistent as feminists have argued that pageants reify patriarchal idealizations and unattainable female beauty standards, which are judged predominantly in heterosexist terms through a patriarchal lens that objectifies women as symbols and not thinking, feeling human beings.

Not all beauty queens are the same, however; both queens and pageants vary widely. Large, pyramidal pageants (in which women graduate after winning local, regional, national, and worldwide contests) often have very narrow definitions of beauty, generally premised on White, Western, industrialized ideals, underpinned and promoted by large cosmetic companies intent on expanding their markets, particularly in the developing world. Other, more local pageants—Miss Cherry Blossom in Honolulu, Hawaii, for example—use the beauty queen to draw people to festivals, to celebrate local culture, and to define collectively their identity in symbolic terms. Local beauty queens are often judged not solely on the attractiveness of their faces and bodies, but also on their cultural competence (usually measured through talent performances), educational achievements, service to the local community, and speaking ability.

Local differences may be reflected in the eligiblity rules that determine who can and cannot participate in a pageant. Most pageant contestants must comply with rules that require them to be unmarried, childless, of a certain age (typically eighteen to twenty-six), and sometimes of a certain racial/ethnic background or blood quantum. For example, until 1998, the Cherry Blossom Queen pageant in Honolulu, Hawaii, required that contestants be of 100 percent provable Japanese ancestry. With increasing rates of interracial marriage in the Japanese American community, the pageant currently requires contestants to be of 50 percent Japanese ancestry, as do most other Japanese American pageants. These rules send strong messages about the image that the chosen beauty queen must undertake such as sexual purity, youth, beauty, and racial authenticity, but they are also ways that groups who chose queens to represent them define not just the queen but the group itself. As the rules change over time, the criteria by which beauty queens are produced also change to reflect the issues, anxieties, and feelings of the larger community.

Beauty queens themselves undergo an often gruelling, and at times, unappreciated role when they make "visitations" to their public; and they must be trained to be royal by consultants and advisors. At the national or international level, beauty queens often use their "reign" and "visitations" to further their careers in public speaking, newscasting, acting, and clothes modelling. *See also:* Aesthetics; Beauty; Beauty Contest; Chastity; Cosmetics; Diet Culture; Ethnicity; Race.

References: Banet-Weiser, Sarah. *The Most Beautiful Girl in the World: Beauty Pageants and National Identity.* Berkeley: University of California Press, 1999; Cohen, Colleen Ballerino, Richard Wilk, and Beverly Stoeltje. *Beauty Queens on the Global Stage: Gender, Contests and Power.* New York: Routledge, 1996; King-O'Riain, Rebecca Chiyoko. *Pure Beauty: Judging Race in Japanese American Beauty Pageants.* Minneapolis, MN: University of Minnesota Press, 2006; Yano, Christine Reiko. *Crowning the Nice Girl: Gender, Ethnicity and Culture in Hawai'i's Cherry Blossom Festival.* Honolulu: University of Hawaii Press, 2006.

Rebecca Chiyoko King-O'Riain

Belly Dance

Belly dance, also known as Middle Eastern dance, *Raqs Sharqi, Raqs al Bedeli*, Oriental dance, or *dansi*, is a style of dance whose movements tend to emphasize the shoulders, torso, abdomen, hips, and hands. Its movements, usually described as sensuous, can be performed by both men and women, but are more typically performed by women. Its forms are said to mimic childbirth, and the dance is believed to have originated as a means of distracting and encouraging a woman in labor. It is also a dance of celebration that women perform for other women.

In the Middle Eastern countries of its origin, belly dancing is recognized as a traditional women's dance form, most properly performed in a harem or other women-only space. Women began performing the dance for men as a product of colonialism and the voyeuristic tastes of nineteenth-century Orientalists who wished to study the folk arts of the region, even those considered off limits to male spectators aside from the performer's husband or sheik (in the case of concubines performing).

There are many names for belly dance in its North African, East Asian, and West Asian countries of origin, and their repertoire of movements differ to some extent; however, names recognizable to North Americans typically have more to do with costuming styles than with movement forms per se. Some of the common styles in North America are designated "cabaret/night-club," "folkloric," "beledi," "gypsy," "fusion," and "American Tribal Styles (ATS)." Costuming varies from the beaded bra and hip-belt of cabaret to the long, full skirts and full-torso coverage of the "folkloric" styles.

American folklore has it that belly dance was introduced at the Chicago World's Fair of 1893 in the person of "Little Egypt," "a mysterious woman" sponsored by San Francisco businessman Sol Bloom along with other dancers he'd seen perform in London. It is also held (incorrectly) that Mark Twain had a heart attack when he saw her dance. However, it is more likely that the form made its North American debut twelve years earlier in the person of a woman dubbed "Fatima" at the Birdcage Theatre, a bordello in Tombstone, Arizona, in 1881.

The crossing of the traditional gender barrier and its exportation led to consideration of belly dance as a disreputable art; it was accorded little prestige in its originating countries. In the United States, Victorian mores ruling women's bodies combined with racist attitudes regarding Western Asian and North African cultures in general essentially condemned belly dancing's forms and costumes to the vaudeville and burlesque traditions. Given this history, along with Hollywood associations of male-pleasing "harem girls" and professional ecdysiasts (striptease artists), many incorrect perceptions of belly dancing have become entrenched in the U.S. mindset.

In recent years, there has been a renewed interest in belly dance, thanks in part to such popular music stars as Shakira (a Colombian-Lebanese singer-dancer) and Beyoncé (an African American from Houston). It is now common to find classes offered in most major North American cities in schools, gyms, spas, and health clubs. According to a widely distributed feature story in 2004, "The allure of belly dancing in the new millennium lies in its low-impact mix of meditation and workout" (AP 2004). Many women now see belly dance as a way to "spice up" their weight-loss exercise regimens or as a way to gain confidence in their sexuality and appearance, claiming that it "brings out the woman inside." Jamileh Jeanne Handy, an instructor in Brunswick, Maine, counters her students' resistance to the form by explaining that "Belly dancing celebrates the excitement of youth, the pride of motherhood, and the wisdom of age" (AP 2004). A typical belly dance class consists of White, middle-class women of all ages and sizes who often have no knowledge of the feminine cultures from which the form arose or that it ever had a practical function in those cultures. In response to this phenomenon, the Bellydancers of Color Association (BOCA), founded in 2004 by the Washington, DC-based troupe Moor Hips, now holds an annual conference "that educates participants about the history of the dance, as well as teaching some fancy moves" (Johnson: 49).

Having become an element of U.S. popular culture, belly dance is the focus of many new Web sites; they typically provide some history of the form and costuming tips, along with schedules for classes and special events. The Rakkasah Middle Eastern Dance Festival celebrated its twenty-fifth anniversary in 2005 in Richmond, California. This annual festival, with new venues in Salt Lake City, Utah, and New York City (Rakkasah East), features live bands, dance demonstrations, and henna decorating, along with vendors selling swords, costumes, instructional videos, and recordings of Middle Eastern music. *See also:* Childbirth and Childrearing; Diet Culture; Festival; Folk Costume; Folk Dance; Henna Art/*Mehndi*; Popular Culture; Region: Middle East; Spa Culture; Women's Folklore.

References: Al-Rawi, Rosina-Fawzia B. *Grandmother's Secrets: The Ancient Rituals and Healing Power of Belly Dancing*. Trans. Monique Arav. Northampton, MA: Interlink Publishing Group, 2000; Associated Press. "Belly Dancing Seen As a Path to Fitness." November 29, 2004. http://my.earthlink.net/article/hea?guid=20041129/41aaacd0_3ca6_15526200411292124240385 (accessed November 29, 2004); Carlton, Donna. *Looking for Little Egypt*. Bloomington, IN: International Dance Discovery Books, 1995; Djoumahna, Kajira. *The Tribal Bible: Exploring the Phenomena that is American Tribal Style Bellydance*. Vancouver: Black Sheep Press, 2003; Johnson, Tammy. "Shake It 'Til You Make It." *Colorlines* (September/October 2006): 49–51; "Rakkasah Middle Eastern Dance Festival." http://www.rakkasah.com (accessed April 23, 2005); Richards, Tazz, and Kajira Djoumahna, eds. *The Bellydance Book: Rediscovering the Oldest Dance*. San Jose, CA: Backbeat Press, 2000; Salimpour, Jamila. "The Mystery of Little Egypt." n.d.

http://www.suhaila.com/Pages/Articles/LittleEgypt.htm (accessed February 21, 2005); Shira. "The Art of Middle Eastern Dance." n.d. http://www.shira.net (accessed December 26, 2007); Van Nieuwkerk, Karin. *"A Trade Like Any Other": Female Singers and Dancers in Egypt*. Austin: University of Texas Press, 1995; Yasmina. "Yasmina's Joy of Bellydancing." n.d. http://www.joyofbellydancing.com (accessed February 21, 2005).

Andrea Kitta

Best Friend

A best friend is a girl's or a woman's closest, primary friend. In early childhood, girls may go through many "best friends," making and breaking friendships easily, but in adolescence and adulthood, there are usually just one or two people who receive this special designation. In childhood, girls often have a best friend who is a girl of similar age. There are exceptions, of course, especially after adolescence, when a woman's best friend may be a man, whether heterosexual or homosexual.

All friendships have unique characteristics, but in the popular imagination, best friends understand each other, share feelings and secrets, and care for one another. A best friend ideally provides unconditional emotional support and advice; she is reliable in times of crisis and celebration. Often a best friend is described as the first person a woman calls if she needs a ride to an emergency room or a temporary shelter; she can be counted on to host her best friend's bridal shower, for example, or her fiftieth birthday party. A woman's best friend is usually the maid or matron of honor at her wedding, and, if she's Latina, one of the *damas* (maids of honor) at her quinceañera. A Christian woman may honor her best friend by asking her to be a newborn child's godmother, thus entrusting her physical and spiritual welfare.

During childhood, best friends may become "blood sisters" by piercing a finger until it bleeds and touching them together so that the blood merges, representing the merging of their lives. Best friends may create and share a secret language, create their own rituals, and share "inside jokes." In North American cultures, they often attend sleepovers together (wherein girls spend the night at another girl's home), "an important way of establishing emotional and social autonomy from one's parents and transferring feelings of tenderness and affection from parents to age mates" (Oxrieder in Georges and Jones: 249). Best friends will often share clothing—another gesture of trust. They may also exchange jewelry such as rings or "friendship bracelets" (handmade bracelets of woven thread) that indicate a valued and enduring friendship between the wearer and the giver.

In middle school and high school, best friends may exchange handwritten notes in the classroom, perhaps signed or decorated with the phrase "BFF"— "Best Friends Forever." Girls frequently make lists ranking their friends, bestowing the most time and attention on those they place at the top. In adolescence, best friends often hold hands or link arms. Traditionally, the little finger is the finger of friendship; girls may link the little fingers of their right hands together and shake them up and down while saying,

"Make friends, make friends,
Never, never, break friends."

Rituals like this one endear children to one another by symbolically linking a part of one friend with the same part of the other.

Numerous portrayals of the best-friend relationship appear in literature, television, and film. Books intended for young and adolescent girls, such as Lisa Yee's *Millicent Min: Girl Genius* (2004), explore the joys and sorrows of making and losing best friends. Popular U.S. television programs intended for adults, such as *Friends* and *Will and Grace*, also extol the virtues of friendship; and many films—perhaps most famously *Thelma and Louise* (1991)—explore the transformative power of the best-friend bond at critical junctures in women's lives.

One of American history's greatest of best friends were Elizabeth Cady Stanton and Susan B. Anthony, the former, author of the 1848 Seneca Falls Declaration of Sentiments and a married mother of seven children, the latter, a restless and unmarried Quaker. Over the course of an intensely intellectual and emotional friendship that lasted for nearly five decades, they not only pushed and prodded America—and finally the U.S. Congress—to accept the political enfranchisement of women through the vote but created the most enduring civil rights movement in world history: women's movement. Per her instructions, when Stanton died, a photograph of Anthony, surrounded by flowers, was placed near her coffin.

As significant as having a best friend is losing one through physical separation or simply due to the shifting nature of childhood relationships. Feelings of profound loss and/or betrayal are frequently expressed by girls who have lost a best friend. And in adulthood, a change in status from best friend to former best friend—whether because of an argument or simply due to differing life trajectories—can be as emotionally painful as it was in childhood. But a best-friend relationship can also mature from its playful childhood beginnings into a lifelong bond that embodies the power and cohesion of female care and intimacy. *See also: Quinceañera*; Rhymes; Ritual; Women's Friendship Groups; Women's Movement.

References: Apter, Terri, and Ruthellen Josselson. *Best Friend: The Pleasures and Perils of Girls' and Women's Friendships*. New York: Crown Publishers, Inc., 1998; Bronner, Simon J. *American Children's Folklore*. Little Rock, AR: August House, Inc., 1988; Corsaro, William. *We're Friends, Right? Inside Kids' Culture*. Washington, DC: Joseph Henry Press, 2003; Georges, Robert A., and Michael Owen Jones. *Folkloristics: An Introduction*. Bloomington: Indiana University Press, 1995; *Not For Ourselves Alone: The Story of Elizabeth Cady Stanton and Susan B. Anthony*. Dir. Ken Burns. Florentine Films, 1999; Oliker, Stacy J. *Best Friends and Marriage: Exchange Among Women*. Berkeley: University of California Press, 1989; Opie, Peter, and Iona Peter. *The Lore and Language of Schoolchildren*. Oxford: Oxford University Press, 1959; Oxrieder, Julia Woodbridge. "The Slumber Party: Transition into Adolescence." *Tennessee Folklore Society Bulletin* 43 (1977): 128–134; Schappell, Elissa, and Jenny Offill. *The Friend Who Got Away: Twenty Women Tell the True Stories Behind Their Blowups, Burnouts, and Slow Fades*. New York: Doubleday, 2005.

Alina Autumn Christian and Theresa A. Vaughan

Birth Chair

A birth chair can take the form of a stool or modified chair, used historically as an aid in childbirth. A woman would sit on the stool or chair, usually supported by one or more attendants, during the final stage of birth. Evidence for the use of a stool or chair for giving birth goes back to ancient Egypt; there are references to the practice in the Hebrew Bible. Chair designs have changed over time, possibly reflecting developing attitudes toward birth as well as shifts in cultural conventions.

Physically, the birth stool or chair helps support a woman in an upright position with her pelvis open. This allows the laboring women to work with gravity as well as position herself in a way which facilitates giving birth. Early designs of birth chairs were low to the ground to allow the woman to brace her feet against the floor while bearing down during a contraction. By the 1700s, however, the height began to rise and the chairs became more complex, seemingly coinciding with the medicalization of the birth process and the transition from midwife-attended births to doctor-attended births. Advocates of the alternative birth movement (begun in the latter half of the twentieth century) see this change as taking power from midwives and other women in its positioning of women's bodies for the convenience of a doctor rather than the comfort of the laboring woman. Some medical doctors, however, feel that using a birth chair makes birth too rapid and maintaining a sterile field too difficult.

By the 1900s, birth chairs were largely replaced by beds or operating tables. Again, the shift coincides with a decline in midwife-attended births. There has been a minor resurgence in the use of birth chairs, although this seems to be limited to midwives and freestanding birth centers participating in the alternative birth movement. In Europe, where midwives are much more commonly accepted by the medical community, birth chairs are also now employed on a regular basis. This may reflect a general cultural shift in expectations about positions and locations appropriate for childbirth, regardless of the gender of the attending health professional.

Historically, very few birth chairs have been manufactured industrially, but were instead individually built or modified from existing chairs; thus, little standardization exists in examples. Most birth chairs (as opposed to stools) have a seat with an area removed to allow access to the emerging infant. Most birth stools are relatively narrow, presumably for the same reason.

Writing from the perspective of a folklorist interested in material culture, Amanda Carson Banks has done a comprehensive survey of surviving examples of birth chairs in Europe and North America. There are extant examples in museums and hospitals, although she reports that very few are currently in service. *See also:* Childbirth and Childrearing; Home Birth; Midwifery.

References: Ashford, Janet Isaacs. *The Whole Birth Catalog: A Sourcebook for Choices in Childbirth.* Trumansburg, NY: Crossing Press, 1983; Banks, Amanda Carson. *Birth Chairs, Midwives, and Medicine.* Jackson: University Press of Mississippi, 1999; Jordan, Brigitte. *Birth in Four Cultures: A Crosscultural Investigation of Childbirth in Yucatan, Holland, Sweden, and the United States.* Prospect Heights, IL: Waveland Press, 1993.

Theresa A. Vaughan

Birthdays

Birthdays mark the anniversary of a person's birth. Many of today's North American birthday rituals have their origins in Europe, related as they are to the ancient Greeks' celebrations of the birthdays of the gods. "The Greeks believed that everyone had a protective spirit or daemon who attended his [or her] birthday and watched over him in life" (Linton 8). The belief was that malevolent spirits are likely to be especially dangerous on such occasions as one's birthday; the giving of gifts and best wishes was intended to ward off these evil spirits. However, in ancient patriarchal societies, the birthdays of women and children were not considered important enough to be worthy of note.

Many of the birthday traditions of today have their origins in nineteenth-century Germany with children's birthdays known as *kinderfeste*. Candles were placed around the edge of a child's dinner plate in the belief that if a child blows out all the candles in one breath, her accompanying wish would be granted. The "Happy Birthday" song often associated with this ritual today was composed in 1893 by the American sisters Patty Smith and Mildred Hill. The giving of birthday cards began in England in the early twentieth century and has since spread internationally.

A birthday ritual that can be found in many parts of the world relates to softening up the body as a new year of life begins; done by intimates of the person whose birthday it is, it can take the form of bumps, punches, smacks, spanks, or ear pulling. Iona and Peter Opie describe a ritual in Britain in which "they take hold of the arms and legs, lift him [or her] as high as they can and bump him on the ground, repeating it according to the number of years old he is" (324–325). The traditional belief is that it is bad luck if the birthday celebrant is not spanked because it was believed to soften up the body for the tomb. Similar rituals are carried out in Ireland, Scotland, Canada, and Argentina.

From Canada comes the tradition of greasing the nose with butter, making the birthday child too slippery for bad luck to catch her. In Latin American cultures a girl's fifteenth birthday, known as a *quinceañera*, marks a girl's passage into adulthood. Many of these celebrations are as elaborate as the Sweet Sixteen parties discussed below, and some are the equivalent of a debutante ball. Chicano and Mexican birthdays feature a papier mache *piñata* suspended from the ceiling; the birthday celebrant hits it with a stick until goodies such as small toys and candy are dispersed. Russian children are presented with pies inscribed with birthday wishes, and Chinese children may expect to be served special noodles at a birthday lunch. In North America's Japanese families, children who turn seven, five, and three are considered special and may take part in the Shichi-go-san Festival (whose name literally translates into the numbers "seven-five-three"). First Nation peoples tend to place more significance on milestones such as a child's first steps and first words than on birthdays.

American girls may participate in lavish Sweet Sixteen birthday celebrations, which can include restaurant visits, sleepovers, theme, and pool parties involving hours of complex planning and preparation and much expense. Elaborate parties for relatives and friends are becoming more common for women when they celebrate milestone birthdays, especially at forty and fifty. *See also: Quinceañera*; Rites of Passage; Ritual.

References: BirthdayCelebrations.net. "Traditions from Around the World." n.d. http://www.birthdaycelebrations.net/usabirthdays.htm (accessed January 5, 2007);

Linton, Ralph, and Adelin Linton. *The Lore of Birthdays*. New York: Henry Schuman, 1952; Opie, Iona, and Peter Opie. *The Lore and Language of the Playground*. Oxford, England: Oxford University Press, 1959.

Janice Ackerley

Blind Folklore

Commonly held American beliefs about blindness and the blind have changed over time, but they frequently center around two ideas familiar to historians of disability: morality and illness. Beliefs circulated about blind girls and women are particularly laden with social anxieties about vulnerability and virtue.

In the nineteenth century, Victorian-era beliefs about the blind (like those of the poor) were two-pronged. On the one hand, charitable associations presented the blind as tragic figures who nonetheless embodied the American ideals of willingness to work and desire to achieve independence. At the same time, stereotypes persisted of the blind as lazy, incapable, and jealous of sighted people. The Victorian taste for sentimentality embraced the image of the blind girl in ballads and folksongs, many simply titled "The Blind Girl," or such variations as "The Lament of the Blind Orphan Girl." The heroine of these songs was virtuous, pathetic, often orphaned, and usually doomed. In the German folk song "The Blind Child's Prayer," a widowed father listens to his daughter's bedtime prayers on the night before he remarries:

And as he turned to leave the room
One joyful cry was given.
He turned and caught the last sweet smile.
The blind child was in heaven.

They buried her by her mother's side
And raised a marble fair.
And on it graved the simple words,
"There'll be no blind ones there."

Following the internationally celebrated accomplishments of Helen Keller (1880–1968), social assumptions about blindness began to change. Keller became famous for her educational and social attainments, despite the fact that she was blind and deaf from birth. Keller's extraordinary achievements were actually anteceded by those of Helen de Kroyft (1818–1915), and Laura Bridgman (1829–1889). Due largely to these women's advances, the popular image of the blind person, and particularly the blind woman, began to include ideas of independence, sophistication, and even erudition.

In the twentieth century, blind and visually impaired people gained greater control of their own public image by means of national organizations such as the American Foundation for the Blind, the National Federation of the Blind, and the Americans with Disabilities Act (ADA) of 1990. At most levels of society, it is no longer acceptable to stereotype the blind negatively, although blind people report that some negative beliefs persist. In academe, for instance, visually impaired people report superstitious fears of blindness in colleagues among people for whom loss of vision would be professionally devastating. Despite greater understanding, fears persist that blindness may be somehow contagious. At the same time, blind and visually impaired people also encounter the attitude that they are privileged by legislation such as the ADA and underqualified for the work they do.

A widely held folk belief is that blind people enjoy heightened sensitivity in their remaining senses. This notion informs many representations of the blind in popular culture. Movies such as *Wait Until Dark* (1967), *Scent of a Woman* (1992), and *Daredevil* (2003) represent blind characters as able to navigate in some, or even all, situations better than sighted people. These beliefs show a tendency to treat blindness as a mere inconvenience, or even as an advantage within the context of a sighted society.

A conflation of physical blindness with lack of insight or understanding is a longstanding conceptual association in Western culture. Ironically, this belief exists simultaneously with one that attributes extraordinary perceptions to the blind. Thanks to the increasing popularity of the genres of personal-experience narratives and memoirs, blind authors are now more able to tell their own stories. One recurring theme in works by the visually impaired is the desire for sighted people to "get it right"—that is, to dispel the many erroneous beliefs and stereotypes the sighted have about blindness. *See also:* Activism; Ballad; Deaf Folklore; Folk Belief; Folk Music and Folksong; Folklore About Women; Occupational Folklore; Personal-Experience Narrative; Superstition.

References: Deutsche Volkslieder. "The Blind Child's Prayer." n.d. http://ingeb.org/songs/theytell.html (accessed June 1, 2005); Freeberg, Ernest. "The Meanings of Blindness in Nineteenth-Century America." *Proceedings of the American Antiquarian Society*, vol. 110, no. 1 (2000): 119–152; Kent, Deborah. "Views From Hollywood: Recent Portrayals of Blind People in Film and on Television." *Journal of Visual Impairment and Blindness*, vol. 93 (June 1999): 392–394.

Karen Munro

Bloody Mary

Bloody Mary (or Mary Whales) is an adolescent's game in which girls stand in front of a bathroom mirror and invoke a violent ghost by chanting a predetermined phrase a specific number of times.

There are variants of the game, as is the case with most folklore. In most versions, one or more girls stand in the dark in front of a bathroom mirror. Each girl pricks a finger with a pin, then all press their bloodied fingers together. The girls then repeat a specified chant, often "I do believe in you," or "Bloody Mary show your fright / show your fright this starry night," or they simply repeat the name "Bloody Mary" a specified number of times (three, ten, 100). Sometimes the chant is done with eyes closed, and sometimes the chanter must turn around in a circle each time the phrase is spoken. Upon opening her eyes, the chanter is supposed to see Bloody Mary in the mirror or, in some versions, Bloody Mary will reach out and scratch the chanter's face with long fingernails or shards of mirror. At this point the girl(s) will usually run screaming from the bathroom, but in some variants one of the girls must remember to first flush the toilet to get rid of Mary.

In some cases, the Bloody Mary game is fused with the Vanishing Hitch-hiker legend, in which an innocent passerby picks up a girl who stands on the side of the road in the rain. The driver takes her to the address she specifies, but upon arriving there, s/he finds that the girl has disappeared, sometimes leaving a wet spot or a scarf on the backseat. The driver then learns from the girl's distraught parents that it is the anniversary of their daughter's death. Mary is also sometimes conflated with *La Llorona*.

Janet Langlois notes that the girls shift from passivity to action as they play the game. When combined with the Vanishing Hitchhiker legend, Bloody Mary is a passive victim, killed by violence; she then disappears only to reappear in a mirror from which she herself acts as a killer of girls when she reaches out to scratch (kill) her summoner(s).

Alan Dundes interprets the game as a ritual associated with menarche, the onset of menses. His analysis begins by noting that the players are girls who are at or near the age of menarche (first menstruation), that the game takes place in the bathroom and involves a sudden appearance of blood, and that flushing the toilet makes Bloody Mary go away. He also reports that girls sometimes refer to themselves as "Bloody Mary" when they are menstruating. *See also:* Folk Belief; Girls' Folklore; Girls' Games; *La Llorona*; Legend, Supernatural; Legend, Urban/Contemporary; Menarche Stories; Menstruation; Rites of Passage; Superstition.

References: Dundes, Alan. *Bloody Mary in the Mirror: Essays in Psychoanalytic Folkloristics.* Jackson: University Press of Mississippi, 2002; Langlois, Janet. "Mary Whales, I Believe in You." In *Indiana Folklore: A Reader*, ed. Linda Dégh, 196–224. Bloomington: Indiana University Press, 1980; Summers, Wynne L. "Bloody Mary: When Ostension Becomes a Deadly and Destructive Teen Ritual." *Midwestern Folklore* 26, no. 1 (Spring 2000): 19–26.

Sarah Catlin-Dupuy

Body Modification and Adornment

Women's body modification and adornment refers to practices of permanent or semipermanent alterations of the body, usually non-medically prescribed, for reasons ranging from the aesthetic to the transformative. The practices most commonly seen in contemporary North America are tattooing, piercing, and scarification, including cutting/cicatrization and branding. In much of the world, these methods are historically folkloric, and remain so today. Many of the skills involved in safely and aesthetically adorning the body are learned largely through firsthand interactions, informal training, apprenticeships, workshops, seminars, and body-arts festivals. Women whose bodies are thus adorned often develop a strong sense of belonging to a folk group, either because their adornment practices allow them to feel that they are part of an ongoing tradition, or because they perceive that the dominant culture views their practices as deviant. In present-day North America, however, the sight of a young woman with a tattooed ankle or pierced nose has become commonplace.

Body piercing is the practice of inserting an object through the skin to create a hole in which jewelry may be worn for aesthetic reasons or to intensify sensation. It is a semipermanent form of body modification: the jewelry may be removed, but a scar will mark the site of the piercing. Protruding and "public" body parts, such as the nostrils and nasal septum, ears, and lips, are most commonly pierced; however, the navel, tongue, nipples, and genitalia may be pierced as well. Less common are surface piercings, which use a bar with a ball on either end, creating a barbell shape. The bar runs under the surface of the skin, anywhere from the forehead to the hand. Each end of the rod projects from the skin and has the balls screwed on to it. Women's piercings range from the socially acceptable (earlobes) to the rebellious (safety pin in a nostril) to the sexually stimulating (labial or clitoral piercings).

Scarification is the practice of intentionally creating or exacerbating a scar, usually by burning or cutting the skin, to achieve aesthetic and/or sensory results. Scarification is a permanent body modification; without plastic surgery, which also leaves scars, most scarifications cannot be removed. Intentional scars may be made on every body region from the limbs and torso (common in North America) to the genitals and face. Scarification is viewed as a more dangerous body-modification practice than tattooing or piercing because the practitioner has less control over the results. Some people scar lightly; others develop keloids, raised, fibrous scar tissue.

Together with tattooing, these practices form the bases of contemporary body modification. The current North American body-modification movement, known as body play, body art, or bodywork, arose in the 1970s in the gay leather S&M (sadism and masochism) scene in San Francisco. Jim Ward, Fakir Musafar, and Doug Malloy's (Richard Simonton's) experiments with piercings and jewelry were primary influences on the way body piercing is practiced today, including the development of an apprenticeship system. Today, a typical piercing is performed with a hypodermic needle (never with a piercing gun). Jewelry, usually made of surgical steel, niobium, or titanium, is secured with a captive bead if it is ring-shaped, or with a screw-on bead if it is shaped like a barbell or a semicircle.

Body piercing has been practiced in human cultures since antiquity; the contemporary upsurge in its popularity draws on historical styles. A female figurine from Iran (ca. 3500–2900 BCE) has multiple ear piercings. Labrets (piercings through the lower lip) are part of traditional women's cultures in the subarctic region, Africa, and South America. Labrets, like earlobe piercings, can be gradually stretched to permit the insertion of larger and larger plugs or plaques. Piercing of the nostrils was common in ancient India, and some claim nipple piercings began as early as fourteenth-century Europe. A prohibition in Leviticus 19:28 admonishes, "You shall not make any cuttings in your flesh for the dead, nor tattoo any marks on you: I *am* the LORD," but may be contradicted in Genesis 24:22 in which Abraham's servant gives a nose ring (also translated as "earring") to Rebekah, the future wife of his son Isaac. Examples of cuttings practiced by African women can be found in ethnographic sources and in issues of the popular *National Geographic* magazine. Many contemporary North American women refer to such ancient or "exotic" examples of "tribal" or "primitive" body modification when discussing their reasons for being pierced, cut, branded, or scarred. Such references enable them to feel centered in a tradition.

Branding and cutting are the most common methods of scarification. Branding burns the skin to leave a scar. Common methods include strike branding, in which small, thin pieces of metal are shaped, heated with a propane torch, and briefly pressed against the skin one at a time to form a pattern, and cautery or laser branding, in which a medical cautery tool is used to draw the brand onto the skin. Because the resulting scar expands to several times the width of the original burn, brands tend to be constituted by broad lines and simple shapes. With the notable exception of those brands common to some contemporary African American fraternities, whose members are sometimes marked with a symbol of their brotherhood, brands have been used historically primarily as a form of punishment, or as a mark of ownership, or both. Women's participation in aesthetic branding is a recent phenomenon.

Cutters in the body-modification movement differentiate their practice of cutting designs into the skin from an increasingly common medical condition that compels young women to repeatedly cut themselves (self-mutilation). In aesthetic cutting, cuts do not penetrate the skin to the muscle tissue. A variant practice is skin removal, in which small to large patches of skin are cut away to leave larger scars. Ink rubbing is a practice that arose in the S&M lesbian community: tattoo ink or another colorant is rubbed into the cut to give the scar color. As the wound heals, much of the color falls out along with the scab, though the scar remains. Keloiding is often desirable, and many wearers of cuttings and/or brands rub irritants into the wound or irritate it with a toothbrush or steel wool to create a large, raised scar. This practice was appropriated from African traditions in which clay is rubbed into a wound to raise ornamental keloids. In North America, tattooing has been practiced more often by White people, and scarification through cutting by persons of African descent; scar tissue is more visible than are tattoos on dark skin.

Among the permanent practices of body modification and adornment, tattooing has perhaps the longest history among North American women. Tattooing involves adding designs and color to the body with ink or another pigment through a process of repeatedly puncturing the skin with a needle or needles or, less commonly, with another sharp tool. The word "tattoo" derives from the Tahitian word *tattau* or *ta-tu* and came into use in Europe following the eighteenth-century voyages of James Cook. The practice gained popularity among European sailors. Later, upper-class Europeans adopted the practice, originally restricting it to men, but soon spreading to women. Tattooed royalty have included Queen Olga of Sweden, Princess Waldemar of Denmark, and the mother of Winston Churchill, Lady Randolf Churchill, who had a snake tattooed on her wrist. While tattooing certainly existed in Native North and South America as well as among the Japanese (where it is known as *irezumi*), it was European tattoo fashion that spread to the United States in the later 1800s with the advent of the first electric tattoo machine.

By the turn of century, and well into the 1920s, society women were getting small decorative tattoos and even cosmetic tattoos now known as "permanent makeup." The art's mainstream popularity didn't last, however;

views of the practice were again associated with the subcultures of sailors, and later with bikers and punks. For decades, women who sported tattoos were displayed as curiosities in carnival "freak shows." For them, tattoos served as means to make an independent living, while for others, tattooed by their husbands, they were a sign of male ownership. Tattooed women rarely had ink on their faces and hands, and thus were often able to present themselves as "normal" in public; many invented stories in which they were kidnapped by "savages" or criminals and forcibly tattooed in order to avoid the stigma of immorality associated with visible tattoos.

Although tattooing came into the mainstream in the 1980s and 1990s, contemporary women's tattooing still retains some of its historical stigma. Until recently, women's tattoos tended to involve mild subjects such as flowers, and were done on private areas such as a breast, hip, or buttock. Just as piercing has become more mainstream, so has tattooing; women and girls with tattooed arms or ankles are no longer unusual. For many women, the choice of design and placement of a tattoo may appear at first be aesthetically based, but continuing pleasure in (or sometimes aversion to) body modification is often linked to the emotional and physical sensations that occurred during the tattooing process.

Women bring designs of their own choosing to tattoo shops, pick from the work a proprietor-artist has done in the past, or choose from the shop's "flash," brightly colored stencils posted on its walls. Traditional women's flash includes roses, hearts, small animals, and Celtic knotwork. A woman may choose a flash tattoo because it fits her notion of how a tattoo should look (adding to her feeling of inclusion in a folk group), because getting a tattoo was a last-minute decision, or because she did not realize she could ask to be tattooed with a design of her own making.

A tattoo design is transferred onto the body with a washable ink stencil, which both gives the artist an outline and shows the client what it will look like on her body. Contemporary artists use a grouping of three needles to create a fine outline and groupings of five to seven needles for wider lines or to fill color in a large space. A single needle might be used for extremely delicate designs. Tattooing needles are mounted on a "gun" and go in and out of the skin about 3,000 times per minute.

In contemporary North America, many women both wear permanent and semipermanent adornments on their body and participate in these traditions as body artists themselves. Due to the sensitive nature of many of the sites at which women choose to permanently adorn themselves, women tattoo customers often specifically seek a female artist. Their reasons for being tattooed, pierced, cut, branded, or scarred include aesthetics, rites of passage/personal meaning, sexual or tactile stimulation, shock value, sense of affiliation, and reclaiming the body from trauma. *See also:* Aesthetics; Beauty; Coding; Cosmetics; Fashion; Folk Group; Hair; Henna Art/*Mehndi*; Initiation; Rites of Passage.

References: Demello, Marge. *Bodies of Inscription: A Cultural History of the Modern Tattoo Community.* Durham, NC: Duke University Press, 2000; Duerr, Hans Peter. *Dreamtime: Concerning the Boundary Between Wilderness and Civilization.* Trans. Felicitas Goodman. New York: Basil Blackwell, 1985; Featherstone, Mike, ed. *Body*

Modification. London: Sage Publications, 2000; Myers, James. "Non-mainstream Body Modification: Genital Piercing, Branding, Burning, and Cutting." *Journal of Contemporary Ethnography*, vol. 32, no. 3 (October 1992): 267–306; Rubin, Arnold, ed. *Marks of Civilization: Artistic Transformations of the Human Body*. Los Angeles: Museum of Cultural History, University of California, Los Angeles, 1988; Sanders, Clinton R. "Memorial Decoration: Women, Tattooing and the Meanings of Body Alteration." *Michigan Quarterly Review* 30 (1991): 146–57; Serra, Richard, ed. *Pierced Hearts and True Love: A Century of Drawings for Tattoos*. New York: The Drawing Center, 1995; University of Pennsylvania Museum of Archeology and Anthropology. "Body Modifications Ancient and Modern." Near East Collection. n.d. http://www.museum.upenn.edu/new/exhibits/online_exhibits/body_modification/bodmodpierce.shtml (accessed December 26, 2007); Vale, V., and Andrea Juno, eds. *Modern Primitives: An Investigation of Contemporary Adornment and Ritual*. San Francisco: Re/Search Publications, 1989; Wojcik, Daniel. *Punk and Neo-Tribal Body Art*. Jackson: University Press of Mississippi, 1995.

Camilla H. Mortensen

Borden, Lizzie

Legendary for the two brutal murders she was alleged to have committed, Lizzie Borden takes her place as one of relatively few women counted among America's most notorious criminals. The fact that she was tried and acquitted of these homicides has done little to counter the memory of Borden as an infamous hatchet murderer. The controversy surrounding both killings and their alleged perpetrator persists, along with a singsong children's rhyme still heard on playgrounds in the United States today:

> Lizzie Borden took and axe and gave her mother forty whacks.
> When she saw what she had done, she gave her father forty-one.

Some matters are not in dispute. As grisly crime scene photographs attest, there is no question that Lizzie Borden's father and stepmother, Andrew and Abby Borden, met horribly violent deaths. Discovered on August 4, 1892, in the private residence they shared with thirty-two-year-old Lizzie in Fall River, Massachusetts, both bodies bore the marks of repeated blows from an axe or similarly sharp object.

But other aspects of the events have become the subject of extended debate. Was Borden in fact guilty of the murders? (She claimed to have been in the barn at the time.) Who else, such as Bridget Sullivan, the Borden family's housemaid, might have had sufficient access and motive to commit the crimes? What was the household's untold story? What torments might compel someone, particularly a family member, to such intense physical violence? The deep controversy surrounding Borden likely owes to the crime's affront to Victorian-era sensibilities about womanhood and propriety. A hatchet murder would draw attention in and of itself, then or now, but the notion that a woman, and otherwise unremarkable "spinster" (Borden was single) could be implicated in double-parricide and, in its commission, in acts of brazen mutilation, was almost impossible for the public to fathom.

The trial itself is the subject of lore, particularly because, despite incriminating circumstantial evidence, Lizzie Borden was acquitted in both the deaths of her father and his second wife. Although legally exonerated of the crimes, Borden would find herself identified with the murders for the rest of her life, and was stigmatized by accusations that she was responsible for brutally ending two innocent lives. She finished up her own life as a pariah at the age of sixty-seven, still living in the Hill District of Fall River, neither vindicated in public perception nor forgiven by her community.

Borden remains a recognizable figure within popular culture, and the deeds she is said to have committed still capture the nation's imagination. Contemporary retellings of the Borden tale abound, from spooky stories passed among children, to novels, films, plays, operas, and ballets dramatizing Borden's life and dismal end. Angela Carter's (1986) short-story rendition of the tale told from Borden's perspective is especially remarkable.

As with other macabre tales, the Borden incident also finds its way into tourism, with eerie sites opened in Fall River, such as the "Lizzie Borden Bed and Breakfast" and its accompanying museum. Guests may stay overnight in the house where the murders occurred; more squeamish visitors, however, may opt to take the daytime tour.

Lizzie Borden is, likewise, the subject, predictably enough, of many Web sites. At least one "virtual Borden house" invites online guests to graphically experience the bloody scene of the crimes. Other Web sites, somewhat less sensational and morbid in purpose, offer digital archives of trial evidence, and serve as curricular units for students posing as historical detectives sleuthing for the truth. That search continues. *See also:* Local Characters; Rhymes; Rumor; Violence.

References: Bellesiles, Michael A., ed. *Lethal Imagination: Violence and Brutality in American History.* New York: NYU Press, 1999; Carter, Angela. "The Fall River Axe Murders." In *Saints and Strangers*, 7–31. New York: Viking Penguin, Inc. [King Penguin], 1986; Kent, David, and Robert A. Flynn. *The Lizzie Borden Sourcebook.* Boston: Branden, 1992; Williams, Joyce. *Lizzie Borden: A Case Book of Family and Crime in the 1890s.* Bloomington, IN: TIS Publications, 1980.

Linda S. Watts

Breastfeeding

Breastfeeding is the act of nourishing an infant at the breast of its mother or another lactating woman. Until the early twentieth century, breastfeeding was nearly always essential to the survival of an infant, and is still considered by both biomedicine and most vernacular traditions to be the healthiest way to feed a baby.

While breastfeeding is a natural, physiological process, it is also a social and cultural one. Customs dictating the duration and practice of breastfeeding have varied widely in different places and eras. Who breastfeeds whose baby, what constitutes wholesome or unwholesome milk, how and when babies are weaned, and how breastfeeding is valued all vary. Although a natural process, breastfeeding is also a skill that must be learned by both the mother and her newborn, and thus it is highly sensitive to cultural norms.

Since breastfeeding is a cultural as well as a natural act, it follows that there is a complex relationship between traditional wisdom regarding its practice and what is now understood about the physiological process of lactation. For instance, in many cultures around the world, women have been advised to delay the start of breastfeeding until the milk comes in several days after birth, since colostrum (an important source of antibodies and nutrients) is perceived as unhealthy. It is widely held that the quality of breast milk can be harmed by the mother's emotional state, to the degree that an anxious woman may be encouraged to wean her baby. Among Haitian women, it is commonly believed that strong emotions can generate bad blood, which can contaminate breast milk. The mother's diet is often restricted; women may be advised to avoid spicy foods, broccoli, onions, or chocolate. Many African American women avoid any food they were unable to tolerate during pregnancy. Alternatively, to improve breast milk, women may be encouraged to eat spicy foods, garlic, or, in the case of Ozark women observed by Vance Randolph, raw onion (209).

There is also traditional wisdom regarding the best time to wean, such as by zodiac signs or phases of the moon, and the best age to wean, which can vary greatly. A widely held folk belief with some physiological justification holds that breastfeeding provides protection against pregnancy. Breast milk is commonly considered to have benefits other than infant feeding, and is used as a treatment for eye infections and other ailments. Various herbal and other remedies have been used to increase or decrease milk supply and to soothe engorged breasts and sore nipples. For example, fenugreek, first known to have been used in Ayurvedic medicine, is still used in many parts of the world, including North America, to increase the milk supply. Applying cabbage leaves to the breasts to relieve engorgement is likewise a widely distributed practice that is present in North America.

Breastfeeding rates declined precipitously throughout the twentieth century in the United States and in much of the world as the birthing and rearing of children came to be seen as a scientific enterprise to be managed by experts. For the first time in human history, many of the women becoming mothers, particularly in North America, had not themselves been nursed, may have never seen a woman nurse a baby, and had no breastfeeding peers to turn to for advice and support. Much of the traditional wisdom regarding breastfeeding had been lost. Those who did choose to breastfeed their babies often received such poor medical advice that their milk supply dwindled. In the mid-twentieth century, it was commonly believed that most women could not produce enough milk to feed their babies. The numbers of breastfed babies in the United States declined to 18 percent in 1966 (WHO statistics cited in Carter: 4).

In 1956, Catholic mothers in Illinois started La Leche League, an organization dedicated to providing mother-to-mother support, and it quickly became an influential organization. In the 1970s, paralleling the rise in natural childbirth, breastfeeding rates began to rise again. Currently, the majority of babies are breastfed in their first month of life, and numbers have increased in the first decade of the twenty-first century, although attitudes toward breastfeeding in North America remain highly ambivalent. The first years of the new century have seen the rise of "lactivists," nursing mothers who fight for the right to breastfeed their babies in public by organizing "nurse-ins" in locations where this right has been denied. *See also:* Activism; Childbirth and Childrearing; Herbs; Mothers' Folklore; Nature/Culture; Old Wives' Tales.

References: Baumslag, Naomi, and Dia L. Michels. *Milk, Money, and Madness: The Culture and Politics of Breastfeeding.* Westport, CT: Bergin & Garvey, 1995; Carter, Pam. *Feminism, Breasts and Breast-feeding.* New York: St. Martin's Press, 1995; Farmer, Paul. "Bad Blood. Spoiled Milk: Bodily Fluids as Moral Barometers in Rural Haiti." *American Ethnologist,* vol. 15 no. 1 (1988): 62–83; Friedman, Albert B. "Grounding a Superstition: Lactation as Contraceptive." *Journal of American Folklore,* vol. 95, no. 376 (1982): 200–208; Hand, Wayland D., ed. *Popular Beliefs and Superstitions from North Carolina. Volume VI of the Frank C. Brown Collection of North Carolina Folklore,* Newman Ivey White, general ed. Durham: Duke University Press, 1961; Harmon, Amy. "'Lactivists' Taking Their Cause, and Their Babies, to the Streets." *New York Times,* June 7, 2005. http://www.nytimes.com/2005/06/07/nyregion/07nurse.html?ex=1275796800& en=0c55cf357d95bd30&ei=5088&partner=rssnyt&emc=rss; Huggins, Kathleen. *The Nursing Mother's Companion.* Third revised edition. Boston: Harvard Common Press, 1995; Humphrey, Sheila. *The Nursing Mother's Herbal.* Minneapolis: Fairview Press, 2003; Maher, Vanessa, ed. *The Anthropology of Breast-Feeding: Natural Law or Social Construct.* Providence, RI: Berg Publishers, 1992; Randolph, Vance. *Ozark Superstitions.* New York: Columbia University Press, 1947; Snow, Loudell F. *Walkin' Over Medicine.* Detroit: Wayne State University Press, 1998; Ward, Jule DeJager. *La Leche League: At the Crossroads of Medicine, Feminism, and Religion.* Chapel Hill: University of North Carolina Press, 2000.

Jennifer E. Livesay

Brideprice

Brideprice is the amount given to the bride by the bridegroom prior to marriage. In cultures where this marriage custom exists, the giving of brideprice is a requirement for a valid marriage. In cultures where there is no formal marriage ceremony, the marriage is recognized when the brideprice has been paid. Originally, the groom's family paid the brideprice to the parents of the bride to make up for the loss of their daughter and of the work she performed for them. Today, many cultures recognize the brideprice as the bride's property. In some cultures, the groom or his parents provide goods, services, or work to the bride's family in lieu of the brideprice.

In many instances, brideprice is not regarded as the purchase price of the bride, paid by a suitor to the girl's father for the right to marry his daughter and control her. Rather, it is seen as a gift, a token of respect and kindness toward the bride. It also symbolizes the bridegroom's promise to support his wife. Another of its purposes, if paid in money, is to provide financial protection for a woman should she be divorced or widowed. In some cultures, a woman feels pride and increased status in her community by the payment of a satisfying brideprice by her husband. It gives her the public assurance that she is a person of worth.

Many peoples of African, Australian Aboriginal, Native American, and Semitic descent observe traditions of giving and receiving brideprice, generally given to the bride by the bridegroom and paid in money, goods, and/or services. In ancient Jewish marriage custom, the payment of brideprice is an established law, provided for in the marriage contract called the *Ketubah*, and given to the bride to protect her in the event of divorce or widowhood. This provision of the Ketubah are said to have helped to raise the status of women.

In Muslim cultures, the *sadaq* (brideprice) is given to the bride's parents, but it is established by Koranic law to be the property of the bride. Payment of brideprice is required for a valid Islamic marriage. The value of the brideprice depends upon many factors, such as a woman's beauty, talents, education, the wealth of her parents, and her family's desire to keep her at home. The brideprice for a Muslim virgin is more than that for a widow or divorcee. Among well-to-do families, the brideprice is usually spent on the bride's marriage trousseau of jewelry, furniture, and clothes. These items remain the bride's property during and after marriage by the term of the marriage contract; they give a married woman some insurance against poverty if her husband were to die or divorce her. *See also:* Engagement; Jewish Women's Folklore; Muslim Women's Folklore; Rites of Passage; Wedding.

References: Fielding, William J. *Strange Customs of Courtship and Marriage.* New York City: Hart Publishing Company Inc., 1942; Goodsell, Willystine. *A History of Marriage and the Family.* New York: AMS Press, 1974; Jones, E. O. *Marriage Customs through the Ages.* New York: Collier Books, 1965; Mordecai, Carolyn. *Weddings: Dating & Love Customs of Cultures Worldwide including Royalty.* Phoenix: Nittany, 1999; Murphy, Brian. *The World of Weddings.* New York & London: Paddington Press Ltd., 1978.

Zainab Jerret

C

Calamity Jane

Born Martha Jane Cannary in Princeton, Missouri, on May 1, 1852, there is some speculation that Calamity Jane may have been born as late as 1856. At the age of thirteen, Martha, with her parents and three siblings, began a five-month trek along the Overland Pass. During the journey, Martha spent much of her time riding horses and hunting with the men. She preferred their company and adopted masculine dress, though she was rarely mistaken for a man, as some western lore states. Not long after the family's arrival in Virginia City, Montana, Martha's mother and father died and she began her adventures in the American West.

At sixteen, Martha started a series of masculine jobs: scouting for the army, bull-whacking, and riding for the Pony Express. Though difficult jobs even for most men, Martha excelled at each of them; she is said to have scouted for General George Custer, although there is little likelihood of this. In her autobiography, she claims to have obtained the nickname "Calamity Jane" while on a scouting mission. It seems she stumbled upon soldiers trying to stop a Native uprising when a captain named Egan was shot. He began to fall from his horse and Martha rushed to his aid. "I lifted him onto my horse in front of me and succeeded in getting him safely to the fort. Captain Egan on recovering laughingly said, 'I name you Calamity Jane, the heroine of the plains.'" Captain Egan denied this event ever occurred.

Martha Cannary may also have received her nickname while nursing victims of smallpox in Deadwood, South Dakota, in 1878. The town had been ravaged by the disease, and Martha wanted to help nurse the ill. It is said that due to her selflessness, the townsfolk were able to forget her already-brazen past during this "calamity," and named her Calamity Jane.

Between the 1870s and 1890s, new stories began to emerge about Calamity Jane and her wild adventures in dime novels. Published by Beadle and Adams, Calamity had a costarring role with Deadwood Dick, though in most stories she emerged as the heroine. Calamity fought Natives, villains, and in many episodes, saved Dick from death. She was "... a dare-devil ... the most reckless buckaroo in these Hills" (Faber: 38). With her popularity and reputation growing, tourists traveled to Deadwood, South Dakota, to meet the "famous" Calamity Jane—a woman whom locals regarded as an alcoholic and a burden to their society was quite popular back East.

According to legend, Calamity married Wild Bill Hickok and may have had a child by him, named Janey, who was given up for adoption. Calamity began to keep a journal that, upon her death, would be given to her daughter. Many doubt the authenticity of the letters, but if they are real, they show a Calamity Jane who is lonely, depressed, and tired of her nomadic life. She longs to meet her daughter and wants to be another person, a better person.

In her later years, Calamity opened a saloon and hurdy-gurdy house. She attempted touring with Buffalo Bill's Wild West Show, but her hard drinking kept her in trouble. After being kicked out of the show, Calamity went home to Deadwood and wrote the previously mentioned autobiography, *Life and Adventures of Calamity Jane by Herself*. Calamity went to a fair in Buffalo, New York, to sell the booklet herself, but it was a disappointing experience; her health failing, Calamity returned again to Deadwood. She passed away two years later on August 1, 1903, due to "inflammation of the bowel." Her funeral is said to be one of the largest Deadwood had ever seen, with mourners including members of its high society. Calamity Jane is buried next to Bill Hickok in Mount Moriah Cemetery in Deadwood, South Dakota. *See also:* Cowgirl; Cross-Dressing, Legend, Local; Local Characters; Popular Culture: Region: United States.

References: Botkin, Benjamin Albert, ed. *A Treasury of Western Folklore*. New York: Crown Publishers, 1951; Faber, Doris. *Calamity Jane: Her Life and Her Legend*. Boston: Houghton Mifflin Company, 1992; Hickok, Martha Cannary. *Calamity Jane's Letters to her Daughter*. San Lorenzo, CA: Shameless Hussy Press, 1976; McLaird, James D. *Calamity Jane: The Woman and the Legend*. Norman: University of Oklahoma Press, 2005; Sollid, Roberta Seed. *Calamity Jane*. Helena, MT: Montana Historical Society Press, 1995.

Tamara Robbins-Anderson

Camplore

Camplore is the folklore of recreational camping and summer camps. It draws on traditions based on the temporary culture of camping trips and summer camps for children, which have become fixtures of U.S. and Canadian culture over the past 150 years. Songs, stories, local legends, and rituals may form part of campers' orientation to a new environment and community, but camplore also emerges among campers and camp staff as they experience living in temporary communities and develop personal histories with distinctive places. The origins of camps can be linked to educational and recreational philosophies that valued folklore for the creation of national identities, recapitulating elements of the frontier experience together with Native American elements that in the late nineteenth century were enlisted to emblematize a distinctive new-world identity.

U.S. and Canadian women were central to the nineteenth-century creation of the camping movement, which emerged both to socialize immigrant and urban children and to benefit the health and social development of children generally. According to the American Camp Association, a majority of camp directors today are women, and about 30 percent of established camps today are for girls only. These camps may foster strong associations, mentor relationships, and peer networks that last a lifetime. Many cross boundaries of education, occupation race, ethnicity, and residence to focus attention on common formative experiences in group living, leadership, risk management, culture creation, and personal and environmental values. Camplore is at the heart of this experience.

There are more than 12,000 established camps in the United States alone. Most are operated by non-profit youth, religious, and educational organizations, but more than 20 percent are run by families who may have owned and operated a summer camp for generations. In Canada, a similar pattern is found. Many children attend "day camp" or "sleep-away" camps (some for up to eight weeks annually). Study of their experiences can illuminate the changing social networks of girls and women in North American societies.

Although there are collections on camp folklore and general camp ethnographies in several archives (for example, at University of California at Los Angeles; Bowling Green University, Ohio; New York Folklore Society; and Utah State University), most published discussions focus on sponsoring organizations and on the social institution of the summer camp in general terms. Some call attention to the conscious appropriation of adapted Native North American themes and motifs, including nomenclature, tipis, woodcraft and nature activities, and dance skills. Others include material on rites of passage, pranks, and other small traditions of subversion, campfire rituals, skits, gift exchanges, music, and storytelling. Abigail Van Slyke's work deals with the architecture of camps as the embodiment of ideas about gender, nature, and childhood; Richard Louv writes about the importance of regular exposure to, confidence about, and competence in the natural environment in ways that may be relevant to further explorations of camplore. *See also:* First Nations of North America; Folk Custom; Folk Drama; Folk Group; Folk Music and Folksong; Foodways; Girl Scouts/Girl Guides; Legend, Local; Rites of Passage; Ritual; Storytelling.

References: Brewer, Teri F. "Why They Went to the Woods: Immigrants and Citizenship in the Nineteenth-Century United States." Unpublished conference paper. Cardiff: Anthropology Wales, 2001; Brewer, Teri F., and Patricia A. Wells *Creating and Maintaining Traditions: Ramifications of Expressive Behavior for Policy.* Unpublished conference paper. Santa Monica, CA: Organizational Folklore, 1983; Chandler, Joan. "Camping for Life: Transmission of Values at a Girl's Summer Camp." In *Children and Their Organizations: Investigations in American Culture,* eds. R. T. Sieber and A. J. Gordon, 67–70. Boston: G. K. Hall and Co., 1981; Deloria, Phillip J. *Playing Indian.* New Haven, CT: Yale University Press, 1998; Eels, Eleanor. *The History of Organized Camping: The First 100 Years.* Martinsville, IN: American Camping Association, 1986; Kahn, Laurie. *Sleepaway: The Girls of Summer and the Camps They Love.* New York: Workman Publishing, 2003; Louv, Richard. *Last Child in the Woods: Saving our Children from Nature Deficit Disorder.* New York: Algonquin Books, 2005; Van Slyck, Abigail. *Manufactured Wilderness: Summer Camps and the Shaping of American Youth, 1890–1960.* Minneapolis: University of Minnesota Press. 2006; Wells, Patricia Atkinson. "The Paradox of Functional Dysfunction in a Girl Scout Camp: Implications of Cultural Diversity for Achieving Organizational

Goals." In *Inside Organizations: Understanding the Human Dimension*, eds. M. O. Jones, M. D. Moore, and R. C. Snyder, 109–17. Newbury Park, CA: Sage, 1988.

Teri Brewer

Charivari/Shivaree

Charivari/Shivaree is a ritual usually linked with marriage in which friends, relatives, and community members gather outside the newlyweds' house or even in their bedroom and make raucous noise by running chainsaws, honking car horns, shooting rifles, banging pots, singing, shouting, and/or playing instruments off-key. Once a social critique of unacceptable marriages, sexual or sex-role deviations, or political actions, charivari (or shivaree) is now practiced in parts of rural Canada and the United States as an affectionate prank. It is usually accompanied by trickery inside and outside the house, such as placing alarm clocks set at untimely hours beneath the couple's bed, removing labels from canned goods, toilet papering the yard, and assembling farm machinery on the barn roof.

In the United States, charivari can be called belling, bull band(ing), calathump, calthump(ian) band, horning, serenade, skimerton, skimilton, tinpanning, or rattle band(ing). In Canada, banjo or saluting are also used, but sometimes the practice is unnamed.

Charivaris were recorded in medieval times. The Italian Renaissance crowd demanded a "ransom" and then punished the couple with cacophony or rewarded their generosity with melodious song. Charivaris drew attention to marriages that fell outside of social conventions, such as between old and old, old and young, or interracial persons, or to "[lampoon] shrewish wives and impotent husbands in the interests of effecting procreation and ensuring the community's future" (Tylus 2000). The focus on procreation symbolically ties charivari's older and newer forms: older charivaris denounced couples unlikely to be fertile or whose children could not be incorporated into a racially segregated society. But in parts of Canada, couples can endure the newer affectionate charivari any number of times until there is evidence that their first child is on the way.

Disapproval charivaris were conducted almost exclusively by men. In an 1804 shivaree in New Orleans, even "very genteel men" took part; "all this comes from an indisposition to allow ladies two chances for husbands, in a society where so few single ladies find even one husband!" (Davis 1984). In the 1840s, "young unmarried males . . . engaged in the practice of charivari, as, in masked disguise, they named and marked with raucous antics those in the community who had violated—through adultery, for instance, or wife-beating, or condescension toward the community—the neighborhood's norms" (Gura 1999).

Some time in the late nineteenth century, most charivaris became a positive comment on the marriage (though the two forms coincided well into the twentieth century). Welcoming charivaris involved women as well as men, and were often cross generational. Women's participation often included bringing lunch (a cold meal of sandwiches and sweets) in expectation of being invited into the house. These charivaris usually close with a community celebration in the newlyweds' home. *See also:* Folk Custom; Marriage; Ritual; Wedding.

References: Davis, Natalie Zemon. "Charivari, Honor, and Community in Seventeenth-Century Lyon and Geneva." In *Rite, Drama, Festival, Spectacle: Rehearsals toward a Theory of Cultural Performance*, ed. John J. MacAloon, 42–57. Philadelphia: Institute for the Study of Human Issues, 1984; Greenhill, Pauline. "Welcome and Unwelcome Visitors: Shivarees and the Political Economy of Rural-Urban Interactions in Southern Ontario." *Journal of Ritual Studies* 3 (1989): 45–67; Gura, Philip F. "America's Minstrel Daze." *New England Quarterly: A Historical View of New England Life and Letters*, vol. 72, no. 4 (1999): 602–616; Morrison, Monica. "Wedding Night Pranks in Western New Brunswick." *Southern Folklore Quarterly* 38 (1974): 285–297; Tylus, Jane. "Theater and Its Social Uses: Machiavelli's Mandragola and the Spectacle of Infamy." *Renaissance Quarterly*, vol. 53, no. 3 (2000): 656–686.

Sarah Catlin-Dupuy

Chastity

The concept of chastity (from the Latin *castus*, "pure") has deep roots in the sexual politics of the ancient Mediterranean world, especially since the rise of Christianity. Today, its historically accumulated cognate meanings include sexual and emotional modesty, restraint, virtue, abstinence, renunciation, celibacy, divinely or officially sanctioned sexual behavior, without sin, and holy. The notion that a human body-mind has the capacity for "purity" in thought, word, and deed implies that it also has the capacity for its opposite: a temporary or permanent state of being sullied or stained. Originating in Platonic and Manichaean philosophies, the concept of chastity reveals a fundamental split in Western thought between matter (from the Latin *mater*, "mother"), deemed inherently evil because it inevitably changes, dies, and decays, and disembodied mind, spirit, or soul, deemed inherently good because it is unchanging and immortal. Given this formulation, chastity is an expression of the belief that "abstinence from sex [is] the most effective technique with which to achieve clarity of soul" (Brown: 78); it is also a conceptual construct that generates what has become known as the madonna/whore dichotomy as a characterization of "the nature of women."

Chastity—historically and in the present—presents a paradox for women for three reasons. First, associated with the realm of matter in the Western imagination, women have come to represent (hetero) sexuality itself (men *have* sexuality; women *are* sexuality). Therefore, "good women" (madonnas) abstain from illicit sexual expressions for the sake of men, whose souls are endangered by their mere presence, and also for the sake of their own souls' redemption from the "sin of Eve," that is, original sin. Second, procreation, particularly socially sanctioned procreation, as every Roman matron knew, is necessary for the orderly continuity of society. If a woman chooses to abstain altogether from expressing her sexuality, she leaves herself open to the charge that she has transgressed not only against the stability and order of society, but against her own nature. Finally, long-accepted metaphorical associations between a woman's mouth and her vagina (both have "lips" and are potentially dangerous when open) mean that chastity in word implies women's silence (closed lips).

She may, therefore, correctly choose chastity only within the bounds of (quiet) married sex, once she is widowed, or as a renunciate nun. If her sexuality finds expression in other contexts, she falls into the whore category, where her sexuality becomes the sole mark of her personhood.

Patriarchy maintains its control of female sexuality primarily because its regulation ensures continuity of male inheritance patterns and because it reflects upon the reputations of its male guardians. Hence, during the European medieval period, a departing crusader insisted that his wife wear a chastity belt while he was away, or so the stories go. Chastity belts are more fictive than factual, but it is in the idea that he must somehow restrain and secure her naturally vagrant sexuality for himself that their importance lies.

But while chastity may seem like an old-fashioned ideal in these post-*Sex-and-the-City* days, its foundational ideology remains essentially unchanged. Women, particularly upper- and middle-class women, whose unchaste sexual behavior results in the births of "illegitimate" children, may still be sent to homes for unwed mothers, a very hush-hush and shame-filled operation. Historically, abortions were life-threatening, back-alley procedures; as of this writing, it remains to be seen if they will remain legal, safe, and available in the United States. The idea that raped women are "asking for it" by wearing immodest dress persists in some sectors. And "blushing" brides dressed in white are still "given away." The classic pattern of heterosexual gender relations in which good men are expected to be aggressively initiating and sexually experienced while good women giggle, blush demurely, and passively comply with male desires, are colored by historical notions of the pure, virtuous, modest, chaste female.

Current evangelical Protestant abstinence campaigns in England and North America encourage young women and men to abstain from sexual intercourse until marriage and to mark their commitment to chastity by wearing a "chastity ring" or "purity ring" on the fourth finger of the left hand ("Silver Ring Thing"). Due to poor sex education, however, especially in the United States, studies show that abstinence pledgers are up to six times more likely to have oral and anal sex, resulting in sexually transmitted disease rates that coincide with those of their non-pledging peers. In other traditions, chastity is marked variously by the wearing of habits, head- and/or bodyscarves, special underwear (in the case of Mormons), chastity belts (in the case of sadism and masochism adherents), and in its most extreme form, by surgically removing the clitoris and/or closing the vaginal lips through female genital cutting. *See also:* Eve; Female Genital Cutting; Helpmate; Sexuality; Veiling; Virginity; Wedding.

References: Associated Press. "Study: Abstinence Pledgers May Risk STDs." *Arizona Daily Sun*, March 19, 2005, http://www.azdailysun.com/non_sec/nav_includes/story. cfm storyID=105330 (accessed March 19, 2005); Brown, Peter. *The Body and Society: Men, Women, and Sexual Renunciation in Early Christianity.* New York: Columbia University Press, 1988; Classen, Albrecht. *The Medieval Chastity Belt: A Myth-Making Process.* New York: Palgrave Macmillan, 2007; Silver Ring Thing. http://www.silverringthing.com (accessed June 29, 2007); Theiss, Janet M. *Disgraceful Matters: The Politics of Chastity in Eighteenth-Century China.* Berkeley: University of California Press, 2004.

Jessica Grant Jørgensen and Liz Locke

Cheerleading

Cheerleading is an adolescent-driven cultural production combining folk dance—patterned and rhythmic movement—with folk poetry—memorized shouts and chants in rhyming or blank verse. The practice has developed its own trappings, vocabulary, theatrics, and organizational structures. Though originally American, cheerleading has been exported around the world. Its elements are traditional, patterned, and symbolic. While boys and men are incorporated into many teams, especially in the extensively developed U.S. technical cheerleading competitions, the custom is primarily associated with and dominated by girls and women.

Since the early 1970s, through national media and organizational structures, the vernacular practice of cheerleading has been extracted from its local ceremonial contexts and developed for staged presentations. Cheerleading was once viewed only as vigorous sideline encouragement to keep both players and spectators enthused about winning at community sporting events like high school basketball and university football games. It now occurs in a variety of contexts and for various purposes—from its original function as sideline entertainment at sports events to elaborately staged championships in which teams of cheerleaders compete. This self-conscious alteration has transformed the auxiliary nature of the form into an activity recognized as a sport in its own right, not simply as an accessory to male-dominated sports events.

While some high-powered teams have professional choreographers who groom them for national championships, commonly team captains are responsible for teaching cheers and dances to new cheerleaders. Knowledge of the practice and of the cheerleader role and social image are passed down through generations of girls, primarily through oral transmission. In the United States, it is transmitted from experts to novices within individual squads over school years marked by cheerleading's calendrical rituals. Among these, tryouts (experienced as a chance for initiation into an elite clique) and competitions are especially vital.

Cheerleading's processes of firsthand transmission take place in two major arenas: first, during the learning and teaching of cheers within one team, and second, at gatherings of cheerleaders at camps and competitions. The latter events gather passionate participants who demonstrate and share routines that remain remarkably consistent across time and space. Specific cheers are rarely transmitted between squads at these brief occasions, yet the rules of performance are influenced, shaped, and reinforced by the intense communal experience. Cheerleaders explicitly refer to "spirit" as a core value; they strive to embody it through elements that combine the unofficial and spontaneous with the formalized and ceremonial.

This traditional body of knowledge finds a forum for exchange and validation in the context of the competition. Cheerleading competitions, in the United States and elsewhere, are grand conventions of scantily uniformed, coiffed, and glittered girls presenting their routines in screaming, synchronized teams. Costumes, cosmetics, hairstyles, facial expressions, preparations, and customs on- and offstage are stylized and imitative.

At standard competitions, each team has two and a half minutes to perform on a brightly lit stage. Routines can include human pyramids and other stunts, dancing to recorded music, and required verbal cheer elements. These singsong chants, accompanied by choreographed movements, handclapping and foot-stomping, feature complex rhythms and syncopations. They typically incorporate suggestive pelvic movements and symbolic gestures that illustrate (often with militaristic imagery) the accompanying lyrics. Common elements include clenched fists, punching and chopping motions, kicks and jumps that reveal the crotch area, and defiant stances with legs spread. The hip-thrusting and gyrating mimic more consciously seductive styles of dance. Such choreography is a requisite element of contemporary cheerleading performance, but the increasing sexualization of the genre troubles some critics. As troubling is the marked increase in injuries sustained by competitive cheerleaders, especially in recent years.

The amalgamation of other styles of movement—for example, hip-hop and martial arts—into American cheerleading has not significantly altered the genre's basic vocabulary, including its repertoire of gestures, jumps, and formations, its body of textual material, and its accompanying accessories, such as pom-poms and poodle socks. Cheerleading squads from around the United States, convening at competitions, share a common repertoire of cheers that have been passed down often virtually unchanged for fifty years.

See also: Clique; Cosmetics; Folk Dance; Folk Poetry; Girls' Games; Hair; Initiation; Sorority Folklore; Tradition.

References: Adams, Natalie Guice, and Pamela J. Bettis. *Cheerleader!: An American Icon.* New York: Palgrave MacMillan, 2003; Hanson, Mary Ellen. *Go! Fight! Win!: Cheerleading in American Culture.* Bowling Green: Bowling Green State University Popular Press, 1995; Kurman, George. "What Does Girls' Cheerleading Communicate?" *Journal of Popular Culture* 20 (1986): 57–64; Lesko, Nancy. "We're Leading America: The Changing Organization and Form of High School Cheerleading." *Theory and Research in Social Education* 16 (1988): 263–278; Miller, Montana. "Radiant Smiles: The International Spread of American Cheerleading." Paper presented at American Folklore Society annual meeting, Salt Lake City, Utah, 2004; Pennington, Bill. "As Cheerleaders Soar, So Does the Danger." *New York Times*, March 31, 2007. http://www.nytimes.com/2007/03/31/sports/31cheerleader.html?_r=1&adxnnl=1&oref=slogin&adxnnlx=1198430036-kLr8 e4Spe6KlV7EiCGCupw (accessed December 23, 2007).

Montana Miller

Childbirth and Childrearing

Childbirth is the act or process of giving birth (parturition), and childrearing the acts or processes of protecting, caring for, feeding, and otherwise facilitating the development of offspring from infancy to relative self-sufficiency.

For the majority of human history in both Western and non-Western societies, the practices of childbirth, midwifery, and early infant care have been shaped by societal issues and beliefs and have undergone great changes, new understandings, and different practices. Influences on childbirth and childrearing practices have included advances in medical knowledge, industrialization and urbanization, the rise of the middle class, changes in belief patterns and structures in both organized religions and in community-based household or folk religions, and new scientific and cultural understandings about women's bodies, health, and roles.

In the nineteenth century, early folklorists and antiquarians began to collect what they regarded as survivals (relics of the past, particularly traditions and beliefs common to rural areas). Examples associated with pregnancy, childbirth, and infancy included notions about dietary intake and prenatal marking, including pica (the desire to eat non-food items, such as ice, chalk, ashes, or starch, and particularly geophagy—dirt-eating during pregnancy); divination practices regarding the sex of the fetus; practices and styles of delivery; methods of pain relief and postures; customs and rituals of birth chambers and attendants; and societal attitudes and beliefs regarding general birthlore and early infant care. These were recorded in large collections of folkways and rural practices. Fanny Bergen's *Current Superstitions: Collected from the Oral Tradition of English Speaking States* (1996) and Charles Skinner's *Myths and Legends of Our Own Land* (2003) are examples.

In contrast, histories of birth presented by members of the medical profession were based on cultural evolutionary ideas involving projections of progress toward social ideals; in the main, they advocated and described cultural advances and technological developments. Conventional histories, however, did not capture or discuss the experiences of the vast majority of women giving birth, the role and beliefs of the community in the birth process, or the practices, traditions, and beliefs of midwives.

More recent efforts to create a history of birth from a folklife or social historical perspective placed traditions and practices within chronological periods. Typically, early histories describe a period in the deep past when women were highly involved in delivery as midwives and assistants practicing a non-interventionist approach that was centered on serving mothers. A second period in Western Europe and in North America is seen as beginning in the mid-1700s with the growing professionalization of medicine, an increase in the study and practice of midwifery by males, and the definition of birth as a disease state. A third period, from the mid-nineteenth century until the present day, is characterized as a period of consolidation of medical control over birth, with a counter-movement to reclaim birth as a female-centered, natural event, and a glorification of the early period of what is now called "social birth."

In the first period of social birth, from the early years of America until the mid-1700s, the process of labor and delivery was a community event. Childbirth was viewed as a normal process, and community members were content to allow nature to follow its course. The predominant practices, material objects, and language associated with birth were predicated upon this understanding and approach. Intervention was rare, and doctors were called only in the case of an impossible delivery, the death of the mother, or the death of the child in utero (as yet unborn).

Near the time of delivery, the neighborhood midwife was alerted that her services would be required in the days to come. When the moment arrived, the father, a child, or a neighbor was sent to fetch her to the pregnant woman's home to assist in the delivery. The midwife would bring along the tools of her trade—twine, scissors, cloth, and perhaps a birth stool or chair. The latter would be assembled and the expectant mother would spend her labor talking with her friends and neighbors who had gathered. When she reached the point of delivery, she would sit upon a birth chair, makeshift stool, or the lap of attendants, and deliver her child. Fathers participated if needed; doctors were seldom present.

A diary account from 1677 by Samuel Sewall of Massachusetts portrays such a visit by a midwife:

> April 2, 1677. Father and I sitting in the great Hall, heard the [summoning] child cry.... Went home with the Midwife about 2 o'clock, carrying her Stool, whose parts were included in a Bagg. Met with the watch at Mr. Rocks Brew house, who baid us stand, enquired what we were. I told the Woman's occupation, so they baid God bless our labours, and let us pass (Banks 1999: 6).

American midwives were high-ranking members of their communities, consulted for their advice on birth, but also on conception, pregnancy, abortion, childrearing, and all elements of community health care. In addition to their practical expertise in delivery, midwives had knowledge—passed on through oral communication and informal apprenticeships—of herbal treatments, including the use of ergot, a wheat fungus that stimulates labor (later marketed and used as a medical drug), herbs to cause the contraction of the uterus (for delivery or abortion), and aids for relaxation. In the seventeen century, only the poorest of the poor delivered their children in hospitals, lying-in societies, or the medical area of the poorhouse. These were the only cases a doctor might have occasion to observe, although the vast majority of these deliveries were also attended by midwives. By the late nineteenth century, Dr. Charles Zeigler was complaining in the *Journal of the American Medical Association*, "It is at present impossible to secure cases sufficient for the proper training in obstetrics, since 75 percent of the material otherwise available for clinical purposes is utilized providing a livelihood for midwives" (Ehrenreich 1989: 95).

In early American settlements, church authorities were involved in approving or certifying midwives, because they were required by law to baptize children, often in utero, in the event of a difficult or fatal delivery so the infant could be absolved of original sin prior to death. In addition, part of a midwife's duties, as dictated by church authorities, included determining the identity of the father of an unmarried woman's child, and informing authorities if an abortion had been performed after a report of quickening (first movement of a fetus in utero perceived by the mother).

Despite their high status within the community, midwives also bore the burden of suspicion. Various Christian doctrines loosely supported the interpretation of illness or death as the will of God or the result of sin or association with the Devil. Midwives were therefore vulnerable to charges of witchcraft upon failure to deliver a perfect child. Suspicion was also attached to their free access to body parts long considered magical: the placenta, the umbilical cord, and the caul (the embryonic sac when it covers the head at birth). In 1555, Würzburg regulations for midwives forbid them to take away the placenta and required that they throw it in running water. As late as 1711, Brandenburg regulations forbade midwives to give away or sell remains of birth, such as the membranes, caul, or umbilical cord (Forbes 1966: 118). The first person executed in the Massachusetts Bay Colony in 1648 was Margaret Jones, a midwife accused of witchcraft (Williams 1992: 152). The decline of the influence of the institutional Protestantism and Catholicism after the American War of Independence served to lessen charges of witchcraft; midwives continued to practice throughout the American colonies and states.

Colonial women bore children on an average of every two and a half years—about twelve pregnancies in a lifetime. Approximately one birth in every twenty-four resulted in stillbirth or death within the first days of life, and about seven children in each family survived infancy and early childhood. Colonial Americans generally regarded the rearing of offspring as an exercise in taming children's innate sinfulness and training them to be productive citizens. Many New England Puritans beat their children, seeking to break their willfulness, and took them to see corpses or hangings as a warning against the consequences of sin.

The vast majority of colonial and early republican American families lived on farms and depended on the labor of every family member. By the age of six or seven, farm children had specific responsibilities. Considered miniature adults, their rearing was built on received gender roles: girls were schooled in household chores, boys on the farm, in the family business, or apprenticed out to a neighboring industry. By ten or twelve, sons were working at men's tasks and daughters were helping their mothers with cooking, washing, spinning, and milking, or taking over certain areas of home and garden care completely. Boys and girls were often fostered out between the ages of seven and fourteen as servants or apprentices. Titles of conduct books by Louisa Caroline Huggins, one of the first women in the United States to write for and about children, are representative of the belief in separate gender spheres: *I Will Be a Lady: A Book for Girls* (1845) and *I Will be a Gentleman: A Book for Boys* (1846). It should be noted, however, that there was no single American way of childrearing; Native Americans, African Americans, and White colonists had different traditions.

After the Revolutionary War, the growing influence of physicians' guilds and colleges, the increase in the numbers of doctors being trained and practicing, and the discovery of possibilities for profit in midwifery threatened the practice of traditional midwifery and the livelihood of female midwives in the United States. By increasingly defining birth as a dangerous, pathological crisis, the medical profession undermined society's belief in the skills of midwives, thereby increasing doctors' incomes. In 1820, Walter Channing, professor of obstetrics at Harvard, wrote, "Women seldom forget a practitioner who has conducted them tenderly and safely through parturition. . . . It is principally on this account that the practice of midwifery becomes desirable to physicians. It is this which insures to the permancy [sic] and security of all their other business" (Banks 1999: 40).

Physicians developed and substantiated a definition of pregnancy and birth as disease states. Displacing traditional folk medicine in order to supply a specific etiology (cause) and catalogue of symptoms, they offered elaborate birth-chair designs and began to innovate invasive practices and the liberal use of technologically advanced tools. Forceps, crochets, and hooks, previously only utilized as a last resort to save the life of the mother, the child, or both, became commonplace. Changes in the folk practices of delivery and in the beliefs and attitudes that had supported them are most evident in changes in styles and postures for delivery—from upright in a birth chair to recumbent in a bed (necessary for tool use); in the sex of the birth attendant—from female to male; in attitudes toward laboring women; and in language regarding pregnancy and birth. Terms such as "teeming" and "breeding" were replaced in nineteenth-century diaries, literature, and other texts with terms like "sick," "confined," and, tellingly, "ill."

Midwifery manuals gave way to obstetrical texts, and in the titles of these works, pregnancy and birth were increasingly referred to as the "diseases of women." Advice booklets appeared which instructed women as to proper behavior during pregnancy exams and birth, and provided general guidance for the selection and use of doctors. This portrayal of birth as a disease state fed the growing conception within society of the fragility of women. As Dr. Mary Putnam Jacobi stated in 1895, "I think, finally, it is in the increased attention paid to women, and especially in their new function as lucrative patients, scarcely imagined a hundred years ago, that we find explanation for much of the ill health among women, freshly discovered today" (Banks 1999: 41).

The actual practice of childbirth was also affected by other significant societal changes, including shifts in the general attitude of the populace about femininity and womanhood, industrialization, changing economic structures, and the emergence of the middle class. Women were eventually understood to be as weak and fragile as doctors and scientists thought they were. Exertion and activity were regarded as dangerous to their health and general well-being. If a woman did not experience illness as a result of such activities, she must not be "truly female." Thus, fragility and ill health became acceptable and common indications of a refined sensibility and high social status.

The cultivation of upper-class women's ill health as a sign of status and civilized behavior further contributed to the growing conception that the whole process of childbearing was well beyond a refined woman's capability. If a woman was "civilized," it was believed, she needed medical help in delivery. As members of the growing middle class sought to emulate the wealthy classes in all ways, it became critical for them to show that the active economic participation of their wives and daughters to provide for the family's welfare was unnecessary. Female idleness, once considered sinful, was now a status symbol.

Yet in the nineteenth century, birth in some ways became more difficult. Life in the industrialized city and standards of fashionable dress made the image of unhealthy women into reality. Years of use of supports such as corsets and strait lacing seriously altered a woman's anatomy. Malformed torsos and pelvic areas made delivery difficult or impossible, and fetuses were damaged when women continued to wear fashionable undergarments throughout pregnancy.

By the late nineteenth century, the practice of delivery was strikingly different from what it had been 100 years earlier. The strong bonds of female community, particularly noticeable through women's earlier participation in the delivery of a community member, were weakened by popular migration to cities where friends, family members, and neighbors were no longer available. Knowledge about pregnancy and childbirth declined as these topics became increasingly unacceptable in polite conversation; when people did speak of them, they used euphemisms and told fictional stories about where babies come from (for example, brought by the stork or found in a cabbage patch). Even practitioners used such euphemisms when advertising their services.

Drugs were used to hasten delivery, bloodletting was practiced, and obstetrical tools were extensively employed to remove the infant mechanically from the mother. Birth-chair design was first radically altered, and then the chairs themselves gradually were dismissed as archaic items; horizontal delivery in bed was preferred. Such changes may have made doctors physically more comfortable and enhanced their feeling and appearance of control, but they increased the actual burden on the mother and removed control of the event from her. The elements and practices associated with the earlier, more natural approach came to be regarded with apprehension and dread, representing a period before treatment was available.

The nineteenth century also saw the development of the cult of motherhood in the United States, with the glorification of "true womanhood" and the invention of childhood as a distinct stage of life. In her separate domestic sphere, a wife as full-time homemaker and mother was valued as a nurturer, not as a worker. More children were kept at home into their late teens because they were no longer considered economic assets who could be employed in household industries or bound out as child apprentices. Children were treated as beings in emotional and social formation instead of as miniature adults to be trained in the skills and necessary tasks of society (Kertzer and Barbagli 2002).

By the middle of the nineteenth century, these changes in the view of children had spread from the elite to the urban (and largely Protestant) middle class. Books, magazines, poetry, and fiction were being written especially for children who now enjoyed prolonged childhoods. Parents eagerly read advice books on how best to rear children. Merchants began offering dolls, trains, and other children's playthings, and stores specializing in games, toys, and children's goods opened in larger cities. Attitudes about children's early learning also changed. As late as the 1830s and 1840s, infant schools in the northern states enrolled children as young as three years; reading at an early age was encouraged. Elizabeth Palmer Peabody established the first formally organized kindergarten in Boston in 1860. Influenced by German educational experiments, Peabody sought to offer children learning activities such as clay modeling and papercutting, rather than specific instruction in reading or writing, or training in the chores and tasks of their elders as in the past. The former activities, she argued, stimulated children's educational development; the latter merely exploited and broke them (Mann and Peabody 1869).

Unfortunately, not all children lived such a privileged existence. Although urban middle-class families could prosper without having to put their children to work, for most families a child was still a necessary economic asset. Children of the poor, the indentured, and the enslaved were still sent out to work in fields, mines, and mills until the enactment of child-labor laws, beginning in 1916. Children were expected to contribute to the well-being and support of the family and work the same hours as adults; they could be prosecuted and punished under the same laws.

While maternity hospitals or lying-in centers were first used only by poor women who were delivered free of charge in exchange for their use as test cases for medical students, birth in hospitals among women of the upper classes and paying customers rose sharply following the introduction of obstetrical anesthesia, known as "twilight sleep," at the turn of the twentieth century.

Delivery in hospitals took place in operating rooms or theaters, with women highly anesthetized on flat tables or hospital gurneys with arm straps, shoulder straps, and stirrups with leg restraints, attended by licensed medical personnel. Birth was a medical procedure conducted by doctors on the unconscious woman. Texts on childbirth available to and intended for women were treatises on home economics: advice on mothering, scientific housekeeping, diapering, and tips for the care and nurturing of children. Little information about becoming pregnant and the processes of gestation and delivery was made available; women were instructed to speak about their condition to no one but their doctors. S. Weir Mitchell of Philadelphia stated in 1888, "Wise women choose their doctors and trust them. The wisest ask the fewest questions" (Banks 1999: 49).

In the early years of the twentieth century, midwives, already radically compromised, increasingly lost access even to indigent women as clients. Hired by governments and municipalities, midwives performed home visits following delivery to check on the mother and to monitor the infant's progress, but were infrequently, if ever, participants in the actual birth process. Only in very rural areas or among the very poor were midwives still the primary birth practitioners. While in the past, midwives had been cast as witches, in the early twentieth century, practicing midwives were assumed to be abortionists.

The widespread commonality of experience due to the surge in childbirth in North America from the mid-1940s until the early 1960s ("the baby boom"), combined with massive family movement to the suburbs, provided new forums for contact and community among women. These new circumstances created contexts in which the topic of birth was once again considered acceptable for discourse. As women discussed birth in general and the actual details of the delivery process, they questioned the standard medical approach to childbirth, debated whether medicalized birth in hospitals was really the best approach to delivery, and expressed concern over the absence of the laboring woman in the event.

Bolstered by information about the growing popularity in Europe of methods of birth like *accouchement sans douleur* (birth without pain, the Lamaze method), women in North America sought not only to reduce unnecessary intervention in their deliveries but also to defeat the patronizing attitudes of professional medicine toward women. From this renewed dialogue on the topic of delivery, the movement for alternative birth began. Encompassing a wide variety of natural, alternative, and non-interventionist practices, the movement placed value on the mother's role and strove for practices that worked in concert with birth, rather than attempting to dictate and manipulate it. This movement looked to traditional practices, to the era of social birth, and to the growing trend toward self-care for models of practice. Newer approaches such as underwater birth were introduced, and older practices were revived—birth chairs, use of midwives and community women (doulas), and the birth act as a communal event. With the growth of the alternative birth movement, midwives began to take on greater roles in delivery, practicing in hospitals as certified nurse-midwives and certified professional midwives, legally licensed and recognized in some states. Midwives and advocates of natural birth established freestanding birth centers. In an effort to meet the demands of their lucrative clientele, hospitals responded by creating specialized birthing suites that offered a more "homey" atmosphere yet maintained the pathological definition of birth.

Building on the nineteenth-century cult of motherhood and the glorification of childhood, progressive-era reformers from the 1890s to the 1920s stressed new scientific understanding of child development (as well as scientific housekeeping, cooking, and motherhood). These reformers urged that children be removed from the labor force, age-segregated, protected from adult concerns, and shepherded through systematic stages of growth by nurturing mothers and/or trained experts dedicated solely to the needs of their children. By the 1920s, this new style of childrearing had been adopted by most families with sufficient resources, although many others still lacked the means to create and maintain such child-centered households. While parents or guardians were expected to provide their children with moral guidance and oversee their education and training for an occupation, meeting the needs of children, even inventing new needs, became important elements of the consumer economy.

The symbolic leader in this era was pediatrician Dr. Benjamin Spock, following the publication in 1946 of his manual *Baby and ChildCare*. Throughout the twentieth century, social, cultural, political, and economic emphases on children, childhood, and childrearing grew by leaps and bounds. Scholarly attention has been brought to bear on the folklore of children, children as a lucrative market, the special vulnerabilities of children, and specialized entertainment, diversions, and activities for children, including camps, educational programs, sports, clubs, clothing, and the burgeoning toy industry. In the early twenty-first century, the children of the poor are included and their futures implicated in consumer-oriented childrearing. *See also:* Abortion; Birth Chair; Doula; Folk Custom; Folk Medicine; Herbs; Home Birth; Lullaby; Midwifery; Mothers' Folklore; Pregnancy; Witchcraft, Historical.

References: Arnup, Katherine, Andre Levesque, and Ruth Roach Pierson, eds. *Delivering Motherhood: Maternal Ideologies and Practices in the 19th and 20th Centuries.*

New York: Routledge, 1990; Banks, Amanda Carson. *Birth Chairs, Midwives, and Medicine*. Jackson: University Press of Mississippi, 1999; Davis-Floyd, Robbie E. *Birth as an American Rite of Passage*. Berkeley: University of California Press, 1992; Ehrenreich, Barbara. *For Her Own Good: 150 Years of the Experts' Advice to Women*. New York: Anchor Books Doubleday, 1989; Forbes, Thomas Rogers. *The Midwife and the Witch*. New Haven: Yale University Press, 1966; Haines, Michael. "Fertility and Mortality in the United States." *EH.Net Encyclopedia of Economic and Business History*, ed. Robert Whaples, 2005. http://www.eh.net/encyclopedia (accessed July 22, 2005); Hoffert, Sylvia. *Private Matters: American Attitudes Toward Childbearing and Infant Nurture in the Urban North, 1800–1860*. Urbana: University of Illinois Press, 1981; Kertzer, David, and Marzio Barbagli, eds. *Family Life in the Long Nineteenth Century, 1789–1913: The Rise of the European Family, Volume 2*. New Haven, CT: Yale University Press, 2002; Leavitt, Judith Walzer. *Brought to Bed: Childbearing in America, 1750–1950*. London: Oxford University Press, 1988; Mann, Mary Tyler Peabody, and Elizabeth P. Peabody. *Moral Culture of Infancy, and Kindergarten Guide: With Music for the Plays*. New York: J. W. Schemerhorn, 1869; Stearns, Peter N. *Anxious Parents: A History of Modern Childrearing in America*. New York: New York University Press, 2003; Welter, Barbara. "The Cult of True Womanhood, 1820–1860." *American Quarterly*, vol. 2, no. 1 (1966): 151–174; Williams, Selma R., and Pamela Williams Adelman. *Riding the Nightmare: Women & Witchcraft from the Old World to Colonial Salem*. New York: Harper Perennial Editions, 1992.

Amanda Carson Banks

Cinderella

"Cinderella," meaning "ash-girl" (Italian *Cenerentola*, French *Cendrillon*, German *Aschenputtel*), is perhaps the best-known folktale in the world. Its earliest known variant dates to ninth-century CE China. The most influential European versions are in magic tale collections from oral sources by Neapolitan Giambattista Basile (1634–1636), Parisian Charles Perrault (1697), and the German philologists Jacob and Wilhelm Grimm (1812); the first English printing was a 1729 translation of Perrault. Interpretations focus on variations and meanings in the heroine's initial persecution, her magic helpers, her encounter with the prince, proving her identity, and their marriage. The Walt Disney animated film, which debuted in 1949, is one in a long line of reworkings/retellings of this ever-popular story.

British folklorist Marian Roalfe Cox's 1893 study of 345 variants of "Cinderella" and Swedish folklorist Anna Birgitta Rooth's 1951 *Cinderella Cycle*, based on almost 700 versions, attest to the tale's historic and geographic range. Virtually unknown in the West until 1932, the Chinese Cinderella Yeh-hsien appears in a book by Tuan Ch'eng-shih (ca. 850), who identifies the teller as a former servant, "originally a cave man of Yung Chow [who] remembered very much about the strange stories of the south" (Jameson in Dundes 1982: 77). Chinese folklorist Nai-tung Ting's 1974 study of Cinderella in China and Indochina includes twenty-one versions. The Chinese practice of foot-binding girls to create a form of ideal beauty may be origin for the shoe-test to prove Cinderella's identity, as in some versions of the tale.

The earliest European reference is in a sermon delivered at Strasbourg, France, in 1501; a tale text appears in an early 1570s edition of Bonaventure des Périers's *Novel Pastimes and Merry Tales*. "The Cat Cinderella" is the sixth "diversion" on the first of five days during which ten women each tell one story in Basile's *Il Pentamerone*, originally called *The Story of Stories or the Entertainment of the Little Ones* when it was published in the Neapolitan dialect; it was translated into Italian in 1747. Perrault's "Cendrillon" in his 1697 collection *Tales of Past Times, with Lessons*, better known by its alternate title *Tales of My Mother Goose*, was first translated from French into English in 1729. Ash Girl ("Aschenputtel") is in the first volume (1812) of the Grimm brothers' *Children's and Household Tales*. Perrault's version, which introduces the glass slipper, has proved the most popular.

Marian Cox identifies two major versions of "Cinderella" (Tatar 1999: 103–104): one involves an "ill-treated heroine (with mothers, stepmothers, and their progeny as victimizers)"; the other involves an "unnatural father," Victorian wording for an importunate "father's perverse erotic attachment . . . or . . . insistence on a verbal declaration of love." The former are called Cinderella tales, the latter, Catskin tales. Some Catskin plots combine both: the heroine, persecuted by her father, becomes a Cinderella "obliged to spend her days in domestic servitude under the supervision of a despotic cook or a queen."

The Chinese Cinderella Yeh-hsien is assisted by a long-haired man in coarse clothing who comes down from the sky to tell her how to pray to the bones of the magically growing fish beheaded by her stepmother. Basile's Cat Cinderella is helped by magical gifts from the dove of the fairies on the Island of Sardinia; Perrault's Cendrillon is assisted by her fairy godmother; and the Grimms' Aschenputtel has the aid of a white bird who three times a day alights on the tree that grows on her mother's grave. British historian and writer Marina Warner suggests that the absent mother in Cinderella and other magic tales is replaced by the good fairy who may also herself be the narrator of the story and thus, "if she is offering herself as the benevolent wonder-worker in the lives of the story's protagonists, . . . may be reproducing within the tale another historical circumstance in the lives of women besides the high rate of death in childbirth or the enforced abandonment of children on widowhood: she may be recording, in concealed form, the antagonism between mothers and the women their sons marry, between daughters-in-law and their husbands' mothers" (1994: 217). In *Kissing the Witch*, Irish novelist, playwright, and historian Emma Donoghue ends "The Tale of the Shoe" with Cinderella fleeing the prince's marriage proposal, tossing away the shoe, and going home with the helpful woman stranger old enough to be her mother.

Greek folklorist Photeine P. Bourboulis (Dundes 1982) seeks origins for Cinderella's encounter with the prince in the "bride-show custom." She documents how in Byzantium, Russia, and China an imperial bachelor selected a bride from among eligible girls assembled before him. Cinderella's true identity is not revealed at this first meeting and must be divined by the fit of a finger-ring, a shoe of whatever material, or by some other means. In Nazi Germany, magic tales like Cinderella were retold and reinterpreted in anti-Semitic terms. According to one Aryan interpreter, "The prince finds the genuine, worthy bride because his unspoiled instinct leads him, because the voice of his blood tells him that she is the right one" (Zipes 1983: 140).

Cinderella's marriage to the prince and her stepsisters' failure to marry him has been interpreted in terms of social class. For example, American folklorist and German Studies scholar Jack Zipes (1983) sees fairy tales as important elements in the nineteenth-century rise of the urban-industrial bourgeoisie from the agrarian feudalism evident in many of the tales' accounts of nobility and peasantry. Tale collections served to socialize children to meet changing domestic and public normative expectations. In the Grimms' "Aschenputtel," American folklorist Elisabeth Panttaja finds the conflict between Cinderella and her stepmother and the stepsisters and their mother evidence of "the discord between feudal and bourgeois values, attitudes, and aesthetics." In the end, the stepsisters are severely punished and the old "aristocratic order" prevails because "unlike many other tales which reward the cunning upstart, 'Cinderella' prizes innate nobility over striving, and reserves the happy ending for the daughter of the 'pure' past instead of the daughters of the aspiring middle class" (1993: 94).

Greek-born lesbian poet and translator Olga Broumas's Cinderella laments her token status in a household of pretentious men and longs to return to her sisters' hut and her "wet canvas shoes" (Mieder 1985: 85–86). The hugely popular American film, *Pretty Woman* (1990), uses the conventions of the folktale to romanticize contemporary sex work as an unfortunate detour on the inevitable path that all "pretty women" take toward happy marriages with wealthy men. The Cinderella of American children's literature is influenced by the Horatio Alger "rags-to-riches formula," according to Jane Yolen (Dundes 1982: 296), herself an American author of children's books. This "American creed ... that even a poor boy can grow up to become president" and its "unliberated corollary that even a poor girl can grow up and become the president's wife" is "ironic:" "'Cinderella' is *not* a story of rags to riches, but rather riches recovered; *not* poor girl into princess but rather rich girl (or princess) rescued from improper or wicked enslavement." It is "that [American] story" of strike-it-rich, working-class people who win sweepstakes, chance to marry wealth, or collect large insurance settlements which poet Anne Sexton (1971) "transforms" in her retelling of the Grimms' "Cinderella."

Walt Disney produced several silent animated films adapting magic tales with his collaborator Ub Iwerks, one of which was "Cinderella" (1922). His Hollywood studio's 1949 animation, an enormous box-office and merchandising success, is from Perrault. Jack Zipes encapsulates Disney's "spell" or successful "formula for feature-length fairy tales, [which] he never abandoned" from 1934 on: "Instead of using technology to enhance the communal aspects of narrative and bring about major changes in viewing stories to stir and animate viewers, he employed animators and technology to stop thinking about change, to return to his films, and to long nostalgically for neatly ordered patriarchal realms" (Tatar 1999: 352).

Feminists have vigorously debated the kind of socialization into gender roles fostered by the tales' passive and active heroes and heroines. For example, in "'Some Day My Prince Will Come': Female Acculturation through the Fairy Tale," American Marcia K. Lieberman finds magic-tale heroines like Cinderella "not merely passive ... but frequently victims and even martyrs as well"; a "child who dreams of being a Cinderella dreams perforce not only of being chosen and elevated by a prince but also of being a glamorous sufferer or victim" (Zipes 1986: 194).

Such arguments were field-tested by Canadian folklorist Kay Stone, who interviewed women, men, girls, and boys about their perceptions of and memories about the tales (1975, 1985). She found that both females and males at some point in their lives "clearly view fairy tale heroines and heroes as providing different kinds of idealized behavior," with women continuing to be involved even after childhood: "For women, the problem-creating aspect of the tales is the attempted identification with the ideal woman, or the guilt if one fails to identify with her, and the expectation that one's life will be transformed dramatically and all one's problems solved with the arrival of a man ... [and they may] continue to reinterpret their responses at various ages, but often without solving the problem" (1985: 143). This supports views of these "classic tales" as "both 'parables of female socialization' *and* stories that ultimately call 'women forth to an awakening'" (Haase 2000: 37).

The concept of voice, whether studied editorially or ethnographically, is important to a more complex understanding of Cinderella tales. American scholar Ruth B. Bottigheimer has analyzed "Aschenputtel" in the Grimms' editions of 1812, 1819, and 1857 to see how instances of direct speech and thought by the various characters were reduced, altered to indirection, or silenced by the editors (1987: 57–70). In the final edition, Cinderella has lost virtually all direct voice and thus appears more passive and isolated. Karen E. Rowe (in Bottigheimer 1986) and Marina Warner (1994) both argue for the importance of viewing magic and other tales as originating primarily among women storytellers such as the ten women narrators in Basile's *Pentamerone*. Their concerns as women inhabiting particular sociohistorical positions influence their narrations' portrayal of mothers, fathers, stepmothers, daughters, and suitors.

Ethnographic studies of "Cinderella" as told on specific occasions by named tellers show the range of interpretations. Told by grandparents and grandchildren during a traditional hearthside evening in Tuscany, "Cinderella" illuminates the competition between women and men, old and young (Falassi in Dundes 1982). In eastern Iran, Ismaili Muslim women recount "Cinderella" as part of an all-women food offering and ritual meal to honor Mohammed's daughter Fatima, who is petitioned to fulfill wishes (Mills in Dundes 1982). In rural Spanish villages, where folktales like "Cinderella" are integral to the courtship and marriage process, women and men tell different versions reflecting their divergent views of romantic love as illusory, ambivalent, and sometimes very dangerous (Taggart 1990). Conversational versions of and allusions to "Cinderella," whether humorous or serious, also need study to complement the cross-cultural, literary, and popular texts in order to fathom the longstanding, widespread, collective, and individual appeal of this heroine. *See also:* Beauty; Courtship; Daughter; Folktale; Housework; Marriage; Old Wives' Tales; Princess; Red Riding Hood; Sleeping Beauty; Stepmother.

References: Bettelheim, Bruno. *The Uses of Enchantment: The Meaning and Importance of Fairy Tales.* New York: Alfred A. Knopf, 1978; Bottigheimer, Ruth B., ed. *Fairy Tales and Society: Illusion, Allusion, and Paradigm.* Philadelphia: University of Pennsylvania Press, 1986; ———. *Grimms' Bad Girls & Bold Boys: The Moral & Social Vision of the Tales.* New Haven and London: Yale University Press, 1987; Donoghue, Emma. *Kissing the Witch: Old Tales in New Skins.* New York: Joanna Cotler Books, HarperCollins, 1997; Dowling, Colette. *The Cinderella Complex: Women's Hidden Fear of Independence.* New York: Summit Books, 1981; Dundes, Alan. *Cinderella: A Folklore Casebook.* New York and London: Garland Publishing, 1982; Haase, Donald. "Feminist Fairy-Tale Scholarship: A Critical Survey and Bibliography." *Marvels & Tales: Journal of Fairy-Tale Studies,* vol. 14, no. 1 (2000): 15–63; Mieder, Wolfgang, ed. *Disenchantments: An Anthology of Modern Fairy Tale Poetry.* Hanover and London: University Press of New England for University of Vermont, 1985; Panttaja, Elisabeth. "Going Up in the World: Class in 'Cinderella'." *Western Folklore* 52, no. 1 (1993): 85–104; Sexton, Anne. *Transformations.* Boston: Houghton Mifflin Company, 1971; Stone, Kay. "Things Walt Disney Never Told Us." In *Women and Folklore: Images and Genres,* ed. Claire R. Farrer, 42–50. Prospect Heights, IL: Waveland Press, 1986 [1975]; ———. "The Misuses of Enchantment: Controversies on the Significance of Fairy Tales." In *Women's Folklore, Women's Culture,* eds. Rosan A. Jordan and Susan J. Kalčik, 125–45. Philadelphia: University of Pennsylvania Press, 1985; Taggart, James M. *Enchanted Maidens: Gender Relations in Spanish Folktales of Courtship and Marriage.* Princeton, NJ: Princeton University Press, 1990; Tatar, Maria. *Off with Their Heads!: Fairy Tales and the Culture of Childhood.* Princeton, NJ: Princeton University Press, 1992; ———. ed. *The Classic Fairy Tales: Texts, Criticism.* New York and London: W. W. Norton & Company, 1999; Ulanov, Ann, and Barry Ulanov. *Cinderella and Her Sisters: The Envied and the Envying.* Reworked and expanded edition. Einsiedeln, Switzerland: Daimon, 1998; von Franz, Marie-Louise. *The Feminine in Fairytales.* New York: Spring Publications, 1972; Warner, Marina. *From the Beast to the Blonde: On Fairy Tales and Their Tellers.* New York: The Noonday Press, Farrar, Straus and Giroux, 1994; Zipes, Jack. *Fairy Tales and the Art of Subversion: The Classical Genre for Children and the Process of Civilization.* New York: Wildman Press, 1983; ———. ed. *Don't Bet on the Prince: Contemporary Feminist Fairy Tales in North America and England.* New York: Methuen, 1986.

Marta Weigle

Class

The word "class" refers to a person's position in the social hierarchy. Broadly speaking, people occupy three main classes in North America: the upper, middle, and lower classes. One's class identity is based on the three interdependent factors of wealth, educational attainment, and occupational status. Ethnicity and length of residence in the United States, Canada, or Mexico also impinges upon perceptions of class status. A lower-class woman, for instance, is limited in her choices of what to study and in the kind of career she has because she has few economic resources at her disposal, a situation made worse if she belongs to a non-dominant ethnicity or does not have full citizenship status. This, in turn affects the relative influence she has not only in her own social sphere, but also in the larger society.

Each class tends to develop a "class culture." The conditions of lower-class work and living are understood to be less desirable than those of the middle class, which are understood to be less desirable than those of the upper class. Lower- and middle-class occupations, for instance, imply working for someone, whereas upper-class occupations imply working for oneself, with colleagues, or managing or employing other workers. Lower- and middle-class neighborhoods tend to demonstrate greater uniformity and have fewer amenities than do upper-class neighborhoods. Persons with less access to social resources and fewer opportunities for upward mobility depend more on others, while greater socioeconomic class privilege allows a higher degree of independence from and/or subjugation of others. World- wide, women are far more likely to be poor than men, and in the United States, women over the age of sixty-five are twice as poor as men in the same age group.

A majority of Americans regard themselves as members of the middle class and operate as if the middle class were the most influential sector in society. Those at the bottom and the top of the American middle class, however, exhibit great disparities in both material conditions and social power. For this reason, Dennis Gilbert (2003) recalibrated and renamed the tripartite class system in the United States. Using census data from 1950–2000, Gilbert iden- tifies those at the very top of the socioeconomic hierarchy as belonging to the privileged classes. This group can be further divided into a capitalist class, whose income is derived from returns on assets, and an upper-middle class, whose income is derived from work. Members of capitalist households might be heirs to large fortunes, investors, and top-level executives. They comprised 1 percent of the total U.S. population in 2000. In that year, a capi- talist earned upward of $2 million a year. Members of the upper-middle class are usually highly educated professionals, medium-sized business owners, and upper managers. They comprised 14 percent of the total U.S. population in 2000 and earned upward of $120,000 a year.

In the past, the middle class was contrasted with the working class in order to distinguish between those who performed mental as opposed to physical labor. The labels "blue collar" and "white collar" are sometimes used in the same way to distinguish dirty or outdoor work from clean or indoor work. If one considers economic earnings, however, an electrician who engages in skilled physical labor may earn a great deal more than a teacher, who performs mental/managerial labor. Nevertheless, the teacher possesses more occupational prestige than the electrician because her job requires a college degree. The label "pink collar" is a gendered addition to this way of distinguishing jobs based on their prestige or desirability. Pink- collar service-industry workers constitute a largely female sector of the workforce. They do not necessarily get dirty or work outside, yet they enjoy little to no occupational prestige and receive very low wages. This group constitutes a kind of servant class in a technological age.

Gilbert identifies the middle and working classes as two segments of what he calls the majority classes. Thus, these two classes are grouped to- gether, even though they exhibit some distinctions in educational attain- ment and earning power. The 30 percent of U.S. households that are middle class in this schema often have completed some college, earned about $55,000 a year in 2000, and work in semiprofessional, lower-management and non-retail sales jobs. The 30 percent of U.S. households that are working class have a high school education, earned about $35,000 a year in 2000, and work in manufacturing, clerical, and retail-sales jobs. One can easily perceive that as one descends the economic order, the difference in earnings between class subgroups diminishes.

Gilbert identifies the remaining 25 percent of U.S. households in 2000 as belonging to the lower classes. This group can be further divided into the working poor and the underclass. The working poor have completed some high school, earn about $22,000 a year, and work as laborers, factory, clerical, and service workers. The underclass is made up of individuals who participate only sporadically in the official workforce. They may be unemployed, working part-time, and/or dependent on government assistance. Typically, they have completed some high school and earn about $12,000 a year. Thus, Gilbert renames the traditional categories of upper, middle, and lower classes the privileged, majority, and lower classes. He divides these categories into six distinct groups: capitalist, upper-middle, middle, working, working poor, and underclass.

What is obscured when we speak of a middle-class majority is the important role played by the very few at the top of the social hierarchy in directing social life in the United States. Stephen Rose (2000) demonstrates that the 7 percent of people earning more than $300,000 annually have exponentially greater wealth than the 72 percent whose earnings place them in the middle class (in this case, a combination of Gilbert's upper-middle, middle, and working classes). The concentration of wealth at the top of the hierarchy, which is further concentrated in the hands of fewer individuals since Rose conducted his study (DeNavs-Walt, et al), correlates with the greater influence this tiny upper class has over society at large. The leaders of business and government come from this class; they provide a vision of the social good that is likely to serve their own interests; however, while this class is powerful, its influence does not go unchallenged. Class conflict is the result of disparities in wealth, access to opportunity, and worldview.

For women, the notion of class as a function of wealth, educational attainment, and professional status remains problematic because women's earnings continue to lag behind White men's regardless of educational attainment. On average, American women earn 80 percent of what men earn one year after college graduation; after ten years, that figure falls to 69 percent (CNN/Reuters). Black and Latino men also fare worse than do White men, but disparities are compounded for Black and Latina women. To complicate matters further, many women participate in the paid workforce only part-time or intermittently over their lifetimes as a consequence of childrearing and other household obligations. At a glance, this work pattern appears similar to that of Gilbert's underclass. A housewife may be highly educated and have no independent income. Alternately, she may have a high school education, yet have access to considerable wealth through her ties to a professional husband. Since men continue to contribute more earnings than do women in the majority of American families, a married woman's class identity is usually dependent upon her husband's earnings, occupation, and educational attainment.

American historian John Bodnar (1987) has traced the relation between social class and success among early twentieth-century immigrants to the

United States. He finds immigrants who were middle class in their countries of origin were able to accomplish the American Dream of upward mobility over time, even if they suffered a period of downward mobility as a consequence of their emigration. On the other hand, immigrants who were working-class or impoverished in their countries of origin were more likely to join the permanent underclass in the United States. These findings indicate aspirations, values, and adaptive capacities tied to one's class can play a powerful role in perpetuating one's class identity in changed circumstances.

When one examines the class positions of women, however, the picture becomes more complicated. Christine Grella (1990) discovered that middle-class women who divorce generally experience downward mobility. This situation creates dissonance between a woman's subjective sense of middle-class identity (acquired and/or maintained through her association with her former husband) and her actual experience of material impoverishment. Those who remain single heads of households redefine themselves as poor or lower-middle class over time. Grella's study indicates social class for women is not a rigid identity category but may change with changing economic circumstances.

While the assignment of class identity is based on wealth and social influence, it is marked by other factors as well. Where you live, how you move your body, how you speak, what you value, what you eat, wear, drive, and even what kind of sports you enjoy can signal your class identity. Louis Alvarez and Andrew Kolker explore the American class system in their documentary video, *People Like Us: Social Class in America* (2001). They demonstrate how each social class exhibits a set of preferences that become deeply ingrained in individual members through a process of informal learning or enculturation. Members who violate these preferences are sanctioned by others of their class. For example, a woman who marries above her class is as likely to be sanctioned as one who marries below her class. In this sense, members of all classes are in some ways limited by their class identity in what they can and cannot do. This is what is meant by "class culture."

Alvarez and Kolker's earlier documentary, *American Tongues* (1987), demonstrates the influence of class-based dialects on women's opportunities outside their communities of origin. A working-class woman from Appalachia who migrated to Ohio states that she has to work twice as hard to demonstrate her competence because her coworkers disparage the way she speaks as ignorant. Another from Brooklyn, New York, attempts to "unlearn" her dialect in order to get people from outside her own neighborhood to take her seriously in the business environment. While a working-class identity may involve having one's opportunities limited, talents overlooked, and personal integrity distrusted, it may also engender and/or project qualities that are valued by members of all classes: sincerity, unpretentiousness, and loyalty to friends and family.

Class cultures are often intertwined with regional and ethnic cultural complexes. Patricia Hill Collins (2000) introduced the word "intersectionality" to describe how multiple dimensions of oppression shape a person's lived experience. Folklorist Richard Bauman's earlier phrase, "differential identity," refers to multiple dimensions of identity without special reference to oppression. For instance, the experience of being Black is not uniform across the African American population. Instead, racial identity intersects with other aspects of one's social identity and lived experience: being female, being reared in a rural setting, being homosexual, being deaf or disabled, and/or being lower class. These sources of oppression cannot simply be tallied to determine a sum total. Rather, the various aspects of lived experience interact to produce unique and multifaceted effects.

As a case in point, Maxine Baca Zinn (1989) interrogates the various explanations scholars and policymakers have created to explain the continuing existence of a largely Black, central-city underclass. She finds the link between family dissolution and middle-class women's impoverishment does not hold for lower-class Black women. Black women who become single heads of household appear to experience no significant downward mobility because they were usually already impoverished as married women. Such data contests the notion that a high rate of broken families in lower-class Black communities is a cause of poverty. Rather, household dissolution is more likely to be an adaptive response to limited opportunities. Baca Zinn points to structural conditions such as the decline of well-paying, low-skill manufacturing jobs and their shift in location from city to suburbs as a cause of Black male joblessness and impoverishment. However, she rejects the recommendation to develop secure, well-paying, low-skill jobs for men in order to allow them to reassert themselves as patriarchal providers for Black families. Such a solution would not reduce independent Black women's impoverishment, whereas universal childcare and equal pay for equal work might.

Feminist theorist bell hooks (2000) uses her personal life story to explore the important and often overlooked dimension of class in African American culture. Throughout her published work, hooks expresses a continuing nostalgia for the rural folk culture she experienced as a child while visiting her maternal grandmother. This integrated, self-sufficient way of life existed in some ways outside the class system and allowed its members to avoid challenges to their integrity in the American South prior to passage of the Civil Rights Act of 1964. In her own journey to class consciousness, hooks reveals the white face of class privilege in America. She contrasts contemporary attitudes in African American and progressive communities—living simply, in solidarity with the poor—with powerful and pervasive social messages that encourage greed and ruthlessness. By continually circling back to her own autobiography to mine the lessons of a lower-class upbringing, hooks demonstrates that much is to be gained by retrieving and celebrating the perspectives of lower-class, Black folk culture even as Americans aspire to ascend the social hierarchy.

The class structure in Canada, while not equivalent to that of the United States, follows the general model for postindustrial, developed nations. In contrast, the class structure of Mexico is marked by even greater disparities in wealth and opportunity than its northern neighbors. These disparities are related historically to the concentration of land ownership in the hands of a few. Despite recent democratizing trends, a ruling class combined with a small middle class maintains control of both political and economic power, whereas the vast majority of both urban and rural Mexicans live in poverty. Moreover, a legacy of internal colonization besets those regions in Mexico that are home to large Indigenous populations. Indigenous groups find themselves at the very bottom of the social hierarchy, alternately despised and exoticized by majority *mestizos* (people of mixed European and Native ancestry) and ruling *criollos* (Mexican descendants of the Spanish colonizers). Rosario Castellanos' (1925–1974) brilliant novel, *The Book of Lamentations* (1998), about an Indigenous uprising in Chiapas, Mexico, provides a sobering view of this society in the early part of the twentieth century. In it, she describes how local elites, descended from Spanish conquistadors, mistreated Indigenous workers with impunity, and how gender oppression permeated the society at all levels. In the 1990s, Chiapas once again erupted in violence as Zapatista revolutionaries defended Indigenous peasants against increasing incursions by business interests and the state.

After World War II, a period of strong economic growth in Mexico allowed for the expansion of its middle class, which now includes about 20 percent of all households. This group changed the course of Mexican government by overthrowing the ruling one-party system and installing opposition candidate Vicente Fox in 2000 (Gilbert 2007). During the 1940s, thousands of landless peasants from rural Mexico participated in the U.S. guest-worker program, initiating the migrant stream that continues to spark debate on both sides of the U.S.-Mexico border. Folklorist María Herrera-Sobek (1979) explores the image of these *braceros* ("laborers") in elite and folk literature in Mexico. She discovers that elite writers, inspired by virulent nationalism, ignore the entrenched exploitation of peasants in their own country to highlight the indignities and injustices of migrant life in the United States. When Herrera-Sobek collected stories from the migrants, she found that they painted a less ideologically charged picture of their situation, recognizing and comparing opportunities and challenges on both sides of the border. More recently, cultural theorist Nestor García Canclini (1993) explored how Indigenous producers fit into Mexico's contemporary capitalist market. He argues that those at the bottom provide symbolic capital for Mexican national identity, but they continue to miss out on economic rewards. For García Canclini, the folklorist's role is not only to promote the products of folk culture but also to assist the folk in maintaining control over the fruits of their labor.

As in Mexico, folklore studies in the U.S. have focused more commonly on the cultural traditions of the lower classes than on those of the middle and upper classes. This preference is partly motivated by the recognition that folk cultures in some ways resist purely economic forms of evaluation. Folklorists have extensively studied groups such as Appalachians, central-city dwellers, non-English speakers, and male prisoners because their social isolation from the mainstream has enabled them to preserve alternative lifestyles, knowledge, and social and aesthetic forms. At the same time, folklorists have found it easier to discuss ethnic and regional identities than class identities; to speak openly of class would be to recognize the folklorist's own privileged position, as a professional and an academic, with respect to the people she studies.

In an internal critique of folklore's class dynamics, Rosan Jordan and Frank de Caro (1996) trace the origins of folklore study in Louisiana to a group of privileged White Creoles whose regional identity was being threatened by assimilationist pressures. Previous American folklorists had been especially interested in collecting the lore of Black, French-speaking, former slaves. Whereas such a focus may seem benign compared with the brutal violence directed at Louisiana Blacks from other quarters, Jordan and de Caro demonstrate that the act of collecting became a way for early folklorists to assert their enlightened superiority over their interlocutors. They constructed a highly romanticized vision of a former plantation society in which Blacks and Whites lived harmoniously. In this case, members of a privileged social class used folklore collecting to reassert their benevolent authority over an underclass simultaneously distinguished by race. In the process, the folklore of formerly enslaved Blacks became the folklore of White Creoles.

David Whisnant's study of the politics of culture in Appalachia (1983) similarly explores the dynamics of cultural preservation in that region in the early twentieth century. By examining three such efforts—the Hindman Settlement School in Eastern Kentucky, Olive Dame Campbell's work in western North Carolina, and the Whitetop Festival in southwest Virginia—Whisnant uncovers a class dynamic in which mostly female, privileged outsiders worked simultaneously to reform the manners and customs of poor Appalachian families and to preserve what they viewed as this groups's vanishing folkways. While Whisnant shows that cultural preservationists were well intentioned, they were also highly selective in their activities; the resulting images of Appalachian culture were more representative of the romantic ideas of the cultural interventionists than of the region's residents. To add to this irony, funding for these efforts came from the same capitalist industrialists who were wreaking havoc on local economies by exploiting the region's timber and mineral reserves. Not only does Whisnant provide a cautionary tale for contemporary cultural preservationists, he also reveals the intersecting dimensions of class and gender in cultural interventions.

Feminist folklorists insist that the exchange between an informant and a researcher is always embedded in relations of power. In reflecting on her work with impoverished Brazilian women, Daphne Patai (1991) points out that systematic inequalities between first-world researchers and third-world narrators make collecting such women's oral narratives fit the typical pattern of first/third-world exchange. That is, raw materials (in this case, oral histories and personal-experience narratives) are extracted from the third-world community for subsequent refashioning, packaging, and sale to a distant consumer in the first world. Patai concludes that under such circumstances, ethical research is impossible. She admonishes feminist fieldworkers to cultivate humility and to recognize that our research does not improve the lives of those we study, no matter how fervently we wish it to be so.

Since work is one of the defining elements of class identity, occupational folklore ought to provide some insight into questions of women and class; unfortunately, this subfield has been overwhelmingly oriented toward male-identified professions and masculine artistry. Studies of office lore tend to focus on how the informal verbal and material products of the modern office environment (water-cooler stories and photocopy lore, for example) express workers' frustration with corporate culture. Their gender-neutral focus ignores class and gender hierarchies within the corporate setting in order to emphasize the struggle of the individual against the organization.

Among the few folkloristic essays that do take gender into account is Michael J. Bell's (1989) examination of the occupational performances of women bartenders in a Black middle-class neighborhood in West Philadelphia. In pointing out that much occupational folklore deals with the artistic and verbal byproducts of particular professions, he emphasizes that tending bar, which involves the self-conscious adoption and manipulation of dramatic roles, is itself an expressive performance. Owners and patrons alike expect a barmaid to create or facilitate a social scene at her bar while simultaneously maintaining a certain distance—to engage with patrons, but not to become a patron in the process.

Labor lore and labor history provide a wealth of interesting possibilities for the student of women and class. Yet, here again, folklore scholarship has focused, with a few notable exceptions, on masculine trades and traditions. Susan Davis (1982), for example, provides a fascinating picture of nineteenth-century Christmas revelry on the part of largely unemployed, White, working-class young men, but laments the absence in the record of information about working-class women's customs. In the course of their merrymaking, masked young men invaded Philadelphia's city center, threatening businesses and theatergoers with noisemaking, shooting, drinking, and fighting. They also assaulted Black residents and members of rival gangs. Davis points out that, on the one hand, lower-class youth challenged city authorities with their violent disorder. On the other, their derogatory masking—particularly as women and in blackface (a particularly onerous form of racist minstrelsy)—united them with the city's middle- and upper-class leaders in an assertion of White male privilege.

In stark contrast, Davis also identifies an emerging middle-class complex of customs centered on the home, family, and children. Interestingly, these customs were propagated largely by the middle-class women. She concludes that, whereas nineteenth-century working-class celebrations were gendered male, middle-class celebrations were gendered female. This kind of historical coupling of divergent class and gender identities still permeates American folkloristics.

Oral histories of factory workers provide useful insights into the class culture of the working poor. Victoria Byerly's collection of oral histories from female cotton mill workers (1986) includes the voices of Black and White union and non-union workers from the turn of the twentieth century to the 1980s. Each woman's story is distinctive, but they share common experiences: going to work at an early age, earning low wages, marrying young, bearing children, and being subjugated by fathers, brothers, husbands, and sons. Yet, despite their memories of hardship and their awareness of unfavorable views about mill workers prevalent in the larger society, these women remember their old mill communities fondly. They eloquently recall positive aspects of working-class culture, reflecting the ambivalence many lower-class people feel about their distinctive folkways and lifestyles.

Herbert Biberman's classic labor film *Salt of the Earth* (1954) dramatizes the complexity of women's participation in a miner's strike against the New Jersey Zinc Company in Bayard, New Mexico, in the early 1950s. Unusual then in documentary filmmaking, most of the actors were Chicanos playing themselves in their struggle for wage parity with Anglo coworkers. More surprisingly, Biberman chose to dramatize the decisive role the wives of strikers played in the strike, even when faced with their husbands' resistance to their activism. Thus, it contains an early and powerful feminist message about equality, respect, and solidarity across gender lines. More recently, Connie Field's documentary film *The Life and Times of Rosie the Riveter* (1989) focuses on women industrial workers during and after World War II. Her film follows the stories of several White and Black women who answered the call to join the U.S. labor force while most able-bodied men were fighting overseas. The women speak passionately about their work lives, the pleasure they took in learning new skills, building ships and airplanes, and receiving hefty paychecks. After the war, however, their narrow window of opportunity for high-paying industrial jobs closed as the men—along with virulent gender discrimination—returned to the industrial workplace.

Housekeeping, an occupation consistently linked to women, has been severely understudied from a folkloristic perspective. In her pathbreaking article, Judith Levin (1993) points out that, on the surface, housework lacks many of the characteristics traditionally associated with creative expressivity. Commonly portrayed as "trivial, repetitive, and invisible," it is performed in isolation from others, remains unpaid and rarely results in a product (287). Levin borrows a process orientation from Michael Owen Jones— "a feeling for form"—to discover how women derive aesthetic pleasure from doing housework.

Another excellent source for exploring the intersection of women and class is Pierrette Hondagneu-Sotelo's (2001) sociological examination of domestic workers in the Los Angeles area. Hondagneu-Sotelo explores how the overwhelmingly female, immigrant, women of Color in the American "pink-collar" workforce experience their roles as paid housekeepers (*domésticas*). She notes that the doméstica makes visible the profound inequality in the conditions and rewards of labor for women of different social classes, sparking a painful ambivalence toward them in their largely female, professional employers. Hondagneu-Sotelo reveals just how much an affluent lifestyle depends upon the subjugation of others.

Finally, investigative journalist Barbara Ehrenreich reports on her experiment in adopting the lifestyle of the working poor (2001). Ehrenreich gave up her comfortable professional lifestyle for a year to learn firsthand what life is like for those who live at the bottom of the socioeconomic hierarchy in the United States. She traveled from Florida to Maine to Minnesota, working as a waitress, hotel maid, cleaning woman, nursing home aide, and Wal-Mart sales clerk. Along the way, she discovered smart, hardworking coworkers who nevertheless were barely able to make ends meet. For the majority of Americans, one job doesn't pay enough to get by, and, just because they are poor, workers endure indignities ranging from mandatory drug testing to being treated as if they were children. In a forceful challenge to the rhetoric of contemporary welfare system reformers, Ehrenreich eloquently reveals just how much class continues to matter in America. *See also:* Beauty; Deaf Folklore; Folk Speech; Glass Ceiling; Housekeeping; Immigration; Photocopylore; Wage Work; Women's Work.

References: Alvarez, Louis, and Andrew Kolker, director and producer. *American Tongues.* Center for New American Media, 1987; ———. *People Like Us: Social Class in America.* Center for New American Media, 2001; Bauman, Richard. "Differential Identity and the Social Base of Folklore." *Journal of American Folklore*, vol. 84, no. 331 (January–March 1971): 31–41; Bell, Michael J. "Tending Bar at Brown's: Occupational Role as Artistic Performance." In *Folk Groups and Folklore Genres: A Reader*, ed. Elliott Oring, 146–157. Logan: Utah State University Press, 1989; Biberman, Herbert. *Salt of the Earth.* Independent Productions: International Union of Mine, Mill, and Smelter Workers, 1954. http://www.archive.org/details/salt_of_the_earth (accessed June 22, 2007); Bodnar, John. *The Transplanted: A History of Immigrants in Urban America.* Bloomington, IN: Indiana University Press, 1987; Byerly, Victoria, and Cletus E. Daniel. *Hard Times Cotton Mill Girls: Personal Histories of Womanhood and Poverty in the South.* Ithaca, NY: ILR Press (Cornell University School of International Labor Relations imprint), 1986; Castellanos, Rosario. *The Book of Lamentations.* New York: Penguin Classics, 1998 (1962); Collins, Patricia Hill. *Black Feminist Thought: Knowledge, Consciousness, and the Politics of Empowerment.* New York: Routledge, 2000; CNN Money.com (Reuters). "On payday, it's still a man's world." April 23, 2007. http://money.cnn.com/2007/04/23/news/economy/gender_gap/index.htm (accessed June 22, 2007); Davis, Susan G. "'Making Night Hideous': Christmas Revelry and Public Order in Nineteenth-Century Philadelphia." *American Quarterly*, vol. 34, no. 2 (1982): 185–199; DeNavas-Walt, Carmen, Bernadette D. Proctor, and Jessica Smith. "Income, Poverty, and Health Insurance Coverage in the United States: 2006." Issued August 2007. http://www.census.gov/prod/2007pubs/p60-233.pdf (accessed August 10, 2008) Ehrenreich, Barbara. *Nickle and Dimed: On (Not) Getting By in America.* New York: Henry Holt and Company, 2001; Eisler, Riane. "The Feminine Face of Poverty." AlterNet, April 19, 2007. http://www.alternet.org/rights/50727 (accessed August 10, 2008); Field, Connie, director. *The Life and Times of Rosie the Riveter.* Clarity Films, 1989; García-Canclini, Nestor, and Lidia Lozano. *Transforming Modernity: Popular Culture in Mexico.* Austin: University of Texas Press, 1993; Gilbert, Dennis. *The American Class Structure in an Age of Growing Inequality.* Sixth edition. Belmont, CA: Wadsworth, 2003; ———. *Mexico's Middle Class in the Neoliberal Era.* Tucson: University of Arizona Press, 2007; Grella, Christine E. "Irreconcilable Differences: Women Defining Class after Divorce and Downward Mobility." *Gender and Society*, vol. 4, no. 1 (1990): 41–55; Herrera-Sobek, María. *The Bracero Experience: Elitelore versus Folklore.* Los Angeles: UCLA Latin American Studies Publications, University of California, Los Angeles, 1979; Hondagneu-Sotelo, Pierrette. *Doméstica: Immigrant Workers Cleaning and Caring in the Shadows of Affluence.* Berkeley: University of California Press, 2001; hooks, bell. *Where We Stand: Class Matters.* New York: Routledge, 2000; Jordan, Rosan, and Frank de Caro. "In This Folk-Lore Land Race, Class Identity, and Folklore Studies in Louisiana." *Journal of American Folklore*, vol. 109, no. 431 (1996): 31–59; Levin, Judith. "Why Folklorists Should Study Housework." In *Feminist Theory and the Study of Folklore*, eds. Susan Tower Hollis, Linda Pershing, and M. Jane Young, 285–296. Urbana: University of Illinois Press, 1993; Patai, Daphne. "U.S. Academics and Third World Women: Is Ethical Research Possible?" In *Women's Words: The Feminist Practice of Oral History*, eds. Sherna Gluck and Daphne Patai, 137–154. New York: Routledge, 1991; Rose, Stephen J. *Social Stratification in the United States.* New York: The New Press, 2000; Whisnant, David E. *All that is Native and Fine: The Politics of Culture in an American Region.* Chapel Hill: The University of North Carolina Press, 1983; Zinn,

Maxine Baca. "Family, Race, and Poverty in the Eighties." *Signs: Common Grounds and Crossroads: Race, Ethnicity, and Class in Women's Lives*, vol. 14, no. 4 (Summer 1989): 856–874.

Katherine Borland

Clique

A clique is a relatively small, exclusive folk group, an elitist clustering formed within a larger, encompassing social network. Cliques can be formed and found in all folk groups, large and small—in families, workplaces, governments, social clubs, sports teams, and councils, for example. But the term "clique" is most often used to reference elitist groups in schools, particularly in North American middle school and high school settings.

Social exclusivity demands delineations regarding the inclusion and exclusion of members—its two most powerful functions; its rules of acceptance/rejection are marked by symbolically powerful coding that signals clique members' interests, preferred locales for gathering, bodily adornments, speech patterns, behaviors, decision-making, associations, consumption habits, and musical preferences, among others—all of which may be summed up as their "style." In essence, a clique is something like a preferred marketing brand, a mark that signifies more than a tangible product but a way of living and being.

It is tempting to classify all folk groups—with their initiatory rites and jargon, their esoteric ways of doing and being—as cliques, but cliques, especially in the school setting, possess an enigmatic quality known as "popularity," and popularity equals power. While the youth culture of any North American high school is comprised of many differing folk groups, each with an identifying label and style—including but not limited to jocks and cheerleaders (male and female athletes), headbangers (heavy-metal music enthusiasts), greasers (members of Latino or White street gangs), plastics (haughty, well dressed girls), nerds (intellectuals), geeks (computer whizzes), punks (ostentatious rebels), skate rats (skateboard enthusiasts), and stoners (marijuana smokers)—cliques occupy different niches in the social hierarchy, forming alliances as necessary, setting and enforcing behavioral and attitudinal expectations for members, and generally reifying the social pecking order. Each group excludes those who occupy positions lower in the hierarchy as well as those higher up.

Teenage girls, particularly those identified in a spate of recent books as "mean girls," play a critical role in upper-echelon clique formation and maintenance, utilizing such boundary-enforcing skills as rumormongering, backbiting (speaking ill of a person not present), ostracism, pointed group giggling, verbal and physical bullying, studied indifference, and a certain capriciousness in making someone or something "in" (attractive, cool, popular) one day and "out" (unattractive, passé, unpopular) the next. While cliques are often passionately disparaged by non-members, they do provide a kind of social safety net by making a large school environment seem smaller and its assortment of denizens more manageable. Emotional insecurity is a condition of adolescent youth in most cultures; an all-consuming desire to "fit in" emboldens and empowers clique members. Wearing the "right" clothes, being seen at the "right" places, saying the "right" things, and hanging out with the "right" crowd means modifying oneself in order to "fit" its prescribed norms. The insular and whimsical nature of cliques does mean, though, that fitting in can be forever elusive: one's skin color and socioeconomic class, for example, are not susceptible to modification.

Cliques are featured prominently in hundreds of books, films, and television programs catering to teenagers. A few examples are Susan Eloise Hinton's widely read *The Outsiders*, Canadian television's *Degrassi High*, most of John Hughes' films (*The Breakfast Club*, *Sixteen Candles*, etc.), the disturbing *Carrie* and *Heathers*, the comic *Clueless*, and recently, *Mean Girls*. Each offers a representation of adolescent culture focused on the influence of prevailing social hierarchies.

The serious consequences of belonging to teenage cliques in North American schools have been much-discussed in recent years, especially in light of several tragic school shootings, acts committed by marginalized and deeply troubled White males. Increased reports of teens bullied to suicide have also laid bare the potential violence of cliquishness, illuminating the deep psychological scarring it can induce. *See also:* Class; Fashion; Folk Group; Girls' Folklore; Popular Culture.

References: Aufferman, Kyra. "Mean Girls?: A Culture of Cliques." *BCHeights.com: The Independent Student Newspaper of Boston College*, March 21, 2005. http://media.www.bcheights.com/media/storage/paper144/news/2005/02/21/Features/Mean-Girls.A.Culture.Of.Cliques-871128.shtml (accessed June 30, 2007); Goodwin, Marjorie Harness. *The Hidden Life of Girls: Games of Stance, Status, and Exclusion* (Blackwell Studies in Discourse and Culture Series). Malden, MA: Wiley-Blackwell, 2006; Hebdige, Dick. *Subculture: The Meaning of Style*. London: Methuen, 1979; Jansen, William Hugh. "The Esoteric-Exoteric Factor in Folklore." In *The Study of Folklore*, ed. Alan Dundes, 43–51. Englewood Cliffs, NJ: Prentice, 1965; Wiseman, Rosalind. *Queen Bees & Wannabes: Helping Your Daughter Survive Cliques, Gossip, Boyfriends & Other Realities of Adolescence*. New York: Three Rivers Press, 2002.

Jessica Grant Jørgensen

Coding

In the sense in which folklorists use it, "coding" means communicating through a set of signals—words, forms, behaviors, and signifiers of some kind—in situations where some members of the audience may be competent and willing to decode the message, but others are not. In the context of complex audiences, strategic coding can protect its creator from the consequences of openly expressing particular messages. When we speak of coding as a strategic folk process, we distinguish the term from more general use in which it designates the system of language rules through which communication is possible.

Not all forms of coding are surreptitious, nor are all forms of coding undertaken in situations of high risk; it is also not always clear that coding is in fact (or intentionally) taking place. Coding may be undertaken for a variety of purposes, from pleasure and play to the deliberate attempt to prevent outsider understanding, from protection against mild anxiety to protection against threat to one's life. At one pole, children may delight in devising expressions or languages (such as pig Latin) that adults cannot understand, or lovers may devise private terms of address; in such instances, a "cracking" of the code may cause embarrassment or discomfort but has no serious consequence. In these situations, having outsiders aware that coding is taking place might even enhance the satisfaction derived from the act. At the other pole, codes may take the form of highly secret signals for, say, rescue operations that put many lives at risk. In this case, not only the message but the very fact that coding is occurring must be concealed. It is important, therefore, to distinguish a range of contexts, forms, and practices in which coding may occur.

The bicultural (in this case, dual-gendered) context created by the association of men and women in North America creates many opportunities for women's coding. Although women's experiences and material circumstances vary from culture to culture, from community to community, and from individual to individual, in most societies, women have developed a set of common signifying practices (beliefs, understandings, behaviors, and rituals) whose meanings are not necessarily accessible to men of the same group. These practices derive from separation between men's and women's traditional areas of activity—separate domains usually marked not only by difference but by subordination. Because women are often socially, economically, and emotionally dependent upon the good will of men, their attitudes and understandings cannot always be openly acknowledged, and women are therefore especially likely to express themselves, and to communicate with other women, through coded means.

We can distinguish three forms of coding: explicit, complicit, and implicit. Because the boundaries between these kinds of coding strategies are not hard and fast, it is best to think of them as stages along a continuum.

In cases of explicit coding, the presence of a code is obvious even to those who cannot decipher it. Explicit coding tends to challenge an audience to decode its message, and thus it may have various effects. Pig Latin, for example, may be used playfully to tease, but the vivid displays of the Clothesline Project, using colors to encode T-shirts representing different types of gender-related violence, are intended to educate and to inspire change. In situations of risk, however, explicit coding can be dangerous precisely because it constitutes an announcement that coding is taking place; it broadcasts the idea that the outsider is not *meant* to understand, and thereby opens the possibility that the "wrong" receiver will crack the code and decode the message.

Complicit coding, arguably the most common form, is consciously employed among members of a folk group who are united both by shared culture and a shared sense of threat. Situations of complicit coding are not obvious to outsiders, but as in explicit coding, they require definite, comprehensible signals. Such signals may be agreed upon collectively beforehand (for example, symbols, code names, or a sheet hanging on a clothesline to indicate a safe house on the Underground Railway) or drawn from inside knowledge and adopted on the spot (for example, mentioning a significant name to signal membership in Alcoholics Anonymous, or wearing particular clothing to indicate group membership). Young Islamist women in Turkey encode in the pastel shades of their raincoats their membership in a particular *tarikat* (a banned religious order). This kind of coding is also common among lesbians in the United States. Informants mention "the L. L. Bean look" as a clue to lesbian identity, for example, and one woman explained how her lesbian friends at a particular Navy base managed to discuss their evening plans in front of other members of the company: "Are you going out *star gazing* tonight?"—alluding to a local discotheque called Star's. In complicit coding, what has been communicated may seem odd to the outsider, its significance uncertain, but the fact that the outsider is not *meant* to understand is not made obvious.

Moreover, complicit coding—a folk art with many functions—often has playful as well as protective purposes. In lesbian culture, for instance, the signals and double entendres adopted for complicit coding in the presence of straight people—or other signals, that would not be deemed appropriate for use among heterosexuals—are used in exclusively gay settings as a means of consolidating and celebrating group identity.

Although both explicit and complicit acts of coding are undertaken knowingly and purposefully, not all coding is deliberate. In the third type, implicit coding, even the existence of a coded message is arguable and may be denied by the creator, and the signals are not collectively determined. Implicit coding is covert, and its purposes may not be consciously recognized even by the encoder herself.

This raises complex questions about intentions and interpretations that may be constructed both by original signal-receiver(s) and by outside observer-analysts such as folklorists. A quilter who sews a patch in which the traditionally sweet Sunbonnet Sue figure is swallowed by a snake may dismiss her creation as "just a joke," but persons viewing the quilt may ignore her assertion and interpret it as an encoded message of feminist resistance to traditional stereotypes. Obviously, the interpretation of implicit coding presents a dilemma, but with careful and respectful scholarship grounded in the specific cultural context of the performance, it is feasible to posit at least the possibility that an act of coding has occurred.

A context for concealed coding (complicit or implicit) exists when, for a particular individual or folk group, there exists a situation of oppression, dominance, or risk; when there is some kind of opposition to this situation that cannot safely be made explicit; and when there is a community of potential "listeners" from which one would want to protect oneself. However, the identification and interpretation of implicit coding must ultimately remain an act of inference—inference that has potentially serious consequences for individuals and communities and hence should be undertaken with great care. In the absence of clear information from the encoder, interpreting implicit coding remains an ambiguous project, not only uncertain but often highly charged.

Coding in individual texts and performances is frequently ambiguous, and different audiences may disagree as to their interpretation. But it is possible to identify certain common strategies, often occurring in combination.

The first of these is appropriation, the act of adapting forms or materials normally associated with the dominant culture to the purposes of an oppressed culture. Strategic appropriations may simply borrow and refashion dominant cultural forms. For example, Irish storyteller Peig Sayers, who learned her stories from her father and other male relatives, retold those tales with major changes of pace, tone, and emphasis to focus attention on the hard lot of women. More extreme appropriations may constitute parodies or subversions: lesbian commitment ceremonies, for instance, may playfully adapt features of heterosexual weddings (for example, one spouse wears a tuxedo; two bride dolls crown the wedding cake). As women move into roles that have previously belonged to men, appropriation can be an effective tactic, as with African American women rappers who gained airtime in the predominantly male rap music industry of the 1980s by adopting the "hard" performance mode of male rappers, but injected into their work significant rebuttal of negative male attitudes toward women.

Juxtaposition is the ironic arrangement of texts, artifacts, or performances so that they develop additional levels of meaning. For example, a quilt created by a group of women as a bridal gift for one of their members may represent an ironic coded message when it covers her marriage bed; symbolic of the group's intimacy, it becomes a reminder that the bride has been removed from that intimacy by her new primary duties to her husband.

Distraction is a coding strategy that drowns out or draws attention away from the subversive power of a message. A mother may voice and simultaneously disguise her deepest fears in the lyrics of a soothing lullaby ("Hush, little baby, don't you cry, / You know your mama's bound to die ..."). Pentecostal women preachers may draw attention away from the fact that they are moving into a normally male position of power by describing their pastoral duties in maternal terms, and emphasizing their obedience to God's call.

Indirection refers to the many ways in which, as Emily Dickinson put it, one can "tell all the truth but tell it slant." Perhaps the most common strategy of coding, indirection includes metaphor, impersonation, metonymy (substitution of a part for the whole), and hedging. For example, Mexican American women tell legends of vaginal serpents as metaphoric expressions of sexual fears; Kentucky mountain women sing traditional Euro American ballads as impersonal lessons about how to outsmart men; lesbians may use metonymy to inquire about a stranger's sexual orientation by asking if she has been to the Michigan Women's Music Festival. Hedging—almost saying something, but not quite saying it—encompasses a range of verbal strategies that have been identified by some linguists as characteristic of "women's language" or the "language of the powerless," including passive constructions, euphemisms, and qualifiers.

Minimization or trivialization strategies understate, minimize, or "normalize" the subversive power of a message, usually by employing forms that the dominant culture considers to be unimportant, innocuous, or irrelevant. The claim that "it's only a joke" disguises criticism, prejudice, anger, and other risky feelings. The seriousness of women's communication and knowledge is likewise trivialized by traditionally disparaging labels— "gossip," "woman talk," "old wives' tales."

The last common coding strategy is incompetence. Here, the encoder of a message expresses resistance to the dominant culture's expectations by claiming or demonstrating incompetence at activities conventionally associated with her oppressed culture. Strategic incompetence is often a tactic of underclasses whose labor power is being exploited, as, for instance, in some of the African American folktales of the slave John and Old Massa in which John manages to be excused from onerous duties by feigning inability. Women who profess or display incompetence at conventionally feminine activities—such as cooking, sewing, or cleaning—may be expressing their resistance to patriarchal expectations; were they to refuse these duties outright, they might run considerable risks, but incompetence, though frowned upon, is not usually regarded as blameworthy. *See also:* Feminisms; Folk Group; Gossip; Hip-Hop Culture/Rap; Housekeeping; Humor; Lesbian Folklore; Old Wives' Tales; Sunbonnet Sue; Vaginal Serpent.

References: Babcock, Barbara, ed. *The Reversible World: Symbolic Inversion in Art and Society.* Ithaca, NY: Cornell University Press, 1978; Buhler, Sarah. "'I Chose Some Cups and Saucers': Gender, Tradition, and Subversive Elements in my Grandmother's Life Stories." *Ethnologies,* vol. 21, no.1 (1999): 47–63, 303–04; Hollis, Susan Tower, Linda Pershing, and M. Jane Young, eds. *Feminist Theory and the Study of Folklore.* Urbana and Chicago: University of Illinois Press, 1993; Jordan, Rosan A. "The Vaginal Serpent and Other Themes from Mexican-American Women's Lore." In *Women's Folklore, Women's Culture*, eds. Rosan A. Jordan and Susan J. Kalčik, 26–44. Philadelphia: University of Pennsylvania Press, 1985; Lawless, Elaine J. "Access to the Pulpit: Reproductive Images and Maternal Strategies of the Pentecostal Female Preacher." In *Feminist Theory and the Study of Folklore*, eds. Susan Tower Hollis, Linda Pershing, and M. Jane Young, 258–76. Urbana and Chicago: University of Illinois Press, 1993; McDowell, Margaret B. "Folk Lullabies: Songs of Anger, Love and Fear." *Feminist Studies*, vol. 3, no.1 (1977): 205–218; Radner, Joan Newlon, ed. "The Woman Who Went to Hell: Coded Values in Irish Folk Narrative." *Midwestern Folklore*, vol. 15, no. 2 (1989): 49–51; ———. *Feminist Messages: Coding in Women's Folk Culture.* Urbana and Chicago: University of Illinois Press, 1993; Shuman, Amy. "Gender and Genre." In *Feminist Theory and the Study of Folklore*, eds. Susan Tower Hollis, Linda Pershing, and M. Jane Young, 71–88. Urbana and Chicago: University of Illinois Press, 1993; Taggart, James M. *Enchanted Maidens: Gender Relations in Spanish Folktales of Courtship and Marriage.* Princeton, NJ: Princeton University Press, 1992; Williams, Brett. "Why Migrant Women Feed Their Husbands Tamales: Foodways as a Basis for a Revisionist View of Tejano Family Life." In *Ethnic and Regional Foodways in the United States: The Performance of Group Identity*, eds. Linda Keller Brown and Kay Mussell, 113–26. Knoxville: University of Tennessee Press, 1984; "Women and Storytelling." Special issue of *Women and Language*, vol. XIX, no. 1 (Spring 1996).

Joan Newlon Radner

Consciousness Raising

Consciousness raising is one of the primary methods of encouraging self-awareness enacted by those in the women's liberation movement, whereby women share personal-experience narratives that link their experiences to those of other women, recognizing these experiences not as personal idiosyncrasies but as evidence of systematic oppression. Consciousness raising demonstrates the feminist adage that "the personal is political."

There is some debate about the origins of consciousness raising as a feminist strategy, some link it to the civil rights movement's slogan "tell it like it is"; others, like Alice Echols, associate it with Chinese peasants' practice of "speaking bitterness." Regardless of its genesis, consciousness raising played a central role in the women's liberation movement of the late 1960s and early 1970s. Proponents of consciousness raising argue that by sharing their personal-experience narratives, women gain an awareness of their oppression and realize that problems they believed were personal are actually socially constituted. Solutions to these problems therefore require a political movement, not just individual transformation.

Consciousness raising occurs in small group sessions (CR groups) of varying size and frequency in which women's personal-experience narratives are shared and analyzed. These narratives typically deal with topics such as sexuality, health, marriage, motherhood, and employment. Many groups discourage outright leadership, although some appoint facilitators to suggest topics or monitor discussion. As frequently occurs in storytelling performances, one personal-experience narrative elicits another, and everyone present is encouraged to speak.

In her article "'. . . like Ann's gynecologist or the time I was almost raped': Personal Narratives in Women's Rap Groups," Susan Kalčik (1975) argues that the narratives told in CR groups are structurally fluid. A recurring type of narrative is what she calls the kernel story, "a brief reference to the subject, the central action, or an important piece of dialogue from a longer story." She reports that because the women who participate in CR sessions often have similar experiences to describe, stories known to the group become touchstones for common experience, needing to be evoked only by "kernel" allusions upon which others may elaborate. While women are frequently stereotyped as being unable to tell stories "correctly," CR groups foster creativity and competence, providing women a space in which to share their stories in a supportive environment without fear of derision.

For many second-wave feminists, consciousness-raising sessions were meant to provide a starting point from which participants could move on to other political projects. However, these sessions were criticized by some for encouraging only talk while actually discouraging action. Consciousness raising also came under fire for being monopolized by middle-class women with bourgeois values. Although it was premised on the notion of identifying the common oppression shared by women, consciousness raising often minimized women's differences, such as race, class, and sexual orientation.

According to Lisa Maria Hogeland, consciousness-raising groups faded from use among feminists by the mid-1970s, replaced largely by the solitary act of reading feminist literature. However, consciousness raising arguably continues in Women's Studies classrooms, in Internet chat rooms, and in women's homes to the present day. *See also:* Activism; Feminisms; Oral History; Personal-Experience Narrative; Politics; Storytelling.

References: Echols, Alice. *Daring to be BAD: Radical Feminism in America, 1967–1975.* Minneapolis: University of Minnesota Press, 1989; Hogeland, Lisa Maria. *Feminism and Its Fictions: The Consciousness-Raising Novel and the Women's Liberation Movement.* Philadelphia: University of Pennsylvania Press, 1998; Kalčik, Susan. "'. . . like Ann's gynecologist or the time I was almost raped': Personal Narratives in Women's Rap Groups." *Journal of American Folklore*, vol. 88, no. 347 (1975): 3–11; Stahl, Sandra Dolby. *Literary Folkloristics and the Personal Narrative*. Bloomington: Indiana University Press, 1989.

Audrey Vanderford

Cosmetics

Cosmetics serve an aesthetic purpose, usually in the form of applied toiletry, makeup, clothing, wigs, or surgical intervention designed to beautify the body or complexion. The application of cosmetics to the male or female face, hair, and body should also be understood by anthropologists and folklorists as a ritual communicative act deeply imbued with meanings determined by historical moment, tradition, and cultural context.

Historical cross-cultural studies of cosmetics trace their use by women and men from ancient Egyptian and Mesopotamian cultures (kohl eyeliner, malachite eye shadow, lip and cheek rouge/stain, and face powder date to about 10,000 BCE) to ancient China (nail polish dates to about 3000 BCE). Perhaps the oldest cosmetic is henna, used in Asian, African, Middle, and Far Eastern cultures in *mehndi* skin art and as hair dye and nail stain.

Cosmetics have been used for ceremonial and everyday purposes and by various classes and castes of people to communicate attractiveness, sex appeal, and fertility, but they also signify ancient tradition and cultural values, identity, and community. Cosmetics are a powerful communicative medium.

Industrialized Western cultures have developed cosmetics as part of their technologies of beautification. Outpacing most other industries, the cosmetics and personal care industry expects global sales of its products to exceed $270 billion in 2008. Historically, many female inventors and businesswomen found their fame and established their fortunes in the manufacturing and distribution of cosmetics. It is disputed as to which African American inventor and cosmetics entrepreneur was the first Black millionaire in the United States: Madame C. J. Walker (Sarah Breedlove McWilliams Walker), who sold her grooming products door to door in the 1910s, or her colleague Annie Minerva Turnbo Malone, who made her fortune selling products and apparatus for relaxing and growing hair in the 1920s.

The cosmetics industries have always provided women with opportunities for professionalization, and have been used as vehicles for class ascension. Today, the Mary Kay Cosmetics empire and the globally reaching Avon Cosmetics company are two corporations that employ large numbers of women and encourage entrepreneurial spirit and personal empowerment through selling and using their beauty products. These conglomerates are so successful as to have become cultural icons—the "Avon Lady" and the pink Cadillacs driven by Mary Kay agents have widespread recognizability.

Other key figures in the Western history of cosmetics production include Estée Lauder, Helena Rubenstein, Max Faktor (Factor), Elizabeth Arden, Charles Revson (Revlon), Eugene Schueller (L'Oreal), and Frank Toskan (MAC). Each of these inventors is associated with an innovative product, signature style, look, or "face," such as Factor's "bee-stung lips"; a cosmetically enhanced "look" is often made famous through its use by a celebrity figure in advertising.

Prior to the establishment of federal standards regulating the manufacturing of cosmetics in the United States and Canada, many unsafe products caused their wearers irreparable damage, and in some cases proved fatal. The history of innovations in cosmetic use and manufacturing includes cases such as the dangerous and corrosive effects of lead in white face paint and power, corrosive skin lightening and bleaching products marketed by and for Black women and men, and Lash-Lure mascara, which caused blindness in the 1930s. However, some useful innovations and breakthroughs include the quest by manufacturers to produce a durable "kissproof" lipstick; a widely influential and unpatented formula for indelible lip stains was finally realized by American chemist Hazel Bishop.

Professional makeup artists practice cosmetic application for print and television advertising, and in theater, film, and the fashion industry. Some of these professionals gain notoriety and launch their own product lines, as did Bobbie Brown and Sonia Kashuk. Hollywood and its spectacularly made-up stars have greatly influenced trends in makeup. For example, actors Clara Bow, Greta Garbo, Bette Davis, and Marlene Dietrich each had a "trademark face" achieved through intricate makeup artistry.

Aestheticians and makeup artists also participate in the culture of beauty shops and retail cosmetic counters. During the early twentieth century, employment in beauty salons provided essential income for Black women, whose options for paid work were otherwise largely restricted to domestic service. Ethnographic studies of Western hairdressing and beauty salons document these sites as key arenas for the creation and maintenance of women's communities; at some historical moments, they served as rare public spaces in which women could connect to discuss life and politics.

As integral components of the beauty industry and the cult of femininity, cosmetics are used by women for reasons of vanity, but also as a form of pleasurable and playful experimentation, an opportunity for creativity and artistry. Socially and health-conscious female consumers today demand strict cosmetic production regulations, often preferring the use of environmentally friendly and organic or natural ingredients. Responding to public outcries about animal testing in cosmetics research has proved the key to success for many cosmetic companies, including Aveda, Prescriptives, and The Body Shop, which proudly proclaim that their products are "cruelty free." *See also:* Aesthetics; Beauty; Fashion; Film; Hair; Henna Art/*Mehndi*; Magazines, Women's and Girls'; Mass Media; Popular Culture; Ritual; Sexuality; Spa Culture; Women's Work.

References: Ash, Mary Kay. *Miracles Happen: The Life and Timeless Principles of the Founder of Mary Kay Inc.* New York: Perennial Currents, 2003; Basten, Fred E., Robert Salvatore, and Paul A. Kaufman. *Max Factor's Hollywood: Glamour, Movies, Make-Up.* Los Angeles: Stoddart, 1995; Blackwelder, Julia Kirk. 2003. *Styling Jim Crow: African American Beauty Training During Segregation.* College Station: Texas A&M University Press. 2003; Corson, Richard. *Fashions in Makeup: From Ancient to Modern Times.* London: Peter Owen Publishers, 2004 [1981]; Global Cosmetics Industry (GCI)

Homepage. http://www.globalcosmetic.com/mediakit (accessed August 8, 2008); Pallingston, Jessica. *Lipstick: A Celebration of the World's Favorite Cosmetic*. New York: St. Martin's Press, 1998; Riordan, Teresa. *Inventing Beauty: A History of the Inventions That Have Made Us Beautiful*. New York: Broadway, 2004; Roddick, Anita. *Body and Soul: Profits with Principles—The Amazing Success Story of Anita Roddick & The Body Shop*. New York: Crown, Three Rivers Press, 1994 [1991]; Woodhead, Lindy. *War Paint: Madame Helena Rubinstein and Miss Elizabeth Arden, Their Lives, Their Times, Their Rivalry*. Hoboken, NJ: John Wiley & Sons, 2004.

Sidney Eve Matrix

Courtship

Courtship is the premarital relationship between a couple involving a wide variety of traditional practices from rhymes to rituals. From childhood, women are prepared for their role in courtship, with the expectation that it will ultimately lead to marriage. Even preschool children may have opposite-sex boyfriends and girlfriends before they are aware that, in adulthood, the terms will invariably signify sexual relationships. Once in grade school, the preparation begins in earnest. The playground becomes the location where early role-modeling takes place. Little girls—and sometimes boys—jump rope to rhymes such as:

Policeman, policeman
Do your duty
For here comes Delinda (or other child's name)
The bathing beauty.
She can wiggle
She can waddle
She can do the kick
And I bet you all the money
She can do the split (Bronner: 72).

The rhyme describes provocative behavior by girls or women, suggesting its aim is to attract men's attention. Another, implicating pregnancy, is

Mother, mother I am ill
Send for the doctor
Over the hill
First comes the doctor
Then comes the nurse
Then comes the lady with the alligator purse (Bronner: 73).

Kissing tag encourages boys to assume their traditional role of pursuer, and Valentine's Day is a time for little boys and girls to declare that they love each other, at times resulting in mock weddings on playgrounds during recess. Both boys and girls model the behavior that they know from home or from various media. In North America, little girls may become caught up in perceiving themselves as princesses waiting for their prince to come. They are encouraged to take this role into adulthood; for example, Disney counts on the lure of childhood fantasies to sell its line of "Princess" wedding dresses. Cinderella gowns are "classic glamour;" Snow White is "sweet elegance;" Ariel and Jasmine, on the other hand, are "considerably racier" (Marr).

Adolescence is a time of transition from the games of childhood to eventual commitment as adults. Activities like "hanging out" (large groups of both sexes, no pairing) or "hooking up" (pairing up and engaging in a physical relationship) are practiced both by high school age and older adolescents. Among heterosexual couples, the man is expected to initiate dating, though it is now permissible and not unusual for women to take that role.

The culminating courtship event of adolescence is the prom (a formal dance event), and "for some young women, the prom is seen as a dress rehearsal for weddings" (Best: 61). Prom memories are often highlights of adolescence for those who choose to participate. Adolescence is a period of liminality—a state of being between childhood and adulthood—which is reflected in the prom. "While the prom is resolutely a space of constraint, it is also a space of infinite possibility and self-(re)invention, a rich tapestry of spectacle and pageantry. Proms are spaces of performance and often emerge as meaningful sites in which to express a range of confrontational youth stances" (Best: 11).

Older adolescents, including college students, fine-tune the art of hanging out and hooking up, although for most, the latter requires no exclusivity or commitment. While different terminology applies for relationship statuses, "dating" usually implies an exclusive relationship. Those with multiple partners and/or no exclusivity are considered "single."

At some point, usually during the late twenties or early thirties, most individuals look for a spouse or partner. This is where the years of preparation and courtship-like events begin to pay off. When considering their path from courtship to marriage, most "Americans think in reverse, revising the past on the basis of what happened later, replacing coincidence with destiny" (Zeitlin et al.: 91–92) in stories identifiable as the "family romance" (94).

When a couple gets engaged, generally marriage has already been discussed. The asker, usually the man in heterosexual partnerings, is secure in the knowledge that he will be accepted. In fact, it is not uncommon for some wedding planning to take place before the official engagement. While flowers and champagne or sparkling cider are still familiar parts of the engagement process, the settings have broadened. A formal atmosphere is no longer expected. Engagements may take place in the mountains, in parks, or on a beach, as well as in a variety of other informal places. For some, engagements can be very public. "Will you marry me?" may flash across a scoreboard at a football game, an entertainer may do the asking for someone in the audience, or the asker may hire a plane to fly overhead with a banner saying "Will you marry me?" and the name of the (usually) woman.

Similarly, weddings, the culmination of courtship, are in mainstream North America becoming more elaborate. Weddings are big business. With paraphernalia from planners to favors, weddings and receptions average around $25,000. Churches, hotels, reception centers, and homes are only a few of the choices for wedding venues. Some couples create "destination" weddings. They and their guests fly to designated "romantic" locations and enjoy a week of celebration. These might celebrate the couple's love of the outdoors and the activities they enjoy there, or may simply display their wealth and opportunities for conspicuous consumption.

However, not all Euro North Americans see courtship and marriage as the ultimate aim of their lives. Feminists have been particularly critical of heterosexual courtship's enforcement of patriarchal patterns and male dominance. Self-proclaimed spinster-for-life Jaclyn Geller states that her purpose in writing *Here Comes the Bride* is to "dissuade many would-be wives from draping themselves in white and walking down the aisle" (71). For example, criticizing Gloria Steinem's decision to marry for the first time at the age of sixty-six, Geller argues "that choosing to uphold an institution rooted in the barter of women as property, an institution that devalues friendship and envisions female existence in terms of a romantic narrative of male redemption, is not valid, not right at any age" (71). Though most heterosexuals in the United States expect their courtship will lead to marriage, many individuals now seek new courtship practices that may not culminate in a wedding. *See also:* Engagement; Jump-Rope Rhymes; Rhymes; Rites of Passage; Ritual; Valentine's Day; Wedding; Wedding, Mock.

References: Best, Amy L. *Prom Night.* New York: Routledge, 2000; Bronner, Simon J. *American Children's Folklore.* Little Rock: August House, 1988; Geller, Jaclyn. *Here Comes the Bride.* New York: Four Walls Eight Windows, 2001; Marr, Merisa. "Fairy-tale wedding? Disney can supply the gown." *Deseret Morning News,* Salt Lake City, March 4, 2007; Zeitlin, Steven J., Amy J. Kotkin, and Holly Cutting Baker. *A Celebration of American Family Folklore.* New York: Pantheon Books, 1982.

Kristi A. Young

Couvade

From the French *couver*, to brood or hatch eggs, couvade refers to gestation and birth customs involving the father, particularly his lying-in at the time of delivery, and more generally to beliefs about male pregnancy and parturition. The custom is first mentioned in Apollonius of Rhodes's epic *The Argonautica* (ca. 260 BC), citing Tibareni on the Euxine (Black) Sea: "When a woman is in childbirth, it is the husband who takes to his bed [and] lies there groaning with his head wrapped up and his wife feeds him with loving care" (Dundes 1987). The term first appears in print in Charles de Rochefort's 1665 "natural and moral history"of West Indies Carib Natives (*Antilles Histoire naturelle et morale des Iles Antilles de l'Amérique*). Anthropological use "to refer to a widespread custom whereby fathers or men about to become fathers ritually went through the motions of confinement and childbirth" began with British anthropologist Edward B. Tylor's 1865 *Researches into the Early History of Mankind.* Western medical literature identifies couvade syndrome among some fathers-to-be with various gastrointestinal disorders and/or psychological symptoms.

British amateur Egyptologist Warren R. Dawson's 1929 compendium *The Custom of Couvade* geographically surveys worldwide evidence for "related customs" which "require that the father of a child, at or before its birth and for some time after the event, should take to his bed, submit himself to diet, and behave generally as though he, and not his wife, were undergoing the rigors of the confinement," but offers little analysis. Many anthropologists have related couvade to the ritual establishment or recognition of paternity (for example, Douglas 1975), others to male protection for the mother and/or child by symbolically diverting attention to themselves during a vulnerable period.

Couvade syndrome manifests clinically with physical symptoms similar to pregnancy discomforts like morning sickness and/or psychological ambivalence toward the mother or child. Freudian psychoanalyst Bruno Bettelheim saw this as "womb envy:" "Women, emotionally satisfied by having given birth and secure in this ability to produce life, can agree to the couvade; men need it to fill the emotional vacuum created by their inability to bear children" (1962). Jungian analytical psychologist Nor Hall (1989) considers male "brooding" part of the preparation for fatherhood and bonding with the child.

Greek mythology depicts the Olympian god Zeus as a father who swallows his pregnant first wife, the goddess Metis, and "gives birth" to a fully formed daughter, Athena, through his head. It is also Zeus who carries the fetus of his son Dionysus sewn into his thigh until proper delivery time because the latter's mortal mother, Semele, was immolated by beholding her lover in immortal form. From the latter eleventh century, European cathedral iconography showed a pregnant Adam with a mature Eve halfway out of his side while God oversees the "birth"; there is a complex of European Catholic folklore associated with Eve, Adam, and other pregnant, parturient males (Zapperi 1991, Dundes 1987). Alchemy and some contemporary reproductive technologies also may be viewed as types of male or male-managed pregnancy. *See also:* Childbirth and Childrearing; Eve; Pregnancy.

References: Bettelheim, Bruno. *Symbolic Wounds: Puberty Rites and the Envious Male*. New York: Collier Books, 1962; Dawson, Warren R. "Introducing the Custom of Couvade [1929]." In *Broodmales: A Psychological Essay on Men in Childbirth*, ed. Nor Hall, 3–44. Reprint edition. Dallas: Spring Publications, 1989; Douglas, Mary. *Implicit Meanings: Essays in Anthropology*. London and Boston: Routledge & Kegan Paul, 1975; Dundes, Alan. *Parsing through Customs: Essays by a Freudian Folklorist*. Madison: The University of Wisconsin Press, 1987; Zapperi, Roberto. *The Pregnant Man*. Trans. Brian Williams. Chur, Switzerland: Harwood Academic Publishers, 1991.

Marta Weigle

Cowgirl

Women with athletic mastery of horses and a penchant for working with livestock are known in the United States as cowgirls. Evoking images of courage, self-reliance, and hard work, cowgirls had their primary origin on the frontier family ranches of the American West. Sometimes identified as the "cowboy's female counterpart" or the "cowboy girl," cowgirls ride and frequently rope animals because it is a necessary part of their working lives, just as it is for men. During the settlement of the western states, women performed jobs typically held by men and were expected to participate in all aspects of life, from housekeeping to castrating cattle. Cowgirls often worked for their families, but unlike cowboys, they usually were not paid.

The image of the cowgirl began to develop in the late nineteenth century with casually organized rural festivals or ranch-versus-ranch rodeos in which women and girls demonstrated their expert handling of horses and livestock alongside the men. Despite the fact that women had long had experience with ranching and rodeos, it wasn't until the Wild West shows of the 1880s that the word "cowgirl" was used—its coining credited to Theodore Roosevelt—both nationally and internationally.

The public persona of the cowgirl grew from her appearances in Wild West shows and dime novels, and more recently in films and on television. Cowgirls typically performed and competed alongside cowboys in shooting events, trick riding, and bull-dogging (steer wrestling), and, like cowboys, women also rode buffaloes and played equestrian football. Between 1830 and 1930, traveling Wild West show cowgirls like Annie Oakley, Laura Mulhall, and Ruth Roach drew large audiences to their exuberant performances in Europe as well as in the United States.

Performance and competition in rodeos contributed to the cowgirl's identity as a confident, competent participant in the building of the American West. Many women took part in rodeo competitions just as they do today. Rodeo stars such as Tad Lucas, Fanny Sperry Steele, and Mabel Strickland were not only expert horsewomen, but were famous for their talent with the lariat, bull riding, relay racing, trick riding, Roman racing, and steer tying. However, by the 1930s, equestrian skill, a well-groomed horse, and the cowgirl's own beauty had become the overriding factors in the judging of rodeo cowgirls in competitions. This double standard in judging criteria led in part to the exclusion of women from a number of rodeo events. However, by 1941, cowgirls had organized the Women's Professional Rodeo Association, and thereby reinstituted many rodeo competitions previously barred to them. Barrel racing, a timed race around a cloverleaf course of three barrels, was established specifically for cowgirls.

Early dime novels popularized the image of the cowgirl as eminently capable. But referred to as a "sport" or "the pard" (partner) in early twentieth-century fiction, the cowgirl eventually came to be seen as less competent than the cowboy, and even subservient to ranching men. With the rise of the Western film genre, real cowgirls were allowed to participate as actors and stuntwomen, displaying strength and agility on horseback, but with minor exceptions, movie cowgirls played secondary roles to the films' male heroes. Dale Evans, one of television's most famous cowgirls, performed on the *The Roy Rogers Show*, which ran from 1950 to 1957. In her cowgirl persona, Evans demonstrated courage and independence when chasing villains, but was more often shown serving coffee and food to Roy Rogers and his friends back at the café.

Today, throughout the American West, many cowgirls work on ranches and compete in rodeos. As a tribute to cowgirls of the past and present, the National Cowgirl Museum and Hall of Fame opened in 2002 in Fort Worth, Texas. *See also:* Occupational Folklore; Women's Work.

References: Armitage, Shelley. "Rawhide Heroines: The Evolution of the Cowgirl and the Myth of America." In *The American Self: Myth, Ideology, and Popular Culture*, ed. Sam Girgus, 166–81. Albuquerque: University of New Mexico Press, 1981; Flood, Elizabeth Clair, and William Manns. *Cowgirls: Women of the Wild West*. Santa Fe, NM: ZON International Publishing Company, 2000; Fragnito, Skawennati Tricia, and Marilyn Burgess. "Indian Cowgirls." n. d. http://www.moa.ubc.ca/Exhibitions/Online/Other/Indian Cowgirls/cowgirl.html (accessed May 27, 2005); Jordon, Teresa. *Cowgirls: Women of the American West*. Lincoln and London: University of Nebraska Press, 1992; LeCompte, Mary Lou. *Cowgirls of the Rodeo: Pioneer Professional Athletes*. Urbana and Chicago: University of Illinois Press, 1993; Redden, Paul. *Wild West Shows*. Urbana and Chicago: University of Illinois Press, 1999; Riske, Milt. *Those Magnificent Cowgirls: A History of the Rodeo Cowgirl*. Cheyenne, WY: Frontier Printing, 1983; Roach, Joyce Gibson. *The Cowgirls*. Texas: University of North Texas Press, 1990; Russell, Don. *The Wild West*. Fort Worth: Amon Carter Museum, 1970; Savage, Candace. *Cowgirls*. Vancouver and Toronto: Greystone, 1996; Stoeltje, Beverly J. "Gender Representations in Performance: The Cowgirl and the Hostess." *Journal of Folklore Research*, vol. 25, no. 3 (1988): 219–241; Wallis, Sue. "Spirit of the Cowgirl." In *Cowgirls: Commemorating the Women of the West*, ed. David R. Stoecklein, 17–29. Ketchum, ID: David R. Stoecklein Photography and Publishing, 1999.

Kristin M. McAndrews

Crafting

Crafting is a term used in English-speaking North America to refer to the creation of decorative items, often from household scraps or commercially produced kits. Crafting is distinguished from other types of creative production traditionally associated with women (such as quilting, needlework, knitting, and so forth) in that crafting projects are normally quickly and easily accomplished; they are, in fact, usually advertised as fast or easy, requiring no special skill or training on the part of the creator to complete.

Crafted items include decorative innovations on practical items, or items which are intended to be only decorative. Projects are usually accomplished using a mix of techniques combining some traditional folklife activities and materials (mentioned above) with some characteristics of fine art. Product descriptions frequently employed in advertisements for commercially produced kits refer to the creation of "museum quality" art with inexpensive materials. Faux finishes, or surface decoration meant to mimic more expensive materials, are popular.

Projects are often described in women's magazines, in crafting magazines, and on television how-to or domestic-living programs directed at female audiences. The last twenty years have seen the rise of profitable crafting stores, often very large and stocked with silk flowers, fabric paint, glue guns, frames and furniture to decorate, colored paper and ribbons, and other supplies used to produce simple decorative items.

Often crafting is a social activity. Women gather in groups to do projects, compare notes, and trade materials. Scrapbooking is especially popular in this regard. Many crafting activities are also geared toward sharing with or teaching crafting to children. This is in keeping with historic women's traditions such as quilting bees, in which the participants gathered socially to talk, watch and teach children, and accomplish a creative task together.

Crafting is not well respected among most women who consider themselves adept in the fine arts or at traditional crafts that require a great deal of practice to master. Nevertheless, crafting is a very popular creative outlet for women who have not the time, inclination, training, or confidence to explore more demanding, elite, or traditional art forms. Crafting may have gained in popularity as women moved out of the multigenerational family settings in which more complex activities and techniques are usually learned. The increased number of women in the workforce who consequently cannot accomplish time-consuming creative tasks is undoubtedly also a factor in the value and popularity of crafting. *See also:* Folk Art; Material Culture; Sampler; Scrapbooks; Women's Friendship Groups.

References: Vaughan, Theresa A. *Art and Community: A Community Art Center in Norman, Oklahoma.* Diss., Indiana University, Bloomington, 1999.

Theresa A. Vaughan

Crime-Victim Stories

Personal-experience prose narratives that deal with crime victimization are told to inform, entertain, frighten, and to impart street smarts about city life to the listener or audience of other urbanites. In this type of modern storytelling, the narratives are formulaic and have an identifiable form. They often embed themes such as bystander apathy and fear of the city and function in a didactic way, such as reinforcing one mental map of a city or neighborhood and identifying "safe" and "unsafe" territory based not only on empirical evidence but often by subjective observations that are presented within these stories.

The stories reveal that women often believe that they are targets of crime because they "were in the wrong place at the wrong time." Women often say, for example, that they should have followed their intuition and crossed the street when they realized they were being followed. Women share their stories about muggings and rapes, whether with a counselor at a rape-counseling center or at women's social gatherings. While crime-victim stories can be told in any city and by any group, they are particularly common among people who live in New York City and reveal a particular type of New York humor.

Today, it is common and acceptable for women to talk about their experiences as crime victims, especially at rape-crisis centers, where personnel often encourage women to get medical attention and social and psychological support after experiencing rape. However, in the early days of the feminist movement of the 1960s, women first started "revealing" their experiences about crime-victim events, especially rape, in women's consciousness groups. In the past, the sharing of women-centered narratives was not encouraged; women were expected to remain silent about rape, or to reveal their experiences only to family members because victims were often perceived as the instigators of rape via their choices of venue or dress. The recounting of crime-victim stories among women provides a way for them to feel empowered about situations in which they feel otherwise powerless.

Incarcerated women narrate their experiences from a different perspective and may reveal their firsthand accounts of murder and other violent crimes as well as their "vision" narratives of belief. Through these stories, women restore their self images, reshape their lives, and learn to cope with their status as crime victims or perpetrators. *See also:* Consciousness Raising; Humor; Personal-Experience Narrative; Rape.

References: Brunvand, Jan. H. *The Vanishing Hitchhiker: American Urban Legends and Their Meanings.* New York: Norton, 1986; Burke, Carol. *Vision Narratives of Women in Prison.* Knoxville: University of Tennessee Press, 1993; Cody, Cornelia. "Only in New York: The New York City Personal-Experience Narrative." *Journal of Folklore Research: An International Journal of Folklore and Ethnomusicology*, vol. 42 no. 2 (2006): 217–244; Wachs, Eleanor. *Crime-Victim Stories: New York City's Urban Folklore.* Bloomington: Indiana University Press, 1988.

Eleanor Wachs

Croning

Croning, an invented tradition that has arisen in North American women's groups since the early 1980s, refers to a rite of passage, a ceremony marking either menopause or a woman's transition into midlife. A woman is considered eligible for croning at or around the age of fifty, but there is no absolute agreement as to the proper age. Based on the idea that women's lives consist of childhood, child-bearing, and postmenopausal stages (corresponding to the three aspects of the archetypal Triple Goddess—maiden, mother, and crone), croning marks women's passage into the third stage of life, wherein they become elders, or "crones."

As North American women active in the second wave of the feminist movement have entered midlife, they have created age-related support groups, online communities, Web sites, publications, and conferences. Claiming that older women were revered in pre-Christian, matriarchal societies, and that the crone aspect of the Triple Goddess was once worshipped, the croning movement draws upon ideas from liberal feminism, feminist spirituality, and Jungian psychology. It seeks to overturn Christian and patriarchal demonization of the crone and to win back for older women the respect they formerly enjoyed by reclaiming negative stereotypes, such as that of the crone.

Jungian psychologists assert that the psychological work of navigating life changes requires a ritual (for example, Prétat 1994: 17–18). Traditional rituals to mark menopause or the transition to later life are very rare; hence, women have created their own. Some individuals design their own ceremonies, usually involving women friends and family. However, most ceremonies are created and enacted by women's groups such as support groups and feminist witchcraft circles, and professional groups such as the Women's Section of the American Folklore Society. Croning ceremonies may initiate a single woman or a group of women. Men are sometimes included, and in a few groups, men may also be eligible to become crones. A Chicana ceremony, the *cincuentañera*, has recently evolved to celebrate a fifty-year-old woman's life and accomplishments, often including elements reminiscent of those employed in the *quinceañera* ("fifteenth year") coming-of-age ritual.

The form of croning ceremonies varies widely. Some new crones receive homemade crowns or other headdresses (from the spurious but often-repeated etymology of the word "crone" from "crown") to mark their new status. Elder crones in a group often initiate newly eligible women into crone status. A ceremony for an individual woman usually includes some commemoration of her life, either by herself or by her friends, for example in a "memory book." Croning ceremonies also celebrate older women in general: one group prays to "the grandmothers," while another includes representations of women pioneers in their field. Groups borrow and freely recombine ideas from each other; elements from modern witchcraft rituals are common (such as casting a circle or calling upon the four elements of Earth, air, fire, and water), as are rituals from other religious traditions, such as Native American practices like smudging.

On the personal level, croning ceremonies are instruments of conscious aging, and may help individuals come to terms with the changes that accompany later life. Politically, the croning movement seeks to reverse Western society's fear and denial of aging, especially in women. Cross-culturally, the status and quality of life for women usually improve when they reach midlife. Although status improvements do occur in less-marked forms in industrialized societies, the croning movement emphasizes that society despises women who are no longer young, sexually attractive, and capable of childbearing. Croning ceremonies attempt to reverse this trend by arguing that older women should be respected as sources of wisdom and moral authority. *See also:* Aging; American Folklore Society—Women's Section; Goddess Worship; Maiden, Mother, and Crone; Menopause; *Quinceañera*; Rites of Passage; Wicca and Neo-Paganism; Women's Groups.

References: Brown, Judith K. "Cross-Cultural Perspectives on Middle-Aged Women." *Current Anthropology*, vol. 23, no. 2 (1982): 143–56; ———. "Lives of Middle-Aged Women." In *In Her Prime: New Views of Middle-Aged Women*, ed. Virginia Kerns and Judith K. Brown, 17–32. Second edition. Urbana: University of Illinois Press, 1992; Cantú, Norma E., and Olga Najera-Ramirez, eds. *Chicana Traditions: Continuity and Change*. Urbana: University of Illinois Press, 2002; Dresser, Norine. *Multicultural Celebrations: Today's Rules of Etiquette for Life's Special Occasions*. New York: Three Rivers Press-Random House, 1999; McCabe, Janice. *Morphing the Crone: A Critical Ethnography of Crone Consciousness, Culture and Communities, a Feminist Participatory Action Research Project*. PhD diss., York University, 2005; Mantecon, Valerie H. "Where Are the Archetypes? Searching for Symbols of Women's Midlife Passage." *Women and Therapy*, vol. 14, no. 1 (1993): 77–88; Prétat, Jane R. *Coming to Age: The Croning Years and Late-Life Transformation. (Studies in Jungian Psychology by Jungian Analysts)*, 62. Toronto: Inner City Books, 1994; Radner, Joan N. "Coming of Age: The Creative Rituals of Older Women." *Southern Folklore*, vol. 50, no. 2 (1993): 113–25; Rountree, Kathryn. "The New Witch of the West: Feminists Reclaim the Crone." *Journal of Popular Culture*, vol. 30, no. 4 (1997): 211–29; Walker, Barbara G. *The Crone: Woman of Age, Wisdom, and Power*. San Francisco: Harper and Row, 1985.

Moira Smith

Cross-Dressing

Women cross-dress as men and take on male social roles in virtually every culture and time period, with varying purposes and degrees of social acceptance. Cross-dressed warrior women are perhaps the most common and widely approved. Those who sail away or ride out to join and/or rescue husbands and/or lovers who have gone to war appear frequently in European ballads and their North American descendants. A cross-dresser in balladry may end up pregnant and/or dead, but as often as not, she marries the man who discovers her true identity. Distaste for cross-dressers in Christianity is exemplified by legends about the ninth-century pontiff, Pope Joan (John VIII), who in some variants died giving birth to the Antichrist in the streets of Rome. Goddess figures around the world assume men's roles and clothing, frequently remaining perpetually virginal, which serves to limit and contain their masculinized femininity.

Two-spirited persons (*berdaches*) in many North American First Nations perform the social roles and adopt the traditional dress associated with the opposite sex. In some traditions, women may live some or even most of their lives gendered as men. Some even marry women and adopt children. Cultures have varying requirements for legitimizing the practice, including a woman's age, marital and social status, motivation, type of dress, and willingness to return to gender-appropriate clothing once her goal has been met. In folklore, disguising oneself for the sake of another is far more likely to meet with success than is doing so solely for personal gain.

In contemporary North America, cross-dressed women have moved into popular culture, where they may achieve both success and heterosexual romance without the unfortunate side effects of unwanted pregnancy or death. Examples include Marlene Dietrich's tuxedo-clad torch singer in *Morocco* in 1930, Julie Andrews' female impersonator ("a woman pretending to be a man pretending to be a woman") in *Victor/Victoria* in 1982, and Whoopi Goldberg's role in the American remake of *The Associate* in 1996, in which, rather than working for White men, she "becomes" one to succeed on Wall Street. Like most folkloric heroines, cabaret performers Dietrich and Andrews give up their careers after finding the love of good men; however, Goldberg's character ultimately unmasks herself to affirm her identity as an unattached, successful Black woman. But dressing in men's clothes for the sake of one's religious beliefs is presented in a less positive light than are other motives. For example, in *Yentl* (1983), Barbra Streisand's character dresses as a male rabbinical student to avoid the trap of marriage after her father's death. She finds both scholarly and romantic success in the short term, but abandons both when she realizes that, if discovered, her deception will result in ostracism both for herself and her friends.

Clinical psychologists use the term "transvestism" to describe the practice of cross-dressing as a sexual fetish. Statistically, males are more prone to transvestism than are females, but more likely to be socially chastised for it. Within the sexualized contexts of patriarchy, men who genuinely aspire to femininity are more likely to be seen as deviant for taking on what is perceived as a submissive role (for example, a serial killer in *Silence of the Lambs*, 1991) than are women who aspire to higher, masculine status. Folklore and popular cultural genres generally represent cross-dressing men less positively than their female counterparts. They are portrayed as less capable at women's work, as in the 1983 film *Mr. Mom* and the folktale "The Old

Man and Woman Who Switched Jobs," both of which portray wives as far more competent in performing "men's work" than are their husbands in completing traditionally female tasks. The film portrays an inventively disastrous day of housekeeping; the folktale's role-switching results in, among other things, burned bread and a hanged cow. Two film characters are notable exceptions: in *Mrs. Doubtfire* (1993), Robin Williams transforms himself into his own children's beloved nanny, and in *Tootsie* (1982), Dustin Hoffman wins fans as a female soap-opera character.

Men often cross-dress to flee from capture—in *Some Like It Hot* (1959), Jack Lemmon and Tony Curtis join a women's musical group to escape the mob after witnessing an execution; in *Willow* (1988), Val Kilmer's warrior character comically takes on women's clothing to escape the wrath of a cuckholded husband. Or men may cross-dress to commit murder—in the urban legend, "The Hairy-Handed Hitchhiker," a killer disguises himself as a female hitchhiker, only to be given away by his hairy hands. However, even when portrayed in a positive light, cross-dressed women are generally deemed dangerously subversive, while cross-dressed men are simply not taken seriously. *See also:* Ballad; Film; Folklore About Women; Folk Music and Folksong; Folktale; Gender; Legend, Urban/Contemporary; Popular Culture; Transgender Folklore; Women Warriors; Women's Work.

References: Baring-Gould, Sabine. *Curious Myths of the Middle Ages.* New York: Oxford University Press, 1978; Boureau, Alain. *The Myth of Pope Joan.* Trans. Lydia G. Cochrane. Chicago: University of Chicago Press, 2001; Courlander, Harold, ed. *Hopi Voices: Recollections, Traditions, and Narratives of the Hopi Indians.* Albuquerque: University of New Mexico Press, 1982; Dugaw, Dianne. *Warrior Women and Popular Balladry, 1650–1850.* Cambridge: Cambridge University Press, 1989; Greenhill, Pauline. "Neither a Man Nor a Maid: Sexualities and Gendered Meanings in Cross-Dressing Ballads." *Journal of American Folklore*, vol. 108, no. 428 (Spring 1995): 156–177; Hymes, Dell. *In Vain I Tried to Tell You: Essays in Native American Ethnopoetics.* Philadelphia: University of Pennsylvania Press, 2004 [1991]; Jordan, Rosan A., and Susan J. Kalčik, eds. *Women's Folklore, Women's Culture.* Philadelphia: University of Pennsylvania Press, 1971; Lewis, C. S. *A Horse and His Boy.* New York: Harper Collins, 1954; Pratchett, Terry. *Monstrous Regiment.* New York: Harper Collins, 2003; Radner, Joan Newlon, ed. *Feminist Messages: Coding in Women's Folk Culture.* Chicago: University of Illinois, 1993; Roscoe, Will. *Changing Ones: Third and Fourth Genders in Native North America.* New York: Palgrave Macmillan, 1998; ———. "What are Two-Spirits/Berdaches?" n.d. http://www.geocities.com/westhollywood/stonewall/3044/berdache.html (accessed August 10, 2008).

Julia Kelso

Curandera

Curandera ("folk healer") is an umbrella term that encompasses various folk-healing modalities, such as *partera, hierbera, sobadora,* and *huesera*—midwife, herbalist, folk massage therapist, and chiropractor—and seers and card readers as well as those who practice the black arts (sorcery) in Mexican American, Mexican, and U.S. Latino communities. As a folk-healing practitioner in the United States, she fulfills a vital function for the well-being of individuals and communities. The curandera is an experienced seer or spiritual counselor and often specializes in a particular healing practice;

parteras, for example, are specialized health practitioners who may or may not engage in the traditional activities of the curandera.

The origin of the curandera of folk-healing traditional lore can be traced to the Indigenous roots of mestizo culture, and to the folk-healing practices of Spain and Africa. The traditional women healers of Puerto Rican and other Caribbean cultures, known as hierberas or *babalaos*, may practice within the religious context of Santería or espiritismo; they also heal with herbs and with rituals. *Susto* (fright or soul loss) and *limpias* (general soul cleansing) are but two conditions curanderas and hierberas attend to. In both traditions, herbal baths, teas, and particular rituals may be prescribed. The *botánica*, the *yerberia*, or *hierberia* (herb store) provides a much-needed service by making the various necessary utensils, herbs, images, and other accoutrements available for the patient and the healer. The store is a community focal point, serving as a meeting place for healers, who may advertise their services to the neighborhood by leaving a business card or handwritten note on a bulletin board at the establishment.

The curandera belief system holds that there must be balance between hot and cold, and that four conditions determine health: the physical, the mental, the spiritual, and the emotional. Curanderas believe that the balance among these four aspects determines illness or good health in a body. Thus, they treat holistically, looking for imbalance when diagnosing an ailment that may or may not be recognized by Western medicine, such as cancer, heart disease, chronic fatigue syndrome, migraine, a broken heart, susto, or *bilis* (rage).

The figure of the curandera appears often as a stock character in Chicano/a and Latino/a literature; portrayed as a wise and revered member of the community, she is also satirized to provide comic relief. *See also:* Divination Practices; Folk Medicine; Fortune-Teller; Herbs; Tradition-Bearer.

References: Avila, Elena, and Joy Parker. W*oman Who Glows in the Dark: A Curandera Reveals Traditional Aztec Secrets of Physical and Spiritual Health.* New York: Penguin/Putnam, 1999; Fernandez Olmos, Margarita, and Lizabeth Paravisini-Gebert. *Healing Cultures: Art and Religion as Curative Practices in the Caribbean and its Diaspora.* New York: Palgrave MacMillan, 2001; Kay, Margarita A. *Healing with Plants in the American and Mexican West.* Tucson: University of Arizona Press, 1996; Paredes, Américo, and Richard Bauman. *Folklore and Culture on the Texas-Mexican Border.* Austin: University of Texas Press, 1993; Trotter, Robert T., and Juan Antonio Chavira. *Curanderismo: Mexican American Folk Healing.* Second edition. Athens: University of Georgia Press, 1997.

Norma E. Cantú

Cursing

Cursing maintains separate but linked meanings in folklore. It can involve the utterance of words or phrases generally considered objectionable in mainstream society, also called "swearing" or "profanity." In Euro North America, this type of curse takes three main forms: obscenity—sexual references, as in "Fuck you!"; blasphemy—religious references, such as "Holy Mary, Mother of God!"; and abjection—materials or processes that break through bodily boundaries and are thus found disgusting, like "Shit!" Swearing and profanity connect with a second, often implicitly magical, form of cursing, that of using language to manipulate negative supernatural forces against another person or persons. Though sometimes supported by powerful objects, such curses most commonly form simple verbal charms or spells. Thus, a swearing curse like "Fuck you!" can be understood as a verbal invocation by the curser of what is implicitly a negative act against the recipient. Conversely, "Holy Mary, Mother of God!" invokes that venerated figure's protection of the speaker herself or another person, making it also similar to a charm or spell. The latter two forms—cursing as profanity and cursing as magical speech—can be enacted by both women and men. However, both often have marked associations with women or take specific forms when women use them. A third form of curse, unquestionably women-centered, is what is called "the curse" in the vernacular— menstruation, which is also associated with the abject, menstrual blood.

In Euro North American society, swearing and profanity as linguistic forms are thought to be employed primarily by men, particularly by those of the working class. Foundational feminist linguistic research connected women's need to elevate their social position with their language use. Since cursing is impolite, it is unfeminine. Women and girls are encouraged to be ladylike, and their language as well as their postures and actions should reflect their femininity. However, though women are normally expected to avoid curse words, in extreme circumstances, they are informally licensed not to censor their speech. Thus, mild expressions like "Oh fudge, my hair is on fire," or "Dear me, did he kidnap the baby?" (Lakoff: 246) are considered inapt in the extreme circumstances.

Further, Euro North American women in aggravated and painful circumstances like childbirth (another process associated with abjection) often find themselves extricated from everyday social constraints. They often express that freedom in an informal license to curse. Parturient women were "surprised when they found themselves yelling loudly, cursing, complaining, giving orders, or 'losing control'"—all symptoms of a social liberty usually denied them (Martin: 66). Under some circumstances, however, women are culturally enjoined to otherwise problematic language. Brides in some Chinese cultures are supposed to lament their loss of youth, freedom, and natal family by cursing their parents, the matchmakers, and their future husband's family. Similarly, women undergoing "the curse," or who are premenstrual or postmenopausal, may find they can access the verbal freedom of cursing because they are thought to be less in control of themselves at that time. Feminist theorists suggest that women take full advantage of such license to express the anger and frustrations with politics, work, family, and society that they may feel on a daily basis but should not show for fear of condemnation, or even legal and/or medical intervention. This temporary freedom of expression is often a source of immense pleasure for women.

Magical cursing comprises a significant element of many traditional narratives. For example, older folktale witches regularly curse younger women, whether the stepmother in "Snow White," jealous of her stepdaughter's beauty, or the bitter uninvited guest at the christening of the baby who will become Sleeping Beauty. This form of cursing, like its swearing counterpart, is a weapon of the weak, used by those who cannot directly attack those who may threaten them. But cursing can be a most effective weapon, if only temporarily, as folktale cursers and others demonstrate.

Indeed, cursing can be an effective weapon in actual communication. In Turkish culture, women use curses precisely because they lack power and because of their inability to use physical force, particularly against men. "Under such circumstances, cursing remains the only way to demonstrate emotional reactions such as anger, or hatred of unfair treatment" (Vanci-Osam: 75). Women's curses, called *beddua*, differ from men's curses, called *küfür*, which are "ruder, more derogatory, and often an initial step toward violence or the use of physical force" (ibid.). Beddua include: "May their tongues be covered by boils. May the boils be eaten by worms" (ibid.: 79), "May you suffer at the hands of judges and doctors," or "May dead crows gouge out your eyes" (ibid.: 81). These texts clearly demonstrate the links between magical cursing and swearing. It is doubtful that the women who invoke beddua actually believe that they will bring boils, judges, doctors, or dead crows to punish individuals who have done them wrong. Instead, beddua offer their users a remarkably poetic, creative, and allusive outlet for anger.

In traditional Jewish culture, women may curse one another, despite the possibility that it will bring shame to their families. Predictably, curses are "weak" or "strong," that is, associated respectively with women and men. "Weak" curses include "'May you break your neck,' 'May you become blind,' [and] 'May you die young'" (Shai: 43). When used by men, they are considered negatively effeminate. Though sometimes seen as ignominious, a woman may curse "to bring her problems to the attention of the wider community, since if the act should bring shame on herself it may also bring shame to the extended family" (ibid.: 44). Women's cursing, which may look like an uncontrolled outburst, may actually be a strategy to air in public, and thus to resolve, grievances with others. "The expression of dissatisfaction quickly mobilizes local people to bring about reconciliation. For this reason, cursing in a direct form may lead to a state of repaired relationships between individuals" (ibid.: 45).

Women in all-female contexts may feel more comfortable cursing, particularly in heterosexist cultures where a negative judgement from men is more serious than one from other women. Thus, in women's self-defense classes, consciousness-raising groups, or other homosocial organizations, women may curse more freely. However, women may also be the recipients of cursing from men as a form of sexual harassment, for example, when they enter non-traditional fields of employment. *See also:* Consciousness Raising; Folktale; Gender; Menstruation.

References: Black, C. Fred. "Death and Abuse in Marriage Laments: The Curse of Chinese Brides." *Asian Folklore Studies*, vol. 37, no. 1 (1978): 13–33; Lakoff, Robin. "Extract from Language and Women's Place." In *The Feminist Critique of Language*, ed. Deborah Cameron, 242–252. Second edition. London: Routledge, 1998 [1975]; Martin, Karin A. "Giving Birth Like a Girl." *Gender and Society*, vol. 17, no. 1 (2003): 54–72; Shai, Donna. "Public Cursing and Social Control in a Traditional Jewish Community." *Western Folklore*, vol. 37, no. 1 (1978): 39–46; Vanci-Osam, Ülker. "May You Be Shot with Greasy Bullets: Curse Utterances in Turkish." *Asian Folklore Studies*, vol. 57, no. 1 (1998): 71–86.

Pauline Greenhill

Cyberculture

Cyberculture studies focus on the cultural origins and evolving legacies of computing technologies, and include the study of their related scientific, technological, and philosophical contexts. Cyberculture encompasses early automata and calculating machines, computing machines (those capable of manipulating data according to instruction), robotics (the science of complex machines), cybernetics (the science of complex systems), virtual environments (artificially generated, non-material environments), the Internet, artificial intelligence (AI), and, at its broadest, the philosophical concept of "simulation."

As an expression of the basic human drives for building and for navigation, cyberculture is closely tied to folklore, myth, and fiction. In *The Cybercultures Reader* (2000), Timothy Leary uses the term "cybernaut" to describe all engineers, architects, explorers, and cartographers in virtual and/or physical geographies, comparing the voyages of both Renaissance explorer, Marco Polo, and fictional hero of Greek epic poetry, Odysseus, with the midnight activities of teenage hackers engrossed in online gaming. Such terminology captures a primary conflict that has characterized the development of cyberculture, one of particular importance to the student of folklore: a violent striation between the concerns of authoritative rule on the one hand and populist practice on the other. At the same time, stereotypical and hierarchized categories of "male" and "female," "controller" and "machine," and "creator" and "created," have tended to be reduplicated in all areas to do with computing technologies, both in official discourse and in computing subcultures.

Perhaps unsurprisingly, published histories of early computing have largely championed the accomplishments of men. When female pioneers in the field are included, gender stereotypes detract from public perception of their contributions. The portrayal of computing progenitors Charles Babbage and Lady Ada (Byron) Lovelace speaks directly both to the perpetuation of gender stereotype in established histories and to cyberculture's competing claims of authority and populism. Babbage's Analytical Engine (1840) is widely cited as the first modern analog computer. Lady Lovelace constructed what has been described as the first computer program, a set of instructions for the Analytical Engine intended to be utilized in a manner similar to the cards of Jacquard's loom. She also published *A Sketch of the Analytical Engine* (1845), a treatise describing in prophetic terms the potential use to which such a machine might be put. Officially, Babbage envisioned the Analytical Engine performing sophisticated astronomical calculations for the British Navy. However, Lady Lovelace envisioned the machine generating musical combinations, pieces of text, and other representational output.

The more colorful biographies also record the pair's fondness for horse racing and speculate that the Analytical Engine's calculating potential fuelled their dream of a reliable, predictive system of betting based on mathematical probabilities. Yet Lovelace's significant contribution has been forgotten or seriously downplayed. While Babbage has been presented by computing historians as the authoritative inventor of the machine, the scientist interested in astronomy and naval procedure, and a risk-taker intent on cracking the mathematics of random variables, Lovelace has been characterized as "Babbage's muse," as a "dreamer" predicting computer-driven art and music, and as an opium addict who lost a fortune "on the ponies." Yet the Analytical Engine's presumed transposition from naval research to entertainment (art, music, and horse racing) did foreshadow the evolution of the computer in the twentieth century, as government-directed supercomputing gave way to the personal computer (PC) and brought the technology into the feminized realm of popular culture and mass consumption.

Advances in computing architectures and programming in the 1950s, 1960s, and 1990s retraced the mythic ambitions of the field's earlier pioneers: the creation of "life" and cheating fate. The military context of microcomputer development paradoxically bequeathed a legacy of secrecy and restriction while enabling the structures and devices that would grant access to this technology by the general populace. E-mail developed in the 1960s and 1970s from the need for U.S. Department of Defense personnel to communicate electronically. It soon filtered down through the military to academic institutions, although it would be decades still before it was available to Jane and John Doe on the street. Similarly, the Internet originated from ARPANET, the corporate communication network of Xerox PARC (Palo Alto Research Center) computer scientists. Downsized after military cutbacks at the end of the Cold War, PARC group scientists moved from military to corporate funding while vehemently retaining a 1960s counterculture ethic; they were responsible for key innovations that would bring about the widespread distribution of computer communication networks (today referred to as the "democratization of the 'Net'"). The established histories often describe the transition of computing from a military context to the realm of democratic practice through a rhetoric of iconoclastic male heroes who rescued a passive, general population from governmental control or the perceived threat of AI. Science fiction firsts such as *Forbidden Planet* (1956) and the hugely successful television series *Buck Rogers* (1950) form unofficial parallels in popular culture to the official vision of these histories, both offering decidedly male-centered narratives.

At the same time, the science of cybernetics, theorized by Norbert Wiener in 1948, fundamentally reconceived of complex systems in ways that eschew ideas like "authoritative" and "centeredness" in favor of concepts such as "distributed" and "part function." Wiener generalized and expanded the concept of cybernetics to describe all complex systems of interacting parts, whether the human body, a building, or a computer network, and suggested that they be defined not by physical arrangement and boundaries, but through the processes of information flows. Similarly, in the late 1960s, a group of four architects using the name Archigram developed an "architecture of lightness," a mode of conceptualizing buildings as open to networks of communications technologies, and as portable—even disposable. The Microsoft Windows catchphrase, "Where do you want to go today?" nicely encapsulates what Archigram envisioned for cities of the future: people, machines, and buildings capable of roaming and linking up in various arrangements, at various times, in fluid relationships, and with fluid purposes. Such decenteredness and flexibility promised much for an egalitarian vision of computing technologies, in terms of both public usage and gender identity.

However, the dream of nomadically empowered populations has proven difficult to achieve, as current conflicts between proprietary software and corporate licensing on the one hand and public demand for free access and unlimited information upgrade on the other have inevitably resulted from the dual impulses that structured the late 1960s and early 1990s explosions in computing technologies. Such conflict reaches a popular apotheosis in the blockbuster film *The Matrix* (1999). Played out in terms that emphatically restate the symmetries between naval, architectural, physical, and virtual territories, the film stages an epic confrontation between authoritative control with Agent Smith, a sentient program or AI, and the iconoclastic hacker-hero Neo. Despite the liberatory potential envisioned in the very malleability of simulated worlds and digital relations, a masculinist rhetoric amenable to military and corporate warfare has reasserted itself in cybercultures with amazing resilience; the impulses of technological egalitarianism have not included women as a specific group.

Primary categories of cyberlore reveal aggressive gender polarizations: hacker culture and its mythologies center around the lone, teenage male; video games feature both militarized combat sequences and hypersexualized female avatars (on-screen player icons), playing, like hacker culture, to the teenage male audience; online shopping sites, although statistics attest to the generality of their demographic, are perceived as feminized "space" marked by excesses of consumption, frenzied bargain hunting, and purchase for leisure rather than necessity; chain e-mails, invariably of the "joy-luck" variety ("send to five friends; break the chain and misfortune will follow"), are overwhelmingly targeted at and distributed by women; and chat rooms have spawned activities with decidedly sexual content that are potentially dangerous spaces for women and children. As Nina Wakeford remarked, much of the Internet still functions as a "lawless wild west world," controlled by "console cowboys" (Wakeford 91).

Frontier justice, largely underpinned by conspiracy theory, has been described as the motivational calling card of self-styled techno-subversives— "hackers." A hacker's perception that authorities not only have complete, regulated control of network technologies but are withholding vital information from the populace, presents him or her with the irresistible challenge to infiltrate restricted databases and cause anarchic havoc. As Andrew Ross details, the media constructs teenage hacking as a threat to both corporate hegemony and national security, thereby perpetuating its romantic counter-culture mythology; "the dominant representation of the hacker is that of 'rebel with a modem'" (Ross: 256). Note that although it is aimed against institutional authority, hacking is still clearly regarded as a form of skilled combat. Moreover, cultural productions from news headlines to online humor confirm that hacker culture is clearly coded male.

Frequently linked in the popular imagination with hacking, videogaming, too, is perceived as a pastime for teenage males. Numerous games adopt militarized scenarios, whether single-player or MMPORG (massive multi-player online role-playing games) in design. The exaggeratedly masculine avatars of games like *Duke Nukem* and *Doom* are easily intelligible in this context, while the use of female avatars has generated considerable debate. Role-playing games, originating from early Dungeons and Dragons groups and online MUDs (multi-user dungeons, domains, or dimensions), appeared initially to offer considerable flexibility in character construction and ample opportunity to reenvision gender roles. However, as these games evolved into popular console versions and MMPORGs, commercial interests and user demand combined to produce fairly rigid generic protocols for gendered playable characters.

The video game character Lara Croft, adapted for the *Tomb Raider* films (2001, 2003), serves as a good example of the gender debate. While Lara takes on the role of action hero within the game and even combines masculine and feminine attributes in her hypergendered signature look of big breasts and guns, the sexualization of her character and its alignment with soft-core pornography is demonstrated by the fan lore that surrounds her. Lara fans have created entire backstories and supporting paraphernalia, including the infamous "nude Lara" patch, a modification that strips the avatar of her clothing. Combat-hardened video vixens like Lara may have come a long way from the passive prostitutes in *Duke Nukem* who beg, "Kill me, kill me," but feminist critics argue that the difference is one of degree, not kind. The ease with which video games translate between militarized and pornographic scenarios is obvious in a game such as *Leisure Suit Larry*, in which the object of game play is to maneuver Larry into positions of sexual intercourse with several female characters—much like shooting down as many space invaders as possible—within a given time limit.

Online, women have grouped toward activities involving consumption and private or domestic communication, spaces already culturally coded as female, particularly online shopping malls, e-mail, and blogs (Web-published diaries). Online malls have consistently tailored site graphics and navigation designs to evoke physical shopping malls, with female-targeted items such as clothing, shoes, and purses in the most visibly noticeable locations, heavy usage of female models with the products, and female-oriented catchphrases such as "Discover the softer side of Sears." Likewise, chain e-mails—one of the first Internet genres to capture the attention of folklorists—are mass-produced, but stealthily invade the space of private e-mail addresses. These e-mails promise love or good luck as a result of sending a copy of the letter to five or more friends within a designated time limit. While the address to "friends" encourages erasure of the border between the virtual, generic address and the recipients' actual friends through the nature of their intended distribution, chain e-mail also functions, like the shopping mall, as public inscription of private space. Graphics included with such e-mails are often female-oriented and content-themed, with prominent displays of roses, babies, and butterflies. The association of femininity with friendship, love, and the private sphere versus the warrior's code of videogaming and the publicity of lone-male hacking suggests just how stereotyped computing lore and practice remains.

Further, many commentators believe that the potential for virtual gender play that feminist critics had envisioned so positively in the heady first days of Internet expansion has been curtailed through both authoritative and populist mechanisms. The economic realities of niche marketing, from video games to the online auction mall eBay, have resulted in products and associated advertising that exaggerate gender stereotypes. Unofficial online practice has also reinforced rigid gender identity in many subcategories, from chat-room humor that makes gender masquerade a staple comic subject to the use of e-mail and chat-room space for pornography distribution. Certainly, cyberspace has offered women new access to public expression, with many sites dedicated to the publication of women's writing about women's concerns, along with online versions of feminist magazines like *Bitch*, which have a wider virtual than print readership. However, cybercultures have failed to bring gender-egalitarian principles to the mainstream, and have more easily translated standard gender roles from the physical world to the digital. *See also:* Film; Gender; Magazines, Girls' and Women's; Popular Culture.

References: Bell, David, ed. *An Introduction to Cybercultures*. London: Routledge, 2001; Bell, David, and Barbara Kennedy, eds. *The Cybercultures Reader*. London: Routledge, 2000; *Bitch* Magazine. n.d. http://www.bitchmagazine.org (accessed July 13, 2007); Colomina, Beatriz. *Sexuality and Space*. New York: Princeton Architectural Press, 1992; Haraway, Donna. *Simians, Cyborgs, and Women: The Reinvention of Nature*. New York: Routledge, 1991; ———. "A Manifesto For Cyborgs: Science, Technology, and Socialist Feminism in the 1980s." In *The Gendered Cyborg: A Reader*, 50–57. New York: Routledge, 2000; Hayles, N. Katherine. *How We Became Posthuman: Virtual Bodies in Cybernetics, Literature, and Informatics*. Chicago: University of Chicago Press, 1999; Kirkup, Gill, Linda Janes, Kath Woodward, and Giona Hovenden, eds. *The Gendered Cyborg: A Reader*. New York: Routledge, 2000; Leary, Timothy. "The Cyberpunk: The Individual as Reality Pilot." In *The Cybercultures Reader*, eds. David Bell and Barbara Kennedy, 529–539. London: Routledge, 2000; Lupton, Ellen. *Mechanical Brides: Women and Machines from Home to Office*. New York: Princeton Architectural Press, 1993; Palumbo, Maria Louisa. *New Wombs: Electronic Bodies and Architectural Disorders*. Basel, Switzerland: Birkhauser, 2000; Ross, Andrew. "Hacking Away at the Counter-Culture." In *The Cybercultures Reader*, eds. David Bell and Barbara Kennedy, 254–267. London: Routledge, 2000; Toole, Betty Alexandra. *Ada, the Enchantress of Numbers: Prophet of the Computer Age*. Mill Valley, CA: Strawberry Press, 1998; Wakeford, Nina. "Networking Women and Grrrls with Information/Communication Technology: Surfing Tales of the World Wide Web." In *Processed Lives: Gender and Technology in Everyday* Life, eds. J. Terry and M. Calvert, 52–66. London: Routledge, 1997.

Andrea Austin

D

Daughter

The female child of parents of any gender—biological, adopted, foster, or stepoffspring—is their daughter. The relationship combines emotional, sociocultural, and legal aspects. Parents are expected to provide for their daughters and sons until a legally mandated age that differs from one nation and/or state to another. Required provisions often include the basics of life and formal education to some level. However, it is usually the emotional and social aspects of the relationship between parents and daughters that are explored in traditional and popular culture.

Parents, especially fathers, are often represented in ballads as excessively controlling of their daughters' relationships with men. Fathers' scrutiny of daughters' sexuality and, ultimately, of their choice of marriage partners, goes beyond mere solicitousness and care for the women's future happiness. Anthropologist Gayle Rubin argues that the exchange of women, that is, fathers offering their daughters to the sons of their male allies to cement a connection between the men, is fundamental to the development of the system of patriarchy in human cultures. Thus, a folksong like the Newfoundland lyric "The Star of Logy Bay" is not simply a lament by a lover that his girlfriend's father has sent her far away to prevent the two marrying; it is an expression of the power of the patriarchal rule that fathers have over their daughters.

Indeed, relationships between fathers and daughters are frequently the motivating force behind Anglo American ballad stories. A standard pattern is that the father refuses to let his daughter marry the man of her choice. She rebelliously follows her lover anyway, with varied results. Sometimes, particularly when the woman has shown great boldness by dressing as a man to pursue her lover, the outcome is happy. If the daughter doesn't marry the man she originally went after, she gets another, even better choice. Instead of one of her peers, she may marry the wealthy ship's captain or the rich landowner. Sometimes, however, the results are tragic, and the lovers die together. The ballad's metaphorical result is often a plant, which grows on their contiguous graves and twines together "in a true love's knot" over their resting places. The implication is that though they could not be together in life, they are joined in death. Sometimes this evidence of the couple's love makes parents remorseful of their actions toward their daughter.

The relationship between mothers and daughters isn't usually central to the plots of traditional ballads; however, these bonds are a primary motivating force in folktales. Also in contrast to ballads, father-daughter folktale links are positive. In "Beauty and the Beast," Beauty saves her father, and indeed her family, by taming the Beast, who threatens to kill him. Youngest daughters are especially obedient and reliable, and often seem to be the main support of their family. But stepdaughters in particular have a hard time in the Grimms' folktales (even though it is doubtful whether the lack of blood relation is traditional or part of the Grimm brothers' inability to conceive of biological mothers acting cruelly toward their children). In one famous tale, the mother overvalues her biological children (Cinderella's two ugly stepsisters) and makes her own stepdaughter act as their servant or slave. In many variants, even after the daughter's relationship with the prince who courts her is established, the daughter remains kind and caring toward her stepmother and stepsisters.

Oral histories of pioneer life in nineteenth- and early twentieth-century North America show that mothers and daughters invariably relied upon each other for emotional support, and also in conducting domestic labor and maintaining social relations. Daughters remembering their mothers invariably cite their deep admiration for the older women's resiliency and caring, but also their sense of mutual responsibility. Feminist scholar Eliane Silverman calls this situation "a mother-daughter web of obedience and obligation" (39). She points out that the web extends through the generations to granddaughters and also to daughters-in-law.

In contemporary Euro North American societies, the lack of affordable health care often turns daughters into live-in caregivers for their elderly parents. Eldercare is an extension of women's expected unpaid domestic labor. In this situation, the cultural presumption that daughters should rely on their parents is reversed. Daughters may find themselves providing all the necessities of life to those who once provided the same to them when they were young. The resulting bond is a complicated one. Given the difficulties of relationships between daughters and their parents, it's not surprising that this arrangement can be extremely trying for all involved while it can be mutually rewarding and nurturing. *See also:* Ballad; Elder Care; Family Folklore; Folktale; Oral History; Women's Work.

References: Abel, Emily K. "Adult Daughters and Care for the Elderly." *Feminist Studies*, vol. 12, no. 3 (Fall 1986): 479–498; Rubin, Gayle. "The Traffic in Women." In *Toward an Anthropology of Women*, ed. Rayna Reiter, 157–210. New York: Monthly Review Press, 1975; Silverman, Eliane. "In Their Own Words: Mothers and Daughters on the Alberta Frontier." *Frontiers: A Journal of Women's Studies*, vol. 2, no. 2 (Summer 1977): 37–44; Stewart, Polly. "Wishful Willful Wily Women: Verbal Strategies for Female Success in the Child Ballads." In *Feminist Messages: Coding in Women's Folk Culture*, ed. Joan Newlon Radner, 54–73. Urbana: University of Illinois Press, 1993; Tatar, Maria, ed. *The Annotated Brothers Grimm*. New York: W. W. Norton, 2004; Westkott, Marcia. "Mothers and Daughters in the World of the Father." *Frontiers*, vol. 3, no. 2 (1978): 16–21.

Pauline Greenhill

Deaf Folklore

As a North American folk group, the Deaf community includes deaf and hard-of-hearing individuals of all classes, genders, and ethnicities who identify themselves as sharing a common language (American Sign Language or ASL) and culture; the term "Deaf" is a mark of that cultural identity while "deaf" marks only a physiological condition. Rather than a single-characteristic description of people who are physically incapable of perceiving the sounds of speech, Deaf culture includes those who identify themselves and are accepted by other members of the community as part of that group. Thus, individuals who are deaf but do not use ASL are not considered members of Deaf culture. Deaf culture can also be recognized in the formal institutions and structures shared by its members (for example, Deaf Women United, Gallaudet University, the National Association of the Deaf, and community groups), in its material culture (for example, telecommunication devices known as TDDs, and flashing alarm clocks and doorbells), and in its normative tendency to endogamous marriage (Deaf people almost exclusively marry other Deaf people). Written English is a second language for many individuals in the Deaf community, and, not surprisingly, visual representations of English, rather than auditory/oral forms, are the preferred means of its transmission (for example, television closed-captioning). Through contact with other Deaf individuals, deaf children born into hearing families have the potential to become members of a cultural group different from that of their own parents. A modern ASL/English bilingual Deaf identity is the product of generations of a collective experience of being deaf in a predominantly hearing society (Humphries 2004).

Deaf folklore, unique in numerous respects, includes riddles, jokes, games, legends, folktales (see Padden and Humphries 1988), and a variety of other genres transmitted through ASL. It functions, like all folklore, to help define and maintain social identity, to facilitate developmental adaptation, to navigate the frustrations and injustices that are part of the experience of living in the hearing world, and to provide humor and entertainment. Distinctly Deaf folklore includes sign puns, number stories, and ABC stories. An ABC story is a story or poem that begins with the finger-spelled letter A and proceeds through the alphabet, finally ending with the letter Z. As each letter is used, the storyteller must use the handshape of the manual alphabet in the signs or motions conveying the story. For example, the handshape for the letter A, if moved in a circular fashion in front of the chest, represents the phrase "I'm sorry," but the same gesture held in a stationary position indicates knocking on a door. Given the high degree of linguistic play the genre involves, good ABC storytellers must display great creativity in signing.

Deaf folklore is not translatable into the linear structures of written language. ASL makes it possible, for example, to convey more than one idea simultaneously by signing them with different hands, or by signing one with one hand and spelling the other with the other hand. Because it frequently involves physicality for the full expression of an idea or emotion, ASL storytellers use facial expressions and movements to communicate nuanced emotions or to embody a character. The audience knows who is "speaking" by a stance, a cocked eyebrow, or a change of gait. Consequently, it was only with the relatively recent advent of videotape technology that Deaf folklore came to be recognized as an art form; today, it can be communicated within Deaf culture and preserved for study by outsiders in this and other visual media.

Deaf Women United (DWU) held its seventh national convention in the United States in 1999. Its activist mission statement sets goals of "empowerment, enrichment, and networking":

> Deaf women are key members in this era of social change by being involved in the shaping of this world and our respective communities.... [yet] successful Deaf women have not made front page headlines or been recognized for their contributions. We currently have a small number of Deaf women leaders at the helm of some very important organizations and institutions; yet we do not have complete access to services and opportunities that are available to hearing women. It is this equal access that ensures an individual the right and ability to lead full and productive lives. (DWU 2000)

The subversive potential of Deaf culture forcefully entered the perception of the hearing world in 2004, when Natalya Dmitruk, an anchorwoman-interpreter for Ukraine's state-owned television station, and the hearing daughter of Deaf parents, signed to her audience that the night's election results were fraudulent. The community of Laurent, South Dakota, is designed around ASL users and planned for full occupation by 2018. Everyone who lives there—from restaurant workers to the members of the town council—will be expected to communicate in sign language. *See also:* Childbirth and Childrearing; Coding; Consciousness Raising; Feminisms; Fieldwork; Film; Folk Belief; Folk Group; Folk Poetry; Humor; Joke; Material Culture; Politics; Storytelling.

References: Davey, Monica. "As Town for Deaf Takes Shape, Debate on Isolation Re-emerges." *The New York Times*, March 20, 2005; Davis, Lennard J. "Deafness and the Riddle of Identity." *The Chronicle of Higher Education*, B6–8. January 12, 2007; Deaf Women United (DWU). n.d. http://www.dwu.org (accessed June 22, 2005); Humphries, Tom. "The Modern Deaf Self: Indigenous Practices and Educational Imperatives." *Literacy and Deaf People: Cultural and Contextual Perspectives*, ed. B. J. Brueggemann, 29–46. Washington, DC: Gallaudet University Press, 2004; Padden, Carol, and Tom Humphries. *Deaf in America: Voices from a Culture*. Cambridge, MA: Harvard University Press, 1988; Peters, Cynthia L. *Deaf American Literature: From Carnival to the Canon*. Washington, DC: Gallaudet University Press, 2000; Rutherford, Susan. *A Study of American Deaf Folklore*. Burtonsville, MD: Linstock Press, 1993; Schreck, Carl. "Ukraine Journalist Stages Silent Revolt." *The Moscow Times*, November 29, 2004. http://www.themoscowtimes.com/stories/2004/11/29/002.html (accessed August 10, 2008).

Melanie Zimmer

Death

The end of a human life is a social and spiritual transition in which women play a multitude of roles. Women are extensively implicated spiritually, ritually, practically, and in narrative traditions, with others' deaths. In the mythic traditions of many cultures, humanity was created immortal—or at least born to be reborn after death, like the seasons—but at some point, people made a choice (or a mistake) which led to permanent mortality. As often as not in mythology, women are assigned the role of making that choice. In Judeo-Christian-Muslim tradition, Eve chose to eat an apple from the Tree of Knowledge, an act which led to humankind's loss of access to the Tree of Life as well as to its exile from the Garden of Eden. Eve's action is not described as a conscious choice for mortality; however, in other cultures, women have been deliberately responsible for the coming of death.

Female characters often serve as gods of death. In most cultures, they are morally neutral characters; they take the dead, judge them, tend to them, and sometimes punish them, but have no personal stake in their deaths or in their souls, and, with few exceptions, never kill. In Norse mythology, warrior-women called the Valkyries choose the men who will die on the battlefield so that these dead warriors can fight in Ragnarok, the war which will bring the end of the world. Goddesses of the dead are also often responsible for the introduction of mortality into human life, but it is cross-dressed Loki, a Trickster god, who brings permanent death into the Norse world. He kills the god Balder, and then, in contrast to the significant roles women play in lament traditions, refuses to cry, even when the death-god, Hel, Loki's daughter, makes Balder's return to life conditional on all things in the world weeping for him.

Ereshkigal was the death goddess of Sumer; ancient Egypt's was Isis. Isis became associated with the world of the dead when she rescued her brother-husband Osiris by gathering his scattered body parts and putting them back together so that he could take his place as judge of the dead. Greek myths tell that when Persephone (Kore) was kidnapped by Hades and taken to the underworld to be his wife, her mother, Demeter, caused the Earth to become barren in her mourning. When her daughter was returned, she rejoiced, returning generative life to the human world. But, in a common folkloric trope, Persephone had eaten the food of the dead, and therefore had to return to Hades' realm. In a compromise negotiated by the male gods, Persephone spent three months underground with her husband, and the rest of the year with her mother on Earth.

Kali, an Asian god of destruction and rebirth, is commonly associated with battlefields and war. She wears a necklace of human skulls and dances on the bodies of the dead. She was sometimes propitiated through human sacrifices, and had a cult of assassins as followers. Another divine figure revered in Asian Indian tradition is Sati or Suttee. In the ultimate expression of love and loyalty, she threw herself on the pyre of her husband Rama when he died. This led to a long-standing tradition of women voluntarily (or not) throwing themselves on their husband's pyres in funeral ceremonies, despite the practice having been officially outlawed in the present day. Women's mourning, the notion of an eternal connection between spouses, and the burial of royal wives and concubines with their husbands (so that they may serve and honor their male partners in the afterlife) are long-standing expressions of connections attributed to women with deaths not their own.

Doña Sebastiana appears frequently in New Mexican art and folktales, sometimes conferring healing powers on those who treat her well. Her life-sized image was drawn through the streets by Catholic Penitentes during Holy Week processions. Death also held a significant place in the Mexico's ancient civilizations. Among the Aztecs, for example, it was considered a blessing for a woman to die in childbirth; such a death, like dying in battle or as a human sacrifice, assured a desirable afterlife. In the folklore of *Dia de los Muertos* (the Mexican "Day of the Dead"), death is always personified as a woman—*La Catrina* ("Fancy Lady"), *La Pelona* ("The Bald One"), *La Flaca* ("The Skinny One"), *La Huesuda* ("The Boney One"), *La Calaca* ("The Skeleton")—just as she is in the *calaveras*, satirical songs and poems written for the living on the Day of the Dead (Palfrey 1995; Hernandez 2002).

Jean Cocteau's 1949 film *Orphée* anthropomorphizes death as a woman, as do Neil Gaiman's *Sandman* graphic novels. In the latter, modeled after musician Tori Amos, she is one of the seven Deathless (the others being Destiny, Destruction, Desire, Despair, and Delight, and Dream), and one of the most popular characters in the series. In the Marvel Comics universe, Hela, based on the Norse death-god Hel, functions not only as the ruler of the underworld, but as an enemy of the hero-god Thor. She has been reinterpreted here to give us an evil creature who actually causes death rather than one who merely collects and jealously guards the dead.

Female figures may also function as harbingers of death. The Morrigan of Celtic mythology stands across streams combing her hair on the eve of battle as a forewarning of the deaths to come. Her bird, the raven, feasts on the dead. In Ireland, Brittany and elsewhere, the banshee, said by some to be an aspect of the Morrigan, cries at the houses of those about to die.

One theory about the close connection between women and death is that menstruation ties them to mortality. The misogynist saying, "I don't trust anything that bleeds for seven days but doesn't die," holds a powerful and sometimes frightening image. With its blood, physical risk, and connection to the cycles of nature, the act of childbirth also brings women closer to death. Birth, like death, has long been considered unclean, not only for reasons of hygiene, but because the process of being born places the (otherwise pure) human spirit into a body that will inevitably decay, necessitating the separation from society of persons who have had contact with either one. In medieval Europe, for example, the blood of the afterbirth was believed to attract demons, combining fertility with death.

In some European traditions, women who died while pregnant were believed to continue to gestate the child. As a result, they were buried with swaddling and other items they would need to properly care for their child after death. Women who died pregnant or in childbirth were buried with special precautions or at particular locations; like other unquiet European dead, they were buried at crossroads or in unhallowed ground to keep them and/or the dead child from walking the land.

Purportedly physical connections between women and the world of the dead may explain the dual nature of so many folkloric entities. Demeter and Persephone, like Isis and Osiris, trade their time between the dead and the living. In a similar motif, fairy queens are generally soulless and apparently unable to conceive; they steal children and convey a limited and treacherous immortality on men they choose to bring into their worlds. For example, a prince is taken by the Fairy Queen and after three days desires to return home. He is allowed to leave only the condition that he swears he will return and is admonished not to let his feet touch the ground. He discovers that 300 years have passed, his family is dead, and his kingdom has fallen. He falls from his horse in sorrow, quickly ages, and dies.

In practical matters that mark ritual transitions from life to death, women may wash the dead and prepare a body for burial, including wrapping and/ or dressing the corpse. Women also mourn the dead, and may be hired as official or professional mourners (moirologistres) in cultures from Ghana to Ireland to China to Mexico. Their job is to express the family's and community's grief by singing laments, beating their chests, rending their clothes, and sometimes cutting their own skin to express communal sorrow and loss.

In many European, African, and Asian cultures, women are expected to lament the dead loudly and publicly; they may be paid to do so. While the ritual honors the deceased, the noise of keening and chanting may drown out their complaints that the dead person was cruel or unkind; the ritual provides professional mourners and those who hire them the opportunity to criticize the deceased without suffering any consequences.

Women's connection with death has also been expressed in the restrictions placed on them regarding the deaths of those around them. In the Victorian era in Britain, following the queen's example, a married woman was required to mourn for a year after her husband died. This included dressing only in black and strictly limiting her socializing. After the mourning period, especially if her financial status was not secure, she was strongly encouraged to seek out another husband as soon as possible. Daughters, sisters, mothers, and other female relatives of a high-status dead male also had strict clothing codes; after varying periods, they were allowed to wear clothing with white borders of strictly regulated sizes, and eventually dark colors other than black.

Female figures in various states of undress are used to adorn European and North American cemeteries. Sculpted women crouch, kneel, and sprawl especially across the graves of men. With their clothing apparently discarded in distress, they reflect actual patriarchal expectations for women to mourn extravagantly and publicly upon the death of a beloved man.

Women frequently provide for the informal rituals associated with death. In rural North American Catholic and Protestant church basements, women provide a repast of sandwiches and dainties (small sweet cakes and bars) after a funeral service. "El duelo" ("the duel") in Mexican American tradition offers a similar meal, sometimes in the home of the dead person's family, provided by friends and relatives, especially women, who arrive to offer their condolences bearing gifts of food. As in the Jewish tradition of "sitting Shiva" ("seven days of mourning"), the idea is that the family is so bereft that its members cannot cook for themselves. In Mexican tradition, *pan dulce* ("sweet bread") and cookies, foods that remind the family to trust again in the sweetness of life, are served at the funeral home; in Jewish tradition, hard-boiled eggs and lentils are served, symbols of the cyclical nature of life and the immortality of the soul. In early modern China, it was customary for the married daughters of Taoist and Confucianist families to provide pork for family funeral services to sympathetically imbue the corpse with *yin* energy, thereby helping to balance their energies for the afterlife.

Men and women share some death-related roles equally. In balladry and legendry, both are capable of excessive mourning, which can cause harm to themselves or to others. Legends, folktales, and ballads concerned with disproportionate mourning demonstrate the dangers inherent in unhealthy levels of grief and clinging too tightly to the memory of the dead. Women are abducted by dead lovers; women who have been killed or abducted by fairies return to their homes to visit husbands and children; grieving widows and mothers are visited by dead loved ones with warnings and portents. The consequences for excessive grief, for the living as well as for the dead, can be dire. *La Llorona* of Mexican folklore is one such legend.

In the ballad "The Wife of Usher's Well," a mother prays for her dead sons to return to her, until they finally do—to force her to accept their death. In "The Cruel Mother," the title character refuses to acknowledge the deaths of children she herself killed, but is finally punished when they return to denounce their murderer. The idea that parents will be unable to reconcile themselves to the death of a child, and may wish for her or his return under any circumstances, is represented in W. W. Jacobs' "The Monkey's Paw," which concerns a mother who so desires her dead son's return that she wishes him alive without considering that he was horribly mutilated when he died. The same motif occurs in Stephen King's novel and film *Pet Semetary*, which involves the return of a child from the dead in a changed and evil form. An inversion of the motif, in which a young girl attempts to return her dead mother to life, is portrayed in an episode of the television series *Buffy the Vampire Slayer*. Nor is there any shortage, in legend and popular culture, of attractive, sexually desirable, female revenants who seek living men to help solve their murders or help them exact revenge. *See also:* Ballad; Banshee; Cross-Dressing; Graves and Gravemarkers; Lament; *La Llorona*; Legend, Supernatural; Menstruation; Myth Studies; Nature/Culture; Region: Mexico; Rites of Passage; Women Warriors.

References: Bennett, Gillian. *"Alas Poor Ghost!"* Logan, UT: Utah State University Press, 1999; Bourke, Angela. "More in Anger Than In Sorrow: Irish Women's Lament Poetry." In *Feminist Messages: Coding in Women's Folk Culture,* ed. Joan Newlon Radner, 160–182. Urbana: University of Illinois Press, 1993; Davidson, Hilda R. Ellis, and W. M. S. Russell, eds. *The Folklore of Ghosts.* Totowa, NJ: D. S. Brewer, 1981; Hernandez, Aracely. *Northern Notes.* "Dia de los Muertos." DeKalb: Northern Illinois University, 2002. http://www3.niu.edu/newsplace/nndia.html (accessed August 10, 2008); King, Steven. *Pet Semetary.* New York: Doubleday, 1983; Narvaez, Peter, ed. *The Good People: New Fairylore Essays.* Lexington: University Press of Kentucky, 1991; Noxon, Marti, writer and director. "Forever." *Buffy the Vampire Slayer,* Season Five, Episode 17. Premiered April 17, 2001; Palfrey, Dale Hoyt. 1995. *Mexico Connect.* "The Day of the Dead." http://www.mexconnect.com/mex_/muertos.html (accessed August 10, 2008); Palmer, Greg. *Death: The Trip of a Lifetime.* Collingdale, PA: Diane Publishing, 1993; Pentikainen, Juha. "The Dead Without Status." *Nordic Folklore: Recent Studies,* eds. Reimund Kvideland and Henning K. Sehmsdorf, 128–134. Bloomington: Indiana University Press, 1990; Thomas, Jeannie Banks. *Naked Barbies, Warrior Joes, and Other Forms of Visible Gender.* Urbana and Chicago: University of Illinois Press, 2003; "Understanding the Tradition of Shiva." Toronto: Benjamin's Park Memorial Chapel, 2005. http://www.benjamins.ca/Static/shiva_background.htm (accessed May 21, 2005) Yolen, Jane, ed. "Youth Without

Age, Life Without Death." *Favorite Folktales from Around the World*, 457–465. New York: Pantheon Books, 1986.

Julia Kelso

Diet Culture

Diet culture comprises all customs and practices associated with losing, or attempting to lose, body weight. It includes narratives, customs, and beliefs. Dieting is widely practiced in North America; women and girls particularly experience pressure to achieve and maintain a low body weight. Mainstream cultural judgments of women overvalue their physical appearance and favor underweight female bodies as most attractive. Thus, dieting is ubiquitous for contemporary North American women. Countless books, articles, television programs, advertisements, and films explore the alleged problem of overweight and give purported solutions through diets, proprietary food and vitamins, exercise regimens, and psychological techniques. It is nearly impossible to separate cultural aspects of dieting from reputable medical evidence about the dangers of excess weight, since physicians themselves suffer from bias against overweight women.

Folklorist Jean Renfro Anspaugh, in *Fat Like Us* (2001), reports on interviews she conducted with dieters at the Rice House at Duke University in Durham, North Carolina. As a dieter herself, she portrays sympathetically the trials of those who wish to lose weight, their frustrations when they are unable to do so, and their joys at success. She shows that the narrative that accompanies weight loss reflects struggle and changing self-identity. Anthropologist Mimi Nichter, in *Fat Talk: What Girls and Their Parents Say About Dieting* (2000), notes crucial differences between White and Black teenagers' communications about body image. White teenagers verbally criticize their own and others' weight and body shape, and talk extensively about dieting. However, they talk about dieting much more than they actually practice it. This "fat talk" seems to be a pivotal element of their socialization process. Black girls talk much less of dieting than do their White counterparts, and show greater acceptance of body weight and shape. For them, projecting attitude and self-confidence, not simply being thin, is the paramount factor of attractiveness.

Stories of new diets spread rapidly and informally through word of mouth and the Internet, much as do urban/contemporary legends. Those based in folklore include the grapefruit diet, in which one eats a half grapefruit or drinks a glass of grapefruit juice with each meal; the cabbage soup diet, in which one consumes almost nothing but cabbage soup; and the negative-calorie diet, in which one consumes only those foods, such as celery, which purportedly require more energy to digest than they provide in calories. Less serious takes on the practice are the cotton ball diet, in which one eats cotton balls to experience a feeling of fullness and thus consume less actual food; or the amputation diet, in which one loses weight by amputating a limb.

Feminists have long pointed out that the social pressure to diet stems from patriarchy's need to symbolically and literally control women. Thin females take up less space and are less imposing, and a single-minded focus on weight can drain their energy and distract attention from worthwhile activities. Feminist scholars like Susan Bordo note that in North American mainstream society, weight preoccupation inflicts impossible goals on women. Media images of women have become progressively thinner. Fashion models, for example, must maintain such low body fat that they retain the look of prepubescent girls, but they also risk serious health problems from osteoporosis to heart failure. Societal pressures are often blamed for women and girls developing eating disorders such as anorexia and bulimia. Girls face contradictory pressures: surrounded by, and internalizing, the drive to be thin, while simultaneously besieged by a culture of food abundance. Women perceived as overweight are too often presumed to be unable to control their urges and behavior around food, which is translated into a moral failing comparable to that which stigmatizes women who fail to repress their sexual urges. Still, movements for fat acceptance—such as the National Association to Advance Fat Acceptance—have arisen in response to these pressures. *See also:* Beauty; Fashion; Feminisms; Folk Custom; Folk Medicine; Foodways; Magazines, Women's and Girls'; Popular Culture; Sexuality.

References: Anspaugh, Jean Renfro. *Fat Like Us*. Durham, NC: Windows on History Press, Inc., 2001; Bordo, Susan. *Unbearable Weight: Feminism, Western Culture, and the Body*. Second edition. Berkeley: University of California Press, 2004; National Association to Advance Fat Acceptance. n.d. http://naafa.org (accessed August 10, 2008); Nichter, Mimi. *Fat Talk: What Girls and their Parents Say About Dieting*. Cambridge, MA: Harvard University Press, 2000.

Theresa A. Vaughan

Divination Practices

Divination refers to the ascertaining of otherwise unknowable information through extraordinary means, such as via dreams or visions, trance states, supernatural contact, by the use of magical tools or devices, or through the intuitive interpretation of phenomena in the natural world. Diviners strive to answer questions that fall outside the range of ordinary methods of scientific-rational inquiry. Typically, practioners pose questions about future events; past disasters whose causes cannot be explained; things unknown, hidden from sight, or removed in space; appropriate conduct in critical situations, including the healing of illness; determining the times and modes of religious worship; and making decisions about when to perform particular tasks.

Divination practices are numerous and range from simple binary devices such as flipping a coin or acknowledging the appearance of omens to more complex pictographic systems requiring oral narrative interpretative methods such as the medieval European tarot system and the Chinese oracle, *I Ching*. The *I Ching* is one of the most complex, as well as the most studied, of divination tools; today it is used worldwide, including by many North Americans.

American anthropologist Barbara Tedlock considers divination as an alternate, rather than an inferior, mode of cognition, one in which individual creativity operates, and "meaning emerges as a result of experiential immersion in the expressive patterns of the symbolic medium, which is grasped intuitively" (191–192). Seen in this light, women who practice certain types of skilled divination may be understood as exploring and mastering an intuitive way of receiving, representing, and transmitting knowledge and healing.

Modern divination is often conducted in personal, informal settings, but many historical oracles required the cooperation of skilled specialists, support staff, and a dedicated sacred space for the performance of divination as ritualized theatrical enactments. The Old Nordic *seidr*, for instance, required a chorus of singers to help induce the trance state of the *volva*, or female diviner, who imparted information about agricultural outcomes and the personal destinies of the men and women in the audience.

Anthropologists have attempted to classify divination according to various criteria. Zeusse's well-known typology posits three major categories into which divination practices fall: intuitive divination, possession or trance-mediated divination, and wisdom or systematized divination. Intuitive forms include the interpretation of dreams, visions, and omens, and tend to occur spontaneously in natural folk settings. Possession is traditional in institutionalized divination settings, such as that undertaken by the ancient Greek oracle, known as the Pythia, at Delphi. Likewise, séance mediums and others who enter into involuntary states often make contact with supernatural entities that may convey oracular insight. Other trance mediums claim to channel non-corporeal entities.

By far the largest category, systematized divination practices include techniques such as sortilege (random selection) that employ devices, tools, or other means to perform a reading, often in conjunction with an interpretive commentary. Systematized divination methods include astrology (reading the stars via a horoscope), chiromancy (palm reading), haruspicy (studying the internal organs of sacrificed animals), tasseography (reading tea leaves), bibliomancy (interpreting random selections from sacred scriptures and other books), runes, dowsing (interpreting the movements of a divining rod or other object to locate water, precious metals, and other hidden things), numerology, the tarot, African Ifa divination (involving a wide variety of ritual practices designed to gain guidance and knowledge of the future), and the *I Ching*. An interpreter may use various and eclectic traditional means to interpret the results of a divination session.

Divination practitioners often employ a number of different techniques to achieve a result. For example, numerological and/or astrological calculations might be incorporated into a tarot reading to divine pertinent information about the querent in order to better understand the characteristics of her personality and its role in her unfolding destiny. Importantly, as a necessary means of propitiating mysterious forces at work in disease or misfortune, the practice of divination often extends beyond mere diagnosis; a diviner may prepare medicines and/or talismans and/or prescribe or perform ritual expiations to promote the process of healing or to reverse bad luck.

Divination has long been associated with women. The stereotypical fortune-teller and her crystal ball, for instance, and the modern conflation of romance and astrology come to mind. While such images of women as psychics and palm readers are hardly representative of the scope of divination practices or of the diversity of its practitioners, historically, in fact, in many peasant societies, women dominated personal and household divination, interpreting domestic omens and family members' dreams. They also acted as folk healers, curers, and midwives, and often included divination in these activities.

Divination by women is not confined to rural circumstances, however. In the nineteenth and early twentieth centuries, young women in North America, England, and parts of Europe used traditional spells and formulae on specified occasions to divine a vision of a future husband or to determine who would next marry. In modern times, this type of love-and-marriage divination survives in the popular, "He loves me, he loves me not" daisy-petal counting formula and in a popular wedding tradition in which unmarried women guests line up to catch the bride's bouquet; the one who catches it will be the next to marry.

American New Age healers use a variety of oracles to address women's concerns, including using a pendulum to determine the sex of an unborn child or employing the *I Ching* or tarot cards to divine the cause of psychic discord. Professional psychics may also enter a trance state to obtain hidden information for their clients regarding love, health, relationships, and careers, as well as for conveying spiritual guidance.

North American popular culture has successfully coopted divination practices in combination with women's interests in terms of magazine and newspaper horoscopes, astrology Web sites that calculate life purpose and romantic compatibility, and telephone hotlines for consulting psychics. Commercial versions of divination such as these may be perceived as less efficacious than traditional means. In any case, divination is commonly seen as a way of access to magical or supernatural explanations for our most cherished, basic, and ordinary concerns. *See also: Curandera*; Folk Belief; Folk Medicine; Fortune-Teller; Midwifery; Sex Determination; Wedding.

References: Blacker, Carmen, and Michael Loewe. *Oracles and Divination*. Boulder, CO: Shambhala Publications, Inc., 1981; Mair, Lucy. "Divination" in *Magic, Witchcraft, and Religion: An Anthropological Study of the Supernatural*, eds. Arthur C. Lehmann and James E. Myers, 262–269. Fourth edition. Mountain View, CA: Mayfield Publishing Company, 1985; Nunez, Luis Manuel. *Santeria: A Practical guide to Afro-Caribbean Magic*. Woodstock, CT: Spring Publications, Inc., 1992; Parke, H. W. *Sibyls and Sibylline Prophecy in Classical Antiquity*. London and New York: Routledge, 1988; Peek, Philip M. *African Divination Systems: Ways of Knowing*. Bloomington and Indianapolis: Indiana University Press, 1991; Tedlock, Barbara. "Divination as a Way of Knowing: Embodiment, Visualisation, Narrative, and Interpretation." *Folklore*, vol. 112, no. 2 (October 1, 2001): 189–197; Thiselton-Dyer, T. F. *Folklore of Women as Illustrated by Legendary and Traditionary Tales, Folk-Rhymes, Proverbial Sayings, Superstitions, Etc*. Chicago: A. C. McClurg & Co., 1906; Von Franz, Marie-Louise. *On Divination and Synchronicity: The Psychology of Meaningful Chance*. Toronto: Inner City Books, 1980; Wigzell, Faith. *Reading Russian Fortunes: Print Culture, Gender and Divination in Russia from 1765*. Cambridge: Cambridge University Press, 1998.

Alina Autumn Christian

Divorce

Divorce is the legal dissolution of a state-sanctioned marriage. With the increase in the divorce rate in North America in recent decades, the divorce process has come to be acknowledged in many quarters as a contemporary rite of passage. Although still generally considered a mark of personal failure to make a marriage "work," the announcement of an impending or completed divorce is now more often met with remarks like "Congratulations," rather than "I'm so sorry to hear it."

During the colonial period in the United States, men and women could be granted a divorce on the grounds of adultery or desertion. If a married person was discovered having an extramarital affair, or if one spouse had abandoned the marriage bed for at least two years, a divorce could be granted; only the man was legally permitted to remarry. Women rarely obtained any economic benefit from divorce, and were more likely impoverished by it, while men profited from having fewer expenses. Since obtaining a divorce was such an ordeal, women often opted simply to desert unfaithful or abusive husbands to live as well as they could on their own.

After the American Revolution, more states granted divorce for cruel treatment in addition to adultery and abandonment. Divorced women (with or without children) were not usually provided financial support, and were stigmatized as persons "fallen from the married estate" due to some failing of their own. Canada permitted divorce on the grounds of sexual impotence, along with desertion and adultery in the 1700s. However, by 1867, divorce was possible only with proof of adultery.

After the two world wars of the twentieth century, North American divorce rates rose dramatically, despite the fact that divorce was still relatively difficult to obtain. For middle-class and upper-class women, who had benefited by becoming part of the workforce while their male partners were away at war, greater financial independence inspired confidence to seek independence from unhappy or abusive marriages. By and large, heterosexual North American women were beginning to view men in a different light, and divorced women were becoming more readily accepted by society because divorce was more common. Especially among the White, Protestant middle class, marriage came to be viewed not solely as an economic relationship maintained for the survival of the partners and their children, but as a source of personal fulfillment. Hence, divorce came to be seen in some quarters as a personal remedy rather than as a social or spiritual illness.

Divorce became common during the last half of the twentieth century, especially in the United States, Canada (legalized in 1968), the countries of the European Union, Japan, and Korea. The Roman Catholic Church disallows divorce as a matter of doctrine because it breaks the sacramental bond of marriage. As a consequence, it was not until 1997 that divorce became legal in Ireland, and not until 2004 in Chile; as of 2005, it was still illegal in Malta and the Philippines. While some segments of North American society continue to push for stricter divorce laws, evidence points to the conclusion that divorced women are better off emotionally than those who remain in troubled marriages. An American study published in 1985 revealed that five years after divorce, two-thirds of women are happier with their lives; similar results were obtained by British researchers in 2005.

Currently, the primary reasons for divorce in North America are adultery and desertion; provided sufficient evidence, most states also permit divorce on the grounds of non-support, gross neglect of duty, alcohol and drug addiction, bigamy, and physical or mental cruelty. Of U.S. divorce proceedings, 55 to 60 percent are initiated by the wife. Her action, however, is frequently precipitated by the husband's request. Coincident with the rise of the women's movement, no-fault divorce emerged during the 1970s and 1980s, allowing couples to dissolve marriages without apportioning blame. Many individuals concerned over the apparent ease of divorce started to blame the women's movement for the destruction of the family. Politicians increasingly encouraged women to remain in their marriages.

The late 1980s saw increased social hostility toward women who sought to live independently from husbands to pursue their own careers. The NBC network ran a report that proposed that the more a woman achieved in her career, the greater were her chances for divorce. Television dramas such as *thirtysomething* and sitcoms like *Kate and Allie* portrayed divorced women as embittered and career-driven, suggesting they would be much happier as soon as they remarried. The television networks went so far as to marry off the lead females in *Kate and Allie* and *Moonlighting* to bland characters in order to demonstrate the network's belief in marriage. Cultural critics and politicians labeled mothers who divorced their husbands as irresponsible, a danger to their children, and a detriment to society. The film *Kramer vs. Kramer* (1979), based on an actual couple's experiences, vilified the mother for leaving her child. *The War of the Roses* (1989) portrayed a couple attempting divorce finally driven to murder one another. In the 1990s, *The First Wives' Club* (1996) involved three women who financially supported their husbands at the start of their marriages supplanted by younger women. In it, the older women are advised by Ivana Trump, playing herself, who tells them: "Don't get mad, get everything." *See also:* Class; Consciousness Raising; Feminisms; Film; Folklore About Women; Marriage; Popular Culture; Rites of Passage; Sexism; Women's Movement.

References: DiCanio, Margaret. *The Encyclopedia of Marriage, Divorce, and the Family.* New York: Facts on File, Inc., 1989; DiFonzo, J. Herbie. *Beneath the Fault Line: The Popular and Legal Culture of Divorce in Twentieth-Century America.* Charlottesville: University Press of Virginia, 1997; Faludi, Susan. *Backlash: The Undeclared War Against American Women.* New York: Random House, 1995; Frith, Maxine. "Women happier than men after divorce, study shows." *The Independent* (UK), July 4, 2005. http://www.independent.co.uk/news/uk/this-britain/women-happier-than-men-after-divorce-study-shows-497550.html (accessed August 9, 2008); Phillips, Roderick. *Putting Asunder: A History of Divorce in Western Society.* Cambridge: Cambridge University Press, 1988.

Claire Dodd

Dolls

Human-like figures made for ritual, amusement, and educational purposes, dolls have been frequently associated with the domestic training of female children. Scholars have begun to debate whether these objects could be religious articles or children's toys, but perhaps not both. Recent work on play and fertility ritual utilizing African sculpture, Hopi kachinas, and dolls in Alaskan Native cultures project a continuum of community involvement with dolls that may begin in childhood but does not end there. Dolls appeal across ages and genders in folktales, foodways, music, dance, ritual, popular beliefs, mass culture, and craft.

In regard to folktales, Stith Thompson's *Motif-Index of Folk-Literature* lists dolls who prompt forgetful fiancés to remember their brides; act as "magic statues" in Irish, Italian, Jewish, Chinese, and Eskimo tales; answer for fugitives in Greenland; hold kings in their clutches; furnish treasure in Italian tales; and marry humans or become fairies in Indian tales. In Europe, the merging of the confection dolls of medieval and Renaissance Europe with tales of passion resulted in stories like "The Sugar Puppet," which tells of an Italian princess, who, fearing her husband's rage, leaves a life-sized doll made of candy in her bed. The prince stabs it, repents, and the couple reunites. Sexual tension often accompanies the folkloric use of dolls in Anglo American tales.

In an example that draws on foodways, music, dance, and ritual in Native American culture, male and female adults clothe and feed Hopi kachinas, and specific communities address the figures for divine intervention. Clifford Geertz (1987) notes that in the Sa'lakwmanawyat ceremony, the Sa'lako dolls, or "the two little girls," dance to the "Grinding Song" with the help of their handlers. "Then, when the two little girls have ground their sweet-corn meal fine, they scoop it onto small wicker plaques and pass it among the people, so they may partake of it," in what he calls "an act of communion," a "sacred blessing" intended to reinforce community values and bring happiness to the audience, the performers, and the dolls' caretakers. Those who provide the meal for the ceremony do so with the hope that their grandchildren will learn to grind maize, regarded as a crucial female contribution to traditional Hopi society.

In Latino communities, dolls can also assume magical properties; *brujas* (witches) may work magic or put a hex on someone via homemade dolls, as is more commonly associated with Voudon ("voodoo"). Also among Latinas, in the rite of passage called the *quinceañera*, the final doll that a girl receives from her *madrina* (sponsor) symbolizes her passage from girlhood to young adulthood. While dolls remain culturally linked to concepts of the feminine, especially in North American cultures, dolls have not existed solely to impress caretaking skills onto young girls. In fact, Miriam Formanek-Brunell (1993) finds that middle-class Anglo girls in the United States in the late nineteenth century actively resisted such training by "staging frequent doll funerals."

Although some female children have performed rituals to rid themselves of domesticated dolls, American adults of both sexes have attributed power to dolls they possessed. Wendy Lavitt (1982) tells of a Union soldier, who, upon finding a rag doll on a Southern plantation, kept it as a talisman, carried it throughout the war, and returned safely home with it. Wayland Hand (1981) reports that dolls appeared in U.S. popular beliefs in mid-twentieth-century Ohio: a Metropolitan Opera baritone propped a battered "mascot" on his dressing table during all of his performances for good luck, and a woman noted that, if an old doll kept in a dresser was moved in any way, she experienced misfortune.

Popular belief about the power of dolls to benefit or harm humans continually reappears in American mass culture via movies and television. Jacqueline Fulmer (2003), examining the 1995 horror film *Tales from the Hood*, notes that it borrows elements from African American folklore, including dolls. A doll carrying the spirit of a murdered slave kills an African American public relations man in retribution for his laughter at a Klansman's racist jokes, and then, along with an army of other spirit-inhabited dolls, eats the Klansman himself. Ruth Bass (1990) notes that dolls have connections with the dead in African American lore—doll heads, small cups, or toy animals used to be placed on the graves of small children to assuage those who died young, much like the murdered slaves in *Tales from the Hood*. As with the dolls in *Tales*, such objects serve to inspire deference in the living as much as to placate the dead.

The notion of dolls coming to life, either as the benign Hopi "little girls" or as the vengeful slave dolls in *Tales from the Hood*, echoes the Jewish legend of the Golem and has inspired films such as *The Devil Doll* (1936), *Dolls* (1986), *Child's Play 1, 2*, and *3* (1988, 1990, and 1991), culminating in *The Bride of Chucky* (1998), all of which involve dolls coming to life to take the lives of humans. Ovid's story of Pygmalion, of a man's desire to create the perfect woman, also reappears in popular culture: window-dressing models come to life in *One Touch of Venus* (1948), *Mannequin* (1987), and *Mannequin Two: On the Move* (1991). A little girl's longing for her dead mother in *Life-Size* (2000) brings to life a fashion doll, played by real model Tyra Banks.

Reflecting popular culture, yet not mass-produced, KISS (Kisekae Set System) digital paper dolls, software originating with male Japanese computer programmers, emphasize the erotic manipulation underlying the Pygmalion theme. By clicking a mouse, users undress and re-dress dolls—drawn as schoolgirls, pixies, dominatrixes, anime (Japanese animation), or Western cartoon characters, but most posed as pinup girls—on a computer screen. As described in Steven Heller's *Sex Appeal: The Art of Allure in Graphic and Advertising Design* (2000), "the open-ended play of paper dolls shifts into a game of interactive striptease." KISS consumers interact and exchange dolls on Web sites, a very different form of folk community than that of the Hopi Sa'lako dolls, but nonetheless a community of adults finding a kind of fulfillment through the creation and manipulation of dolls.

Dolls in folklore reflect more than childhood amusement and education; they also mirror adult sexuality from a variety of angles. From the nineteenth century onward, wedding-cake dolls, miniature bride-and-groom pairings—first created with flour paste, then manufactured in pipe cleaners, bisque, celluloid, and plastic, sometimes dressed by family members—celebrate heterosexual marriage at the intersection of foodways, handicraft, and mass culture. In the United States, hobbyists of varying sexual orientation repaint Barbie dolls to become "Trailer-Park Barbie," or Ken dolls to become "Kendra," thereby blurring distinctions between class, gender, and folk art versus mass-production. *See also:* Barbie Doll; Folk Belief; Folk Group; Folktale; Foodways; Gender; Graves and Gravemarkers; Marriage; Popular Culture; *Quinceañera*; Ritual; Sexuality.

References: Ashliman, D. L. *A Guide to Folktales in the English Language.* New York: Greenwood Press, 1987; Bass, Ruth. "Mojo." *Mother Wit from the Laughing Barrel: Readings in the Interpretation of Afro-American Folklore,* ed. Alan Dundes, 380–377. Jackson: University Press of Mississippi, 1990; Cameron, Elisabeth L. *Isn't S/He a Doll?: Play and Ritual in African Sculpture.* Los Angeles: UCLA Fowler Museum of Cultural History, 1996; Faraone, Jim. "Steven Pim/Grant Salminen/Jennifer Scaff King." *Fashion Doll Makeovers III: Learn from the Artists,* 62–63. Cumberland, MD: Hobby House Press, 1999; Fulmer, Jacqueline. "Men Ain't All": A Reworking of Masculinity in *Tales from the Hood,* or, Grandma Meets the Zombie." *Journal of American Folklore,* vol. 115, nos. 457/458 (2002): 422–442; Geertz, Armin W., and Michael Lomatuway'ma. *Children of Cottonwood: Piety and Ceremonialism in Hopi Indian Puppetry.* Lincoln: University of Nebraska Press, 1987; Hand, Wayland D., Anna Casetta, and Sondra B. Thiederman. *Popular Beliefs and Superstitions: A Compendium of American Folklore.* Boston: G. K. Hall and Company, 1981; Heller, Steven, ed. *Sex Appeal: The Art of Allure in Graphic and Advertising Design.* New York: Allworth Press, 2000; Lavitt, Wendy. *American Folk Dolls.* New York: A. A. Knopf, 1982; Lee, Molly C., ed. *Not Just a Pretty Face: Dolls and Human Figurines in Alaska Native Cultures.* Fairbanks: University of Alaska Museum, 1999; Page, Linda Garland, and Hilton Smith. *The Foxfire Book of Toys and Games: Reminiscences and Instructions from Appalachia.* New York: E. P. Dutton, 1985; Thompson, Stith. *Motif-Index of Folk-Literature.* Bloomington: Indiana University Press, 1955.

Jacqueline Fulmer

Doula

A doula is a woman professionally trained to support and comfort another woman during pregnancy, childbirth, and the postpartum period. She may also give nutritional advice to the mother during her pregnancy. *Doula,* a Greek word, means "servant-woman." In North America, there are two main types of doulas—those who assist women during labor, and those who attend to the new mother in her home for up to several weeks after the birth. A doula differs from a midwife in that she does not generally perform any medical tasks and is responsible only for emotional and spiritual aid to the mother.

Historically, the role of assisting a woman during childbirth with care, support, and comfort belonged to family members, close friends, or midwife assistants. The popularity of paid, professionally trained doulas in North America coincides with the rise of the alternative-birth movement of the 1970s, a response to the twentieth century's increasingly medicalized birth procedures, in which a woman labored alone with intermittent nursing and was usually drugged for the delivery.

Doulas feel that their role is to provide some of the assistance traditionally given by female friends and family, increasingly absent in industrialized societies. Their work provides a much more positive birth experience for the mother than the allopathic medical system offers. They generally encourage the presence of the father, but feel that they offer both parents a calm and experienced presence in what can be an extremely stressful situation. Doulas may have strong opinions about medical intervention in the birth process. Most feel that their role is to serve as advocates for laboring women. They know and can clearly state the woman's needs and preferences when she may have difficulty articulating them, whereas the medical profession may not always be counted upon to be so respectful. Many doulas have the skills to catch babies, but this is not properly part of their role; they are usually trained in non-medical and non-pharmacological forms of pain relief, such as massage, aromatherapy, and visualization and relaxation techniques. Postpartum doulas help the family in the days immediately following birth. They may aid with establishing breastfeeding, cleaning, cooking, and tending the new baby or other children. They are also present to answer questions that the new mother may have about childcare, and seek to provide reassurance, help, and much needed rest for her.

Becoming a doula does require certification, akin to midwifery; the relationship between doulas and the medical profession in North America is somewhat ambivalent, although an increasing number of medical doctors feel that doulas offer important maternal support without excessively challenging medical care decisions. In this respect, doulas are generally better accepted by the medical profession than are midwives. Various major studies have shown that the presence of a trained doula during birth significantly reduces length and complications of labor and improves both physiological and psychological outcomes. While some midwives perceive doulas as a threat to their own supportive role, most midwives welcome them and the continuous emotional and physical support they provide. *See also:* Breastfeeding; Childbirth and Childrearing; Folk Medicine; Midwifery; Pregnancy.

References: Campera, L., C. Garcia, C. Diaz, O. Ortiz, S. Reynoso, and A. Langer. "'Alone, I wouldn't have known what to do': A Qualitative Study on Social Support during Labor and Delivery in Mexico." *Social Science and Medicine*, Vol. 77, no. 3 (1998): 395–403; DONA International. n.d. http://www.dona.org (accessed August 10, 2008); Klaus, M. H., J. H. Kennell, and P. H. Klaus. *Mothering the Mother: How a Doula Can Help You Have a Shorter, Easier, and Healthier Birth.* Reading, MA: Addison-Wesley, 1993.

Theresa A. Vaughan

Dowry

The dowry consists of the objects a woman takes with her to her husband's house after marriage (in patrilocal societies). These goods may include textiles, jewelry, money, and household items. In many parts of Europe, a woman, in preparation for her marriage, would accumulate useful things for her dowry chest. In Europe, it was considered custom, not law, for the bride's family to give her a marriage gift, and the tradition remained among European immigrants to North America. In the late eighteenth and early nineteenth centuries, for example, Pennsylvania German brides customarily received a wooden chest that was often painted with their names or initials. This personal piece of furniture was most likely filled with clothes, and also with pots and pans, cutlery, and fabrics to be used in her new home.

While old Pennsylvania German chests survive, scholars can only speculate about the kinds of objects that were placed within them. The contemporary dowry traditions of Turkey, however, provide us with an instance in which the contents of the dowry chest are well documented. When a wedding takes place in a Turkish village, the dowry chest is ceremoniously carried from a woman's natal home to her new husband's. A bride's chest is filled with her handcrafts, such as scarves with tatting along the edges, embroidered kitchen and bathroom towels, and pillowcases. Village women also add rugs that they have woven with their sisters, mothers, or female companions, and saddlebags to be carried by their future husbands to market, displaying the women's weaving skills for all to admire. The pile of rugs displayed in a young woman's home signals her productivity, artistry, and availability for marriage.

As in many dowry traditions, in Turkey a girl prepares herself for her marriage by engaging in the creation of items to be used in her future home. Her dowry chest contains items made by her, purchased objects, and even heirloom pieces received from previous generations. Most women make decisions as to which of these things to use in the home, which to keep and pass on to their daughters, and even which to sell if the need for emergency cash arises. Rugs and other textiles passed from one dowry chest to another provide a wonderful resource of traditional designs for weavers.

Among women in India, and, to some extent, Indian immigrants in North America, the generic term "dowry" encompasses three distinct kinds of gifts, all referred to as dowry. Customarily, two principal gifts go from the bride's family to the groom's house: the sacred gift of a virgin—their daughter—and the secular gift of a negotiated dowry in return for the acceptance of the daughter as a bride. In addition, the bride receives from her parents a trousseau—a personal gift of clothing and jewelry that is not technically part of the dowry, but is colloquially called "dowry" as well. When a union is being negotiated among the parents in an arranged marriage, one of the key questions to be settled is the amount the groom's family expects to receive. Many people, especially those living in villages, will state a sum of cash, and they may add other items, such as livestock or appliances. The assumption is that the husband will provide his new wife with food and shelter for the rest of her life, through his own earnings and his family's assistance. Since the woman will not work outside of the home (though she will surely work hard inside of it), her monetary contribution to the household arrives with her in the form of the dowry provided by her parents.

One rationale for giving one's daughter a dowry that includes expensive pieces of jewelry is to pass on to the daughter her share of the family wealth, since the ancestral home, the furnishings, and other property will generally be given to the sons. It is common for families to marry off their daughters before arranging the marriages of their sons. The reason for this is to show that the family is prosperous enough to accumulate and give away multiple dowries—one for each daughter—before receiving any dowry from the families of their sons' brides. Less-affluent families will recycle bits of the dowry, marrying a son first to be able to marry a daughter next.

Parents give their daughters gold jewelry, which may be liquidated in case of an emergency. Other items included in the dowry also serve the bride, though indirectly. Parents hope to buy a respected social position for the daughter in her new home by sending with her things for the family to enjoy, such as a refrigerator, a stove, or a color television set. The groom's family commonly requests a bicycle, a motor scooter, or, more rarely, a car. Expensive dowry items tax the financial capacity of the bride's family: the more the household items cost, the less money there is to buy jewelry for her. Although the bride may receive immediate gratification by arriving with many coveted gadgets, these are not (like her jewelry) hers exclusively, and, most importantly, she may not sell them for immediate cash. Appliances and vehicles, unlike gold jewelry, devalue with time and cannot be secretly sold.

The Indian example shows that the parents are responsible for providing their daughters with the household necessities for married life. While this was the case in the United States when conventional European dowry traditions were still followed, now friends, not family, are the providers of the items needed for the new life. Guests at a bridal shower give a woman the kinds of personal items usually received as part of her trousseau, and guests at the wedding give the new couple the household items historically received in the dowry: linen, cutlery, and crockery, in addition to small appliances. *See also:* Brideprice; Class; Courtship; Crafting; Daughter; Divorce; Embroidery; Engagement; Folk Art; Folk Custom; Folk Group; Folklore About Women; Gender; Housekeeping; Immigration; Marriage; Material Culture; Needlework; Rugmaking; Sewing; Sexism; Virginity; Weaving; Wedding; Women's Work.

References: Elson, Vickie G. *Dowries from Kutch: A Women's Folk Art Tradition in India.* Los Angeles: Museum of Cultural History, 1979; Fabian, Monroe H. *The Pennsylvania-German Decorated Chest.* New York: Universe Books, 1978; Fruzzetii, Lina M. *The Gift of a Virgin: Women, Marriage, and Ritual in a Bengali Society.* New Brunswick, NJ: Rutgers University Press, 1982; Glassie, Henry. *Turkish Traditional Art Today.* Bloomington: Indiana University Press, 1993; Goody, Jack, and T. J. Tambiah. *Bridewealth and Dowry.* Cambridge: Cambridge University Press, 1987.

Pravina Shukla

E

Elder Care

Elder caregiving is defined as providing assistance for senior citizens who cannot care for themselves. The contributions of women in mothering children are universally recognized. The role of women in caring for elders, however, is less celebrated; even more than for their roles in childcare, women have been responsible for providing care for their aging parents and in-laws, even in cultures that designate sons as responsible for elder care. Traditionally, the needs of elders were handled first by wives, then by daughters, daughters-in-law, and other female relatives or close friends. One of the most well-known folkloric caregivers is a granddaughter, Red Riding Hood, whose adventures begin when she takes a meal to her infirm grandmother. But as more women enter the workforce and the elderly population grows, the social and economic impact of elder care on women is becoming more complex; it is also becoming better understood.

Elder-care duties range from simply providing companionship, emotional support, or recreational activities, such as taking someone for a walk, to providing personal care and hygiene such as bathing, dressing, grooming, and home-based medical treatments. In many folk groups, caregiving women assist family members in their spiritual preparations for death. Caregiving often extends to other services such as housekeeping, food preparation, shopping, home maintenance, and providing transportation. In extreme cases, such as with persons suffering from dementia, the caregiver also handles legal and financial matters on behalf of the aged individual.

According to the U.S. Department of Health and Human Services' Administration on Aging (AOA), 75 percent of elder caregivers are women. An AOA study found that women caregivers spend 50 percent more time helping older family members than do men. More than half of the women are employed outside the home, and often find that their caregiving responsibilities adversely affect their jobs. Elder-care issues are more prominent, albeit little researched, in North American minority populations as women in these cultures participate more frequently and more intensively in caring for their aging relatives than do members of the dominant culture, who increasingly rely on nursing homes and other for-profit institutions to provide the daily care and support their elders need. Even with this increasing reliance upon professionals, a great many women family members are still involved in providing emotional care for elderly relatives.

And, despite or because of the increasing reliance on professionals to care for the elderly, there is a growing body of folk narrative about various experiences of dealing with elderly parents. Personal-experience narratives emerge in practice, as one person relates her experiences either to a friend who has just begun the process or to friends who function as the caregiver's support network; narrators and listeners—as in other informal therapeutic networks such as those for breast cancer survivors—exchange tales, providing support and empathy by example, as well as laughter and tears.

Another neglected source of the folklore of elder care is professional caregivers, who have their own networks and sites for exchanging information, stories, and experiences about their clients, the medical system, and social services bureaucracies. The exchange of personal-experience narratives provides critical information as well as emotional support during extended periods of caregiving. Such exchanges also occur frequently among professional and family care providers, who, in the optimal situation, provide support for each other as well as for an elder.

Medical developments in the United States and Canada are producing societies of people who not only live longer, but who suffer from chronic rather than acute medical conditions. Unlike acute conditions, chronic medical conditions are expensive, prolonged, and frequently interfere with a person's daily activities. Care of the chronically ill requires more than dedication. Women commonly face the burden of simultaneously caring for aging parents, their own children, and employment commitments. Consequently, women caregivers commonly suffer from stress conditions brought on by guilt, time limitations, financial costs, and serving multiple social roles. Women caregivers experience a higher incidence of depression and other health disorders than do women in the general population. On the other hand, women often report that despite the hardships, the experience is enriching. Cultural and personal attitudes about caregiving range from invocations of the biblical injunction to "Honor thy father and thy mother" (Exodus 20:12) to expression in pessimistic folktales of women's resignation to their fates (see Ashliman). For many caregivers, the folk saying "It's a blessing in disguise" has acquired new and vivid meanings. Deborah Hoffman's Academy Award-nominated documentary film, *Complaints of a Dutiful Daughter* (1994), for example, is a superb illustration of a caregiver's efforts to retain her good humor as her mother falls victim to Alzheimer's disease.

The well-being of caregivers is an evolving area of social concern, evidenced by a proliferation of research studies on and an increasing number of organizations and support groups, many of which are accessible on the Internet. Public policy is changing as evidenced in the United States by the passage of the Older American Act of 2000, which established the National Family Caregiver Support Program, and in Canada by the passage in 2003 of British Columbia's Community Care and Assisted Living Act. *See also:* Aging;

Daughter; Folktale; Grandmother; Healing; Nursing; Personal-Experience Narrative; Red Riding Hood; Women's Work.

References: Abel, Emily K. *Hearts of Wisdom: American Women Caring for Kin, 1850–1940.* Cambridge: Harvard University Press, 2000; Ashliman, D. L. "Aging and Death in Folklore." n.d. http://www.pitt.edu/~dash/aging.html (accessed May 24, 2007); Elder Care Online. n.d http://www.econline.net/ (accessed June 20, 2006); Family Caregiver Alliance (FGA): National Center on Caregiving. "Caregiver Heath: A Population at Risk." http://www.caregiver.org/caregiver/jsp/content_node.jsp?nodeid=1822 (accessed August 9, 2008); Hoffman, Deborah. *Complaints of a Dutiful Daughter.* P.O.V. Independent Directors Series. Boston: WGBH Television (PBS), 1994; McCleod, Beth Witrogen, ed. *Caregiving: The Spiritual Journey of Love, Loss, and Renewal.* Second edition. Hoboken, NJ: John Wiley & Sons, 2000; ———. *And Thou Shalt Honor: The Caregiver's Companion.* Emmaus, PA: Rodale, 2002.

Gilda Baeza Ortego

Embroidery

Embroidery enriches textiles using needle and thread, occasionally with a full complement of accessories and magical materials such as shells, mirrors, feathers, beads, quills, buttons, sequins, and coins. Embroidery styles tend to be decorative and more aesthetically determined than is the basic ground fabric. Embroidery is an inexpensive and adaptable art form. Women can stitch in between household tasks, can embroider at night after finishing daily duties, and can carry their embroideries with them. Due to the individualistic nature of stitching, along with the limitations of needlework conventions, embroidery is often classed as a minor genre relative to weaving and sewing. Its alliance with domesticity and enduring association with decorative "women's work" further separate it from mainstream scholarly interest. General discussions of embroidery ordinarily emphasize description and technique over theoretical possibilities and aesthetic analysis. As a universal medium with a rich stylistic and symbolic repertoire, however, embroidery is well-suited for studying women's cultural expressiveness within the sphere of women's folklore.

Most embroiderers are women, but men and women do collaborate in cases where men weave and women apply the distinctive embroidery that gives the material its particular identity and aesthetic form (for example, Central African Kuba textiles).

As a cultural expression, embroidery indicates lineage and status, is spiritually and symbolically potent, and visibly manifests tradition, innovation, and change. It can be prescribed yet mutable; for example, religious patterns cross over into secular pieces, thus disseminating the arcane and elevating the domestic. In some non-European traditions, separate bands of embroidery with magical properties offer protection against evil forces during rites of passage when participants are most vulnerable; talismanic designs are placed on clothing to shield susceptible points of entry for spirit possession at the head, neck, chest, and back. In seventeenth-century Dutch art, spinning and weaving symbolize industry and virtue while embroiderers were depicted as both virtuous and lascivious. According to patriarchal Protestant morality, embroidery represented a condemnable luxury criticized for its opulence, sensuality, vanity, and foolishness, which, by association, extended to embroiderers' behavior as well.

Embroidery belongs to post-loom decoration, in which threads are either counted or "free." Counted stitches follow obvious right-angled warp and weft grids by calculating number of stitches to determine size, direction, and pattern (for example, cross-stitch, running, or counted satin stitch). Embroidery stitches also move freely across the surface, thus defying basic structural constraints such as grid lines, fabric width, and seams. Freestyle embroidery creates curvilinear motifs using stitches that bend and undulate, including chain stitch, satin stitch, long stitch, and short stitch. Dense, lush patterns that entirely cover the ground fabric with little waste on the underside resemble weaving and tapestry, while other embroideries highlight the contrast between clusters of complex ornamental patterns and areas of unadorned fabric.

Embroidery's relevance to the study of material culture and gender is critical to the interplay of context, aesthetic choice, and social interaction; it provides a vehicle for the exploration of issues of creativity as well as a basis for the interpretation of views about stitching held by insiders and outsiders. *See also:* Folk Art; Needlework; Sampler; Women's Work.

References: MacAulay, Suzanne P. *Stitching Rites*. Tucson: University of Arizona Press, 2000; Paine, Sheila. *Embroidered Textiles: Traditional Patterns from Five Continents*. London: Thames & Hudson, 1990; Parker, Rozsika. *The Subversive Stitch and the Making of the Feminine*. London: The Women's Press, 1984; Schneider, Jane. "The Anthropology of Cloth." *Annual Review of Anthropology* 16 (1987): 409–448; Weiner, Annette B., and Jane Schneider, eds. *Cloth and Human Experience*. Washington, DC: Smithsonian Institution Press, 1989.

Suzanne P. MacAulay

Engagement

Engagement is a formal declaration of the intention to marry. Becoming engaged (betrothed, affianced) is usually publicly announced by a couple or by their parents. Engagement is regarded as a binding act and a forerunner to marriage.

In patriarchal cultures, it is generally expected that a man will ask for the "hand" of the woman he wishes to marry from her father or other male guardian of her sexuality. If he receives permission, he is then free to ask the woman herself; traditionally, he does so in a half-kneeling posture, enlisting some variant of the formula, "Will you marry me?" His proposal of marriage is often accompanied by his presentation to her of an engagement ring; alternatively, he may wait for her affirmative response before giving her an engagement present. Since the advent of modern feminism, it is no longer unheard of for a woman to propose marriage to a man—or to another woman in locales where same-sex marriage is legal (a few U.S. states and throughout Canada)—but it is possible that his acceptance of her proposal will come back to the couple in the form of taunting or disparaging jokes about his (or her) "manliness" later in the marriage.

The act of becoming engaged can be an elaborate affair in which the giver tries to surprise his or her intended with a ring hidden in food or drink, or in multiple boxes, which the recipient must open until the smallest box reveals the gift. To further add to the recipient's delight, the ritual may be enacted in an exotic location (an expensive restaurant, for example) or in a very public place (at a football game, perhaps, or on television). But sometimes becoming engaged is more subtle and private, particularly if there is a chance that a marriage proposal might be refused.

The giving (usually by a man) and receiving (usually by a woman) of an engagement ring are symbolic of the couple's commitment to marry; when a North American woman wears a diamond ring on the fourth finger of her left hand in public, she is announcing her impending status as a bride. In some countries, both members of a betrothed couple are expected to wear such a ring; however, the marketing to and wearing of engagement rings by men is a recent phenomenon. In contemporary North America, an engagement ring most frequently consists of a single, clear diamond mounted on a gold band; however, in European countries, colored gems or plain bands are more popular. The customary use of clear diamonds for engagement rings resulted from a massive advertising campaign in the 1940s by a private South African corporation, De Beers (now 45 percent owned by Anglo Americans), the world's largest diamond-mining and brokerage company. The engagement ring may double as a wedding ring.

The history of engagement rings may go back to ancient times, but can most reliably be traced to the late medieval period in Europe, when the Roman Catholic Church's Second Lateran Council in 1139 decreed a mandatory waiting period between betrothal and marriage—the engagement period—ostensibly to help couples to avoid making a lifelong, monogamous commitment to one another (the dissolution of which could cost them their immortal souls) under the influence of sexual passion. In some Christian denominations, "banns"—formal and repeated announcements of a couple's intent to marry—are an essential step to a religiously sanctioned marriage. This custom also originated in medieval Europe, where such public announcements were deemed necessary to determine that there were no other claims on a betrothed person, either because of a secret marriage or another, previous, or privately exchanged promise to marry.

An engaged woman might receive handcrafted items, clothes, and/or foodstuffs instead of an engagement ring. In some cultures, engagement is seen as the beginning of marriage; hence, if an engaged woman were to decide to break her engagement, she would be required to file for divorce. In this case, if the man to whom she is engaged dies, she is expected to mourn his death as his widow. In others, a ring (or other object or objects of substantial value) is given to the bride in lieu of a dowry. And in other cultures, the engagement present is understood as a financial investment (or insurance) for the woman to cash in if her husband divorces her or if she becomes a widow. In such cases, if a woman decides to break her engagement, she is expected to return the engagement ring to the man who gave it to her; however, this custom has been legally challenged in recent years as some women claim the gift is theirs to keep. Such challenges represent an interesting intersection of legal practice and social custom.

Engagement celebrations are meant to bring together families and friends to announce the engagement publicly. Friends and family members congratulate the couple and/or toast them as a sign of their recognition of the couple's changed social status. Such celebrations might involve not only eating and drinking, but also singing, dancing, and gift-giving, usually of items that the couple, especially the bride-to-be, will use in their household when they are married. Some engagement parties are large and elaborate, involving caterers and live bands paid to perform in a hired hall. Others are more intimate and less expensive. Today, a North American couple's engagement may also be announced in the couple's community's newspapers. Following the engagement party, the couple's relationship is expected to exclude other suitors.

In all cultures that mandate or acknowledge an engagement period before marriage, it symbolizes a serious promise of commitment on the part of two individuals, and often two families, to merge. While many people view engagement as a testing period for the love and commitment of the intended couple, most engagement customs actually stem from concerns about the couple's—and their families'—economic and social status rather than about the fostering and protection of romantic love. *See also:* Dowry; Folk Custom; Marriage; Rites of Passage; Ritual; Wedding.

References: Ballard, Linda May. *Forgetting Frolic: Marriage Traditions in Ireland.* Belfast: The Institute of Irish Studies in association with the University of Belfast, 1988; Charsley, Simon R. *Rites of Marrying.* Manchester and New York: Manchester University Press, 1991; Laverack, Elizabeth. *With This Ring: 100 Years of Marriage.* London: Elm Books, 1979; Mordecai, Carolyn. *Weddings: Dating & Love Customs of Cultures Worldwide including Royalty.* Phoenix, AZ: Nittany, 1999.

Zainab Jerret

Erotic Folklore

Erotic folklore comprises the traditional practices that express love, sex, various sexualities, and the sociosexual power relations that are played out in and across those sexualities. Depending on one's political, moral, and aesthetic values, erotic folklore may be distinguished as romantic, bawdy, vulgar, obscene, pornographic, or simply "dirty." Erotic expressive forms include the heart-shaped valentine presented to the beloved on Valentine's Day; the disparaging sexual gesture made with mouth, hand, or hips; the singing of sentimental love ballads and rollicking bawdy songs; the performance of bawdy rhymes, riddles, and limericks; the belief that certain foods enhance sexual arousal; and the sexual acts that people engage in when aroused. Additionally, people tell a wide range of stories concerning the pleasures and dangers that can accompany sex (personal-experience narratives, legends, folktales, and jokes).

Folk speech enlists an erotic lexicon that, depending upon the performance context, can range from the sweetly intimate to the derisively distant. Male genitalia include "a set of balls" that may be described metaphorically as "the family jewels," and a penis that may be referred to variously as a "prick," "pecker," "cock," "whang," "shaft," "wiener," "tallywhacker," or "dick." In turn, female breasts become "boobs," "boobies," "tits," and "knockers," and the parts of female genitalia are named variously as a "pussy," "gash," "cherry," "cunt," the "nether regions," or simply "down there." Similarly, engaging in sexual intercourse may be as formal as "copulating," "having conjugal relations," or "fornicating," but frequently it is "sleeping together," "making love," "fucking," "grinding," "knocking boots," "getting it on," or simply "doing it."

As children, girls explore sex and its primary biological ramification (pregnancy) through the sharing of folk beliefs about the body, sexual jokes, and traditional rhymes:

> (Girl's name) and (boy's name) up in a tree
> K-I-S-S-I-N-G
> First comes love
> Then comes marriage
> Then comes (girl's name) with a baby carriage.

Later, as adolescents, girls continue sexual exploration by means of such games as "Spin-the-Bottle" and "Truth-or-Dare," in which girls or girls and boys are required to perform a sexual act and/or tell personal-experience narratives about sexual acts they have performed. The sharing of personal-experience narratives of heterosexual and lesbian encounters continues into adulthood as a major genre through which women explore and define the erotic possibilities of the biological and social body.

Frequently, the biological and social dangers associated with sex are explored through the telling of urban legends. For example, the legend "The Stuck Couple" is about a heterosexual couple who are involved in an extramarital affair. While engaging in sexual intercourse, usually in a small sports car, the couple becomes physically "stuck" in mid-coitus; they are eventually discovered by a passing police officer or motorist who calls for help. In order for a doctor to be able to disengage the stuck couple, a wrecking crew must partially dismantle the car, and the woman is left worrying about how she is going to explain the condition of the car to her husband. And while, in legend, heterosexual sex with a partner may prove embarrassing and/or a danger to the social self, sexual performances that, in one way or another, are viewed as aberrant may prove to be deadly.

If legend is a means to explore sexual danger, song is frequently used to attest to sexual pleasure. Historically, female military personal and college sorority sisters have had access to a corpus of rollicking bawdy songs (for example, "Roll Me Over in the Clover, Roll Me Over and Do It Again") to be performed during bouts of social drinking. Similarly, women blues singers like Bessie Smith have sung the bawdy blues:

> I woke up this morning / with an awful aching head
> My new man had left me / just a room and an empty bed
> Bought me a coffee grinder / got the best one I could find
> So he could grind my coffee / because he had a brand new grind
> He's a deep-sea diver / with a stroke that can't go wrong
> He can touch the bottom / and his wind holds out so long
> He knows how to thrill me / and he thrills me night and day

He's got a new way of loving / almost takes my breath away
Lord he's got the sweetest something / and I told my gal friend Lou
By the way she's raving / she must have gone and tried it too. (Taft 1983: 237)

Such wordplay is also endemic to women's erotic humor, whether in the form of a quick one-liner spoken by a grandmother to her granddaughters, "Before you marry any ol' hairy-legged boy, be sure to look carefully into his genes (jeans)," or as a joke about male sexual incompetence, as in the case of a tale about a sailor who is on shore leave and visits a prostitute but is too drunk to perform sexually:

As he huffed and puffed in his efforts to get his money's worth, he asked how he was doing.
"Oh, about three knots," replied the lady.
"Three knots?" he asked.
"Yeah," she said. "It's not hard. It's not in. And you're not gonna get your money back."

Through their performances of erotic folklore, women become active agents engaged in a social dialogue about the female body as both a biological entity and as a product of ongoing sociocultural construction. *See also:* Folk Belief; Folk Music and Folksong; Folktale; Foodways; Girls' Games; Humor; Joke; Legend, Urban/Contemporary; Personal-Experience Narrative; Sexuality; Valentine's Day.

References: Green, Rayna. "Magnolias Grow in Dirt: the Bawdy Lore of Southern Women." *Southern Exposure*, vol. 4, no. 4 (1977): 29–33; McEntire, Dee L. "Erotic Storytelling: Sexual Experience and Fantasy Letters in *Forum* Magazine." *Western Folklore* 51 (1992): 81–96; Paros, Lawrence. *The Erotic Tongue: A Sexual Lexicon.* Seattle: Madrona Publishers, 1984; Randolph, Vance. *Roll Me in Your Arms: "Unprintable" Ozark Folksongs and Folklore, Vol. I: Folksongs and Music* and *Blow the Candle Out: "Unprintable" Ozark Folksongs and Folklore, Vol. II: Folk Rhymes and Other Lore*, ed., G. Legman. Fayetteville: University of Arkansas Press, 1992; Taft, Michael, ed. *Blues Lyric Poetry: An Anthology.* New York: Garland Press, 1983; Whatley, Mariamne H., and Elissa R. Henken. *Did You Hear about the Girl Who ... ?: Contemporary Legends, Folklore, and Human Sexuality.* New York: New York University Press, 2000.

Cathy Lynn Preston

Ethnicity

Often confused with or considered synonymous with the term "race," ethnicity is defined in terms of historical or national origin, distinctive cultural traits and practices, and/or a community created around ethnic or cultural identification factors such as language, culture, and religion. Ethnicity can be plural and/or contextual. For example, a person may be English among French speakers; English Canadian among Canadians; and Canadian among North Americans.

Ethnicity first came into focus in discussions of feminism during its second wave, in which feminists of Color critiqued liberal and radical feminism as ethnocentric and color-blind. The Combahee River Collective (1986), a group of Black feminist theorists formed in 1974, asserts that feminism must address the concerns of women of Color, and that the only advocates for women of Color are indeed women of Color themselves. The collective argues that those who share an ethnic or cultural identity with others will become one another's best allies based on these cultural characteristics.

Identity and ethnicity mark differences among feminists, giving birth to debates about identity politics, a position that demands that women and men ask and answer the question, "With what aspect of my identity *should* I identify? With which community does my allegiance, based upon this question of identity, lie?" An activist social-justice critique is implicit in this question. However, as feminist philosopher Linda Martin Alcoff argues, identity politics is vague and nowhere defined by either its detractors or advocates. How does identity formation matter in terms of political, social, and cultural constructs?

Further, problems specific to women arise when values ascribed (rightly or wrongly) to the group conflict with women's concerns (such as pressure from male leaders to not use birth control and to have large numbers of children). Too often, recognition and support for women's issues is absent from male leaders' understanding and discourse, and women feel they must choose between ethnic and gender loyalty. Some women explicitly reject feminism for this reason; they feel that their ethnic allegiance is primary. Others reject the sexism in their ethnic movement and feel more comfortable as feminists. Still others, like politician Rosemary Brown in Canada, or theorist bell hooks in the United States, refuse to be coopted by feminist White women or ethnic men, and work to ensure recognition of the intersections of oppressions, not only by race/ethnicity and gender, but also by sexual orientation, class, ability, and a myriad of other aspects.

Folklorists and anthropologists have long recognized a distinction between endogenous identity—a group's own notion of itself—and exogenous identity—created and referenced by those not of the group. For example, the term "Native American," referring to the Indigenous or Native peoples of the United States (Canadians use "Aboriginal," "First Nations," "Indigenous," "Native," and, in legal contexts, "Indian") is exogenous: their homogenous identity is externally constructed. "American Indian" (and later "Native American"), an apparently unified ethnic category, actually incorporates thousands of peoples of varying languages, cultures, religions, and worldviews. To divide and conquer the tribal power of Indigenous peoples, the U.S. government created legislation to forcibly remove many Native peoples from their ancestral homelands into marginal rural areas called reservations or *rancherias*, and, later, to urban areas, with promises of jobs and security. Urban relocation in the 1950s and 1960s was the culmination of government policies designed to assimilate Natives into mainstream culture, further isolating families and communities. Colonization has created a diaspora of Native Americans within the borders of the mainland United States as well as in Hawaii, Alaska, and other areas where the U.S. government has exerted its influence. However, tribal peoples continued to connect with one another and created social-cultural networks that would later give birth to the pan-Indian movement.

Even the formation of tribal identity itself is problematic at best. Traditionally, tribal clan systems defined their own membership and identity.

Now, the U.S. government makes the final decision. Endogenous definitions are often very different from those imposed by outsiders. In many cases, including those of the Muskogee (Creek) and Laguna people, Native American societies are matrilineal (that is, lineage is defined through women), matrifocal (kinship systems are focused on matrilineal descent), and traditionally gynocratic (women make principal decisions; see Gunn Allen 1992). The colonizing powers of the United States and Canada not only imposed their own definition of "Indian," but also framed its significance in patriarchal, patrilineal, and sexist terms. In Canada, under the notorious Indian Act Section 12(1)(b), First Nations' women lost their "Indian" status and right to live on their family and community reserves if they married White men. Protests, political actions, and national and international court cases eventually led to Bill C-31, which, like its predecessor, treats First Nations' women differently than their brothers, but has at least removed the most sexist and colonialist provisions.

In most tribal cultures, self-identity comes first from family, second from clan, and finally from tribal or national identification. For example, in the Muskogee Nation, one identifies oneself by tribal town, clan affiliation, tribal affiliation, then by Native ancestry. Only rarely would an individual self-define as "American Indian." Indigenous Hawaiian peoples have a long tradition that enjoins one, when meeting others in a group setting, to relate through song/chant the ancestral formation of identity by repeating the names and deeds of ancestors, identifying the place of birth, the ancestor's place of birth, and the relationship to the landscape from which one is formed. Ancestral identity, language, landscape, and genealogy form Indigenous Hawaiian self-identification; the designation "native Hawaiian" is given in subjection by the colonizing power. Traditional Indigenous Hawaiian and traditional Muskogee identities, therefore, predate their subjection.

Ethnicity also plays a role in the lives of women who self-identify and/or are identified by mainstream cultures as White. Among North American Jews, for example, Sephardic and Ashkenazi women view one another differently. Some Jews do not view themselves as White at all. No longer affiliated with land or language—or even ancestry—"ethnic" is a word that has become for many Whites a designator for "non-White." When asked about their ethnicity, they may think in terms of "ethnic clothing," "ethnic music," or the "ethnic foods" aisle in their supermarkets, not about the fact that they have Belgian, Swedish, Welch, Dutch, German, and/or English heritages. Young White Americans, in particular, may not know their family histories beyond two or three generations; but ethnicity does not cease to be complex when it is denied or forgotten. Other and perhaps older White North Americans retain a strong sense of their ethnic identities, each for her own reasons, and will respond to the same question without hesitation: Sicilian, Ukrainian, Irish, Norwegian, Spanish, Cajun, Gullah, or Basque, for example. Yet other White groups with different histories feel stigmatized in North America, among them Poles, Appalachian Scots-Irish, and Newfoundlanders.

Members of the Caribbean, Mexican, and South American diasporas in North America, on the other hand, express amazement that White

Americans seem not to understand the difference between a Dominican and a Haitian, or between a Guatemalan and an Argentine. A widely told joke relates that a Latina can be Cuban in Miami, Chicana in San Diego, Puerto Rican in New York, and Mexican in Texas—all while knowing herself to be Salvadoran—because as long as she is speaking in a Spanish accent, it makes no difference to White people. Asians in North America voice similar complaints when Koreans are mistaken for Japanese, for example, or Hmong for Chinese.

Different generations of women may also experience ethnicity differently. White North American notions of childrearing, which consider the development of individuality and independence a requirement, may conflict with expectations from the home country. Immigrant women in North America, often without access to learning English, can be isolated in their homes, or at best, in ethnic community enclaves where they can provision their families and maintain their houses in their original languages and foodways. Sometimes their children acquire considerable power because they must translate for their mothers during school visits, medical appointments, and interactions with government officials. The children, in turn, particularly girls, feel pressure from their parents to maintain family and ethnic honor as defined in their original culture, most often associated with chastity and modesty, directly at odds with the styles and expectations of mainstream North Americans. Further, in patriarchal and patrilineal societies (which trace kinship and ancestry through the male line), a man marrying outside of his ethnic group brings to it his wife as a new member, along with their children. Women, however, are pressured to marry within the group, because a woman marrying outside the group is considered lost to the community, whatever her personal feelings may be.

Studies of ethnicity often ignore women's contributions to identity, especially when male or female fieldworkers identify public male culture as normative. Recently, work on areas of tradition such as foodways has rectified to an extent the underrepresentation of women's ethnic cultures. Studies of foodways often show the remarkable creativity of women in producing foods that follow their families' tastes, sometimes in the face of the lack of availability of foodstuffs used in their native or ancestral countries.

The complex interrelations of sexism, scholarship, and ethnicity can be seen in the tradition of Morris dancing, brought to the United States and Canada and extensively popularized by English immigrants of the 1960s. Historic scholarship on this practice from England suggests that it is a male tradition, and sees the extensive participation in North America of female Morris dancers as an indication of non-tradition at best, and as a betrayal of the practice at worst. In fact, however, research has shown that women danced Morris in England from its early history, and continued to do so (albeit as a minority of dancers) to the present. Thus, North American women Morris dancers are an extension of an ethnic tradition, not a deviation from it.

Ignorance about the complexities of ethnicity in the early twenty-first century has contributed to wars, genocides, and mass migrations; the ideological myth embodied in its trivialization and dismissal is pernicious in a world where most people use the categories of ethnicity to structure their lives. As Judith Butler (1997) argues, "Power imposes itself upon us, and, weakened by its force, we come to internalize or accept its terms. What such an account fails to note, however, is that the 'we' who accept such terms are fundamentally dependant on those terms for our existence" (2). Women in ethnic groups understand this relationship with power because they must live it daily. *See also:* Feminisms; Fieldwork; First Nations of North America; Folk Dance; Folk Group; Foodways; Humor; Immigration; Politics; Race; Tradition; Violence.

References: Brodkin, Karen. *How Jews Became White Folks and What That Says about Race in America.* New Brunswick, NJ, and London: Rutgers University Press, 1998; Brown, Rosemary. *Being Brown: A Very Public Life.* Toronto: Random House, 1989; Butler, Judith. *The Psychic Life of Power: Theories in Subjection.* Palo Alto, CA: Stanford University Press, 1997; Combahee River Collective. "Black Feminist Organizing in the Seventies and Eighties." http://www.buffalostate.edu/orgs/rspms/combahee.html (accessed August 10, 2008); Greenhill, Pauline. *Ethnicity in the Mainstream: Three Studies of English Canadian Culture in Ontario.* Montreal: McGill-Queen's University Press, 1994; Gunn Allen, Paula. *The Sacred Hoop: Recovering the Feminine in American Indian Traditions.* Second edition. Boston: Beacon Press, 1992; hooks, bell. *Feminism Is For Everybody: Passionate Politics.* Cambridge, MA: South End Press, 2000; Jacobs, Beverley. "Gender Discrimination Under the Indian Act: Bill C-31 and First Nations Women." In *Feminism, Law, Inclusion: Intersectionality in Action,* eds. Gayle MacDonald, Rachel L. Osborne, and Charles C. Smith, 175–199. Toronto: Sumach Press, 2005; Le Espiritu, Yen. "'We Don't Sleep Around Like White Girls Do': Family, Culture, and Gender in Filipina-American Lives." *Signs,* vol. 26, no. 1 (2001): 415–440; Minh-ha, Trinh. *Woman, Native, Other: Writing Postcoloniality and Feminism.* Bloomington: Indiana University Press, 1989; Mohanty, Chandra Talpade, Anne Russo, and Lourdes Torres. *Third World Women and the Politics of Feminism.* Bloomington: Indiana University Press, 1991; Moraga, Cherrie L., and Gloria E. Anzaldua. *This Bridge Called My Back: Writings by Radical Women of Color.* New York: Kitchen Table—Women of Color Press, 1983; Stern, Steven, and John Allan Cicala. *Creative Ethnicity: Symbols and Strategies of Contemporary Ethnic Life.* Logan: University of Utah Press, 1991.

Carolyn Dunn and Liz Locke

Eve

In Jewish, Muslim, and Christian religious traditions, Eve is the first woman created by God. Her name is derived from the Hebrew, meaning "living," and she is considered the mother of all humankind.

The first chapter of Genesis presents two versions of the creation story. In the first (1:26–28), "God created man [sic] in his own image; ... male and female he created them." In the second version (2:4–24), God created the first human, Adham (or Adam), from "the dust of the ground." Declaring that "It is not good that the man should be alone," God caused him to sleep and removed one of his ribs to form a woman. This second version is frequently cited as justification for the subordination of women, both within the church and in daily life. The first version is favored by those (notably Jews and Muslims) who prefer a more egalitarian interpretation.

God placed Adam and Eve in Eden, a garden in which grew "every tree that is pleasant to the sight and good for food." In the midst of this garden stood the Tree of Life and the Tree of the Knowledge of Good and Evil. God told Adam and Eve that they could eat freely from any tree except for these two, from which they would die. A serpent, usually interpreted as a personification of evil, told Eve that she would not die from eating the fruit of the Tree of the Knowledge of Good and Evil, that instead, "your eyes will be opened and you will be like God, knowing good and evil." Eve ate the fruit and gave some to Adam. Their eyes opened, they saw that they were naked, and they covered themselves. God confronted them, cursed them for their disobedience, and drove them from Eden.

The role of Eve in the creation story has had a profound influence on Judeo-Christian attitudes toward women. Eve is blamed for bringing mortality, sin, and evil into the world. Although her "original sin" was disobedience, later interpreters such as Augustine argued that all humankind has inherited a sinful nature through subsequent acts of sexual intercourse. The association of sin with a woman and with sex permeates many Western religious denominations.

In Greek mythology, Pandora is similarly blamed for unloosing evils into the world through disobedience. In contrast, Prometheus is celebrated as a culture hero (a mythological figure that teaches a group its cultural patterns, "how to be the people") for disobeying the gods and bringing fire to the people of the Earth. The creation stories of other cultures, including Native American groups, frequently include a female figure whose fecundity and generosity produces life on Earth. Some scholars suggest that the recorded tale of Eve is a deliberate and monotheistic attempt to counter earlier creation stories featuring female deities, particularly the Babylonian epic *Enuma Elish*. "No other text has affected women in the Western world as much as that found in the opening chapters of Genesis" (Kvam et al.: 1). *See also:* Goddess Worship; Helpmate; Jewish Women's Folklore; Legend, Religious; Lilith; Muslim Women's Folklore; Sexuality.

References: Deen, Edith. *All of the Women of the Bible.* New York: Harper & Row, 1955; Kvam, Kristen E., Linda S. Schearing, and Valarie H. Ziegler, eds. *Eve & Adam: Jewish, Christian, and Muslim Readings on Genesis and Gender.* Bloomington: Indiana University Press, 1999; Moyers, Bill. *Genesis: A Living Conversation.* New York: Doubleday, 1996; Murphy, Cullen. *The Word According to Eve: Women and the Bible in Ancient Times and Our Own.* Boston: Houghton Mifflin, 1998; Pagels, Elaine. *Adam, Eve, and the Serpent.* New York: Random House, 1988; Trible, Phyllis. *God and the Rhetoric of Sexuality.* Philadelphia: Fortress Press, 1978.

Laurel Horton

Evil Eye

The evil-eye belief complex stems from the notion that the stare of a particular person has the power to convey harm to a person or other object of its gaze. Despite variations in causes and effects, evil-eye practices and expectations have in common the belief that "having the evil eye" refers to individuals who are perceived to have had more than their fair share of bad luck and ill health and consequently possess the uncanny ability of projecting harm onto others and the possessions of those whom they envy.

Belief in the evil eye, also known as the "malevolent eye," is ancient and widespread, spanning the cultures of the Indo-European and Semitic world, the Near East, the Mediterranean, South Asia, northern Europe, and north and east Africa. In all instances, the evil eye is singular and primarily connected with women, pregnancy, and fertility, but its targets are also commonly associated with domestic animals, fruit trees, and crops, that is, all things fecund.

This belief complex requires that traditional precautionary behaviors be enacted in order to avoid, discourage, and/or negate the effects of the evil eye, including specific gestures such as spitting, and the wearing of round or horn-shaped amulets and talismans, the most common of which is a blue pendant (called *nazarliklar* in Turkey) enclosing a miniature reproduction of a human eye. As other apotropaic strategies (those designed to avert evil), Azerbaijani elders recommend the wearing of a cutting from a plant locally known as *uzarlik* (*Peganum harmala*), and Asian Indian women may draw black lines around their eyes, not only to shield themselves from the evil eye, but to prevent themselves from inflicting it on others. Wearing images of animals with unusual eyes—such as foxes, grasshoppers, snakes, fish, snails, toads—may offer protection; colonial Americans were partial to wearing heart-shaped lockets as insurance against the evil eye.

The evil-eye belief complex has raised curiosity and inspired scholarship dating from classical antiquity, through the European Renaissance, and into the present day. It is generally acknowledged that whether voluntarily or involuntarily, the evil eye is motivated by envy, and thus steeped in what anthropologist George Foster dubbed "the image of limited good" (1979). The notion of "limited good," generally identified with a culture's agricultural peasantry, articulates a worldview in which there is always a finite amount of a resource, whether it be luck or life force, exemplified by the notion that the gain of one inevitably comes at the expense of another. Casting the evil eye is, therefore, considered a powerful means of attempting to redistribute limited resources through its capacity to drain the good luck and sap the life force possessed by a family or an individual in order to benefit its envious practitioner. The belief complex explains the paradoxical behavior of parents and grandparents who appear to treat their precious children harshly, when, in fact, they are purposely taking preventative measures so as not to attract the evil eye to them.

In "Wet and Dry, the Evil Eye: An Essay in Indo-European and Semitic Worldview," Alan Dundes (1980) identifies an innate accommodation of the concept of limited good in his analysis of a substratum of folk belief in which all life depends upon liquids, and the loss of liquids corresponds with loss of life. Thus, fluids, especially the non-eliminative bodily fluids—milk, semen, and blood—have fundamental significance, and are often the perceived targets of the evil eye, which is believed to be cast especially on breasts and testicles. Hence, the evil eye is frequently blamed for the drying up of livestock's milk supply and lack of fecundity in bulls. According to Dundes, the traditional apotropaic gestures of tugging the earlobes (an expression of upward displacement performed by both males and females), women covering their breasts, and men touching their genitals are unconscious efforts to symbolically counter the evil eye's curse of sterility and other forms of bad luck. *See also:* Cosmetics; Cursing; Farm Women's Folklore; Folk Belief; Pregnancy; Superstition.

References: Dundes, Alan. "Wet and Dry, the Evil Eye: An Essay in Indo-European and Semitic Worldview." In *Interpreting Folklore*, 93–133. Bloomington: Indiana University Press, 1980; ———. ed. *The Evil Eye: A Folklore Casebook*. New York: Garland Publishing, 1981; Foster, George McClelland. "The Image of Limited Good." In *Tzintzuntzan: Mexican Peasants in a Changing World*, 122–52. New York: Elsevier, 1979; Gravel, Pierre Bettez. *The Malevolent Eye: An Essay on the Evil Eye, Fertility and the Concept of Mana*. New York: Peter Lang Publishing, 1995; Holmes, Hannah. "The Skinny on the Evil Eye." *Discovery Online*, April 24, 1997. http://www.discovery.com/area/skinnyon/skinnyon970425/skinny1.html (accessed August 9, 2008); Maloney, Clarence, ed. *The Evil Eye*. New York: Columbia University Press, 1976; Onians, Richard Broxton. *The Origins of European Thought*. Salem, NH: Ayer Company, Publishers, 1987; Peterson, Jean, and Arzu Aghayeva. "The Evil Eye: Staving Off Harm—With a Visit to the Open Marketplace." *Azerbaijan International*, 8.3 (Autumn 2000). http://www.azer.com/aiweb/categories/magazine/83_folder/83_articles/83_evil.html (accessed February 16, 2005).

Maria Teresa Agozzino

F

Family Folklore

Family folklore comprises traditional expressive behavior and its products transmitted by family members to other family members. Topics include relatives, family events, and family ways of being and doing. Families include people united by blood, marriage, civil union, and adoption, as well as those who love and care for one another. Family folklore includes stories, jokes, and songs about family members and events as well as the ways family members share them with one another; festivals the family celebrates, such as religious and national holidays; festivals that celebrate family, such as weddings, reunions, and funerals; festivals that individual families invent for themselves and pass on through the years; foods, cooking instructions, ways of eating, and methods of gathering to eat as a family; family naming traditions; a family's ways of dancing; expressions and gestures a family uses; visual records of family life, such as arrangements of items inside and outside the home, photographs, photograph albums, videotapes, computerized albums, embroideries, and quilts; tombstone design and cemetery decorations; occupational, song, story, and craft traditions carried on within a family; and fieldwork methods used within family settings.

Folklorists have long been welcome in the homes of families. Once back at their desks, however, most professional and amateur folklorists in North America before the 1970s discussed the material they collected in families as regional or ethnic, religious or occupational folklore. They approached the family as a source of folklore materials, not as the subject of their study. Several, though, published a family story or two as "family folklore," usually without analysis, in local journals. In 1958, Mody Boatright called on folklorists to collect "an important source of living folklore"—the "family saga," individual stories with a variety of themes that preserved a family's way of seeing itself in history. Interested in a generic approach, Boatright asked what forms and motifs made up the family saga. A second mode of inquiry, a small-group approach, came soon after from Kim Garrett, who suggested that every family who recognizes itself as a unit has its own traditions, including stories, taboos, and expressions.

In the late 1960s and early 1970s, the study of family folklore burgeoned. Folklorists' growing interest in folklore as communication within and between small groups, and their consideration of more privatized forms of folklore such as personal-experience narratives; feminists' focus on women's lives and concerns; African American scholars' explorations of personal identity and their reevaluation of earlier assessments of the Black family; and Alex Haley's *Roots*, the exploration of his African American family's history, all contributed to an increased interest in studying the family as the subject of its own folklore.

Women folklorists took the lead in family folklore studies as they turned their gaze toward their own families. In her 1966 study of her family's legends about their ancestor Caddy, Kathryn L. Morgan showed what collecting family stories had to offer folklorists. Asking questions about family stories' functions, she suggested that her African American family's stories operated as buffers against the ravages of racism and served as an alternative system of education since Black history had been ignored by the schools. Karen Baldwin, in her 1975 dissertation on her central Pennsylvania mountain family, gave family folklorists a theoretical foundation for their work when she declared the family to be "the social base of folklore." The family, she showed, is not just a group that generates its own traditions; rather, it is the "first folk group, the group in which important primary folkloric socialization takes place and individual aesthetic preference patterns for folkloric exchange are set." Margaret Yocom in her 1980 dissertation on her Pennsylvania German family detailed the issues involved in personal-family fieldwork. In her 1983 dissertation, Marilyn White analyzed interracial and intraracial relationships in rural Virginia from 1865 to 1940 as seen in her African American family stories.

Male folklorists who worked in the first years of the family folklore field turned to the study of multiple families. In 1975, Stanley Brandes published family narratives of lost fortunes that are told by White, lower-middle, and working-class citizens of the United States. He found that the tellers of such stories deflect onto ancestors the anxiety they feel for not achieving top economic success in a capitalist country that maintains that all individuals can become economically successful. And Steven Zeitlin in 1978 published his dissertation on the stories of families throughout the United States, discovering common themes that sweep through family stories in the United States, themes that revolve around the characters of family members (heroes, survivors) and the transitions in family histories (migrations, courtships).

Fieldwork was an early concern, especially since the first family folklorists chose to work with their own families. Earlier discipline-wide and regional fieldwork guides often described family folklore fieldwork as ideal for the novice because it was easily conducted, but as more and more folklorists began working with their own families, the discussion about such personal-family fieldwork deepened. Baldwin, Morgan, Yocom, and Susan Sherman with her Jewish relatives detailed concerns particular to such fieldwork among intimates. With other scholars, they challenged the notion of objectivity, recognizing it not only as an impossible goal but also a counterproductive one for personal-family fieldworkers in particular. These scholars have discussed the importance of including oneself in family activities as a member of the group as well as the necessity for exploring and using one's involvements; later discussions about reflexivity and reciprocity, as well as feminist reminders that the personal is political, have all reinforced family folklorists' positions on the challenges of such fieldwork that cuts close to the bone. Questions about fieldwork among family members continue to interest folklorists, as the work of Kim Miller and Susan Scheiberg shows.

As the study of family folklore continued, it engaged with questions that lay at the heart of Folklore as a discipline. Folklorists are interested in how traditional materials are passed on to others: what are the characteristics of this process of transmission? Lucille Burdine and William B. McCarthy in their study of an extended Ozark family, for example, showed how folklore is not handed on "en bloc" from person to person, generation to generation, but rather that each element of folklore finds its own sympathetic channel of transmission in different members of a family. Other studies by Baldwin, Yocom, and Jane Beck discussed gender differences in transmission as well as attitudes of ownership and deference between generations.

Folklorists have puzzled over the generic nature of folk narratives, and family scholars began to ask how the individual stories related to the whole of a family's repertoire. Family stories, often brief and often elliptically told, usually do not take the form of legend, folktale, or memorate. Boatright and William Wilson saw family stories as anecdotes that together comprise a larger saga or novel, and emphasized that each anecdote must be heard in light of other anecdotes for the larger story to be understood. Baldwin emphasized that a family's "narrative is a composite of changing and interchangeable parts," that since no one person is the ultimate source, many must be heard so their piece of the narrative composite can be included.

Folklorists have been concerned about the ways gender intersects with folklore, and family folklorists have turned to evidence of gender-role stratification in storytelling, material culture, and more. Baldwin and Yocom, for example, studied how family stories and storytelling differ among men and women in their Anglo American and Pennsylvania German families. While they found women's telling in these specific contexts to be more collaborative, interruptible, and filled with information and genealogy, men's telling is often uninterrupted and more competitive, their story beginnings and endings are formally marked, and their stories make a point worth telling. Yocom explored gender differences in the transmission of woodcarving and knitting skills in an extended Anglo and French Acadian family in Maine. And Thomas Adler's 1981 study of gender and family food preparation found that men's cooking traditions in the family are often limited to one or two celebratory meals a week—often Sunday breakfast—or to outdoor meals with meat, while women cook the mundane, everyday, diversified meals.

Also from the 1980s to the present, family folklore study has engaged with multiple social issues, including economic stress on families, abuse in families, "family-values" discourses, and the multiple forms of the contemporary family. Phyllis Scott Carlin, for example, has written about the narratives families tell who are swept up in ongoing economic crises as many are forced to give up the way of life that has sustained them for generations. Alan Dundes, Janet Langlois, and Ed Walraven have considered parent-child interaction, influenced by changing economic and social factors, as it is configured in dead-baby jokes, stories of violence against children, and legends of *La Llorona* in a garbage dump.

In her 2001 study of the narratives women tell as they leave abusive relationships, Elaine Lawless documented a painful side of family life. She shows how slowly becoming able to tell their stories helps women heal and regain power in their own lives. The work of Steven Zeitlin and others in the Family Folklore Section of the Smithsonian Institution's Festival of American Folklife explored how families experiencing divorce or abandonment by one parent use ritual and storytelling in the reconstruction of their single-parent families. Elizabeth Stone, interviewing families across the United States, recorded family members' stories of abuse and abandonment and how individuals transformed stories about hurtful relatives into stories that could lead them down new and healthier paths of life.

Scholars of family folklore also have contributed to the current American melée over "family values" (a politically charged phrase often used to signal the "conventional, heterosexual family") by writing about folklore in the multiple forms that contemporary families take. Family folklore scholars understand that since no one family pattern is statistically dominant, contemporary families are increasingly diverse, including single-parent, two adults of any gender with or without children, households of single adults united by their care for each other, and more. Folklorists' research with adoptive, blended, and stepfamilies, for example, has led them to investigate such practices as "Gotcha Day," a yearly festivity that a family holds to celebrate the day their adopted child arrived. In his 1993 research of gay male families, Joseph Goodwin discussed the structure of gay families as that based almost totally on levels of closeness and the families' use of nicknames, jokes, stories, and ritual. Folklorists have documented ceremonies of commitment and Vermont's civil unions, as well as the legal marriage ceremonies of gays and lesbians in Denmark and Norway. They have also turned to the family traditions that have grown up around the Names Project's AIDS quilt and other memorial processes surrounding the AIDS pandemic. Folklorists also have explored how family members, given their different families of origin, and often given their different religions, ethnicities, races, or places of birth, negotiate their various traditions, creatively blending them into new versions of old practices that can sustain their new families.

Family folklorists interested in folklore and literature have often turned to the work of poets; fiction writers; writers of creative non-fiction, biography, and autobiography; and professional storytellers who incorporate family folklore in their presentations. Michael Ondaatje's description of a day's storytelling in his Ceylonese family provides a taste of the possibilities:

[W]e will trade anecdotes and faint memories, trying to swell them with the order of dates and asides, interlocking them all as if assembling the hull of a ship. No story is ever told just once. Whether a memory or funny hideous scandal, we will return to it an hour later and retell the story with additions and this time a few judgments thrown in … [A]ll day my Aunt Phyllis presides over the history of good and bad Ondaatjes and the people they came in contact with. Her eye … will suddenly sparkle and she will turn to us with delight and begin "and there is another terrible story …" (1984: 26) *See also:* Courtship; Divorce; Festival; Fieldwork; Folk Group; Folk Photography; Foodways; Graves and Gravemarkers; Joke; *La Llorona*; Marriage; Naming Practices; Personal-Experience Narrative; Ritual; Storytelling; Tradition; Tradition-Bearer.

References: Adler, Thomas A. "Making Pancakes on Sunday: The Male Cook in Family Tradition." *Western Folklore*, vol. 40, no. 1 (1981): 45–54; Baldwin, Karen. "'Woof!' A Word of Women's Roles in Family Storytelling." In *Women's Folklore, Women's Culture*, eds. Susan Kalčik and Rosan Jordan, 149–162. Philadelphia: University of Pennsylvania Press, 1985; Beck, Jane. "Newton Washburn; Traditional Basket Maker." *Traditional Craftsmanship in America*, ed. Charles Camp, 72–76. Washington, DC: National Council for the Traditional Arts, 1983; Boatright, Mody C. "The Family Saga as a Form of Folklore." *The Family Saga and Other Phases of American Folklore*, eds. Mody C. Boatright, Robert B. Downs, and John T. Flanagan, 1–19. Urbana: University of Illinois Press, 1958; Brandes, Stanley. "Family Misfortune Stories in American Folklore." *Journal of the Folklore Institute*, vol. 12, no. 1 (1975): 5–17; Burdine, Lucille, and William B. McCarthy. "Sister Singers." *Western Folklore*, vol. 49, no. 4 (1990): 406–417; Carlin, Phyllis Scott. "'That Black Fall': Farm Crisis Narratives." *Performance, Culture, and Identity*, eds. Elizabeth C. Fine and Jean Haskell Speer, 135–157. Westport, CT: Praeger, 1992; Dundes, Alan. *Cracking Jokes: Studies of Sick Humor Cycles and Stereotypes.* Berkeley, CA: Ten Speed Press, 1987; Garrett, Kim. "Family Stories and Sayings." In *Singers and Storytellers.* ed. Mody C. Boatright, 273–281. Publications of the Texas Folklore Society, Vol. 30. Dallas: Southern Methodist University Press, 1961; Goodwin, Joseph. "My First Ex-Lover in Law: You Can Choose Your Family." *Southern Folklore* 51 (1994): 35–47; Haley, Alex. *Roots: The Saga of an American Family.* New York: Delta, 1977; Hirsch, Marianne. *Family Frames: Photography, Narrative and Postmemory.* Cambridge: Harvard University Press, 1997; Langlois, Janet. "Mothers' Double Talk." In *Feminist Messages*, ed. Joan Newlon Radner, 80–97. Urbana: University of Illinois Press, 1993; Lawless, Elaine. *Women Escaping Violence: Empowerment Through Narrative.* Columbia: University of Missouri Press. 2001; Miller, Kim. "All in the Family: Family Folklore, Objectivity and Self-Censorship." *Western Folklore*, vol. 56, nos. 3/4 (1997): 331–46; Morgan, Kathryn L. *Children of Strangers: The Stories of a Black Family.* Philadelphia: Temple University Press, 1980; Ondaatje, Michael. *Running in the Family.* London: Picador, 1984 [1982]; Scheiberg, Susan L. "A Folklorist in the Family: On the Process of Fieldwork among Intimates." *Western Folklore*, vol. 49, no. 2 (1990): 208–14; Sherman, Sharon R. "'That's How the Seder Looks': A Fieldwork Account of Videotaping Family Folklore." *Journal of Folklore Research*, vol. 23, no. 401 (1986): 53–70; Stacey, Judith. *In the Name of the Family: Rethinking Family Values in the Postmodern Age.* Boston: Beacon Press, 1996; Stone, Elizabeth. *Black Sheep and Kissing Cousins: How Our Family Stories Shape Us.* New York: Penguin, 1988; Sullivan, Maureen. *The Family of Women: Lesbian Mothers, Their Children, and the Undoing of Gender.* Berkeley: University of California Press, 2004; Walraven, Ed. "Evidence for a Developing Variant of 'La Llorona'." *Western Folklore*, vol. 50, no. 2 (1991): 208–17; White, Marilyn M. "'We Lived on an Island': An Afro-American Family and Community in Rural Virginia, 1865–1940." PhD diss., Austin: University of Texas, 1983; Wilson, William A. "Personal Narratives: The Family Novel." *Western Folklore*, vol. 50, no. 2 (1991): 127–149; Yocom, Margaret R. "Family Folklore and Oral History Interviews: Strategies for Introducing a Project to One's Own Relatives." *Western Folklore*, vol. 41, no. 2 (1982): 251–274; ———. "'Awful Real': Dolls and

Development in Rangeley, Maine." In *Feminist Messages*, ed. Joan Newlon Radner, 126–154. Urbana: University of Illinois Press, 1993; Zeitlin, Steven. "'An Alchemy of Mind': The Family Courtship Story." *Western Folklore*, vol. 39, no. 1 (1980): 17–33; Zeitlin, Steven J., Amy J. Kotkin, and Holly Cutting Baker. *A Celebration of American Family Folklore: Tales and Traditions from the Smithsonian Collection.* Cambridge, MA: Yellow Moon Press, 1993 [1982].

Margaret R. Yocom

Fans, Language of

The language of fans refers to messages conveyed by manipulating the positions of hand-held fans, a form of communicative coding practiced in many cultures throughout modern history, but especially by upper- and middle-class European women during the Victorian era.

Thought to have come to China from Korea sometime between the tenth and fourteenth centuries, hand fans are made in a variety of shapes from a wide assortment of materials. By the eighteenth century, they were considered essential accessories in a woman's wardrobe in Europe and North America. Their use to encode non-verbal messages was common when social norms disallowed open conversation, particularly between men and women.

One early system of fan language developed in Spain, where it consisted of about fifty different gestures. Its codification passed through a series of translations; by the time it was available in English, the list was reduced to thirty-three movements. Among these are carrying a fan in the right hand in front of the face to mean "Follow me"; twirling it in the left hand to mean "We are watched"; holding a shut fan to the heart to mean "You have won my love"; resting a shut fan on the right eye to mean "When may I be allowed to see you?"; and shutting a fully opened fan very slowly to mean "I promise to marry you."

Some researchers claim that common European use of "language of the fan" originated as a publicity ploy by a Parisian fan maker, Duvelleroy, who included a French translation of the truncated list of actions and their meanings with every fan that he sold. The use of fan gestures was sufficiently widespread in Europe during the eighteenth century that satirical artist William Hogarth included images of women conveying a variety of fan messages in his paintings and engravings. Despite the fact that young women's academies of the Victorian era in London and Paris offered instruction in advanced fan-language technique, much of the communication made possible by a fan is easy enough to interpret; peeking over the edge of a fan to indicate coyness or snapping it closed to indicate refusal are actions that do not require instruction to interpret.

Due in part to the increased availability of air conditioning, the use of hand fans has declined markedly in most parts of the world in recent decades. Anyone familiar with the language of fans today is unlikely to encounter many contemporaries with whom to share its nonverbal messages. Yet, interest in the topic has not completely disappeared. The fan itself as an art form is the subject of occasional exhibitions, and still appears from time to time in the performing arts, notably dance and opera. Classes in the language of fans are sometimes offered in summer camp programs for young girls, as a matter of historical and aesthetic interest; and the topic is revisited from time to time in the popular press through feature articles and in advertising material published by manufacturers and sellers of decorative fans. *See also:* Coding; Fashion; Flowers, Language of; Folk Dance; Gender; Girl Scouts/Girl Guides; Material Culture.

References: Delorey, Barbara. "Creating an Image: The Evolution of 18th-Century Dress Beginning with our Bicentennial or Is There Life After Simplicity?" http://www.18cnewenglandlife.org/18cnel/delorey1.htm (accessed August 9, 2008); "Girl Scouts Get the Low Down on Juliette Low." In *Family News* (Winter) 6. Girl Scout Council of Cumberland Valley, Nashville, TN, 2004; "Have You Noticed?" *Newsletter of Imperial Society of Teachers of Dancing: Latin American Faculty News,* June 2003. http://www.istd.org/latin/facultynews/june2003/haveyounoticed.html (accessed August 10, 2008); Kwon, Nancy. "European, East Asian Fans on Exhibit." *iArt News,* 2002. http://www.artseoul.net/artnews/news02/e08asianfan.html (accessed August 10, 2008); McMath, Meredith Bean. *Inquire Within: A How-to Guide of Victorian Entertainment.* Purcellville, VA: Run, Rabbit, Run Productions, 2003; Rosenthal, Angela. 2001. "Unfolding Gender: Women and the 'Secret' Sign Language of Fans in Hogarth's Work." *The Other Hogarth: Aesthetics of Difference,* eds. Bernadette Fort and Angela Rosenthal, 120–141. Princeton, NJ: Princeton University Press, 2001; "The Uses of Fans." In *Cool Breezes: Handheld Fans in Twentieth-Century American Folk Art, Fashion, and Advertising* (Program Guide). Kansas City: Mid-American Arts Alliance and ExhibitsUSA, n.d.

Julia Arrants

Farm Women's Folklore

Once called "farmer's wives," farm women have long been devalued as workers, even though their labor, usually unpaid, has been an essential part of most agricultural operations. Since men were traditionally considered heads of households, women usually gained access to land only through marriage. In the past century, however, an increasing number of North American women have farmed without men.

In the United States, from frontier times to the present, women have taken part in the hard work of farming, including decision-making and bookkeeping. Depending on the season and mode of production, farming has required traditional skills and activities of the entire family, with men and women typically having interdependent spheres of work. Women's roles have always been critical and multiple, ranging from fieldwork, animal husbandry, household management, food production and preservation, to child rearing, family and community building, and "making do"—providing as much year-by-year economic stability as possible within such a risky enterprise.

As a result, the productivity of farm women has resulted not only in a substantial body of lore, but also in a multitude of recognizable narratives, generated both within and without the group. Bawdy jokes about "the farmer's daughter" can serve as an example of one type of lore promoted about women in agriculture, although most certainly not by farm women themselves. Rather, the experiences of farm women support personal narratives that emphasize strength in the face of adversity, reflections on the rewards and pitfalls of country life, stories of cleverness and industry, and a plethora of lore about ways to manage household and farmyard affairs: predicting weather; doing laundry; planting vegetable and flower gardens; nursing with herbs and other home remedies; and handling unruly animals, children, and men. Farm women often see themselves as the heroes in their stories, and rightly so.

In the past, farm women often functioned as "petty entrepreneurs," earning income from auxiliary enterprises, such as selling eggs, making butter, raising and selling flowers or fruit such as strawberries, or by boarding hunters or schoolteachers. This so-called "egg and butter money" might keep the farm running in lean times, or allow for extra comforts in more prosperous years. Farm women's income was a fundamental, if invisible, part of the family budget.

Women's farm work has often included tending animals, especially cows and chickens. The significance of women as poultry raisers was demonstrated by the prevalence of cotton print bags for poultry feed from 1940–1960. Poultry feed manufacturers hired New York fabric designers to create prints that would entice their women customers, who reused the bags for clothing and other household needs. The feed bags themselves became important items for exchange and sale. Women made up such a large part of their customer base that manufacturers also sponsored national feed bag sewing contests.

Farm women often joined extension clubs, which taught and promoted programs on food safety, health, and other issues of special concern to women. Extension clubs also guaranteed regular and welcome social activity.

In the United States, women's farm labors began to shift in the early part of the twentieth century. Until then, even non-farm women in villages still raised their own chickens, pigs, cows, and vegetables in kitchen gardens, responsibilities that have become increasingly rare. In rural towns, as homes were modernized, women's duties changed to emphasize their role as consumers rather than producers; in the countryside, women's farm responsibilities became less socially valued. By the 1940s, farm women began to feel self-conscious about outdoor chores, often leaving field and tractor work to their husbands.

In the past sixty years, the number of farms in the United States has declined from about 6 million to 2 million. Similarly, in Canada, farm numbers have steadily decreased over the last five decades, losing 55 percent of its farms between 1951 and 1991, and continuing to lose more than 10 percent during the last decade. Currently, as reproductive duties and other household chores have decreased, North American farm women have begun spending more time in the fields and barns, replacing other farmworkers. Conversely, farm women have for years taken off-farm work to finance costly health insurance and provide steady income for their families.

There is a global trend toward the "feminization of agriculture." For example, women have increasingly participated in the Community Supported Agriculture (CSA) movement of the past decade or so. CSAs consist of small agricultural operations that market a variety of produce directly to consumers, who generally purchase a "share." The share system underwrites the risk involved in any agricultural venture in exchange for several months of fresh vegetables, fruits, and sometimes eggs, meats, flowers, or herbs. As women purchase shares from CSAs, another level of social reciprocity can develop from these local operations—recipe exchanges, potlucks, and the like—further contributing to the building of community infrastructure.

Elsewhere in the world, women are also deeply involved in agriculture. In Mozambique, for example, for every 100 men in agriculture, there are 153 women. In parts of sub-Saharan Africa, women grow 70 percent of all food for family and local consumption. Although there have been large differences worldwide in the lives of farm women, as women in agriculture strive to participate in a shifting marketplace, the era of globalization now begins to coalesce at least some of their economic and environmental concerns. *See also:* Gardens; Region: Sub-Saharan Africa; Sewing; Wage Work; Women's Clubs; Women's Work.

References: Adams, Jane. "Farm Women, Class, and the Limits of Nostalgia." *Journal of Illinois State Historical Society*, vol. 92, no. 4 (Winter 1999/2000): 325–48; Fairbanks, Carol, and Bergine Haakenson, eds. *Writings of Farm Women, 1840–1940: An Anthology*. New York: Garland Publications, 1990; Jones, Lu Ann. *Mama Learned Us to Work: Farm Women in the New South*. Chapel Hill: University of North Carolina Press, 2002; McMurry, Sally. *From Sugar Camps to Star Barns: Rural Life and Landscape in a Western Pennsylvania Community*. University Park: Pennsylvania State University Press, 2001; Neth, Mary. *Preserving the Family Farm: Women, Community, and the Foundations of Agribusiness in the Midwest, 1900–1940*. Baltimore: The Johns Hopkins University Press, 1995; North Central Regional Center for Rural Development. "Community Supported Agriculture (CSA): Supporting Women and Communities." Women in Agriculture Conference, April 6–7, 2006. http://www.ncrcrd.iastate.edu/projects/csa/womeni nag.pdf (accessed February 1, 2007); Schmidt, Kimberly D. "'Sacred Farming' or 'Working Out': The Negotiated Lives of Conservative Mennonite Farm Women." *Frontiers: A Journal of Women Studies*, vol. 22, no. 1 (2001): 79–102; Van de Vorst, Charlotte. *Making Ends Meet: Farm Women's Work in Manitoba*. Winnipeg: University of Manitoba Press, 2003; Walker, Melissa, ed. *Country Women Cope with Hard Times: A Collection of Oral Histories. Women's Diaries and Letters of the South*. Columbia: University of South Carolina Press, 2004; Weber, Devra Anne. "Raiz Fuerte: Oral History and Mexicana Farmworkers." *Oral History Review*, vol. 17, no. 2 (1989): 47–62.

Ruth Olson

Fashion

A popular style of dress, manners, and living prevailing in a culture or subculture, fashion can be understood as a practice of production and consumption as well as a form of material culture. In societies experiencing rapid change such as now prevails in the economic Northern Hemisphere, it can be conservative and retrogressive in its social effects. However, it can also offer its users, particularly women, opportunities to recognize their power to create while resisting domination.

Fashion is not exclusively a modern Western practice. Fashion's processes of comparison, emulation, and differentiation are also found in stable social settings. The archaeological record provides evidence that systematic changes in style have sporadically happened historically and across cultures, suggesting fashion has always been a part of the human experience. Researchers debate whether changing uses of ornamentation to indicate identity and social contrast can be defined as "fashion." However, a more inclusive definition places emphasis on sociocultural and economic analysis rather than on any moralizing comparison of modern fashion's supposed superficiality with traditional dress or costume's supposed authenticity.

In the past, scholarship on fashion defined exclusively as Western and capitalist was limited by its focus on psychological factors and social status. Without questioning the assumption that men's clothing was outside of fashion codes, women were seen as the exclusive followers of fashion. Taken out of the context of patriarchy, a woman's pursuit of fashion was viewed as an emotional abnormality in need of explanation, and/or as the display of her husband's wealth and strivings for social status. Because of patriarchal obsessions with women's appearance and homemaking functions, then, fashion "has served traditionally as the cultural sign of the feminine" (Benstock and Ferriss 1994: 4), passive and irrational.

As consumer capitalism and practices of accumulation become more pronounced and permeate everyday life to a greater extent, the dynamics of fashion are complex, requiring more nuanced analysis and critique. Assuming that clothing and ornament found outside Western consumerist fashion systems are unchanging representations of historical practice overlooks the conscious choice to differentiate that people make in a globalizing world. In the economic South, dress may remain relatively stable in direct resistance to pressure from international capital. For Indigenous peoples, recovery of historic clothing, particularly if it has been subject to suppression by missionaries or colonial rulers, may be embraced as a marker of "authentic" identity. Only rarely, however, is this fashion completely unchanged from its precolonial forms. Newer functional and decorative elements may be borrowed or strategically deployed. A woman may wear Western trousers at home for comfort, and more traditional skirts and dresses to market when selling her wares to Western tourists, emphasizing the public and private contexts for materializing identity. On the other hand, conversion to conservative forms of Christianity or Islam may lead to rejection of precolonial dress on the grounds it is "backward" or "obscene." Women bear the brunt of such perceptions: their dress becomes indicative of community piety and their bodies a site for moral debate.

There is an important distinction between the actual everyday wear of ordinary people and the codification of national costumes during the era of nation building. Such costumes are invented traditions based on historical styles but are frozen, ritualized, and primarily used to legitimize the nation-state. Images of the half-clad Marianne of revolutionary France and the more respectable Britannica and Miss Canada symbolized collective yearnings while real women were largely disenfranchised. Typifying non-dominant peoples on the basis of costume was a projection of nationalist thinking onto colonized peoples; the resulting image of the Other as strange and exotic was then used to consolidate identity in the centers of North America and Europe. This logic exemplifies now-debunked theories of unilineal cultural evolution (evolutionary racism) wherein the wearing of fewer clothes, while tittilating, is equated with a lower level of cultural development or social evolution.

More recently, fashion designers from the economic North have appropriated traditional folk dress for economic gain. Taken out of context, such clothing may simply figure in rapidly shifting fads. Their wearers, seeing them purely in aesthetic terms, remain ignorant of the local cultural codes embodied in the styles. Such appropriation may be well meaning: an item of clothing or jewelry such as a Palestinian scarf or Norse Pagan rune may be worn as a sign of political solidarity or spiritual identification by middle-class North American women.

In fully capitalized societies where identities are strongly marked by commodified forms of dress, reflexivity has made fashion's codes more nuanced and layered. While once it was possible for designers to dictate styles from above, now they often look to the urban folk culture of the street for inspiration. Young, creative women play on meanings already inherent to styles and items to construct a unique, distinctive look that resists their cooptation into the mainstream fashion system. A good example of this phenomenon is the Doc Marten: a comfort shoe originally made for postwar German women, its patented sole was used in men's work boots in the United Kingdom by the 1960s. Soon after, disenfranchised White working-class young men appropriated the boot into a look intended to threaten the middle classes and non-White immigrants. In the 1970s, the punk movement picked up the Doc and gave it an international cachet of rebellion. Gay men wore Docs to perform masculinity, while grrrls—the progeny of the grunge movement—combined Docs with ultrafeminine items such as lace camisoles and skirts to confuse the codes of gender.

Fashion design has long been a medium for talented and business-savvy women such as Coco Chanel and Donna Karan to succeed. But it can have wider-ranging effects. For example, the Freedom Quilting Bee, a group of poor, Black women in Wilcox County, Alabama, capitalized on the elite fashion for quilts and quilting designs in the 1960s to form a cooperative. They simultaneously supported the civil rights movement, stimulated economic growth in their community, raised members' living standards, fostered interest in the art of quilting, and inspired other cooperatives.

Similarly, Coast Salish knitters of southern Vancouver Island, mostly women, have produced Cowichan sweaters for more than a century. While their products are recognized around the world, the Aboriginal women who make them remain largely invisible. These resourceful women continue to provide for their families by knitting, but increasingly they are refusing to be exploited by buyers who purchase their goods cheaply and then sell them at inflated prices in urban Canada and the United States. *See also:* Folk Costume; Knitting; Material Culture; Quilting.

References: Benstock, Shari, and Suzanne Ferriss, eds. *On Fashion.* New Brunswick, NJ: Rutgers University Press, 1984; Brydon, Anne, and Sandra Niessen, eds. *Consuming Fashion: Adorning the Transnational Body.* Oxford: Berg Publishers, 1988; Crane, Diana. *Fashion and Its Social Agendas: Class, Gender, and Identity in Clothing.* Chicago: University of Chicago Press, 2000; Holland, Samantha. *Alternative Femininities:*

Body, Age and Identity. Oxford: Berg Publishers, 2004; Palmer, Alexandra, ed. *Fashion: A Canadian Perspective*. Toronto: University of Toronto Press, 2004.

Anne Brydon

Female Genital Cutting

Female genital cutting (FGC) designates a range of customs that involve modifying, and/or removing external female genitalia for non-therapeutic purposes. Sometimes referred to as "female circumcision" or "female genital mutilation" (FGM), these practices are currently most prevalent in parts of Africa, the Middle East, and areas of Central and South America, although they have been recorded at various times throughout the world. Most girls who undergo FGC are between the ages of four and twelve, although performing the surgery on teenage women is not unheard of; the surgeon is usually a female elder with no medical training. Current estimates place the number of women worldwide who have undergone some form of FGC at between 100 and 160 million; statistics generally exclude girls who have undergone intersexual genital cutting because they were born with ambiguous genitalia.

The World Health Organization (WHO) classifies FGC into four types, of which three are primary. In the least invasive, the prepuce or hood around the clitoris is removed. Most common in Muslim countries, this form is sometimes referred to as "Sunna circumcision" and is considered parallel with male circumcision, required of all Muslim men. A second form of FGC is excision, the removal of the clitoris and often parts of the labia minora. Clitoral removal can be the procedure's goal, or a consequence of an improperly performed operation. A third form is infibulation, removal of the labia minora and sometimes part of the labia majora, with the remaining labia majora sewn together, leaving a vaginal opening that may be as small as the width of a matchstick. This type of FGC is sometimes called "Pharaonic circumcision" and is traditionally held to have been practiced in ancient Egypt. Women who are infibulated usually undergo circumcision and excision as well. Non-primary types of FGC include cauterization of the clitoris, and piercing or stretching of the clitoris and/or labia.

Reasons/rationales for the custom of FGC vary. Practitioners cite hygiene, aesthetics, control of female sexuality, increased submissiveness and/or obedience to a husband, and/or insurance that the recipient will remain a virgin until marriage, thereby maintaining her family's honor. In many cultures, FGC, as an integral part of puberty rites, marks a girl's transition to womanhood. In others, including Kenya, Uganda, and some West African countries where a woman may be expected to prove her fertility by delivering a child before marriage, she may undergo FGC postpartum.

FGC has received sharp criticism in the global North since the early twentieth century. Many view the practice as a brutal assault on girls that results in fear, pain, denial of sexual pleasure, lifelong suffering, and significant health consequences. The prevalence of AIDS in some areas where FGC is practiced heightens concerns about the transmission of HIV during the procedure. All forms of FGC can result in infection, cysts, abscesses, chronic pain, scar tissue, and increased risk of infertility. Excision permanently interferes with female sexual response and destroys a woman's ability to achieve orgasm. Infibulation can result in incomplete elimination of urine and/or menses, leading to chronic infection and pain. Infibulated women must have the fistula (the opening left for drainage of urine and menses) forcibly enlarged for first sexual intercourse and for childbirth. In the cultures that practice infibulation, a woman's labia are often resewn when her husband is away, after childbirth, or to heighten her husband's sexual response.

Numerous charities and educational outreach organizations work toward halting FGC through educational and legal means. Sweden outlawed all forms of FGC in 1982, the United States in 1996, and Canada in 1997; Mexico has no legislation concerning the practice. FGM is explicitly condemned in the United Nations Declaration on the Elimination Against Violence Against Women (1993), the Declaration and Platform for Action of the Fourth World Conference on Women (1995), and the African Charter on Human and People's Rights and its Protocol on Women's Rights (2003).

Though outlawed for many years in locations such as Sudan, FGC continues to be widely practiced because laws are not enforced. Among countries and/or ethnic and cultural groups that perform FGC, attitudes are mixed. Some women and men condemn the custom. Increasingly, successful grass-roots movements are working to change pro-FGC ideas. Their members may agree in part with outsiders' criticisms, but insist that permanent change can come only from within, using indigenous terms and concepts, rather than from imposed foreign values. In Egypt, the reported death of a girl from a botched circumcision brought the topic out in the open for discussion. Publicizing an event normally kept hidden has helped people to question the practice. Most North Americans were unaware of FGC until Stephanie Walsh won the Pulitzer Prize in 1996 for her photograph of a FGC rite in Kenya, although African American author Alice Walker explored the topic her 1992 novel *Possessing the Secret of Joy*.

Those who support FGC argue for its supposed health benefits (although evidence does not indicate any medical benefit) and necessary role in the transition of girls to adulthood. Folklore often supports its continued practice. For example, some African peoples, such as the Igbo of Nigeria, believe that uncut women will conceive the children of spirits, rather than their husbands', with dire repercussions for the community. Some argue that outsider assertions that excision destroys female sexual response are based upon inaccurate or ethnocentric understandings of human sexuality.

Evidence suggests that change will take several generations. Reports abound of parents who condemn the practice, and forbid it for their daughters, only to find that grandparents or older community members have had the procedure performed in order to conform to cultural norms. Indeed, some who disapprove allow their daughters and granddaughters to undergo FGC out of fear that the girls will be considered aberrant non-adults and be stigmatized within their communities. Additionally, parents and grandparents are concerned that girls who do not undergo FGC will be unable to find a marriage partner within their local communities, and thus will eventually move far away.

FGC is a social custom, not a religious practice and, as such, was commonly practiced in Anglo North America during the nineteenth century and well into the twentieth. Though both male and female sexual impulses were considered immoral and offensive, women's sexuality was seen as particularly dangerous; women were considered ideally asexual. Doctors sometimes prescribed excision (especially clitoridectomy) as a cure for masturbation, promiscuity, and nymphomania—uncontrollable female sexual desire—which could be diagnosed in women showing any sexual response or desire whatsoever. Indeed, as recently as the 1950s, physicians in Europe and North America used clitoridectomies to treat hysteria, epilepsy, mental disorders, depression, and lesbianism.

Clitoridectomies and other forms of FGC are currently imposed on intersexed newborns—those born with genitals corresponding to both male and female binary norms, or with ambiguous genitals—in Europe and North America. In these cases, the adverse effects of FGC are complicated by the secrecy that invariably follows such operations; parents and physicians alike seek to conceal the facts of their surgery from children and adults. Further, the default location for gender assignment is often female, justified by the saying "You can make a hole, but you can't build a pole" (Chase 2006: 302). Intersex activists oppose this procedure, arguing that sex-assignment operations should be performed only on adults, and only when they request assignment to one sex or the other. *See also:* Androgyny; Daughter; Folk Belief; Gender; Grandmother; Marriage; Sexuality; Transgender Folklore; Violence.

References: "Broken Bodies, Broken Dreams: Violence Against Women Exposed." n.d. http://brokendreams.wordpress.com/2007/01/18/female-genital-mutilation-part-2/ (accessed August 10, 2008); Chase, Cheryl. "Hermaphrodites with Attitude: Mapping the Emergence of Intersex Political Activism." *The Transgender Studies Reader*, eds. Susan Stryker and Stephen Whittle, 300–314. New York: Routledge, 2006. Originally published in *GLQ: a Journal of Lesbian and Gay Studies* 4, no. 2 (1998): 189–211; Female Genital Cutting Education and Networking Project. n.d. http://www.fgmnetwork.org/index.php (accessed August 10, 2008); Moen, Elizabeth. "The Sexual Politics of Female Circumcision." n.d. http://www.etext.org/Politics/Progressive.Sociologists/authors/Moen.Elizabeth/The-sexual-politics-of-female-circumcision.EMoen (accessed August 10 2008); Prazak, Miroslava. "Introducing Alternative Rites of Passage." *Africa Today*, vol. 53, no. 4 (Summer 2007): 19–40; Sexuality Education Resource Centre Manitoba. n.d. http://www.serc.mb.ca/SERC/content/article/femaleGenitalCutting/view?market=SP&topic=WA&subject (accessed August 10, 2008); Slackman, Michael. "Voices Rise in Egypt to Shield Girls from an Old Tradition." *The New York Times*, September 20, 2007. http://www.nytimes.com/2007/09/20/world/africa/20girls.html?ex=1347940800&en=05458b185d64b2fc&ei=5090&partner=rssuserland&emc=rss (accessed August 10, 2008); World Health Organization. "World Health Organization Factsheet on Female Genital Mutilation." n.d. http://www.who.int/mediacentre/factsheets/fs241/en/ (accessed December 23, 2007).

Theresa A. Vaughan

Feminisms

Folklore about feminism includes all discourses about feminism and feminists: the individuals and movements struggling against White capitalist heteropatriarchy at all levels—personal, institutional, and global. Feminist theorist bell hooks argues that "feminism is a movement to end sexism, sexist exploitation, and oppression," and cautions that it is not "always and only about women seeking to be equal to be men," nor is it "anti-male".

Feminist perspectives rarely get popular attention, but when they do it is usually only one form, radical feminism, that is highlighted, albeit in a distorted mode. In fact, feminism draws upon a wide variety of theoretical perspectives, some of which are intrinsically women-centered, and others of which draw upon perspectives like liberalism, Marxism, and psychoanalysis. Before we can fully appreciate the folklore-related content of various forms of feminism, it is important to note that these philosophical orientations have similarities and differences.

Liberal feminisms subscribe to ideas that most self-described social conservatives in North America would support. For example, they hold that reason and education are primary resources for improvement in the world; therefore, correcting misconceptions about women will improve their lot. Contemporary liberal feminists feel that the rights and privileges traditionally granted to men should be extended to women. They seek change through formal structures like politics, the law, and education, and their watchword is equality. Liberal feminists have certainly gained new opportunities for some women (mainly White and middle-class) as well as a more developed public consciousness about women's inequality. However, liberal feminism lacks an analysis of the ways in which institutionalized (structurally "traditionalized") forms of inequality based, for example, on class, race, ethnicity, disability, and sexuality, are difficult to dislodge through reasoning alone. Further, liberal feminisms presume a strong distinction between the public and private spaces of women and men, without necessarily recognizing the ways in which those spaces interact.

Socialist and Marxist feminisms are particularly valuable for their attention to those interactions. They locate the economy as a primary source of women's oppression, and are particularly attentive to the ways in which labor is divided into men's waged production outside the home and women's unpaid reproduction inside it. They see the traditional family household as propping up an exploitative capitalist system by reproducing wage-earner men and caregiver women, while supporting the wage-earning potential of men by making the care of men and children the responsibility of women. Socialist and Marxist feminisms describe how women serve as a reserve army of labor to be called upon when they are needed (for example, in wartime) to work in production, but to be sent back to the home once men are again available. They also note that women's work—traditionally unpaid or lower paid because of the fiction that women work only for extras and that there is a male breadwinner at home to provide for children—also serves to keep wages low overall, particularly when women move into hitherto male-dominated professions. This division of labor serves capitalism by setting wage-earning women against wage-earning men rather than uniting them against an economic system that exploits both.

Radical feminists have critiqued socialist/Marxist feminism's reliance upon traditional family structures; they see the oppression of women as fundamental to society, as a model for understanding all other forms of oppression. Not surprisingly, they have been critical of concepts of gender—the sociocultural deployment of sex—as well as noting the apparently biological inequities between women and men. Thus, reproduction itself—making babies—is seen by some radical feminists as the source of women's oppression. Their solution, however, is not to eliminate heterosexual reproduction altogether, but to value mothering as a central institution in society. They also note, contra liberal feminism, that the state (as much as individual men) is the source of violence against women and other forms of male control over female sexuality.

Anti-racist feminisms challenge the notion that differences between women and men are fundamental sources of oppression, noting that the state and individuals also foster inequities between people of Color and others through immigration policies and race-specific notions of appropriate behavior between the sexes. They have been particularly critical of the absence of women of Color and their concerns from feminist agendas and feminist organizations alike.

Psychoanalytic feminisms suggest that women need to better understand both the political and the personal dimensions of their lives though an awareness of the role of the unconscious in shaping experience and knowledge. Many see psychoanalysis's famous foreparent, Sigmund Freud, not as a male chauvinist asserting fundamental female and male differences, but instead as a cultural anthropologist giving an account of the ways in which patriarchal society processes women to be subordinate through an arcane but effective system of unconscious indoctrination. Psychoanalytic feminisms concentrate in positive ways upon mothering, sexual pleasure, and femininity.

More recent feminisms challenge other viewpoints for proffering big theories and seeking objectivity and universality, which they see as illusory. They view all humans in culture as socially constructed, multiply identified, and inherently contradictory. This perspective, sometimes called "post-feminism," has been criticized from other feminist positions as a patriarchal ploy to ensure that now that women have gained some measure of progress against oppression, they are returned to a space wherein claims about gender, patriarchy, and women have no basis. Others feel that postmodern feminisms ask that feminism itself become self-critical rather than relying upon its critics to define it: feminism must become more attentive to what we can and cannot know about the world, and what kinds of claims we can and cannot make about ourselves and others.

In the first wave of feminism, which began in Canada and the United States in the early nineteenth century, feminists sought access to education and to political processes including, but not limited to, the vote. Even during this period of strenuous political and social activism, feminists deployed humor among other tools for change. In 1914, feminists from Manitoba, the first Canadian province to give women the vote (1916), went to the Legislative Assembly asking to be enfranchised. They were refused. The next day, they presented a show at a local theater, featuring a "mock Parliament" and "a humble delegation of men, pleading for the vote," only to learn that "*nice men* don't want the vote" (Grant, 432). The performance was not only a successful fundraiser for the cause of women's suffrage, it also "set the whole province laughing at the old conception of chivalry ... as a substitute for common, old-fashioned justice" (ibid., 433).

Feminism's dour reputation blossomed during its so-called second wave, beginning in Canada and the United States in the 1960s and focusing in-depth on the social and cultural inequities women face. The source of this manifestly erroneous belief in humorless feminists may be in attempts by purveyors of sexism to excuse their behavior and words by suggesting that they were merely joking. For example, sexual harassers often try to thus explain away their displaying posters of naked women or telling jokes that stereotype women as stupid, hypersexualized, and/or incompetent. Feminists' refusal to accept these actions as humor, recognizing their underlying controlling and othering purposes, finds a parallel in the current widespread acceptance in North America that racist, and to a lesser extent classist, ableist, and homophobic behaviors and words are not only unacceptable, but also, under some circumstances, illegal. Countering such sexist acts and words, feminist humor and other forms of its folklore involve confronting negative aspects of people's characters and personalities that they can change, such as hypocrisy and racism, but is often misunderstood because it is fundamentally ironic.

Although the third wave of feminism in the 1990s and later has actively rejected the stereotype of feminism as hyperserious and feminists as self-obsessed, their discourse has had little impact on popular and media discourse. One stereotype implicit in this idea is the belief that feminism is fundamentally limited to endless discussion of trivial matters, that it is purely academic. The mainstream media in Canada and the United States foster the idea that feminists are all talk and no action, often by publicizing feminist concerns but not feminist solutions. They offer the impression that we are ivory-tower dreamers, unable to deal with reality and action.

Some newcomers to feminism, particularly those who identify as third wavers, are concerned that so much time and energy has gone into the efforts of feminists to define their differences. They often suggest that all feminists should agree on a series of aims that we would sequentially fight and win. This idea may seem initially attractive, yet feminists also need to recognize that women and other marginalized groups have different experiences and varying needs across the world. What may seem crucial for White middle-class women in Toronto or Atlanta may seem outlandish to Palestinian women living in occupied Gaza. Multicultural, global, and post-colonial feminisms draw attention in particular to the concerns of folk who have traditionally been marginalized not only by mainstream cultures and politics in the economic North, but also by feminism itself.

"How many feminists does it take to screw in a lightbulb?"
"That's not funny!"

Some Euro North Americans believe that feminists lack a sense of humor. Regina Barreca recalls her own folklore about feminists:

I thought being a feminist meant I couldn't wear lipstick or crave men with small behinds. I thought that "feminist" meant I couldn't send *Peanuts* cards to guys who I was afraid wouldn't call back, or buy stockings with seams.

I thought "feminist" meant no more steamy flirtations or prolonged shopping trips. I thought it meant braided hair and short nails, maybe mandatory tofu. I certainly associated feminism with humorless, dour, and—worst of all—unblinkingly earnest women (1991: 174).

The stereotypes Barreca alludes to remain current, especially in mainstream media, but fail to do justice to the multiplicity of feminists and feminisms.

"How many feminists does it take to screw in a lightbulb?"
"Eleven. One to screw in the bulb, and ten to form a consciousness-raising group to discuss the sexist implications of the word 'screw.'"

The stereotype that feminists are anti-sex—indeed, that we would rather discuss sex than have sex—has a multiplicity of implications for feminists and feminism. Regina Barreca's "boyfriend, relatives, professors, and other disreputable sources" told her that feminists

were ambitious, sharp-tongued, a little too smart for their own good. They told me that only women who couldn't get laid got political. They told me what was perhaps the biggest and most interesting lie of all: that independence and ambition were unattractive in a woman (1991: 174).

The idea that only lesbians are feminists—and further, that women are lesbians only because we can't persuade a man to have sex with us and/or that lesbian sex isn't sex because no penis is involved—simultaneously dismisses both the political and personal aspects of feminism. American evangelist Pat Robertson's definition of feminists and feminism—articulated in a fund-raising letter attacking the proposed Iowa Equal Rights Initiative, but often said to have been put forth at the 1992 Republican Convention—is now an item of folklore: "Feminism is a socialist, anti-family political movement that encourages women to leave their husbands, kill their children, practice witchcraft, destroy capitalism, and become lesbians" (see Moi 2006). Such disdain for politically progressive ideas: families comprising something other than a male, a female, 2.5 children, and a dog; reproductive choice; religions other than Protestant Christianity; and any sexuality other than hetero, is not shared by feminists. Many appropriate his definition to indicate that we celebrate all in feminism that anti-feminists spurn.

"How many feminists does it take to screw in a lightbulb?"
"One, to write a thesis."

Without suggesting any disrespect to privileged academic feminists in Euro North America, it must be recognized that feminism is a worldwide, multilevel movement, with multiple theories, analyses, and perspectives. Even within North America, multiple feminisms flourish. Aboriginal and Chicana feminisms, for example, focus on developing anti-colonialist as well as anti-patriarchal knowledge, recognizing the need for making space for women to use their original languages and to have a voice that is not dependent upon the ability to communicate in the mainstream language—English. And Black feminists or womanists (a term that has its origin in Alice Walker's 1983 collection of essays, *In Search of Our Mothers' Gardens:*

Womanist Prose), compelled by a different history in North America, have developed a literature distinct from those of second-wave liberal, Marxist, existentialist, and psychoanalytic feminisms; the radical force of womanist concerns is conveyed by Walker's phrase, "Womanist is to feminist as purple to lavender."

Feminism is a philosophy, a method, a politics, a worldview, and a way of life by no means limited to women, the academy, or a particular people, place, or time; nor does it lack in action or practical concepts for change—what is lacking is mainstream reports and support of those alternatives. *See also:* Activism; Class; Consciousness Raising; Folklore About Women; Gender; Humor; Joke; Politics; Race; Sexism; Sexuality; Wage Work; Women's Folklore; Women's Work.

References: Barreca, Regina. *They Used To Call Me Snow White ... But I Drifted: Women's Strategic Use of Humor.* New York: Penguin Books, 1991; Bhavnani, Kum-Kum, ed. *Feminism and "Race."* London: Oxford University Press, 2001; Cotera, Maria. "Feminism: The Chicana and Anglo Versions: A Historical Analysis." In *Twice a Minority: Mexican American Women,* ed. Margarita B. Melville, 217–234. St. Louis: C. V. Mosley Co., 1980; Grant, Diane. "Nellie McClung and the Redlight Theatre." *Canadian Women's Issues.* Vol. 1: *Strong Voices,* eds. Ruth Roach Pierson et al., 430–434. Toronto: James Lorimer and Co., 1993; Greenhill, Pauline. "Folklore." In *Encyclopedia of Feminist Theories,* ed. Lorraine Code, 211–212. New York: Routledge, 2000; Hernandez, Daisy, and Bushra Rehman. *Colonize This!: Young Women of Color on Today's Feminism.* New York: Seal Press, 2002; hooks, bell. *Feminism is for Everybody: Passionate Politics.* Cambridge, MA: South End Press, 2000; Locke, Liz. "Folklore and Feminism." *Folklore Feminists Communication,* 1997. http://www.temple.edu/isllc/newfolk/ffc.html (accessed August 10, 2008); Moi, Toril. "'I Am Not a Feminist, But ...': How Feminism Became the F-Word." *PMLA* vol. 121, no. 5 (October 2006): 1735–1741; Moraga, Cherrie, and Gloria Anzaldua. *This Bridge Called My Back: Writings by Radical Women of Color.* Third edition. Berkeley: Third Woman Press, 2002 [1981]; Ouellette, Grace J. M. W. *The Fourth World: An Indigenous Perspective on Feminism in Aboriginal Women's Activism.* Halifax: Fernwood Publishing, 2002; Shakhovtseva, Elena. "'The Heart of Darkness' in a Multicolored World: The Color Purple by Alice Walker as a Womanist Text." 2000. http://spintongues.vladivostok.com/shakhovtseva2.htm (accessed February 12, 2005); Walker, Alice. *In Search of Our Mothers' Gardens: Womanist Prose.* Reprint edition. New York: Harvest Books (Harcourt), 2003 [1983].

Pauline Greenhill and Liz Locke

Festival

Festivals are special events, almost always involving revelry and merry-making, that celebrate an event, person, or specific interest important to a body of like-minded individuals. Thousands of festivals are held by North Americans each year, and many of them celebrate women and aspects of women's and girls' lives. From film and music festivals, to regional cuisine and quilting festivals, and saints days' processions, and from the International Yukon Storytelling Festival in Whitehorse, to the Midwest Mime and Clown Festival in Indiana, to Mardi Gras in New Orleans, and *Semana Santa* (Holy Week) among the Raramuri (Tarahumara) people of northwest Mexico, festivals are many-splendored undertakings requiring the time, energy, dedication, and money of many individuals.

Festivals provide entertainment and serve the social needs of the groups who identify with whatever is being feted. They allow people who may have only a single thing in common—a love of chocolate, perhaps, or of motorcycles, or of a saint—to feel a sense of belonging and of self-celebration, but they also mark the boundaries between those who identify from an insider's perspective with a festival's theme and activities and those who come from outside to observe. With few exceptions, festivals simultaneously educate outsiders and bring communities together, all in a celebratory context in which everyone can enjoy themselves.

Festivals are generally classified as either calendrical or interest-specific. Calendrical festivals are occasions for celebration that recur at regular calendar intervals. Religious festivals usually fall into this category. For example, a ten-day pan-Mexican celebration of the Virgin Mary begins every December 3 and culminates on December 12, the day of her appearance to Juan Diego on Tepayac in 1531. While tourists are offered services and goods to satisfy their needs during the festival, the core of the celebration is experienced only by Mexican people for whom the Virgen de Guadalupe is a marker of Catholic religious identity, since the miracle was not only that the Virgin appeared but that she appeared to a Native person.

An interest-specific festival is generally an organized matrix of performances constructed around a single idea, person, event, or item of material or oral culture enacted to celebrate or promote a region, folk group, sport, story, occupation, skill, art, musical genre, food, local hero, political cause, or historical period, to name a few. Governments, private institutions, community groups, activist groups, and businesses often sponsor festivals in this category.

Increasingly aware of the economic and social issues provoked by cultural tourism, folklorists and anthropologists are producing ever more debate and scholarship regarding festival production and presentation. Most commercially marketed cultural festivals exhibit tensions between the sponsor's need for economic success and its desire to represent the specific folk group's identity in ways that satisfy its members. In a commercial festival designed largely for the pleasure of outsiders, the intended audience dictates what happens; in a festival intended to be community-centered, those attending will not differ greatly from those planning or performing at the event. Publicly funded folklife festivals, sponsored and organized by local, state, federal, and not-for-profit organizations in the United States, tend to mediate between commercial and in-group events with performances, discussions, demonstrations, and talks specifically designed to explain, educate, and showcase cultural traditions for a mixture of audiences.

Although a festival is technically distinct from a fair, carnival, rodeo, parade, heritage day, or other community celebration, any such celebration that includes a performance stage is likely to be described as a festival by visitors, performers, and organizers alike. Fairs composed mainly of competitions and demonstrations commonly host a festival stage for musical performances, storytelling, and dance associated with the community. Conversely, performance festivals often include workshops, exhibits, live demonstrations, and craft sales and displays. Agricultural festivals usually feature livestock, vegetable produce, music, and cooking competitions. The International Rice Festival of Crowley, Louisiana, for example, hosts a frog jump, a football game, the crowning of a queen and king, musical stages, and a livestock show. The Southern Womyn's Music Festival in Unadilla, Georgia, includes workshops, craftswomen, and a pet show. Festivals can be housed during a weekend in temporary tents, placed in a rural field, use existing city buildings over the course of a month, or fall anywhere between in terms of location and duration.

Many festivals, particularly those associated with religious traditions, incorporate some form of procession. At the week-long *vela* (harvest festival) held in Jalapa, Mexico, to honor Saint Sebastian, for example, a young woman is crowned queen by the mayor at the culmination of a procession of women in long, hand-embroidered dresses. On the second day of the vela, women on foot and men on horseback process to the Chapel of Saint Sebastian, where the women leave offerings of flowers and food at the feet of his statue.

Religious festivals, also known as holidays ("holy days"), may have relatively few organized performances, consisting instead of a primary activity presented by a religious leader and selected participants. Pageants in festivals at Christmas, Eid, Purim, and other holy days often enlist children as the main performers. Such presentations are not necessarily rehearsed; rather, members of a congregation or religious group view them as affirmations of community beliefs. Such pageants function to signify and create inclusion and thus community. Outsiders may be welcomed, but they will see an event presented on the community's own terms, not one designed for their entertainment.

The holding of festivals predates written records. Euro North American festivals owe much to their Greek and Roman predecessors. Since ancient times, festivals have functioned not only as community entertainments, but as rites of reversal, mechanisms for the controlled release of pent-up frustration, anger, and potential rebellion by encouraging temporary subversions and reversals of the normative social order. The ancient Athenian Thesmophoria (Festival of Demeter), a three-day festival at which citizen-wives slept in makeshift huts on the Pnyx Hill, for example, rigorously excluded men. It was probably the only time in which upper-class Athenian women were allowed to take time away from their homes and families. In a society notoriously famous for its radical gender bipolarity, "For this short period, the men were displaced, and the women took over their position at the core of the city's civic life" (Blundell, 164). And in honor of the legendary fifth-century Argive warrior-poet Telesilla, who led Argos's young women to victory against Spartan invaders, the Argives celebrated Hybristika (Festival of Impudence) on the anniversary of the battle, putting the women into men's tunics and cloaks and the men in women's dresses and head-coverings (Lefkowitz and Fant, 129).

The Roman Empire had its many public pageants, games, and gladiatorial contests, often called spectacles, to distract and entertain its citizens. But it also celebrated the annual preplanting Festival of Bona Dea (Good Goddess) at the homes of the city's generals, praetors, and consuls, who had to go away while their wives and other women took over to celebrate at night "with great amounts of festivity in the revels and music as well" (Lefkowitz and Fant, 292–293). Later, medieval European Catholics celebrated the bawdy and irreverent Feast of Fools in late December at which "license [was] permitted ... because it was customary of old among the Pagans that during this month slaves and serving-maids should have a sort of liberty given them, and should be put upon an equality with their masters, in celebrating a common festivity" (Thurston). In this and similar festivals, a beggar might be crowned king for the day, an ass might be "worshipped" in church, and the rich would serve food and give coins to their less fortunate neighbors.

Today, festivals continue to provide opportunities for people to poke fun at, even to renounce for a limited time, otherwise sacrosanct cultural values. Frequently these involve cross-dressing in a subversion of gendered norms. Dia de los Locos (Day of the Crazies) in Mexico, for instance, is a contemporary rite of reversal. During this annual celebration of spring, men not only dress in women's clothing but fully disguise themselves as women and girls. At the Farmer's Ball in Asheville, North Carolina, for reasons no longer remembered, men traditionally wear skirts to the contra dance. And at the Festival of Saint Sebastian mentioned above, at dusk the women climb the saints' chapel's bell tower to pelt the men below with fruit and party favors ranging from T-shirts to soft household gadgets such as Tupperware in a rite that some interpret as an act of their assertion as the matriarchs of the community. During Cajun Mardi Gras in Louisiana, rural women turned this centuries' old tradition on its head to create their own *courirs* (runs), during which they mask, costume, and "cut up" in order to receive money and ingredients for community gumbo dinners.

Contemporary women's festivals often accommodate discussion groups and venting sessions as part of this "safety valve" function of festival. The three-day Women's Voices Festival at Bean Town Ranch in Plantagenet, Ontario, celebrated in July since 1997, for example, provides a festival setting in which women may explore issues especially important to them through the arts, crafts, music, and comedy.

Women's roles in public festivals tend to fall into three broad categories, the importance of which have waxed and waned over time. Historically, women and girls prepared foods considered significant to community identity, sometimes demonstrating how edibles were made, and almost always selling refreshments to hungry crowds. Women produced and sold handicrafts, particularly needlework. And women were enlisted as symbols of fertility—a pregnant woman would walk at the head of an agricultural parade, or the newest mother and child would portray the Virgin Mary and infant Jesus in a performance. In most regions of North America, women representing fertility have been a smaller part of festival history than in Europe; where such roles are found in contemporary North America, they tend to be associated with a European or Latin American precedent.

After World War II, women's overt roles as fertility symbols all but disappeared in the festival context until the rise of women's festivals in the 1970s. Among the reasons for this near-extinction were the increase in women of reproductive age working outside the home, and therefore distanced from the site most commonly associated with motherhood; the rise of second-wave feminism, which encouraged women to think of themselves as more than reproductively fertile; and concerns over associations between traditional folk symbols and the abuses of folklore perpetrated by Nazi publicists. In Christian communities, doctrinal differences between Catholic and Protestant Christian theologies and between Pagan and Christian beliefs also determined when and where women may celebrate themselves or be celebrated as fertility symbols. Many Jewish women have revived the monthly Rosh Chodesh (new moon) ceremony, traditionally a women's celebration. The reclamation of the Lambda symbol (λ) at women's festivals focused on lesbian, bisexual, and transgender cultures is but one example of renewed interest in women's fertility symbolism in the festival context. Modern uses of women's fertility symbolism, however, contrast radically with previous historical and cultural assumptions in that they now connote assertions of female autonomy in matters of sexuality and fertility. Workshops, storytelling about births, and fertility rites revived and revised from pre-Christian goddess worship are some examples of the ways in which many women's festivals currently celebrate female fertility.

Women are increasingly conspicuous as both festival headliners and as organizers and administrators. The Kerrville Folk Festival and the Smithsonian's Festival of American Folklife, to take two examples, have female directors and board members. The first U.S. National Folk Festival was set up by Sarah Gertrude Knott in 1934. In Canada, the Winnipeg Folk Festival and other such events are coordinated largely through the efforts of female administrators, and women run many smaller community-focused festivals. At the oldest and perhaps best-known women's event in the United States, the Michigan Womyn's Music Festival, the governing board and all volunteer workers are female; and Canadian musician Sarah McLaughlin, who ran Lilith Fair from 1997–1999, did so on behalf of women in the pop, rock, and folk music industries.

There has been a recent proliferation of women's film festivals run by and for women, although not exclusively. These include the International Women's Film Festival held in St. John's, Newfoundland, each October; the Madcat Women's Film Festival, held in San Francisco's Bay Area in September; and Women's Video and Visionarte, a lesbian film festival held in Mexico City each August.

The Pinkster Festival, which began in New York's Hudson Valley in 1737 as a market festival for enslaved Africans in Dutch society, today acknowledges the oppression of slavery in New York and the triumph over it. African American women lead the festival's storytelling activities to honor to the matriarchs of African history. And at the Essence (magazine) Music Festival, held in New Orleans in July, seminars such as "Take Back the Music" offer forums for the discussion of the sexual exploitation of Black and other women in the music industry.

Each May, Canada holds a wide variety of Asian Month Heritage Festivals, which may include Japanese tea ceremonies, Indian classical dance performances, Chinese folk dancing, Hmong stand-up comedy, Filipino poetry;

Vietnamese puppetry, Korean musical performances, and Taiwanese story-telling, to name a few genres on display. The Asian Pacific Islander Cultural Center of San Francisco has since 1998 held its annual six-week-long United States of Asian America Festival, which showcases the talents of Bay Area cultural performers in theater, film, literature, dance, and the visual arts. Mexico City's annual Puerta de las Americas ("Gateway to the Americas") Festival hosts Mexican, Japanese, and Korean cultural events at dozens of venues throughout the city.

Some festivals, such as Native American powwows in Canada and the United States, and festivals celebrating the Hindu, Sikh, and Muslim faiths, may have certain gender-specific activities. Men may be excluded from watching particular dances performed by women and vice versa, or partici-pants may be prohibited from taking a role designated to another gender in a religious ceremony. But for the most part, there are few festival activities that actively discourage women's participation.

Rather than being confined to women-only presentations and perfor-mances, as was so often the case in the past, women have become integral to activities across the wide array of genres that festivals present. At the September Pamplonada in Mexico, for example, young women jump the barriers set up in the streets to run with the bulls—and with the men. In the southern United States, competitions at old-time and bluegrass music festival, traditionally the purview of White males, show marked increases in female competitors. In 1935, Galax, Virginia's Old-time Fiddlers Convention had a female winner only in the dulcimer competition. In 2006, women placed in the top-ten ranking in all nineteen categories, excepting Dobro, mandolin, and bluegrass banjo. Even Morris dancing, a performance art exclusive to men since the Victorian era, has begun to see a resurgence of interest from female performers. Canada and the United States host several all-female Morris dance teams or "sides" in addition to mixed-gender sides.

Likewise, male participation has begun to increase in festival genres pre-viously considered female domains: beauty and popularity pageants. The crowning of a king and queen, or the bestowing of some other honorary title—"Miss Bunny" at the Rabbit Festival in Louisiana, for example—now embraces male as well as female participants. Although there are still some festivals where the queens—usually women aged sixteen to twenty-four—reign alone, men are playing greater roles. And some festivals present rever-sals of the traditional female beauty pageant by auctioning male "slaves" to raise money for charities and political causes, or holding beauty contests in which men in bathing suits saunter across stages for the delectation of female spectators. Such competitions tend to be tongue-in-cheek amuse-ments. In some cases, fund-raising festivals that previously relied on a popu-lar vote or on a panel of judges' adjudication to crown its competition winners have moved to crowning "queen" the woman who has raised the most money.

Recently, North America has seen a rise in beauty contest parodies in fes-tival contexts. The No-Regrets Majorettes and the Menopausal Mafia, among others, dress themselves as beauty queens to march in parades. In Jackson, Mississippi, the Sweet Potato Queens, dressed in large red wigs, fishnet stockings, and sequined costumes fitted with padded hips, breasts, and buttocks, marched in the St. Patrick's Day Parade; these middle-aged women mounted a flatbed truck and threw potatoes at the audience. Humorous gender bending reverses not only stereotypes about female beauty and passivity, but explicitly parodies associations of youthful beauty with the crowning of queens at small-town festivals.

Women's festival participation today covers the gamut from audience to administration. Where their roles were once limited to the arenas of fertility, food, and handicrafts, women are now winning string-band competitions, whooping it up at jam sessions, and leading thoughtful discussions and workshops on everything from breastfeeding to social justice in the festival context. *See also:* Activism; Beauty Contest; Cross-Dressing; Film; Folklife; Folk Music and Folksong; Foodways; Gender; Lilith Fair; Material Culture; Processional Performance; Saints; Sexuality; Storytelling; Virgin of Guadalupe; Women's Music Festivals; Women Warriors.

References: Babcock, Barbara, ed. *The Reversible World: Symbolic Inversion in Art and Society.* Ithaca: Cornell University Press, 1978; Blundell, Sue. *Women in Ancient Greece.* Cambridge, MA: Harvard University Press, 1995; Browne, Jill Conner. *God Save the Sweet Potato Queens.* New York: Three Rivers Press, 2001; Davis, Susan G. *Parades and Power: Street Theatre in Nineteenth-Century Philadelphia.* Philadelphia: Temple University Press, 1986; Demott, Tom. "Jalapa Honors its Saint, Visitors Join the Fun." Festivals in Jalapa, Mexico. n.d. http://www.transitionsabroad.com/publications/magazine/0005/festivals_in_jalapa.shtml (accessed August 10, 2008); Falassi, Alessandro, ed. *Time out of Time: Essays on the Festival.* Albuquerque: University of New Mexico Press, 1987; Lefkowitz, Mary R., and Maureen B. Fant. *Women's Life in Greece and Rome: A SourceBook in Translation.* Second edition. Baltimore: The Johns Hopkins University Press, 1992 [1982]; Scullard, Howard Hayes. *Festivals and Ceremonies of the Roman Republic.* Ithaca, NY: Cornell, 1981; Smith, Melanie, and Kathryn Forest. "Enhancing Vitality or Compromising Integrity? Festivals, Tourism, and the Complexities of Performing Culture." *Festivals, Tourism and Social Change*, eds. David Picard and Mike Robinson, 133–151. Clevedon, North Somerset: Channel View Publications, 2006; Thurston, Herbert. "Feast of Fools." In *The Catholic Encyclopedia.* New York: Robert Appleton Company, 1909. http://www.newadvent.org/cathen/06132a.htm (accessed August 10, 2008); Ware, Carolyn E. *Mardi Gras: Cajun Women and Mardi Gras: Reading the Rules Backward.* Urbana: University of Illinois Press, 2007; Wilson, Joe. *Folk Festivals: A Handbook for Organization and Management.* Knoxville: University of Tennessee Press, 1983; "Women's Voices Festival." Plantagenet, Ontario, n.d. http://guides.hotel book.com/sisp/index.htmfx=event&event_id=27757 (accessed August 10, 2008).

Wendy Welch

Fieldwork

Fieldwork is a research methodology that centers on personal encounters between researchers and the people they consult. It includes many practices, including interviewing, participating in events, observing performances, recording and photographing performances, holding telephone and e-mail conversations, and discussing research texts with consultants. In short, fieldwork is the work of attention to almost every interaction, gesture, statement, and detail of the cultural world under study. It usually involves researchers traveling to the home areas of their consultants. Above all, fieldwork is an intimate activity that can often results in friendships and webs of responsibilities that last a lifetime.

Women folklore fieldworkers have contributed to the growth of the discipline since it was in its infancy in the late 1880s. Since then, women fieldworkers' perspectives have brought to the discipline new materials and groups to study as well as new ways of conducting fieldwork and theorizing the results of their labors in the field. Ideological differences in feminist theoretical perspectives notwithstanding, feminist folklore fieldworkers display genuine interest and commitment to women's causes and concerns. They employ feminist theories and approaches in choosing topics, observing, collecting, analyzing, and interpreting fieldwork data to understand and highlight the experiences, positions, roles, and other social conditions of the people whose traditions they study.

Women folklorists have long been conducting fieldwork and adding to the knowledge of cultural traditions. When folk music collecting began in earnest in New England in the 1920s, for example, women led the way, both as singers and collectors. Although men held positions in North America's academic Departments of Folklore and at the Library of Congress, there were several dedicated, self-taught folk music collectors who assiduously traveled the roads of New England looking for singers, reciters, and other musicians.

Looking back on her 1940s fieldwork, collector and musician Eloise Hubbard Linscott (1897–1978) told journalist Carol Knapton:

> "Lots of things I've done haven't been very ladylike. [I didn't plan on a career but] housework irritates me so. I'd save a nickel at a time from the household budget. I never asked my husband for a cent. When I had enough saved up in the tin box and my husband didn't need the car, I'd map out a route, one way going and another way coming back. I've been all over New England ... to record and write down tunes, words, and dance steps" (*Needham MA Times*, November 11, 1976).

Though laced with irony, the comments of early folksong collectors Fannie Hardy Eckstorm and Mary Winslow Smith in their 1927 *Minstrelsy of Maine: Folksongs and Ballads of the Woods and the Coast* show both the dedication and the challenges that early women folklore collectors faced:

> The editors of this volume fully realized that collecting these songs was a man's job. We knew very well that we could not go into lumber camps and the forecastles of coasting schooners ... where the unprinted, and too often unprintable, songs of the kind we must seek originate and flourish. Had a man been competent to perform the task expressed an intention of preserving these songs, we should not have undertaken the work. But no man appeared steeped in balladry and versed in folk-music, understanding the hearts of the people and wise to interpret what he found in them. The old songs were fast vanishing.... So we volunteered for a service for which we professed no special fitness, and soon we found that it was far from being a forlorn hope. (vii)

Folklorists had long collected materials from women, but both men and women collectors perceived them as regional or occupational, for example, rather than in gendered terms, that is, as folklore performed by women that centered on women's concerns. A significant shift in perspective came as feminist folklorists in the early 1970s began to conduct fieldwork that viewed the folklore women perform as women's folklore and urged others to do likewise.

Women fieldworkers maintain that it is insufficient to simply collect traditional material from women and call it "women's folklore"; instead, fieldwork must be conducted with the goal of focusing on or including women's traditions in meaningful ways. Fieldworkers provide information on the full context of the collected traditions: how and when do women tradition bearers perform their traditions? How have they learned their traditions and how do they teach others? Who may or may not be present when they are performed? What other materials are in their repertoires? What is the history of a traditional performance? Having such information about traditional items and their contexts—including the identities of performers and audiences, interaction styles, performance modes, and physical locations—provides a better understanding of what a tradition means to the individuals or groups involved, how it fits in with major issues in their lives, and why they may have chosen to perform it at this time. Biographical information about research participants, such as age, gender, occupation, and other aspects of personal identity, helps to give a fuller picture of traditional materials and their roles in performers' lives.

Folklore fieldworkers follow a code of ethics outlined by the American Folklore Society (AFS), which includes an obligation to explain the research project fully, to ensure the privacy of consultants who want anonymity, to conduct all interactions with honesty, and to share the collected materials with consultants.

Because women fieldworkers recognize the multiple aspects of women's folklore, they often use multidisciplinary approaches. And because women fieldworkers tend to be intrinsically motivated by their research interests, many have conducted fieldwork with little or no institutional funding. Often, fieldworkers prefer relatively lengthy stays among their research consultants to help better understand a tradition's multiple social contexts. When Kathy Neustadt (1992) conducted her multiple-year field study of a Rhode Island clambake, for example, she worked alongside her consultants at each stage of the event. While in the field, folklorists write down their observations, record performances (audio and video), photograph cultural details, participate in events, and, in general, meticulously document their field site, carefully labeling their recordings and photographs, transcribing their recordings, and translating texts as necessary.

Throughout their fieldwork and research, women fieldworkers usually maintain a feminist viewpoint, that is, they seek to deconstruct previous paradigms constructed by male-only models and also to provide detailed studies on the experiences of women. They ask such questions as how the collected materials express women's identities and their relationships with each other—women and men; what the practice of these materials shows about women and the cultures they live in; and how the materials serve to reinforce restricted images of women, subvert the status quo, or negotiate change. Women's fieldwork provides data on women's experiences that challenge and then rewrite gendered stereotypes and other erroneous cultural concepts. Carol Mitchell (1978), for example, examined joking traditions that have been the focus of other, primarily male, scholars and their male joke-tellers; but she asked about the differences between male and female joke-tellers. And Robbie Johnson (1972) looked at traditions previously ignored—the verbal art of a Texas madam—and discovered how one women used stories and jokes to control her customers and support her women workers.

African American and Chicana fieldworkers have used their fieldwork and analysis to simultaneously challenge their own and their consultants' marginalization on the bases of race, class, ethnicity, and sexuality, as well as gender. Zora Neale Hurston is particularly well-known not only for exposing racism but also for blending genres of fiction and memoir with traditional tales in ways that illuminated her society as well as her texts.

Women's folklore fieldwork and scholarship has both changed prevailing theories and established new ones. Richard Bauman's performance-centered theory, for example, has been central to Folklore Studies since the 1970s, but as Tamara Burk points out, the theory is based on research with male singers and storytellers who perform solo. Burk's essay on collaborative storytelling among women (1996) added a new perspective to performance theory and encouraged other fieldworkers to do the same.

Feminist fieldworkers have also introduced new field methodologies that have resulted in more inclusive ways to analyze and interpret field data. Elaine Lawless developed reciprocal ethnography, a practice whereby fieldworkers and consultants work with each other during each step of the research process, including analysis and interpretation. Because they want their consultants' knowledge and viewpoints to be a major part of their research texts, women fieldworkers rewrite contemporary ethnographic practices by including ample selections of their consultants' voices in their publications. Some reciprocal ethnography experiments have included blends of ethnographic and creative writing.

Gender and marital status are always factors in fieldwork, and women fieldworkers may encounter resistance or face repeated scrutiny in their field sites. Many female performers may be reluctant to perform for anyone but other women, especially if the material is personal or bawdy. Thus, in all-female get-togethers, women fieldworkers can obtain different materials than can their male counterparts, and often note varying genres and performance modes. Unmarried women conducting fieldwork in male-centered societies may encounter uncooperative community members, and sometimes danger. On the other hand, married fieldworkers who have children, for example, may find it easier to establish rapport with married women consultants who also have children. In her study, Ellen Lewin (1995) discovered that lesbian mothers identified more closely with other mothers, heterosexual or homosexual, than they did with single lesbians such as herself.

Fieldwork experiences affect not only those being studied but also those conducting the research, often instilling a new awareness in both parties of the limitations and benefits of their social roles. Women fieldworkers develop confidence in their research abilities. And since feminist folklore studies give interlocutors the opportunity to express their views, they may feel a new worth in both themselves and their traditions.

Many women develop lifelong friendships with their field consultants, and report personal satisfaction and professional growth from long-term associations with consultants who are often as passionate about their traditional materials as the fieldworkers. Often, feminist fieldworkers give back to the communities they study by establishing cultural programs, working gratis for local museums and historical societies, and sometimes becoming social and political advocates for the women they study.

Much more folklore fieldwork remains to be done in areas where, for example, women have crossed occupational gender barriers—among construction workers, firefighters, commercial truck drivers, taxi drivers, medical doctors, and professional wrestlers. Today's women folklorists are increasingly studying such populations. *See also:* Ballad; Feminisms; Folk Music and Folksong; Joke; Storytelling; Tradition; Tradition-Bearer; Women's Folklore.

References: Bourke, Angela. "More in Anger than in Sorrow: Irish Women's Lament Poetry." In *Feminist Messages: Coding in Women's Folk Culture*, ed. Joan Newlon Radner, 160–182. Urbana: University of Illinois Press, 1993; Burk, Tamara. "Collaborative Group Performance Among Three Generations of Women." *Women and Language*, vol. 19, no. 1 (1996): 3–8; Cantú, Norma E., and Nájera-Ramírez, Olga, eds. *Chicana Traditions: Continuity and Change*. Urbana: University of Illinois Press, 2002; Collins, Camilla A., ed. *Folklore Fieldwork: Sex, Sexuality, and Gender*. Lexington, KY: University of Kentucky Press, 1990; Golde, Peggy, ed. *Women in the Field: Anthropological Experiences*. Second edition. Berkeley and Los Angeles: University of California Press, 1986; Hollis, Susan Tower, Linda Pershing, and M. Jane Young, eds. *Feminist Theory and the Study of Folklore*. Urbana: University of Illinois Press, 1993; Hurston, Zora Neale. *Every Tongue Got to Confess: Negro Folk-tales from the Gulf States*. Compiled in the late 1920s. New York: HarperCollins Publishers, 2001; Johnson, Robbie Davis. "Folklore and Women: A Social Interactional Analysis of the Folklore of a Texas Madam." *Journal of American Folklore*, vol. 86, no. 341 (1972): 211–224; Lawless, Elaine J., ed. *Holy Women, Wholly Women: Sharing Ministries of Wholeness Through Life Stories and Reciprocal Ethnography*. Philadelphia: University of Pennsylvania Press, 1993; Lewin, Ellen. "Writing Lesbian Ethnography." *Women Writing Culture*, eds. Ruth Behar and Deborah A. Gordon, 322–335. Berkeley: University of California Press, 1995; Mitchell, Carol. "Hostility and Aggression toward Males in Female Joke Telling." *Frontiers: A Journal of Women's Studies*, vol. 3, no. 3 (Autumn 1978): 19–23; Neustadt, Kathy. *Clambake: A History and Celebration of an American Tradition*. Amherst: University of Massachusetts, 1992; Panini, M. N., ed. *From Their Female Eye: Accounts of Women Fieldworkers Studying Own Communities*. Delhi: Hindustan Publishing Corporation, 1991; Radner, Joan Newlon, ed. *Feminist Messages: Coding in Women's Folk Culture*. Urbana: University of Illinois Press, 1993; Sawin, Patricia. *Listening for a Life: A Dialogic Ethnography of Bessie Eldreth Through Her Songs and Stories*. Logan: Utah State University, 2004; Yocom, Margaret R. "'Awful Real': Dolls and Development in Rangeley, Maine." In *Feminist Messages: Coding in Women's Folk Culture*, ed. Joan Newlon Radner, 126–159. Urbana: University of Illinois Press, 1993.

Zainab Jerret and Margaret R. Yocom

Film

Film here includes folkloristic films and videos about women, the folklore of women in feminist and feature films, and women who make folkloristic films and videos.

Perhaps the best known early and influential female filmmaker to use the theories and methods associated with folkloristics is Maya Deren, whose avant-garde *Meshes of the Afternoon* (1943) includes a shot of Deren in a domestic space staring through a glass into something beyond or within herself. Her reflexive gaze foreshadows the postmodern turn to reflexivity in folkloristics, and many of her films touch on folklore topics. In 1947, she received a Guggenheim fellowship to conduct research on the rituals of Haitian Vodun. Her resultant work includes a book, audio recordings, and *Divine Horsemen: The Living Gods of Haiti* (1985), a posthumously edited film made from footage shot from 1947 to 1954.

While Deren was recognized for her experimental films, ethnodocumentary filmmaker Margaret Mead wanted to capture the ethos of a culture that could not be adequately conveyed without recording its visual dimension. Her *Trance and Dance in Bali* (1952), made with Gregory Bateson and Jane Belo, is especially noteworthy for folklorists; it records a ritual as a complete event, an approach that would not become theoretically significant in folklore scholarship until much later.

Another early female filmmaker was the controversial Leni Riefenstahl, who staged the 1934 Nazi Party Congress at Nuremburg using thirty-six cameras carefully angled to capture the action for *Triumph of the Will* (1935). Less well-known are her contributions to the "mountain films," intended to capture the "spirit of the folk" during the Weimar cinema era that preceded the Third Reich. The romantic images of mountain people in a towering landscape were meant to highlight their allegedly natural purity via a somewhat simplistic notion of "man against nature," thereby embodying conceptions about tradition and folklore as rural and nationalistic.

Most early folkloristic films tend to document folklore perceived as an entity, evidenced, for example, by Bess Lomax Hawes' *The Georgia Sea Island Singers* (1974/1963), made with Edmund Carpenter and Alan Lomax. Staged against a dark background and shot outside of the usual performance context, the performers sing four songs for posterity (Hawes in Sherman 1998: 67). Using films to document textual data in a new way came about, in part, because of a theoretical shift to emphasize context. Hawes changed her style for *Pizza-Pizza Daddy-O* (1969), which documents twelve African American girls performing eight singing, handclapping, and line-dance songs on a Los Angeles playground. Its textual bias is revealed by editing that cuts out most of the girls' interaction between games, but the filmmaker's move toward event studies is clear. Also in 1969, Sharon Sherman used an event model for *Tales of the Supernatural* (1970), which includes a group of teenagers telling tales that, years later, would be labeled urban legends. In a sense, her film is a test of theories about narrating as process, interaction, and event. In 1983, Sherman again emphasized event over entity with *Passover: A Celebration*, a video that focuses on a Seder (ritualized dinner) and family folklore.

Many other female filmmakers have documented folklore topics. Judy Peiser, with Bill Ferris, created *Fannie Bell Chapman, Gospel Singer*, an intimate portrait of a faith healer and singer in Centerville, Mississippi (1975). Twenty-five years later, she produced *All Day and All Night:*

Memories from Beale Street Musicians (1990), a slice of blues performances and remembrances in Memphis, Tennessee. Folklorists Elaine Lawless and Betsy Peterson (with filmmaker John Winninger) made *Joy Unspeakable* in 1981, a video about Oneness Pentecostals in southern Indiana; and Elaine Eff revealed the artistry of *The Screen Painters* (1988) as they decorated the screen doors of homes in Baltimore, Maryland. Marjorie Hunt and Paul Wagner documented the community of *The Stone Carvers* (the 1985 Academy Award Winner for Outstanding Short Documentary), the men who built the National Cathedral in Washington, DC; the film highlights the significance of ethnicity, occupation, and family.

Jennie Livingston's *Paris is Burning* (1990) depicts gay, cross-dressing African American and Latino men who attend balls in New York City dressed as they might in the White middle-class that has rejected them; they live in "houses" (informal families), have their own lingo, and attempt to be "real" (to dress and walk so as to copy their mainstream counterparts as closely as possible). Livingston's documentary calls attention to itself as a film while presenting a performative subject. Susan Levitas's *The Music District* (1996) portrays four styles of music played by men in the neighborhoods of Washington, DC: a rhythm-and-blues quartet, a go-go group, a brass "shout" band, and a jubilee-style gospel quartet.

Feminist films often document women's folklore that has been devalued or disregarded. Much of women's art, for example, is folk art. In *The Painted Bride* (1990), Amanda Dargan and Susan Slyomovics present a henna artist who creates elaborate designs on the hands and feet of a bride-to-be in the *mehndi* tradition of India and Pakistan. With her partner Irving Saraf, Allie Light produced films that honor two female visionary artists: *Grandma's Bottle Village: The Art of Tressa Prisbrey* (1982) and *The Angel that Stands By Me: Minnie Evans' Paintings* (1983). Pat Ferrero is well-known for documenting the personal significance of quiltmaking in *Quilts in Women's Lives* (1980); she used quilts to tell the story of women's social history in the nineteenth century in *Hearts and Hands* (1987). As a symbolic visual representation, quilts are ubiquitous in feminist films. For example, Elizabeth Barret's *Quilting Women* (1976) shows the special artistry and affinity Appalchian women enjoy at a quilting bee; and Sharon Sherman's *Kathleen Ware, Quiltmaker* (1979) examines the relationship between a quiltmaker's repertoire and personality, and quilting and economics. The quilt is both literal and symbolic in feature films such as *How to Make an American Quilt* (1995), which weaves together the stories of women who create a quilt for a wedding present.

Women who make films tend to concentrate on art in women's everyday lives. One such film, made by a non-folklorist but widely screened in Women's Studies, Film Studies, and Folklore courses, is *Clotheslines* (1981) by Roberta Cantow. How women use laundry as expressive behavior is brought to the screen in a series of images and voice-overs that reveal the social implications of doing the wash. By women and about women, *Clotheslines* is a self-examination of women's lives. Another look at women's concerns, *Union Maids* (1976), by Julia Reichart, James Klein, and Miles Mogulescu, juxtaposes on-camera interviews with archival footage as three women discuss the roles of female workers and union organizers, thereby highlighting both feminist issues and women's folk history. In a similar vein, Jenny Cool draws upon personal-experience narratives to examine the pressures society places on women in a commuter culture; in their housing development outside of Los Angeles, women discuss the destructive effects of suburban living in *Home Economics: A Documentary of Suburbia* (1994).

As already noted, women also document the folklore of men. Sharon Sherman looks at a chainsaw carver in *Spirits in the Wood* (1991), and at a male garage/funk/pop music band in *Kid Shoes* (2001). Likewise, there are many men's film topics of interest to or about women. For example, Tom Davenport's *When My Work Is Over: The Life and Stories of Miss Louise Anderson, 1921–1994* (2000) portrays a talented African American storyteller; John Cohen's 1981 film *Sara and Maybelle* documents the founding sisters-in-law of country music's influential Carter Family; and Les Blank, with Mauren Gosling, folklorist Chris Simon, and Susan Kell, study *Gap-Toothed Women* (1987), which explores the feminist issue of what beauty means for the members of a folk group who share only two things in common: being female and having gapped teeth.

As a rule, feminist film attempts to disentangle images of women as objects for the gaze of men from their agency as women. When more women gained access to film schools in the late 1960s, they began to claim a sense of self through film. Documenting the lives of ordinary women whose stories had been ignored by the still-male-dominated film industry, their early works served especially well as vehicles for consciousness raising. As feminist filmmakers stretched the limits of documentary film practice by personalizing their work, often presenting their tales through experimental editing, Women Make Movies, a multicultural, multiracial, non-profit media arts organization (and today a major distributor of women's films) was born. Filmmakers Elisha Miranda, Sofía Quintero, and Sonia Gonzalez have since founded Chica Luna ("Girl Moon") Productions, a company dedicated to challenging stereotypical images of women of Color. Their projects include F-Word (the F is for "feminism"), a multimedia project in New York City that trains young women (sixteen to twenty-five years of age) "across the racial, sexual, economic, and linguistic spectrum" in the filmmaking arts and sciences of screenwriting, directing, producing, cinematography, editing, and working with actors; their selected films are shown at Chica Luna's annual short film festival (Rice, 50–51).

Reflexivity, a strategy that acknowledges the filmmaker's presence in the film itself, frequently prevails in documentaries made by women (Ruby 1982; Sherman 1986). For *Not a Love Story* (1981), director Bonnie Klein and ex-stripper Linda Lee Tracy conduct fieldwork in the pornography industry to create a journey narrative of their responses, demonstrating again that, for women, the personal is political. As a result of this experience, Tracy became a filmmaker. For *Zulay, Facing the 21st Century* (1993), Argentine filmmakers Jorge and Mabel Preloran develop a relationship with Zulay, an Otavaleña, who first shows them rituals, dances, and other activities in her region of Ecuador, and then comes to visit them several times in Los Angeles. The film becomes a dialogue as Mabel and Zulay, more and more deeply connected as women and as immigrants, take over, and Zulay herself begins to edit the film. In *Stranger with a Camera* (2000), Elizabeth Barret examines the killing of a Canadian filmmaker in Kentucky in 1967; she questions her home community as both a member and as a filmmaker, weaving her personal story into the substance of the film.

In feature films, domesticity, sexuality, ritual, and celebration continue to inform films about women. As stories that bring these elements of women's lives together, many focus on weddings, as do *Steel Magnolias* (1989) and *My Big Fat Greek Wedding* (2002). Feature films may also employ biographical studies of women. For example, *Songcatcher* (2000) bases its story loosely on the life of folksong collector Olive Dame Campbell. *Prey for Rock 'n Roll* (2003) draws upon a play written by Cheri Lovedog, a tattoo artist, rock singer, and songwriter from Los Angeles. As lead actor and front person for Clam Dandy, actress Gina Gershon sings Lovedog's songs written during the 1980s heyday of punk rock. We watch as her "chick band" tries to "make it" while the seedy side of rock 'n' roll comes to the forefront, as do tattooing as a folk art and rock bands as folk groups. This semiautobiographical feature film is certainly a reflexive enterprise for Lovedog, but Gershon becomes reflexive as well when she makes a television documentary series about touring with a band while promoting the film.

Feature films often stereotype women as either dangerous or weak. Witch figures appear repeatedly, from *The Wizard of Oz* (1939) to *The Witches of Eastwick* (1987) to *Bewitched* (2005). Women and girls are frequently characterized by mainstream film as damsels in distress; the woman-in-jeopardy plot is commonplace, but especially typical of animated films based on folktales, as in Walt Disney's *Snow White and the Seven Dwarfs* (1937) and *Cinderella* (1950). The smart woman also makes appearances in feature films. In *Candyman* (1992), for example, a female graduate student conducts research on the combined urban legends of "Bloody Mary" and "The Hooked-Arm Man," a figure who has scared teenagers in lovers' lanes for decades.

In the past, women directed films but did not shoot them; today, with advances in digital technologies, the camera is often in the hands of a woman. And more educational film facilities are available. Appalshop, for instance, makes films about Appalachia; the University of Oregon Folklore Program trains students in how to make films about folklore subjects; and a number of summer institutes offer film and videomaking courses. From films and videos about such traditional topics as folk dancing, midwifery, and weaving to those that examine Neo-Pagan folklore, drum circles, hot-air balloon enthusiasts, and topless dancers, the topics women choose to document are personal, political, and constantly evolving. *See also:* Beauty; Body Modification and Adornment; Consciousness Raising; Family Folklore; Fieldwork; Folk Art; Folk Group; Gullah Women's Folklore; Handclapping Games; Henna Art/*Mehndi*; Jump-Rope Rhymes; Laundry; Legend, Urban/Contemporary; Mass Media; Personal-Experience Narrative; Popular Culture; Quiltmaking; Wedding; Women's Movement.

References: Erens, Patricia. "Women's Documentary Filmmaking: The Personal is Political." *New Challenges for Documentary*, ed. Alan Rosenthal, 554–65. Berkeley: University of California Press, 1988; ———. ed. *Issues in Feminist Film Criticism*. Bloomington: Indiana University Press, 1990; Georges, Robert A. "Toward an

Understanding of Storytelling Events." *Journal of American Folklore* 82 (1969): 313–28; Juhasz, Alexandra J., ed. *Women of Vision: Histories in Feminist Film And Video.* Minneapolis: University of Minnesota Press, 2001; Kaplan, Anne E., ed. *Feminism and Film.* Oxford and New York: Oxford University Press, 2000; Mulvey, Laura. "Visual Pleasure and Narrative Cinema." In *Movies and Methods, Vol. 2*, ed. Bill Nichols, 303–315. Berkeley: University of California Press, 1985; Rice, LaVon. "Mujeres Making Movies: Three Latinas band to change media and the arts." *Colorlines* (July/August 2007): 50–52; Rich, B. Ruby. *Chick Flicks: Theories and Memories of the Feminist Film Movement.* Durham, NC: Duke University Press, 1998; Ruby, Jay, ed. *A Crack in the Mirror: Reflexive Perspectives in Anthropology.* Philadelphia: University of Pennsylvania Press, 1982; Sherman, Sharon R. "That's How the Seder Looks": A Fieldwork Account of Videotaping Family Folklore. *Journal of Folklore Research*, vol. 23, no. 401 (1986): 53–70; ———. *Documenting Ourselves: Film, Video, and Culture.* Lexington: University of Kentucky Press, 1998; Women Make Movies. n.d. http://www.wmm.com.

Sharon R. Sherman

First Nations of North America

In most Indigenous societies of North America, the role of women is complementary in nature but equal in importance to that of men. Female power, wisdom, and labor are all necessary to maintain the balance and harmony that characterize Aboriginal life.

Women often play an essential role in the origin and creation stories of many First Nations. In the Iroquois account, creation is set in motion by a woman who falls from the Sky World onto a turtle's back. She suggests to the animals who come to her aid that if they can find some dirt, she will cause it to grow into the Earth. When one of them succeeds in bringing up a small amount of soil from the bottom of the ocean, she walks around it until the Earth is formed. For the Hopi, a Pueblo people of the southwest, it was two female spirits who first created the animals, and then Spider Woman who created pairs of men and women to people the Earth.

Women are honored in most creation stories as the origin of life. Even when they are not the prime movers, they may be present and actively involved in creation. For the Navajo (Diné), it was First Man and First Woman who brought the world into being, and who discovered Changing Woman, the ancestor of the Navajo people. For the Acoma, a Pueblo people of New Mexico, the world begins with the birth of two sisters in a dark, underground place. Guided by a spirit who teaches them to pray and sing, they bring stones, seeds, and animal images upward to the light and together they complete the work of creation.

It is through women that sacred ceremonies as well as means of sustenance are given to the people. White Buffalo Woman brought the Sioux seven great gifts, which include the Sun Dance, the sweat lodge, and the calumet (pipe). She taught them how to live and pray. Selu gave the Cherokee corn and beans, and in her death, taught them how to cultivate both. And it was a woman, the wife of Bull-By-Himself, who helped the Blackfoot men learn how to plant tobacco.

Women's role in sustaining life is recognized not only in myth, but also in traditional practices. Women of the village tribes of the Upper Missouri

River—Mandan, Hidatsa, and Arikara—performed public ceremonies before the planting of corn to ensure a good harvest. Cayuga women had a series of song-and-dance rituals for the success of their corn and bean crops. And in 1826, Henry R. Schoolcraft described a former Ojibwe practice in which, after the corn was planted, a woman walked around the field at night, naked, to ensure a successful crop.

Among the Tigarmiut of northern Alaska, women played an essential role in the success of the whale hunt. In preparation for a coming hunt, the captain's wife took a newly made sealskin float to her husband's boat, where, singing her special songs, she passed it under the bow. Once the whale was sighted, she accompanied her husband to the launching of the boat, positioning herself so that the boat would touch her before it was taken to open water. She then lay down on the ice where the boat had been launched, facing inland. The crew paddled the boat back toward her, the harpooner ready as if to strike. But as they came close, he dipped the harpoon in the water, and the boat turned seaward. The captain's wife returned home without looking back. There, for the entire period of the hunt, she was to do nothing but sit quietly, so that, just as she was motionless, the whale might not resist and give himself to the hunters. It was recognized that her behavior would affect the outcome of the hunt.

Woman's power is inherent; it comes from within, from her very nature as a woman. Perhaps the most respected—even feared—of woman's powers is menstrual power. Nearly all First Nations used to isolate young girls during menarche, using this time to instruct them in their roles as women. Numerous taboos were associated with menstrual isolation, and care was taken that a girl not touch herself, or be in the presence of men's weapons and sacred objects, so powerful was she during this time. Among the Tlingit, for example, a girl of high rank could be isolated for as long as two years; she could drink water only sparingly and through a bone tube; she had to wear a special head covering so that she could not look up at the sky; and she had certain dietary restrictions during this time. Among most First Nations, however, this isolation lasted only four days, at the end of which a feast was given by the family. Navajo girls are still honored with a four-day ceremony known as Kinaalda, in which the girl publicly makes the transition to womanhood by learning to grind corn and make a perfect *alkaan*, or corn cake, and has her body and spirit molded into a more beautiful form. On the final day of the ceremony, her power is so great that she shares it with others by blessing them one by one.

Pregnancy is also a time of great power and innumerable taboos. Pregnant women were sometimes secluded from the rest of the community because of their potentially harmful power. Among the Ojibwe, expectant mothers were told not to roll over in bed, not to look at a corpse or a deformed person, and not to lie around, but to do hard work. Food taboos included turtle, porcupine, berries, and entrails. Violations of any of these prohibitions would have physical or emotional effects on the child.

Women's power might also be acquired either in a dream or by receiving it from someone who possessed that power. These powers are most often seen in medicine women, who have knowledge of specific herbs or treatments and are sought by tribal members for their healing powers. These women know precisely where to go to find the medicine needed, and how to use the medicine for which they have power.

One medicine woman of great power was Essie Parrish, a Kashaya Pomo of California who died in 1979. At the age of eleven, she dreamed her power and song to heal people and used them both, along with ritual sucking, to draw out sickness. Later, she became leader and dreamer of the Bole Maru, the dream dance of the Pomo.

Some women who have power are afraid to use it because it is greater than they are. Those who have power, any power at all, do not advertise it, do not speak of it, and are often in awe of it. It is only when they use that power that others become aware of it. Respect for power remains one of the essential marks of the North American Aboriginal person.

Women could also be conduits of power for their husbands. The Mandan as well as other nations of the northern plains practiced ritual sexual intercourse, by which either spiritual power or membership in men's societies could be transferred from an older man to the woman's husband. Women were also important in the ceremonial life of Aboriginal people. For the Blackfoot, the opening of most sacred bundles required the participation of the bundle owner's wife. Furthermore, the Blackfoot Sun Dance had to be vowed and given by a holy woman, that is, one who had always been faithful to her husband.

Among most First Nations, women's role was distinct from that of men. They were responsible for the lodge, which they usually owned. They gathered and prepared food. They collected—and sometimes chopped—firewood. The fields and agricultural pursuits were generally their domain. They also scraped and prepared hides, a difficult job made easier because it was a communal work. Women can be portrayed as facing inward, toward the camp or village circle; men faced outward, to the world beyond. Hunting, warfare, and politics were their domain. It was a balance not always evident to outsiders, but one necessary to the well-being and continuance of the people. Women and men each fulfilled essential roles in the life of the community.

In the political realm, men may have had the most visible and active role, but that is not to say that women were silent. Among the Iroquois, a matrilineal society, the clan mothers could select and depose chiefs. Women also had their own council which served to advise the chiefs, and they could influence a decision on going to war by withholding necessary supplies. The Cherokee had their Beloved Women, such as Nancy Ward (ca. 1738–1822 or 1824), who advocated for the Cherokee to stop selling their land to Whites, and whose proven wisdom and experience earned a dominant role in community affairs and council decisions for Cherokee women.

A Blackfoot story tells of Napi, the Creator-Trickster, and his wife Old Woman, who were making some decisions about how humans would live. "Well," said Napi, "I am to have the first say in everything." "Fine," replied Old Woman, "as long as I have the second say." And that how it has been ever since; women have the final say. Or as Paula Dove Jennings (Niantic-Naragansett) has expressed it, it is right for men to stand in the forefront, and it is right for women to stand behind men, but it is right so that they can tell them where to go (*The Native Americans: Northeast* 1994).

Stories of women who distinguished themselves in battle are found in many Aboriginal groups. It was not unusual for women to accompany war parties, but it was rare, and often by accident, that a woman participated in a battle. The daughter of Na-nong-ga-bee, an Ojibwe chief of Lac Courte Oreilles in Wisconsin, had accompanied her father and her brother to the signing of the Treaty of 1854. On the way home, they were ambushed by the Sioux. Both men were killed, but the daughter picked up her father's rifle and killed and scalped two of the enemy. On her return to La Pointe, she was honored as a warrior. She married and lived until 1919. The Piegan warrior woman Running Eagle led many war parties to avenge her husband's death at the hands of the Crow. She herself was killed leading a horse-stealing raid against the Flatheads.

A woman's role at the center of tribal life made her the bearer of culture, and in this role, she also created objects that were both useful and beautiful. At various times in almost all Aboriginal societies, she made and decorated clothing, pottery or baskets, mats or rugs. Like Spider Woman, Navajo women still weave rugs, Pueblo women still make pottery, and one only has to see a powwow to know that women of the First Nations are still making beautiful clothing, remain powerful in their dance, and continue to share in the work of creation. *See also:* Herbs; Initiation; Menarche Stories; Menstruation; Myth Studies; Politics; Pregnancy; Ritual; Tradition-Bearer; Warrior Women.

References: American Indians, The. 21 vols. Alexandria, VA: Time-Life Books, 1992–96; Erdoes, Richard, and Alfonso Ortiz, eds. *American Indian Myths and Legends*. New York: Pantheon Books, 1984; Hilger, M. Inez. *Chippewa Child Life and Its Cultural Background*. St. Paul: Minnesota Historical Society Press, 1992; Kehoe, Alice B. "The Function of Ceremonial Sexual Intercourse among the Northern Plains Indians." *The Plains Anthropologist*, vol. 15, no. 3 (1970): 99–103; Mason, Philip P. *The Literary Voyager or Musseniegun*. Michigan State University Press, 1962; *Native Americans, The: Nations of the Northeast*. Dir. John Borden and George Burdeau. Turner Broadcasting Corporation, 1994; Peters, Virginia Bergman. *Women of the Earth Lodges: Tribal Life on the Plains*. Norman: University of Oklahoma Press, 1995; Perdue, Theda. *Cherokee Women*. Lincoln: University of Nebraska Press, 1998; Rainey, Froelich G. "The Whale Hunters of Tigara." *Anthropological Papers of the American Museum of Natural History*, vol. 41, part 2 (1947): 231–283; Sturtevant, William C., gen. ed. *Handbook of North American Indians*, vols. 5–15. Washington, DC: Smithsonian Institution Press, 1978–2004; Wissler, Clark, and D. C. Duvall, eds. *Mythology of the Blackfoot Indians*. Lincoln: University of Nebraska Press, 1995.

Theresa Schenck

Flowers, Language of

The language of flowers refers to meanings attached to different types of flowers, primarily during the Victorian era. With their beautiful forms and sweet smells, flowers have been appreciated by all cultures that encounter them. They are mentioned in some of the earliest writings of humankind, and their images appear on pottery and other extant art from the earliest eras. Flowers have been valued for their beauty and perfume, and sometimes for their medicinal properties. During medieval times in Europe, flowers were commonly used to flavor both food and drink.

Historically, it has been common to associate certain flowers with symbolic meanings. For example, in North America today, it is common to associate roses with love. That symbolism is further elaborated by color value: red roses symbolize passion, white roses a pure and chaste love, and yellow roses symbolize friendship. In France, chrysanthemums are associated with death, and any hostess would be shocked to receive them at a dinner party. Lilies are celebratory at Easter and grim at funerals; the French exchange lilies-of-the-valley on May Day.

At perhaps no time, however, was flower symbolism as highly elaborated as it was during Queen Victoria's reign in England. In the mid- to late-1800s, numerous books were written on the meanings associated with flowers. One of the most popular, published in 1885 and still reprinted today, is *The Language of Flowers* by Kate Greenaway. Codes for understanding the language of flowers were usually presented in books of etiquette and proper social and business behavior. All well-comported middle- and upper-class women were aware of flower symbolism and its use in social interaction. One could send a message to a friend or lover through careful choice of flower types in a bouquet. This era saw a number of covert ways of expressing sentiment—more direct means of communication were considered in poor taste, or otherwise socially prohibited. The Victorians also had an elaborate language for the use of hand-held fans and for the disposition of stamps on envelopes.

Flower meanings include examples such as these: bachelor button for celibacy; calendula for joy; forget-me-not for true love; gardenia for secret love; purple hyacinth for sorrow or apology; larkspur for fickleness; orange blossom for wisdom; snapdragon for deception; sweet pea for departure; and zinnia for thoughts of friends. Finality was bequeathed to relationships with a bouquet of wilted flowers, a very clear statement of displeasure and loss of affection. Appropriate flowers to convey an intended message were gathered into bouquets known as "tussie-mussies" and exchanged as gifts.

Students of Victorian culture continue to disseminate information on the language of flowers, although it must be said that the use of this language is quite rare today. Still, it has made its way into North American popular culture and remains there, enlivened by etiquette writers such as Judith Martin, a syndicated columnist known as Miss Manners. *See also:* Coding; Gardens; Gender; Language of Fans; Popular Culture; Pottery; Tradition.

References: Greenaway, Kate. *The Language of Flowers.* New York: Dover Reprint, 1993 [1885]; Laufer, Geraldine Adamich, and Ockenga, Starr. *Tussie-Mussies: The Victorian Art of Expressing Yourself in the Language of Flowers.* New York: Workman Publishing, 1993; Robinson, Nugent. *Collier's Cyclopedia of Commercial and Social Information and Treasury of Useful and Entertaining Knowledge.* New York: P. F. Collier, 1892.

Theresa A. Vaughan

Folk Art

Folk art has multiple meanings dependent on context and use. For the purposes of this entry, "folk art" will be used to refer to those traditional arts falling under the category of material culture, as opposed to performance, beliefs, knowledge, etc. The term "folk" embodies the collective, communal, and traditionally social aspects of creative expression, while "art" alludes to the aesthetic, symbolic, solitary, and imaginative spheres of artistic practice. "Folk" coupled with "art" offers the broadest sweep of cultural and aesthetic conventions corresponding to individual or group creative sensibilities, subject to the forces of tradition as well as catalysts for change. Folk art defined as a process emphasizes the dynamics of creativity and the transformative power of artistic action performed in a cultural context. Such a flexible definition highlights the sociocultural interplay among layers of artistic transmission and preservation, religious beliefs, ritual enactments, local aesthetic systems, and creative invention.

During the early Renaissance, art conceptually separated from the cluster of folk arts, popular arts, and craft. The latter were considered subordinate to "fine art," and a majority of them were associated with domestically produced "women's work." Thus, women's creative activities were doubly segregated in terms of space and importance. Although women are among some of the most prolific and innovative folk artists, particularly in the field of textile production, they often play a secondary role to male artists or, in the commercial domain, to men acting as purveyors for the marketing and distribution of folk art objects. Both male and female artists are active in the traditional areas of non-commercial, culturally based folk arts, but within this category, the domestic arts (for example, spinning, weaving, basketry, sewing, cooking, baking, and family photography) are still more likely to be considered typical of women's creative efforts.

In the past, many academics, particularly art historians, judged folk art to be fixed and static representations of societal values, created by untutored individuals with little choice but replication, who performed automatically, or unquestioningly, within the constraints of unchanging traditions. Nevertheless, due to folk art's evident resilience and adaptability, a few scholars, especially folklorists using a performance theory or ethnography of speaking perspective, looked beyond "instinctual expressions" and "dying traditions" to identify a different dynamic at work: change, which they regarded as a creative stimulus rather than as an agent of annihilation or extinction. Proponents of this view further suggest that traditional art forms and cultural realities simultaneously feed into each other in a round of reciprocal stimulation and creation. This attitude is more consistent with the inventiveness and diversity characteristic of folk art; it recognizes the innate human desire for creative expression channeled through history and tradition into a vibrant aesthetic of the everyday.

Discussion about differences among folk art categories is less productive in the long run than is an examination of creative behavior in cultural contexts. Such terms as "outsider art" with its subsets of visionary, naïve, and self-taught artists, as well as "peasant," "popular," "ethnic and tourist," "vernacular," "primitive," and "traditional" arts, tend to be more useful for classification and analysis. Maintaining a focus on the dimensions and energies of the creative process avoids the pitfalls of such limiting boundaries in order to minimize categorical distance for the sake of relationship and meaning. There are several genres that fall under folk art in its most inclusive sense.

The primary ones are painting, pottery, textile arts, carving, sculpture, basketry, furniture, jewelry, foodways, and environmental art (for example, yard installations, shrines, and buildings). Some of these are historically allied with women's creativity, while others are crossovers that both contemporary male and female artists practice. For instance, the Lopez family of wood carvers from Córdova, New Mexico, is indicative of a trend wherein daughters and granddaughters join sons and grandsons to perpetuate family carving traditions. In traditional rural communities, men and women sandwiched their art-making between the all-consuming chores that were their livelihood, embroidering at night or sculpting during rest breaks. For others, like Navajo weavers, art was their main occupation, and women dominated the field.

Painting is one of the more idiosyncratic of expressive media. For this reason, it is also the most problematic folk art genre. Folklorists tend to position aesthetic actions relative to key social values and communal traditions rather than identify them with eccentric fringe or marginal elements. Painting often leads to highly individualistic creations, but if viewed in relation to historical and sociocultural contexts, then a framework exists for judging creativity and innovation in cultural terms, that is, within specific rules and boundaries. It also helps, as in the case of Anna Mary Robertson Moses, "Grandma Moses," when iconography, symbolism, and imagery are inspired by local scenes and traditions. The term "memory painting" refers to the way a folk artist channels the past into the present by reactivating memories through form, color, and image.

The biographies of other folk artists attest to similar circumstances: a background of continuous employment, even hard labor, transmuted into ceaseless creative activities upon retirement. For instance, the Finnish folk painter Tyyne Esko was a single parent who embroidered her children's clothing as a creative antidote to the persistent health problems and intolerable poverty of a harsh working life. Upon compulsory retirement due to back trouble and severe allergies, she diverted her creative energy into the production of more than 250 paintings, many of which depict themes connected to her own stories of privation and neglect exacerbated by blatant governmental prejudice and patriarchal bureaucratic disregard.

Other folk artists created their work as a form of self-therapy. For example, Theora Hamblett, a Southern artist, painted childhood scenes as well, but used her art to sublimate emotions stemming from a personal history of family trauma. She was a driven artist who claimed that she could paint any subject any day of the week, excepting Wednesdays, which she reserved for dreams and visions.

The work of Navajo painter Sybil Yazzie and Pablita Velarde, a painter from New Mexico's Santa Clara Pueblo, exemplifies the "naturalistic style" of Native American painting prior to the 1960s. Images of ceremonies, dances, reservation life, and material culture, rendered in a characteristic two-dimensional style, were emblematic of certain expectations applied to a Native American "aesthetic" resulting from the promotion of southwestern tourist or ethnic arts beginning in the 1930s. Although the majority of these paintings depict cultural enactments, their representational style relates to an assimilation of dominant Anglo art methods adapted by a subordinate minority, especially in the manipulation of space, composition, and other formal elements. As tradition-bearers in their respective societies, Sybil Yazzie and Pablita Velarde, however, are more akin to ethnographic memory painters who fashion their narrative elements from a myriad of cultural details in the name of remembrance.

A salient characteristic of folk painting is the number of visual particulars, images, and complex designs present in one composition to convey the richest possible story line without sacrificing any details. Works of some folk artists teem with motifs that appear to completely fill all available space with a sense of *horror vacuo* (fear of the void), banishing emptiness in favor of overabundance. In Native American painting, groups of moving figures are rhythmically placed against plain backgrounds, so that despite the profusion of elements, there is a feeling of infinite spaciousness as well as a timeless quality. This mood is common to "Indian painting" of that era and evolved from the visual synthesis of religious and temporal components. Similarly, Grandma Moses' compositions are replete with a surfeit of detail that relates to an array of narrative possibility according to the degree of visual documentation necessary for a kind of total pictorial "recall." There is something "homely" about her compositional arrangements, suggesting a feminine sensibility and an observant eye attuned to a theater of the rural-domestic.

Folk painting generally involves a flat, two-dimensional, non-illusionistic style that does not try to replicate nature or reproduce "what the eye sees;" rather, it depicts "what the imagination knows." Representational elements are important for narrative truth, but are portrayed abstractly with flat applications of color, no shading or modeling, an emphasis on linearity and color edges, and exaggerations or distortions in relation to scale. Figures and background meld into the frontal picture plane, negating a sense of depth. Perspective is frequently interpreted through the vertical alignment of formal components piled up and trapped in shallow spaces. There is no suggestion of recession in space, but only an arrangement of elements suspended across the painting's surface, held there by the internal logic of the composition. The notion of bodies physically occupying space is implied by overlapping figures rendered in profile or three-quarter view. In this way, the painter artistically communicates as much visual information as possible without having to contend with the complexities of illusionism's proportioning and foreshortening techniques. Relationships among figures are often represented symbolically through a hierarchical scale that stresses importance (the largest being the most important) rather than the reality of actual size. Many of Tyyne Esko's mini-self portraits stress her self-perception as a politically powerless but nevertheless obdurate and persistent social critic. This impression is conveyed in the way she continually and astutely inserts a wry mini-representation of herself into each painting. Through the creative process, Esko reclaims her power as an artist-witness, affirming her personal values by painting these scenes of inequity and injustice.

The genre of pictorial narrative is not restricted to painting. Embroidery has also been used, chiefly by women, in different parts of the world to create commemorative scenes and utopian dreams, to portray cultural enactments, to satirize politics, and to record myths and legends. Because of its fluid, plastic nature, embroidery, like painting, is more susceptible to individualistic impulse and free invention than are other types of textile creations. Unlike most functional embroidered pieces, at least in Western European cultures, the primary subject matter of narrative embroidery indicates that it is intended to be displayed and "framed" in some way—placed on a wall, a bed, or clothing—and intended to be "read." Many such compositions are signed, which is still more common in the fine art world of museums and galleries. To sign one's work counteracts the prevalent notion of the "anonymous" and interchangeable folk artist, an idea long circulated among certain art professionals.

Unlike the dominant two-dimensionality of folk painting, embroidery, with its dense rows of stitches, presents a surface thick with color and tactility. The selection of a wide variety of stitches enhances visual and narrative interest in the textural detail and three-dimensional qualities of embroidered compositions. Aesthetic decisions about formal elements such as perspective, shadow, texture, and surface highlights, transform embroidering pictorial compositions from replication to artistic action. The uneasy course of decision-making is riddled with risk and experimentation, ultimately tempered by the folk artist's creative engagement with the artwork. An artistic form emerges from an internal crossfire of questions and responses operating within the artist's mind and executed by her hand. The highly complex process of creative choice-making that infuses these pieces is reflected in the intensity of their artistic expressiveness.

Some folk artists who are positioned as both insiders, members of a particular community, and outsiders, by virtue of their dedication to art practice as well as by their unique or visionary worldviews, frequently benefit from the creative advantage of their dual perspective. Such artists have intimate native knowledge combined with a critical distance necessary to conceptualize the familiar "from afar." This is apparent in the embroidered pictorial narratives of Josephine Lobato, a folk artist in Colorado's San Luis Valley. The self-conscious synthesis of internal and external viewpoints within the context of her art work validates Lobato's artistic mission to serve as a type of cultural commentator or tour guide to her own Latina/o culture. She is a prolific artist whose themes encompass aspects of the cultural landscape, ceremonial enactments, religious observances, myths and legends, and pictorial maps of significant sites dotted with portraits of local personalities. The majority of Lobato's embroidered images and narrative scenes derive from her memories of the post-World War II 1940s, a transitional period for Latina/o people in the American Southwest. Her choice of such imagery, with its diverse pictorial content, provides clues to the folk artist's process of evaluating acts of remembrance and cultural transformation in relation to tradition, change, and discontinuity.

Folk artists like Lobato are compelled by ongoing creative restlessness that keeps generating ideas for new work while still engaged in creating its antecedents. Ulla Nordin, a Swedish embroiderer, is another such artist. She describes her inspirations, also derived from childhood reminiscences, in terms of her head "swarming with images" that come to her all of the time, triggering chain reactions of creative response.

Tradition is the yardstick against which continuity and creative innovation are measured. The culturally determined legacy of borrowing and cross-fertilization in the evolution of Navajo weaving places it within the tradition of ethnic folk arts. Because of its adaptability and eclecticism, however, over time Navajo weaving has also been responsive to the creative interventions and impulses associated with folk art. These are generated by dynamic artistic and cultural processes as well as historic forces (for example, the wool trade, interactions with Anglos and Spaniards, marketability, commercial versus traditionally prepared dyes, color preferences, changing symbolic repertoire, pictorial compositions, etc.). Early in the eighteenth century, during the Spanish colonial period, the nomadic sheepherding Navajo learned weaving from their sedentary Pueblo Native neighbors. Unlike the Pueblo, the majority of Navajo weavers are women, who pass on their techniques and aesthetic standards through a female-directed line of cultural transmission from generation to generation. Since the 1700s, weavers have traded their wool blankets and rugs while, in turn, their engagement with the marketplace has catalyzed the cycles of innovation and experimentation that characterize the lively history of these textiles.

The aesthetic orientation of many Navajo weavings derives from women's experience of living close to the natural world, observing the gradations in a light-suffused sky from dawn to dusk, its horizon lines, colors, and cloud patterns, and the features of the land. Portable looms permit weavers some freedom to locate themselves at various spots on the landscape, to work surrounded by family, or alone on a mesa, perhaps with sheep for company. Another constellation of weaving designs draws from Navajo storytelling traditions of creation myths, ancestor stories, ceremonies, and sacred songs or chants. Many older textiles subtly display an underlying compositional structure correlating to sets of prayers or chants, which are visually symbolized in paired lines of motifs contrasted with varying configurations alternately repeated across the design field. Her familiarity with weaving and prayer composition prompted ethnologist Gladys Reichard to identify these formal arrangements as the "visual rhythm" of Navajo textile motifs, their aural counterparts echoed in the metrical patterns of prayer chants. Since prayers are considered intrinsic to the weaving process, the designs on Navajo blankets and rugs represent a spiritual belief system together with an aesthetic view of reality.

Creative exchanges between Navajo weaving and Latina/o (Hispanic) Rio Grande textile traditions continue today in the work of women such as Eppie Archuleta, a contemporary southwestern weaver living in Colorado. Descended from an ancestral mother-line of Navajo and Latina weavers, Archuleta's art represents an ongoing synthesis of styles, with injections of inspiration culled from magazine illustrations, museum collections, and textiles exhibits at the annual Santa Fe Spanish Market. Her work and the weavings of many of her contemporaries exemplify the vibrancy of an internal artistic dialogue that embraces revival and innovation as viable alternatives to the oft-cited dichotomy between the "authentic" and the "fake," or non-traditional.

Quilts are another genre of folk art that encompasses the functional and the decorative. They are the creative products of groups of women cooperatively creating and working together in quilting bees. Originally pieced from recycled scraps of clothing, sometimes appliquéd, and then quilted through long hours of conversation and camaraderie, quilts are an assemblage of tangible traces of personal biographies and collective histories. While piecing is often an individual effort, or one in which an older relative might guide a younger one, the actual quilting frequently is a communal folk process, and quilts as composite aesthetic forms have much to say about the social nature of women's and girls' creativity and the potency of artistic activity vis-à-vis societal norms. Folklorists Joyce Ice and Judith Shulimson wrote about this social process in 1979. The notion of ethnoaesthetics or folk aesthetics (how groups judge its work and the values they assign to it) is vital to maintaining internal creative expressiveness within the quilting group; further, it guides quilters in their mutual reactions to and appraisals of finished quilts.

Quilting is an amalgamation of European sewing methods inventively adapted to local aesthetics and materials (although imported trade fabrics were originally used). For example, while European and American missionaries taught many Indigenous women Western European sewing techniques, these women adapted and sometimes changed those techniques for already extant traditions of fabrication and design, whether hide-binding in North America, barkcloth construction in the Pacific, or African strip-weaving. This stylistic integration is notable in Cook Islands' *tivaevae*, African American pieced quilts, and Hawaiian and Native American pieced and appliquéd quilts. Borrowing and assimilation characterize the burgeoning relationship between Amish quilters and refugee Hmong needleworkers in Pennsylvania. Instead of a minority group incorporating and adapting the stylistic features of a dominant society, Hmong and Amish textiles share some technical and aesthetic affinities (for example, intricate hand-quilting skills, use of borders, or a preference for linear geometrical forms and solid colors), but quilters also appropriate particular aspects of their art from one another, for example, the distinctive color blocks on Amish quilts and Hmong virtuoso appliqué and reverse appliqué techniques.

Hmong women traditionally create *paj ntaub*, "flower cloth," with a combination of appliqué, geometric reverse appliqué, complex embroidery, and profuse fields of cross-stitch. Hmong "story cloths," which document cultural traditions as well as the Vietnam War, emerged as a genre in Thai refugee camps. Missionaries encouraged this art form as a way to pass the time and create a saleable product for which women use traditional embroidery stitches to tell their tales. Men and boys, however, who learned to read and write, generally were the ones who drew the original designs for the stories. Over time, story cloths have acquired words in both Hmong and English, and women now make them in more "modern" colors, which appeal to their mostly American purchasers.

Before the period of enforced migration from Asia, these ornamental panels were not only affixed to clothing, but served as showpieces to impress suitors with evidence of the stitcher's skill, which would be critiqued to determine her suitability as a marriage partner. Children's clothing was especially embellished with geometric maze-like patterns used as protection against malevolent spirits. Complicated apotropaic (evil-averting) designs were believed to deter bad spirits by trapping them within their convoluted, overlaid, and densely stitched decorations lacking any "escape routes." The protective magical properties of African American strip quilts were based on similar symbolic trickery. African American quilters created bold, intricately fashioned patterns to attract evil forces, disorient them in a profusion of shapes and colors, and entrap them, depriving them of their ability to cause harm.

Coding is another form of non-verbal symbolism found in women's folk arts. Differing from the practices of protective and sympathetic magic previously described, coding reconfigures conventional imagery in a way that defiantly subverts common meanings in order to mask or camouflage political ideas that if blatantly expressed may threaten the dominant culture. Familiar examples of these strategies of subversion and transformation appear, for instance, in parodies of the traditional Sunbonnet Sue quilt patterns. Through a rich syntax of visual language, folk textiles have always been vehicles for encoded meanings; they are felt to embody magical forces and symbolic inversions that creatively negate and contradict official cultural codes, sustain artistic license, and challenge social norms.

Pottery easily lends itself to the folk artist because clay is readily available, relatively inexpensive to work with, and a ceramicist can be as social or solitary as she likes, potting by herself or with others in a studio. Pottery maintains strong traditions, whether in the Appalachians, the American South, or the Southwest, yet it also offers opportunities for invention and creative change, as in the case of Helen Cordero (1915–1994) of Cochiti Pueblo in New Mexico, who revived a nearly moribund tradition of pottery at Cochiti in the 1950s. Folklorist Barbara Babcock notes how Cordero reinvented and personalized a line of effigy storytelling figures inspired by memories of her grandfather telling stories to her and her cousins. Cordero invigorated and enhanced a now-popular figurative genre that extends to other pueblos and continues to generate endless creative variations, for example, grinning bears, tourists slung with cameras, men smoking, even a Navajo-style storyteller.

In the case of Georgia Blizzard (1919–2002), clay was the only traditional contribution to her ceramic art. Her vessels and sculptures are characterized by a visual vocabulary drawing from nature, particularly its harshness and unpredictability. Her signature "woman pots" blend pre-Columbian fertility symbols with autobiographical elements. Blizzard empathized with future owners of her pots when she designed her hand-built "arks" to hold not only physical objects, but also ineffable experiences, emotions, memories, and ideas; hence, her work has strong poetic appeal. The importance of communicating to and connecting with others through one's artistic expressiveness is also revealed in environmental works in which folk artists create installations from found objects. The scale and accumulation of recycled material in these art spaces is frequently impressive, reflecting the artist's choice-making in vivid, complex arrangements, and always intended to be viewed and experienced by others. Wisconsin artist Mary Nohl (1914–2001) spent years transforming her family home and yard on the shores of Lake Michigan into a shrine to lost underwater worlds. Each fresh layer of sediment added to her installations generated new interactions and another round of involvement and appreciation. Tressa Prisbrey transformed her anguish over the loss of most of her family at age sixty into an intricate "Bottle Village" where she greeted visitors by asking if they were alone in the world; she then sympathetically invited them into her alternate universe, one that offered them solace.

Folk art revivals are more than salvage or rescue operations. Whether a tradition is revered or altered, revitalizations of folk art genres have proven themselves to be powerful ways in which the past emerges freshly in the present. Training in techniques such as spinning, weaving, embroidery, and pottery in locales where these art forms have historical associations can invigorate and extend the possibilities of the present. Women tend to benefit from such projects not merely for the economic gain and the flexibility of working at home in the midst of families, but also for the boost in self-confidence, the discovery that their creations are valued, and the sense of empowerment. Many women confirm that the most successful revival projects are consonant with their present lifestyles, provide a modicum of self-sufficiency, and offer a broad range of artistic expectations and goals. In all of the folk arts, external and internal forces spin around within the folk artist, each of whom attempts to resolve and finalize slippery concepts such as tradition, authenticity, and change. The most open-ended view of folk art opts for interpretations that are highly sensitive and responsive to the changeability of human nature and that honor the transcendent character of art-making as inherent to all peoples' struggles and accomplishments. *See also:* Aesthetics; Coding; Embroidery; Folk Photography; Folklife; Foodways; Material Culture; Piecework; Pottery; Quilts; Sampler; Tradition; Weaving.

References: Babcock, Barbara. *The Pueblo Storyteller: Development of a Figurative Ceramic Tradition.* Tucson: University of Arizona Press, 1990; Glassie, Henry. *The Spirit of Folk Art.* New York: Harry N. Abrams, Inc., 1989; ———. *The Potter's Art.* Bloomington: Indiana University Press, 1999; Ice, Joyce, and Shulimson, Judith. Beyond the Domestic: Women's Traditional Arts and the Creation of Community. *Southwest Folklore* 3 (1979): 37–44; Jones, Michael Owen. "How Do You Get Inside the Art of Outsiders?" In *The Artist Outsider: Creativity and the Boundaries of Culture*, eds. Michael D. Hall and Eugene W. Metcalf, 312–30. Washington, DC, and London: Smithsonian Institution Press, 1994; Klein, Barbro, and Mats Widbom, eds. *Swedish Folk Art: All Tradition is Change.* New York: Harry N. Abrams, Inc., 1994; Pershing, Linda. "'She Really Wanted to Be Her Own Woman': Scandalous Sunbonnet Sue." In *Feminist Messages: Coding in Women's Folk Culture*, ed. Joan Newlon Radner. Urbana and Chicago: University of Illinois Press, 1993; Radner, Joan Newlon, ed. *Feminist Messages: Coding in Women's Folk Culture.* Chicago: University of Illinois Press, 1993; Wahlman, Maude Southwell. *Signs and Symbols: African Images in African American Quilts.* East Rutherford, NJ: Studio Books, 1993; Zug, Charles G. III. "Folk Art and Outsider Art: A Folklorist's Perspective." *The Artist Outsider: Creativity and the Boundaries of Culture*, eds. Michael D. Hall and Eugene W. Metcalf, 144–161. Washington, DC, and London: Smithsonian Institution Press, 1994.

Suzanne P. MacAulay

Folk Belief

Folk belief includes a wide range of performances, both oral and material, founded in faith, cultural knowledge, or popular tradition. It refers to an idea, but usually takes the form of an expression or behavior that describes or communicates how a person or group conceives of or relates to a range of social structures from everyday life to religious belief to natural systems and more. The observable expression of a folk belief is only part of its meaning, which can be explored only in its original context. The contexts of women's folk belief include the realms of foodways, folk medicine, religion, parenting, and the supernatural, among many others.

Particularly in the past, many folklorists failed to address whether the people they worked with actually believed the traditions they described. Without information about the social contexts in which particular examples are expressed, practiced, or performed, it is difficult to understand belief. Exceptionally, Canadian folklorist Helen Creighton opens her autobiography with the question, "Was it prophetic that I was born with a caul?" She gives a good indication of her varying levels of belief in her explanation that in Nova Scotia and elsewhere, infants born with portions of the placenta covering their face "will inherit second sight or at least a sixth sense, and *this is true in a slight degree in my case*" and that "a person so born need never worry. Things would always work out for them, and *this has always been true for me*" (emphases added, 1975: 1). Creighton's case shows clearly how a more sympathetic understanding of belief and knowledge—often associated with women fieldworkers—can positively influence research results.

However, "folk belief" is too often used in a pejorative sense to describe the allegedly irrational fears or misconceptions of rural, uneducated, and naïve people. Folklorists' attempts to redefine the term and/or to rename the genre have remained unsuccessful. Folk belief remains nearly synonymous with the even more loaded term "superstition," generally connoted as a backward, uneducated belief in superhuman or supernatural powers.

Contemporary folklorists are careful to note that while many folk beliefs are conscious, imaginative, and purposeful, others express cultural knowledge and understanding rather than belief, and some may be spoken or performed by people who don't actually believe in them. At the same time, folk belief continues to be construed as a type of knowledge that is not verifiable or measurable by scientific or quantitative methods—which is not to say that folk belief is the opposite of knowledge (or knowledge misconstrued). Rather, it is a different way of knowing. Some folklorists and others would argue that Euro North American scientific understanding is itself extensively based upon beliefs, and the designation "belief"—as opposed to "knowledge"—for vernacular understandings is thus multiply problematic. What makes modern medicine, for example, different from magic is that Euro North Americans believe it to be knowledge rather than belief. Feminists argue that women's understanding is often similarly dismissed as belief while men's is approvingly termed knowledge.

Folk beliefs are not only abstract expressions or symbolic actions; they may also shape actual behaviors and everyday practices. For example, a rhyme circulated especially by college-age students suggests that drinking "beer before wine, feeling fine; liquor before beer, nothing to fear; beer before liquor, never been sicker." The verse may influence what the drinker consumes, but also the order in which she imbibes. Such verbal expressions reveal folk beliefs that result in actual behaviors.

Many beliefs describe or prescribe North American women's experiences and lives. They may concern women's sexuality, domestic life, character, behavior, anatomy, physical ability, intellect, social roles, professional practices, and relations to men, family, nature, and deities, among other areas. Others reflect and reinforce beliefs about women. Prescriptions include a requirement for brides to wear "something old, something new, something borrowed, and something blue." Similarly, many male-dominated (or formerly male-dominated) occupations hold beliefs that women negatively influence their work—that women bring bad luck on boats or into mines, for example. These ideas are effectively prescriptive in discouraging women from the activities described, and make it all the more difficult for women to break into such occupations.

Beliefs can work for or against women. Ideas about witchcraft, for example, have been used by women positively to influence their own situations—to ensure that they are cared for by their family or community, who fear the witch's curse. But witch beliefs can also be used against women by individuals who seek to control what they see as excessive feminine power, who may enact anti-witching spells or even pursue legal and religious charges against a purported witch.

Similarly, women may draw on fairy beliefs to express themselves, but may be victims of violence if their power becomes too threatening. Irish folklorist Angela Bourke notes that fairy-abduction stories served women as alibis against problems with their children that might otherwise be blamed upon them, including: "sudden infant death, failure to thrive, birth defects, and a variety of congenital disabilities" which "correspond to the descriptions of babies taken away, or 'swept,' [by fairies] and replaced by mute, wizened, hairy creatures, or lifeless images" (571). For twenty-six-year-old Bridget Cleary, murdered by her family in 1895 in rural Tipperary, Ireland, however, the "narrative of fairy abduction may have empowered [her] for a while but then become a rationale for her torture and killing" (ibid.: 573).

Several notable female scholars have extensively contributed to folklorists' understanding of folk belief. British folklorist Gillian Bennett's *Traditions of Belief: Women and the Supernatural* deals with British women's narratives of paranormal experiences. In *Alas, Poor Ghost! Traditions of Belief in Story and Discourse*, she argues that two cultural options—rationalist and supernaturalist—are available to the women she studied for interpreting their experiences. The supernaturalist believes that her perceptions offer a faithful account of an event. In contrast, the rationalist view interprets supernatural encounters as dreams, hallucinations, or as the result of creative imagination. Rationalists generally employ this discourse in ridiculing persons who report such experiences, a standard response born out of pejorative attitudes toward folk belief.

But Bennett very trenchantly points out that rationalism is a folklore tradition itself, adhering to inherited patterns of explanation and thought that compete with supernaturalist discourse. She argues that rationalism and supernaturalism are ultimately competing discourses, and that neither is more nor less "superstitious" than the other. Bennett also suggests that her subjects' belief in the supernatural as a valid form of knowledge has a relationship to the gender roles they perform as middle-class, older British women. Bennett's contribution to belief scholarship holds value both for its emphasis on the experiences of women, and for its basis in folklore fieldwork as a process of interpretation of belief-in-context.

Folklorist Linda Dégh conducted an extremely detailed study of one particular legend-teller, Janet Callahan, analyzing a remarkable document produced by Callahan herself that attests to her own extrasensory perception and visionary experiences. Careful not to impose her own concepts upon Callahan's knowledge, Dégh says "My role is to present her self-image, her legends and her meanings with suggestions concerning their socio-cultural, religio-ideological connections and relevance" (115). The resulting essay holds implications for women's autobiography as well as for narrative, religion, and belief studies.

For an ethnographic and semiotic perspective on folk belief, Elaine Lawless' work on women preachers and women religious leaders is indispensable. She explores the practices of belief among Pentecostal women preachers and others within their communities, focusing on the relationships between spiritual expressions and the construction of identities. Her work shows that women need not be simply subjected to beliefs; they can in fact actively construct knowledge and ideas in order to positively influence their situations. Canadian Pamela E. Klassen similarly shows that a profound religious belief need not preclude a woman from acting forcefully, even in ways that seem contrary to traditional belief's expectations, as in the example of Mennonite Agatha Janzen preaching from the pulpit. Similarly, American folklorist Margaret K. Brady argues that, for Mormons, "elements of folk belief within established religious systems both manipulate and are manipulated by women in an attempt to find power and meaning in their lives" (461).

Lawless' work has also crucially addressed the profound relationship between fieldworkers and those they work with. Empathy and understanding on the researcher's part can immeasurably enhance research experiences, particularly when dealing with issues of folk knowledge and belief, where the insider may fear that the outsider will not understand, or may even ridicule her. Lawless' solution is dialogue, respect, reflexive ethnography, and reciprocal ethnography. Understanding that knowledge and belief are held by both ethnographer and subject, she concludes, "The final phase of the hermeneutic circle, then, demands that we subject our interpretations to the interpretations of our subjects" (1992: 313).

An excellent example of such reflexive belief scholarship is Jeanne Favret-Saada's exploration of the cultures of witchcraft in France, *Deadly Words: Witchcraft in the Bocage*. Also methodologically compelling is Diane E. Goldstein's work, "The Secularization of Religious Ethnography and Narrative Competence in a Discourse of Faith," which discusses how an ethnographer's belief system affects all belief-studies scholarship, suggesting that "ethnographic secularization" tends to cause scholars to focus on the form, aesthetics, and structure of an expression of belief, rather than on its more crucial functions and meanings.

A particularly useful exploration of the concept of folk belief is Marilyn Motz's "The Practice of Belief." She calls for combining performance studies with the study of folk belief to create a theoretical and methodological framework for investigating "the practice of believing as a way of knowing" (339). Motz contests academics' negative evaluation of folk belief's "presumed inferiority" (341) as a way of knowing, common since the ascendance of Enlightenment thought. She traces how Cultural-Studies theorists discuss belief and traditional modes of knowledge as important sites for agency or subversion of a dominant system.

Motz similarly sees the study of belief at the center of political practice, since such knowledge is the point of intersection for the individual and the group, the private and the public, the abstract and actions. As folklorists have long studied both hegemonic and counter-hegemonic beliefs, they know how crucial it is to consider the overall politics and power structures as well as the more individualizable features of artistic performance. But Motz also suggests that the criteria for considering the aesthetics of an expression of belief lie in the degree to which a given expression is useful for illustrating a belief within a group or for an individual. The combination of examining small groups and artists, politics, and art makes folklorists' studies of belief respectful, insightful, and important. *See also:* Assault, Supernatural; Childbirth and Childrearing; Folk Medicine; Foodways; Gender; Personal-Experience Narrative; Politics; Popular Culture; Superstition; Witchcraft, Historical; Women Religious.

References: Bennett, Gillian. *Traditions of Belief: Women and the Supernatural.* New York: Viking Penguin, 1987; ———. *"Alas, Poor Ghost!" Traditions of Belief in Story and Discourse.* Logan: Utah State University Press, 1999; Bourke, Angela. "Reading a Woman's Death: Colonial Text and Oral Tradition in Nineteenth-Century Ireland." *Feminist Studies*, vol. 21, no. 3 (1995): 553–586; Brady, Margaret K. "Transformations of Power: Mormon Women's Visionary Narratives." *Journal of American Folklore* 398 (1987): 461–468; Cardozo-Freeman, Inez. "Serpent Fears and Religious Motifs among Mexican Women." *Frontiers: A Journal of Women Studies*, vol. 3, no. 3 (1978): 10–13; Creighton, Helen. *Bluenose Magic: Popular Beliefs and Superstitions in Nova Scotia.* Toronto: Ryerson Press, 1968; ———. *A Life in Folklore.* Toronto: McGraw-Hill-Ryerson, 1975; Dégh, Linda. "The Perceptional Life of Janet Callahan." *Western Folklore*, vol. 55, no. 2 (1996): 113–136; Favret-Saada, Jeanne. *Deadly Words: Witchcraft in the Bocage.* Trans. Catherine Cullen. New York: Cambridge University Press, 1980; Goldstein, Diane E. "The Secularization of Religious Ethnography and Narrative Competence in a Discourse of Faith." *Western Folklore*, vol. 54, no. 1 (1995): 23–36; Lawless, Elaine J. "'Your Hair is Your Glory': Public and Private Symbology of Long Hair for Pentecostal Women." *New York Folklore*, Vol. 12, nos. 3–4 (Summer-Fall 1986): 33–49; ———. "Brothers and Sisters: Pentecostals as a Religious Folk Group." In *Folk Groups and Folklore Genres: A Reader*, ed. Elliott Oring, 99–113. Logan: Utah State University Press, 1989; ———. "'I Was Afraid Someone like You ... an Outsider ... Would Misunderstand': Negotiating Interpretive Differences between Ethnographers and Subjects." *Journal of American Folklore*, vol. 105, no. 417 (1992): 302–314; Klassen, Pamela E. "Speaking Out in God's Name: A Mennonite Woman Preaching." In *Undisciplined Women: Tradition and Culture in Canada*, eds. Pauline Greenhill and Diane Tye, 242–249. Montreal: McGill-Queen's University Press, 1997; Mullen, Patrick B. "Belief and the American Folk." *Journal of American Folklore* 113 (2000): 119–143; O'Connor, Bonnie Blair. *Healing*

Traditions: Alternative Medicine and the Health Professions. Philadelphia: University of Pennsylvania Press, 1995; Rieti, Barbara. *Strange Terrain: The Fairy World in Newfoundland*. St. John's: Institute of Social and Economic Research, Memorial University of Newfoundland, 1991; ———. "Riddling the Witch: Violence Against Women in Newfoundland Witch Tradition." In *Undisciplined Women: Tradition and Culture in Canada*, eds. Pauline Greenhill and Diane Tye, 77–86. Montreal: McGill-Queen's University Press, 1997; Simpson, Jacqueline. "Witches and Witchbusters." *Folklore* 107 (1996): 5–18.

Jacqueline L. McGrath

Folk Costume

In the past, the term "folk costume" referred to clothing, hairstyle, headgear, footwear, and accessories worn by Euro North Americans for special or traditional occasions such as weddings, festivals, and parades, or to the everyday wear of non-industrialized, non-Western, and/or Indigenous people. Today, scholars of material culture prefer to think of costume as part of the broader genre of "dress." Dress includes not only objects worn, but also hair, jewelry, makeup, and other additions and modifications made to the human body. Given this formulation, folklorists understand that all groups have dress traditions, even if they are designed by a formal institution such as a school, religious, or governmental agency. Exemplars in popular culture may also inspire dress customs. Any group may also have costume or extraordinary dress for special occasions, including performance contexts. Bridal outfits, Asian Indian saris, African inspired clothing, and dresses for *quinceañeras* (fifteenth birthdays) in Latin American cultures are some examples of unique clothing worn for both ceremony and fashion displays. Feminine dress in contemporary North America ranges from Girl Scout and Girl Guide uniforms (with one or more merit badges sewn onto the sash to identify a girl's accomplishments) to square dance costumes designed by a dance school leader or by a dancer herself, from a business pants suit to T-shirts sporting logos or colors in support of social causes such as breast cancer research.

Women have always played important roles not only in the design, creation, and wearing of dress but in developing and maintaining its aesthetic. Some immigrant and Indigenous North American women, especially those who are members of highly observant religious groups, continue to wear traditional dress. For example, Orthodox Jewish women often wear scarves and/or wigs in observance of tradition, as well as make sure that sleeves and skirts cover their elbows and knees; Muslim women may wear the *hijab* (headscarf) or the full-length *chador* (body scarf); women in Pentecostal and Amish groups wear lace caps, long hair, long sleeves, and long skirts; and many Asian Indian women wear *saris* long after their menfolk have taken up wearing European-style suits.

Costume serves to illustrate personal, community, and cultural identities, and because women are often—consciously and unconsciously—tradition-bearers, both actually and symbolically, folkways that celebrate group cohesion and loyalties generally fall into their domain. A notable exception is *haute couture*, that is, exclusive fashions designed for upper-class women, increasingly designed by women, but still more often by men. Most women wear traditional costumes—clothing whose designs are handed down from previous generations—when they participate in cultural performances (such as weddings, musical, processional, or dance events) both as fashion and as symbols of group identity as well as in affirmation of their connection with previous generations. Women in certain occupational groups—flight attendants working on international flights or clerks in upscale hotels patronized by westerners, for example—may wear a version of traditional dress in accord with company policy. Immigrant women who have adopted conventional Euro American dress in their daily lives in North America may attend events of political or cultural significance wearing traditional clothes as emblems of national or clan identity. Conversely, Euro American women often temporarily adopt the dress of the regions they visit as tourists in order to identify with the people they encounter there. And folklorists and anthropologists sometimes wear clothing from the cultures they study to affirm their solidarity with those groups.

Women from all cultural groups and ethnicities participate in the design, construction, and/or assemblage of clothing for performance and display. The seamstresses who sew the costumes that North American performers wear, however, often reside in the home country. For example, most Mexican American dance groups rely on costumes made in Mexico. Irish step dancers in the United States may design their own costumes, but nearly all import them from Ireland. Both classical and folk dancers from Asian Indian communities purchase costumes made in India. Lao and Vietnamese classical dancers in the United States either import their costumes (elaborate versions of everyday wear back home) or rely on local seamstresses within their own ethnic communities, as do children's dance groups from those cultures.

Weaving, sewing, knitting, dyeing cloth, embroidery, and lacemaking are still employed for traditional dress long after a group has stopped using these textile arts for the manufacture of everyday clothing. Examples of folk dress techniques encountered in North America include the bead and leather work of some First Nations groups, elaborately embroidered baby carriers among the Hmong, the art of sewing dancers' bodies into their costumes among Thai immigrants, and the head wraps and loosely fitting garments favored by West African immigrants. Some North American women of African descent enjoy wearing brightly colored Ghanaian *kente* cloth—associated in the United States with the rise of the Black nationalist movements of the 1960s and 1970s—as fashion, a political statement, or both.

Hairstyles, wigs, headgear, jewelry, makeup, and other bodily decorations also serve as everyday identity markers and for special cultural performances; some of these traditions are changing in the North American context and some remain stable. Irish American step dancers, for example, may curl their hair into ringlets following instructions provided by dancer-maintained Web sites. Mexican *folklórico* dancers wear traditional makeup and jewelry, but today, they also often wear hair extensions. Asian Indian brides in North America apply henna tattoos (*mehndi*) to their hands in preparation for their weddings to indicate their change in status from single to married women, a practice that some Euro American and Canadian women have adopted purely as fashion. Among the highly assimilated Scandinavians of the American Midwest, however, the tradition of an eldest daughter wearing a white dress and a crown of candles on Saint Lucia's Day (December 13) to herald the opening of the Christmas season has remained unchanged since the fifteenth century.

Other dress traditions are not limited to women from a particular ethnic or cultural group. Anti-war and other activist groups such as CODEPINK Women for Peace use dress, specifically the color pink, to symbolize their collective political power as women. In recent years, women who have attained the age of fifty may wear red hats and purple clothes to signal membership in the Red Hat Society, a folk group inspired by Jenny Joseph's poem "Warning," which encourages older women to work against social constrictions. While dress and folk costume have been heavily documented as art and symbol for centuries, the study of women's dress and costume is in its infancy. Much work remains to be done to discover how women use these forms to express identity, solidarity, rebellion, conformity, and pleasure. *See also:* Activism; Body Modification and Adornment; Fashion; Girl Scouts/Girl Guides; Hair; Jewish Women's Folklore; Material Culture; Muslim Women's Folklore; Occupational Folklore; *Quinceañera*; Tradition-Bearer; Wedding; Women's Friendship Groups.

References: Eleuterio, Susan. *Irish-American Material Culture: A Directory of Collections, Sites, and Festivals in the United States and Canada.* Westport, CT: Greenwood Press, 1988; ———. "Irish, Chicago." *Encyclopedia of American Folklore*, 631–633. Armonk, NY: M. E. Sharpe, 2006; Hardwick, Patricia Ann. "The Spirit of Fiesta: Costume and the Performance of History, Community and Identity during Santa Barbara's Old Spanish Days." In *Dress, Costume, and Bodily Adornment as Material Culture*, ed. Pravina Shukla. Special Issue of *Midwestern Folklore*, vol. 32, nos. 1/2 (Spring/Fall 2006): 67–82; Hertz, Carrie. "The Uniform: As Material, As Symbol, As Negotiated Object." In *Dress, Costume, and Bodily Adornment as Material Culture*, ed. Pravina Shukla. Special Issue of *Midwestern Folklore*, vol. 32, nos. 1/2 (Spring/Fall 2006): 43–46; Saliklis, Ruta. "The Dynamic Relationship between Lithuanian National Costumes and Folk Dress." In *Dress, Costume, and Bodily Adornment as Material Culture*, ed. Pravina Shukla. Special Issue of *Midwestern Folklore*, vol. 32, nos. 1/2 (Spring/Fall 2006): 211–234; Shukla, Pravina, ed. *Dress, Costume, and Bodily Adornment as Material Culture*. Special Issue of *Midwestern Folklore*, vol. 32, nos. 1/2 (Spring/Fall 2006); Welters, Linda, ed. *Folk Dress in Europe and Anatolia: Beliefs About Protection and Fertility.* New York: Berg, 1999.

Susan Eleuterio

Folk Custom

A ubiquitous and well-documented genre, folk customs are traditional and repeated practices that typically cluster around life cycle and calendar events, signifying some form of transition of a folk group member from one state of being to another. Sometimes called folkways, folk customs serve to facilitate, celebrate, commemorate, and commiserate across a broad spectrum of human relations, ranging from the personal (for example, henna markings and body piercings) to the familial (for example, the timing of the evening meal) to the international (for example, celebrations of New Year's and Midsummer Day).

In a foundational work, *Rites of Passage*, Arnold van Gennep (1909) explained that customs and ceremonies accompanying life change or crisis revolve around three major phases, which he labeled separation, transition, and incorporation (or schism), and that ritual accompanies the middle stage, such as occurs at the end of one year and the start of the new. Victor W. Turner further described the transitional or liminal ("threshold") stage as a time removed from normative social structuring in which homogeneity and camaraderie prevail. Such generalized social bonding also applies to calendrical rites, which involve large groups or even whole societies coming together at a crucial liminal time.

Thus, folk customs may be enacted by specific groups and/or whole communities. Life events marked by folk customs include transitions such as pregnancy, childbirth, baptism, initiation, graduation, courtship, marriage, divorce, retirement, death, and burial, and are demonstrated by traditions like throwing the bridal bouquet, placing a knife under a woman's bed during labor to cut the pain, and Sadie Hawkins' Day, the twenty-ninth of February, on which women are permitted—and even expected—to ask a man out on a date. Preferred settings for folk traditions such as dances, games, pranks, storytelling, and the manufacture of folk crafts are generally customary, including community halls, children's playgrounds and hearths.

Calendar customs are generally associated with the natural or agricultural calendar and often overlap with major events in the life cycle (for example, New Year weddings). In many instances, seasonal changes are acknowledged by festivals, which can be fixed (for example, El Dia de los Muertos, Carnival, Midsummer's Day, and Kwanzaa) or moveable (for example, Cherry Blossom time, harvest, ice festivals, and Spring Break) and oftentime glossed with religious influence and appropriations, such as Halloween, St. Brigid's Day, and Purim (the feast of Esther).

Holy days and the anniversaries of historical events have long been favored as charters for traditional gatherings, and include performances of many and varied folk customs, such those associated with U.S. Independence Day (viewing fireworks, eating black-eyed peas); Hanukkah (lighting candles, playing dreidel games); Cinco de Mayo (playing mariachi music, breaking piñatas); Thanksgiving (eating turkey and pumpkin pie); Ramadan (applying henna, distributing sweets); Christmas (decorating the tree, crèche building); Labor Day weekend (boating, picnicking); and Super Bowl Sunday in the United States (boisterously eating and drinking in front of the television set). Many of these traditions specifically locate women as food preparers and hostesses; however, there are also growing traditions in North America in which women and girls participate in Take Back the Night marches on U.S. Independence Day, and gather to watch and discuss advertisements aired during the football game on Super Bowl Sunday, especially during halftime.

Because folk customs generally signify a conclusion or renewal of a period of time or stage in life, they are frequently accompanied by complementary superstitions, which manifest as symbolic measures to appease, prevent, and protect their enactors. For every celebration, there is potential and/or perceived disappointment; therefore, many customs have evolved through efforts to offset the feared bad consequences of a life or calendrical crisis, such as with the varied running-yellow-traffic-signal responses to lining one's pocket with coins and/or paper money at New Year. Folk customs, then, are often overdetermined reactions to liminal periods, often revealing or reflecting a substratum of folk belief and latent magic.

Invaluable collections of folk customs have been amassed, largely due to the salvage strategies employed by folklorists and anthropologists during the nineteenth and twentieth centuries, such as those by Violet Alford (1937) and Mary Macleod Banks (1937–1941; 1946). Contemporary scholarship, including works by Margaret Bennet (1992), Margaret Coffin (1976), Venetia Newall (1989), and Ethel Urlin (1990), abounds with domestic and calendrical folk custom descriptions

Meanwhile, the appeal of traditionality has inspired many folk custom revivals, particular in festivals such as May Day celebrations (Maypole dances, garlanding) and at Renaissance fairs (open markets, juggling). Technically speaking, revivals fall under the rubric "folklorismus" because they lack continuous practice or performance; nevertheless, whether constant or contrived, folk customs are replete with social, cultural, economic, and political content and commentary; they function as sanctioned tension reducers while upholding cultural norms and maintaining conformity to accepted patterns of behavior; and they help to confirm social identities by validating the beliefs and justifying the rituals and institutions of and to those persons who perform them. *See also:* Beauty Contest; Charivari/Shivaree; Childbirth and Childrearing; Courtship; Divorce; Engagement; Evil Eye; Festival; Folk Belief; Folk Dance; Folk Group; Foodways; Graves and Gravemarkers; Henna Art/*Mehndi*; Initiation; Marriage; Material Culture; Menarche Stories; Pregnancy; *Quinceañera*; Rites of Passage; Ritual; Roadside Crosses; Sexuality; Storytelling; Tradition; Wedding.

References: Alford, Violet. *Pyrenean Festivals: Calendar Customs, Music and Magic Drama and Dance.* London: Chatto & Windus, 1937; ———. *Introduction to English Folklore.* London: G. Bell and Sons Ltd., 1952; Banks, Mary Macleod. *British Calendar Customs: Scotland,* three volumes. Publications of the Folklore Society 100, 104, 108. London: William Glaisher Ltd., 1937–1941; ———. *British Calendar Customs: Orkney and Shetland.* Publications of the Folklore Society 112. London: William Glaisher Ltd., 1946; Bascom, William R. "Four Functions of Folklore. In *Contributions to Folkloristics,* Folklore Institute, 40–64. Meerut, India: Archana Publications, 1981 [1954]; Bennett, Margaret. *Scottish Customs from the Cradle to the Grave.* Edinburgh: Polygon, 2004 [1992]; Brunvand, Jan Harold. *The Study of American Folklore: An Introduction.* 4th ed. New York: W. W. Norton and Company, 1997; Coffin, Margaret M. *Death in Early America: The History and Folklore of Customs and Superstitions of Early Medicine, Funerals, Burials and Mournings.* New York: E. P. Dutton, 1976; Newall, Venetia. "Two English Fire Festivals in Relation to Their Contemporary Social Setting." *Western Folklore,* vol. 31, no. 4 (1972): 244–276; ———. "Up-Helly Aa: A Shetland Winter Festival." *Arv* 34 (1978): 37–97; ———. "Masking in England." *New York Folklore* 11 (1985): 205–29; ———. "A Note on the Chinese New Year Celebration in London and its Socio-Economic Background." in *Western Folklore,* vol. 48, no. 1 (1989): 61–66; Turner, Victor W. *The Ritual Process: Structure and Anti-Structure.* Chicago: Aldine Publishing Company, 1969; Urlin, Ethel L. *A Short History of Marriage: Marriage Rites, Customs, and*

Folklore in Many Countries in All Ages. Farmington Hills, MI: Gale Group, 1990; Van Gennep, Arnold. *The Rites of Passage*, trans. Monika B. Vizedom and Gabrielle L. Caffe. Chicago: University of Chicago Press, 1960 [1909].

Maria Teresa Agozzino

Folk Dance

Folk dance involves structured, often rhythmic movement, usually to instrumental music and/or voice accompaniment. Folk dance is an expressive form in which both women and men participate as performers, choreographers (creators of dance-movement patterns), and audience members. Historically, folklorists' and anthropologists' tendency to study culture from male perspectives has led them to neglect the more private domain in which many women's expressive forms are found. Folk dance is a Public Folklore genre; however, perhaps due to its frequent association with the feminine domain, folk dance research is a relatively new phenomenon.

Women scholars have dominated the field of folk dance research. Theresa Buckland, Adrienne Kaeppler, Joann Kealiinohomoku, and Anya Peterson Royce are among those who have helped to define folk dance and dance ethnography. Academic attention to traditional dance has increased since the mid-1980s, as folklorists, anthropologists, and other cultural scholars have considered the genre of folk dance useful for illuminating gender roles, identities, and politics. But even with the emergence of Dance Studies, and the field's interest in the anthropology of the body, "the study of moving bodies remains on the periphery" (Reed, 504). More than twenty years after Adrienne Kaeppler's articulation of what she calls "structured-movement systems," few studies have analyzed the specifics of movement, much less in the context of female-dominated traditions and events.

But there are exceptions. Jill Drayson Sweet, for example, describes gender-role reversals in San Ildefonso Navajo dance, though her emphasis on inter-tribe relations and attitudes toward marriage do not particularly focus on the experience of women. In this performance, forty women dancers play female and male roles, half of them dressing as men. Meanwhile, the men of the village dress as women, care for the children, and bring lunch to the dancers.

Barbara LeBlanc studied Acadian dance forms and corresponding social relations in the Maritime Provinces of Canada. She conducted extensive research on traditional step dances in that region, including interviews with members of the Cape Breton Irish community. In the late 1700s and early 1800s, immigrants from all over the British Isles began to settle in the eastern half of the island of Cape Breton. These settlers handed down to their children the traditions of Scotland, including the art of step dancing, which many consider an extension of the Irish tradition. Movement and choreography in step dancing prioritizes footwork, with the upper body and arms held relatively rigid. Though debates persist about origins, the traditional music, song, and dance of Cape Breton are generally perceived as unique to the island and still central to its identity.

Historian Linda Tomko attributes the increased visibility of folk dancing around the turn of the twentieth century to its use as a tool for assimilating immigrants from Eastern and Southern Europe. In progressive-era America, members of the dominant middle class used the institution of the settlement house to socialize young immigrant women in the proper roles, behaviors, and values of American society. Women put themselves and their bodies at risk for the sake of suffrage and labor rights at a time when their ambitions were growing beyond the confines of housework and motherhood. In this early era of American modern dance, female leaders were influential; woman-run institutions such as New York City's Henry Street Settlement and Chicago's Hull House sponsored artistic events and seasonal festivals.

These phenomena occurred in the context of a separate sphere in which certain social institutions mediated folk dancing as a performative activity. In doing so, they took on the pedagogical mission of instilling in working-class girls a sense of pride and pleasure in their bodies, giving them an alternative site to integrate the arts into their everyday lives, away from the morally questionable dance hall and the honky-tonk. Through the settlement house movement, women drew on folk dance traditions that had originated in Western Europe to form new vocabularies of movement. Thanks to the women of this era, dance became an important and accessible means for Americans to establish a sense of national heritage; that immigrant-driven expressive tradition remains powerful today.

Canadian feminist folklorist Pauline Greenhill studied the practice of Morris dancing in Ontario, Canada. This allegedly "English," "male," "traditional" "dance" has taken distinctive North American forms, is now and has always been practiced by women as well as men, has incorporated extensive innovation as well as time-honored moves, and is associated with a full congeries of practices—performances, celebrations called "ales," and extensive socializing within groups formed specifically for the purpose of doing Morris.

Until recently, most English scholars' definitions of Morris have asserted that it is a masculine practice. Historically, women Morris dancers were certainly in a minority. However, too many scholars went on to dismiss evidence of women performing identical steps to identical music as being outside the realm of Morris, using the circular argument that since Morris was a male dance, if women performed it, it was not Morris. They often bolstered this notion with arguments about the dance being "strong," "aggressive," "rough," and so on, qualities usually more associated with masculine than with feminine pursuits. Further, groups of Morris dancers are called "sides" or sometimes "teams," terminology more connected with sports (presumptively masculine) than with dance (presumptively feminine). However, like other homosocial (single-sex) events once associated primarily with men, women have made extensive inroads into contemporary Morris in North America. There are now mixed (male and female) and all-female sides as well as queer and transgender Morris, such as the White Rats of San Francisco, self-described as "the world's first queer/pervert/leather Morris team" ("White Rat's History").

Another form of step dancing, more popularly known as "stepping," has its origins in traditional African dance and has developed into a flourishing form over the past fifty years among fraternities and sororities of traditionally African American colleges. This phenomenon has been studied by

Elizabeth Fine and by Jacqui Malone. In competitive African American step shows, fraternities and sororities "step off" against each other as teams performing synchronized routines. Although a step (a rapid-fire routine of rhythmic vocals and body percussion) can be set to music, some performers do "straight step," which involves only the sound of the dancers clapping and stamping out a beat. The goal is to create a collective rhythm, not to showcase the virtuosity of individual performers.

While this form of stepping echoes an evident heritage of African movement and communication patterns, the contemporary tradition took shape on college campuses. The ritual performance of stepping in Black fraternities and sororities may have developed from African American Masonic rituals. This form of dance has an extensive history and evolution, including the recent explosion of fraternity and sorority step shows. Their choreography dates back to the public dance contests of slave times, popular minstrel shows, 1920s Harlem cabaret performances, and Motown groups performing stylized moves. Elements of stepping also reflect drills practiced by Black men in the military during World War II and vaudeville tap routines. Stepping incorporates all of these cultural influences as well as children's games, cheerleading, martial arts, and hip-hop moves. Step's popularity burgeoned during the 1980s; Spike Lee's 1988 film *School Daze* includes scenes of fraternity stepping.

Few scholars have isolated forms of folk dance associated exclusively or primarily with women. For example, while practices such as belly dancing have received some attention, such analyses have mainly treated techniques and individual practitioners, rather than traditional folkloric forms in context. However, with a contemporary perspective, we can identify various emerging traditions of female-dominated movement that constitute a flourishing of the women's folk dance genre. *See also:* Activism; Belly Dance; Cheerleading; Class; Ethnicity; Folk Costume; Gender; Sorority Folklore; Tradition.

References: Buckland, Theresa J., ed. *Dance in the Field*. New York: St. Martin's Press, 1999; Fine, Elizabeth C. *Soulstepping: African American Step Shows*. Champaign: University of Illinois Press, 2002; Greenhill, Pauline. *Ethnicity in the Mainstream: Three Studies of English Canadian Culture in Ontario*. Montreal: McGill-Queen's University Press, 1994; Kaeppler, Adrienne. "Structured Movement Systems in Tonga." In *Society and the Dance*, ed. Paul Spencer, 92–118. Cambridge: Cambridge University Press, 1985; Kealiinohomoku, Joann Wheeler. "Folk Dance." *Folklore and Folklife: An Introduction*, ed. Richard M. Dorson, 381–402. Chicago: University of Chicago Press, 1972; LeBlanc, Barbara. "Changing Places: Dance, Society, and Gender in Cheticamp." In *Undisciplined Women: Tradition and Culture in Canada*. Pauline Greenhill and Diane Tye, eds. Toronto: McGill-Queen's University Press, 1997; Malone, Jacqui. *Steppin' on the Blues: The Visible Rhythms of African American Dance*. Urbana: University of Illinois Press, 1996; Reed, Susan A. "The Politics and Poetics of Dance." *Annual Review of Anthropology* 27 (1998): 503–532; Royce, Anya Peterson. *The Anthropology of Dance*. Bloomington: Indiana University Press, 1977; Sweet, Jill Drayson. "Play, Role Reversal and Humor: Symbolic Elements of a Tewa Pueblo Navaho Dance." In *Dance Research Journal* 12.1 (1979–80); Tomko, Linda. *Dancing Class: Gender, Ethnicity, and Social Divides in American Dance, 1890–1920*. Bloomington: Indiana University Press, 1999; "White Rat's History." http://www.whiteratsmorris.org/history.html (accessed August 9, 2008).

Montana Miller

Folk Drama

A folk drama is a scripted performance involving mimicry and the distribution of roles among two or more players transmitted by traditional means among members of a folk group. The foregoing definition of folk drama works well enough in theory and for the North American traditions on which this volume focuses, but in practice there are important relationships among drama per se, dance, festival, spectacle, and related traditional display forms. Traditional dance and drama, however, reveal the greatest degree of overlap. In fact, in many world cultures the two genres are sufficiently intertwined to render distinctions between them little more than an academic exercise. A set of working distinctions is useful, however. While both dance and drama are ensemble activities—they involve the coordinated efforts of two or more people in the performance—dramas require narrative development. They have a plot; they tell a story. In order for this to occur, there must be conflict between a central figure or figures and others that seek to block the goals of the central character(s). Such conflict can be developed only when character roles are distributed among two or more players, whether the players are humans or, for example, puppets. Dance, of course, may be narrative in nature, but this is not a requirement.

In order to accomplish the ensemble activities seen in both genres, the actions of individuals must be coordinated. In dance, coordination is accomplished at its most fundamental level by rhythmic accompaniment. Some forms, such as the square dance, go to even greater lengths and therefore provide the best examples of coordinated action in dance. In this case, the movements of dancers are not merely suggested by musical rhythms, but are dictated by the words of the square dance "calls." On the other hand, in drama, the coordination of the ensemble is accomplished by means of the script: a set of directions (written or oral) encompassing both words and actions. Dance, as is frequently noted, is choreographed, while drama is scripted.

Folk drama is customarily associated with festivals—those events that commemorate points of special significance to a celebrating community (for example, Ramadan, Christmas, and Passover). The reasons for the connection between drama and festival are very clear in some cases. The Christmas plays of the Hispanic Southwest, *Los Pastores* ("The Shepherds"), also known as *La Pastorela*, and *Las Posadas* ("The Inns") are representative. Los Pastores, an often-elaborate reenactment the adoration of the Christ Child by shepherds (including a conflict between the archangel Michael and one or more devils who try to impede the shepherds' travel), logically falls into the Christmas season and fits the working definition of folk drama presented above. Las Posadas, derived from St. Luke's account of Joseph and Mary's search for shelter on the nine nights from December 16 through December 24, dramatizes the sacred events commemorated by the holiday, combining the features of drama and procession and utilizing sung dialogue. New Mexican folk plays, *Los Comanches*, date back to the late 1700s and reflect the conflict that arose during the Spanish Conquest of the area. In the Christmas-based Los Comanches, Comanche people have kidnapped the Christ Child; the Mexican characters chase after them until all is resolved when the Comanche chief returns the child and offers gifts. While these plays suggest the range of folk plays proper, both are thematically consistent with the festival that provides the focus of events.

On the other hand, the mummers' plays of British and Anglo American Christmas tradition seem to have no connection to the occasion being celebrated. The plays get their name from the fact that they are brief dramas ("skits") performed by groups of people (usually adolescent boys and young unmarried adult men) called "mummers" who traditionally travel in disguise from house to house begging refreshment within a community during the Christmas season. Today, most mumming performances have moved to pubs and street corners in the United Kingdom. The tradition has lapsed in North America, although there are notable exceptions. Herbert Halpert and G. M. Story document historical performances in Newfoundland, and Marie Campbell witnessed a play, "The Turkish Knight," on Christmas Eve 1930 in Gander, Kentucky, that had been revived to honor her Christmas sojourn to that Appalachian community.

In the British Isles—where folk drama traditions have received the most scholarly attention—direct female participation (as actors in the plays) is extremely rare and seems confined to modern revival performances. When the casts are not all male, the female members who do appear are characteristically used as a last resort to "fill out" the cast; they are commonly relatives of male cast members (Russell). Various explanations have been provided for the lack of female actors historically, one of the more popular theorizing that the plays descended from "men's ceremonials" (Brody). More reasonable explanations for the gender bias involve "traditional strictures of behavior in the English countryside [that] forbade" public performance by women (Tillis). Moreover, the disorder associated with a mumming troupes' perambulations, especially when alcohol was provided, could include fights with rival troupes and rough pranks on travelers encountered on the road. Direct female participation in the Anglo-influenced Western Hemisphere, then, was curbed by customary behaviors that attended the actual performances of the plays. In contrast, in the Hispanic tradition of the American Southwest, female actors have been documented not only in roles such as Gila, a young female shepherd, but in the part of the archangel Michael.

The absence of female actors in British-derived New World traditions does not correlate with a lack of female characters. Female characters are common in the mummers' dramas conventionally labeled "The Hero Combat" and "The Wooing Play," cross-dressed in the conventional disguises characteristic of mumming house visits, and in the "Womanless Wedding," a traditional drama performed as a North American community fundraiser well into the twentieth century. Characters such as Besom Betty (that is, Betty with a Broom), Dirty Bet, Bessie Brownbags, Dame Dorothy, and the Bride and Bridesmaids of the "Womanless Wedding" are less imitations of women than parodies of men parodying women. That is, the actors tapped to play women's and girls' roles are those males least likely to pass as female owing to male secondary sexual characteristics (for example, facial and body hair or a protruding Adam's apple). The result is a deliberate collision of gender traits, a form of play consistent with the overall licensed, topsy-turvy behavior associated with festivals. The predominance of confusion as a motif, rather than cross-dressing per se, is underscored by stock characters such as "the Young Lady or Bride [who] exhibited a cow's tail beneath the flounces of a starched petticoat" (Dean-Smith 1958, 253) and the Bessy of Appalachian tradition who—as a man with a cow's face, horns, tail, and bells—not only create cross-gender dissonance, but cross-species dissonance as well.

The preferential bias of folk drama toward male actors as a tradition in the British Isles and Anglo America notwithstanding, when analyzed in context, it becomes clear that women play a crucial role in performance events. Dean-Smith notes that in the performance proper, the players' costumes provided by wives and sweethearts became vehicles for female creativity and even competition (1958). Moreover, while expressive license is widely reported for the mummers' perambulations, their disorder is confined primarily to the roads; when festival play goes indoors (as in house performances), unruly elements become more subdued. Thus, from a broader interactional perspective, as agents of order in the homes to which traveling troupes appeal for a "stage" and refreshments (in Newfoundland, at least, the kitchen usually provides both), women exercise considerable control over the behavior of male folk drama performers.

Outside the context of performance, women scholars have made significant contributions to folk drama studies as theoreticians, analysts, and collectors. Many of the earliest analyses of the genre, inspired by the work of Sir James George Frazer, sought to explain myth, ritual, and drama via reconstructions of "primitive" fertility magic, especially those rites based on an agricultural subsistence base. During the early decades of the twentieth century, classicist Jane E. Harrison (1850–1928) sought magical connections among Greek myth, ritual, and drama, while Jesse L. Weston (1850–1928), in *Ritual to Romance*, her analysis of the Arthurian Grail cycle, pursues similar arguments with regard to the mummers' plays, sword dances, and Morris dances.

Beginning in the 1920s, British scholars Violet Alford and Margaret Dean-Smith turned their energies to the study of the folk play in the British Isles and North America as well as to stimulating interest in reviving lapsed traditions. Their work tended to prefigure today's emphases on broader generic connections. Therefore, beyond adding to our knowledge of the plays, their work reinforced ideas about the interrelatedness of festival, dance, drama, song, and ritual.

Violet Alford, like many of her colleagues, was drawn to folk drama material through an interest in traditional dance, but this focus inevitably became more distributed, resulting in works such as *Pyrenean Festivals Calendar Customs, Music and Magic, Drama and Dance* (1937) and a European survey of animal-masked performances, *The Hobby Horse and Other Animal Masks* (1978), that underscore the interdependence of display traditions. She eventually emerged as one of the leading authorities on sword dancing, although her major work on the subject, *Sword Dance and*

Drama (1962), espouses a controversial hypothesis that links sword-dancing traditions with the customary rituals of miners and metal workers. In addition to her scholarship, she actively encouraged the revival and practice of the traditions she documented, most notably the Marshfield mummers play in the 1930s.

Increasing disenchantment with the analysis of folk texts in isolation from traditional performance contexts in the latter decades of the twentieth century tended to lead scholars away from the old texts that intrigued the likes of Edmund K. Chambers, Alford, Dean-Smith, and others of their generation. Instead, the borders of the dramatic expanded, yielding to studies such as Anne C. Burson's analysis of skits based on recurrent models rather than traditional texts, and Ian Russell's consideration of the impact of martial arts films, advertising, and other influences of the mass media on a traditional mumming team.

Of course, textual treatments have not disappeared entirely. An interesting example from the late twentieth century is Christine Herrold's 1998 analysis of the standard Hero Combat play texts through the psychological lens of neo-Jungian feminist critical theory. For the most part, however, speculations about texts and origins, following the advice of Georgina Smith (1981) to look to social bases of folk drama rather than to ritual origins, have given way to the analysis of folk dramas as performance events and to consideration of their functions in contemporary contexts. *See also:* Cross-Dressing; Festival; Folk Custom; Folk Dance; Folk Group; Mass Media; Text.

References: Alford, Violet. *Pyrenean Festivals Calendar Customs, Music and Magic, Drama and Dance.* London: Chatto & Windus, 1937. ———. *The Hobby Horse and Other Animal Masks.* London: Merlin Press, 1978; ———. *Sword Dance and Drama.* London: Merlin Press, 1962; ———. Brody, Alan. *The English Mummers and Their Plays: Traces of Ancient Mystery.* Philadelphia: University of Pennsylvania Press, 1970; Burson, Anne C. "Model and Text in Folk Drama." *Journal of American Folklore* 93 (1980): 305–316; Campbell, Marie. "Survivals of Old Folk Drama in the Kentucky Mountains." *Journal of American Folklore* 51 (1938): 10–24; Cawte, Edwin C., Alex Helm, and Norman Peacock. *English Ritual Drama: A Geographical Index.* London: Folk-lore Society, 1967; Chambers, Edmund K. *The English Folk-Play.* Oxford: Clarendon Press, 1933; Dean-Smith, Margaret. "The Life-Cycle Play or Folk Play: Some Conclusions Following the Examination of the Ordish Papers and Other Sources." *Folklore* 69 (1958): 237–253; Green, Thomas A. "Folk Drama: Introduction," in *Journal of American Folklore* 94 (1981): 421–432; Halpert, Herbert, and G. M. Story, eds. *Christmas Mumming in Newfoundland: Essays in Anthropology, Folklore, and History.* Toronto: Published for Memorial University of Newfoundland by University of Toronto Press, 1969; Harrison, Jane. *Themis: A Study of the Social Origins of Greek Religion.* Cambridge: Cambridge University Press, 1912; Herold, Christine. "The English Mummers as Manifestations of the Social Self." *Société Internationale pour l'Étude du Théâtre Médiéval. Ödense,* 1998. http://www.sdu.dk/Hum/SITM/papers/christine_herold.html (accessed August 10, 2008); Russell, Ian. "In Comes I, Brut King: Tradition and Modernity in the Drama of the Jacksdale Bullguisers." *Journal of American Folklore* 94 (1981): 456–485; Smith, Georgina. "Social Bases of Tradition: The Limitations and Implications of 'The Search for Origins'." *Language Culture and Tradition.* A. E. Green and J. D. A. Widdowson, eds., 77–87. CECTAL Conference Paper Series, No. 2. Sheffield: Centre for English Cultural Tradition and Language, 1981; Tillis, Steve. *Rethinking Folk Drama.* Westport, CT: Greenwood Press, 1999; Weston, Jessie L. *From Ritual to Romance.* London: Cambridge University Press, 1920; Wheat, John. "'Los Pastores': Continuity and Change In a Texas-Mexican

Nativity Drama." *Journal of Texas Catholic History and Culture* 5 (1994): 47–52; Woodside, Jane. "The Womanless Wedding: An American Folk Drama," PhD diss., University of North Carolina at Chapel Hill, 1987.

Thomas A. Green

Folk Group

Although the definition of the term "folk group" has been highly contentious among folklorists since the founding of the discipline in England in 1848, in North America today a folk group is considered any group of people who share at least one common linking factor, such as an awareness of a shared tradition, whether defined by country, region, community, ethnicity, gender, family, school, occupation, religion, or any subgroup or interest thereof. Folk groups, then, may be as large as a nation or as small as a pair of siblings. Persons may both change groups and belong to several groups at any given time, usually according to their stage in life, habits, hobbies, and the day's schedule. For example, an American teenager may go from belonging to a high school sports team to a college study group, and from being a Madonna fan to sharing in the customary life of a college Drama Department within a single year, maintaining meaningful contact with the members of all four groups. Likewise, a mother may simultaneously belong to a women's friendship group, a union, an exercise class, a community service organization, and a carpool, all the while maintaining membership in various gender, family, ethnic, regional, and religious groups.

The definition of a folk group was not always as broad as the one posited by Alan Dundes in 1980 and discussed above, and its simplicity has been strenuously contested. From the early days of folklore collecting by eighteenth-century antiquarians and myth-ritualist and literary folklorists, and most explicitly by the anthropological "survival" school of folklorists championed by Edward Burnet Tylor, the folk were consistently identified as rural, uneducated peasants. This equation persists in some quarters. However, in the first half of the twentieth century, the Italian political activist Antonio Gramsci suggested a combination of the conservative view of the folk, that is, peasants, with a Marxist notion of the folk as persons occupying the lowest stratum of society, thus extending the definition of a folk group to the urban equivalent of rural, uneducated peasants, the urban proletariat.

Every folk group has its own forms of lore that endow its traditions. Each operates simultaneously as a vehicle for the transmission and communication of a collective identity and as a "function of shared identity." Folklorists often specialize, choosing to focus their research on a particular folk group, such as Appalachian folklore, children's folklore, Chicano folklore, entertainment folklore, medical folklore, Mormon folklore, gay and lesbian folklore, or women's folklore. Numerous notable studies focusing on specific folk groups have been undertaken, from Iona and Peter Opie's pioneering collections of children's folklore (1944 onward) to Sabina Magliocco's breakthrough *Witching Culture: Folklore and Neo-Paganism* in America (2004).

According to Jan Brunvand, female folk groups traditionally cluster around the domestic sphere, and include genres such as foodways, handicrafts, folk medicine, and family lore. However, Margaret Mills cautions against such a "distorted and limited folklorists' view of both folklore and folkloristics." After all, contemporary women's and girls' participation in groups ranging from cheerleaders to riot grrrls and from political organizing to covens, along with their roles in religious institutions, sororities, consciousness-raising groups, popular culture, academia, government, and nearly all branches of the armed forces would seem to indicate that the number and scope of female-specific folk groups cannot be limited by these characterizations. *See also:* Activism; Cheerleading; Clique; Consciousness Raising; Croning; Farm Women's Folklore; Foodways; Girls' Folklore; Jewish Women's Folklore; Military Women's Folklore; Muslim Women's Folklore; Occupational Folklore; Popular Culture; Sorority Folklore; Tradition; Wicca and Neo-Paganism; Women Religious; Women's Clubs; Women's Friendship Groups.

References: Bauman, Richard. "Differential Identity and the Social Base of Folklore." *Journal of American Folklore* 85 (1971): 31–41; Brunvand, Jan Harold. *The Study of American Folklore: An Introduction.* 4th ed. New York: W. W. Norton and Company, 1987; Dorson, Richard M. *The British Folklorists: A History.* London: Routledge, 1999 [1968]; Dundes, Alan. "Who Are the Folk?" In *Interpreting Folklore*, 1–19. Bloomington: Indiana University Press, 1980 [1977]; ———. "Defining Identity through Folklore." *Folklore Matters*, 1–39. Knoxville: The University of Tennessee Press, 1989 [1983]; ———. ed. "Introduction to Gramsci, Antonio. Observations on Folklore." In *International Folkloristics: Classic Contributions by the Founders of Folklore*, 131–36. Lanham: Rowman and Littlefield Publishers, Inc., 1999; Mills, Margaret. "Feminist Theory and the Study of Folklore: A Twenty-Year Trajectory toward Theory." *Western Folklore* 52 (1993): 173–192; Oring, Elliot. *Folk Groups and Folklore Genres: An Introduction.* Logan: Utah State University Press, 1986.

Maria Teresa Agozzino

Folk Medicine

Folk medicine may be defined as any unofficial health practice or belief. Folk medical beliefs may work apart from or in conjunction with whatever official medical system is in place within a society. Folk medical practices include acts done to heal or prevent illness (for example, eating garlic to cure a cold or not going outside with wet hair) and religious themes (for example, praying to prevent or treat disease). Folk medicine practices and beliefs are part of a complex system of beliefs, attitudes, and values that are ultimately personal and work with the logic of the individual.

Historically, the study of folk medicine has focused on herbal remedies and traditional healers. As in other areas of Folklore Studies, scholars tended to collect their data from persons of low socioeconomic status, members of specific cultural and ethnic groups who transmit their information primarily through oral tradition (for example, root workers, curanderas, and herbalists), and rural residents, since it was believed that folk medicine would not be in evidence where scientific biomedicine was available and affordable. This idea is today known as the functional fallacy of folk medicine. A 1993 study in the *New England Journal of Medicine* found that 34 percent of Americans had used "unconventional intervention" within the previous twelve months. Unconventional interventions included herbs and spiritual healing, but not prayer, suggesting that the numbers actually might be much higher. This survey also found that the use of unconventional interventions *increased* with a person's level of education (Eisenberg et al. 247–252).

"Official" is a relative term. Rooted in cultural context, it generally refers to approaches and practices that are authorized in a formal way. In the American context, scientific biomedicine is sanctioned medicine, regulated by a body of official intuitions, such as the Office of the Surgeon General and medical schools. Since folk medicine has no official standing with these institutions and frequently does not possess a formal authoritative body of its own, many of its forms are considered "unofficial" despite the endorsement of research, clinical trials, and personal-experience narratives.

In spite of folk medicine's lack of formal authoritative bodies, it does operate as a coherent system of knowledge. Such systems include consensus among a group of individuals who attest, for example, to the health benefits of Tai Chi or yoga. Even the personal health beliefs and practices of an individual practitioner, an herbalist, or a massage therapist, for example, are internally coherent. Because beliefs and practices are interdependent, one cannot consider one aspect of a health belief system in isolation. In general, the greater the number of relationships among the parts of a health belief system, the more stable it will be. If an individual's personal health belief system is challenged, she will often construct a logic that accommodates new information without destroying the existing system.

Due to the cost of medical-health insurance in the United States as well as in other countries, folk medicine may be a less expensive alternative. Many people feel that folk medical practices, such as the use of herbal remedies, are more "natural" for the body. Others, especially those faced with life-threatening diseases such as cancer, may enlist folk medical practices as means for combating the harsh side effects of chemotherapy and other treatments, or may turn to folk medicine in hope of a cure.

The use of folk medicine in conjunction with official medicine often causes distress for medical professionals since many folk treatments have not undergone official medical testing or clinical trials, and the possibility of interaction, depending on the type of folk medical intervention used, may be a concern. Many patients who supplement treatment with folk medicine feel that medical practitioners are not open to alternative practices, and so do not inform doctors of their treatment plans for fear of rebuke. More frequently, however, individuals do share official medical test results with their alternative or folk health care practitioners.

Folk medicine is frequently considered both a first and last resort. Over-the-counter medicines (OTC) or folk remedies are often used to combat the first signs of illness, and only after those methods do not work will a patient seek another's advice, be it a doctor, folk medical practitioner, or a member of her folk group, including friends and family. Typically, after a patient has gone as far as she can through the official health care system, she will resort to alternative or folk medical practices for relief of her disease or symptoms.

Women, especially those who suffer from menopause, frequently turn to alterative therapies or folk medical practices when they feel that their symptoms are not being taken seriously by medical professionals. Women report that symptoms such as rage during menopause are often overlooked or undertreated simply because no medical studies have been conducted to address them. When no conclusive evidence exists, when a woman's symptoms are not typical, or when a woman does not trust the treatments official medicine suggests, she typically turns to oral tradition or the Internet to find others who have experienced similar symptoms. She looks for other methods of last resort, which often include folk medical practices.

Women frequently make the medical decisions in a family, be it to see a doctor or other health care provider, apply a poultice, brew a tea, or enforce bed rest. Since women typically arrange appointments and oversee treatments for all family members, better understanding their decision-making processes, real concerns, and health beliefs is useful for health care professionals. *See also: Curandera*; Folk Group; Herbs; Menopause; Old Wives' Tales.

References: Adler, Shelley R. "Integrating Personal Health Belief Systems: Patient-Practitioner Communication." *Healing Logics: Culture and Medicine in Modern Health Belief Systems*, ed. Erika Brady, 115–128. Logan: Utah University Press, 2001; Brady, Erika. *Healing Logics: Culture and Medicine in Modern Health Belief Systems*. Logan: Utah State University Press, 2001; Eisenberg, David M., Ronald C. Kessler, and Cindy Foster. "Unconventional Medicine in the United States." *New England Journal of Medicine*, vol. 328, no. 4 (1993): 247–252; Gevitz, Norman, ed. *Other Healers: Unorthodox Medicine in America*. Baltimore: The John Hopkins University Press, 1988; Goldstein, Diane. "'When Ovaries Retire': Contrasting Women's Experiences with Feminist and Medical Models of Menopause." *Health*, vol. 4, no. 3 (2000): 309–323; ———. "Competing Logics and the Construction of Risk." in *Healing Logics: Culture and Medicine in Modern Health Belief Systems*, ed. Erika Brady, 129–140. Logan: Utah State University Press, 2001; Hufford, David. "Traditions of Disbelief." *New York Folklore*, vol. 8, nos. 3 and 4 (1982): 47–56; ———. "Introduction." *Southern Folklore* 54 (1997): 1–14; Kirkland, James W., Holly F. Matthews, C. W. Sullivan III, and Karen Baldwin, eds. *Traditional Medicine Today: A Multidisciplinary Perspective*. Durham, NC: Duke University Press, 1991; Mattingly, Cheryl, and Linda C. Garro. *Narrative and the Cultural Construction of Illness and Healing*. Berkeley: University of California Press, 2000; O'Connor, Bonnie Blair. *Healing Traditions: "Alternative" Medicines and the Health Professions*. Philadelphia: University of Pennsylvania Press, 1994.

Andrea Kitta

Folk Music and Folksong

Folk music is generally understood by folklorists as orally transmitted, unwritten songs and instrumental pieces performed by nonprofessional musicians. Its repertoires are generally specific to a region or ethnic group, and are passed down from generation to generation through personal interactions rather than by written notation or formal instruction. Folk music is the more inclusive term, comprising instrumental as well as solo and accompanied vocal pieces, the latter being termed "folksong." Contemporary folk music can include materials transmitted through the mass media, but tends to follow the musical and textual styles of more traditional works.

Women have always been central to the collection, composition, and performance of folk music in North America.

Defined by its uncomplicated melodies, plain-speaking lyrics, and universal themes, folk music expresses and reaffirms the values, traditions, and life experiences of people from a specific region, ethnicity, community, or folk group, especially those based in rural rather than urban settings. The particular combination of melodic structure, instrumentation, lyrics, and subject matter is unique to the folk music of a specific locality or folk group, but due to its oral nature, folk music travels from one place to another with musicians and singers, and is shared with others through their musical performances. As a result, folk music evolves as it is transmitted from one person to another or is used in different contexts and for different occasions. Folk music, then, is something of a paradox, for although it is a highly personal and localized art form created and maintained by a particular community or social group, its oral essence and high level of mobility renders it a collective and universal form as well.

Folk music performed in the United States and Canada is generally simple in form and most may be classified by its binary and ternary structures. Music in binary form has two sections that differ from one another melodically and lyrically; usually each section is repeated. Ternary forms have three sections: the first section is followed by a contrasting one, then by a repetition of the first section. Folksongs that narrate a story are most commonly performed as a ballad, lyric song, or epic. The ballad is perhaps the most common form found in North American folksongs of European origin; composed in stanzas, its lyrics comprise several verses, each employing the same melody, followed by a refrain or chorus. Lyric songs may be structurally similar to the ballad, with verses and refrains, but are thematically different; less frequently coherent narratives, they focus on the attitudes and emotions of the narrator. Epic refers to longer musical works that arrived in North America with emigrants from the Balkans, Scandinavia, Asia, Africa, and the Middle East; they are usually accompanied by a musical instrument and sung to a melody that varies throughout the work.

Communities throughout the United States and Canada—from Indigenous North American peoples to recent emigrants from Russia, South Asia, and the Middle East—create and sustain their own folk music traditions. Ethnic folk music traditions are identifiable through their particular use of instrumentation, melodic and vocal range, subject matter, and musical texture, as well as the contexts in which they are performed and the social significance that they acquire through them.

What the recording industry today calls the "ethnic" folk music traditions of the United States and Canada include Native North American powwow music; Hispanic North American *corridos* and *mariachi* music; Jewish *klezmer* music; African North American spirituals, blues, and gospel music; Euro North American dance music tune types such as the jig, reel, polka, hornpipe, quadrille, waltz, *schottische*, *springar*, *polska*, and *mazurka*; Greek *bouzouki* ensemble music; Japanese *taiko* drumming ensembles; Russian *balalaika* ensemble music; and South Asian *bhangra* music.

Hybridized folk music forms emerged in the United States and Canada resulting from musical collaboration among various ethnic groups residing—often for the first time—in close proximity to one another. Hybrid genres in North America are numerous, and include *Cajun* and *zydeco* music of the Louisiana-Texas border, which developed from cultural contact between Franco-Canadian (Acadian) immigrants and African Americans; "hillbilly" (bluegrass) music of the Appalachia region, which combined British and Irish folk ballads and fiddle tunes; the blues music of southern African Americans; southern religious hymns; *conjunto*, a Texas-Mexican music form that melds musical traditions from German and Hispanic settlers residing in Texas from the mid-nineteenth century; and Canadian *Métis* music, which combines Irish, Scottish, and French tunes with Plains First Nations dancing and rhythmic structures.

Although the instruments used in folk music vary according to the group from which it emanates, some of those most commonly used in Euro North American folk music include the voice, fiddle, banjo, flute, whistle, dulcimer, accordion, guitar, harmonica, mandolin, bagpipe, washboard, Jew's harp (or jaw harp), bones, spoons, musical bow, and, in recent times, piano. The musical instruments transplanted to North America from various regions of the world are countless, but include zithers such as the Finnish *kantele*, dulcimers such as the Hungarian *cimbalom*, bowed instruments such as the Yugoslavian *gusle*, lutes such as the Hawaiian ukulele, unfretted instruments such as the Japanese *shamisen*, and flutes such as the Middle Eastern *nai*.

Traditional folk music often accompanies activities such as work, life-cycle events, rituals, social gatherings, and dances. Folksongs cover a wide range of subject matter and suit many purposes, including work songs, prison songs, war songs, lullabies, religious devotional songs, children's songs, love songs, and protest songs.

Women have been central to the creation, dissemination, and performance of folk music from its earliest origins. In particular, women were vital for music transmission in domestic spaces where, for example, they sang lullabies to children, hummed tunes to dull the drudgery of housework, and held kitchen parties to entertain each other. However, some women also attained broader recognition and performed for audiences of women and men in more public locations.

Folksong lyrics have both defined and contested the roles and sociocultural positions of women throughout history. Many traditional songs paint lyrical portraits of women as household servants and domestics, decorative accoutrements to men, symbols of evil and temptation, or sources of diversion and entertainment. Many folksongs, however, can be read as oblique or coded commentaries that resist convention and offer alternatives. Numerous contemporary female folk musicians and singers have directly challenged stereotypical images of women by writing folksongs that present images of women as powerful, vital members of society on an even footing with men.

Throughout the twentieth century, women have been essential in folk music's development from a genre revolving primarily around community and family to one that is also firmly situated in the North American popular music milieu. Countless women have promoted and advanced the genre. Their activities have ranged from collecting and analyzing, to performing, to composing folk music.

Many female scholars were vital to late nineteenth- and twentieth-century folk music scholarship, including Alice Cunningham Fletcher (1838–1923), Frances Densmore (1867–1957), Natalie Curtis Burlin (1875–1921), and Helen Heffron Roberts (1888–1985), all pioneering figures in Native American song research. Other significant scholars in the field were Dorothy Scarborough (1878–1935), who collected in Virginia and North Carolina; Olive Dame Campbell (1882–1954), who researched in the Appalachian Mountains; Helen Creighton (1899–1989), who collected 4,000 songs from Gaelic, Acadian, Mi'kmaq, English, German, and African musicians residing in the Maritime Provinces of Canada; and Sidney Robertson Cowell (1903–1995), who organized and directed a California Works Progress Administration project intended to document musical traditions in Northern California. Edith Fowke (1913–1996) gathered Canadian folksongs from such singers as LaRena Clark (1904–1991), an Ontario-based folksinger whose repertoire included British ballads, country and western songs, and lumbering songs.

Two families of scholars, musicians, and composers—the Lomaxes and the Seegers—were vital to the establishment of American folk music scholarship and folk music performance in the twentieth century. Their work demonstrates the link between traditional folk music performed within and for small communities and contemporary folk music and song, often inspired by traditional forms but recently composed and dealing with current issues. The folk revival brought traditional forms to public attention.

John Lomax (1867–1948) and his children Alan Lomax (1915–2002) and Bess Lomax Hawes (b. 1921) were pioneering figures in folk music archiving, collecting, and recording. John and Alan Lomax produced numerous songbooks and field recordings that helped define the folk music genre, and inspired numerous budding folk music performers. Folksong collector, educator, and folk music advocate Bess Lomax Hawes earned a reputation as one of the best folk music instructors in the United States in the 1940s, and, in collaboration with Jacqueline Steiner, wrote "M.T.A." (better known as "Charlie on the M.T.A." about a subway fare increase by Boston's Metropolitan Transit Authority), later recorded by the Kingston Trio. The Lomaxes promoted and recorded several notable female folk singers, including Almeda Riddle (known as "Granny Riddle," 1898–1986), a folk balladeer from Arkansas renowned for her repertoire of more than 600 songs; Vera Hall (1902–1964), who was one of the greatest singers of folksongs, blues, and spirituals in Alabama of her time; and Bessie Jones (1902–1984), a legendary singer based on the Georgia Sea Islands. Alan Lomax is also credited with assisting the career of Jean Ritchie (b. 1922). Ritchie was a member of a huge musical family who first settled in the Cumberland Mountains of Kentucky in the 1700s. She performed and recorded material from her family's massive and far-reaching repertoire, produced original pieces, and published a number of folksong collections, including *The Singing Family of the Cumberlands* (1955).

The academic research of married couple Charles Seeger (1886–1979) and Ruth Crawford Seeger (1901–1953) created access to folk music resources that influenced and stimulated the careers of numerous folk musicians, particularly their own children—acclaimed folk singers Pete Seeger (b. 1919, Charles Seeger's son from a previous marriage), Mike Seeger (b. 1933), and Peggy Seeger (b. 1935). In her early career, Ruth Crawford Seeger was a highly successful classical composer and pianist, but from the mid-1930s to her death, she devoted much of her work to folk music. Crawford Seeger incorporated American folksongs into children's music education, collaborated with Alan and John Lomax on several folksong collections, and published her own collections, including *American Folk Songs for Children in Home, School and Nursery School: A Book for Children, Parents and Teachers* (1948).

Members of the Seeger family are credited with fostering the careers of Hazel Dickens (b. 1935) and Elizabeth "Libba" Cotten (1895–1987), a folk singer from North Carolina who worked in the Seeger home for a number of years. Cotten was recognized as the source of the renowned "Freight Train" (*Freight Train and Other North Carolina Folk Songs and Tunes*, Folkways Records, 1989). Cotten performed throughout the 1950s and 1960s at folk music concerts and festivals (including the Newport Folk Festival) and released a number of albums, including *Elizabeth Cotten Live!*, which won a Grammy Award for best folk recording in 1984.

During the late nineteenth century and throughout the twentieth, all kinds of music and song became accessible to audiences beyond the immediate communities of their performers through dissemination in songbooks and as commercial music recordings. As the recorded music industry grew, folk music changed from a form created and enjoyed only in its communities of origin to an identifiable genre distinct and separate from other styles, such as country, blues, and various ethnic music traditions. Distinctive genres became more pronounced as record companies and radio stations attempted to increase their profitability by producing music that would appeal to specific commercial audiences, thereby to sell more recordings and attract more radio listeners. As a result, within the commercial recording industry, the term "folk music" most frequently came to refer to folksongs accompanied by acoustic instruments, while instrumental folk music without vocal accompaniment became identified as "ethnic" or "traditional" music.

As a byproduct of this process of commercialization, folk music and song came to be associated with social change and leftist politics. In the late 1920s and 1930s, North America was experiencing an economic depression and political activists were looking for an artistic medium that could articulate the hardships of the times. Union organizations began to appropriate folksongs for use at rallies, and numerous folk singers wrote protest songs that spoke eloquently of the need for social and political reforms to remedy unjust living and working conditions. Notable female balladeers of this era include Ella May Wiggins (1900–1929), an ardent union member who was shot by anti-union demonstrators. Her best known folksong is "The Mill Mother's Lament:"

We leave our homes in the morning,
We kiss our children good-bye,
While we slave for the bosses,
Our children scream and cry ...

How it grieves the heart of a mother,
You everyone must know.
But we can't buy for our children,
Our wages are too low....

But understand, all workers,
Our union they do fear.
Let's stand together, workers,
And have a union here. (Alloy, 1976)

Other female folk singers of the time whose works detailed the miner's condition include Mary Magdalene Garland (1880–1960), a coal miner's wife from Kentucky who spoke out about miners' working conditions, sang at union meetings and on picket lines, and later recorded songs for the Library of Congress, and her half-sister Sarah Ogun Gunning, who also sang folksongs addressing the miners' plight.

More sedate folk music was popular with middle-class American audiences throughout the 1940s and early 1950s. However, two groups, the Almanac Singers and the Weavers, were key to the continued propagation of folk music during these decades. The Almanac Singers featured a frequently changing collective of musicians, including Pete Seeger (b. 1919, as noted above), Woody Guthrie (1912-1967), Lee Hays (1914-1981), Millard Lampell (1919-1997), Burl Ives (1909-1995), Butch Hawes (1919-1971), and Bess Lomax Hawes (b. 1921). They were the most recognizable and popular folk music group throughout the late 1930s and early 1940s, performing traditional folk music, anti-war ballads, and union songs at hootenannies (informal gatherings of musicians and their guests) during their heyday. The group disbanded shortly before the onset of World War II, when patriotic ideology linked to the war effort supplanted the socialist agenda the Almanac Singers expressed.

Folk music boomed in popularity by the late 1950s and early 1960s. The increased interest signaled the onset of the North American folk music revival, a movement spurred by middle-class, college-educated musicians disillusioned with the political and social climate of America who looked to the past—albeit a romanticized one—to find solutions to contemporary problems. Because folk music had been associated with leftist politics and political dissent since the 1920s, it was a logical choice of musical genres in a newly emerging climate of social unrest.

Folk music groups began to enjoy large-scale success in the commercial music milieu. These included the Weavers, a postwar quartet that featured Pete Seeger, Fred Hellerman (b. 1927), Lee Hays (1914-1981, as noted above), and singer Ronnie Gilbert (b. 1936); the Kingston Trio, whose "Tom Dooley" topped the pop charts in 1958; and the award-winning trio of the mid-1960s, Peter, Paul, and Mary, which featured the voice of Mary Travers (b. 1937). Other musicians, most notably Bob Dylan (b. 1941), first discovered America's folk music on recordings such as the Smithsonian's monumental *Folkways Anthology of American Folk Music*. They felt compelled to perform works from those albums as well as to compose music of their own in a similar vein.

Folk music performances thrived in the United States and Canada in the 1960s. Coffeehouses from Cambridge, Massachusetts, to Berkeley, California, to Montreal, Quebec, to New York City's Greenwich Village often showcased folk musicians. Several festivals, most notably the Newport Folk Festival (founded 1959) and the Mariposa Folk Festival (founded 1961) headlined folk music performers. The revival was a rediscovery of North America's musical roots, with folk music metamorphosing into the soundtrack for the large-scale political and social movement that was taking place at the time.

The civil rights movement, anti-war protests, and women's struggles for equality shaped the 1960s, and folk music spoke to the climate of the times. Reminiscent of the 1920s, folk music was once again treated as a viable and forceful medium for voicing political and social dissent. Many folk singers, such as Woody Guthrie, Bob Dylan, Buffy Sainte-Marie (b. 1941), and Joan Baez (b. 1941) held strong political convictions and wrote protest ballads and other political songs modeled on traditional folk music. Canadian-born, Native American folk singer Sainte-Marie was one of the first female folk singers involved with the Vietnam War protest movement, and her song "Universal Soldier" (*Illuminations*, Vanguard Records, 1969) became a rallying cry for protestors against the war.

The 1960s women's movement attracted women songwriters and performers in the folk revival, and the careers of a number of them were fostered by the social climate of the times. Peggy Seeger (b. 1935) of the acclaimed Seeger family was one of the first women prominent on the folk scene in the 1950s and 1960s. In songs such as "I'm Gonna Be an Engineer" (*Different Therefore Equal*, Folkways Records, 1979), which became one of the anthems of the women's' movement, Seeger excelled at singing ballads from a feminist perspective.

Female musicians such as folk-blues singer Odetta Felious (b. 1930), Rosalie Sorrels (b. 1933), Caroline Hester (b. 1937), Hedy West (b. 1938), Judy Collins (b. 1939), Sylvia Fricker (b. 1940) of the duo Ian and Sylvia, Kate Wolf (1942–1986), Maria Muldaur (b. 1943), Jackie DeShannon (b. 1944), and Mimi Fariña (1945–2001) were also vital players in the folk revival scene. Many of these musicians enjoyed commercial and critical success in a variety of musical styles for decades to come.

Joan Baez emerged at the 1959 Newport Folk Festival as the first female folk musician of the 1960s to become a star. She released her first album in 1960, and it was an immediate hit. In 1962, Baez appeared on the cover of *Time* magazine, signaling her rise in status to the undisputed "queen of folk." Throughout her five-decade career, Baez has been highly visible and vocal as a political activist, beginning with her now-famous appearance on stage with Marin Luther King, Jr., at the 1963 march on Washington, DC, where she sang "We Shall Overcome." Toward the end of the 1960s, Baez's style began to gravitate toward country music, but she remained one of the most popular folk artists of the decade. Baez has continued to record and perform into the new millennium, with her music sometimes bordering on country, pop, and rock music.

Folk musicians of the revival often interspersed self-penned music with folk standards in their live performances, but traditional folk music was the primary draw for most audiences. As the 1960s drew to a close, many performers who had first made names for themselves as folk musicians were now garnering press and attracting audiences based on the merits of their original compositions. From roughly 1968 to 1977, a singer-songwriter era developed, characterized by highly personal, often autobiographical lyrics. Rock, pop, folk, and gospel musicians alike worked within this format.

Canadian Joni Mitchell (b. 1943) was the first folk-oriented female singer-songwriter to gain commercial success, and she is widely credited for blazing a path for struggling women singer-songwriters. Throughout her enduring and highly successful career, Mitchell's body of work always featured poetic sensibilities, innovative guitar techniques and tunings, the integration of divergent musical styles, and deeply introspective and imaginative lyrics.

Many other acclaimed singer-songwriters of this period melded folk in varying degrees within their own music, including Carole King (b. 1942), Carly Simon (b. 1945), Kate McGarrigle (b. 1946), Anna McGarrigle (b. 1944), Linda Ronstadt (b. 1946), Laura Nyro (1947–1997), Holly Near (b. 1949), Joan Armatrading (b. 1950), and Rickie Lee Jones (b. 1954). The singer-songwriter style waned in the late 1970s as pop, disco, punk, and rock music grew to dominate commercial music, but the musical aesthetics of the singer-songwriter remained part of the popular music scene in North America throughout the late 1970s and early 1980s, even if it was not commercially central.

Throughout the 1980s, metropolitan areas in the United States, such as New York City, Washington DC, and Boston were once again centers where many folk singers earned commercial exposure. *Sweet Honey in the Rock,* an African American female a cappella ensemble, was founded in Washington, DC, in 1973. The group has musical roots in various African American genres, including spirituals, hymns, gospel music, jazz, and the blues. Performing first as a quartet and later as a sextet, Sweet Honey in the Rock has featured more than twenty musicians during its thirty-plus-year career. The group won a Best Traditional Folk Recording Grammy award in 1989 for its version of Leadbelly's "Grey Goose."

The Fast Folk Cooperative, a singer-songwriter organization established in New York City in 1982, was a means for songwriters to release their first recordings. Fast Folk's initial goal was to document the folk music scene centered in Greenwich Village during the 1980s, but over the next two decades it grew to include a record label, a concert series, a touring live revue, and a community of folk musicians who performed regularly and released their own recordings. Female folk musicians who got their start on the Fast Folk record label include Shawn Colvin (b. 1956), Julie Gold (b. 1956), Suzanne Vega (b. 1959), Lucy Kaplansky (b. 1960), Michelle Shocked (b. 1962), and Tracy Chapman (b. 1964).

Folk music again came into the spotlight in the late 1980s largely due to the remarkable success of a handful of musicians. The overwhelming commercial success and critical acclaim of these four—Emily Saliers (b. 1963) and Amy Ray (b. 1964) of the Indigo Girls, as well as Suzanne Vega and Tracy Chapman—ushered in a new wave of record-company investment in female singer-songwriters. Suzanne Vega came to prominence in 1985 with the hit single "Marlene On The Wall" from her self-titled debut, followed by the top-ten-selling single "Luka" from her 1987 album *Solitude Standing,* which went on to sell millions of copies. Tracy Chapman's 1988 self-titled debut album sold more than ten million copies worldwide, had the hit singles "Fast Car" and "Talkin' 'Bout a Revolution," and earned Chapman three 1988 Grammy Awards. The Indigo Girls' self-titled first album sold more than a million copies, contained the chart-reaching single "Closer to Fine," and earned the duo a Grammy for Best Contemporary Folk Recording in 1989.

Female musicians with roots in folk music came to control a portion of the commercial music scene, signaling the beginning of a music style known as the "nu folk revival," "folk roots revival," and "new folk movement." Artists who had struggled to make names for themselves throughout the 1980s, such as Lucinda Williams (b. 1953), Nanci Griffith (b. 1954), and Shawn Colvin finally earned the recognition they deserved.

The success of the nu folk movement offered inspiration for women musicians who wanted to express themselves through music that freely and unabashedly crossed the boundaries of pop, rock, punk, and country music, creating hybridized music forms such as folk-rock, folk-pop, folk-country, and folk-punk music. Musicians working in these hybridized genres sought to create highly personal and unique music. Although their music encompasses a wide variety of styles, they share an overriding desire to create "authentic" music, shown by their use of acoustic instruments, uncomplicated costumes and minimal makeup, quirky or eccentric personas, and autobiographical lyrics and spare musical forms.

Throughout the twentieth century, folk music and folksong changed to suit modern performance contexts and new technological advancements, in part by appropriating stylistic elements from other music genres with which it came into contact. Contemporary folk music defies categorization and often cuts across musical styles; rock, pop, rhythm and blues, and country musicians frequently compose music that could be defined as folk music. However, certain qualities continue to thread through folk music, such as confessional lyrics, a lack of overt reliance on electronic amplification, and a thematic focus on common life experiences. *See also:* Activism; Ballad; Folk Group; Lullaby; Occupational Folklore; Politics; Tradition; Tradition-Bearer; Women's Movement.

References: Alloy, Evelyn. *Working Women's Music: The Songs and Struggles of Women in the Cotton Mills, Textile Plants, and Needle Trades, Complete with Music for Singing and Playing.* Somerville, MA: New England Free Press, 1976; Ammer, Christine. *Unsung: A History of Women in American Music.* Portland, OR: Amadeus, 2001; Briscoe, James R. *Contemporary Anthology of Music by Women.* Bloomington: Indiana University Press, 1997; Burns, Kristine Helen, ed. *Women and Music in America Since*

1900: An Encyclopedia. Westport, CT: Greenwood Press, 2002; Cantwell, Robert. *When We Were Good: The Folk Music Revival.* Cambridge, MA: Harvard University Press, 1996; Cohen, Ronald D. *Rainbow Quest: The Folk Music Revival and American Society, 1940–1970.* Amherst: University of Massachusetts Press, 2002; Grattan, Virginia L. *American Women Songwriters.* Westport, CT: Greenwood Publishing, 1993; Pendle, Karin *Women and Music: A History.* Bloomington: Indiana University Press, 2001; Whitely, Sheila, ed. *Sexing the Groove: Popular Music and Gender.* New York: Routledge, 1997.

Erin Stapleton-Corcoran

Folk Photography

Folk photography is concerned with photography—an artistic and documentary element of both material and popular culture—as it is used by ordinary people to document everyday life. The commercialization and technological democratization of photography for non-elite consumption has made photography a shared life experience and presence for most North Americans, as well as an expressive medium strongly associated with women, families, and the domestic sphere. If not from photography's arrival in 1839, certainly since the latter part of the nineteenth century with the introduction of the Kodak camera and the rise of amateur photography, photographs have chronicled the lives of common persons. As an artifact that resides in a context—a literal and figurative frame—the photograph should be considered for both its surface qualities and the more subtle information it holds about the human condition.

By treating photography customarily as a flat art, photographic scholarship has privileged surface analysis, accomplished exclusively by scrutinizing its composition and other formal characteristics of the picture plane. While this is one appropriate level of appreciation and understanding of photos, in considering folk photography it is equally necessary to adopt methods for the contextual study of photographic images, in which women would represent not merely the subject matter for, or the creators of, images, but the chief (though not exclusive) guardians of generational stories catalogued in photograph files, albums, scrapbooks, slideshows, and, most recently, household items featuring digitized images, ranging from personalized calendars to customized mousepads.

Photographs act as visual cues for the behavior of persons connected with them; that is, they frequently encourage an intimate viewer to engage in a dialogue specifically corresponding to the imagery. Pictures may serve as a catalyst to the viewer-listener's sharing of narrative memories, or even tangentially related stories, as is common in the ritual act of presenting the contents of a family album to a guest as after-dinner entertainment. However, if not fastidiously tended, family photographs risk becoming pedestrian, devoid of emotional meaning, and become artifacts, collections of images whose specific importance resides in their function within social and historical memory.

Because photography is a relatively new phenomenon, the context of its making sometimes remains accessible, at least in part. Often, the photographer or others linked directly to the photographic event are still available to researchers. Interviews, oral histories, and other records of personal contact may then accompany visual scholarship. With good fieldwork, the student of photography and its lore can capture and preserve interactions between people and their contexts through material images. Daniel Wojcik's study of photographs purportedly representing apparitions of the Virgin Mary is a good example.

While photography receives explanation and embellishment from verbal expression, it is a language in itself. Every photographic image has a surface and a deep structure. The communication of a photographic message is coded, containing a subtle set of rules for the transmission and reception of visual information. People assign their own meanings to images, and yet, when viewed in large numbers, snapshots begin to resemble each other, falling into recognizable categories. Photographic images are, therefore, generalizable, signaling social and aesthetic meanings using consensually agreed upon patterns (for example, obligatory smiles, the group shot with an identifying placard placed in front) and visual tropes (newlyweds with all the reception guests, the new baby peering from beneath a crib blanket), at once showing the unique faces of family members and the familiar poses and occasions American viewers have come to regard as emblems of a family's history.

In this sense, the study of photographs concerns itself with the history of everyday life. Once the hand-held camera had freed photographers from costly and cumbersome tripods and flash units, shooting in more remote locations and with quicker exposure times became achievable. The revolution in technology inevitably influenced both choices of photographic subjects and their manner of representation. Prints became affordable and plentiful, and thus less formally posed. Marianne Hirsch and Jerald Maddox, among others, approach homemade photography as a folk medium, concerned more with documenting vernacular culture than with technological savvy or pretensions to art. To the extent that women have traditionally been charged with the role of culture-bearer, they are similarly the keepers of most homemade photographic images. Whether generating, arranging, displaying, or exchanging photographs, women preserve the images, and with them the memories, that have become mainstays of family folklore. However, since few well-developed studies on women and folk photography are available, the field remains open to further study. *See also:* Family Folklore; Film; Oral History.

References: Adams, Timothy Dow. *Light Writing and Life Writing: Photography in Autobiography.* Chapel Hill: University of North Carolina Press, 1999; Coke, Van Deren, ed. *One Hundred Years of Photographic History.* Albuquerque: University of New Mexico Press, 1975; Hirsch, Marianne, ed. *Family Frames: Photography, Narrative, and Postmemory.* Cambridge: Harvard University Press, 1997; ———. *The Familial Gaze.* Hanover, NH: University Press of New England, 1999; Ohrn, Karen Becker. *Dorothea Lange and the Documentary Tradition.* Baton Rouge: Louisiana State University Press, 1980; Sayre, Maggie Lee. *"Deaf Maggie Lee Sayre": Photographs of a River Life.* Ed. Tom Rankin. Oxford: University Press of Mississippi, 1995; Wojcik, Daniel. "'Polaroids from Heaven': Photography, Folk Religion, and the Miraculous Image Tradition at a Marian Apparition Site." *Journal of American Folklore* 109 (1996): 129–148.

Linda S. Watts

Folk Poetry

Rhythmic and/or rhyming texts, intended for reading, chanting, recitation and/or singing, including local compositions as well as traditional verse, often highly symbolic and relevant to a community's knowledge, beliefs, and views, are considered folk poetry.

Folk poetry is an extremely diverse genre. It can include verse for or by children—nursery and skipping rhymes; materials related to particular occupations from peddlers' cries and military cadences to cowboy poetry; written short verses communicated in graffiti and autograph books; lyric, narrative, and epic song texts; traditional as well as event-specific recitations, including African American toasts; and written verses for family and community circulation. Arguably, many kinds of folk poetry—ballads, lyric folksongs, epics, and newer forms like rap—are distinctive because of the integral importance of tunes and musical accompaniment. However, folklorists have often considered together verses intended for singing, recitation, and reading, and the line between them is a particularly difficult one to draw in current societies, as it was in literate cultures of the past. The texts or the rhymical/verse structures of songs may be the bases for both serious and parodic folk poetry for singing, reciting, or reading, suggesting that the distinctions between them may be detected primarily in terms of performance. And the same tunes can be used for entirely different song texts, suggesting a less-than-unbreakable link between music and verse content.

Folk poems of various types—original and traditional, irrespective of performance mode—say a great deal about the perspectives of women and men on their society, and about sociocultural organizations of gender in general. Many religious poetic texts like the *Ramayanas* of India are recited, and probably also authored, by men. In Iran, historical battle poetry is associated with men, dirges and laments with women, and wedding verse is recited by both sexes. Seven of the fifteen "amateur poets" whose gender could be identified in Cynthia Lamson's collection of Newfoundland counterprotest verse about seal hunting are women; one used a feminine pseudonym "Minnie Ha-Ha." However, in the additional categories of published, performer, and public-figure poets, only one woman is found, leaving a maximum of nine out of twenty-six writers who could be women.

Though some Eastern European folk poetic traditions have historically been restricted to male bards, many others are strongly associated with women. Women often perform ritual songs associated with weddings, funerals, and calendar customs—Christmas, Easter, Saints' Days, etc. In Brazil, the broadside *literatura de cordel* is almost exclusively masculine, since it is a professional activity requiring literacy and conflicting with women's traditional roles. But many forms traditionally associated with men, and misogynist lyrics like those found in many forms of male rap, also offer sites wherein women can express themselves.

The gendering of folk poetry can be deceptive. It might seem that cowboy poetry, relating to a quintessentially masculine occupation, would not be written or performed by women; however, they are performers as well as audience members at cowboy poetry gatherings in Canada and the

United States. In the Canadian province of Alberta, women and men write and perform poetry about pioneer life—farming and homesteading—more than about ranching. Much of what is called "cowboy" poetry in the United States may similarly refer to any and all aspects of life on the western plains.

The groups or communities to which folk poetry is directed are extremely diverse. They may be ethnic groups, rural communities, age groups, religious congregations, or special populations like prisoners, friends, families, and so on. Folk poetry is read, recited, or sung because of its expression of ideas and sentiments that the poet or presenter feels will be useful to the community or group to which it is directed. Since gender relations are pervasively significant in all cultures, folk poetry often says a great deal about women and men and their interactions with one another. Take, for example, this song text from nineteenth-century Iran:

> Daughters? One is enough.
> If there are two, well, Mother is not without help.
> If there are three, the ceiling beams will break down.
> If there are four, calamity is complete.
> If there are five, it is a deep darkness.
> If there are six, send out a crier.
> If there are seven, think of husbands.
> Still, may God bless the girls;
> Still, may God's name protect the girls (quoted in Soroudi 1990: 552).

Folk poetry may at times reflect social relations, but it may sometimes also address them adversarially, as in this Brazilian *folheto*, based on the Jorge Amado novel, *Tereza Batista*, in which the male author counters conventional views of sex workers:

> The prostitute is a human being
> like any other,
> Therefore, if treated with respect
> she can tomorrow lead
> a more honorable life as wife
> and mother, no longer dimming
> the radiance of the Immaculate
> Virgin-Mother of Christ (quoted in Slater 1982: 157).

While not the most progressive view imaginable, this perspective counters the notion that all sex workers are irredeemably damned.

Not all folk poetry by men shows women in a negative light, but such presentation is not uncommon, as in Texas prisoner Johnny Barone's poem about his life experiences:

> Once in jail he came to know,
> Of his wife and best friend Joe,
> She told his sons that he was dead,
> Married Joe and shared his bed (quoted in Burns 1993: 45).

The poet makes his wife directly responsible for most of the evil in his life. However, as Roger Renwick noted, folk poets may extol the conventional virtues of women too, as in verses composed to nurses as thank-you's after a hospital visit, praising their nurturance, kindness, and so on.

A Macedonian wedding text speaks eloquently about the bride's situation:

Give me your blessing, Oh darling father,
for I must leave you for a strange household,
for a strange household, and for strange people.
Though not my father, I'll call him father,
I'll call him father, he'll not say daughter.
Though not my mother, I'll call her mother,
I'll call her mother, she'll not say daughter (quoted in Sazdov 1991: 193).

Many ritual occasions call for focus upon particular female participants. In Luri (Macedonian) wedding verse, the mother-in-law is an ambivalent figure:

O girl, get up, get up, it is better there than here.
The mother-in-law you'll have is sweeter than sugar.
O girl, get up, get up, it is better here than there.
The mother in law in store for you is worse than a viper (quoted in Amanolahi and Thackston 1986: 108).

The above text also reflects the structuring of much folk poetry in terms of parallels and opposites, as will be discussed below. Luri dirges also reflect gender relations between women:

A mother dies, and a daughter next to her
Spreads her black tresses over the body.

Or:

A daughter and her mother are at the riverbank
When they do not see each other they pine for each other.

And between the sexes:

My grave is narrow, for no brother dug it.
The mourning for me is cold, for no sister wailed.

Or:

Girls with fathers sit in honor;
Girls without fathers welter in blood.

There are often touching commentaries on the importance of women:

Mother, mother, I shall never call you mother again.
You have left me behind like a mountain ewe's lamb.

Cross-culturally, women are frequently placed in the role of mourners, often as semiprofessionals extemporizing chanted dirges and/or mourning songs. Irish Gaelic lament poetry—keening—allows a mourning woman to express praise for the deceased. But a woman can also direct anger against a priest who tells her to accept her lot as a widow, against her husband for dying and leaving her, or against the abuser she is burying:

You used to give me
The thick end of the stick,

The hard side of the bed,
The small bit of food,
—That was all I expected (quoted in Bourke 1993: 174).

Much folk poetry paints a bleak picture of women's lives. Ingrian (Finnish/Russian) wedding songs advise the groom to beat his wife, but not to injure her excessively, and indoors rather than publicly. Women ethnographers often un/dis/cover resistance in verse-making traditions. Lila Abu-Lughod shows that Bedouin women's poetry does not indulge in the stereotypical representations of compliant, invisible Islamic women. She cites a Bedouin wedding verse that offers a negative view of polygyny:

Better death, blindness, poverty, and destitution
than a match with a married man (quoted in Abu-Lughod 1986: 217).

Folk poetry about heterosexual relationships is abundant cross-culturally. The Serbian "Death of Omer and Merima" is a tale of family opposition to lovers which ends, as so many of this story type do, with their deaths. In one version, the parallels so often evident in folk poetry take another form familiar cross-culturally—plants growing from the lovers' graves which link the two:

When just a little time had passed,
From Omer springs a young green pine,
Another springs from Merima:
About young Omer's Mera's wreathes,
Like silky thread a nosegay binds;
About both trees, the wormwood climbs (quoted in Zimmerman 1986: 141).

Indeed, much love poetry expresses misery:

Tears won't bring your sweetheart
endure your malady patiently
Tears won't bring your sweetheart
pay no mind and be quiet (quoted in Abu-Lughod 1986: 263).

Or:

The wounds, oh beloved, of your love
heal some days then open again.…
My wounds were just about healed
and today oh my torment, they tore open (ibid.: 264).

But heterosexual relationships are not always unhappy. "Maiden of Kosovo" is about lovers reunited on the battlefield because he recognizes the gold ring he gave her, and she recognizes the gold shawl she gave him.

Misogyny is rampant in folk poetry, especially that which is composed and/or presented by men. But alternative visions are also possible. Dianne Dugaw found cross-dressing ballads throughout Anglo European and North American traditions, in which bold women become sailors, highway robbers, and soldiers. Though these songs appear to be particularly popular with women singers, men also perform them. Indeed, the almost exclusively male-performed Brazilian *literatura de cordel* includes many texts with a woman-warrior theme. But the attitudes expressed toward such women in these songs cannot be generalized; one singer and audience member might see them as personal role models, where another finds them abhorrent and unfeminine.

In a genre as diverse as folk poetry, it is difficult to locate specific common qualities. Indeed, folk poetry's symbolic and communicative aspects make it richly interpretable. For example, a series of verses which appear in as diverse a group of genres as ballad, lyric folksong, and African American blues, are these:

Who's gonna shoe your pretty little foot,
Who's gonna glove your hand,
Who's gonna kiss your ruby red lips,
Who's gonna be your man?

Papa's gonna shoe my pretty little foot,
Mama's gonna glove my hand,
Sister's gonna kiss my ruby red lips,
And I don't need no man (Greenhill 1997).

This traditional Euro North American song text exemplifies the repetitive and paralleling structures that make folk poetry so easy to remember, but it also says much about gender assumptions and relations in Euro North American society. Most readers/listeners would assume that the first speaking persona is male. He is probably addressing a woman who is his lover or some other relative, questioning her about her economic situation, but also about her sexual availability. The woman's response in the second verse implies familial dependence but sexual autonomy—or even lesbianism.

Folk poetry is highly adaptable to circumstances. Note the extreme semantic shift when the identities your/my are reversed (as is frequently the case in traditional versions of this text):

Who's gonna shoe my pretty little foot,
Who's gonna glove my hand,
Who's gonna kiss my ruby red lips,
Who's gonna be my man?

Papa's gonna shoe your pretty little foot,
Mama's gonna glove your hand,
Sister's gonna kiss your ruby red lips,
And you don't need no man.

Now the first speaker is female, and her questions have become somewhat plaintive, while the second speaker could be male or female, the tone either dismissive or reassuring. The structures of folk poetry make it not only memorable, but also multiply interpretable. *See also:* Ballad; Folk Music and Folksong.

References: Abu-Lughod, Lila. *Veiled Sentiments: Honor and Poetry in a Bedouin Society.* Berkeley: University of California Press, 1986; Amanolahi, Sekandur, and W. M. Thackson. *Tales from Luristan: Tales, Fables and Folk Poetry from the Lur of Bâlâ-Garîva.* Cambridge, MA: Harvard University Press, 1986; Bourke, Angela. "More in Anger than in Sorrow: Irish Women's Lament Poetry." In *Feminist Messages: Coding in Women's Folk Culture*, ed. Joan Newlon Radner, 160–82. Urbana: University of Illinois Press,

1993; Dugaw, Dianne. *Warrior Women and Popular Balladry.* Cambridge: Cambridge University Press, 1989; Greenhill, Pauline. *True Poetry: Traditional and Popular Verse in Ontario.* Montreal: McGill-Queen's University Press, 1989; Greenhill, Pauline, ed. Special Issue: Folk Poetry. *Canadian Folklore canadien*, vol. 15, no. 1 (1993). Also see *intra* Richard A. Burns, "Prison Folk Poetry: The Barone Trilogy," 41–53; Greenhill, Pauline. "'Who's Gonna Kiss Your Ruby Red Lips?': Sexual Scripts in Floating Verses." In *Ballads Into Books: The Legacies of Francis James Child,* eds. Tom Cheesman and Sigrid Rieuwerts, 225–36. Berne: Peter Lang, 1997; Lamson, Cynthia. *"Bloody Decks and a Bumper Crop": The Rhetoric of Sealing Counter-Protest.* St. John's, NF: ISER, 1979; Renwick, Roger. *English Folk Poetry: Structure and Meaning.* Philadelphia: University of Pennsylvania, 1980; Sazdov, Tome. "Macedonian Folk Poetry, Principally Lyric." *Oral Tradition,* vol. 6, nos. 2/3 (1991) 186–199; Slater, Candace. *Stories on a String: The Brazilian Literatura de Cordel.* Berkeley: University of California Press, 1982; Soroudi, Sorour S. "Folk Poetry and Society in Nineteenth-Century Iran." In *Proceedings of the First European Conference of Iranian Studies,* eds. Gherardo Gnoli and Antonio Panaino, 541–52. Rome: Instituto Italiano Per Il Medio Ed Estremo Oriente, 1990; Zimmerman, Devrnja. *Serbian Folk Poetry.* Columbus Ohio: Kosovo Publishing, 1986.

Pauline Greenhill

Folklife

Folklife comprises the traditionary culture of a group and the study of that culture. The combination "folk" and "life" (and its equivalent in Scandinavian languages and German) appears in nineteenth-century documents. As a specialized term, the English word is derived from twentieth-century Swedish usage *(folkliv),* and suggests a particular approach toward the study of traditional culture. Folklife, like all aspects of culture, tends to be strongly gendered. The distinction between women's folklife and men's folklife in a particular culture generally corresponds to the sociocultural distinctions between women and men, and between the feminine and the masculine as defined by that culture. One important aspect of women's folklife today is the way in which women use traditional communicative forms to express and sometimes to contest their positions in their cultures.

The distinction between the terms "folklife" and "folklore" tends to be one of emphasis rather than one of subject matter. Current usage is quite diverse. Some sharply distinguish an older approach to folklore from a newer approach to folklife. But many scholars combine the terms— "folklore" and "folklife"—regarding them as more or less synonymous or as referring to identical materials from only slightly different perspectives.

Folk Studies began as the study of items that could be recorded on paper. Texts of tales and ballads attracted by far the most serious and consistent attention, and folklore centers collected them in folklore archives and published them in folklore journals. As other materials came under consideration, they were denominated by new coinages, "folk music," "folkways," "folk art," "folk architecture," etc. Emphasis was on the materials themselves. Analysis tended to be comparative or historical, seeking answers to the questions 1) what does this item tell us about the lost culture of this people? or 2) what is the original form of this item and how has it migrated from culture to culture? North American folkloristics continues to place much emphasis on folk materials. Jan Brunvand's popular textbook

American Folklore (1998, fourth edition) for instance, is largely organized into chapters with titles such as "Folktales," "Superstitions," "Folk Gestures," and "Folk Costumes." By the late 1800s, however, a more integrated approach to folk materials emerged in Sweden with the establishment of Skansen, the great outdoor folk museum in Stockholm. There, traditional buildings from throughout Sweden were rebuilt and grouped to exhibit the way of life of those who had lived and worked in them. The emphasis at Skansen was on the past, but in time Swedish researchers came to realize that materials and activities like those they studied not only survived in contemporary times, but continued to have a functional role in their own social life and that of their contemporaries. In other words, folkliv was a part of modern everyday Swedish culture.

Folklife Studies thus began with the realization that there are traditional materials that have a functional place in the researchers' own contemporary culture. The emphasis shifted from comparative patterns of a particular genre across cultures to the place of the genre in the overall pattern of a particular culture, and from what the item revealed about the lost past to what it revealed about the lively present. This more holistic approach also heralded a change in focus from items to the people in whose lives those items functioned. Thus, folklife shifted study from the history of items to the ethnology or ethnography of item-producers. Consequently, Folklife Studies became more anthropological than literary or historical, more concrete than abstract, and more concerned with process than with product. The communities studied were no longer just the rural, agricultural, and unlettered—so-called "folk cultures." Gradually the urban and even the middle class came into the folklife specialist's purview. The folklife specialist could study culture from the insider's perspective, while the folklorist was usually an outsider studying material that was culturally or at least socially foreign. Folklife studies also have tended to focus on the executors of arts, crafts, and subsistence skills, rather than on oral traditions or music.

The folklife approach, with its emphasis on process and producer, facilitated the emergence of the field dubbed "public folklore," perhaps more properly called "public folklife." Public folklife specialists work with state and national governments and private foundations to promote folklife. Since many traditional artists are women and/or come from families, communities, and ethnic groups that are financially pressed and/or politically marginalized, public folklife has exhibited a strong social and political thrust. The shift in emphasis from folklore to folklife has also proved a boon to feminist scholars who seek to foreground the skill and genius of traditional women and their contributions to folk culture and to culture as a whole.

An early description of American folklife appeared in *Scribner's* in 1930. There, Ruth Suckow created a remarkably detailed and perceptive evocation of the common folklife of older English-speaking White communities across much of the United States. She wrote about the language, manners, architecture, festivity, crafts, livelihoods, games, dances, songs, values, foodways, aesthetics, and communal gatherings of what she termed "just common ordinary Americans." Suckow even used the term "folklife" to refer to the whole, rich, varied cultural expression she observed.

However, Suckow's essay makes no reference to Scandinavian folklife studies. Credit for introducing the Scandinavian approach to the United States usually goes to Alfred Shoemaker of the University of Pennsylvania. He had learned about folkliv when he first visited Folk Studies centers in Sweden and elsewhere in the 1930s. He realized that an approach to studying folk culture that emphasized folk arts, crafts, and subsistence skills was ideal for someone like him who was interested in studying and promoting his own Pennsylvania Dutch cultural milieu.

Folklife Studies outside of Pennsylvania did not make much headway in North America until the 1960s, when restless young scholars both there and abroad saw in folklife a less elitist and more relevant approach to Folk Studies. At the same time that students were taking folklife as their starting point in approaching folk materials, however, three movements in the field began to converge; and each has its proponents today. One was the "text and context" movement, which sought to establish and study the context or *sitz in leben* of the folklore item—its real-life situation and the persons in the real-life situation who produced it. A parallel movement involving the performance-oriented study of expressive culture emphasized the action that produced the item and the person who produced it. A third movement considered the repertoire of a folk performer as a whole, asking what that repertoire revealed about the art, the artist, and the process of transmission—often cross-generational. Representing a convergence of influences from European Folk Studies and from within American folkloristics, the folklife approach had become dominant in American Folk Studies by the turn of the twenty-first century.

Folklife is often described as "expressive culture." This aspect of folklife inspires celebratory rhetoric. Mary Hufford, for instance, writes:

> Folklife is community life and values, artfully expressed in myriad forms and interactions. Universal, diverse, and enduring, it enriches the nation and makes us a commonwealth of cultures.... Today the study of folklife encompasses all of the traditional expressions that shape and are shaped by various communities.... The traditional knowledge and skills required to make a pie crust, plant a garden, arrange a birthday party, or turn a lathe are exchanged in the course of daily living and learned by imitation. It is not simply skills that are transferred in such interactions, but notions about the proper ways to be human at a particular time and place. Whether sung or told, enacted or crafted, traditions are the outcroppings of deep lodes of worldview, knowledge, and wisdom, navigational aids in an ever-fluctuating social world.... [c]onferring on community members a vital sense of identity, belonging and purpose (2002: 238–241).

Furthermore, as Hufford also points out, the people of a community, by living their folklife in a particular place, make that very place expressive—for example, in the way they celebrate its streams in their dances, or plant trees reminiscent of the old homeland, or in the way, through religious ritual, "the passion of Christ is annually mapped onto urban landscapes in the Good Friday processions" (2002: 241).

In a formulation useful for the study of gender in small, relatively stable, traditional societies, Ivan Illich (1982) describes gender as a system of "dissymmetric complementarity" that extends to every aspect of traditional life: subsistence, art, and ritual. For example, some food activities are women's and some are men's; some of the work of turning material (animal skin, flax, cotton, or wool) into clothing is women's work, and some men's; and some tools are reserved for women, and some for men—or women handle a tool one way and men another. Women walk differently, use their hands differently, and speak and sing differently from men. Family resources may be divided, for instance, with the children belonging to women and the animals to men. Traditional space, too, is gendered: women avoid men's spaces and vice-versa, though a plaza that belongs to the women in the morning might belong to the men in the late afternoon. This complementarity is dissymmetric because some elements on one side of the divide may have no corresponding elements on the other. If women do the buying and selling in the market, for example, one cannot necessarily point to an aspect of men's lives that corresponds to that activity.

In this view, the domains of women and men in such systems may be absolutely separate, but each is equally essential to the functioning of the society. Nevertheless, there are no universals. Women generally care for young children and prepare the daily family food, and men, generally speaking, hunt and make war; but almost any activity might be the domain of either sex. There are cultures in which women are expected to engage in what Euro North Americans think of as masculine activities, such as handling all trade and financial transactions, serving as high chief, or officiating at public religious functions. Conversely, activities Euro North Americans might think of as feminine fall into men's domains in some cultures. Though weaving, for instance, is women's work among the Navajo, among the neighboring Hopi, it is men who weave for their people, including weaving the traditional blanket dresses of Hopi women.

Strongly gendered societies and cultures are not necessarily unfair to women and girls. While they may limit potential realms of female activity, they restrain male activity just as rigidly. Moreover, patriarchal societies in particular can create oppressive positions for both women and men, however disproportionately. Nevertheless, in matrilineal societies especially, social privilege may be equitably distributed. And in some patrilineal societies as well, such as the Newfoundland outport society described by Hilda Chaulk Murray (1979), an equitable and satisfactory apportionment of labor, resources, and happiness may be attainable for all its members.

In the differentiating and industrializing cultures of the West, as Illich notes, the underlying gender system has been eroding for a thousand years. Nevertheless, folklife—and popular culture, too—still tend toward gendering most, if not all, aspects of cultural life.

In the gendered cultures that we have inherited, there are traditional elements that constitute a distinct "women's world." First among them is the home, especially the kitchen. Therefore, women's folklife includes foodways, recipes, and the preparation of staple foods for later consumption, including churning, cheese making, sauerkraut making, and grinding corn and coffee. Women also observe traditional ways of apportioning space in the home, arranging the kitchen and other rooms, and raising vegetables and flowers.

In recent years in mainstream North American culture, gardening has become regendered, with men usually raising the vegetables and women the flowers. This change may be a direct result of the "victory gardens" of World War II. At that time, families who had not practiced vegetable gardening were encouraged by the federal government to take up the growing of food. The tending of those new "war gardens" usually fell to the father or grandfather who was still at home. After the war, vegetable gardening remained a men's hobby.

Traditional women's crafts are those connected with providing clothing, sundries, and comforts for the family and the home. These include spinning, weaving, and sewing, often using traditional patterns; needlework and embroidery, including samplers; knitting and crocheting; lacemaking, beadwork, quilting, rugmaking, and pottery and basketmaking. They include creating utilitarian items for everyday use as well as fancier items for the parlor, for Sunday or holiday best, or for a daughter's trousseau. The aesthetic observable in these crafts reflects the folklife of the whole culture out of which such crafts emerge. Sometimes, too, a particular craft such as quiltmaking becomes the focus of the aesthetic energies of an individual woman or her community.

An annual cycle takes place within traditional homes and communities involving women both as women and as members of their families. Home customs for holidays such as Christmas, Valentine's Day, Easter, winter nights, and summer days are part of women's folklife. Seasons and festivals sometimes require special decorations or the establishing of home altars, which are traditionally the responsibility of the women of the house. Within the home and family, women also carry out customs for all the stages of life (rites of passage), including birth, breastfeeding, childrearing, menarche, adolescence, courtship, marriage, menopause, aging, and death. Historically, North American women have cared for the ill and the aged and laid out the dead. They are often a source of traditional medical beliefs and practices, some purely magical, some consistent with scientific-medical practice. Women's storytelling, particularly informal storytelling in all-woman groups, includes many anecdotes about home, family, and events associated with the stages of life.

Women have had customary niches in community life as well. In church, school, and community, they organize festivals, cook spaghetti dinners, and hold bake sales and rummage sales. In the late nineteenth and twentieth centuries, at White community dances in Appalachia, the American heartland, and as far east as the Canadian Maritimes, the fiddlers and guitar players were likely to be men, while women might have provided backup and rhythm on piano.

In other communities and ethnic groups, women's music-making might be confined to the home, draw upon a different repertoire, or exhibit a style different from men's music-making. In traditional Greek communities, for instance, all church music was provided by men. Similarly, in bars and at dances, the band was composed of men, though there might be a woman singer or belly dancer. In the home, women sang lullabies, songs for children, and other traditional songs, both solo and a cappella. In other communities, women had opportunities for public performance more or less equal to those of men and shared in a single community repertoire and style. In traditional Black churches, for instance, both women and men have had many opportunities as musicians.

In North American cultures, women have held certain traditional occupations, including midwife, nurse, schoolteacher, secretary, pieceworker, waitress, nursemaid or nanny, farm wife, prostitute, and preacher. Each occupation embodies a wealth of traditional beliefs and practices. In much of North America, as in much of the world, the traditional occupations of divination, fortune-telling, curing, and performing of or instructing in rituals to enhance luck—good and bad—are also linked with women.

Practices connected with the female body are another important element of women's folklife. In addition to fashion and costume, these may take the form of body adornment with henna art, scars, brands, or tattoos, or hairstyles such as cornrows, braids, or the coils of uncut hair typical of members of certain Protestant evangelical denominations. Women's folklife also includes beliefs about the female body, its functions and sexuality, attitudes regarding the female body, and complementary or opposing beliefs and attitudes regarding the male body.

It is important to remember that the character of women's folklife, whether in the home or community, depends upon the ethnicity, class, and regional group or groups to which women belong. Women's folklife on a Navajo reservation differs from that of a West Virginia mining camp, as does the folklife of a university professor from that of the laborer who cleans her house.

Of course, in contemporary North American culture, there are many individuals and families who ignore or violate inherited gender codes, whether by choice or by necessity. For example, automobiles are traditionally associated with men and the male domain (though often affectionately given women's names), but a single mother who must rely on an old car to get her back and forth to work must of necessity learn to keep the vehicle running. A woman who grew up working in her father's Midwestern small-town garage, but who marries a man from New York City whose family never owned a car, may find that both expertise and inclination make her the family auto mechanic.

Contemporary women likewise continue to create new traditions or adapt older traditions in folk or folk-like ways. These include the *quinceañera,* menarche parties, lesbian commitment ceremonies, processional performances, croning, women's friendship groups, and bachelorette parties and divorce parties. Especially interesting is the way that folklife traditions have been adopted for humanitarian and political purposes. A paradigmatic instance of this impulse was the 20,000-woman march on Washington, DC, on August 4, 1985, recalling the fortieth anniversary of the U.S. attack on the cities of Hiroshima and Nagasaki, in protest against the proliferation of nuclear armaments. A major feature of the march was a fifteen-mile-long ribbon exhibiting women's needlework in its many forms, which was wrapped around the Pentagon and other federal buildings.

This event combined two forms of folklife that have often been drawn upon for humanitarian and political purposes. Mass marching has a long tradition in American life, surfacing whenever the voiceless have demanded to be heard. The most famous occasions of regular mass marches in twentieth-century U.S. history are the miners' (and the miners' wives') marches in the southern Appalachian coal fields in the 1920s and 1930s and the Black civil rights marches of the 1960s. In recent years, women have used mass marches to serve political ends, such as the Million Mom March on Washington, DC, in May 2000 (to demand gun control), and to serve humanitarian ends, such as the annual nationwide walks known as Making Strides Against Breast Cancer (to raise money for cancer research) and Take Back the Night (to promote awareness of rape).

Needlework—especially quilting—for ceremonial purposes also has a long tradition. Women have made quilts to mark occasions in their lives or more commonly in family life. A quilt might be made for a wedding, for a birth, to celebrate a life, or even for the acquisition of the first family dog. Lakota and Sioux women create star quilts for use in ceremonial events such as welcoming a new child, performing a healing, honoring an individual, or burying the dead. And on the Fort Peck Reservation in Montana, basketball-star quilts honor the coaches and families of basketball players. But the creation of quilts as political or humanitarian statements is relatively new. Many of the units that made up the 1985 fifteen-mile ribbon were quilts. In 2000, the International Year for the Culture of Peace, an American group created a quilt known as the Cloth of Many Colors. This nearly mile-long quilt was presented at the United Nations and also wrapped around the Pentagon. The AIDS Quilt, with blocks sewn in memory of those who have died from the disease, continues to grow, and portions of it tour the United States; it is displayed on football fields or in gyms of large university field houses.

After the attacks of September 11, 2001, American women, schoolchildren, and people from around the world spontaneously created quilts that they sent to the Pentagon. Initially, these quilts were hung in the Pentagon, but the number grew so great that a foundation was created to curate them. The World Trade Center Memorial Quilt Project was organized to create quilts with contributed blocks to be sewn into five quilts honoring the deceased at the World Trade Center, the Pentagon, Bedford County, Pennsylvania (where one of the hijacked planes crashed), and New York City's fire and police departments, respectively. Blocks came in from forty-seven states and fourteen countries. The finished quilts, though of different sizes, averaged almost ninety square feet apiece in size.

Not only are North American women living their folklife—they are drawing upon it in ways that are simultaneously deeply traditional and brilliantly innovative. *See also:* Aesthetics; Ballad; Body Modification and Adornment; Class; Folk Art; Folk Custom; Folk Music and Folksong; Folktale; Foodways; Gardens; Gender; Processional Performance; Public Folklore; Quiltmaking; *Quinceañera*; Rites of Passage; Sexuality; Storytelling; Women's Work.

References: Bronner, Simon J. "Alfred Shoemaker and the Discovery of American Folklife." In *Following Tradition: Folklore in the Discourse of American Culture,* 266–312. Logan: Utah State University Press, 1998; ———. *Folk Nation: Folklore in the Creation of American Tradition.* Wilmington, DE: Scholarly Resources, Inc, 2002; Cantwell,

Robert. *Ethnomimesis: Folklife and the Representation of Culture.* Chapel Hill: University of North Carolina Press, 1993; Hufford, Mary. *American Folklife: A Commonwealth of Cultures.* Washington: American Folklife Center, Library of Congress. Reprinted in Bronner 2002: 237–247; Illich, Ivan. *Gender.* New York: Pantheon, 2002 [1982]; MacDowell, Marsha L., and C. Kurt Dewhurst. *To Honor and Comfort: Native Quilting Traditions.* Santa Fe: Museum of New Mexico Press, 1997; Murray, Hilda Chaulk. *More than Fifty Percent: Woman's Life in a Newfoundland Outport, 1900–1950.* St John's, NF: Breakwater Books, 1979; Suckow, Ruth. "The Folk Idea in American Life." *Scribner's Magazine* 88 (September 1930): 245–255. Reprinted in Bronner 2002: 145–160.

William Bernard McCarthy

Folklore Feminists Communication

Folklore Feminists Communication (FFC) is a Web-based American publication begun as a printed newsletter in 1973 to facilitate the exchange of ideas and information relevant to the study of women's folklore.

With the rise of feminism in the 1960s and 1970s (and feminist scholarship by the early 1970s), women trained as professional folklorists in the United States organized the Women's Section of the American Folklore Society to discuss areas of special concern to women in the academic field of Folklore. They adopted as the section's official newsletter *Folklore Feminists Communication*, which had already begun circulating ideas relating to women as folklorists and to women's folklore as an exciting new field of study.

The Women's Section's concerns were several. First, women wanted a venue to meet and converse with other women folklorists about feminist scholarship and the problems associated with participating in the male-dominated field of Folklore in particular and academia in general. Second, they began to assess the implications of feminist theory and scholarship in the work that male and female folklorists had been doing, or had been failing to do, as a result of patriarchal bias in the field. From these concerns would spring much of the recent American scholarship focused on women as academic, public, and community folklorists, and as cultural actors in general, as well as scholarship focused on those areas of folklore and folklife traditionally associated with women (embroidery, quilting, pregnancy and childbirth, and elder care, among others) as legitimate areas of inquiry and study in the field of Folklore.

Folklore Feminists Communication has, over the years, been a place for short articles about folklore and feminism; communication about the concerns and achievements of members of the American Folklore Society Women's Section; meeting information and minutes from annual meetings; commemoration of group rituals (such as the triannual "croning" of section members who have passed their fiftieth birthdays); and other matters of concern to section members.

Folklore Feminists Communication currently operates as a Web-based information site and can be accessed through the American Folklore Society (http://www.afsnet.org). Paper copies of past issues are held by a many university libraries in the United States, and permanent archives exist at the

Utah State University Fife Folklore Archives. *See also:* American Folklore Society Women's Section; Croning; Feminisms; Women's Folklore.

References: "Women's Section of the American Folklore Society." http://www.artlore.net/ffc.html (accessed August 9, 2008).

Theresa A. Vaughan

Folklore Studies Association of Canada

The Folklore Studies Association of Canada/Association canadienne d'ethnologie et de folklore (FSAC/ACEF), founded 1976, encourages research and education in Folklore/Ethnology in Canadian universities, museums, and archives. Its multidisciplinary, international membership comprises academics, researchers, curators, archivists, and students as well as libraries, museums, archives, and universities. FSAC/ACEF operates bilingually in Canada's official languages. Its use of both the English word "folklore" and its French counterpart "ethnology" recognizes the double heritage of Folklore/Ethnology Studies in Canada.

FSAC/ACEF acts to develop excellence, increase competence, and support study, education, and research, as well as to promote, publish, and disseminate it. FSAC/ACEF belongs to the Humanities and Social Science Federation of Canada, and normally holds annual meetings with its Congress of Social Sciences and Humanities, where members present formal papers, hold workshops and roundtables for professional development, and discuss current issues. Several have been held jointly with the Canadian Women's Studies Association, offering additional opportunities for feminist collaboration.

FSAC/ACEF publishes an annual bulletin containing meeting abstracts and schedules, minutes, and executive reports, and (with funding from the Social Sciences and Humanities Research Council of Canada and Fonds québécois de la recherche sur la société et la culture) the refereed biannual journal *Ethnologies* (formerly *Canadian Folklore canadien [CFC]*). Many of its academic papers, book, film, record reviews, and research notes are feminist and women-centered, but related thematic issues include Women and Tradition/Femmes et traditions (15#2, 1993), Masculinities/Masculinités (19#1, 1997), and Wicca (20#1&2, 1998). FSAC/ACEF's Web site provides an executive list, calls for papers for FSAC/ACEF events and publications, consultations, announcements of prizes, and links to relevant sites.

From FSAC/ACEF's beginnings, women have been active and visible. One-third of its presidents—Catherine Jolicoeur, Nancy Schmitz. Edith Fowke, Carole Carpenter, Kay Stone, Jocelyne Mathieu, Vivian Labrie, Diane Tye, and Barbara LeBlanc—and two of the five editors of *CFC/Ethnologies*—Carole Carpenter and Nancy Schmitz—have been women. In 1990, FSAC/ACEF established the Luc Lacourcière Memorial Scholarship Fund, awarded to the top student in Folklore/Ethnology Studies at the end of his or her first year of graduate studies at a Canadian university. The majority of winners have been female. From 1978 to 1984, FSAC/ACEF gave the Distinguished Canadian Folklorist award, the first going to Edith Fowke, and three other women also received it (Helen Creighton in 1981, Carmen Roy in 1982, and Simonne Voyer in 1983). In 1985, reflecting its interest in supporting and encouraging all kinds of work in folklore/ethnology (not only academic), FSAC/ACEF began awarding the Marius Barbeau Medal. Again, the first recipient was a woman, the Acadian composer and singer Edith Butler. In 1987, it went to LaRena Clark, a remarkable source singer (that is, directly connected with the tradition and not a revival performer) from Ontario with a repertoire of more than 500 songs; in 1995 to Dorothy Burnham, a museum textile specialist and author; in 1999 to dance ethnologist Simonne Voyer; and in 2002 to Nancy Schmitz, retiring professor of Anthropology at Université Laval, Québec and outgoing editor of the *Bulletin* and *Ethnologies*. *See also:* Region: Canada; Women Folklorists.

References: Canadian Folklore canadien 1 (1979)–19 (1997); *Ethnologies* 20 (1998–); Folklore Studies Association of Canada/ Association canadienne d'ethnologie et de folklore. http://www.celat.ulaval.ca/acef (accessed August 10, 2008)

Pauline Greenhill

Folktale

Translating the German *Volksmärchen* (the people's "little story" or "news"), the term "folktale" refers to one of the main prose narrative genres that folklorists study. In contrast to belief narratives like myth and legend, the folktale features fictional characters in culturally meaningful situations, centers on the ordinary, and is primarily for entertainment. Classified into tale types by the Finn Antti Aarne and the American Stith Thompson in the early twentieth century, the folktale groups a number of subgenres, including the animal tale, religious tale, joke, and formula tale. But the most prominent is the "tale of magic"—the *Zaubermärchen* in German or *conte merveilleux* in French—also known in English as the "wonder tale" and more commonly as the "fairy tale." Women—as characters, tellers, writers, listeners, and readers—have historically engaged with and been powerfully associated with this particular kind of folktale, found in both oral and literary traditions.

While for the most part folktales were collected for print in the nineteenth century and later, they also were part of much older and classic literary texts ranging from the *Panchatantra* and the *Arabian Nights* to Apuleius's *The Golden Ass* and the Italian *Pentamerone*. Nowadays, a few old-world folktales featuring female protagonists such as Snow White, Cinderella, Little Red Riding Hood, Sleeping Beauty, and Rapunzel are particularly popular in North America thanks to books and films for children. But the range of female folktale characters is much broader and includes more resourceful and wise, though less-known, female heroes from the oral traditions of Europe, Appalachia, Native America, and Africa.

While "fairy tale," from the French *conte de fées*, is a misnomer in that fairies are scarce in these stories, magic does play a distinctive part in them. "Once upon a time" signals that a story—some will call it a folktale, others a fairy tale—is coming our way and we should suspend disbelief because, whether told or printed, this story will not conform to realism. But the

German and French terms, Volksmärchen and conte de fées, also point to different genealogies: the folktale is firmly rooted in orality and a group's traditions and aesthetics, while the fairy tale is identified with printed texts that may or may not emerge from an oral tradition and are often signed by an author. This is undoubtedly a significant distinction. Clearly, when a literary fairy tale has no counterpart in oral tradition, it is not a folktale. However, the oral traditions of storytelling and the literary traditions of authored texts have been intertwined throughout history, which has made it problematic to draw a sharp distinction between "authentic" folktales and "inauthentic" literary tales. For example, "Cinderella" is a widely told folktale—classified as ATU 510 by folklorists—with hundreds of versions recorded all over the world, but it has also been part of literature since Giambattista Basile's sixteenth-century *Pentamerone*. Most modern performances and adaptations of it are based on the French literary version by Charles Perrault. In common usage, the boundaries between folktales and fairy tales are often blurred. And increasingly in scholarship, that blurring is accepted and results in a fruitful probing of the dynamic relationship between folklore and literature.

While the expressions "old wives' tales" and "Mother Goose" point to women as the traditional tellers of folktales, it is through collections edited by men like Charles Perrault in France, Jacob and Wilhelm Grimm in Germany, Andrew Lang in England, and through Walt Disney's movies that these tales are now best known. Feminist writers and scholars have worked to expand and transform this limited canon wherein "persecuted heroines" abound by producing more woman-centered anthologies, recognizing the varied and coded art of women storytellers, rediscovering neglected women writers of fairy tales, reevaluating and revising well-known tales, and performing and writing new ones. Continuing to serve both normalizing and emancipatory social functions and articulating diverse aesthetics, the folktale keeps on performing magic—especially for women—into the twenty-first century in different media. Thus, following a few observations about the overall genre and about tales of magic in North America, this entry focuses on the tales of magic or fairy tales in *both* oral and literary traditions; and on the tales' relation to women and to feminist scholarship primarily in a European and American context.

Usually set in distant times and generic places, tales of magic most commonly tell the story of a rather unpromising male or female hero who, often aided by a magic helper, overcomes extraordinary challenges and is rewarded, at times with royal marriage. Think Jack or Cinderella. Within these tales' worlds, a mix of the supernatural and the ordinary is accepted as natural, and the hero's magically achieved success coincides with the restoration of a naturalized order. Leaving home is often required for the test to begin; at other times something is missing and must be found. "Departure" and "lack" are two of the narrative "functions" that the formalist Vladimir Propp identified as constitutive of folktale plots. The journey is transformative, like rites of passage. Protagonists are often children or young men and women who assume a "new" social role and sense of being once they have proven themselves.

Symbolism and transformation are key elements that allow for imagining change *and* for recognizing hidden resources. This paradox works on multiple levels of meaning, from the psychological to the social, so that—in different historical or cultural contexts and in specific performances or retellings—a tale may tip toward either subverting or reproducing stock social arrangements; however, wonder and convention are both consistently at play. Recognizing the dynamics of variation and tradition has been a challenge that folktale scholars have addressed in a range of ways. But there is a long-standing consensus among folklorists that a credible analysis will be based never on just one, but on a number of versions of a tale or plot. More recently, attention to performance—its emergent quality or situated dynamics—has productively supplemented text-based studies and emphasized the artistry and contextualized elements that pertain to individual tellings.

Folklorists have relied on two important reference tools for the basic study of folktales and more specifically of "tales of magic." The Aarne-Thompson (AT) *Types of the Folktale: A Classification and Bibliography* (1910; 1928 and 1961) catalogued Indo-European folktales based on plot, identified tales of magic as tale types AT 300–749. It was revised in 2004 into the more comprehensive *Types of International Folktales: A Classification and Bibliography*, edited by Hans-Jörg Uther (ATU). Stith Thompson's six-volume *Motif-Index of Folk-Literature* (1932–1936; second edition 1955–1958), identified small but significant narrative units recurring in folklore and across tale types. While specific categories and headings for tale types and motifs have been criticized by women scholars as embodying a male view of the world, useful regional and national indexes for tale types and motifs have since appeared.

Starting in the nineteenth century, the collection, study, and classification of folktales dominated European folkloristics for a long time. Scholars have persuasively shown how this interest in folktales—of which the collection *Kinder- und Hausmärchen* (*Children's and Household Tales*, 1812, 1815) by Wilhelm and Jacob Grimm is a foremost example—was tied to the rise of nationalism, the establishment of bourgeois values, the increasing domestication of women, and the production of childhood. Whether studying multiple versions of a tale type or a range of folk and literary tales in a specific context, scholars of folktales in the 1970s became increasingly attentive to their variable social and ideological functions.

Feminist scholarship has played a crucial role in this development. Such studies often incorporate elements from other well-established approaches to folktales in Psychology, Sociology, Linguistics, Literary Studies, Myth Studies, and Children's Literature programs. Recent significant texts that attest to the general vitality of folk- and fairy-tale studies are the *Enzyklopädie des Märchens* (see entries like "Frau," "Frauenmärchen," "Die geschwätzige Frau," "Erzählen, Erzähler," "Mädchen," "Mädchen ohne Hände," or "Mutter"); the *Oxford Companion to Fairy Tales: The Western Fairy Tale Tradition from Medieval to Modern* (2000); the *Arabian Nights Encyclopedia* (2004), edited by Ulrich Marzolph and Richard van Leeuwen; and *Marvels & Tales: Journal of Fairy-Tale Studies*, edited by Donald Haase and Anne Duggan.

Most people in the United States today, however, accept folktales and fairy tales without giving them much thought. They identify the tale of magic with Walt Disney movies and illustrated children's books featuring canonical texts associated with the Grimm brothers, Charles Perrault, or Hans Christian Andersen. These stories are thus loosely understood to be for children—which then translates into the tales being escapist or trivial fantasies—and to be inescapably tied to the Old World. Vivid metaphoric images from folktales, such as the red cap, magic mirror, and gingerbread house, and stock expressions like "golden goose," "prince charming," and "fairy-tale wedding" permeate contemporary American culture and have become part of everyday language, but they do not in most cases originate with American folk traditions.

Tales of magic did, nevertheless, have a place in the American oral tradition, and thanks to oral recordings in Appalachia dating back to the 1930s, as well as to the comparative work of scholars, we can identify these stories' distinctive features. In American magic tales, as Carl Lindahl explains in *American Folktales from the Collections of the Library of Congress*, opening formulas include the abbreviated "One time"; characters often inhabit mountain cabins and farms rather than castles; the hero receives less magic help than her/his European counterpart; the giant is the most common opponent, while the dragon is extremely rare; and marriage is not as commonly a part of the happy ending.

Furthermore, as Kay Stone asserted in "Things Walt Disney Never Told Us" (1975), just as the apparently simple but quick-witted Jack acquired specific traits as a story hero in the new world, female heroes in the American folktale tradition were and are more resourceful and active than in those popularized by Disney and Perrault. Regrettably, they are scarcely known to the general public; Tom Davenport's film *Ashpet: An American Cinderella* (1990), for example, tells a story based on Appalachian versions that are unfamiliar to most contemporary American viewers.

As powerfully symbolic stories, magic tales have not had the same impact on men as on women. While gender and class socialization is an important ideological ingredient of the genre, scholars agree that, as adults, it is primarily women who continue to engage with fairy tales. This may be related to the romance themes that are associated in contemporary culture with fairy-tale plots, but more generally tales of magic script a range of relationships—between mother and daughter, siblings, father and daughter, older women and coming-of-age girls—that do not involve heterosexual courtship and romance exclusively and are more broadly familial and social.

Inspired by feminism, North American women's discussions in the 1970s focused on fairy-tale protagonists as positive *or* negative role models for modern girls and women: did identifying with fairy-tale heroines encourage women to be passive and dependent (Marcia Lieberman) or to be active and resourceful (Alison Lurie)? But it was soon clear that such polarization could not do justice to the variety of folktale heroines and folktales. For every self-effacing and docile Beauty and Cinderella, there was a brave Kate Krackernuts who frees her stepsister and a sleeping prince from their respective spells, or a "wise girl" who could solve riddles and unmask injustice. Disobedience and wit as well as submission and silence can be positive attributes for folktale heroines. Woman-centered anthologies such as *Tatterhood and Other Tales*, edited by Ethel Johnston Phelps (1978), Angela Carter's *The Virago Book of Fairy Tales* (London, 1990; reprinted as *The Old Wives' Fairy Tale Book* in the United States, 1990), and Kathleen Ragan's *Fearless Girls, Wise Women & Beloved Sisters: Heroines in Folktales from Around the World* (1998) provide a range of possibilities for self-reflection that demonstrates how folktales and tales of magic are, to quote Kay Stone in her article, "Misuses of Enchantment," both "problem-creating" and "problem-solving" narratives for women (1985: 133).

Furthermore, some oral versions of "Little Red Riding Hood" portrayed a clever girl who escaped the wolf by using her wits; others depicted her as defenseless, a devoured victim, or one in need of rescue. In *The Trials and Tribulations of Little Red Riding Hood: Versions of the Tale in Sociocultural Context* (1983), Jack Zipes showed how interpreting a tale and its representation of gender, sexuality, and violence gained tremendously from considering its many versions, each in relation to social and ideological milieus. Ruth B. Bottigheimer's and Maria Tatar's studies of the production of gender and childhood in the Grimms' tales also proved how the Brothers' editing, and not the women tellers, worked to silence female protagonists. And Kay Stone's reception-based research revealed that, regardless of the versions they have been exposed to, women often refashion the most passive heroines' plots to reinterpret them in a more positive light.

When analyzing the folktale in North America, ethnic and cultural diversity also make a difference. Tales from the British and Irish traditions were popular in Appalachia, but circulating in oral and printed form we find African American folktales—animal tales especially—in the South, and also Native American, Mexican American, French Creole, and Italian American tales. However, with Native traditions, the Western classification of narratives as "folktales" in contrast to "legends" or "myths" is especially problematic. For the African American tradition, the work of women folklorists and retellers—for example, Zora Neale Hurston's *Mules and Men* (1935) and Virginia Hamilton's *Her Stories: African American Folktales, Fairy Tales, and True Tales* (1995)—has been significant in making these stories known where the damsel in distress is not typical, and humor plays an important role in heterosexual relations.

Scholars of folk and fairy tales have also given much consideration to the role of gender in both the tellers and the audience of folktales. The narrator Sheherazade from the *Arabian Nights*, the famous Arabic-language collection that in its first 1704 European translation became an influential Orientalist example of exotic fantasy, has as the female trickster *par excellence* more recently been the focus of much feminist analysis of gendered telling. When nineteenth-century male scholars collected oral tales from women, these tellers were primarily seen as bearers of a tradition, not of knowledge. Their "uneducated" words were then edited and interpreted within an aesthetics and narrative of history that demanded the "disenchantment of the world" for the sake of modernity. The confinement of "old wives' tales" to the premodern meant that they held a privileged spot as records of the past, but were nevertheless trivialized and othered.

In contrast, folktales collected in the 1870s by Laura Gonzenbach in Sicily from mostly female storytellers exemplify how narrative repertoire, performance, themes, and meaning are affected when women are telling stories to other women. Spoken in Sicilian dialect, printed in high German, Gonzenbach's collection was subsequently translated into standard Italian and thoroughly researched by folklorist Luisa Rubini, and only recently made available in English as *La Bella Angiola* and *The Robber With a Witch's Head* by Jack Zipes. These tales exemplify at once the potential for women's cross-cultural communication with one another and their difficult negotiation of class and national differences.

The appropriation of women tellers' authority by male authors has a long history in the Western narrative tradition going back, in Karen Rowe's and Martha Weigle's accounts, most emblematically to Ovid's taking over as master "talespinner." In his poetic retelling of the weaving and storytelling contest between the divine Minerva/Athena and the human Arachne, the woman in etiological fashion is then transformed into the first spider by the goddess she dared to challenge. In her fascinating and sweeping study of narrative and visual culture, *From the Beast to the Blonde: On Fairy Tales and Their Tellers*, Marina Warner points to the often derided Mother Goose as having Sybil as well as Saint Anne and the Queen of Sheba as forgotten authoritative antecedents. Establishing this genealogy then allows Warner to read both gossip and silence in connection to fairy tales as "stratagem[s] of influence" and self-assertion (1994: xxv).

While women's voices have been muffled—by being labeled as dangerous, or literally silenced, or dismissed as trivial—folk and fairy tales as told by women nevertheless can deliver what Joan N. Radner notably called "coded" messages to a listener, reader, or scholar whose epistemological framework is woman-centered. In widely different cultural contexts, Margaret Mills' *Rhetorics and Politics in Afghan Traditional Storytelling* (1991), Isabel Cardigos' *In and Out of Enchantment: Blood Symbolism in Portuguese Fairy Tales* (1996), and Lee Haring's "Creolization as Agency in Woman-Centered Folktales" from the Indian Ocean (*Fairy Tales and Feminism* 2004) exemplify methodologies for collecting tales whose performance relies on complex gendered mediation and produces different meanings for women and men. Significantly, these studies and others emphasize the centrality of women's bodies and embodied experiences to the tales' production of meaning in performance.

Two contemporary storytellers in North America have written eloquently about such dynamics in their own lives and performances. Susan Gordon, a professional storyteller from Maryland, works mostly in therapeutic settings ("The Powers of the Handless Maiden" in *Feminist Messages*). Kay Stone, a folklorist and storyteller in Winnipeg, Manitoba, wrote *Burning Brightly: New Light on Old Tales Told Today* (1998), which considers the revival of storytelling in a range of American and Canadian communities, and traces her own interpretive journey over the years with the performance of a specific tale, "The Curious Girl."

Contemporary women writers in North America have also taken inspiration from folk and fairy tales in a range of ways. Among the best known is

Jane Yolen with, for instance, *The Girl Who Cried Flowers and Other Tales* (1974). Author of the insightful study *Touch Magic* (1986), Yolen has written fiction for adolescents and children that is rooted in the folktale tradition (including the Holocaust-related novel *Briar Rose* in 1993) and seeks to revise its gender bias (see the humorous *Sleeping Ugly* in 1981). Like Yolen, Terri Windling has authored fairy tales, written about women and fairy tales, and edited collections of traditional and retold tales. Among the many volumes Windling coedited with Ellen Datlow are *Snow White, Blood Red* in 1993 and *A Wolf at the Door and Other Retold Fairy Tales* in 2001. The connection of folktales and fairy tales with fantasy as well as the specific focus on adolescents as readers are imaginatively at work in the writing of Susan Fletcher (whose 1998 *Shadow Spinner* imagines the intervention of a crippled young girl in the storytelling that frames *The Arabian Nights*), Los Angeles-based Francesca Lia Block (*The Rose and the Beast: Fairy Tales Retold* [2000]), and Caribbean Canadian Nalo Hopkinson (whose *Skin Folk* [2001] collects exuberant creole retellings of "Red Riding Hood" and "The Kind and the Unkind Girl").

These collections are but the tip of the iceberg for twentieth-century North American fairy-tale fiction and poetry that put women at center stage. Others have included not only *The Wonderful Wizard of Oz* by Frank Baum (1900), which in folktale fashion features young Dorothy's quest and the quintessentially good fairy and evil witch, but also Anne Sexton's acerbic anti-Grimm poems in *Transformations* (1971), Robert Coover's provocative retelling of "Snow White" in "The Dead Queen" (1973) and haunting novel *Briar Rose* (1996), Margaret Atwood's many "Bluebeard" fictions, including *Bluebeard's Egg* (1983) and *The Robber Bride* (1993), and Chitra Banerjee Divakaruni's *Mistress of Spices* (1997)—a magic-filled novel that is also a strong indictment of violence against women.

In England, Angela Carter's extraordinary collection *The Bloody Chamber and Other Stories* (1979) provides multiple permutations of the "Beauty and the Beast" theme in well-known fairy tales focused on heterosexual relations, courtship, marriage, and the experience of menarche. Irish scholar and fiction writer Emma Donoghue bends the heterosexual fairy-tale plots to tell about women's solidarity, desire, and love for one another in *Kissing the Witch: Old Tales in New Skins* (1997), a collection of short stories centered on the multiple valences of orality. *Disenchantments: An Anthology of Modern Fairy Tale Poetry* (edited by Wolfgang Mieder in 1985) and *The Poets' Grimm: 20th Century Poems from Grimm Fairy Tales* (edited by Jeanne Marie Beaumont and Claudia Carlson in 2003) offer a wide sampling of English-language fairy tale and anti-fairy tale poetry, much of which plays on tales with women protagonists and on the theme of women's acculturation.

If marriage, procreation, and transformation have been at the heart of the tale of magic since Apuleius's "Cupid and Psyche" and the *Arabian Nights*, these themes have also been central to women's literary tradition of fairy-tale writing at least since the emergence of the French *conte de fées* in the late seventeenth century, best exemplified by the elegant and fanciful tales of Marie-Catherine d'Aulnoy and in contrast to the better-known fairy tales by Charles Perrault. In particular, together with studies of Madame Le Prince de Beaumont's 1757 "Beauty and the Beast" and of Victorian literature, the scholarly recovery and revaluation of women's French and German fairy tales (for English-language translations, see Jack Zipes' 1991 *Beauties, Beasts, and Enchantment*, and Shawn C. Jarvis's and Jeannine Blackwell's 2001 *The Queen's Mirror: Fairy Tales by German Women, 1780–1900*) have illuminated creative efforts to establish a female narrative voice and style in the literary fairy tale, then an emerging and increasingly male-dominated genre. Even though the tales' extravagance was labeled as ridiculous by the French academy of the time, and their ideological inflections vary widely, politics—both of the state and of the body—figure prominently in these women's texts. While Cristina Bacchilega's *Postmodern Fairy Tales: Gender and Narrative Strategies* (1997) analyzes late twentieth-century English-language fictions (Atwood's and Carter's especially) that revision well-known fairy-tales with a focus on the production of women's subjectivity and sexuality, Elizabeth W. Harries' excellent *Twice Upon a Time: Women Writers and the History of the Fairy Tale* (2003) has a much fuller historical scope.

Many believe that the folktale and fairy tale are a genre of the past, hopelessly tied to premodern economies and nineteenth-century gender arrangements. However, well-known tales continue to permeate Western popular culture. Film provides many examples, and here too woman-centered and romance-focused texts—though not necessarily their feminist interpretations—dominate the scene. Jokes and soap operas are, Angela Carter asserted, *the* twentieth-century folktales, the "invisible luggage" that we carry and repack. Cathy Lynn Preston's essays "'Cinderella' as a Dirty Joke: Gender, Multivocality, and the Polysemic Text" (*Western Folklore* 1994) and "Disrupting the Boundaries of Genre and Gender: Postmodernism and the Fairy Tale" (*Fairy Tales and Feminism* 2004) offer a perceptive analysis of recent "Cinderella" texts, including the movie *Ever After* (1998), television shows, and advertisements at women.com (also known as http://www.ivillage.com). The blurring of fiction and nonfiction in contemporary "fairy-tale" texts that JoAnn Conrad noted in "Docile Bodies of (Im)Material Girls: The Fairy-Tale Construction of JonBenet Ramsey and Princess Diana" (*Marvels & Tales* 1999) has, in Preston's assessment, at least some potential for social transformation that includes shifts from stereotypical gender relations associated with the Perrault and Grimm tradition.

The sexual politics of folk and fairy tales as well as their representations of gender will continue to surprise given that such narratives are still emerging in new contexts and media, and our knowledge of oral and literary traditions—especially when it comes to women's—is limited. Edited by Donald Haase, *Fairy Tales and Feminism: New Approaches* (2004) offers an up-to-date bibliography of English-language critical studies on the topic, provides a thorough overview of feminist fairy-tale scholarship, and includes essays that promise to expand the scope of research on women and tales of magic. In addition to the mirror images of Snow White and her crafty (step)mother, folktales have offered to their readers powerful fairies, bold maidens, brave sisters, bawdy wives, wise girls, and older women for self-reflection. In the 1998 collection edited by Kate Bernheimer, *Mirror, Mirror on the Wall: Women Writers Explore Their Favorite Fairy Tales*, there are a range of perspectives on how tales of magic have framed and invigorated contemporary women's writing in English; and among the many Internet fairy-tale resources, SurLaLune Fairytales.com includes annotated tale texts as well as essays and a lively site for discussion that often has a woman-centered or feminist bent. As narratives characterized by "pleasure in the fantastic" and "curiosity about the real" (Warner 1994: xx), folk and fairy tales have over the centuries and in different social contexts offered an imaginative outlet for desire while maintaining a strong grip on ordinary social life. Women have much to say and much at stake both in the reevaluation of "old wives' tales" and in the ever-multiplying transformations of the genre. *See also:* Cinderella; Coding; Courtship; Feminisms; Gender; Gossip; Joke; Marriage; Menarche Stories; Mother Goose; Mothers' Folklore; Myth Studies; Old Wives' Tales; Red Riding Hood; Rites of Passage; Sleeping Beauty; Tradition-Bearer.

References: Aarne, Antti, and Stith Thompson. *The Types of the Folktale: A Classification and Bibliography.* Second revision. Helsinki: Suomalainen Tiedeakatemia, 1961; Bacchilega, Cristina, and Steven Swann Jones, eds. *Perspectives on the Innocent Persecuted Heroine in Fairy Tales.* Special issue of *Western Folklore*, vol. 52, no. 1 (1993); ———. *Postmodern Fairy Tales: Gender and Narrative Strategies.* Philadelphia: University of Pennsylvania Press, 1997; Benson, Stephen. "Craftiness and Cruelty: A Reading of the Fairy Tale and Its Place in Recent Feminist Fictions." *Cycles of Influence: Fiction, Folktale, Theory,* 167–246. Detroit: Wayne State University Press, 2003; Bottigheimer, Ruth B. *Grimms' Bad Girls and Bold Boys: The Moral and Social Vision of the Tales.* New Haven: Yale University Press, 1987; Cardigos, Isabel. *In and Out of Enchantment: Blood Symbolism and Gender in Portuguese Fairy Tales.* Helsinki: Academia Scientiarum Fennica, 1996; Haase, Donald, ed. *Fairy Tales and Feminism. New Approaches.* Detroit: Wayne State University Press, 2004; Harries, Elizabeth E. *Twice Upon a Time: Women Writers and the History of the Fairy Tale.* Princeton, NJ: Princeton University Press, 2003; Jarvis, Shawn C. "Feminism and Fairy Tales." *Oxford Companion to Fairy Tales,* ed. Jack Zipes, 155–159. Oxford and New York: Oxford University Press, 2000; Lindahl, Carl. *American Folktales from the Collections of the Library of Congress.* Armonk, NY: M. E. Sharpe, 2003; Marzolph, Ulrich, and Richard van Leeuwen, eds. *Arabian Nights Encyclopedia.* Vols. 1–2. Santa Barbara, CA: ABC-Clio, 2004; Mills, Margaret. "A Cinderella Variant in the Context of Muslim Women's Ritual." In *Cinderella: A Casebook,* ed. Alan Dundes, 180–199. New York: Wildman Press, 1982; Radner, Joan Newlon. *Feminist Messages: Coding in Women's Folk Culture.* Urbana and Chicago: University of Illinois Press, 1993; Rowe, Karen E. "To Spin a Yarn: The Female Voice in Folklore and Fairy Tale." In *Fairy Tales and Society: Illusion, Allusion, and Paradigm,* ed. Ruth B. Bottigheimer, 53–74. New Haven: Yale University Press, 1986; Shoaei Kawan, Christine. "A Masochism Promising Supreme Conquests: Simone de Beauvoir Reflections on Fairy Tales and Children's Literature." *Marvels & Tales: Journal of Fairy-Tale Studies* 16 (2002): 29–48; Stone, Kay. "Things Walt Disney Never Told Us." *Journal of American Folklore* 88 (1975): 42–50. Reprinted in 1975, 42–50, in *Women and Folklore,* ed. Claire R. Farrer. Austin: University of Texas Press; ———. "The Misuses of Enchantment: Controversies on the Significance of Fairy Tales." In *Women's Folklore, Women's Culture,* eds. Rosan A. Jordan and Susan J. Kalčik, 125–145. Philadelphia: University of Pennsylvania Press, 1985; ———. *Burning Brightly. New Light on Old Tales Told Today.* Toronto: Broadview Press, 1998; SurLaLune Fairytales.com. n.d. http://www.surlalunefairytales. com/index.html (accessed June 16, 2005); Tatar, Maria. *Secrets beyond the Door: The Story of Bluebeard and His Wives.* Princeton: Princeton University Press, 2004; Uther,

Hans-Jörg, ed. *The Types of International Folktales, a Classification and Bibliography.* Based on the system of Antti Aarne and Stith Thompson. FF Communications no. 284. Helsinki: Suomalainen Tiedeakatemia, 2004; Warner, Marina. *From the Beast to the Blonde: On Fairy Tales and Their Tellers.* New York: Farrar, 1994; Windling, Terri. "Women and Fairy Tales." *The Endicott Studio Forum*, 1995. http://www.endicott-studio. com/forwmnft.html (accessed 16 June 2005); Zipes, Jack, ed. *Don't Bet on the Prince: Contemporary Feminist Fairy Tales in North America and England.* New York: Methuen, 1986; ———, ed. *Oxford Companion to Fairy Tales.* Oxford: Oxford University Press, 2000.

Cristina Bacchilega

Foodways

Foodways refers to the network of activities and beliefs surrounding food. Food is a source of both power and oppression for women. Through food, women love, nurture, display competence and artistry, construct relationships, and strengthen social ties; through food, women also find themselves tied to the garden and home, restricted by the daily routine of preparing meals. For many women, food itself is a source of both great delight and of much consternation. Many folk traditions and beliefs concerning women and food have emerged from these complexities. Women's folklore of food refers to food traditions associated with women and to the ways in which women use food as an informal, unofficial medium through which they communicate artistically and construct meaningful connections with their pasts, places, and other people. Among folkloristic approaches to exploring women, food, and folklore are women's foodways as gendered foods and food practices; forms of folklore related to women's foodways; and food as a medium for communication and power.

Historically, many aspects of foodways have been considered women's work. Food products (the raw materials, the ingredients, and the dish itself) are informally gendered in dominant U.S. culture—salad, quiche, and lighter foods are associated with femininity. The labor involved in procurement of food was traditionally divided by gender: men were hunters of large, potentially dangerous game, while women trapped smaller animals (rabbits, opossum, and birds) and fished from local streams or ponds. Men farmed the large fields and cash crops, while women tended herb and vegetable gardens near the home (kitchen gardens) for the family table and medicines; men butchered the larger animals, while women frequently took on the indoor work (rendering the fat, creating smaller cuts of meat, and making sausage). Women usually ran the henhouse, collected the eggs (or asked children do it), butchered poultry, milked the family cow, and gathered wild berries and nuts. In the United States today, where most food is procured from supermarkets, women still tend to take primary responsibility—at least for generating the shopping list, if not for actual shopping. Preservation of food (canning, freezing, and drying), if they are done at all, remain women's chores.

Historically, the kitchen was a woman's domain. She was allowed and expected to rule the household from this room. It was frequently the gathering place for close friends and family members, the emotional center of the household; yet, it also physically separated women from the rest of the family. Cooking was a necessary household skill, and a marketable one for securing a husband. Today, cooking is recognized as potentially artistic and financially lucrative. As its status has risen, so has the number of male cooks. (This phenomenon may reflect a shift in childrearing and homemaking responsibilities among some men, as well as other factors.) "And he can cook, too!" is a declaration of approval for a man being considered for the role of romantic partner. Although the professionalization of cooking brought more respect to the activities of food preparation, there is still a tendency to call men "chefs" and women "cooks." Women's cooking tends still to be the everyday, routine variety—simple meals consisting of plain dishes—while men's cooking tends to be more celebratory, lucrative, and public.

Presentation in foodways refers to the physical appearance of prepared food. Women are expected to make table decorations and to present meals in an attractive way, in short, to add "a feminine touch." Women are expected to eat daintily, not to "shovel it in" as men do. Cleaning up after a meal tends to be a women's responsibility. Although men and children may help out, women tend to be blamed for a messy kitchen; such a kitchen is perceived as a reflection of her incompetence or intentional rebellion.

Foodways' material forms include kitchens, cookware, cookbooks, recipes, and other tangible items associated with food preparation and consumption. As Meredith Abarca claims, "when women define the kitchen as their *space,* they engage in their own everyday acts of agency" (22). Cooking equipment (stoves, tables), kitchen tools, and eating implements often carry memories and may be treasured as heirlooms passed down by relatives. Dishes, silver tea services, and silver tableware are traditional wedding gifts. (Silverware is also a traditional gift for a couple's twenty-fifth wedding anniversary.) Cookbooks and written recipes are vivid documents of women's foodways—and lives. Recipes are passed down from family and friends; artistically rendered recipe cards may be given as gifts. Many women treasure their mothers' and grandmothers' handwritten recipes and keep them in special boxes or scrapbooks.

Oral forms of women's foodways include sayings related to food, personal-experience narratives, and spoken recipes ("a pinch of this, a pinch of that"), all of which may reflect underlying assumptions about both food and gender relations. For example, many girls are taught early that the "way to a man's heart is through his stomach." Once a husband is secured, his responsibility as "breadwinner" means that he "brings home the bacon," while the proper place of women is "barefoot and pregnant and in the kitchen." And if a wife allows her husband too little independence, she is said to keep him "tied to her apron strings." Anecdotes and personal-experience narratives about food are a significant part of women's conversation. Women tell such stories to teach, comfort, create bonds, and entertain. Generally dismissed as "kitchen gossip," such tales offer critiques of women's lives and relationships with men, children, and other women.

Women use food as means to nurture themselves and others: chicken soup for a cold, hot toddies for chills, and poultices and herbal teas for healing. Women's customary foodways lore also includes rituals, celebrations, and practices that are distinctive to and representative of women's traditions, such as croning parties, bridal showers, and *quinceañeras*. Food is oftentimes the focal point of women's social events and an excuse for gathering at "coffee klatches," tea parties, and dinner parties. Such customs help to create community as well as shape personal relationships. Food-related rituals and beliefs may mark a woman's passage through life: girls are generally expected to make cookies to distribute to schoolmates on special occasions, hold tea parties for friends, and play "mother's helper" in the kitchen, all of which focus their attention on relationships and the domestic sphere.

The role of food in shaping an adolescent girl's body—and therefore her social standing and physical attractiveness—is a major source of folklore. Traditions of dieting, along with folk beliefs and narratives concerning weight loss or gain, frequently become an integral part of women's lives by the time they reach puberty. Folk groups develop around specialized diets (such as vegetarian, vegan, or gluten-free) and dieting—especially since the advent of the Internet—and official organizations for dieting and fitness encourage members to develop personalized cooking and eating rituals (prepare a dessert if you want it, for instance, or light a dinner candle when you eat alone).

Menarche comes with a number of food traditions. In the past, custom kept most menstruating women away from their usual domestic routines: their touch purportedly made fruit trees barren, mayonnaise curdle, bread fail to rise, wine turn to vinegar, meat rot, jam fail to set, and preserves spoil. Other menstrual foodways are attempts to ease dysmenorrhea, such as eating no salt or consuming large quantities of milk or soy products during the week before menstruation. Latina girls are warned that eating certain foods such as avocados and hot peppers will cause cramping.

With adolescence also comes the role of food in romance. A gift of chocolates from a male (or female) admirer on Valentine's Day is a public symbol of love. During courtship, the feminine role of nurturer is reversed with the expectation that suitors will pay for women's meals on dates. On the other hand, a girl may state her independence or lack of romantic interest by insisting on paying her own way, by "going Dutch." Food also plays a role in failed romances: girls and women are generally forgiven for "drowning" their disappointment by overeating foods usually forbidden to the diet-conscious female—quarts of ice cream, bags of cookies or potato chips, or whole jars of peanut butter at a single "meal." Romances leading to marriage are also marked by food traditions—bridal showers and luncheons, the wedding rehearsal dinner, the reception, and, most significant of all, the wedding cake. Although the standard wedding cake is a multitiered white cake with white icing and delicate decorations, including bride and groom dolls on top, variations on the theme may reflect a bride's personal identity and interests. As ephemeral art, cakes as material objects may embody both cultural and personal preferences.

As the foregoing attests, sexuality and food are closely connected in women's folklore. This is also true of much folklore about women. In many cultures and throughout history, countless metaphors in common parlance suggest that women can be cultivated and consumed in the same way that food is (see Henry 1992 on ancient Greece and Parker 1991 on contemporary Brazil). Femaleness and food are sometimes conflated, and attractive women are described by myriad food terms—honeybun, cupcake, hot tamale, Georgia peach, sugar, dish, tart, and hot tomato. Tradition identifies some foods—chocolate, oysters, ginseng, asparagus, and chili peppers—as aphrodisiac; it also suggests the eating of specific foods in sexually provocative ways (eating a firm banana may be seen to mimic fellatio; eating a juicy peach may be thought to mimic cunnilingus). Foodlore also plays a role in contraception and conception; certain foods are believed to have particular effects. These beliefs may appear in urban legends, such as one in which a woman sues a spermicide manufacturer because she became pregnant despite eating contraceptive "jelly," and another that claims that douching with Coca-Cola is an effective way to prevent pregnancy.

Pregnancy carries its own food traditions. Some concern the effects of certain foods on the fetus—caffeine and alcohol may cause fetal abnormalities and/or delivery complications (corroborated by allopathic medicine); too much chocolate, sugar, and spicy food may predispose an infant to hyperactivity. Other traditions concern the mother's health and comfort: tomato sauce causes heartburn; expectant mothers should drink extra milk for the calcium; and red meat provides needed iron. Folk remedies for morning sickness suggest nibbling on crackers throughout the day; having someone else do the cooking; and eating whatever the pregnant body craves, lest the baby be born with a birthmark—that is, if the mother craves shrimp, the baby may be born with a birthmark in that shape. This last has led to many anecdotes about searching for particular foods that are out of season or hard to obtain and about odd food combinations—in the United States, "pickles and ice cream" has become emblematic of pregnancy. Some women develop pica (cravings for non-food items such as chalk or ashes). In accord with a custom thought to originate in Africa, where people might eat the enzyme-rich, white clay in termite mounds, some pregnant Black women in the rural American South practice geophagy (earth-eating).

Breastfeeding has given rise to a great deal of folklore. Techniques for getting an infant to nurse are passed down through oral tradition, as are beliefs about particular foods to eat (drinking milk or beer helps the milk to flow; chili peppers, tomato sauce, and spicy foods turn the milk sour). Stories (frequently humorous) about breast milk are common: it is intentionally or unintentionally used as coffee creamer, in puddings, ice cream, or baked goods. Breastfeeding in public is associated with a material culture of clothing and folklore about how to arrange both clothes and baby so as to hide one's breasts or the act of nursing. Foodlore is also associated with menopause. Certain foods (currently flax and soy among Euro Americans and Canadians) are believed to help relieve hot flashes, night sweats, insomnia, and other discomforts.

Recent terminological distinctions attest to an increasing interest about how, what, and why we eat. The term "gastro-politics" refers to differential access to food production, distribution, and consumption based on class, ethnicity, gender, and locale. For example, historically, one of the few means women had for earning money was through food—as cooks in affluent homes, as caterers, or as cottage-industry food producers. "Egg-and-butter money" was the cash earned by farm women's entrepreneurship. The "cultural politics of food" refers to the power to define what is healthy, nutritious, or appropriate food. Within the home, mothers and grandmothers generally have that power; however, within the larger society, it belongs to the medical and scientific establishments and to food production and marketing companies, many of which are male-centered and male-dominated. Women tend to have more control over "commensal politics," power concerning eating together: deciding on menus, portion sizes, choice of recipes, selection of ingredients, and presentation of food in the home.

As sugar-laden "fast foods" have become ubiquitous in the dietary lives of most Americans, they have taken a particular toll on Indigenous Hawaiian and Native North American populations, in which diabetes is 2.6 times more likely to occur than among Whites; girls and women are especially prone to develop this disease. Noting the 50 percent increase in diabetes rates among Native peoples over the last decade, Wynona Duke and Margaret Smith of the White Earth Reservation in Minnesota and Terrol Dew Johnson of the Tohono O'odham Reservation in Arizona have revitalized the dietary and cultural importance of indigenous foods, especially tepary beans (eaten plain or in stews), wild rice, and cholla (cactus) buds. Johnson explains by saying that when Coyote was running with a bag of tepary beans, he tripped and the white beans flew into the sky, creating the Milky Way. "You're not just seeing these beans. You're seeing the whole culture. That bean holds our language, our songs, our history" (Hernandez, 26). Along with efforts to convince Natives to eat less fry bread (seen by many as contributing to negative stereotypes), the tepary bean may be the key to many Aboriginal cultures' survival.

Food is also a medium for resistance to social norms or individual circumstances or relationships. A refusal to cook can be a blatant and intentional "rebellion," as in the case of former presidential wife Hilary Rodham Clinton's 1998 statement that she doesn't bake cookies or in the case of a Latino wife whose husband was granted a divorce because she refused to make him labor-intensive and time-consuming homemade tamales. Women can also show disdain for stereotyped gender assumptions by "chowing down," that is, by heartily enjoying their food. In this context, women's eating disorders (especially anorexia and bulimia) are interpreted as a bid for power.

Resistance through food can also be coded expressions of sentiments or opinions that would be unsafe or unwise for a woman to voice publicly. These "feminist messages" are read and can be interpreted correctly only by other members of her group. Joan Radner suggests five coding strategies. Trivialization uses activities considered innocuous and innocent to convey meaningful and significant information and opinions, such as holding a bake sale to support anti-war activism. Incompetence is a claim or demonstration of inability at conventionally feminine activities as a way of resisting social expectations. For example, burning food when making dinner may express a woman's resistance to the social norm that women do the cooking. Appropriation is the borrowing by women of male-associated activities, as in businesses managed by women hosting parties through informal networks, such as Tupperware parties. Gender-role inversion in foodways can also be a form of women's resistance, when, for example, a woman carves the Sunday roast or holiday turkey, oversees cooking on an outdoor grill, drinks beer, or relaxes while her husband prepares a meal and cleans up afterward. *See also:* Aphrodisiac; Breastfeeding; Coding; Courtship; Croning; Diet Culture; Engagement; Farm Women's Folklore; Gardens; Gender; Gossip; Herbs; Housekeeping; Legend, Urban/Contemporary; Menarche Stories; Menopause; Menstruation; Personal-Experience Narrative; Pregnancy; *Quinceañera*; Recipe Books; Scrapbooks; Sexuality; Tradition; Wedding; Women's Friendship Groups; Women's Work.

References: Abarca, Meredith E. *Voices in the Kitchen: Views of Food and the World from Working-class Mexican and Mexican American Women.* College Station: Texas A&M University Press. 2006; Avakian, Arlene Voski, ed. *Through the Kitchen Window: Women Explore the Intimate Meanings of Food and Cooking.* New York: Berg, 2005 [1997]; Avakian, Arlene Voski, and Barbara Haber, eds. *From Betty Crocker to Feminist Food Studies: Critical Perspectives on Women and Food.* Amherst: University of Massachusetts Press, 2005; Bower, Anne L. ed. *Recipes for Reading: Community Cookbooks, Stories, Histories.* Amherst: University of Massachusetts Press, 1997; Counihan, Carole M. *The Anthropology of Food and Body: Gender, Meaning, and Power.* New York: Routledge, 1999; ———. "Food as Women's Voice in the San Luis Valley of Colorado." In *Food in the USA: A Reader*, eds. Carole M. Counihan and Penny Van Esterik, 295–304. New York: Routledge, 2002; Counihan, Carole M., and Steven L. Kaplan. *Food and Gender: Identity and Power.* Amsterdam: Harwood Academic Publishers, 1998; Henry, Madeleine M. "The Edible Woman: Athenaeus's Concept of the Pornographic." *Pornography and Representation in Greece and Rome*, ed. Amy Richlin, 250–268. New York and Oxford: Oxford University Press, 1992; Hernandez, Daisy. "Got Tradition?: American Indians use native foods to fight diabetes and revive Indian culture." *Colorlines* (Summer 2005): 24–27; Inness, Sherrie A. *Kitchen Culture in America: Popular Representations of Food, Gender, and Race.* Philadelphia: University of Pennsylvania Press, 2001; Inness, Sherrie A., and Clifford Ashby. *Dinner Roles: American Women and Culinary Culture.* Iowa City: University of Iowa Press, 2001; Lanser, Susan S. "Burning Dinners: Feminist Subversions of Domesticity." In *Feminist Messages: Coding in Women's Folk Culture*, ed. Joan Newlon Radner, 36–53. Urbana and Chicago: University of Illinois Press, 1993; Long, Lucy M. "Holiday Meals: Rituals of Family Tradition." In *The Meal*, ed. Herbert Meisselman. Gaithersburg, MD: Aspen Publishers, 2000; Mikkelson, Barbara. Snopes.com. "Killer Sperm." http://www.snopes.com/cokelore/sperm.asp (accessed August 10, 2008); Parker, Richard G. *Bodies, Pleasures, and Passions: Sexual Culture in Contemporary Brazil.* Boston: Beacon Press, 1991; Shapiro, Laura. *Perfection Salad: Women and Cooking at the Turn of the Century.* New York: Farrar, Straus and Giroux, 1986; ———. *Something From the Oven: Reinventing Dinner in 1950s America.* New York: Viking, 2004; Schenone, Laura. *A Thousand Years Over a Hot Stove: A History of American Women Told through Food, Recipes, and Remembrances.* New York: W. W. Norton & Co., 2005; Theophano, Janet. *Eat My Words: Reading Women's Lives Through the Cookbooks they Wrote.* New York: Palgrave Macmillan, 2002; Turner, Kay, and Suzanne Seriff. "'Giving an Altar to St. Joseph': A Feminist Perspective on a Patronal Feast." In *Feminist Theory and the Study of Folklore*, eds. Susan Tower Hollis, Linda Pershing, and M. Jane Young, 89–117. Urbana and Chicago: University of Illinois Press, 1993; Williams, Brett. "Why Migrant Women Feed Their Husbands Tamales: Foodways as a Basis for Revisionist View of Tejano Family Life." *Ethnic and Regional Foodways in the United States: The*

Performance of Group Identity, eds. Linda Keller Brown and Kay Mussell, 113–126. Knoxville: University of Tennessee Press, 1984.

Lucy M. Long

Fortune-Teller

A fortune-teller is a divination specialist consulted about the future or problems in the present, who may or may not be paid for the service and is often self-described as a "reader" or "advisor." Fortune-telling, along with other methods of divination such as the Chinese *I Ching*, Celtic runes, and Greek oracles, reflects the human desire for meaning and order, as well as anxiety regarding the unknown. Traditional divinatory activity involving women has often been concerned with childbirth and marriage. Dactyliomancy is one method used to predict the sex of an unborn child. In one variant, a ring is tied to a string and held over a pregnant woman's belly. Circular movement of the ring indicates that she is carrying a girl, while a boy is forecast if the ring moves back and forth like a pendulum. Numerous rituals are employed for predicting a woman's marriage prospects. These include passing a small piece of bridal cake through a wedding ring, then placing the cake under the woman's pillow to prompt dreams of her future husband.

In the North American context, the term "fortune-teller" generally encompasses astrological counselors and palm, tarot card, and tea-leaf readers, among others, who may be consulted in both informal and professional settings. Although fortune-telling as an income-generating activity has expanded from traditional settings to mass-mediated forms, including newspapers, television, and the Internet, the interstitial nature of fortune-telling as an occupation has made it a popular home-based enterprise for women. Romani ("Gypsy") women have traditionally told fortunes to help support their families, leading to the stereotypical image of the fortune-teller adorned with scarves and jewelry, gazing into a crystal ball. Unfortunately, police officials promote this image, along with the admonition that all such persons are charlatans and criminals. Popular culture does a serious disservice to both Roma and non-Roma with such portrayals. While consumer awareness of psychic services is important, stereotypes and ethnic slurs advance racist attitudes while obscuring core issues of belief, control, and the complexity of regulating paranormal commerce.

In both domestic and commercial fortune-telling, an important part of the dyadic process is the ability to "read" clients psychologically, whether consciously or unconsciously. Generalized, formulaic statements such as, "You have had trouble with a family member in the past," help to establish rapport, encouraging the client to speak more freely about herself and the issues for which she seeks counsel, and to apply the fortune-teller's generalizations to her specific situation. (This is often referred to as the "Barnum effect.") Such aspects of fortune-telling have led to debate regarding the degree, and even the existence, of psychic or precognitive ability. However, as with any such vocation, practitioners manifest a wide range of skills, ethical commitments, and spiritual inclinations. *See also: Curandera*; Divination Practices; Folk Medicine.

References: Andersen, Ruth E. "Romano Drabarimos in Pennsylvania: The Marketing of Tradition." *Keystone Quarterly*, vol. 2, nos. 1–2 (1983): 46–57; Aphek, Edna, and Yishai Tobin. *The Semiotics of Fortune-Telling*. Philadelphia: John Benjamins Publishing Company, 1989; Benes, Peter. "Fortunetellers, Wise-Men, and Magical Healers in New England, 1644–1850." In *Wonders of the Invisible World: 1600–1900*, ed. Peter Benes, 127–48. The Dublin Seminar for New England Folklife Annual Proceedings 1992. Boston: Boston University, 1995; Rusted, Brian. "'The Palm at the End of the Mind,' or Narrative Fortune Telling as Urban Folk Therapy." *New York Folklore*, vol. 10, nos. 1–2 (1984): 21–38.

Holly Everett

G

Gardens

Gardens, especially those associated with private homes, are often considered a woman's domain, providing a space for various activities appropriate for and associated with the female gender. Women have been able to express their artistry, guarantee their importance to the domestic economy, and assert their ability to nurture and heal through their cultivation and use of plants from their gardens.

From earliest times, the gathering and cultivation of plants was associated with women, as hunting was associated with men. Images such as Mother Earth or fertility goddesses draw connections between the fecundity of nature and the reproductive power of women. In patriarchal societies, this association is frequently cast in negative terms, as the unconstrained disorder of the natural world contrasted with the strictures of civilization and the rationality of the man-made environment.

Flower and other ornamental gardens have long been considered an outlet for aesthetic expression particularly appropriate for women. Flowers beautify the home, traditionally the primary sphere of female influence. Therefore, the cultivation of flowers outside, as well as their arrangement in bouquets within the home, fell to women as a part of their traditional homemaking work. Especially with the development of the "cult of domesticity" during the Victorian era, in which a woman's role was to create a tranquil oasis where her husband could escape the rigors of the workaday world, a woman's skill in creating beautiful gardens was considered essential to a tranquil home life. In Western societies, the art of flower arranging is an offshoot of this appreciation for fine gardening, and is similarly considered a feminine art, whether practiced by men or women.

Throughout the nineteenth and twentieth centuries, gardens containing vegetables and other useful plants were also a part of the home, particularly the kitchen, and therefore women's responsibility. Gardens that provided food, seasonings, and medicinal plants contributed to the domestic economy, and gave women a modicum of economic power, even in times and cultures in which such power was considered the prerogative of males. Among economically disadvantaged populations, a woman's garden could be a significant addition to a family's income, producing food to eat or sell. Canning competitions, common at county fairs all over the United States, are community festival events that reflect the importance of women's roles in providing for the family through the cultivation and preservation of foodstuffs.

Home-garden cultivation and the use of medicinal plants in folk medicine practices can enhance women's power in male-dominated societies. Generally, the power of plants to heal disease and relieve pain is associated with magic, putatively granting women who hold that power the role of priestess or witch. The figure of the *curandera* in Latino cultures demonstrates this ambiguity. A curandera, a woman skilled in healing and medicinal plants, was an honored member of frontier Hispanic societies, and the practice of consulting such women for relief from illness has not entirely disappeared from contemporary Latino communities. But the ability of these women to wield the power of life and death is also viewed with suspicion in strongly patriarchal cultures; the line between the curandera (healer) and the *bruja* (witch) frequently marks a distinction without a difference. *See also:* Aesthetics; *Curandera*; Family Folklore; Festival; Flowers, Language of; Folk Medicine; Herbs; Mother Earth; Nature/Culture; Women's Work.

References: Burgess, Karen E. *Home is Where the Dog Is: Art in the Back Yard.* Jackson: University Press of Mississippi, 1996; Goldsmith, Raquel Rubio. "Seasons, Seeds, and Souls: Mexican Women Gardening in the American Mesilla, 1900–1940." *Women of the Mexican Countryside, 1850–1990*, eds. Heather Fowler-Salamini and Mary Kay Vaughan, 141–56. Tucson: University of Arizona Press, 1994; Gundaker, Grey, and Tynes Cowan, eds. *Keep Your Head to the Sky: Interpreting African American Home Ground.* Charlottesville: University Press of Virginia, 1998; Kitchner, Amy. *Windows into the Past: Mexican-American Yardscapes in the Southwest.* Senior thesis. University of Arizona, 1987; Ortner, Sherry. "Is Female to Male as Nature Is to Culture?" in *Women, Culture and Society*, eds. Michelle Z. Rosaldo and Louise Lamphere, 67–88. Palo Alto, CA: Stanford University Press, 1974; Waldenberger, Suzanne. "Barrio Gardens: The Arrangement of a Woman's Space." *Western Folklore*, vol. 59, nos. 3 and 4 (2000): 232–245; Westmacott, Richard. *African-American Gardens and Yards in the Rural South.* Knoxville: University of Tennessee Press, 1992.

Suzanne Waldenberger

Gender

"Gender" is a term used to distinguish socially transmitted norms about masculinity and femininity from "sex" by those distinctions that are understood to be inherent in biology. Sex in binary (male versus female) symbolic systems is generally determined by categorizing genitalia as male, female, or ambiguous; sexual orientation refers to the direction of one's sexual interest toward members of the same (homosexual), different (heterosexual), or both sexes (bisexual). Gender is the set of characteristics and behaviors determined by society to be appropriately masculine or feminine. Any conflation of them in this binary system is generally labeled androgynous (from Greek, "man-woman"), with connotations of greater or lesser stigmatized deviance depending on prevailing social norms. Gender is constructed in each culture and era to normalize what is appropriate and inappropriate for men and women to do, wear, think, and say.

Psychologist John Money first used the term "gender" in 1955 to discuss sexual roles (behaviors), later adding the term "gender identity." Anthropologist Ann Oakley took up the term in reference to socially constructed masculinity and femininity in contrast to sex, which she defined as the anatomical and physiological characteristics that express biological maleness and femaleness. Anthropologist Gayle Rubin first used the term "sex/gender system" to emphasize the ways in which sexually differentiated bodies are socially organized to produce ideas of gender difference. U.S. Supreme Court Justice Ruth Bader Ginsberg is credited with coining the legal term "gender discrimination" in reference to cases involving attempts to invalidate laws protecting the civil rights of girls and women.

In an early use of the term in its contemporary sense, physician Alex Comfort, author of *The Joy of Sex*, employed American sexologist Alfred Kinsey's research to explore the childhood acculturation process that distinguishes sex from gender, concluding that gender roles learned by two years of age are usually irreversible, even if they seem to contradict the sex of the subject. In Western cultures, gender roles are taught as an informal part of the socialization process, beginning as soon as parents dress their infant girls in pink and their boys in blue. Although patterns are changing in some segments of society, most homes and schools still offer dolls and domestic items as playthings to girls, and toy trucks, airplanes, and guns to boys. By the time children are old enough to enjoy popular cultural forms like the Walt Disney Company's *The Little Mermaid* (whose heroine is a perfectly passive subject sacrificing herself for the man she loves) or George Lucas' *Star Wars* (in which male figures of all ages, species, and religious persuasions are alternately admired and defied by a single main female character), they have already fully internalized the Mother Goose rhyme, whether they have heard it or not:

What are little boys made of?
"Snips and snails, and puppy dogs tails
That's what little boys are made of!"
What are little girls made of?
"Sugar and spice and all things nice
That's what little girls are made of!"

In North America, the act of choosing which public restroom to enter, for example, employs numerous gender-conditioning components. The women's restroom door displays a picture of a person in a skirt, and the men's has a picture of a person in pants; as intended, we take these pictures as cues. Men in kilts don't enter the "skirt washroom," nor do trousered women enter the "pants" one. These deceptively simple icons encode an extremely complex system of unspoken assumptions. They indicate not only that there are two types of bathrooms which precisely match two traditional gender choices, but they also tell us the types of clothing choices expected of women and men.

Conventional wisdom teaches, for example, that biology has determined that men are stronger than women and that women have a greater tendency to tears than men, when in reality, some women are stronger than most men, and many men cry on a regular basis and some women do so only rarely. Although not all human societies have such strictly enforced rules, in most cultures the normal socialization of boys and girls inculcates anxiety, embarrassment, and fear in people who cross gender divides. North American girls who display the gender characteristics of boys—playing sports, fighting, talking loudly—are often labeled "tomboys." Boys who play with girls or enjoy playing with dolls are dubbed "sissies." Parents have long been warned that such behaviors are predictors of homosexuality or transgenderedness, despite the prevalent rejection of this notion in the fields of psychiatry and sociology.

A further indication of the separability of sex and gender lies in the fact that gender roles and characteristics change over time and within cultures based on class perceptions, ethnic and cultural status, and religious or regional traditions. Nineteenth- and twentieth-century middle- and upper-class North American girls were conditioned to aspire to grow up to become housewives and mothers; the ideal role for adult women was to be a married, stay-at-home mother, rather than a single woman, one who worked outside the home, or a lesbian. But in areas of Ireland during the same period, normative women's roles included becoming a nun, a woman expected to neither marry nor bear children. In the 1950s in the United States, the use of cosmetics was considered a gender characteristic of heterosexual girls and women. In the 1980s and 1990s, however, heterosexual men who wore eyeliner were likely signaling their membership in the folk group known as Goths. In some African and Native American cultures, face and body makeup is reserved for warrior men rather than for women.

South Asian culture acknowledges *hijras* (from Urdu for "impotent ones")—androgynous, cross-dressing, queer, or transgendered individuals (not castrated "eunuchs," despite that common mistranslation)—who, though frequently ostracized, function in Indian life as sex workers, entertainers, and mourners. The *Ramayana* epic, in which the god Rama appears as a hijra, is often cited as a charter for their right to exist. Six hijras have won local and state elections in India since 1999, and one holds a seat in parliament. In some Native North American groups, mixed-gendered ("two-spirited") individuals dressed differently from men and women in ways that indicate the acknowledgement of a third gender.

However, even in cultures where the binary sex/gender system is strictly enforced, it changes over time. In recent years, the mass media—especially television—have played significant roles in both shifting and reinscribing North American perceptions of binary gender. The talk-show craze of the 1990s increased the visibility of transgendered individuals, traditionally hidden, ostracized figures; however, they did so, for the most part, by portraying them as socially unacceptable freaks. *Saturday Night Live*'s "Pat" character—whose gender/sex other characters try to divine, without success—simultaneously reinforced the idea that masculinity and femininity should be distinct and recognizable.

The social construction of gender has been central to feminist Anthropology's assertion of the universal subordination of women. Sherry B. Ortner, who first put forth the case in 1972 in an essay entitled "Is Female to Male as Nature is to Culture?" argues that the cross-cultural associations of women with nature (mainly through their connection with biological reproduction and childrearing) and men with culture (that which transcends nature's limitations) explains why women (like nature) are universally devalued in patriarchy. Critics have pointed out that the association of women with nature and men with culture is itself a cultural argument, and that nature is as much a cultural construct as is culture; however, Ortner's argument remains compelling.

Language is a central concern for gender studies. Robin Lakoff, for example, traces women's speech patterns as reflective of their subordinate positions in culture. Some feminist linguists argue for the existence of female linguistic subcultures based on cross-cultural explorations of gendered speech performance; others are convinced that the problem is not only that women and men have different speech styles that can be mutually incomprehensible (as in Deborah Tannen's 1990 book, *You Just Don't Understand*), but that linguistic processing interprets women's and men's language differently, and with inflections of power and hegemony. Consider, for example, the following "floating verses"—stock sections used in different traditional folksongs and ballads:

Who's gonna shoe your pretty little foot?
Who's gonna glove your hand?
Who's gonna kiss your ruby red lips?
Who's gonna be your man? (Greenhill 1997: 225)

Most Euro North Americans hearing these lines probably assume that the speaker is male and his addressee female. The questioner's gender is determined partly by default—in the absence of clear evidence, a masculine speaker is assumed. Men's speech in Euro North American culture is presumed to be directly and baldly expressed, as this is. The text will also be interpreted via a White, middle-class, political economy of heterosexual relationships. The expectations for the exchange of power, services, and activities are governed by gender expectations: "shoe your foot/glove your hand" refers to the necessity of taking care of a woman's material needs (usually by a husband); "kiss your ruby red lips" links this to sexual service exchange, and "be your man" confirms the gender of the supplier. It's impertinent to ask these questions of a man because he's expected to provide for his own material and sexual needs, in the marketplace if necessary.

The response, however, opens up a range of possibilities:

Papa's gonna show my pretty little foot
Mama's gonna glove my hand
Sister's gonna kiss my ruby red lips
And I don't need no man (ibid.).

Many folklorists (mostly men) have persisted in interpreting the response within a heterosexual structure, often ignoring the last line, or explaining it away as "I don't need a man ... till you come home" or "I don't need a man ... except you." Yet readers seeking a queer analysis can point out that the respondent has a woman to see to her needs for affection (a "sister" need not necessarily refer to a biological relative), and that the last line is an unequivocal rejection of the need for men as husbands, lovers, suitors, or erotic partners. Presumptions about sex, gender, and sexuality combine in patterned ways.

This sex/gender paradigm of "gender as social construction"/"sex as biology" has been problematized by several influential scholars, including Judith Butler, Thomas Laqueur, and Anne Fausto-Sterling, who question the sustainability of the category of biological sex. Each argues that sex is at least partially socially constructed in ways that exploit an either/or, male/female conception. They posit that either/or constructions fail to account for the complex relationship of sex to gender; nor do they account for the multiplicity of forms biological sex can take.

The presence of mutable sex in many national folklore traditions indicates a rather fluid understanding of sex as a static biological category. Seamus Deane's novel *Reading in the Dark*, for example, discusses the Irish legend of "Francis and Frances," who were so spiritually connected that they spontaneously exchanged sexes and "paid no notice" to the change. The tale is told to inculcate fear and suspicion of rural people in the young narrator, but it also casts suspicion on our traditional reliance upon the primacy and naturalness of the social characteristics we used to identify with a person's sex. *See also:* Androgyny; Ballad; Childbirth and Childrearing; Cosmetics; Cross-Dressing; Feminisms; Folk Group; Folk Music; Lesbian and Gay Studies; Lesbian Folklore; Mass Media; Mother Goose; Nature/Culture; Popular Culture; Sex Determination; Sexuality; Transgender Folklore.

References: Abelove, Henry, Michele Barale, and David Halperin, eds. *The Lesbian and Gay Studies Reader.* New York: Routledge, 1993; Butler, Judith. *Gender Trouble.* 10th anniversary edition. New York: Routledge, 1999 [1989]; ———. *Bodies That Matter: On the Discursive Limits of Sex.* New York: Routledge, 1993; Comfort, Alex. *Sex in Society.* Originally published as *Sexual Behavior in Society.* London: Gerald Duckworth & Co., 1963 [1950]; Duberman, Martin, Martha Vicinus, and George Chauncey, eds. *Hidden From History: Reclaiming the Gay and Lesbian Past.* New York: Plume, 1990; Fausto-Sterling, Anne. *Sexing the Body: Gender Politics and the Construction of Sexuality.* New York: Basic, 2000; "50 Key Terms: Gender." University of Manchester School of Social Sciences. n.d. http://www.socialsciences.manchester.ac.uk/sociology/course_mate rials/sy2891/_notes/gender.htm (accessed May 23, 2005); Greenhill, Pauline. "'Who's Gonna Kiss Your Ruby Red Lips?': Sexual Scripts in Floating Verses." In *Ballads Into Books: The Legacies of Francis James Child,* eds. Tom Cheesman and Sigrid Rieuwerts, 225–236. Berne: Peter Lang, 1997; Lakoff, Robin Tolmach, and Mary Bucholtz. *Language and Women's Place: Text and Commentaries.* Revised and expanded edition. Oxford and New York: Oxford University Press, 2004 [1975]; Lancaster, Roger N., and Micaela di Leonardo, eds. *The Gender/Sexuality Reader: Culture, History, Political Economy.* New York: Routledge, 1997; Laqueur, Thomas. *Making Sex: Body and Gender from the Greeks to Freud.* Cambridge, MA: Harvard University Press, 1992; Money, John. *Man and Woman, Boy and Girl: Differentiation and Dimorphism of Gender Identity from Conception to Maturity.* Baltimore: The Johns Hopkins University Press, 1972; Nicholson, Linda, ed. *The Second Wave: A Reader in Feminist Theory.* New York: Routledge, 1997; Oakley, Ann. *Sex, Gender, and Society.* London: Temple Smith, 1972; Ortner, Sherry B. *Making Gender: The Politics and Erotics of Culture.* Boston: Beacon Press, 1996; Rubin, Gayle. "The Traffic in Women: Notes on the 'Political Economy' of Sex." In *Toward an Anthropology of Women,* ed. Rayna R. Reiter, 157–210. New York: Monthly

Review Press, 1975; Watson, Paul. "Offering India's Voters a Unique Perspective." *London Times*, May 9, 2004. http://www.apihr.org/AAApercent20Newpercent20'Ohanapercent20News/offeringindia'svotersauniqueperspective.html (accessed May 26, 2005).

Erin Clair

Girl Scouts/Girl Guides

Girl and adult members of a youth organization such as the Girl Guides of Canada/Guides du Canada (GGC), whose membership was 80,000 girls and 20,000 adults in 2007, and the Girl Scouts of the USA (GSUSA), whose 2007 membership was 2.6 million girls and 1 million adults, are members of the World Association of Girl Guides and Girl Scouts (WAGGGS). It's the largest organization of girls and young women in the world with 10 million members in 145 countries. Girl Scouts and Girl Guides have an extremely complex and syncretic folk culture, appearing frequently in caricatures in North American popular culture. Full of tradition and clearly part of mainstream culture, Girl Scouting and Girl Guiding have a history of promoting cultural change by empowering girls and women, and both now recognize an increasingly diverse membership with respect to race, religion, ethnicity, sexual orientation, and ability. Inheritances from female folk culture clearly distinguish them from Boy Scouting, although outsiders sometimes erroneously attribute Boy Scout features and terminology to Girl Scouting and Girl Guiding (as in the misnomer, "Girl Scouts of America").

North American Girl Guiding came to Canada in 1910 and to the United States in 1912, having developed from Robert Baden-Powell's British Boy Scouting and from the Baden-Powell family's British Girl Guiding. American founder Juliette Gordon Low renamed her group "Girl Scouts" in 1913, causing much controversy. Robert Baden-Powell's early military influence is visible in the groups' uniforms, ranks, flag ceremony, and patch (merit badge) programs, but largely disappeared as a driving force during the twentieth century. While Canadian Girl Guiding remains closely related to British Girl Guiding, both GGC and GSUSA possess an inheritance from North American women's service and educational organizations, and transformations of Native American cultures appear in both groups' camplore.

As members of WAGGGS, GGC and GSUSA each have a three-part promise and a ten-part law intended to inspire girl and adult members to embody ideals of character, citizenship, and service. The promise's three parts correspond to service to one's country and religion (flexible wording supports religious diversity), helping others, and living by the Guide/Scout law; these virtues are symbolically represented by the trefoil (a three-leaved icon) and a hand sign (three fingers of the right hand raised together). As national organizations, each encourages patriotism, but the Girl Guiding and Girl Scouting ideal of world friendship promotes patriotism as an active part of citizenship, not as a form of international competition. There is a trend in Muslim communities in the United States, increasingly under scrutiny since the attacks of September 11, 2001, for girls to join troops as a means to visibly express their full participation in mainstream American culture; at the end of 2007, Minneapolis, Minnesota, boasted ten predominantly Muslim

Girl Scout troops. The national organizations encourage consistency of programs and message within their countries, although administrative subdivisions often create local variations.

Girl Scouting and Guiding include many fruitful areas for folklife study such as music, storytelling, play, camplore, foodways, ceremony, ritual, festival, and material culture. Across Girl Guiding and Scouting culture, one may find the themes of female empowerment, friendship (often expressed as "sisterhood"), service, leadership, and love of nature. Popular culture caricatures generally emphasize (and exaggerate) the organizations' slogan ("Be Prepared"), promotion of camping and hiking, militaristic or Native American inheritances, high ideals (the "goody-goody"), achievement programs, and annual cookie-selling fundraiser. However, the complexity of North American Girl Scouting and Guiding cultures, their marginalized status resulting from their affiliation with females and children, and local variations result in significantly different insider and outsider perceptions of the meanings and values they contain and perpetuate. *See also:* Camplore; First Nations of North America; Folk Group; Folklife; Folklore about Women; Gender; Girls' Folklore; Girls' Games; Lesbian Folklore; Muslim Women's Folklore; Popular Culture; Ritual; Women's Friendship Groups.

References: Degenhardt, Mary, and Judith Kirsch. *Girl Scout Collector's Guide.* Lombard, IL: Wallace-Homestead, 1987; Girl Guides of Canada-Guides du Canada. n.d. http://www.girlguides.ca; Girl Scouts of the USA. n.d. http://www.girlscouts.org; Green, Rayna. "The Tribe Called Wannabe: Playing Indian in America and Europe." *Folklore* 99 (1988): 30–55; Groth, Susan and Charles Tuft. "'Here We Sit Like Birds in the Wilderness Waiting for Our Dessert': The Girl Scout Program and Ordering Space in Camp Sacajawea's Dining Hall/Main House." *Children's Folklore Review*, vol. 19, no. 2 (Spring 1997): 3–30; ———. *Scouts' Own: Creativity, Tradition, and Empowerment in Girl Scout Ceremonies.* PhD diss., University of Pennsylvania, 1999; MacFarquhar, Neil. "To Muslim Girls, Scouts Offer a Chance to Fit In." *New York Times*, November 28, 2007. http://www.nytimes.com/2007/11/28/us/28girlscout.html?_r=1&oref=slogin (accessed November 28, 2007); Manahan, Nancy, ed. *On My Honor: Lesbians Reflect on their Scouting Experience.* Northboro, MA: Madwoman, 1997; Tedesco, Laureen. "Making a Girl into a Scout: Americanizing Scouting for Girls." In *Delinquents and Debutantes: Twentieth-Century American Girls' Cultures*, ed. Sherrie A. Inness, 19–39. New York: New York University Press, 1998; Tucker, Elizabeth. *Tradition and Creativity in the Storytelling of Pre-Adolescent Girls.* PhD diss., Indiana University, Bloomington, 1977; Wells, Patricia Atkinson. "The Paradox of Functional Dysfunction in a Girl Scout Camp: Implications of Cultural Diversity for Achieving Organizational Goals." In *Inside Organizations: Understanding the Human Dimension*, eds. M. O. Jones, M. D. Moore, and R. C. Snyder, 109–17. Newbury Park, CA: Sage Publications, 1988.

Susan Charles Groth

Girls' Folklore

Girls' folklore includes the accumulated traditions and the inherited and newly invented products and practices of preadolescent and adolescent women. Children's culture in general is rarely taken seriously by adults, and in patriarchal societies, girls' culture suffers the additional stigma of being associated with females. However, its gravity for its young women participants cannot be overstated.

In Anglo American cultures, much of girls' folklore involves sorting and manipulating a hierarchy of insiders and outsiders, popular and unpopular girls. Other traditions are concerned with the girl's future, often circumscribed in domestic and heterosexist terms. Girls' folklore includes such traditions as divination rituals, affirmations (actions and words to reinforce the truth of a statement), friendship rituals, coded messages, secret languages, ordeals, and rhymes.

The structure of girls' rituals and games changes with the social climate of the times. In the eighteenth century, young maidens played ring- or line-singing games as part of the courting process. Girls in Euro North America today play such games primarily for their entertainment value, but some also use them to influence their social standing in girls' society. Rhymes chanted as part of skipping routines to determine the identity of one's true love and the style in which they may live offer a good example. In divination rhymes such as

Jam, jam, apple tart
Tell me the name of my sweetheart/A B C . . .

and

Does he love me?
Yes, no, maybe so.
Will we get married?
Yes, no, maybe so.
Where will we live?
House, church, garbage can.
How many children will we have?
One, two three . . .

The answer is given when the jumper trips on the rope. Players can leave the result to chance, but skilled skippers can trip at the right moment to ensure the desired end, rope turners can pull on the rope so that the skipper ends up living in a garbage can, and so on.

Other rituals divining a girl's future may be practiced alone, are less subject to manipulation, and include those in which buttons, cherry stones, flower petals, or specks on the fingernails are counted to the chant: "He loves me, he loves me not" or "Tinker, tailor, soldier, sailor, rich man, poor man, begger man, thief." For the most part, girls may be unaware of what a tinker or even a begger man might do or be, but the force of tradition behind such games makes their structure quite stable. Another practice involves a long apple peel thrown over the shoulder which, when it lands on the ground, forms the first letter of the future boyfriend's/husband's name. In yet another technique, the diviner writes out the full names of a pair. After crossing out the letters they have in common with each other, she subjects the remaining letters to a sequence of "Love, hate, marry, adore" to find out the future prospects of potential partners.

Divination can involve other issues. A girl places an eyelash on her fingertip; if it blows off onto the ground, the owner's wish will come true. Even involuntary sensations such as tingling or red ears can have meaning, indicating to a young girl that her lover is thinking of her. If she does not know who he is, tradition has it that she can ask the next person she meets for a number, which, by counting through the alphabet will indicate the initial of her admirer.

Pacts between girls involve routines such as swearing eternal friendship by linking fingers of the right hand, shaking them up and down, and chanting, "Make friends, make friends,/Never, never break friends." Girls will often swear eternal friendship, arrange signs and passwords, exchange clothes or jewelry, and appear inseparable. For reasons often inexplicable to adults, however, they may relatively suddenly not even speak to one another. Once the friendship is over, one or both of the parties may apply the chant, "Break friends, break friends,/Never, never make friends."

Affirmations, or reinforcements of the truth, can also be used by girls to manipulate their social relations with one another, and with adults and boys. They include ritually linking fingers, swearing to God, or making crosses on their body to reinforce the seriousness of the declaration.

Recently in the United States, Norway, and the United Kingdom, adolescent girls have used bracelets as a form of coding relating to friendship and sexual activity. These "sex bracelets" (United States) or "shagging bands" (United Kingdom) are made of a jelly-like rubber substance and each color has a special meaning. One code specifies white for friendship, green for a flower, yellow for a hug, pink for a kiss, orange to make out, red to strip, blue for oral sex, and black for sexual intercourse. Someone who manages to break or rip the bracelet off the wearer, in the game known as "Snap," is entitled to the level of intimacy indicated by the color of the bracelet. For some girls, however, these bracelets serve merely as a fashion accessory; they may be unaware of any alternative meaning. Others suggest that the associations are from contemporary legend rather than actual practice. However, conservative schools in the United States have banned the wearing of these bracelets, reconfirming adult fears about adolescent sexuality.

Girls' secret languages have existed for hundreds of years, passed down through the generations. They allow children to communicate within their groups so that outsiders are unable to understand. They appeal to girls because they promote both commonality and exclusivity. The language may involve slang words, technical terms, codes, and signals. Girls' languages include sexual references, such as "love diamond" and "pencil sharpener" for vagina; "paddle the pink canoe" for female masturbation; "hoovering" for an abortion; and "red route" and "Henry" for menstruation.

Among children, if one does something that others disapprove of, that child may be put through an ordeal as punishment. Historically in Britain and North America, boys tended to use such physical ordeals as running the gauntlet, "bumps," "frog marching," and "piling on." These are now increasingly used by girls also, but most popular among them is "the silent treatment" or isolation tactics. "Sending to Coventry" means that other members of the group will not speak to the offender for a specified length of time.

Girls are also the keepers of traditions of playground rhymes and use them in their play activities and social interactions. They are skilled at maintaining traditions of the past and at the same time innovative enough to adapt the rhymes to suit the times. Clever parodies of adult norms and behaviors and issues relating to taboo subjects are explored through the medium of these rhymes. Examples can be seen in the popular Miss Susie handclapping rhyme:

> When Susie was a teenager she went "Ohh ahh, I left my bra in my boyfriend's car."
> When Susie was a mother she went "1, 2, 3, 4 chuck the baby out the door."

See also: Barbie Doll; Best Friend; Coding; Girls' Games; Handclapping Games; Legend, Urban/Contemporary; Rhymes; Riddle; Sexuality; Tradition-Bearer.

References: Abrahams, Roger D. *Jump-Rope Rhymes: A Dictionary.* University of Texas Press, 1969; Factor, June. *Captain Cook Chased a Chook: Children's Folklore in Australia.* Ringwood, NT, Australia: Penguin, 1988; Gaunt, Kyra D. *The Games Black Girls Play: Learning the Ropes from Double-Dutch to Hip-Hop.* New York: New York University Press, 2006; Goodwin, Marjorie Harness. *The Hidden Life of Girls: Games of Stance, Status, and Exclusion.* Blackwell Studies in Discourse and Culture Series. Malden, MA: Wiley-Blackwell, 2006; Online Dictionary of Playground Slang (ODPS). 2001–2003. http://www.odps.org (accessed July 7, 2005); Opie, Iona, and Peter Opie. *The Lore and Language of School Children.* Oxford: Oxford University Press, 1959; Oring, Elliott. "Children's Folklore." In *Folk Groups and Folklore Genres: An Introduction*, ed. Elliott Oring, 91–120. Logan: Utah State University Press, 1986; Sex Bracelets. 2004. http://www.sex-bracelets.com (accessed August 10, 2008); Sutton-Smith, Brian, ed. *Children's Folklore: A Source Book.* Logan: Utah University Press, 1999; Thorne, Barrie. *Gender Play: Boys and Girls in School.* Buckingham: Open University Press, 1993.

Janice Ackerley

Girls' Games

The general category of girls' games covers the period of middle childhood, between the ages of six and twelve years, and includes games that girls play of their own accord, usually out of doors and away from direct supervision by adults. This type of play is owned and controlled by the children themselves—it is spontaneous, unstructured, and mostly unrestricted. Two main categories of girls' games can be identified as those that use equipment and those that are verbal or activity-based.

Ancient grave goods provide evidence that early toys and games—including miniature dishes, furniture, and toy animals—mimicked the activities of adults and date as far back as 5000–4000 BCE. Handclapping games and skipping games using vines are depicted on Egyptian tombs dating to 1600 BCE. A North American game originating in Africa involves girls flicking stones from a pit in the ground, throwing them into the air, and catching them on the backs of their hands; originally played with cattle or sheep bones, this traditional game is today known as "knuckle bones" or "jacks" and is played with a small rubber ball and plastic or metal "stars". A sixteenth-century painting by Pieter Bruegel shows some 200 children playing eighty children's games, many of which are still played today: in it, girls are playing dolls, knuckle bones, odds and evens, blind man's bluff, "shops," dressing up, and follow the leader.

In the nineteenth century, folklorist Alice B. Gomme recognized two distinct divisions of children's traditional games: dramatic games (for girls) and competitive games (for boys). She attributed this gender division to the verbal ability of girls because their games tend to include singing and dancing. Divination in the form of line- or circle-singing games is probably related to courtship and marriage rituals, and is described by Sutton-Smith as played by very young girls (McMahon and Sutton-Smith: 294). These static games largely disappeared in the twentieth century, replaced by exercise games including skipping, handclapping, and ball-bouncing. However, remnants of the rhymes of early singing games survive in "the Susie saga," a clapping rhyme that traces a woman's life passages from birth to death.

Many of the games of African American girls, often performed in lines or circles, also trace female life passages. Their games reflect other aspects of African and African American culture, in which songs, dances, and a number of ceremonies are performed in lines or circles. These formations enable the positioning of a leader separate from—and yet part of—the group for the traditional call-and-response patterns of many African American songs and games. In some girls' games, there is one leader who gets to be in the spotlight; in other games, especially line games, each of the participants has her turn to be the center of attention as she performs various movements or actions that are dictated by the game or as she chooses to demonstrate her own individuality and creativity. Such games demonstrate flexibility and inclusiveness. If the game is usually performed in two lines, with partners, and someone else wants to join, the girls may change the formation to a circle to accommodate any number of players (Eberein and Hawes).

Despite the absence of physical dividers between the sexes today, self-imposed gender segregation remains current in school playgrounds. Gender-play researcher Barrie Thorne notes that even greater sex integration occurs away from the school playground in home and neighborhood environments. Studies by Elizabeth Grugeon, Barrie Thorne, and others have noted discernable differences (similar to those observed by Gomme) in the play of boys and girls. Girls' play is characterized as more cooperative, with a well-developed communication system and involving physical closeness and intimacy. Girls prefer games in which outcome is less important than process; these are called "on-zero-sum" games (Lindsay and Palmer: 12). This assertion is supported by Norwegian researchers who, having asked children to categorize their own games, report that girls identified marbles as a ball game, whereas the boys classified it as a war game (Roberts and Enerstvedt: 5–28).

There is a perception that children today have lost the art of playing the traditional games of the playground and street. The blame for this loss is divided between child-safety issues, which have resulted in a "bubble-wrapped" generation, and the ever-increasing lure of technology, which takes children away from the social networks of the past. But has the computer age driven children indoors and into largely solitary pursuits in front of a screen? Carole Carpenter (173) notes that girls have largely resisted the lure of the electronic and are increasingly the keepers of traditional games.

Girls' games such as hopscotch, skipping, handclapping, jacks, and elastic and string games are examples of inherited and adapted, centuries-old, global games. Hopscotch demands complex skills of hopping, aiming, and kicking the marker from square to square, balancing, following a sequence, and playing within defined boundaries. Skipping games involve complicated routines and moves for any number of players, often accompanied by chants. Likewise, handclapping games are largely the property of girls and involve complex moves, rhythms, and chants. Jacks or knuckle bones requires skill and dexterity in throwing and catching, as well as perseverance and negotiation skills. String games involve complex finger and hand movements to produce intricate patterns. Elastics are a form of skipping that involves elastic bands being stretched between the ankles and accompanied by intricate feet moves and chants. These games are played almost exclusively by girls, although occasionally boys may step across the gender divide. *See also:* Girls' Folklore; Handclapping Games; Jump-Rope Rhymes; Rhymes; Tradition-Bearer.

References: Carpenter, Carole H. "'Our dreams in action': Spirituality and Children's Play Today." In *Play Today in the Primary School Playground*, eds. Julia C. Bishop and Mavis Curtis, 167–179. National Centre for English Cultural Tradition: University of Sheffield, England, 2001; Eberein, Bob, and Bess Lomax Hawes. *Pizza Pizza Daddy-O*. Anthropology Department, San Fernando Valley State College, Distributed by Media Generation. 1968. http://www.folkstreams.net/film,73 (accessed December 2, 2007); Gomme, Alice B. *The Traditional Games of England, Scotland and Ireland*. Reprint edition. Spectacular Victorian Scholarship Series. New York: Dover Books, 1964 [1894–98]; Goodwin, Marjorie Harness. *The Hidden Life of Girls: Games of Stance, Status, and Exclusion* (Blackwell Studies in Discourse and Culture Series). Malden, MA: Wiley-Blackwell, 2006; Grugeon, Elizabeth. "Gender Implications of Children's Playground Culture." *Gender and Ethnicity in Schools*, eds. Peter Woods and Martyn Hammersley, 13–35. London: Routledge, 1993; Lindsay, Peter L., and Denise Palmer. *Playground Game Characteristics of Brisbane Primary School Children*. Canberra: Australian Government Publishing Service, 1981; McMahon, Felicia R., and Brian Sutton-Smith. "The Past in the Present: Theoretical Directions for Children's Folklore." In *Children's Folklore: A Source Book*, 293–308. London: Routledge, 1999; Roberts, J. M., and A. Enerstvedt. "Categorisations of Play Activities by Norwegian Children." In *Cultural Dimensions of Play, Games, and Sport*, ed. B. Mergen, 5–28. Association for the Anthropological Study of Play Series, vol. 10. Champaign, IL: Human Kinetics Publishers, 1986; Sutton-Smith, Brian, ed. *Children's Folklore: A Source Book*. Logan: Utah University Press, 1999; Thorne, Barrie. *Gender Play: Boys and Girls in School*. Buckingham, UK: Open University Press, 1993.

Janice Ackerley

Glass Ceiling

"Glass ceiling" is a term familiar to women in a variety of professions. It has been used to describe barriers to advancement for scientists, engineers, ministers, politicians, university professors, body builders, and most often, women in corporations, not only in North America but around the world. Coined in 1986, "glass ceiling" refers to the invisible but real barrier to advancement and promotion.

Although hundreds of women have described these barriers to a variety of researchers, including members of a bipartisan U.S. commission in 1995, few actual narratives about the phenomenon have been recorded. Most accounts are summarized in books, articles, and blogs on the Internet, in which respondents rarely use the term "glass ceiling." Adjectives have been added since 1986, such as "stained glass ceiling" to refer to the problems women have advancing as religious leaders; "bottomless pits" in reference to the problems that poor women have; and "marble ceiling" to refer to the fact that there has still not been a woman elected president in the United States. The term has also been employed in recent years to describe barriers to people of Color, for men as well as women.

Sue Hayward, the author of *Women Leading*, argues that while the glass ceiling may be a myth for men, for many women it is a source of real pain; it can potentially represent the end of a woman's career unless she can find a way to break through it. Lisa Belkin, writing for the *New York Times* in late 2007, offers this advice to professional women if they wish to break through the glass ceiling: "Don't get angry. But do take charge. Be nice. But not too nice. Speak up. But don't seem like you talk too much. Never, ever dress sexy." It is highly unlikely that a business writer will ever offer the same advice to professional men.

Some fields have designed training programs to retain women. For example, the Society of Women Engineers created a training video in 1997 to facilitate discussions about gender discrimination against women in engineering. Their work apparently met with some success; Jim Morgan and Denise Martinez's study of engineers in 1998 found virtually no disparity between the earnings of men and women who had entered the field most recently.

A few concerted attempts have been made to address occupational barriers for women in North America, including EMILY's List (Early Money Is Like Yeast), which focuses on raising campaign money for women running for elective office. The White House Project, initiated in 1998, seeks to advance women's leadership in all communities and sectors, including the office of the president. Some women have attained high political offices, and many Americans expect to see a woman president in the near future. But for women in corporate North America, results have been slower in coming.

Glass-ceiling stories remain to be collected as a genre, perhaps because of a sense that many folklorists and ethnographers have that the "ceiling" is actually a luxury for Euro North American women. Susan Hayward notes that "Banging your head against the glass ceiling would probably be welcome in some cultures where women have yet to even get a foot on the first rung of the career ladder" (151). Nonetheless, professional advancement or lack of it remains an important part of women's narratives about themselves and about their gender. *See also:* Gender; Personal-Experience Narrative; Wage Work; Women's Work.

References: Albelda, Randy, and Chris Tilly. *Glass Ceilings and Bottomless Pits: Women's Work, Women's Poverty*. Leicester, UK: LPC Group Capstone Ltd., 1997; Belkin, Lisa. "The Feminine Critique." *New York Times*, November 11, 2007. http://www.nytimes.com/2007/11/01/fashion/01WORK.html?ex=1194580800&en=91feaf95fabced83&ei=5070 (accessed December 30, 2007); Brown, Carolyn M. "Advancing African American Women in the Workplace: new study finds challenges remain despite push for diversity." *Black Enterprise*, June 2004. http://findarticles.com/p/articles/mi_m1365/is_11_34/ai_n6168973 (accessed December 30, 2007); Hayward, Sue. *Women Leading*. New York: Palgrave Macmillan, 2004; Lee, Billi. "The Glass Ceiling is also a Comfort Ceiling: Discrimination against Women and Minorities in Business." *San Diego Business Journal*, vol. 15, no. 24 (June 13, 1994): 23; Morgan, Jim, and Denise Martinez. "Focusing Freshman: Engineering and Design on Women and Technology." Presented at the Women in Engineering Program Advocates Network Annual Conference, Washington, DC, June 2000;

Society of Women Engineers. http://www.swe.org/stellent/idcplg?IdcService=SS_GET_
PAGE&nodeId=5 (accessed December 30, 2007); White House Project, The. http://
www.thewhitehouseproject.org/about/mission (accessed December 30, 2007); Wilson,
Marie C. *Closing the Leadership Gap: Why Women Can and Must Help Run the World*.
New York and London: Penguin Group, 2004.

Susan Eleuterio

Goddess Worship

Goddess worship refers generally to beliefs and rituals associated with
female deities, but herein especially to the feminist theologies and practices of various late-twentieth-century Goddess-centered movements and
spiritualities. Anthropology and feminist theology contributed significantly
to re-visioning worship of the Goddess, sometimes called the Great or
Mother Goddess. Alternative, interrelated spiritualities with Goddess dimensions that developed during the late 1960s and the 1970s include Feminist
Spirituality, Neo-Paganism, Dianic Wicca, Women's Spirituality, and Goddess
Reverence.

Nineteenth-century cultural evolutionists proposed stages for all human
societies' development from "savagery" to "barbarism" to "civilization," with
earlier "social conditions" still evident as "survivals" in later, more complex
societies. In *Mother Right: An Investigation of the Religious and Juridical
Character of Matriarchy in the Ancient World* (1861), Swiss jurist Johann
Jakob Bachofen argued for the primacy of the mother and a matriarchal family in unevolved, "savage" societies and their latter-day "survivals." Fifty years
later, in *The Golden Bough: A Study in Comparative Religion* (1890; 12–
volume edition, 1911–1915), British anthropologist Sir James George Frazer
explored the roots of patriarchal religions in matriarchy and Goddess worship, giving primacy to fertility rites involving a mother-goddess and her
periodically sacrificed "sacred king" son-consort.

Contemporary cultural evolutionism in Goddess-worship paradigms views
the earlier stages of culture as a universal "golden age" rather than a phase
of "savagery." The establishment of patriarchy and the patriarchal worship
of male and female deities spells its downfall, but "survivals" of the earlier
culture remain in both historical and contemporary societies. They form
the basis for reconstructing and revitalizing a women-centered, original, or
"ur" culture (Juliette Wood in Billington and Green 1996).

Archaeological evidence for prehistoric Goddess worship comes primarily
from the European Upper Paleolithic and Neolithic periods (ca. 40,000 to
5,000 years ago). In works like *The Language of the Goddess: Unearthing
the Hidden Symbols of Western Civilization* (1989), Lithuanian archaeolo-
gist and folklorist Marija Gimbutas delineates "Women and Culture in God-
dess-Oriented Old Europe" (Gimbutas in Plaskow and Christ 1989; also in
Spretnak 1982). She proposes that before major incursions by male-centered,
Indo-European steppe (Kurgan) pastoralists, who were "mobile, warlike,
ideologically sky oriented, and indifferent to art," the female-centered, pre-
Indo-European civilization of Old Europe was "sedentary, peaceful, art-loving,
earth- and sea-bound."

Upper Paleolithic and Neolithic female clay figurines are key to the archaeological evidence interpreted by Gimbutas and others influenced by her work, for example, American feminist scholars Merlin Stone (1976), Riane Eisler (1987), and Elinor W. Gaddon (1989). American feminist archaeologists Ruth E. Tringham and Margaret W. Conkey (in Goodison and Morris 1998) have reassessed these two sets of figures: the former found in archaeological sites from France in southwestern Europe east into Siberia, especially those from 26,000 to 10,000 years ago; the latter in sites from the circum-Mediterranean and southeastern Europe around 7000–3500 BCE. They argue that both androcentric (centered on men) and gynocentric (centered on women) interpretations of these figurines are in error because they are circumscribed by contemporary gender ideologies and a too-narrow association of the female with fertility and reproduction. The archaeological, historical, and social context of all such figurines (female, male, and animal) must be analyzed for variability before assigning the supposedly female ones to a single homogenous group as fertility symbols and/or representations of the Goddess used in ritual and worship.

Ethnographic and ethnohistorical evidence for contemporary and historical matriarchal societies is likewise in need of careful contextual assessment. American feminist women and religion scholar Cynthia Eller (2000) reviews that literature for four areas of variability in "other societies, early societies": ideas about reproduction and systems of kinship; what Goddess worship indicates about women's social standing; the economic status of women and their work, particularly in agriculture versus hunting; and the presence of interpersonal violence or peacefulness. She concludes that there is no sound evidence for either prehistoric matriarchies or an invasive patriarchal revolution. Eller also observes the ethnocentrism in the notion of Old European origins, noting Latinas', Native Americans', and African Americans' search for non-European matriarchal prehistory and choosing among her examples texts from two important collections on feminist spirituality (Spretnak 1982; Plaskow and Christ 1989).

American feminist theologians (or thealogians, as they call themselves) Carol P. Christ and Judith Plaskow began their collaboration while both were activist students in Yale University's graduate program in Religious Studies and first edited *Womanspirit Rising*, a collection of contemporary feminist thinking on revisioning religion and its critique "to speak to the experiences of women" (Christ and Plaskow 1979). Among the founders of the Women and Religion Section of the American Academy of Religion, they dedicate *Weaving the Visions*, their "sequel" collection of reconstructive feminist approaches to religion in North America (Plaskow and Christ 1989), to that organization's women members. Contributors to the second collection include Black American feminist theologian Delores S. Williams, who traces the emergence of Womanist Theology among African American Christian "women in church and society [who] have appropriated it as a way of affirming themselves as Black while simultaneously owning their connection with feminism and with the Afro-American community, male and female."

By 1989, Plaskow had "committed herself to the transformation of Judaism," while Christ had resigned a tenured position and moved to Lesbos,

Greece, where she now directs the Ariadne Institute for the Study of Myth and Ritual and offers Goddess pilgrimages to Crete. Widely known for her keynote address, "Why Women Need the Goddess" (in Christ and Plaskow 1979 and Spretnak 1982), at the spring 1978 University of California at Santa Cruz conference on "The Great Goddess Re-Emerging," she has since written about her own and others' transition from Christianity to Goddess and nature spirituality (for example, Christ 1997, 2003).

Feminist Spirituality has roots in the second-wave radical feminism of the late 1960s and early 1970s that grew out of the civil rights movement and anti-war activism. During these countercultural movements, formal religious traditions came to be viewed as oppressive and dogmatic social structures that hinder primary, expressive, and direct relationships to divinity. Like many other diverse spiritualities, Feminist Spirituality has "no official sacred texts, no absolute leaders, no required affirmations of faith, no membership dues, and no undisputed agenda of beliefs and rituals ... [but] encourages and accepts as valid and legitimate the inspirations, dreams, visions, experiences, and interpretations of individual women ... [with] the theological and ritual focus ... the celebration of womanhood" (Sered 1994).

Cynthia Eller (1997; in Griffin 2000) identifies two aspects of secular feminism important to the development of Feminist Spirituality: lesbian feminism and consciousness-raising (CR) groups. The lesbian feminist community, including many separatists, strongly supported *WomanSpirit*, a quarterly magazine edited by partners Jean and Ruth Mountaingrove and published between 1974 and 1984 by a collective in southern Oregon. Considered the first magazine of feminist spirituality, it provided an international forum for women choosing new spiritual identities for themselves and expressing their understandings of the Goddess. Between 1976 and 1983, the Lady Unique Collective in New Brunswick, New Jersey, published six "cycles" (issues) of *Lady-Unique-Inclination-of-the-Night*, edited by American lesbian folklorist Kay Turner. The autumn 1976 inaugural collective statement announces Lady-Unique-Inclination-of-the-Night as an American Moon Goddess with Mayan origins, "She who is our most powerful projection of feminine consciousness": "Women have been denied their right to images which define and promote female power and independence. To reclaim images of the feminine, to share them with each other, and especially, to bring them to the world (i.e., to discover and release the political potential of the spiritual) is a serious task which will continue to involve many women."

Many spiritual feminists evolved what Eller calls an "origin myth" for the movement as having developed from the consciousness-raising groups that were a tactic of second-wave feminism to awaken women to their oppression and recruit for the larger, political women's movement. Originally called "rap" or "bitch" sessions and pioneered by the New York Radical Feminists, by 1972, CR groups were being used as an organizing tool by the National Organization for Women (NOW). Following the credo that "the personal is political," group members took turns speaking about the session's topic without interruption or comment from other members. Shared themes in these personal-experience narratives would then be discussed to illuminate common patterns and suggest collective strategies for feminist political action. Such sharing and discussion came to be considered a ritual occasion by those spiritually awakened.

The Goddess's immanence ("here"-ness) as understood in Feminist Spirituality stands in strong contrast to the transcendence (or "out there"-ness) of the divine in the religions of Judaism, Christianity, and Islam. Sered (1994) finds its "clearest declaration" in lines from Black American playwright-poet Ntozake Shange's 1977 choreopoem *for colored girls who have considered suicide when the rainbow is enuf*: "I found God in myself and loved her fiercely" (also in Spretnak 1982). The immanence of divinity plays a major role in the various Neo-Pagan spiritualities that developed contemporaneously with Feminist Spirituality. For the most part, polytheistic nature religions almost all have elements of Goddess and/or Goddess worship, and none of them worship only male god(s).

Among these is the Church of All Worlds (CAW), which originated in 1961–1962 among Missouri college friends, notably Lance Christie and Tim Zell, and was chartered in March 1968. Taken from Robert A. Heinlein's science fiction novel *Stranger in a Strange Land* (1961), whose hero was born to Earthparents on Mars, reared by aliens, and returned to Earth as an alien with an understanding of the universe, he gave this name to the religion of paradisical communities he founded. Zell is credited with evolving the "central myth" of CAW, "writing about the planet Earth as deity, as a single living organism" from an "eco-religious" perspective (Adler 1986). His first article on this, "Theogenesis [subsequently changed to Theagenesis]: The Birth of the Goddess," was published in the July 1971 issue of *Green Egg: A Journal of the Awakening Earth*, the group's official publication which served as a primary communication between Neo-Pagan groups. Zell points to Paleo-Pagans "veneration of an Earth-Mother Goddess" and calls the planet "a real living Being" with "a Soul-Essence which we can perceive." Like every cell in the human body, "every living plant and creature" shares "the essence of the Whole of Mother Earth [and] to each we can rightly say, 'Thou Art Goddess.'" In re-visioning and celebrating this understanding, CAW members embraced a "cosmic purpose of Neo-Paganism": "to work for [awareness] by supporting all ecologically oriented movements, establishing alternative communities, demonstrating alternate possibilities for survival on the planet, and, ultimately, awakening Gaea, the Goddess, the planetary mind" (Adler 1986).

Dianic Wicca was influenced by British Egyptologist and folklorist Margaret A. Murray, whose first book, *The Witch-Cult in Western Europe* (1921), identified Witchcraft as "the ancient religion of Western Europe," a pre-Christian fertility cult with annual great festivals or sabbats and regular, general meetings of covens or esbats led by Diana, the feminine aspect of a central deity that manifested in female, male, and animal forms. In the United States, where it developed during the 1960s and 1970s, Dianic Wicca has two main groupings. Covens following the Dianic Covenstead of priestess Morgan McFarland in Dallas do not exclude men from their worship of the Goddess, who is seen in three aspects: Maiden-Creatrix, Great Mother, and Old Crone. Covens in the Dianic tradition of high priestess Z. Budapest, who founded the Susan B. Anthony Coven Number One of Los

Angeles in 1971, generally exclude men from their feminist Craft or "wimmin's religion."

Hungarian-born, lesbian-feminist Z. (Zsuzsanna Emese) Budapest's coven's first manifesto states the belief that "to fight and win a revolution" there must be "reliable ways to replenish our energies," and "without a secure grounding in women's spiritual strength there will be no victory" (Adler 1986). In 1974, Budapest and others started The Feminist Wicca: A Matriarchal Spiritual Center selling various Craft-related items in Venice, California. Heir to a Witchcraft tradition through her mother, Masika Szilagyi, Budapest also draws on Hungarian folklore in her feminist Craft books, including *The Holy Book of Women's Mysteries: Feminist Witchcraft, Goddess Rituals, Spellcasting and Other Womanly Arts* (1989).

In the 1970s, bisexual feminist Witch and political activist Starhawk (Miriam Simos) founded two covens in San Francisco and was a founding member of Reclaiming: A Center for Feminist Spirituality and Counseling there. In *The Spiral Dance: A Rebirth of the Ancient Religion of the Great Goddess* (1979), Starhawk dates her non-separatist covens' affiliation to the faery tradition of Stone Age Britain preserved by Goddess peoples uprooted by Warrior God peoples and now adapted to contemporary society. Eller (in Griffin 2000) calls her "a translator and mediator between feminism and Neo-Paganism" who has "evolved away" from gender polarity, "developed convincing thealogical justifications for conceiving of the Goddess as both monotheistic and polytheistic," and "carved out a central, indisputable place for women without excluding men."

Both Z. Budapest and Starhawk are also associated with Women's Spirituality and Goddess Reverence. The former is "a spiritual as well as psychological and political movement emerging in the 1970s and continuing into the 1990s ... [which], while embracing numerous spiritual traditions, focuses on the role assumed by the Divine Feminine in these traditions ... [with] special attention ... to the roles women play within these traditions." Women's Spiritualists practice healing, divination, and magic, "all associated in the popular psyche with wisewomen or witches," and are generally inclusive of lesbian, bisexual, and transgendered individuals (Conner et al. 1997). In *The Women's Spirituality Book* (1987), Wiccan priestess, healer, and activist Diane Stein calls it "a celebration of the lives, lifestyles and values of women, women's participation in the cycles of the Earth and the universe, and women's working toward a better world."

Goddess Reverence acknowledges Budapest, who played a central role in the annual International Goddess Festival sponsored by the organization Goddess 2000, and Starhawk, a licensed minister of the legally recognized church Covenant of the Goddess, as "mothers" of the contemporary movement. In *The Heart of the Goddess: Art, Myth and Meditations of the World's Sacred Feminine* (1990), lesbian "pantheist and pansexual" priestess of Wicca Hallie Iglehart Austen emphasizes Goddess Reverence's search for and celebration of a "unity and wholeness" which is "the birthright and potential of every human being. All of us, all of existence, are the Divine. In order to complete this whole by bringing back that which has been denied, I name the Divine the Goddess." According to Gay Spirituality writers and teachers Randy Conner and David Sparks and their lesbian actor-writer daughter Mariya Sparks (1997): "Creativity expressed in visual art, music, literature, and other art forms plays as important a role as—indeed, perhaps more important than—theology in contemporary Goddess Reverence.... One of the most beautiful contemporary hymns to the Goddess, in which the deity is identified with the Earth, is lesbian writer Susan Griffin's ... 'This Earth' [in Griffin 1978], which includes the words: 'I have known her all my life, yet she reveals stories to me, and these stories are revelations and I am transformed ... This Earth is my sister ... how we admire this strength in each other ... we are stunned by this beauty, and I do not forget what she is to me, what I am to her.'" *See also:* Consciousness Raising; Maiden, Mother, and Crone; Matriarchy; Mother Earth; Personal-Experience Narrative; Ritual; Wicca and Neo-Paganism; Witchcraft, Historical.

References: Adler, Margot. *Drawing Down the Moon: Witches, Druids, Goddess-Worshippers, and Other Pagans in America Today.* Second edition. Boston: Beacon Press, 1986; Ann, Martha and Dorothy Meyers Imel. *Goddesses in World Mythology: A Biographical Dictionary.* New York: Oxford University Press, 1993; Baring, Anne, and Jules Cashford. *The Myth of the Goddess: Evolution of an Image.* London and New York: Penguin Arkana Books, 1991; Benard, Elisabeth, and Beverly Moon, eds. *Goddesses Who Rule.* New York: Oxford University Press, 2000; Billington, Sandra, and Miranda Green, eds. *The Concept of the Goddess.* London and New York: Routledge, 1996; Campbell, Joseph, and Charles Musès, eds. *In All Her Names: Explanations of the Feminine in Divinity.* San Francisco: HarperSanFrancisco, 1991; Christ, Carol P. *Rebirth of the Goddess: Finding Meaning in Feminist Spirituality.* Reading, MA: Addison-Wesley, 1997; ———. *She Who Changes: Re-imagining the Divine in the World.* New York: Palgrave Macmillan, 2003; Christ, Carol P., and Judith Plaskow, eds. *Womanspirit Rising: A Feminist Reader in Religion.* San Francisco: Harper & Row, 1979; Conner, Randy P., David Hatfield Sparks, and Mariya Sparks, eds. *Cassell's Encyclopedia of Queer Myth, Symbol, and Spirit: Gay, Lesbian, Bisexual, and Transgender Lore.* London: Cassell, 1997; Eisler, Riane. *The Chalice and the Blade: Our History, Our Future.* San Francisco: Harper & Row, 1987; Eller, Cynthia. *Living in the Lap of the Goddess: The Feminist Spirituality Movement in America.* New York: Crossroad, 1993; ———. *The Myth of Matriarchal Prehistory: Why an Invented Past Won't Give Women a Future.* Boston: Beacon Press, 2000; Gadon, Elinor W. *The Once and Future Goddess: A Symbol for Our Time.* San Francisco: Harper & Row, 1989; Goodison, Lucy, and Christine Morris, eds. *Ancient Goddesses: The Myths and the Evidence.* Madison: University of Wisconsin Press, 1998; Griffin, Susan. *Woman and Nature: The Roaring Inside Her.* New York and San Francisco: HarperCollins, 1978; Griffin, Wendy, ed. *Daughters of the Goddess: Studies of Healing, Identity, and Empowerment.* Walnut Creek, CA: AltaMira Press, 2000; Leeming, David, and Jake Page. *Goddess: Myths of the Female Divine.* New York and Oxford: Oxford University Press, 1994; Marler, Joan, ed. *From the Realm of the Ancestors: An Anthology in Honor of Marija Gimbutas.* Manchester, CT: Knowledge, Ideas, & Trends, 1997; Motz, Lotte. *The Faces of the Goddess.* New York: Oxford University Press, 1997; Plaskow, Judith, and Carol P. Christ, eds. *Weaving the Visions: New Patterns in Feminist Spirituality.* San Francisco: Harper & Row, 1989; Sered, Susan Starr. *Priestess, Mother, Sacred Sister: Religions Dominated by Women.* New York: Oxford University Press, 1994; Spretnak, Charlene, ed. *The Politics of Women's Spirituality: Essays on the Rise of Spiritual Power Within the Feminist Movement.* Garden City, NY: Anchor Press/Doubleday, 1982; Stone, Merlin. *When God Was A Woman.* New York and London: Harcourt Brace Jovanovich, 1976; Walker, Barbara G. *Women's Rituals: A Sourcebook.* San Francisco: Harper & Row, 1990.

Marta Weigle

Gossip

Originally, gossip referred to the valued, ritually established relationship between *godsibbs* or godparents, but became a generally derogatory designation for ostensibly confidential, moralistic, and speculative talk about persons not present and those who engage in such talk, often associated with women's speech. Middle English usage expanded the Old English *godsiblingship* (a christening was a *gossiping*) to include friends and acquaintances of either sex, especially women in attendance during childbirth. The *Oxford English Dictionary* notes the first gendered definition in 1566: "A person, mostly a woman, of light and trifling character, esp. one who delights in idle talk; a newsmonger, a tattler." Eighteenth-century British lexicographer Samuel Johnson offered three definitions: godparent, a "tippling-companion," and "one who runs about tattling like women at a lying-in" (Spacks 1985). By 1811, gossip as conversation was viewed ambivalently as "idle talk; trifling or groundless rumour; tittle-tattle. Also, in a more favorable sense: Easy, unrestrained talk or writing, esp. about persons or social incidents" (*OED*). Ethnographic studies focus on gossip's informal, usually covert but powerful informational, moralistic, and aesthetic meanings for communities and groups. Sociolinguists have considered it an important aspect of women's talk with each other and a characteristic woman's speaking style in cross-sex talk.

The gossip narrates informal, private, and particular cultures that both challenge and confirm dominant and public group cultures. Many traditional healing systems recognize the gossip as both witch and healer who uses covert and intimate knowledge to disrupt or restore well-being. Into the 1600s, Catholic Church officials denounced women gossips talking together during Mass or "tattling" in all-women groups domestically and at public gathering-places, enjoining them to guard or silence their speech. In Western medicine, midwives and other women gossips attendant during childbirth came to be decried and marginalized by male medical (often surgical) specialists who assumed authority over the birth event.

Because gossip as a form of talk is so discreet, personally/situationally specific, and sometimes potentially harmful if publicized, there are few field studies of its strategic and artful performance. For the most part, it is mentioned in passing and in general. Thus, neither the arts and varieties of gossip by whatever participants nor its universality and/or varying roles in group life can yet be assessed.

Some sociolinguists studying gender differences in language use have considered gossiping an important aspect of women's talk with other women who are not strangers, especially those identified as friends. Using empirical and anecdotal evidence primarily from heterosexual, middle-class American whites, influential sociolinguist Deborah Tannen (1990) has proposed gendered conversational styles—women's "private speaking" rapport-talk (including gossip) and men's "public speaking" report-talk—that complicate cross-sex communication because "women speak and hear a language of connection and intimacy, while men speak and hear a language of status and independence." Others have looked at women's and men's gossip as variant genres of speech. All need a greater range of data from people of differing cultures, race, ethnicity, class, age, and sexual identity before venturing more on the significance and art of women's gossip. *See also:* Best Friend; Midwifery; Old Wives' Tales; Personal-Experience Narrative; Rumor; Scandal; Women's Friendship Groups.

References: Bergmann, Jörg R. *Discreet Indiscretions: The Social Organization of Gossip.* Trans. John Bednarz, Jr., with Eva Kafka Barron. New York: Aldine de Gruyter, 1993; Dunbar, Robin. *Grooming, Gossip, and the Evolution of Language.* Cambridge, MA: Harvard University Press, 1996; Goodwin, Marjorie Harness. *The Hidden Life of Girls: Games of Stance, Status, and Exclusion* (Blackwell Studies in Discourse and Culture Series). Malden, MA: Wiley-Blackwell, 2006; Spacks, Patricia Meyer. *Gossip.* New York: Alfred Knopf, 1985; Tannen, Deborah. *You Just Don't Understand: Women and Men in Conversation.* New York: William Morrow, 1990; Walls, Jeannette. *Dish: The Inside Story on the World of Gossip.* New York: Avon Books, 2000.

Marta Weigle

Graffiti

Writings, drawings, or markings on the walls of buildings are graffiti; a single such mark is a *graffito.* Graffiti is probably as old as handwriting; there are examples from Pompeii and ancient Rome and from early medieval Russia. Four compilations of graffiti were published in England in the 1730s under the title *The Merry-Thought: or, the Glass-Window and Bog-House Miscellany.* The compiler, under the wonderfully contrived pseudonym Hurlo Thrumbo, includes a few items noted as written "in a Woman's Hand." One example, dated February 18, 1725, is "From a Tavern in Fleet-Street":

> Since cruel Fate has robb'd me of the Youth,
> For whom my Heart had hoarded all its Truth,
> I'll never love more, despairing e'er to find,
> Such Constancy and Truth amongst Mankind [*sic*]. (Part II, 12)

Graffiti is usually anonymous, although coded names that identify a "tagger" or "writer" (graffiti artist) may actually constitute the art itself in the work of some contemporary spray-painters who decorate subways, buses, and other public places in blighted urban areas. Women, including "Barbara 62," "Poonie 1," and "Suki," were among the most notorious taggers in New York City in the 1970s (@149st). Since then, the controversial art form is practiced predominantly by men.

Much of the debate surrounding graffiti asks whether it should be considered art or vandalism, but a more interesting approach looks at graffiti as communication. Jane Gadsby has developed a taxonomy of six different types of graffiti, which perform different functions for the writer, whether male or female. Gadsby's classification consists of latrinalia, public, folk epigraphy, historical, tags, and humorous (2005: 2).

What are "women who write on walls" trying to say? Women write both public and private graffiti, and, most typically, their private communications are written in restrooms ("latrinalia"), where laments for love lost are especially common. Emma Otto's 1990 Brazilian study demonstrated that women's main concerns were personal problems, romance, and morality. Gwenda Beed Davey's study of women's graffiti in Australia in the 1990s identified cries from the heart, dialogue and debate about religion, politics and sexual preference, philosophical pronouncements, and advice to the lovelorn. The biggest single group of graffiti included "pronouncements" about the writer's favorite topic, and, like many of the eighteenth-century items published by Hurlo Thrumbo, some are in rhyme. An ode to a mammogram was found attached to this valuable but hated machine in a women's hospital:

> This machine was made by a man
> Of that there is no doubt;
> I'd like to get his balls in here,
> For months he'd go without.

Today, women's informal written public communications are more likely to address public social issues than private romantic ones. British researcher Jill Posener writes that "the feminist movement, No Nukes campaigners, the anti-smoking lobby and anarchists have all become street writers" (1982: 11). Some of their graffiti consists of simple painted slogans such as "Dead men don't rape," but other examples "reclaim" billboard advertisements with rewritten corporate slogans, often to humorous effect. Posener includes, for example, a photograph of a billboard advertising a sports car with the message, "If it were a lady, it would get its bottom pinched." The graffitist has added in spray paint "If this lady was a car, she'd run you down." *See also:* Activism; Feminisms; Folk Art; Hip-Hop Culture/Rap; Humor.

References: @149st. "Female Writers." 2001, 2003. http://www.at149st.com/women. html (accessed January 14, 2007); Bushnell, John. *Moscow Graffiti: Language and Subculture.* Boston: Unwin Hyman, 1990; Cooper, Martha, and Henry Chalfant. *Subway Art.* London: Thames & Hudson, 1984; Davey, Gwenda Beed. *Women Who Write on Walls.* In paperback from http://www.gwendadavey.com, 2007; Gadsby, Jane. "Looking at Writing on the Wall: A Critical Review and Taxonomy of Graffiti Texts," 1995. http://www.graffiti.org/faq/critical.review.html (accessed January 12, 2007); Otto, Emma. "Graffiti in the 1990s: a study of inscriptions on restroom walls." *Journal of Social Psychology*, vol. 133, no. 4 (1993): 589–590; Posener, Jill. *Spray it Loud.* London: Routledge & Kegan Paul, 1982; ———. *Louder than Words.* London: Pandora, 1986; *The Merry-Thought:* or *the Glass-Window and Bog-House Miscellany.* London, J. Roberts in Warwick Lane, 1731–?. Facsimile edition. The Augustan Reprint Society Publication Number 221–222, William Andrews Clark Memorial Library, University of California Los Angeles, 1983; Young, Karl. "Names: The Basis of Graffiti Art." *Free Graphz.* n.d. http://www.thing.net/~grist/lnd/graffiti/tags.htm (accessed January 14, 2007).

Gwenda Beed Davey

Grandmother

A grandmother is the mother of one's mother or father. The English language distinguishes a grandmother on the mother's side as maternal and on the father's side as paternal. In many North American cultures—particularly in those of First Nations and Pacific Islands peoples and those with origins in sub-Saharan Africa, Asia, and throughout the Mediterranean region—grandmothers are revered. In Euro American cultures, grandmothers are, for the most part, independent of their children and maintain their own households. (Ill or elderly grandmothers dependent upon their children or living in nursing homes or long-term care facilities constitute a significant exception, especially in the United States.) According to the 2000 U.S. Census, an increasing number of grandparents, mostly grandmothers, are living with their grandchildren for five years or longer, the highest proportion of which are among Indigenous Hawaiians and Blacks (Law: 28). In these and other already economically burdened cultural groups, older women have taken it upon themselves to rear another generation of children, many of whom benefit from the experiences of their family's primary tradition-bearers; however, it also means that these women have little time to pursue their own interests after their children have left home.

Cultural evaluations of grandmothers are often found in proverbs. Consider, for example, the German saying, "Even the Devil's grandmother was a nice girl when she was young" (Hollister). Grandmothers as specific individuals and as a general category of older women suffer from the negative stereotypes associated with their age group. As women age in societies that overvalue youth as a prerequisite for physical attractiveness in women and selects physical attractiveness as the primary measure of women's value, they are too often seen as no longer worthy of emulation.

Popular images of the grandmother generally take one of two forms. She may be a fussy old woman who likes to meddle in the affairs of the family and control its members. This grandmother may be powerful, but is disliked by her grandchildren and ignored by her children and daughters- and sons-in-law. In folklore, she is usually portrayed as a hag or witch who goes to great lengths to harm young children. Alternatively, the grandmother is the person to whom the entire family enthusiastically rushes for the winter holidays, who listens to everything a grandchild has to say, who gives lots of hugs and kisses, and who always serves the best food. She offers no challenge to anyone in the family or outside it. The grandmother in "Red Riding Hood" is a good example; she is liked and regularly visited by her granddaughter, but is a quintessential victim, eaten by a wolf and rescued, if at all, by a young, powerful male.

Grandmothers themselves are currently working to rehabilitate their reputation. At a Women's Institute meeting in Brampton, Ontario, Canada, in the early 1980s, one member read a poem about contemporary grandmothers who no longer "rock and knit/Tat, crochet, and babysit" but instead exercise, tour, take clients to lunch, ski, and curl (Greenhill: 67). In another poem, several versions of which appeared in local Ontario newspapers, "The Modern Grandmother" has vacated the rocking chair, knitting, and tending babies in favor of ceramics, bowling, bingo, dancing, going to college, and writing a book. But grandmothers also act imaginatively upon the world stage. For example, the originally Canadian "Raging Grannies" has chapters in several countries. Their members perform at peace rallies, presenting humorous and serious parodies of popular songs in protest against war. *See also:* Aging; Croning; Elder Care; Folktale; Red Riding Hood.

References: Greenhill, Pauline. *True Poetry: Traditional and Popular Verse in Ontario.* Montreal: McGill-Queen's University Press, 1989; Hollister, Danielle, ed.

"Grandparent Quotations." Bella Online: The Voice of Women. http://www.bellaonline.com/articles/art23662.asp (accessed August 10, 2008); Law, Violet. "No Retirement Home Here." *Colorlines* (Fall 2005): 27–30; Roy, Carole. "The Transformative Power of Creative Dissent: The Raging Grannies' Legacy." *Expanding the Boundaries of Transformative Learning: Essays on Theory and Praxis*, eds. E. V. O'Sullivan, A. Morrell, and M. A. O'Connor, 257–271. New York: St. Martin's Press, 2002.

Cora M. Bradley

Graves and Gravemarkers

A grave is the place where a body is interred after death, usually signifying burial; the traditionally solemn nature of such a location contributes to the adjectival use of the term "grave" to mean serious, gloomy, and of great consequence. Etymologically speaking, the adjective actually comes through the Latin word *gravis*, "heavy, weighty," and the noun through the Old English verb *grafan*, "to dig." Prior to the evolution of the funeral industry in North America in the nineteenth and twentieth centuries, women were often in charge of preparing the body of the family's deceased for burial and/or for the upkeep of the area assigned to the individual or family gravesite. Women also play key roles in the public display of mourning at graveside.

In the Christian Bible, while it was Joseph who prepared the body for burial, it was Mary Magdalene and Mary, the mother of James and Joseph, who sat graveside until the resurrection of Jesus on the third day (Matthew 27–28). In widely diverse cultures—including but not limited to those of Western Asia (the Middle East), the Balkans, Ireland, mainland China, Myanmar (Burma), Sri Lanka, Tibet, Nepal, Micronesia, Muslim Egypt, and in Iran among the Papi tribe—it is traditional for women to demonstrate grief through loud wailing and ululating, self-mutilation by scratching, and/or by taking part in the performance of mourning songs known as laments. In some cases, women hire themselves out as professional mourners to augment their income. On the other hand, in cultures such as those of Muslim Eritrea and Indonesia, women are prohibited from attending burials altogether in acknowledgement of traditional pollution taboos.

Beyond the rites conducted immediately after death, care of the burial site in North America is often performed by women. It is unclear if this is due to the longer lifespan of women in North America in general or to the traditional societal roles prescribed for them. The permanent features of the graveside landscape—the layout of the contemporary "memorial park" and the uniform character of its grave markers—were initially envisioned and implemented by men. Rules governing these sites often detail limits on floral tributes and other objects used for decorating graves. In the past, cleaning and decorating gravesites on "Decoration Day" was practiced widely in the United States, particularly in the Ozarks, in the South, and in the Hawaiian Islands. The creation of perpetual care funds by the funeral industry also contributed to the elimination of the need for the individual upkeep of graves. However, the decoration of graves continues, often to an extent that defies attempts to maintain a landscape that is uniformly flat (intended to minimize the gloomy aspect of earlier cemeteries with their standing headstones, baroque monuments, and family mausoleums).

In the American Southwest, elaborate decorations are commonly brought to gravesides on almost all holidays, both religious and secular. At Christmas in particular, decorating increases significantly; six-foot-tall Christmas trees are not uncommon, calling viewers to notice individual graves and the names of those buried in them. In the Northeast, even the oldest graveyards may contain steel headstones, ornamented with an inset color photograph of the deceased. The increasingly common placement of plastic garden fences and other types of borders around graves serve to further heighten a sense of separation between the anonymity of the collective and specific individuals.

Male-authored histories dealing with graves tend to focus on the more permanent arts of designing gravestones and cemetery landscapes, while fewer deal with the ephemeral aesthetics of grave decorating overseen by women, much in the same way that they tend to privilege architecture over interior design. Challenges to this traditional gendering and subsequent valorization of the use of memorial space are dramatically revealed in Washington, DC's, most visited memorial site, Maya Lin's Vietnam Veterans Memorial Wall, which embodies a "feminine" aesthetic in a traditionally "masculine" form. From the beginning, her design sprang from a desire to focus on the emotional experience of visitors as much as on the nation's war dead. Its highly polished, flat, reflective surface bears witness more to the grief of loved ones—especially after they spend time there—than it does to the more usual glorification of the state and its war efforts in such monuments. While "The Wall" is large and permanent, it is also changeable and unique to each person who sees her or his passing reflection against the deeply etched names on its unyielding black marble surface. The items visitors and mourners have been inspired to leave at the base of the memorial differ in substance and quantity from those at any other American national monument, and are remarkably consistent with the types of items left at individual gravesites—letters, toys, beer cans, Christmas trees, photographs, and other objects imbued with personal meaning. *See also:* Death; Folk Custom; Lament; Rites of Passage; Roadside Crosses.

References: Farrell, James J. *Inventing the American Way of Death, 1830–1920.* Philadelphia: Temple University Press, 1980; Hass, Kristin Ann. *Carried to the Wall: American Memory and the Vietnam Veterans Memorial.* Berkley and Los Angeles: University of California Press, 1998; Matsunami, Kodo. *International Handbook of Funeral Customs.* Westport, CT, and London: Greenwood Press, 1998; Meyer, Richard E., ed. *Cemeteries and Gravemarkers: Voices of American Culture.* Ann Arbor: University of Michigan Research Press, 1989; ———. *Ethnicity and the American Cemetery.* Bowling Green, OH: Bowling Green State University Popular Press, 1993; Mitford, Jessica. *The American Way of Death Revisited.* New York: Alfred A. Knopf, 1998; Mock, Freida Lee, director. *Maya Lin: A Strong Clear Vision.* Distributed by Tapeworm Video, Valencia, CA. 1994; Montell, Lynwood. "Cemetery Decoration Customs in the American South." *The Old Traditional Way of Life: Essays in Honor of Warren E. Roberts,* eds. Robert E. Walls and George H. Shoemaker, 111–29. Bloomington: Trickster Press, 1989; Posey, Sandra Mizumoto. "Grave & Image: Holiday Grave Decorations in a Southern California Memorial Park." *Folklore Forum,* vol. 29, no. 1 (1998): 51–63; Rakhsha, Masoomeh. "Mourning and Weeping Rites Among Papi Tribe, Lorestan." *Kayhan: A Cultural, Scientific, and Art Monthly* 155 (1999): 26–31; Sloane, David Charles. *The Last Great Necessity: Cemeteries in American History.* Baltimore: The Johns Hopkins University Press, 1991.

Sandra Mizumoto Posey

Gullah Women's Folklore

Gullah (also called Geechee) communities can be found on the Sea Islands off the coast of South Carolina, Georgia, and the northeastern tip of Florida. These numerous flat barrier islands—including Edisto, St. Helena, and Hilton Head—range from small uninhabitable islands to some as large as fifty square miles. The Gullah are descended from Africans brought to the Atlantic coast of the United States in the 1700s as enslaved laborers to work on rice, indigo, and cotton plantations. They originated from the rice-cultivating West African coast, including Liberia, Gambia, Sierra Leone, and Senegal; from Central Africa, including Angola; and from Madagascar, which also provided Americans with rice seed for their plantations. The term "Gullah" is thought to be derived either from "Angola" or from the "Gola" community of Liberia.

During the time of slavery, Gullah people farmed the Sea Islands with little interaction with Whites, with the exception of a few overseers. When they were legally freed in 1863, much of the islands' plantation land was distributed relatively evenly among its formerly enslaved inhabitants. The Gullah continued to live in relative isolation on the barrier islands until the region was developed for resorts beginning in the 1950s, whereupon many—as a result of pressure, deception, or not realizing its true market value—sold their land to mainland developers at relatively low prices. The Gullah community has a distinctive culture and language, and retains more connections with its African roots than any other group of Black Americans whose ancestors were enslaved. However, increasingly, members of the Gullah community are moving off the islands or are working at low-wage service jobs in the resort industry.

Gullah culture embodies a distinctive Creole language; a rich expressive and material culture; and a body of knowledge encompassing the medicinal value of roots and herbs, childbirth practices, and ideas about the natural world, for example. The Gullah are known for their basketweaving, which is primarily a women's craft. Baskets using the same spiral designs are found in Senegal and Gambia. Gullah baskets were a ubiquitous part of daily life in coastal South Carolina and Georgia for more than a century (prized, for example, for winnowing rice). Today, Gullah baskets are highly valued home décor and are sold in the resort areas on Route 17. Gullah woman have played an important role in the Gullah economy, partly because of their role in making baskets, which are a significant market commodity.

Josephine Beoku-Betts has studied Gullah women's role in feeding the family. Women share in hunting game and fishing, although to a lesser degree, and women typically fish with a rod and reel and men with net-casting. However, the work associated with preparing meals is done almost exclusively by women. Beoku-Betts argues that while this may be a reflection of women's subordinate position relative to men within the community, meal preparation becomes an important means through which cultural identity is defined collectively as women work together preparing meals. Women's cooking practice, then, is a means of empowerment for both women and the community as a whole. This resonates with Black feminist thought, which recognizes the home as a site of resistance for African Americans.

Gullah culture is not reflected in mainstream society's institutions, and community members themselves carry and transmit their language and traditions. Women have a critical role in this process. Women teach children Gullah history and folkways through storytelling and example because they are the primary caretakers for children. Gullah women tend to have extensive knowledge of the medicinal uses of Sea Island herbs and roots. Women's folkways of cooking, basketweaving, and strip-quilting are often done collectively or taught to children, and this provides a context for building communal bonds, storytelling, and socializing the next generation. Such folklife is a significant site for producing both material and expressive culture. Importantly, it is a means whereby communal values, knowledge, and history are articulated, negotiated, and defined in a social context. When women work together and tell stories to children, the Gullah language is expressed freely and remains a living language.

The critically acclaimed fictional feature film *Daughters of the Dust* (1991), written and directed by Julie Dash, tells the story of the women in a Gullah family in 1902 as they are about to leave the Sea Islands and migrate north. Dash is from New York, but her father was raised in the Sea Islands where she has extended family. The film depicts Gullah culture as distinctive and significant, but not monolithic. The women negotiate between Gullah and mainstream American culture; among traditional West African religions, Islam, and Christianity; between Gullah identity and their relationships with their lovers who are non-Gullah; and between the past and the future as they seek to survive racism, cultural assimilation, and violence. In the film—as in real life—women's identity and Gullah identity are portrayed as complex, diverse, and nuanced. *See also:* Basketmaking; Ethnicity; Family Folklore; Film; Quiltmaking; Race; Storytelling; Tradition-Bearer.

References: Beoku-Betts, Josephine A. "We Got Our Way of Cooking Things: Women, Food and Preservation of Cultural Identity among the Gullah." *Gender and Society*, vol. 9, no. 5 (1995): 535–555; Dash, Julie, with Toni Cade Bambara and bell hooks. *Daughters of the Dust: The Making of an African American Woman's Film*. New York: The New Press, 1992; Jones-Jackson, Patricia. *When Roots Die: Endangered Traditions on the Sea Islands*. Atlanta: University of Georgia Press, 1998.

Jessica Senehi

H

Hair

Hair on the face, head, and body is encoded with cultural and political significance. Every society has traditions about hair's importance, as well as unique fashions, conventions, and rituals for hair care, display, or elimination. Cross-culturally, as a signifier of identity, the stylization of hair demarcates differences between subjects along lines of race and ethnicity, generation, community or subculture, and gender and sexuality. Hair removal or decoration is also symbolic insofar as it is linked to discourses of health, beauty, sexuality, and social status.

Folktales (for example, Rapunzel), legends (such as Lady Godiva), and myths (for example, Medusa) make explicit links between women's hair and female sexual power. For the ancient Greeks, a woman's loose hair was a mark of her fertility and sexuality; however, patriarchal marriage requires fertility only. Perceived as a threat to patrilineal bloodlines, her sexuality could be separated, displaced, or even eliminated, as the myth of Medusa makes clear. After being raped by the god Poseidon, the once-mortal, seductively tousled Gorgon sister suffers the replacement of her hair with hissing snakes, and then, at her encounter with the hero Perseus, she loses her head.

Religious injunctions about women's hair are also common. For example, the Apostle Paul tells the Corinthians that "a woman's hair is her glory," given to her by God as a covering and a veil; the injunction is for her to pin it up or hide it completely, both to dissociate herself from the first-century Christian image of the ecstatic Pagan female and so as not to obscure the glory of men. During the European witch trials, the bodies of women accused of having supernatural powers were publicly shaved and shamed before being tortured and killed by their inquisitors. Today, many patriarchal cultures' religious conventions require women's hair to be covered or shorn to signify modesty (for example, Muslim and Orthodox Jewish).

Social customs of hair removal (including electrolysis, waxing, bleaching, exfoliation, and shaving) have been practiced globally for millennia. Modern regulatory norms in Western culture link feminine beauty to a hairless body. Contemporary North American mass media have normalized the model of the depilated female body and in the process constructed women's body hair and hairy women's bodies as abject, taboo, unsightly, and unhygienic. For men, hair is associated with virility and strength—the ancient Hebrew myth of Samson is the most famous example, but the current proliferation of treatments for male baldness is an unambiguous contemporary sign—thus illustrating the political significance of hair as a marker of differential social status and power.

As a profession, hairstyling and grooming is predominantly a female activity. Historically, the beauty salon has operated as a key site for female entrepreneurship, an opportunity for paid employment, and a place for community networking—particularly for minority women. In twentieth-century North America, trends in hair fashion ranged from the bob in the 1920s, to finger waves in the 1930s, followed by wartime pin curls in the 1940s. Mid-century, the highly structured bouffants and beehives of the 1950s were replaced by the natural look of long hair or Afros for both sexes in the 1960s. Trendsetter Vidal Sassoon's signature chic angular cuts in the 1970s competed with the infamous mullet. In the 1980s, new wave and punk trends in music ushered in gelled, spiky hair; in the 1990s, hip-hop culture popularized shaved, asymmetrical cuts for men and weaves and extensions for women.

Hollywood's influence on hair trends is responsible for the resilient mythos of the "blonde bombshell," perhaps best represented by the born-brunette film star Marilyn Monroe. Since children with light complexions are often born with tow-tresses (flax-colored hair), some argue that the male preference for women with blond hair is aligned with heteropatriarchal fantasies of female infantilization and sexual passivity. The cultural fascination with fair hair also carries persistent and troubling connections to doctrines of Aryan supremacy. *See also:* Aesthetics; Beauty; Cosmetics; Fashion; Feminisms; Folktale; Hip-Hop Culture/Rap; Magazines; Marriage; Mass Media; Popular Culture; Sexism; Sexuality; Women's Work.

References: Banks, Ingrid. *Hair Matters: Beauty, Power, and Black Women's Consciousness.* New York: New York University Press, 2000; Black, Paula. *The Beauty Industry: Gender, Culture, Pleasure.* New York and London: Routledge, 2004; Blackwelder, Julia Kirk. *Styling Jim Crow: African American Beauty Training During Segregation.* College Station: Texas A&M University Press, 2003; Bryer, Robin. *The History of Hair: Fashion and Fantasy Down the Ages.* New York: Philip Wilson, 2003; Carter, Nancy A. General Board of Christian Ministries. "Paul and Corinthian Women's Hairstyles." 2000. http://gbgm-umc.org/umw/corinthians/hairstyles.stm (accessed May 22, 2005); Corson, Richard. *Fashions in Hair: The First Five Thousand Years.* New York: Peter Owen, 2001; Herzig, Rebecca. "Removing Roots." *Technology & Culture*, vol. 40, no. 4 (1999): 723–746; Ilyin, Natalia. *Blonde Like Me: The Roots of the Blonde Myth in Our Culture.* New York: Touchstone, 2000; Myerowitz Levine, Molly. "The Gendered Grammar of Ancient Mediterranean Hair." *Off With Her Head! The Denial of Women's Identities in Myth, Religion, and Culture*, eds. Howard Eilberg-Schwartz and Wendy Doniger, 76–130. Berkeley: University of California Press, 1995; Pitman, Joanna. *On Blondes.* London: Bloomsbury, 2003; Scranton, Philip, ed. *Beauty and Business: Commerce, Gender, and Culture in Modern America.* New York: Routledge, 2000; Toerien, Merran, and Sue Wilkinson. "Gender and Body Hair: Constructing the Feminine Woman." *Women's*

Studies International Forum, vol. 26, no. 4 (2003): 333–344; Weitz, Rose. *Rapunzel's Daughters: What Women's Hair Tells Us About Women's Lives.* New York: Farrar, Straus and Giroux, 2004.

Sidney Eve Matrix

Handclapping Games

Generally performed by girls, handclapping is a playful activity involving face-to-face interaction. It consists of combinations of complex, formalized rhythms, motions, poetry, and song. Handclapping is usually learned informally during the elementary school years. The activity can be performed on the playground, on the bus, or anywhere girls spend time together.

There is little scholarship focusing specifically on handclapping as its own activity. Possibly due to Folklore's historic emphasis on texts rather than on performances, studies of handclapping have focused mainly on the meaning of the words that accompany the claps. Thus, handclaps often are lumped under the more general category of rhymes or songs and collected or studied alongside children's jump-rope rhymes, songs, parodies, counting-out rhymes, and other formalized verbal expressions. Those seeking handclapping texts may wish to consult the numerous historic and contemporary collections of children's rhymes that do exist (Grider 1980; Sutton-Smith 1999). However, these works may not distinguish between handclap texts and other kinds of texts. Tune, rhyme, rhythm, clapping patterns, and participants are generally overlooked. Notable exceptions include Beverly Stoeltje's *Children's Handclaps* (1978); Simon Bronner's *American Children's Folklore* (1988); and Carol Merrill-Mirsky's "Girls' Handclapping Games in Three Los Angeles Schools" (1986). Written as a guide for teachers, Stoeltje's brief book provides handclap texts and variations; musical notation for tunes; notations of rhythms and stresses; and diagrams of clapping patterns. Bronner gives a short photographic essay of a clapping pattern. Merrill-Mirsky provides hand-clapping patterns, tune notations, rhythms, and other items of children's popular culture as evidence to support her analysis of the roles that creativity and tradition play in children's folklore. In addition to these textual sources, Bess Lomax Hawes' 1968 film *Pizza Pizza Daddy-O* is an excellent portrayal of handclapping games performed by African American girls in Los Angeles and is very useful for instructional purposes.

One primary point that has emerged from the study of handclaps, informed by other types of girls' rhymes, is that handclap texts are generally conservative and highly gendered in nature. Scholars point to overarching concerns about domestic responsibilities, boyfriends, sex and pregnancy, motherhood, and a strong emphasis on traditional roles for and attitudes about women. For example:

I wish I had a nickel
I wish I had a dime
I wish I had a boyfriend
To kiss me all the time.

Marilyn Jorgenson (1980), for example, notes that handclap texts model the various gendered roles which girls might experience over the course of a lifetime: infant, schoolgirl, teenager, wife, mother, and grandmother.

Handclapping as a means of shaping gender ideology has been examined from a functional perspective as well. Mary and Herbert Knapp (1976), for example, suggest that handclapping is a way to advertise social relationships, particularly friendships. They also note that the skills required by traditional girls' games such as handclapping require each player to master patterned motions and responses, emphasizing speed, ability, and skill. They point out that in traditional boys' games, players learn to calculate, make judgments, respond to developing situations, and evaluate consequences for the group as a whole. Such differences may have consequences for child development and gender roles.

On the other hand, recent gaming scholarship suggests that girls' play is more complex than previously thought. Rosemary Lévy Zumwalt (1999 [1995]) points out that an analysis of girls' activities must always take into account that girls themselves are much more flexible, dynamic, and complex than are the texts or even the intricate rhythmic patterns they perform. An emphasis on the creative and innovative nature of the performers and their handclapping, alongside the more conservative elements, offers a more balanced perspective. Since few well-developed studies on handclapping are available, the field remains open to further study. *See also:* Coding; Folk Poetry; Gender; Girls' Folklore; Girls' Games; Jump-Rope Rhymes; Rhymes.

References: Bronner, Simon J. *American Children's Folklore: A Book of Rhymes, Games, Jokes, Stories, Secret Languages, Beliefs and Camp Legends for Parents, Grandparents, Teachers, Counselors, and All Adults Who Were Once Children.* Little Rock, AR: August House, Inc., 1988; Grider, Sylvia Ann. "A Select Bibliography of Childlore." *Western Folklore* 39 (1980): 248–65; Jorgensen, Marilyn G. "An Analysis of Boy-Girl Relationships Portrayed in Contemporary Jump Rope and Handclapping Rhymes." *Southwest Folklore,* vol. 4, nos. 3/4 (1980): 63–71; Knapp, Mary, and Herbert Knapp. *One Potato, Two Potato: The Folklore of American Children.* New York & London: W. W. Norton & Company, 1976; Lomax-Hawes, Bess, and Bob Eberlein, directors. *Pizza Pizza Daddy-O.* Black Americana Series. 1968. Distributed on VHS by the Center for Media and Independent Learning at UC Berkeley; Merrill-Mirsky, Carol. "Girls' Handclapping Games in Three Los Angeles Schools." *Yearbook for Traditional Music* 18 (1986): 47–59; Stoeltje, Beverly. *Children's Handclaps: Informal Learning in Play.* Austin, TX: Southwest Educational Development Laboratory, 1978; Sutton-Smith, Brian, Jay Mechling, Thomas W. Johnson, and Felicia R. McMahon, eds. *Children's Folklore: A Sourcebook.* Logan: Utah State University Press, 1999 [1995]; Zumwalt, Rosemary Lévy. "The Complexity of Children's Folklore." In *Children's Folklore: A Sourcebook,* eds. Brian Sutton-Smith, Jay Mechling, Thomas W. Johnson, and Felicia R. McMahon, 23–47. Logan: Utah State University Press, 1999 [1995].

Lisa Gabbert

Helpmate

To be a helpmate to the male of the human species is, according to the second creation story in Genesis (2:7–25, King James Version), the apparent divine purpose of the human female. Eve/woman is created to assist

Adam/man. "And the Lord God said, It is not good that the man should be alone; I will make him an help meet for him" (Gen. 2:18). The inequality inherent in this protorelationship—with the woman in the submissive, subordinate position of helpmate to, indeed an offshoot of, the man—has had a profound effect on gender relations in Western cultures, justifying and rationalizing patriarchal hierarchies, misogynistic ideologies, and the oppression of women and girls.

Attempts to reconcile the first and more egalitarian creation story in Genesis 1:26–28 with the second in Genesis 1 have resulted in stories asserting that the woman with equal status to Adam created in Genesis 1 is not a subservient helpmate. The most famous of these stories concerns Lilith, Adam's vocal and demanding first wife, who, according to some versions, left him in Paradise after refusing to have sexual relations in the missionary position.

The word, "helpmate," itself stems from the Hebrew word, *ezer*, variously translated as "help," "helper," "helpmate," "partner," or "companion." With the rise of second-wave feminism, the term was deconstructed and ultimately reconstructed as empowering by many feminist biblical scholars. Phyllis Trible, among others, asserts that not only does ezer contain no connotations of inferiority, but, to the contrary, since it is a term often used to refer to divine help throughout the Pentatuch/Old Testament, ezer—Eve and women in general—are on par with God, superior beings whose status is tempered only by the clause, "meet for him," meaning suitable for Adam and fitting for a man. So, at the very least, women, it is argued, are complementary equals and mutual partners. While such a redemptive feminist reinterpretation is admirable, it has not necessarily shaken millennia of misogynistic practices.

If being a helpmate is Eve's raison d'être, the question naturally arises, what sort of help does she, as the prototypical woman, provide? Since Eve is the "mother of all living" (Gen. 3:20) and the first couple has been commanded to "be fruitful, and multiply, and replenish the Earth" (Gen. 1:28), presumably the key to a woman's role as helpmate lies in her womb. In the patriarchies of the ancient world and in early Christianity, male writers expressed the belief that the truest companions and best partners are persons of the same sex; in general, heterosexual relations were only necessary to propagate the species. The term "helpmate" may be a reference to the assumption of an inherent male right of access to the "helpful" female body.

Of special interest to folklorists is Beverly Stoeltje's work on the image of frontier women in American society, which identifies three initial roles for women in the West: the "refined lady," the "backwoods belle," and the "bad woman." She discusses these images in relation to their male counterparts: the cowboy, the cattleman-settler, and the bad man. Initially, the refined lady was identified as a model of ideal womanhood. She brought civilization, order, and respectability to a mostly male environment that lacked these qualities. However, she ultimately proved maladaptive to the harsh realities of frontier life. By combining the refined lady's civilizing, institution-building attributes with the strength, courage, and initiative of the backwoods belle, settlers created a new image, the "helpmate" or comrade. Stoeltje's historical work serves as a ground for understanding the contemporary images available to American women. *See also:* Eve; Gender; Lilith; Region: United States.

References: Clines, David J. A. "What does Eve do to Help? And Other Readerly Questions to the Old Testament." *Journal for the Study of the Old Testament*, Supplement Series 94 (1990): 25–48; Collins, John J. *The Bible after Babel: Historical Criticism in a Postmodern Age*. Grand Rapids, MI: W. B. Eerdmans, 2005; Kvam, Kristen E., Linda S. Schearing, and Valerie H. Ziegler, eds. *Eve and Adam*. Bloomington: Indiana University Press, 1999; Stoeltje, Beverly J. "'A Helpmate for Man Indeed': The Image of the Frontier Woman." In *Women and Folklore: Images and Genres*, ed. Claire R. Farrer, 25–41. Prospect Heights, IL: Waveland Press, 1975; Trible, Phyllis. *God and the Rhetoric of Sexuality*. Philadelphia: Fortress Press, 1978.

Jessica Grant Jørgensen

Henna Art/*Mehndi*

Henna body art in North America is practiced among Hindu and Muslim immigrants from South Asia, Western Asia (the Middle East), and North Africa, and by fashionable urbanites with no prior cultural association with it. Henna, or *mehndi* as it is often called, is applied directly to the skin as a paste to create beautiful designs that last for as long as two weeks. The general process includes taking the leaves of the henna plant, which are dried and ground to a fine powder, and then mixed with boiling water and other additives, such as lemon juice, tea, or coffee, and allowing the mixture to sit for several hours. Once sufficiently set, the paste is applied to the skin of the hands and feet with a cone or painted with a toothpick. A mixture of lemon juice and sugar keeps the henna from drying, increasing the potency of the dye. The henna paste's color ranges from dark green to black when on the skin. However, once it dries completely and is scraped off, it leaves a deep reddish-maroon stain.

Henna is used for various ceremonial occasions in many parts of the world, especially among Hindus and Muslims in India, Pakistan, Morocco, Turkey, Tunisia, and Senegal. In India, for example, the hands and feet of a bride are painted in elaborate, lacy designs to commemorate the vital transitional period in a young woman's life. Henna body art marks the woman as a bride, enhancing the beauty of her hands and feet, complementing the gold and silver jewelry on her body, and adding an auspicious quality to the wedding ceremony. The hands and feet are the only parts of the body, other than the face, that are visible; they are decorated with red stain in the shapes of flowers, paisleys, and peacocks, the special bird of lovers. Whereas Indian brides display henna in such pictorial designs, Moroccan women's designs are cleaner, consisting of a series of dots, and Turkish brides often simply cover the entire palm in dye. Both the bride's and the groom's female relatives, as well as the groom himself, may be decorated with henna, although less elaborately.

Henna has become increasingly prevalent in the United States, particularly in large cities, such as New York and Los Angeles. One may get henna applied at fancy body-art boutiques, or in beauty salons owned by people from the Middle East or the Indian subcontinent. These salons are usually located in ethnic enclaves of big cities. Henna paraphernalia, including the powder itself, can be purchased at stores specializing in South Asian or Middle Eastern groceries.

Besides social function and cultural meaning, the other main differences between henna practices in America and henna in the Old World are in the designs, the parts of the body decorated, and the name itself. The designs that appeal to mainstream Americans are similar to tattoo designs, often consisting of a single motif depicting a supposed Celtic or Bornean neo-tribal element, or a word rendered in a foreign script in Japanese and Chinese characters or in the script of Sanskrit. Due to henna's temporary nature, it is often used as a "trial tattoo," an experiment before a permanent commitment has to be made.

In the United States, henna is displayed on the hands and feet, but it is also found on the upper arms, backs, and stomachs—body parts not usually revealed by traditional Hindus and Muslims owing to different notions of beauty and modesty. When designs appear on the hands, they often consist of asymmetrical, vine-like flowers, flowing from the index finger across the back of the hand. This popular American diagonal design motif can now be found in India on the hands of Bollywood movie stars and local brides.

The application of henna is usually referred to as "henna tattoo" in the United States, a tag that has worked its way back from the diaspora to the motherland. Henna stencil decals, found in the Little India section of New York City, can be bought in a variety of shapes obviously catering to westerners, such as Chinese characters, an "Om" written in Sanskrit, or a whale in mock-Northwest coast Native style. The stencils, produced in New Delhi, bear the following label: "Henna Body Tattoo, Building Trust, World Wide."
See also: Aesthetics; Beauty; Body Modification and Adornment; Folk Art; Muslim Women's Folklore; Region: Middle East; Rites of Passage; Wedding.

References: Genini, Izza, director. *For Eye's Delight.* Morocco. Videotape distributed by Ohra: 16 bis, rue Lauriston, 75116, Paris, France, 1997; Kapchan, Deborah. "Moroccan Women's Body Signs." In *Bodylore,* ed. Katharine Young, 3–34. Knoxville: University of Tennessee Press, 1993; Messina, Maria, "Henna Party." *Natural History Magazine,* vol. 97, no. 9 (1988): 40–47; Roome, Loretta. *Mehendi: The Timeless Art of Henna Painting.* New York: St. Martin's Griffin, 1998; Saksena, Jogendra. *Art of Rajasthan: Henna and Floor Decorations.* Delhi: Sundeep Prakashan, 1979; Slymovics, Susan, and Amanda Dargan, directors. *The Painted Bride.* Videotape distributed by Citylore. New York: Queens Council on the Arts, 1990; Untracht, Oppi. *Traditional Jewelry of India.* New York: Harry N. Abrams, Inc. Publishers, 1997.

Pravina Shukla

Herbs

The use of plants to heal the human body is regarded as one of the most ancient forms of health care known to humans. Many scientists consider a 60,000-year-old Neanderthal burial site located in Northern Iraq as evidence of the earliest known use of herbs. Analysis of the site revealed large quantities of plant pollen in the soil near human bones and contained twenty-eight species of plants, including yarrow, groundsels, grape hyacinth, and St. Barnaby's thistle. The plants had most likely been intentionally placed around a Neanderthal man's grave.

From curing colds, to healing minor injuries, to treating more serious illnesses, such as cancer, all human cultures have depended on their native flora to prevent illness and restore health. Although botanists define herbs as non-woody, low-growing plants, herbalists have traditionally relied upon the entire plant kingdom to create herbal remedies. As a result, the ingredients in many herbal remedies have been gathered not only from flowering plants, shrubs, and trees, but have also been collected from mosses, lichens, ferns, algae, and fungi. Various parts of plants may also be used, including the flowers, seeds, fruit, leaves, stems, twigs, bark, root, and rootstock.

In Folklore Studies, the medicinal use of herbs falls under the rubric of "folk medicine." Historically, women often assumed the role of folk healer, wise woman, midwife, and nurse as they maintained the herb garden, dried herbs, and prepared and administered medicinal remedies. Poultices, salves, ointments, tonics, and teas were created, tested, and used to treat a range of ailments. Herbs, however, not only played a significant role for women from the perspective of healer, but were also a crucial and reliable means by which women could facilitate pregnancy, enable abortion, ease childbirth, practice birth control, and, more recently, complement biomedical treatments for breast cancer.

According to ancient papyrus, Egyptian women practiced birth control using remedies containing acacia gum, dates, and an unknown plant which were mixed together and formed into a vaginal suppository. The acacia was believed to act as an herbal spermicide. Many First Nations groups continue to use herbs as a primary means for healing and maintaining harmony throughout pregnancy and birth. Until recently, Navajo women gave birth on a dirt floor in the *hogan*, or traditional dwelling. They burned cedar to cleanse the air, sipped juniper tea to help the uterus contract after delivery, and mother and child were blessed with corn pollen to help restore *hózhó* ("beauty and balance") following the birth. Among women diagnosed with breast cancer in the United States and Canada, recent studies indicate that the number of women who rely upon Complementary and Alternative Medicine (CAM) to complement their biomedical treatment, including herbal remedies, continues to rise. Many women do so in order to improve their quality of life, reduce tumor size, prevent recurrence, obtain a feeling of control, and decrease the negative side effects of chemotherapy and other cancer treatments.

The World Health Organization estimates that 80 percent of the world's population uses some form of traditional medicine as a primary source of health care, most of which is the reliance upon herbs to treat and prevent illness (Bodeker 1996). In recent years, scientists have become increasingly interested in approaches to health care outside official biomedical practice in the United States. A steady increase in the number of people turning to traditional medicine has motivated the National Institutes of Health to create the National Center for Complementary and Alternative Medicine to record, assess, and analyze these forms of health care in the United States.

Biomedical health care continues to improve, and new drugs are developed every day, but reliance upon herbs for healing, relief, and comfort persists. *See also:* Abortion; Childbirth and Childrearing; First Nations of North America; Folk Medicine; Foodways; Gardens; Graves and Gravemarkers; Old Wives' Tales; Pregnancy.

References: Bodeker, Gerard C. "Global Health Traditions." In *Fundamentals of Complementary and Alternative Medicine*, ed. Marc S. Micozzi, 279–290. New York: Churchill Livingstone, 1996; Gordon, James S., and Sharon Curtin. *Comprehensive Cancer Care: Integrating Alternative, Complementary, and Conventional Therapies.* Cambridge, MA: Perseus Press, 2000; Kirkland, James, Holly F. Mathews, and C. W. Sullivan III, eds. *Herbal and Magical Medicine: Traditional Healing Today.* Durham, NC: Duke University Press, 1992; Micozzi, Marc S. *Fundamentals of Complementary and Alternative Medicine.* New York: Churchill Livingstone, 1996; O'Connor, Bonnie B., and David Hufford. "Understanding Folk Medicine." In *Healing Logics: Culture and Medicine in Modern Health Belief Systems,* ed. Erika Brady, 13–35. Logan: Utah State University Press, 2001; Riddle, John M. *Eve's Herbs: A History of Contraception and Abortion in the West.* Cambridge. MA: Harvard University Press, 1997; Solecki, R. S. "Shanidar IV: A Neanderthal Flower Burial in Northern Iraq." *Science,* vol. 190, no. 28 (1975): 880–881.

Denise Kozikowski

Hip-Hop Culture/Rap

Hip-hop, as a culture, encompasses five unique forms of expression: 1) DJing (disc jockeying or mixing; using turntables to "scratch" or combine sounds); 2) b-boying (or breaking; the dance component); 3) graffiti art ("tagging" or "writing"); 4) "MCing" (master of ceremonies, rapping); and 5) education (knowledge). The fifth element was introduced by Africa Bambaataa's Zulu Nation in 1973 and serves the important function of reminding both hip-hop artists and the larger society that history, politics, economics, and social-justice concerns are central to the hip-hop ethos. While the terms "hip-hop" and "rap" are often used interchangeably, rap music per se is only one aspect of hip-hop culture. Hip-hop is best viewed as a widespread cultural network of artistic expression, a form of communication that includes rap, DJ practice, digital sampling, break dancing, and graffiti art. Hip-hop culture is deeply rooted in African American, African Caribbean, and Latino cultures and history, while rap music has become a multibillion dollar industry, due primarily to its strong appeal to non-Blacks.

Hip-hop purportedly originated in the Bronx, New York, where many of its early MCs (for example, Prince Whipple Whip), graffiti artists (for example, Jean Michel Basquiat), and members of crews that "battled" in break dancing contests (for example, Rock Steady Crew) were Latinos, mostly Puerto Rican. DJs Kool Herc and Clement Coxsone were Jamaican, and Grandmaster Flash came to New York from Barbados. The popularity and globalization of hip-hop culture and rap music has sparked numerous debates concerning the genre's boundaries, functions, and definitions. In her article, "Getting Real About Global Hip-Hop," Yvonne Bynoe makes a distinction between being a "fan" of rap music and being someone who is organically part of a larger network of hip-hop culture. She argues that hip-hop culture is more than just an entertainment vehicle; it is specific to the experiences, values, and stories of African and Caribbean Americans. Quoting Raymond Williams (1962), Bynoe reminds us that culture is "'a particular way of life' that is shared by a community and shaped by its values, traditions, beliefs, material objects, and territory." Bynoe argues that hip-hop culture is primarily informed by a Black perspective and understanding of the world (that is, beliefs, customs, norms, restrictions, and styles). For these reasons, the distinction between hip-hop as a culture and rap music as a global commercial phenomenon is crucial from the perspective of Folklore Studies.

A recent issue of *Entertainment Weekly Magazine* commemorated the "Biggest Moments in Hip-Hop's Last 25 years." According to the writers,

> The rap revolution started at the intersection of serendipity and inspiration. Sylvia Robinson, owner of a failing record label, was just looking for some cake and a good time when she went to a birthday party at the New York City club Harlem World in May 1979. But when she heard something called rap being performed there (by a DJ named Lovebug Starki), she recognized its potential (Anderson et al. 2004: 41)

Other music entrepreneurs followed suit, and by the mid-1980s, the genre had become one of the most vital new popular music forms in the music industry. However, the roots of rap music and hip-hop culture run deeper than twenty-five years of mainstream commodification. Recent hip-hop/rap scholarship has begun to document its deeper origins. Anthony B. Pinn (2003), for example, examines its religious influences:

> At its best, perhaps rap music is a continuation of the creative manner in which meaning is made out of an absurd world by promoting a style of living through which a sense of self and community is forged in a hostile environment. Is there any religious significance in rap music? Long before rap and hip-hop became the global and highly commodified phenomenon that it has become, spirituals were a form of musical expression which represented the beginning of an African American cultural tradition and experience. (Pinn 2003: 3)

Many scholars agree that it was through this cultural expression that enslaved Africans made efforts to express a sense of self in a hostile world. Through spirituals, and later the blues, they incorporated their memories of home with their new existence as a means of humanizing a dehumanizing environment. The music, along with folktales, decorative arts, and visual arts that make up this new Black culture, "represents a style of interpretation, a stylized wrestling with life" (ibid.).

The notion that rap music is associated only with Black males is being revised. Public perception of women's presence in the culture has been largely formed by men; however, Cheryl Keyes, Joan Morgan, T. Denean Sharpley-Whiting, and others challenge the long-held notion that rap/hip-hop music was exclusively created by males. By the mid-1980s, the rap industry had expanded to include a growing number of Black women artists. Like their male counterparts, female artists also rap about aspects of central city life and their desire to be "number one"; however, their lyrics come from their experiences of being women. In 1989, Queen Latifah proclaimed "We are the ones that give birth / To the new generation of prophets" ("Ladies First"). Barbara 62, Eva 62, Lady Pink (the first to tag the Statue of Liberty), Charmin, Stoney, and Lady Heart were a few of the women who played a role in changing the male-dominated world of tagging.

In fact, women have been at the heart of hip-hop's commercial success. In products made by the music industry for mass consumption, thus far and in the main, women have been, as T. Denean Sharply-Whiting notes, "either 'hot pussy for sale' or they were 'pussy for the taking'.... Overexposed young Black female flesh, 'pimpin,' 'playin,' 'sexin,' 'checkin' in videos, television, film, rap lyrics, fashion, and on the Internet, is indispensable to the mass-media-engineered appeal of hip-hop culture that helps to shape a new Black gender politics" (44). Yet as Kyra D. Gaunt reminds us, "women are not incidental to the music ... African American women are more than objectified, self-degrading, video-dancing, sex-crazed, 'gold diggers' or 'skeezers'" (278). Derogatory stereotypes, with which so many Black and Latina hip-hoppers have had to contend, vastly oversimplify their participation in all five elements that constitute hip-hop culture.

Tricia Rose notes that female storytellers in hip-hop have three central concerns: heterosexual courtship, the power of the female voice, and physical and sexual freedom. Rather than being relegated to the margins as backup singers and dancers, the past ten years also have seen female rappers gain considerable recognition and respect as artists and lyricists. Citing feminist musicologist Hazel Carby, Anne O'Connell (2002) reminds us of the power and primary function of female rap music:

> ... in women's blues, African-American women used themselves as sexual subjects through song as a means of empowerment. The lyrics of many early female blues songs subverted the fact that female sexuality was only the object of the male desire. Instead, female sexuality was used to serve other females with a positive and empowered image of themselves, lending to the ability of other women to relate. These women sang of the satisfaction that accompanies the rejection of female subordination and sexual exploitation. Female rap groups follow their predecessors with the use of powerful lyrics in order to dispute traditional gender roles prevalent in our society.

Hip-hop and rap are examples of modern oral performances practiced among contemporary youth cultures in the United States, and increasingly, around the world. At the center of hip-hop culture is a critical storytelling component that functions to impart information via music and performance to larger societies by specific groups of people. Hip-hop speaks to the diversity of experiences of men and women, but particularly to those of Black and Latino youth. Shawn A. Ginwright has explored the loss of faith in "the system" experienced and expressed by young Black and Latino women and men in the United States and concluded that studying the "hip-hop generation" from a political perspective is the key to understanding its identity, both as an artistic folk group and as a social force. In keeping with the spirit of its fifth element (education, knowledge), increasingly informed by feminist/womanist perspectives, hip-hop culture provides "not simply a

voice for disenfranchised youth, but an identity that challenges racist practices, speaks to economic struggles, and sometimes provides a blueprint for
the possibilities of social change" for both men and women (Robin Kelly
1996, quoted in Ginwright 2004). *See also:* Feminisms; Folk Dance; Folk
Group; Folk Music and Folksong; Folklore of Subversion; Gender; Graffiti;
Politics; Race; Sexism; Sexuality; Spirituals; Storytelling.

References: Anderson, Kyle, Bob Cannon, Ryan Dombal, Neil Drumming, Michael
Endelman, Raymond Fiore, Leah Greenblatt, Nancy Miller, Whitney Pastorek, Michele
Romero, Tom Sinclair, and Eric White. "Bring the Noise." *Entertainment Weekly Magazine*, November 19, 2004; Bynoe, Yvonne. "Getting Real About Global Hip-hop." *George-
town Journal of International Affairs*, vol. 3, no. 1 (Winter/Spring 2002): 77–84;
Cushing, Casey "Otter." "A Rough-around-the-edges synopsis of Chuck D on the Five Ele-
ments of Hip-Hop: Flatirons Theatre, Boulder, CO, November 2001." Unpublished notes:
Naropa College, 2001; Gaunt, Kyra D. *The Games Black Girls Play: Learning the Ropes
from Double-Dutch to Hip-Hop*. New York: New York University Press, 2006; Ginwright,
Shawn A. *Black in School: Afrocentric Reform, Urban Youth, and the Promise of Hip-
Hop Culture*. New York and London: Teachers College Press, 2004; Keyes, Cheryl L.
"'We're More than a Novelty, Boys': Strategies of Female Rappers in the Rap Music Tradi-
tion." In *Feminist Messages: Coding in Women's Folk Culture*, ed. Joan Newlon Radner,
203–220. Urbana and Chicago: University of Illinois Press, 1993; ———. "Empowering
Self, Making Choices, Creating Spaces: Black Female Identity via Rap Music Performance." *Journal of American Folklore* 113 (2000): 255–269; Morgan, Joan. *When Chick-
enheads Come Home to Roost: A Hip-Hop Feminist Breaks It Down*. New York:
Touchstone Books, 2000 [1999]; O'Connell, Anne. "A Feminist Approach to Female Rap
Music." Castleton Sate College (Vermont): Communication Department student research,
2002. http://www.castleton.edu/communication/research/femalerap.html (accessed May
23, 2005); Oliveras, Pamela. "Women in Graffiti." *Verbalisms Magazine*, n.d. http://
www.verbalisms.com/mt/mt-tb.cgi/19 (accessed May 24, 2005); Pinn, Anthony B., ed. *Noise
and Spirit: The Religious and Spiritual Sensibilities of Rap Music*. New York and London:
New York University Press, 2003; Rose, Tricia. *Black Noise: Rap Music and Black Culture
in Contemporary America*. Middletown, CT: Wesleyan University Press, 1994; Sharpley-
Whiting, T. Denean. "Pimpin' ain't Easy: hip-hop's relationship to young black women ..."
Colorlines (May/June 2007): 43–46; Thompson, Amanda. "Gender in Hip-hop: A Research
Study." 2004. http://www.humboldt.edu/~soc/2004Thompson.pdf (accessed May 23,
2005); Williams, Raymond. *Communications*. London: Penguin UK, 1962.

Maribel Garcia

Home Birth

Home birth refers to delivery accomplished within the home or in a non-
medicalized setting. In the twentieth century, as doctors increasingly
defined birth as a pathological event, and anesthesia during delivery
increased in popularity, birth became a restricted topic in polite society,
and almost all deliveries moved from home to hospital. However, the widespread commonality of experience resulting from "the Baby Boom" (a surge
in childbirth from the mid-1940s until the early 1960s) combined with the
mass migration of Americans to the suburbs nurtured increased contact and
community among women, creating contexts in which birth was again considered an acceptable conversational subject.

As women discussed the details of the delivery process, they questioned
the standard medical approach to childbirth. A growing number argued that

birth injuries and maternal mortality were actually greater in hospitals because of medicalized definitions and interference in the normal birth process.

An important contribution to this dialogue was Marjorie Karmel's 1959 book, *Thank You, Dr. Lamaze*, detailing the natural approach to childbirth she had experienced in France. Women, bolstered by information about more natural methods of birth like *accouchement sans douleur* (the Lamaze method), sought to reduce medical intervention in their deliveries and to defeat the prevalent patronizing attitudes of professional medical practitioners toward women. A social movement for alternative birth began in North America, one that emphasized a holistic approach and strove to return childbirth to nature and to women. Portrayed as a return of birth literally to the home and the family bed, birth came to be represented as a time of celebration, and not the crisis of "coming down to death's door."

The 1976 publication of Ina May Gaskin's *Spiritual Midwifery* introduced an entire generation of young women to the possibilities of home birth and midwifery. Interest in home births continued to grow as more parents decided they wanted to deliver without drugs and other unnecessary interventions, using natural approaches in a familiar, emotionally reassuring setting.

Today, most home births are attended by direct-entry ("lay") midwives. Certified nurse-midwives and certified professional midwives may also attend non-hospital births (including some births at home). American direct-entry midwives are largely trained through apprenticeship, and their practice is illegal in many states. State authorities and medical associations have made efforts to restrict the activities of direct-entry midwives, in some cases arresting or prosecuting them for practicing medicine without a license. Certified nurse-midwives and professional midwives have also been the target of legal actions and medical associations.

Associations such as the Midwives' Alliance of North America and the American College of Nurse-Midwives work to expand the practice rights of midwives—including developing standards and programs for accreditation and certification of direct-entry midwives—for improved interaction of midwives with the health-care system, and for the legalization of midwifery practice at federal and state levels. These efforts have expanded the occurrence of home birth and the practice of direct-entry and certified midwifery in the United States. Every year, more babies are born into the hands of midwives: the national average in 2004 was 7.4 percent (up from 0.4 percent in 1975); in some states, it is as high as 20 percent. Currently, about 30,000 women each year plan for home births, assisted by approximately 10,000 direct-entry and nurse-midwives. *See also:* Birth Chair; Childbirth and Childrearing; Doula; Midwifery; Rites of Passage.

References: Arms, Suzanne. *Immaculate Deception: A New Look at Women and Childbirth in America*. Boston: Houghton-Mifflin, 1975; Breckenridge, Mary. *Wide Neighborhoods: A Story of the Frontier Nursing Service*. Lexington: University Press of Kentucky, 1981; Davis-Floyd, Robbie. *Birth as an American Rite of Passage*. Berkeley: University of California Press, 1992; Farm, The. http://www.thefarm.org/midwives/index.html (accessed August 10, 2008); Gaskin, Ina May. *Spiritual Midwifery*. Fourth edition. Summertown, TN: Book Publishing Company, 2002; Sullivan, Deborah A., and Rose

Weitz. *Labor Pains: Modern Midwives and Home Birth*. New Haven: Yale University Press, 1988.

Amanda Carson Banks

Homeless Women

A subject of study investigated through fieldwork in communities of homeless people and via the collection of personal-experience narratives from individual homeless women and men, frequently with the aim of aiding persons who, for one reason or another, have lost their homes, or of uncovering causes for and possible solutions to homelessness. Homeless women, in particular, are the focus of a 1990 study by Marjorie Bard, *Shadow Women: Homeless Women's Survival Stories*. Bard writes about the ways in which folklore fieldwork can uncover what homeless women know and believe about family, education, the workplace, their own experiences with domestic violence, and the everyday, ongoing circumstances of homelessness. Bard writes about how just the collection and analysis of such personal-experience narratives can lead some homeless women to discover a greater sense of agency or provoke other kinds of change in their lives; being involved in folklore fieldwork has provided many women the opportunity to articulate and rehearse their self-perceived identities, both within and beyond homelessness. Bard suggests that women's personal-experience narratives are shaped in such a way as to create "narrative kernels," or storytelling foundations, for imagining or composing productive new narratives, or as a problem-solving strategy for resolving an individual woman's state of homelessness.

Homeless women, according to Bard, have often experienced domestic violence, which can be the cause of many of the factors that lead to homelessness. Women may also have less earning potential; in some cases, being abandoned by a spouse precipitated homelessness. Perceptions that homeless women are more susceptible to mental impairment may also lead to incidents of abuse, Bard adds.

Studies that focus on homeless women as subjects or on the personal-experience narratives of homeless women include Meredith Ralston's 1996 *Nobody Wants to Hear Our Truth: Homeless Women and Theories of the Welfare State*; Elliot Liebow's 1993 *Tell Them Who I Am: The Lives of Homeless Women*; and Karen Warner's 1996 article about a community of homeless people titled "Spare Any Change? Power and Discourse in Toronto's Urban Panhandling Subculture."

Most studies of homeless women, however, have been conducted by scholars in social-science fields other than Folklore, or by community activists and public folklorists. Regenia Gagnier, in her important 1999 article "Practical Aesthetics III: Homelessness as an 'Aesthetic Issue,'" traces how discourse about homelessness functions in the popular imagination; she observes that media representations construct homeless people as undesirable "sights" on the public horizon that must be scourged from public space. Robert Desjarlais, in his book *Blues: Sanity and Selfhood Among the Homeless* (1997), writes about the "mythology" of homeless people constructed in popular media of homeless people as "beautiful ruins" or as "matter out-of-place." Other important qualitative or cultural studies of homeless people and communities include *The Homeless in Contemporary Society* (1987) edited by Richard D. Bingham et al.; *The Politics of Ending Homelessness* by Susan Yeich (1994); and *Out of Place: Homeless Mobilizations, Subcities, and Contested Landscapes* (1997) by Talmadge Wright.

Folklorists have yet to pay serious attention to grassroots or faith-based advocacy for homeless people and to the interactions within and among such communities. We would do well to acquaint ourselves better with the writing of Catholic Workers, for example, members of communities of people in the urban United States who live according to the Works of Mercy, who focus on service to homeless men and women. Also, it is time for more scholarly studies of homeless men and women that consider how race, gender, class, sexual identity, and/or region factor into the narrative performances and cultural practices of homeless persons. *See also:* Class; Divorce; Family Folklore; Fieldwork; Gender; Mass Media; Personal-Experience Narrative; Race; Storytelling; Violence.

References: Bard, Marjorie. *Shadow Women: Homeless Women's Survival Stories.* Kansas City: Sheen and Ward, 1990; ———. "Aiding the Homeless: The Uses of Narratives In Diagnoses and Intervention." In *Putting Folklore to Use*, ed. Michael Owen Jones, 76–93. Lexington: University Press of Kentucky, 1994; Bingham, Richard D., Roy E. Green, and Sammis B. White, eds. *The Homeless in Contemporary Society*. Newbury Park: Sage Publications, 1987; Desjarlais, Robert. *Shelter Blues: Sanity and Selfhood Among the Homeless*. Philadelphia: University of Pennsylvania Press, 1997; Gagnier, Regenia. "Homelessness as 'An Aesthetic Issue': Past and Present." In *Homes and Homelessness in the Victorian Imagination,* eds. Murray Baumgarten and H. M. Daleski, 167–186. New York: AMS Press, 1999; Liebow, Elliot. *Tell Them Who I Am: The Lives of Homeless Women*. New York: The Free Press, 1993; Ralston, Meredith. *Nobody Wants To Hear Our Truth: Homeless Women and Theories of the Welfare State*. Westport, CT: Greenwood Press, 1996; Warner, Karen. "Spare Any Change? Power and Discourse in Toronto's Urban Panhandling Subculture." *Canadian Folklore canadien*, vol. 18, no. 1 (1996): 71–93; Wright, Talmadge. *Out of Place: Homeless Mobilizations, Subcities, and Contested Landscapes*. New York: State University of New York Press, 1997; Yeich, Susan. *The Politics of Ending Homelessness*. New York: University Press of America, 1994.

Jacqueline L. McGrath

Housekeeping

The complement of activities that are considered housekeeping may be limited to housecleaning tasks performed within the house (analogous to chores), or may include the multitude of duties related to maintenance of the home in general. It may also be expanded to include paid work that is done in someone else's home. Thus, the home may be viewed as an economic unit as well as the center of family and domestic life. Because it is relegated to the realm of the domestic, housework, although acknowledged as "work," is generally recognized as having no monetary value, despite the 1995 UN Human Development Report, which estimated that the economic value of women's unpaid work worldwide amounted to $11 trillion annually. Rather, housekeeping is seen as reproductive labor; that is, labor that maintains people on a daily and generational basis. Gender is often the focal point of housework studies, including—especially with the increase in North America of dual-income families—the changing roles of men and women in domestic labor.

The so-called "traditional" division of domestic labor features a man working outside the home, and a woman staying in the home as full-time homemaker. However, reality in the twenty-first century means that many households now have both partners working outside the home. This may be by choice or, more frequently, by financial necessity. There are also single-parent families, both male and female-headed, in which the sole adult is responsible for household tasks. Same-sex couples, male homemakers, and blended families each have their own challenges to negotiate when it comes to housework. However, studies have shown that even with these multiple household structures, the majority of the housework still falls to the primary female figure in the home, regardless of whether or not she has paid employment outside the home. Additionally, the woman of the household seems to carry the burden of household manager more often; that is, even if males take on chores, their female counterparts still assume responsibility for assigning tasks and managing what gets done, how, and when.

Scott Coltrane and Randall Collins (2001) outline studies completed in the 1990s in the United States that suggest that a number of factors influence how tasks may or may not be shared in a household. Generally speaking, if a couple deliberately divides up the housework, there will be a more even split. However, if the couple decides to share tasks without a conscious division, the woman will most likely assume the majority of tasks, even if she, too, works outside the home. Bart Landry's statistics on African American wives (2000) indicate that this trend transcends racial categories. Additional elements such as education, gender attitudes, age, earnings, children, and marital status all affect how the burden of housework may be shared.

Housework has become a focus of increased academic study, primarily in the disciplines of Sociology and Women's Studies. Judith Levin (1993) argues that folkloristics has ignored the study of housework by valorizing the very images it connotes. By contemporary definitions, folklore involves the study of creative, expressive, traditional, and skilled endeavors. By contrast, housework is viewed as mindless, boring, and repetitive. However, in the terms of folkloristics, domestic labor can perhaps most readily be examined under the auspices of occupational folklore, as well as family folklore. Folklorists such as Michael Owen Jones (1980) approached mundane occupations as situations in which the worker found a creative niche in these repetitive jobs, thereby establishing aesthetic components in jobs that, by their very nature, lack any personal artistry or skill. In her film *Clotheslines*, Roberta Cantow documents the artistry of washing and hanging clothes on outdoor drying lines by women in late twentieth-century New York City as they discuss how they admire (and judge) other women's clothes-hanging practices, and how they themselves strive to arrange their clotheslines in aesthetically pleasing ways.

While housework may not be seen by all as an enjoyable way to spend time, its importance is always recognized, and satisfaction is often derived from knowing that the completion of domestic chores directly relates to care for a family. As a result, there may be conflicting feelings and attitudes in women and girls who realize the importance of their domestic labor, but do not enjoy completing the actual tasks. Susan Lanser (1993) analyzed domestic incompetence as a form of coding and resistance among women. Since it is expected that women will be good housekeepers, the woman who deliberately burns dinners or neglects housecleaning may be sending coded messages rejecting not only the tasks themselves, but also the female roles attributed with competence at these chores.

Although the study of housework is intrinsically linked to the study of labor, it also does not fit into most models of the economic value of labor. For example, Marxist theory asserts that labor is related to subsistence, which is measured by the market value of the labor required to ensure the wage earner's survival. However, Marx focused on work that was recognized through monetary payment, thereby automatically excluding housework, which is almost always unpaid labor performed by a member of the household. As a means of social reproduction, housework is seen as providing emotional ties to family and community in addition to basic household maintenance. Feminist Marxists see the gendered division of labor as it pertains to the home as favoring men. Men generally do not significantly contribute to the labor in the home, and therefore enjoy the fruits of the woman's work at her expense. Men are thereby able to contribute more to the outside labor force than can their female counterparts. Thus, gender divisions that are promulgated in the outside labor market are reinforced and strengthened in the home. Since women who work outside the home also complete the majority of housework, they tend to suffer more conflict over their roles both within and outside the home.

The production of housework involves prioritizing, organization, and time allocation. Much academic interest in household labor focuses on how time is used, measuring specific tasks and how they are allocated. Several national surveys conducted in the United States concluded that the following household tasks consumed the most time: cooking, housecleaning, shopping for household-related goods, cleaning up after meals, and laundry-related tasks. These are seen as required or necessary duties that must be completed on a fairly rigid and regular schedule. Of course, the techniques by which these and other tasks are completed have changed greatly since the advent of industrialization.

Women's diaries have often been the source for sociohistoric studies on housework. Meg Luxton (1986, 2001 with June Corman) completed a number of studies focusing on the division of time and domestic work from both historical and contemporary perspectives. For example, through an examination of women's diaries in Flin Flon, Manitoba, Canada, in the 1920s and 1930s, Luxton found that not only was there a daily routine that women followed, but a weekly schedule as well. A woman would have regular daily chores, such as cooking, taking care of the children, and basic housecleaning. However, larger tasks such as washing clothes, ironing, and baking would be divided up on a daily basis and take up the better part of each day. "Leisure" time was often spent mending or doing other, less physically taxing chores. A similar study, completed by Meg Luxton in 1984, revealed that female homemakers still completed household tasks throughout the day. However, larger tasks were spread out throughout the week and, indeed, throughout the day. Later generations were more flexible, organizing tasks in different ways. For them, there was no need to devote an entire day to one major household task. Chores were done as needed, one could take a day off, or a daily plan could be followed; no generic pattern could be discerned.

This change in the distribution of chores can also largely be attributed to industrialization and the resultant mechanization of housework. Where earlier generations had to hand wash all clothes, it is now possible to throw a load of clothes into the washing machine, run out and go grocery shopping, and return later to put them into the dryer. Rather than concentrating on one task throughout the day, housework has now shifted to supervising four or five tasks at any one time. "Multitasking" is the common term for this approach. Therefore, housework can now be fit around other duties: domestic, family, or employment-related. Also, the escalated manufacture of clothing and products outside the home and a family's increased ability to purchase store-bought clothing and food meant that the nature of household tasks would inevitably change.

An important but understudied aspect of housework is the dangers that are encountered in performing household tasks. Especially ignored is the issue of environmental pollutants that are prevalent in cleaning products. While homemakers are targeted by advertisers to buy numerous new products to assist in cleaning the home, the hazards of using these cleansers and cleaners are hidden. We associate chemical odors and artificial scents with a "clean" smell, believing that these sophisticated, expensive products work more efficiently than tried-and-true cleansers such as salt, baking soda, and vinegar.

Because the house is a living space for the entire family, the services that household labor provides directly affect the well-being of the household. Also, with the advent and spread of machines and innumerable products to assist with housework, those who complete this work are more and more perceived as marketing targets. Thus, homemakers have a direct relationship with the economy through their consumption practices, which in turn drive the creation of goods that are produced. Because of the overall mundane view of housework, advertising focuses on machines and products that make housework "easier" through increased efficacy and speed.

Increased mechanization in housework may also be seen as a factor in reducing the "craft" aspect of household tasks, as there is no longer a clear and direct relationship between the labor and its end result. Conversely, machines have made housework a far less labor-intensive task, as they have taken the place of the human body in the form of washing machines, sewing machines, vacuum cleaners, and even bread makers. Most homemakers gladly traded personal labor for machines that alleviated certain household burdens. However, it is interesting to note that homemakers didn't necessarily have more free time with new appliances and products. This point is made in the film *Clotheslines*, in which women discuss how the purchase of a washing machine affected their cleaning habits. While a washing machine does clean clothes, its efficacy and efficiency mean that clothes can be washed more often. One woman commented that she began changing her child's clothes three times a day because she was able to wash them much more easily. Laundry remained an endless ordeal.

Although housework is associated with unpaid labor within the home, it also includes paid labor in another person's home. Maids, housekeepers, and other servants were frequently employed in Western countries until their numbers declined in the 1800s. Working-class women then had to labor in the homes of upper- and middle-class citizens, as their husbands did not make enough money on their own to support the family. Middle-class housewives thus took on the role of household managers, directing the activities of the servants. This led to a shift toward viewing the middle-class household as a haven, a place where the role of wife and mother could be emphasized because she was no longer required to perform everyday household tasks. The domestic code was thereby reinforced, as these middle-class women read literature and formed associations, clubs, and charities, while their lower class, often culturally "other" counterparts kept their homes clean and in working order.

While the live-in servant is no longer a common household feature in North America, women are still employed to complete household tasks such as housework and childcare. As middle-class women's participation in the workforce increased, so did the hiring of paid help around the house, most often by minority-status women or other, more recent immigrants. Thus, housework does have a paid-market component. However, domestic workers may experience oppressive conditions, often compounded by immigration issues and/or racial, ethnic, and class stereotyping. As the demand for paid help (whether live-in or daytime) increases, not enough North Americans are willing to take on this job. In a situation similar to that of domestic servants of the nineteenth century, contemporary foreign workers often arrive in Canada and the United States, legally or otherwise, to be employed in those positions that their better-off sisters have eschewed. Thus, the home becomes an economic sphere unto itself, with its own challenges of isolation, commoditization, and opportunity. *See also:* Class; Farm Women's Folklore; Immigration; Laundry; Mother's Day; Occupational Folklore; Sewing; Wage Work; Women's Work.

References: Boydston, Jeanne. "To Earn Her Daily Bread: Housework and Antebellum Working-Class Subsistence." In *Unequal Sisters: A Multicultural Reader in U.S. Women's History*, third edition, eds. Vicki L. Ruiz and Ellen Carol DuBois, 80–92. New York: Routledge, 2000; Cantow, Roberta, director. *Clotheslines.* Buffalo Rose Productions, 1981; Coltrane, Scott. *Family Man: Fatherhood, Housework and Gender Equity.* New York, Oxford: Oxford University Press, 1996; Coltrane, Scott., and Randall Collins. *Sociology of Marriage and the Family.* Fifth edition. Belmont, CA: Wadsworth/Thomson Learning, 2001; Davis, Angela Y. "The Approaching Obsolescence of Housework: A Working-Class Perspective." In *Women, Race and Class,* 222–244. New York: Vintage Books, 1983; Eisler, Riane. "The Feminine Face of Poverty." AlterNet. April 19, 2007. http://www.alternet.org/rights/50727 (accessed June 22, 2007); Glenn, Evelyn Nakano. "From Servitude to Service Work: Historical Continuities in the Racial Division of Paid Reproductive Labor." In *Unequal Sisters: A Multicultural Reader in U.S. Women's History*, third edition, eds. Vicki L. Ruiz and Ellen Carol DuBois, 436–65. New York: Routledge, 2000; Jones, Michael Owen. "A Feeling for Form, as Illustrated by People at Work." In *Folklore on Two Continents*, eds. Nikolai Burlakoff and Carl Lindahl, 260–69. Bloomington, IN: Trickster Press, 1980; Landry, Bart. *Black Working Wives: Pioneers of the American Family Revolution*. Berkeley: University California Press, 2000; Lanser, Susan S. "Burning Dinners: Feminist Subversions of Domesticity." In *Feminist Messages: Coding in Women's Folk Culture*, ed. Joan Newlon Radner, 36–53. Urbana and Chicago: University of Illinois Press, 1993; Levin, Judith. "Why Folklorists Should Study Housework." In *Feminist Theory and the Study of Folklore*, eds. Susan Tower Hollis, Linda Pershing, and M. Jane Young, 285–96. Urbana: University of Illinois Press, 1993; Luxton, Meg. *More than a Labour of Love: Three Generations of Women's Work in the Home*. Toronto: Women's Educational Press, 1986; Luxton, Meg, and June Corman. *Getting By in Hard Times: Gendered Labour at Home and on the Job*. Toronto: University of Toronto Press, 2001.

Kristin Harris Walsh

Humor

Humor—an amusing and/or comic quality—encompasses complex sociocultural and physical expressions such as fun, joking, wit, smiling, laughter, and play. Often involving topsy-turvydom or the ability to hold simultaneous yet contradictory realities in suspension, humor may work best when it imposes a comic image on recognizable truths relating to events, ideas, or objects perceived as absurd, incongruous, or ridiculous. Its performance results in a unique kind of social structure which intensifies communication—sometimes positively, so that it is enhanced, and sometimes negatively, so that it is impaired. Yet humor is also ephemeral, changing shape and tone from performance to performance, from culture to culture, and from one historical period to another. It can serve to express and maintain hierarchy or to subvert it, to establish in-groups and out-groups, and to reinforce boundaries and stereotypes or subvert them. It can be found in all folkloric genres, from the material to the verbal to the ritual. Women are extensively implicated in humor—as its subjects, creators, and audiences—especially in its feminist forms.

Social stereotypes pervade humor. In its Euro North American manifestations, women are too often labeled as fundamentally incompetent—dumb blondes and bad drivers—or as excessively emotional. But much comic material intended as humor simply displays misogyny. Consider these excerpts from a well-circulated photocopy-lore text, "25 Good Reasons Why Beer is Better than Women":

> You can enjoy a beer all month long.
> Your beer will always wait patiently for you in the car while you play baseball.
> When your beer goes flat, you toss it out.
> A beer always goes down easy.
> You always know you're the first one to pop a beer.
> Beer doesn't demand equality.
> A frigid beer is a good beer.
> You don't have to wash a beer before it tastes good.
> If you change beers, you don't have to pay alimony (Greenhill et al. 51–52).

The full text stereotypes women as simultaneously inhabiting both sides of devalued oppositions: oversexed yet sexually unadventurous; slaves to their biological functions yet culturally controlling; possessive yet promiscuous; ever-present yet selectively absent; polluted and polluting; exacting yet unskilled; and valueless yet expensive.

Blonde jokes similarly express power dynamics between women and men, illustrating the same patriarchal strategy of inherent contradiction. Specifically, the women who hear blonde jokes are expected to take them seriously, but also to accept them as funny. For example, brunette Angela Brooks reports discussing economics with a male graduate student in the presence of another male student and a blonde woman. During a pause in the conversation, the male student asked: "What did the brunette between the two blondes say? What brunette?" This joke's purpose was to deny Brooks' right to speak, as she realized:

> The joke was used to suggest that I was stepping out of my place, and that no-one was paying any attention to what I was saying in any case. Nothing I said would make anyone notice me, particularly since there was an attractive blonde woman present who was, appropriately, silent. The joke was a successful ploy to silence me (Brooks in Greenhill et al. 1993: 59).

Women faced with such situations have few options. If she had retorted, for example, "Why are all blonde jokes one-liners? So men can understand them," the first teller could have answered with a blonde joke that was not a one-liner. The repertoire of misogynist jokes is huge; that of feminist jokes is smaller and less accessible. If Brooks had acknowledged the joke as an attack, she would be accused of lacking a sense of humor, and lose the battle. Yet, since the rest of the group laughed, she could not ignore it. Accordingly, she was forced to participate in her own oppression by laughing at a joke explicitly intended to silence and impugn her.

Hatred of women and of feminists is often made indistinguishable, as in a graffito that appeared after the murder of fourteen women, most of them engineering students, at the Universite de Montreal on December 6, 1989. Appearing about a month after the massacre on a poster advertising the location of a graduate course in Women's Studies at an Ontario University, it read: "What do you call 14 dead feminists in Mtl [Montreal]? A Good Start.—the M. Lepine [the killer] Fan Club" (Greenhill 1992: 107). Many of the women killed might not have identified as feminists, though as engineering students they were not following the most traditional social script of stereotypical cultural expectations for women. The threat posed to both women and feminists, however, was quite clear.

Women's humor is in large part a reaction to the images of women presented in humor about them. Because of the absence (until recently) of women's humorous writing in literary anthologies and critical studies, the idea that women did not have a sense of humor became a kind of self-fulfilling prophecy. Until the late 1980s, women's rich use of wit was neglected or inaccessible to popular culture because of social theories that privileged the status quo. Some theories argue that women use concepts typical of male humor, such as superiority, incongruity, aggression, and catharsis. Others suggest that women's humor in general, and feminist humor in particular, is qualitatively different from its patriarchal counterpart. Gloria Kaufman argues that "feminist humor strives to educate both weak and powerful in order to stimulate change in the direction of equity or justice" (Kaufman: ix). For example, in "If Men Could Menstruate: A Political Fantasy," Gloria Steinem imagines how men would coopt menstruation for the benefit of patriarchal culture:

> Men would brag about how long and how much.
> Boys would mark the onset of menses, that longed-for proof of manhood, with religious ritual and stag parties.
> Congress would fund a National Institute of Dysmenorrhea to help stamp out monthly discomforts (Steinem: 110).

Kaufman also explains that women's and feminist humor changes meaning, depending on its location in social power dynamics:

> Humor and power are related in highly complex ways. One the one hand society has recognized the expression (or creation) of humor as an exercise of power and has reacted negatively to women humorists. (Things are changing.) One the other hand, women and other suppressed groups have privately and regularly used humor to empower themselves in order to survive oppression or subversively to resist it. No one doubts that humor is empowering. It is especially positive in dispelling fear. Laughing at our enemies diminishes them and emboldens us (ix).

Women's humor is often explicitly compared with men's. Unsurprisingly, the comparison often follows conventional ideas of women and men as social beings. For example, some theorists have argued that men's humor uses the symbolism of domination and power, with the intention of self-aggrandizement in hierarchical relationships, whereas women's humor is linked to the creation of intimacy and caring.

Often women's humor is expressed only between women with similar cultural boundaries, utilizing what Joan Radner calls coded language. Private expressions have been hallmarks of women's humor, making it less formalized and more personal than its male counterpart. Through humor, women educate an audience by assuming a comic perspective on issues both commonplace and outrageous that may be unrecognizable to the dominant culture. Yet women also use public spaces to create or present comedy. But women's wit often subverts and undermines the very community that seeks to control it. Because of its dangers to women's social status and well-being, this type of humor is not often expressed publicly.

For example, seventeenth-century American poet Anne Bradstreet kept her writing private. Some of her poetry is now read as a humorous critique of the social conventions of Puritan society, especially when she responds to descriptions of women as silent and incapable of writing serious poetry. Emily Dickinson is another American poet whose work has comic power. Her patterns and positions of words, as well as disproportionate and bold images, surprise the reader, evoking amusement, a smile, a giggle, or outright laughter.

Because its creators have been traditionally defined as powerless in male-dominated culture, women's humor has developed its own edge.

Experience provides the foundation for humor, and women's use of it links directly with their inferiorized social position. The performance dynamics operating between participants and their societal roles, subject matter, cultural values, and expectations influence the appropriateness of humor in a particular social setting. Humor connects psychosocial habits, images, values, and norms with the immediate social environment. Knowledge of a culture's verbal and physical patterns is an essential element of humor—communication requiring abstract thinking and other complex cognitive processes.

Humor can serve the status quo by providing those who chafe against it with a safe outlet for their ire. For example, Sigmund Freud argued that aggressive humor—jokes or stories told at an individual's or group's expense—is positive because it offers a socially sanctioned outlet for expressing discontent. In other words, humor can be cathartic. Of course, Freud also claimed that women do not need to use such humor because of their inherently non-aggressive place in culture. Making someone laugh means exerting control, even power. To be funny and thus powerful, one must be recognized by an audience. Because women have been historically marginalized both economically and culturally, aggressive humor has not often been an acknowledged part of their discourse.

Domestic humor functions as an avenue for confronting cultural institutions that keep power from women or control their behavior, exposing stereotypes in subversive critiques on the dominant culture that perpetuates them. Self-deprecation, or humor at one's own expense, is most fully developed in domestic humor. Critics argue that self-deprecation supports negative stereotypes about women's incompetence and perpetuates the status quo. Domestic humorists Erma Bombeck and Jean Kerr, for example, do not threaten mainstream patriarchy by encompassing women's lives inside household space. But their humor contains subversive elements that challenge unrealistic standards for wives, mothers, and daughters, transforming negative experiences into funny ones.

Women create and otherwise participate in spoken, drawn, or sung humor, as reflected not only in traditional culture but in comics, television and film comedies, and more recently (and substantially) on the Internet. In the past as well as today, they use comic performance, pantomime, burlesque, impersonation, caricature, parody, clowning, joke-telling, and comedy. In their day, Josephine Baker and Mae West famously called attention to themselves as clowns or caricatures in order to reveal and subvert cultural norms that defined women of Color and feminine women. Lucille Ball and Debra Messing are known for their use of physical humor to achieve similar ends.

In the years since Lucille Ball and Phyllis Diller paved the way for women's entrance into public performative spaces, women's stand-up comedy repertoires have varied enormously by culture, social background, and theme. Such comics may be outrageous or intellectually subtle. Many have disrupted typical expectations of female behavior and thereby influenced social and cultural attitudes. For example, Mo'Nique, a contemporary Black performer, encourages women to reject physical and emotional expectations that mark traditional female identity. Mo'Nique celebrates her full figure, elegant clothes, and sexuality, insisting on her power without offering further inroads to the objectification of Black women. By calling attention to herself as a successful and sexual woman, she inverts racialized paradigms, thus disempowering them. White women comics—Ellen DeGeneres, Paula Poundstone, and Rosie O'Donnell, for example—also use humor about women's social conditions to challenge the gendered status quo. The comic performances of these women work against the cultural dynamics that frame women's lives.

Twentieth-century writers and performers increasingly used stereotypes about women in humorous ways, turning them back on the culture that perpetuates them. In her 1925 novel *Gentlemen Prefer Blondes*, Anita Loos created the stereotypical dumb blonde, Lorelei Lee. Loos reinforces and extends stereotypes of femininity, subversively revealing the real humor in how power is so easily coopted from men by a seemingly incompetent woman. Penned during the same period, Dorothy Parker's writing is satirical and witty, often enlisting stereotypes of men and women to reflect incongruities, for example, between notions of beauty and social behavior. As one of the founders of *Vanity Fair*, her work fits neatly into dominant North American culture; but by challenging the status quo in humorously stating the obvious, it remains an inspiration for women humorists to this day, especially for those who seek to offer alternative gender models.

Despite ample evidence to the contrary, the idea that women lack a sense of humor continues to inform scholarly discussions. Indeed, on some levels, women's humor may be inaccessible to the mainstream, patriarchal culture because men and women often have contrasting interests and experiences due to the fact that at times they occupy different social spheres. A humorous interaction can succeed only if both parties have the relevant cultural and linguistic knowledge to understand it. Comprehending and laughing at a joke, funny story, cartoon, or stand-up comic's routine depends on the listener's ability to decode its message. Men and boys may have difficulty seeing the humor in women's jokes simply because they lack the cultural context to understand them.

Often categorized as culturally subordinate and passive, until the twentieth century, Euro North American women were not expected to tell jokes or even to laugh out loud. While women have access to both domestic and public spheres, in general, men have left the so-called "private" realm to women. Folklorist Carol Mitchell recalls how female informants discussed how they used humor to deal with everyday sexualized intimidation. They particularly identified with a joke about a woman who puts a flasher in his place. They admired her for her calmness and quick wit. One woman said,

> I could not think of anything to say in a situation like this, so I admire the stewardess who can effectively put the exhibitionist in his place without being flustered. Exhibitionism may be an expression of mental instability, but it is also a means men use to embarrass and frighten women in our society ... I would rather make fun of these people because I dislike being intimidated (Mitchell: 311).

In academic humor and Folklore Studies, the fact that women share experiences and have common sources of conflict has only recently been recognized.

Regarding feminist humor, "for those unsympathetic to feminism, the term feminist humor suggests male-bashing jokes by angry women, a definition that most feminists would reject" (Bing: 22). Anti-feminists might view the following as exemplary of feminist humor: "What's the difference between a man and a catfish? One is a bottom-feeding scum sucker and the other is a fish." Yet even feminists differ on the definition of feminist humor. To some, it is the humor of the oppressed; to others, it is "based on visions of change . . . empowering humor that recognizes the value of female experience" (ibid.). Generally, feminist humor works strategically to gain empowerment for all marginalized peoples, to challenge social institutions with its multilevel meanings and subtexts. It creates images of cultural norms, often satirizing the violence and control used by hegemonic culture, and empowers by subverting and misdirecting its audience. It can be divisive or inclusive in its effects.

Divisive feminist humor accentuates the differences between women and men, rather than working to undermine them. Often, it focuses more upon men's actions than on women's. For example: "How many men does it take to change a roll of toilet paper? We don't know; it's never been done" and "The children of Israel wandered around the desert for forty years. Even in biblical times, men wouldn't ask for directions." Rather than stereotyping women, as do most misogynist jokes, these jokes work because they apply stereotyped Euro North American cultural ideas about men's behavior, turning men into the Other, while women's behavior is the reasonable norm against which male actions (or lack of actions) are compared, to men's detriment. This ploy playfully subverts Simone de Beauvoir's famous dictum that women are the Other because they are socioculturally defined in terms of being not-men. Divisive humor may allow women to vent their frustrations, but it does little to change the world in which they live.

Inclusive humor works somewhat differently. For example, the 1991 film *Thelma and Louise* plays on gender stereotypes, incongruity, and the manipulation of cultural images that subordinate women in American society. Debunking the essentialist notion that women are inherently nonviolent, the film's heroes triumphantly blow up a lascivious truck driver's rig using a stolen gun. It is shocking and yet comic at the same time that women would resort to violence in this way, particularly because it comes in a form often depicted as masculine. The aggressive and humorous scene functions as a transfer of power from the masculine realm to the feminine; it does not divide women from men.

Similarly, Chicana writer Sandra Cisneros reconceives letters written to the saints for intervention in their romantic lives. This passage is from one addressed to San Antonio de Padua, patron saint of lost things:

> Can you send me a man man. I mean someone who's not ashamed to be seen cooking or cleaning or looking after himself. In other words, a man who acts like an adult. Not one who's never lived alone, never bought his own underwear, never ironed his own shirts, never even heated his own tortillas. In other words, don't send me someone like my brother who my mother ruined with too much chichi, or I'll throw him back. I'll turn your statue upside down until you send him to me (Herrera-Sobek: 110).

The speaker reverses the conventional idea of what a "man man" might be, making it clear that he is one who, like a woman, is capable of taking care of his own domestic needs. The presumption is that men have lost their mature self-sufficiency, and the patron saint of lost things is held responsible and will suffer the consequences of not meeting this petitioner's request. His statue will be turned upside down—as the world is turned upside down when men do not behave like full human beings—until he persuades her to right it by locating an available and appropriately responsible partner for her.

Lesbian feminist performance artists Shawna Dempsey and Lorri Millan work extensively with inclusive feminist humor, especially by playing on stereotypes about feminists, as, for example, in their "Mary Medusa":

> A woman out of control
> is a frightening thing.
> She may bite you
> and choke you
> and turn you to stone
> and then—snip! (quoted in Greenhill 1998: 92).

Women's appetites, as discussed by Dempsey and Millan, are out of control from a patriarchal perspective. But when reinterpreted by women themselves, male fear is transformed into the absurd; it becomes funny. Women's purported appetite for chocolate, for example, is noted only because of patriarchal hatred of fat women, who are threatening because they remain outside the purview of a society that judges women solely on their sexual attractiveness to men, and female fat is presumed abhorrent to heterosexual males:

> But bring on the chocolate cake.
> I want chocolate cake now.
> Appetite huge
> inappropriate appetite but she doesn't give a
> fuck, and why should she?
> A woman out of control
> is a frightening thing (ibid.).

Because lesbian feminist humor focuses on women and women's cultures, it may be incomprehensible to outsiders simply because hegemonic perspectives do not recognize its content. For example: "How many lesbians does it take to screw in a lightbulb? Seven. One to change it, three to organize the potluck, and three to film an empowering documentary." This joke plays on lesbian stereotypes about lesbians as invariably communalist and political. Similarly, "What does a lesbian take to a second date? A U-Haul" refers to notions of lesbians as interested more in committed relationships than in sex alone, and thus willing to move in together in what seems to be extreme haste in comparison to heterosexual norms. Feminist humor in Euro North American society may pertain to "weight loss, mammograms, HMOs, depression, disorganization, family trips, support groups, fashion, the information highway, self-help books, Republicans, the flat tax, and the 'true nature of dogs and cats'" (Bing: 30), subjects that don't apparently, or sufficiently, interest men.

Women humorists tend to stand apart from their own realities so they can view them with emotional detachment, a strategy that requires confidence and trust in oneself. Individuality, superiority, and aggressiveness—unfeminine qualities all—are necessary traits in a humorist. But humor can demand a very specific social context and a highly idiosyncratic audience, one that in the case of women's humor might not include men at all. Many have followed the French critical theorist Helene Cixous' call to women to shatter "the framework of institutions, to blow up the law," and to "break up the 'truth' with laughter" (Cixous: 258). *See also:* Coding; Cyberculture; Feminisms; Folklore About Women; Joke; Lesbian Folklore; Sexuality.

References: Bing, Janet. "Is Feminist Humor an Oxymoron?" *Women and Language,* vol. 27, no. 1 (2004): 22–33; Cixous, Helene. "The Laugh of the Medusa." In *New French Feminisms: An Anthology,* eds. Elaine Marks and Isabelle de Courtivron, 245–264. Amherst: University of Massachusetts Press, 1980; Greenhill, Pauline. "'A Good Start': A Graffiti Interpretation of the Montreal Massacre." *Atlantis,* vol. 17, no. 2 (1992): 106–119; ———. "Lesbian Mess (ages): Decoding Shawna Dempsey's Cake Squish at the Festival Du Voyeur." *Atlantis,* vol. 23, no. 1 (1998): 91–99; ———, Kjerstin Baldwin, Michelle Blais, Angela Brooks, and Kristen Rosbak. "25 Good Reasons Why Beer is Better Than Women and Other Qualities of the Female." *Canadian Folklore canadien,* vol. 15, no. 2 (1993): 51–68; Herrera-Sobek, Maria. "Social Protest, Folklore, and Feminist Ideology in Chicana Prose and Poetry." In *Folklore, Literature, and Cultural Theory: Collected Essays,* ed. Cathy Lynn Preston, 102–166. New York: Garland Publishing, 1995; Kaufman, Gloria. "Introduction: Humor and Power." *In Stitches: A Patchwork of Feminist Humor and Satire,* ed. Gloria Kaufman, vii–xii. Bloomington: Indiana University Press, 1991; Mitchell, Carol. "The Sexual Perspective in the Appreciation and Interpretation of Jokes." *Western Folklore* 36 (1977): 303–329; Radner, Joan N., ed. *Feminist Messages: Coding in Women's Folk Culture.* Urbana: University of Illinois Press, 1993; Steinem, Gloria. "If Men Could Menstruate." *Ms. Magazine* (October 1978): 110.

Kristin M. McAndrews

I

Immigration

Immigration is the experience of leaving one's home country and culture, whether by choice or by force, to move to and permanently settle in another. However, most newcomers to the United States and Canada distinguish between refugees (driven from their countries by political, religious, or economic persecution) and immigrants (who elected to leave their home countries). Many refugees dream of returning to their homelands, though they rarely do. Immigrants, in contrast, intend to stay in their adopted countries.

Immigration affects culture, traditions, language, spiritual well-being, and customs. Although finding jobs and housing and sometimes learning to speak a new language (usually English in the United States and Canada) are critical to newcomer women, issues of childrearing, cultural continuity, food, family health, education, cultural identity, and changing gender roles are also crucial. The challenge of living with a multiple cultural identity shapes most activities and decisions in immigrants' lives. Folklore genres such as personal-experience narratives, health and healing practices, cuisine preferences and food preparation, and textile traditions reflect immigrant life experiences. Additionally, it has often fallen to women to militate for social action in terms of immigration policies; the cultural capital that they carry based on these genres becomes invaluable in negotiating the new terrain for themselves and their families.

Women, mostly Chicanas and other Latinas, were instrumental in the huge marches and rallies of April and May 2006 opposing proposed legislation to build a wall along the U.S.-Mexico border. Leaders emerged. The American debate about immigration and immigration reform affects women directly. Much of the work of organizing the protests fell to women whose experience and commitment once again led them to the forefront of the current social movement.

The impact of immigration differs greatly for women and men. The expectation that men will seek extra-domestic employment while women establish the home gives men immediate access to language acquisition and development and exposure to new values, resources, and social systems.

Along the U.S.-Mexico border, however, young women often migrate north to work as nannies or maids or in service-industry jobs. While the effect of moving away from the home culture can be devastating for anyone, for women coming to the United States and Canada from highly traditional societies, the transition can be soul-shattering. Immigrant women often feel isolated, not only by linguistic barriers and lack of social contact, but also because their children, who may be caught up in the fast pace of mainstream life in the United States, often drift away from them. Feminist scholars working with immigrant and refugee women have recognized the need to offer a space for these women's voices, and much of their work is rooted in or draws upon oral history and personal-experience narratives. Debra Shutika's (2007) work with immigrant women in Pennsylvania and Mexico and Christian Zlolniski (2006) and others' work in California attest to the effects of immigration on women and families.

Perhaps due to the vacuum left when women have been de-territorialized through forced or chosen migration, immigrant women's stories often have subversive power to create community, preserve personal dignity, and redefine identity. For example, for some Italian women in North America, bawdy and risqué stories and jokes told only in the presence of other women provide a vehicle for criticizing the status quo without belittling the basic tenets of their culture. Novels, poetry, and essays written by Amy Tan, Julia Alvarez, Chitra Banerjee Divakaruni, Sandra Cisneros, and Eva Hoffman, among others, describe the "double otherness" (Zaborowska) of their experiences as immigrants and as women, and suggest ways in which their acculturation narratives challenge male-centered, dominant models of assimilation and integration. Yareli Arizmendi's work with Sergio Arrau for the film *A Day Without a Mexican* (2004) reminds viewers of the United States' economic reliance on immigrant labor.

Amy Tan's novels describe customs, rituals, folktales, recipes, and stories about intergenerational struggles between Chinese American mothers and their daughters. In *The Opposite of Fate: Memoirs of a Writing Life*, she clarifies that her work should not be construed as emblematic of a "pan-Asian American" experience, but rather as the experiences of one woman who writes about her Chinese American community as she remembers it. Yet, when she describes her mother's experiences with stockbrokers and doctors, noting that bad treatment and lack of respect are the penalty for not speaking English in America, she is describing the experiences of most newcomer women. Most women arrive with skills and education, but find themselves in low-income jobs or secluded at home because they don't speak the language. As a result, lack of respect and misconceptions about their intelligence and abilities tend to permeate their experiences.

One of the most prolific areas for the study of immigrant women is that of health and healing. *The Spirit Catches You and You Fall Down,* Anne Fadiman's (1997) poignant account of one Hmong family's attempt to navigate the allopathic medical system in the United States, draws on personal interviews to reveal not only how language barriers confound a newcomer family's efforts to understand treatment strategies for their daughter, but, more importantly, how cultural values and beliefs about health and healing are so deeply a part of the family's worldview as to make American medical practices unfathomable. Fadiman's ethnographic study offers a provocative look at the responsibilities of Euro North American medical practitioners to pay attention to cultural differences if they are to be effective healers. Subsequent studies draw upon life histories to explore the pluralistic health and illness practices of immigrants, who may have deeply held beliefs about the interconnected nature of a person's mind, body, and soul, a holistic approach relatively absent in medicalized healing practice.

Food and the ability to obtain familiar spices, herbs, and staples in order to feed one's family is a powerful concern for most newcomer women, who seek to maintain continuity, reinforce cultural identity, and ensure the health and well-being of their families. A woman from Ecuador living in Pennsylvania said, "I try to cook the food from my country, but my kids won't eat it. Sometimes I end up eating every day for three days the same thing. I do cry sometimes when I have to eat it myself and they request some American things.... They are rejecting my culture and that makes me so sad" (B. A. Jones). Feminists and other scholars have explored the relationship between foodways and cultural identity, using recipe books as frames for telling stories of arrival and survival in a new country.

In recent years, scholars of feminism have begun to look at the relationships between the feminist movement and ethnicity. Some immigrant women, faced with new cultural and behavioral norms, challenge those of their countries of origin in order to achieve and maintain their autonomy in North America; some maintain or return to their original traditions to support political, religious, or cultural beliefs. For example, prior to the attacks of September 11, 2001, many immigrant Muslim women had put away their head- and body-scarves (*hijab*); some did so because veiling symbolized an older, more conservative perspective on women, and some so as to not stand out in their adopted country. After the attacks, however, many women chose to reclaim the hijab as a statement in support of their beliefs and to educate Americans about the depth and breadth of Muslim culture and religion.

Perhaps also in response to the 2001 attacks, increases in the number of criminal-justice units along the border have resulted in increased militarization of the Mexico-U.S. borderlands. The cultural capital of female agents—more and more of whom make up the ranks of the Border Patrol and Immigration and Customs Enforcement—is often matched against that of immigrant women. As a result of U.S. military interventions in Central America in the 1980s, there was an increase in immigration from that region; the women who were apprehended or survived without being detained often formed alliances and support groups. In San Antonio, Texas, Laura Sanchez, for example, established a community-based immigrant and refugee center to provide assistance to newcomers. Women immigrants have enriched and preserved their traditional arts by becoming tradition-bearers, continuing their cultural traditions' practices and making sure that the young do not forget them. Hmong embroidery, Guatemalan weaving, and other material culture artifacts attest to the strength of the women's commitment to keeping their cultures alive in their new place.

Scholarly treatments of the experiences of newcomer women do provide insights, but novels, poetry, and collections of essays written by immigrant women themselves in their own voices offer powerful narratives that expose both the personal and universal realities of the immigrant experience and chronicle the impact of migration and immigration on traditional cultural expressions. *See also:* Activism; Childbirth and Childrearing; Daughter; Ethnicity; Folk Belief; Folk Custom; Folk Medicine; Foodways; Herbs; Muslim Women's Folklore; Politics; Race; Recipe Books; Storytelling; Tradition-Bearer; Veiling.

References: Alvarez, Julia. *Something to Declare.* Chapel Hill, NC: Algonquin Books, 1999; Bardenstein, Carol. "Transmissions Interrupted: Reconfiguring Food, Memory, and Gender in the Cookbook: Memoirs of Middle Eastern Exiles." *Signs: Gender and Memory*, vol. 28, no. 1 (2002): 353–387; Cisneros, Sandra. *Caramelo.* New York: Knopf, 2002; Danquah, Meri Nana-Ama, ed. *Becoming American: Personal Essays by First Generation Immigrant Women.* New York: Hyperion Press, 2000; Del Negro, Giovanna. *Looking Through My Mother's Eyes: Life Stories of Nine Italian Immigrant Women in Canada.* Second edition. Toronto: Guernica Editions, 2004; Divakaruni, Chitra Banerjee. *The Unknown Errors of Our Lives.* New York: Doubleday, 2001; Donnelly, Nancy D. *Changing Lives of Refugee Hmong Women.* Seattle and London: University of Washington Press, 1994; Fadiman, Anne. *The Spirit Catches You and You Fall Down: A Hmong Child, Her American Doctors, and the Collision of Two Cultures.* New York: Farrar, Straus and Giroux, 1997; Hernández, Daisy. "Missing José: The day California lost its Latinos, and cried about it." *Colorlines* (Fall 2004): 6–7; Jones, B. A., excerpt from interview IRWN-2003-AS-4-DT-2. *Pennsylvania Immigrant and Refugee Women's Network Oral History Collection,* Pennsylvania Folklife Archives. Harrisburg, PA: Institute for Cultural Partnerships, 2003; Marcus, Laura, ed. *In My Country: A Gathering of Refugee and Immigrant Fiber Traditions.* Portland, OR: Immigrant and Refugee Community Organization (IRCO), 2002; Pang, Keum-Young Chung. *Korean Elderly Women in America: Everyday Life, Health and Illness.* New York: AMS Press, 1991; Shutika, Debra Lattanzi. *Beyond the Borderlands.* Berkeley: University of California Press, 2007; Smith, Susan L. *Japanese American Midwives: Culture, Community and Health Politics, 1880–1950.* Urbana and Chicago: University of Illinois Press, 2005; Tan, Amy. *The Opposite of Fate.* London: Penguin Books, 2003; Working Women Community. *Tasking Diversity: A Celebration of Immigrant Women and Their Cooking.* North Vancouver, BC: Whitecap Books, 2003; Zaborowska, Magdelena J. *How We Found America: Reading Gender through East European Immigrant Narratives.* Chapel Hill: North Carolina University Press, 1995; Zlolniski, Christian. *Janitors, Street Vendors, and Activists: The Lives of Mexican Immigrants in Silicon Valley.* Berkeley: University of California Press, 2006.

Amy E. Skillman and Norma E. Cantú

Indian Maiden

The Indian Maiden is one of North America's most cherished cultural icons. Complex, multifaceted, and adaptable, she has captured the imagination of artists, writers, politicians and now filmmakers, since the sixteenth century. Her popularity never wanes; it merely shifts to fit the milieu of the era. And while her various depictions reveal little about the real lives of American Native women, they speak clearly about the cultures that continue to wield her as a representation of conquest and patriarchal power over Native peoples.

The Indian Maiden, like her male counterpart—the noble and ignoble savage—grew out of European colonizers' need to order, describe, and understand the people they met in North and South America. She first appeared in sixteenth-century etchings and imaginings as the American Indian Queen, a feared Indigenous warrior whose exotic beauty and military prowess symbolized the physical threats of the New World and Indigenous resistance to colonialism. As colonial powers dominated North America in the 1700s, the Indian Queen was replaced by the "dusky woodland" goddess, a smaller, gentler, less threatening representation of Native America. This Indian Princess has "played a powerful role in constructing the identities of both Indians and non-Indians" (Valaskakis: 5); the figure's beauty, innocence, and attraction to European culture created a viable political image that became the "first symbol of the United States, representing the Western wilderness reclaimed by civilization," and a romantic narrative strategy to assuage cultural guilt over colonialism (Fiedler: 65). Her most famous personifications are Pocahontas and Sacajawea.

The Queen and the Princess, however, are only a part of the complexity that is the Indian Maiden. The primary components—Princess and Squaw figures—form what Rayna Green calls the "Pocahontas Perplex"—a dichotomy against which Native women of Canada and the United States constantly struggle for recognition (Green 1995). While the Princess represents the goodness and nobility of her people and the possibility of racial assimilation into White North American culture, her darker sister, the Squaw, denotes the negative aspects of Nativeness. She may be beautiful, but she is also crafty and often sexually dangerous—a *femme fatale*—or she may be unattractive, overworked (symbolizing the supposed drudgery of women's roles in Native society), and surrounded by many children. Individually or as an amalgamation of both representations, the Indian Maiden's possible integration through marriage or sexual relations into dominant culture threatens the stability of a White racial hierarchy and religious morality. Both noble and ignoble stereotypes carry iconographic power to exploit the Indian Maiden as a tool for cultural dominance over Native Americans, most effectively illustrated in Hollywood westerns in which her inevitably sacrificial role underscores personal, political, and social attitudes about American Natives and interracial mixing.

The Indian Maiden continues to surface in a variety of twenty-first-century popular culture forms that trap Native Americans in an idealized and sexualized mythic past. Examples range from advertising, to product marketing, to music, and film. They include the Land-O-Lakes Butter girl, Imperial Sugar Company's "Pocahontas Sweet Thing" sugar substitute, Indian Princess Halloween costumes, the sexually garbed background dancers for Outkast's 2004 Grammy performance, Indian Princess Barbie, and Disney's *Pocahontas. See also:* Barbie Doll; Ethnicity; Film; First Nations of North America; Gender; Popular Culture; Princess; Race; Women Warriors.

References: Bird, S. Elizabeth. "Gendered Constructions of the American Indian in popular Media." *Journal of Communication* 49.3 (1999): 61–84; ———. "Tales of Difference: Representations of American Indian Women in Popular Film and Television." In *Mediated Women: Representations in Popular Culture*, ed. Marian Meyers, 91–109. Cresskill, NJ: Hampton Press, 1999; Burgess, Marilyn, and Gail Guthrie Valaskaskis. *Indian Princesses and Cowgirls: Stereotypes from the Frontier.* Montreal: OBORO, 1995; Fiedler, Leslie A. *The Return of the Vanishing American.* New York: Stein and Day,

1968; Green, Rayna. "The Pocahontas Perplex: The Image of Indian Women in American Culture." *Massachusetts Review*, vol. 16, no. 4 (1995): 698–714; Jaimes, M. Annette. "Hollywood's Native American Women." *Turtle Quarterly Magazine* (Spring-Summer 1993): 40–45; Marubbio, M. Elise. *Killing the Indian Maiden: Images of Native American Women in Film*. Louisville: University Press of Kentucky, 2006; Valaskakis, Gail Guthrie. "Parallel Voices: Indians and Others: Narratives of Cultural Struggle." *Canadian Journal of Communication*, vol. 18, no. 3 (1993): 3–13. http://www.cjc-online.ca/viewissue.phpid=22#Guest_Editorial (accessed January 1, 2007).

M. Elise Marubbio

Infertility

Infertility is the condition of being unable to become pregnant, or having great difficulty conceiving. Historically, infertility has been viewed as a woman's problem, and too often, therefore, deemed solely her fault—as the pejorative term "barren" for so long suggested—when, in fact, either partner or both may be responsible. The inability to conceive when pregnancy is desired is frustrating and often deeply painful. Infertility often has grave consequences for women, including loss of respect, marriage, and other forms of social support. However, some women want to control their fertility or look forward to menopause, either because they feel they have enough children or because they do not wish to become mothers. Whether the desire is to achieve or avoid pregnancy, concerns about fertility are common to women worldwide.

Cultures have different ways of interpreting infertility, and all have folk beliefs about its causes and cures. In North America, where many often-expensive medical treatments exist to address the inability to conceive, folk remedies and beliefs about how women can achieve pregnancy abound. In the United States and Canada, infertility is frequently attributed to stress, or to an inappropriately strong focus on efforts to conceive. Most women have heard that they must just relax, and pregnancy will come when they are not trying too hard. Alternative explanations include religious interpretations, such as that a past bad act makes the woman undeserving of pregnancy, or simply that God did not intend for that woman to conceive.

More numerous than beliefs about the causes of infertility are folk remedies for it. All cultures have at least some; they range from rituals, prayer, and visiting sacred sites to exercise and medication. In North America, two distractions/actions that are said to promote pregnancy are taking on responsibilities not compatible with parenthood and adopting a child. Common herbal remedies include vitex (chaste tree berry extract), licorice root, and dong quai. Another common remedy is using cough syrup during ovulation. Some advocate taking baby aspirin, while others insist that douching with egg whites before intercourse helps increase the chance of pregnancy. Many stories circulate about the physical positions to use during and after intercourse. Certain foods are said to increase the likelihood of pregnancy, while others are said to reduce it. A Canadian Web site (http://canada.com) advises women wishing to conceive a girl to eat lots of fish, vegetables, and chocolate, to sleep on the right side of the bed, and to initiate intercourse in a woman-superior position on even days of the month.

Among some Catholics, prayers to Jesus, Mary, St. Jude, St. Gerome, and St. Elizabeth are thought to be effective in promoting conception. Many Protestants rely on prayer to God or rely on faith healing. Jews traditionally pray to God for an end to infertility. Trips to holy places are associated with fertility in most religions, and some, like the shrine to Our Lady de la Leche in St. Augustine, Florida, have particular reputations for curing infertility.

Special days may be associated with fertility. Some Canadians believe that a woman who touches a wild hyacinth flower on March 1 will become more fertile; if she does so on an odd day under a quarter moon, she will conceive a boy. In Taiwan, a summer holiday celebrates the birthday of the Seven Old Maids, daughters of the hearth god. If a woman wishes to become pregnant, she makes a vow during the festival to help her community, gives a banquet for her friends and relatives, and sponsors a puppet show or opera at a local temple. If she conceives, her child will be protected by the Seven Old Maids. *See also:* Childbirth and Childrearing; Herbs; Menopause; Mothers' Folklore; Pregnancy.

References: Canada.com. "Find Out if It's Pregnancy: Fact or Folklore." July 27, 2005. http://www.canada.com/topics/lifestyle/parenting/story.html?id=a6a3a320-d189-4195-b888-24e034ab50e6&k=33019 (accessed August 10, 2008); Ginsburg, Faye, and Rayna Rapp. "The Politics of Reproduction." *Annual Review of Anthropology* 20 (1991): 311–343; McDonald, Margaret Read, ed. *The Folklore of World Holidays.* Detroit: Gale Research Inc., 1992; McLaren, Angus. *Reproductive Rituals: The Perception of Fertility in England from the Sixteenth Century to the Nineteenth Century.* New York: Methuen, 1985.

Theresa A. Vaughan

Initiation

Initiation is one of the rites of passage, those rituals connected with critical transformational and transitional events in human life—others being pregnancy and birth, puberty, marriage, and death. Women play central roles in initiation rituals, as participants, officiators, and audience members. Religious rites such as baptism and ordination into the priesthood are also important examples of initiation, typically signifying the death of an old way of life and rebirth into a new one.

Of course, many instances of initiation are quite a bit less momentous; everything from attending a *quinceñera's* debutante ball to pledging as a sorority sister to getting one's first piercing or tattoo can be treated as a form of initiation. Even the degree-granting process of universities, with their many attendant ordeals and trials, is a form of initiatory passage. Practically any activity that marks a new experience, facilitates a significant transition, or celebrates an important life change is material for the creation of an initiation ritual.

Historically, investigation of women's initiation rituals has been hampered by androcentric ethnographic scholarship that largely ignored women's rites and/or interpreted their meaning through the lens of male ritual patterns and often solely in terms of women's relationship to men as sexual property. The tendency for scholars to analyze women's initiation rituals within the context of other ritual activities, in particular marriage or puberty rites, contributed to the understanding of women as solely reproductive agents—or more precisely, sexual and reproductive objects. Women's varied and multivalent ritual experiences were therefore often missing from or distorted by analyses that purported to develop universal models or patterns of initiation.

Anthropologist Arnold van Gennep set what was to become the paradigm for analysis of initiation rituals in 1909. He coined the phrase "rites of passage" to describe rituals such as initiation that marked territorial passage or movement between one discrete level of social status and the next. Studying mostly male rites of initiation, van Gennep observed both cross-cultural and functional similarities among the rituals and reasoned that they were universal in human life across widely disparate cultures. He further determined that these rituals followed a universally set structure as a linear tripartite model of separation, transition, and reincorporation. While Victor Turner subsequently expanded the liminal (transition) stage of the process, little has challenged its linear and tripartite form until recently.

The term "rites of passage" has since entered the Anglo American English lexicon, as well as popular culture, and van Gennep's tripartite linear model has become the archetype by which initiations are not only evaluated, but even sometimes created—a curious case of life imitating academics, if not quite art. However, careful consideration of women's rites of initiation reveals that van Gennep's paradigm falls far short of universality. Several significant challenges to the archetype focus on questions of women's status and the notion of liminality, the absence of social-status motifs in women's rites, and the etically derived (that is, coming from the perspective of an outsider), unilinear directional progression of van Gennep's model.

Caroline Walker Bynum gets at the limitations of van Gennep's structural model of separation, liminality, and reincorporation through an examination of Victor Turner's theory of dominant symbols, liminality, and social drama within the ritual process. She uses a popular form of medieval narrative, the saint's life, to demonstrate that women's experiences are missing from the universal model. Contrary to expectations of the model, Bynum finds that women's stories are less processual than men's, less about dramatic turning points and inversions of status, and more about continuity and the ordinary. In terms of the universality of the liminal, "one either has to see the woman's religious stance as permanently liminal or as never quite becoming so" (1984: 74).

The problem with Turner's theory is not quite one of scarcity of data—he includes many examples of women's rites—but rather one of a skewed perspective. Turner's theory is rooted in a particular kind of Christianity characteristic of elites in the Western tradition. He does indeed look at women, but he does not look *with* them. In other words, he stands with elites within the dominant group (men) and sees women as liminal. While he attempts to stand with the inferior group (women), his analysis arises from an assumed symmetry of status. Comparison with actual experiences from women's lives reveals the hidden elite and male perspective within the allegedly universal model of initiation or rites of passage. Bynum does not develop a competing universal model, but instead uses women's narratives to suggest the complexity of human experience.

Another prominent challenge to van Gennep's universal model of initiation is in Bruce Lincoln's work. Taking a sampling of rites from five widely divergent societies, geographical areas, and time periods (the Tiyyar of South India, the Tiv of Nigeria, the Navajo of the southwestern United States, the Tukuna of Brazil, and the Eleusinian mysteries of ancient Greece), Lincoln finds combinations of four major types or creative forms of ritual at play within women's initiations: body mutation, identification with a mythic heroine or goddess, cosmic journey, and play of opposites. He problematizes the whole notion of status in women's initiations, noting that because women in many cultures have no status outside of their relationship to male relatives, their status is simplistically reduced in traditional analyses to a matter of sexuality. In contrast, Lincoln finds that women's initiations are not rituals of change in social status, but rites of cosmic transformation in which the entire community participates.

Women's initiation rites also lack the change in place or residence characteristic of male initiation ceremonies in van Gennep's model, beginning with a lack of true separation. While still firmly within the tripartite unilinear process, Lincoln offers a very different understanding of spatiality and movement found in women's initiations, arriving at an alternate pattern of enclosure, metamorphosis, and emergence. The women's initiation rites in Lincoln's study yield a number of tantalizing insights and conclusions, among them: 1) the body as the vehicle or means of personal transformation, 2) the lack of status change for women, 3) the goal of cosmic transformation, and 4) a new model of spatiality and movement within the rite.

The latest and most extensive challenge to van Gennep's linear and tripartite model is from Nikki Bado-Fralick. She employs a reflexive methodology to examine religious initiations performed by a group of Witches (Wiccans) in Ohio. She finds that what is traditionally understood as an isolated ritual moment with simple unilinear directional movement is actually embedded in a long and complex multidirectional process of increasingly somatic learning and practice that involves a shift in perceptual orientation as well as the formation of an intimate community.

Situating herself as both scholar and practitioner, Bado-Fralick enables us to look *with* as well as *at* the participants, revealing the range of possible perspectives and experiences throughout different stages of the process. Familiar themes of separation, liminality, and reincorporation (or enclosure, metamorphosis, and emergence) occur and recur throughout the ritual, but change according to perspective. "Initiation offers shifting sets of multidimensional, multidirectional, and multispatial experiences to its participants, depending on their role at any particular moment in the performance of the rite" (2005: 143) The participants' understanding of the rite will also change in time, as each takes on different roles and new perspectives that were not experienced before. Capturing these shifting roles and perspectives "allows us to see there is no single, unilinear movement to the rite, and no single or uniform understanding of initiation" (2005: 143–4).

Such emic (that is, insider) insights reveal the initiation process as a learning curve in which the initiate becomes attuned to a particular mode of perception necessary for ritual work through the development of what Bado-Fralick calls "the body-in-practice." The body-in-practice is specially trained, achieving a state that represents the mind and body working together to realize the whole person. Initiation is the means through which the natural body is ritually transformed into the body-in-practice. Transformation begins in early stages of the initiation process with increasing amounts of training in what anthropologist Thomas Csordas calls "somatic modes of attention." These provide special ways of attending to and with one's body that enable initiates and "other-than-human persons" such as deities and spirits to perceive, mutually interact with, and affect change in one another (1993: 127).

The initiation ceremony dramatically performs this transformation by ritually unmaking the natural body and then remaking it as the body-in-practice. This is accomplished through the ordeals of symbolic death, the ritual performance of the cosmic journey of the Goddess to the underworld, with its attendant purification by the four elements (air, fire, water, and Earth), and, finally, rebirth as a new initiate. These initiation rites participate in at least two ritual themes identified by Lincoln: identification with a mythic heroine or Goddess and a cosmic journey. But in contrast to what might be expected from his analysis of women's rites, it is identification with the mythic female body that is the transformative catalyst for both female and male initiates in this particular form of Wicca.

Extending Lincoln's conclusions, Bado-Fralick finds that the body—or rather, the particularly trained body—is not merely the vehicle for transformation, but the active agent through which spirit is transformed. The journey of purification—undertaken while the candidate is blindfolded—performs the ritual unmaking of a cultural dependence on what Johannes Fabian (1994) calls "visualism," a strategy of distancing that removes all the other senses and thereby the body from knowledge production. Blindfolding compels the candidate to rely upon those other senses—to rely upon the body—in grasping the lessons of initiation. Death and rebirth, the unmaking and remaking of the new initiate are made real by engagement with and through the body-in-practice. The transformation of initiation occurs with and through the body—as active subject, never passive object—and is made meaningful by embodied and performed identification with the Goddess' journey to the underworld (Bado-Fralick 2005: 129–131).

The strategy of looking with, rather than at, women's rituals enables us to glimpse important and sometimes hidden ways in which the body—specifically the gendered body—performs transformation and creates meaning in ritual. As the site of interaction between a person and the structures of political and cultural power, the body is the active field of negotiation for cultural, sexual, and political tensions.

Conflicting gender and political realities are sometimes literally inscribed on the body through initiation, as they are in the extensive bridal "hinna" (henna) ceremony described by M. Elaine Combs-Schilling. The bride undergoes a lengthy process of having henna applied to her body in ornate designs while she remains completely immobile and dependent upon others. She "cannot eat, drink, or use the bathroom by herself" during the time it takes for the application to fully set, a period that may extend to more than twenty-four hours (1991: 111).

Although this occurs in a festive, relaxed, and even ribald context—the bride surrounded by caring women who attend to her every need, praise her beauty, and crack jokes about men—the ceremony is a rite of submission, with the gendered body as its focal point. The female body is required not only to be passive, but also to learn the "postures and attitudes of submission" that she will henceforth practice as a woman in that culture. The henna ceremony strengthens the "culture's inventions of what it means to be male and female" and makes them real with and through the body (ibid.).

Even when the rite is something that is clearly done to the bride, rather than by her, the body plays an active role. "The ritual gives the bride embodied practice in the body stances, attitudes, and postures that are likely to gain her the most security and status during the early years of marital life. Through multiple senses, through multiple enactments, the bride is rehearsed in being the kind of individual that the society expects her to be and will reward her for being" (ibid.). Although restrained and subdued, the gendered body is still the active agent of transformation—teaching and learning, producing and resisting power.

Women's rituals provide critical information about the gendered nature of ritual processes and the importance of the body in the production of knowledge. Looking with women's bodies, with the multivalent expressions of women's initiations, we see rich and complex ritual patterns that provide suggestions about how we might reframe scholarly models to more accurately express a full range of lived human experiences. *See also:* Death; Henna Art/*Mehndi*; Pregnancy; *Quinceañera*; Rites of Passage; Sorority Folklore; Wedding; Wicca and Neo-Paganism.

References: Bado-Fralick, Nikki. *Coming to the Edge of the Circle: A Wiccan Initiation Ritual.* American Academy of Religion, Academy Series. Oxford and New York: Oxford University Press, 2005; Bynum, Caroline Walker. "Women's Stories, Women's Symbols: A Critique of Victor Turner's Theory of Liminality." In *Anthropology and the Study of Religion*, ed. Robert L. Moore and Frank B. Reynolds, 105–125. Chicago: Center for the Scientific Study of Religion, 1984; Combs-Schilling, M. Elaine. "Etching Patriarchal Rule: Ritual Dye, Erotic Potency, and the Moroccan Monarchy." *Journal of the History of Sexuality* 1 (1991): 658–81; Csordas, Thomas. "Somatic Modes of Attention." *Cultural Anthropology* 8 (1993): 135–56; Eliade, Mircea. *Rites and Symbols of Initiation: The Mysteries of Birth and Rebirth.* Trans. Willard Trask. New York: Harper & Row, 1958; Fabian, Johannes. "Ethnographic Objectivity Revisited: From Rigor to Vigor." *Rethinking Objectivity*, ed. Allan Megill, 81–108. Durham, NC: Duke University Press, 1994; Gennep, Arnold van. *The Rites of Passage.* Trans. Monika B. Vizedom and Gabrielle L. Caffee. Chicago: University of Chicago Press, 1960 [1909]; Hufford, David, ed. "Reflexivity and the Study of Belief." Special Issue of *Western Folklore*, vol. 54, no. 1 (1995): 1–11; Kasulis, Thomas P. *Intimacy or Integrity: Philosophy and Cultural Difference.* Honolulu: University of Hawaii Press, 2002; Lincoln, Bruce. *Emerging from the Chrysalis: Studies in Rituals of Women's Initiation.* Cambridge, MA: Harvard University Press, 1981; Myerhoff, Barbara, and Jay Rubin. "Introduction." *Crack in the Mirror: Reflexive Perspectives in Anthropology*, ed. Jay Rubin, 1–35. Philadelphia: University of Pennsylvania Press, 1982; Turner, Victor. "Betwixt and Between: The Liminal Period in Rites of Passage." In *Betwixt and Between: Patterns of Masculine and Feminine Initiation*, eds. Louise C. Mahdi, Steven Foster, and Meredith Little, 3–19. La Salle, IL: Open Court, 1987 [1967]; ———. *The Ritual Process: Structure and Anti-Structure.* Ithaca, NY: Cornell University Press, 1969.

Nikki Bado-Fralick

J

Jewish Women's Folklore

The story of Jewish women's folklore in North America is one of adaptation and innovation. Jewish immigrants brought with them the folkways and traditions they had practiced in Europe. As many Jews became assimilated into the larger Christian society, especially in the early decades of the twentieth century when the largest immigration of European Jews occurred, they abandoned more and more of the religious practices and customs they had brought. The descendants of mid-nineteenth-century German Jews also encouraged the further acculturation of early twentieth-century Eastern European Jews. These Jews, who were no longer observant of all of the *mitzvot* (613 commandments which, according to tradition, God transmitted to the Jewish people on Mount Sinai through the prophet, Moses) wanted to be perceived more as North Americans and less as Jews—a typical reaction of all immigrant groups of that period. After the catastrophe of the Shoah ("Holocaust"), when European Jewry itself was all but extinguished and first-generation immigrants were dying of old age, the majority of Jews who were no longer orthodox (observant of the mitzvot) had a relatively sparse folk tradition to transmit to their children growing up in the latter half of the twentieth century. Music and food traditions tended to be the major exceptions to this phenomenon.

The women's movement of the 1960s—further fueled by New Age spirituality, the *havurah* movement (small groups of Jews meeting in homes for services without rabbis leading), and the creativity of Jewish lesbians seeking to make their claim on tradition—produced a climate of vitality, questioning, and spiritual searching. "What does it mean to be a woman and a Jew post-Holocaust?" "How does feminism inform Judaism?" "Can I find spiritual meaning as a woman and a Jew?" These questions circulated at the time.

Jewish feminism became fertile ground for a women's folklore to take root and grow. Jewish women began meeting in small study groups. Judaism considers study of the Hebrew Bible (also known as the Torah, "the teachings") to be a sacred act. While study had mainly been the provenance of men, women began to engage in study of Jewish texts as feminism spurred them on to find meaning for themselves.

The ordination of women as rabbis—first in Reform Judaism (1972), then in Reconstructionist Judaism (1974) and Conservative Judaism (1985)— necessitated their expertise with traditional texts as professionals. In the late twentieth century, women cantors (clergy in charge of chanting the religious service and leading congregational singing of traditional texts) became increasingly numerous in Reform and Conservative Judaism. Women composers, such as Debbie Friedman (influenced by Joan Baez and others associated with the folksong revival of the 1960s), have also taken the lead in putting traditional texts to new tunes, which have been popularized at camps, conclaves, and conferences. The twenty-first century has even begun to see a miniscule number of Modern Orthodox women ordained privately. In addition to their acceptance as rabbis and cantors, Jewish women were admitted to the formerly all-male enclave of Jewish Studies in universities as professors of Bible, Talmud, and Jewish history. Once Jewish women had access to texts that had been almost entirely written and interpreted by men for centuries, they discovered a world of knowledge to which they had been outsiders. This was key to the revitalization of Jewish women's folklore in recent times.

The revival of *Rosh Hodesh* ("New Moon festival") is a case in point. It was discovered as a holiday for women in the 1970s, when a New York-based women's study group, *Ezrat Nashim* (Hebrew for "the women's section of the Orthodox synagogue," used ironically in this case), came upon a reference to it in the Talmud. It stated that Rosh Hodesh was given as a reward to women for not contributing their gold and jewelry to the making of the Golden Calf (Exodus 32:1 ff.). A group member, Arlene Agus, wrote an article ("This Month is for You" in *The Jewish Woman: New Perspectives*) and Rosh Hodesh groups for Jewish women started appearing in private homes in the United States and Canada. It is significant that the groups did not, for the most part, meet in synagogues. In the early days, women sensed that they were doing something outside the norm. In fact, they were creating a Jewish experience without a rabbi and outside the synagogue. This paralleled the havurah movement, contemporaneous with Rosh Hodesh, led by knowledgeable men and women in their twenties and thirties who were alienated by the predominance of cathedral-like synagogues where the rabbi stood at a distance from the congregation. Spiritual intimacy was not possible in such environments, they felt, and so they began meeting in homes to conduct services.

Jewish women recognized that Rosh Hodesh gave them an authentic ritual context, one rooted in tradition. Linked to their ancestors all the way back to the biblical mothers Sarah, Rebecca, Rachel, and Leah, Rosh Hodesh provided them with the sacred time and space to pursue their personal and collective journeys as Jewish women. Today, there are women's and girls' Rosh Hodesh groups all over the world. Other Jewish women's groups also formed. Small consciousness-raising groups of feminist/lesbian women made Jewish feminists realize that they had needs and viewpoints that could not be addressed in a secular, non-Jewish setting. Out of these groups came an outpouring of creativity: writing, poetry, and journaling that often connected with the line of Yiddish-speaking women writers in Europe and North America.

The types of revitalized Jewish women's folklore are varied. New lifecycle rituals include those for pregnancy, pregnancy loss, infertility, the birth of a girl, naming of a girl, weaning, menarche, pre-*bat mitzvah*, commitment ceremonies for lesbian couples, separation, alternative divorce rites, menopause, and the wisdom of aging.

The development of new ritual objects includes *Kos Miriam* ("Miriam's cup," used alongside the cup reserved for Elijah at the Passover *seder*, or ceremonial dinner), birth and pregnancy amulets, Miriam's tambourines, bat mitzvah quilts, and baby quilts. Holding a women's seder (frequently on the third night of Passover) and injecting woman-centered texts into the traditional ritual meal have also become popular, and are directly related to a feminist sensibility. In addition, innovations on traditional ritual objects emphasize the full participation of women in every aspect of Jewish life, including their use of *tallit* ("prayer shawl") and *kippah* ("skullcap"), and handling the *bein gavra* ("Torah cover").

The development of new verbal lore includes the revival of traditional *tekhinot* ("prayers for occasions of a woman's life"); the writing of *midrash* (a traditional verbal form where a story is created to fill in a gap in the Bible); and the composition of music such as *niggunim* (wordless chants), songs and chants based on biblical verses, and ballads about biblical and historical Jewish women.

A result of Jewish women's study that has had a mixed impact on women's folklore was the popularization of the mystical concept, *Shekhinah* ("Indwelling Presence"). According to the *Zohar*, a classical thirteenth-century text on Jewish mysticism, the Shekhinah is the feminine aspect of God. The Shekhinah is immanent, residing in all beings, responsive to their pain and suffering, receptive, and concerned with worldly matters. Women have written songs, poetry, prayers, and stories about and addressed to the Shekhinah. However, sometimes these creative expressions impart qualities to the Shekhinah that elevate the concept to Goddess-like stature. The contemporary spirituality movements of Neo-Paganism, witchcraft, and goddess-worship have brought a distinctly non-Jewish element to the meaning of Shekhinah as an aspect of God. However, many Jewish women who have felt disenfranchised by antiquated notions of God as father, king, and lord, as well as by remnants of tradition which still denigrate women, have been relieved to discover that the Jewish God has a feminine side which has been present yet covert until recently.

Jewish women's folklore today exemplifies the fullest meaning of "tradition" as an innovative response to contemporary life that remains rooted in the ways of the ancestors. *See also:* Folk Music and Folksong; Foodways; Politics, Popular Culture; Rites of Passage.

References: Adelman, Penina. *Miriam's Well: Rituals for Jewish Women Around the Year.* New York: Biblio Press, 1990 [1986]; Agus, Arlene. "This Month is for You." In *The Jewish Woman: New Perspectives,* ed. Liz Koltun, 84–93. New York: Schocken Books, 1976; Broner, E. M., and Naomi Nimrod. *A Weave of Women.* Reprint edition.

Bloomington: Indiana University Press, 1985 [1978]; ———. *The Telling: Including the Women's Haggadah*. Reprint edition. New York: HarperCollins, 1994; Kaye/Kantrowitz, Melanie, and Irena Klepfisz. *The Tribe of Dinah*. Revised, expanded edition. Boston: Beacon Press, 1989; Koltun, Liz, ed. *The Jewish Woman: New Perspectives*. New York: Schocken, 1976; Nadell, Pamela, ed. *American Jewish Women: A Reader*. New York: New York University Press, 2003; Plaskow, Judith. *Standing Again at Sinai: Judaism from a Feminist Perspective*. New York: HarperCollins, 1990; RitualWell.org: Ceremonies for Jewish Living. http://www.ritualwell.org (accessed August 10, 2008); Rotkovitz, Miryam. "Kashering the Melting Pot: Oreos, Sushi Restaurants, 'Kosher Treif,' and the Observant American Jew." In *Culinary Tourism*, ed. Lucy Long, 157–85. Lexington: University of Kentucky Press, 2003; Saltzman, Rachelle H. "Shalom Ya'll: The Jews of Memphis." *Southern Exposure*, vol. XI, no. 5 (1983): 28–36; Umansky, Ellen, and Ashton, Dianne. *Four Centuries of Jewish Women's Spirituality*. Boston: Beacon Press, 1992.

Penina Adelman

Jingle Dress

Jingle dresses are garments decorated with objects that make tinkling sounds, most often used as clothing for dancing. The adornment of women's dresses with metal pendants has been noted in ethnographic literature since the early eighteenth century. Tinkling cones, replacing the dewclaws of deer, have long been used as ornamental decoration on clothing, bags, and drums, but the first actual depiction of a jingle dress is found in Karl Bodmer's portrait of a Sioux woman at Fort Pierre in 1833. She is clearly wearing a dress trimmed with metal pieces at the bottom.

It is generally agreed that the jingle dress dance originated among the Ojibwe: some claim its use began in the Whitefish Bay community in southwestern Ontario, while others point to Mille Lacs, Minnesota. In almost all versions of the story, the dress and the dance were revealed to an old man in a dream. The man has an ill daughter or granddaughter, and the dress and dance are given to him so that she might be healed.

The jingle dress itself is usually constructed of brightly colored cloth made even more dazzling by the placement of the cones—often constructed from snuff-can lids shaped into triangular bells and attached to the dress with ribbons—and the movement of the dancer. The garment's form is generally straight and multilayered in order to accommodate the greatest number of cones, which might number 200 to 500 or more.

There can be no doubt that the rhythm and movement of the dance are healing, with the soothing sounds of the cones striking each other in perfect assonance. The basic footwork, which can be straight or side step, keeps the dancer's feet on the ground as her body and the cones move with the unique tempo of the drum. Her body is straight and erect, her steps smooth and flowing, even when a more intricate cross step is used. For many, the dance itself is seen as a prayer, and it is not at all unusual to ask a jingle dress dancer to pray for an ill friend or family member during the performance. *See also:* First Nations of North America; Folk Dance; Folk Medicine; Ritual.

References: Axtmann, Ann. "Performative Power in Native American Powwow Dancing." *Dance Research Journal*, vol. 33, no. 1 (Summer 2001): 7–22; Browner, Tara.

Heartbeat of the People: Music and Dance of the Northern Pow-wow. Urbana: University of Illinois Press, 2002; Goetzmann, William H., David C. Hunt, Marsha V. Gallagher, and William J. Orr. *Karl Bodmer's America*. Lincoln: Jocelyn Art Museum and University of Nebraska Press, 1984; Pearson, Tom. "In the Spirit." *Dance Research Journal*, vol. 79, no. 10 (October 2005): 70–74.

Theresa Schenck

Joke

A joke is a form of artistic communication that, within its performance frame, is meant to be humorous. Jokes are, therefore, theorized as culturally "marked" forms of communication. Not only does the telling of a joke require the performer to negotiate a space in conversation to perform the joke, but once negotiated, that space (or play frame) becomes a licensed domain in which the breaking of rules, whether linguistic or sociocultural, is situated as being not serious or not in earnest. Within this play frame, performers address a wide range of topics (gender, sex, sexuality, marriage, race, ethnicity, class, occupation, region, nationality, religion, politics, health, and technology, as well as ephemeral, contemporary events), sometimes affirming the dominant norms of a cultural group and sometimes contesting and seeking to revise them. Thus, by telling a joke or by listening to and deciding whether or not to laugh at a joke, people not only entertain themselves but also participate in a social dialogue about the nature of their world and their relationships in it. This is as true for women as it is for men, but for women, who, historically, have, at times, lived under a cultural injunction of silence, the telling of a joke and the decision whether or not to laugh at a joke has been fraught with ambivalence—the pleasure of claiming agency by asserting the right to speak and the ability to be funny must be weighed against the danger of being chastised for doing so.

Nonetheless, women have an active sense of humor, exhibiting adroitness with wordplay through witty one-liners and a strong preference for humorous personal-experience narratives, a form of conversational humor that has as its primary goal the construction of intimacy. But women also perform a range of more formally constructed jokes. They tell photocopy, fax, and e-mail verbal jokes ranging in length and style from the riddle or question-and-answer joke.

> Do you know what would have happened if it had been Three Wise Women instead of Three Wise Men?
> They would have asked for directions, arrived on time, helped to deliver the baby, cleaned the stable, made a casserole, and brought practical gifts.

to the longer narrative joke which may take the form of a tall tale, a shaggy-dog story, a comic anecdote, a humorous folktale, or a catch tale (a hoax story):

> Three guys are out having a relaxing day out fishing. Out of the blue, they catch a mermaid who begs to be set free in return for granting each of them a wish.
> Now one of the guys just doesn't believe it and says, "Okay, if you can really grant wishes, then double my IQ."

The mermaid says, "Done."
Suddenly the guy starts reciting Shakespeare flawlessly and analyzing it with extreme insight.
The second guy is so amazed, he says to the mermaid, "Triple my IQ."
The mermaid says, "Done."
The guy starts to spout all the mathematical solutions to problems that have been stumping all the scientists in various fields: physics, chemistry, etc.
The last guy is so enthralled with the changes in his friends that he says to the mermaid, "Quintuple my IQ."
The mermaid looks at him and says, "You know, I don't usually try to change people's minds when they make a wish, but I really wish that you would reconsider."
The guy says, "No, I want you to increase my IQ times five, and if you don't do it, I won't set you free."
"Please," says the mermaid, "You don't understand what you're asking. It will change your entire view on the universe. Won't you ask for something else . . . a million dollars, anything?"
But no matter what the mermaid says, the guy insists on having his IQ increased by five times its usual power.
So the mermaid sighs and says, "Done."
And he becomes a woman.

Yet other forms of jokes rely on pictorial representation, on gesture, or on such forms of play behavior as the tricking of someone through the performance of a practical joke; for example, high-school-age girls have been known to "t-pee" a boy's car using toilet paper and tampons that have been dipped in ketchup.

Interpretations of jokes and joke performances generally fall within three broad categories of humor theory: cognitive-perceptual theory, social-behavioral theory, and psychoanalytic theory. Cognitive-perceptual theory seeks to explain why jokes are funny by focusing on linguistic and semantic incongruity or seeming inappropriateness. When a southern American grandmother comments to a group of girls, "Before you marry any ol' hairy-legged boy, be sure to look carefully into his genes (jeans)," her comment is humorous, in part, because of the pun, "genes/jeans" (a homonym juxtaposing two words that sound alike but that have different meanings). The pun incongruously links frames of reference (biology and costume) that seemingly have nothing to do with each other, although that which is more broadly signified (family genealogy and sexual competence) may have much to do with each other. The grandmother's and the girl's laughter acknowledges and celebrates their respective intellectual acuity in using and understanding the pun as well as their mutual enjoyment at having broken a taboo against women and girls speaking openly, though by means of the ambiguity of a pun about sex.

Social-behavioral theory focuses in part on who can joke with whom and under what conditions as well as what social functions joking serves. Also referred to as disparagement or superiority theory, the social-behavioral approach analyzes joking relationships as a means of identifying social structure. For example, research suggests that women prefer to tell jokes in small intimate groups or in their homes while men enjoy telling jokes to small and large audiences and are more willing than are women to tell jokes to casual acquaintances and in public places. Women also prefer to tell their jokes to other women whereas men willingly tell their jokes to other men, to women, and to audiences consisting of both men and women. And women's joking tends to be more conciliatory than does that of men, who frequently participate in aggressive, competitive joking.

Psychoanalytic theory, also called suppression-repression or release theory, explores jokes and performances of jokes in relation to the human psyche and the ways in which laughter functions as a relief mechanism in stressful situations. Jokes are understood as a means of freeing oneself from social conventions, those of perception, logic, language, and morality. As Sigmund Freud explains, jokes, except when innocent, are either hostile (aggressive, satiric, or defensive) or obscene (functioning as a means of exposure). In general, research suggests that men tell more openly aggressive, hostile jokes and more obscene jokes than do women, particularly in cross-gendered situations and in mixed-gendered audiences. Women's humor when hostile is frequently coded, thereby expressing hostility in a disguised form, and it is used tactically rather than strategically.

While women may at times tell many of the same jokes as men, women's humor frequently addresses the details of women's lived experience in ways that seek to validate that experience rather than to denigrate it. Women's jokes are often revisionary in their attempt to disclose past misrepresentations, contest gender boundaries, rethink textual and cultural scripts, speak the unspeakable, and thereby claim agency for the self. Women's laughter celebrates that claim. *See also:* Class; Coding; Ethnicity; Feminisms; Folklore About Women; Gender; Girls' Folklore; Grandmother; Humor; Personal-Experience Narrative; Photocopylore; Sexuality.

References: Apte, Mahadev L. *Humor and Laughter: An Anthropological Approach.* Ithaca, NY: Cornell University Press, 1985; Barreca, Regina. *They Used to Call Me Snow White ... but I Drifted: Women's Strategic Use of Humor.* New York: Penguin Books, 1991; Crawford, Mary. "Just Kidding: Gender and Conversational Humor." In *New Perspectives on Women and Comedy,* ed. Regina Barreca, 23–37. Philadelphia: Gordon and Breach, 1992; Green, Rayna. "'Magnolias Grow in Dirt': The Bawdy Lore of Southern Women." In *Calling Home: Working-Class Women's Writings: An Anthology,* ed. Janet Zandy, 189–198. New Brunswick, NJ: Rutgers University Press, 1990 [1977]; Mitchell, Carol. "Some Differences in Male and Female Joke-Telling." In *Women's Folklore, Women's Culture,* eds. Rosan A. Jordan and Susan J. Kalčik, 163–186. Philadelphia: University of Pennsylvania Press, 1985; Preston, Cathy Lynn. "Cinderella as a Dirty Joke: Gender, Multivocality, and the Polysemic Text." *Western Folklore* 53 (1994): 27–49; Roemer, Danielle M. "Photocopy Lore and the Naturalization of the Corporate Body." *Journal of American Folklore,* vol. 107 no. 423 (1994): 121–138; Ryan, Cynthia A. "Reclaiming the Body: The Subversive Possibilities of Breast Cancer Humor." *Humor,* vol. 10, no. 2 (1997): 187–205; Thomas, Jeannie B. "Dumb Blondes, Dan Quayle, and Hillary Clinton: Gender, Sexuality, and Stupidity in Jokes." *Journal of American Folklore,* vol. 110, no. 437 (1997): 277–313; ———. *Featherless Chickens, Laughing Women, and Serious Stories.* Charlottesville: University Press of Virginia, 1997.

Cathy Lynn Preston

Jump-Rope Rhymes

Skipping—individual or group rope-jumping play—is often accompanied by traditional verses sung or chanted by the players. Although originally enjoyed by boys, when social changes in the 1900s gave girls greater freedom of movement and released them from the confines of the home, girls became the preservers and developers of jumping rope and of jump-rope rhymes in particular. Girls developed a variety of different games and accompanying rhymes. Examples can be found in collections by folklorists Dorothy Howard, Iona and Peter Opie, Roger D. Abrahams, Simon Bronner, Brian Sutton-Smith, June Factor, Edith Fowke, and Ian Turner.

The main forms of jump rope are termed "single rope," "long rope," and "double Dutch." The last—two long ropes turning in unison—was first developed in the United States after World War II, when young girls used clotheslines for ropes on New York City pavements. However, it was in the school playground that jump rope became a highly prized social activity. Single rope involves both individual and pair-skipping, but the long rope offers apparently endless possibilities.

Girls developed rhymes to emphasize the rhythm of the turning rope and to help the turners keep time. Early examples were simple repetitions of syllables in a rhythmically intoned pattern, for example: "Blue-bells-cockle-shells," "Lip-stick-lip-stick," or "Mickey-Mouse-Donald-Duck." Rhymes also mark the rope's speed. The words "red hot peppers," "hot peppers," or simply "pepper" cue the rope-turners to speed up, as recorded in 1909: "Lay the cloth, knife and fork / Don't forget the salt, mustard, vinegar, PEPPER." Folklorists Elizabeth Grugeon and Alan Dundes noted that jump-rope rhymes often deal with universal issues of growing up—sexuality, parenthood, aging, and death—and sometimes parody adult norms and behavior. They may also address social issues such as racism, sexism, and teen pregnancy.

Several categories of jump-rope rhymes can be identified. The most popular are action chants, in which the jumpers perform the movements dictated by the rhyme: "Teddy bear, Teddy bear, touch the ground / Teddy bear Teddy bear turn around ..." and "One, one eat a plum / Two, two touch your shoe / Three, three bend your knee...." Many rhymes have connections with the past, but change to suit the times. Hence, in the rhyme, "We are the Girl Guides dressed in blue," the girls who used to "Bow to the king and salute the queen" now "show their knickers to the rugby team!"

Other categories involve divination: when a jumper trips on the rope, the girls negotiate a decision together about her supposed future. Traditional "Tinker, tailor, soldier, sailor" rhymes may relate to the name of the skipper's future husband, the style of her wedding, the clothing she will wear, and the number of children she will have. Other kinds of rhymes involve a large number of jumpers moving in and out of the ropes on a particular cue, which might be the jumper's birth month, as in "All in together, girls / never mind the weather, girls / When it's your birthday, please jump in / January, February" or character-based rhymes, such as "In came the doctor / In came the nurse / In came the lady with the alligator purse." Rhyme texts in all categories reveal girls as preservers of tradition as well as innovators of change. *See also:* Divination Practices; Girls' Games; Race; Rhymes; Text; Tradition-Bearer.

References: Abrahams, Roger D. *Jump-Rope Rhymes: A Dictionary.* Austin: University of Texas Press, 1969; Factor, June. *Far Out, Brussel Sprout! A First Collection of Children's Chants and Rhymes.* Melbourne: Brolly Books, 2004 [1983]; Fowke, Edith. *Sally Go Round the Sun: 300 Children's Songs, Rhymes, and Games.* Toronto: McClelland & Stewart, 1969; Gaunt, Kyra D. *The Games Black Girls Play: Learning the Ropes from Double-Dutch to Hip-Hop.* New Yrok: New York University Press, 2006; Goodwin, Marjorie Harness. *The Hidden Life of Girls: Games of Stance, Status, and Exclusion* (Blackwell Studies in Discourse and Culture Series). Malden, MA: Wiley-Blackwell, 2006; Jemie, Onwuchekwa. *Yo' Mama! New Raps, Dozens, Jokes, & Children's Rhymes from Urban Black America.* Philadelphia: Temple University Press, 2003; Opie, Iona and Peter Opie. *Children's Games in the Street and Playground.* Oxford: Oxford University Press, 1969; Sutton-Smith, Brian. *The Folkgames of Children.* Austin: University of Texas Press, 1972; Turner, Ian, June Lowenstein, and Wendy Lowenstein, eds. *Cinderella Dressed in Yella.* Melbourne: Heinemann, 1982.

Janice Ackerley

K

Knitting

Knitting is a craft technique used to create stretchy fabrics or garments. Knitters make fabric using long pointed sticks or "needles" typically made of metal, plastic, wood, or bamboo, and "yarn" made of various spun fibers. By creating loops of yarn on the needles and then interlocking the loops using the sticks, knitted work grows to create finished pieces that range from blankets and sweaters to booties, socks, and scarves. Ingenious techniques for shaping and patterning the fabric are based on variants of two stitches: "knit" and "purl." By changing the colors and textures of yarn, knitters create satisfying aesthetic challenges. Women usually learn the art directly from other women, so knitting is often a social activity. Knitters may also work while traveling, watching television, or listening to music. Knitting is not intrinsically a women's activity, but women have dominated craft knitting and carry most of its folk traditions.

Research on industrial and craft traditions traces knitting back more than 500 years, with probable origins earlier in North Africa and the Middle East. A widespread handcraft by the Middle Ages, it spread into North America with European settlement. Some north Atlantic communities with a traditional economic basis in fishing and wool production—the British Channel Islands, the west coast of Ireland, the coast and islands of Scotland, Scandinavia, the Baltics, Iceland, the eastern coasts of Canada, and Maine—are particularly known for their stitch and color patterns in distinctive sweaters, hats, and mittens. Other countries, such as Greece, Australia, and Peru, where local wool is produced from sheep, goats, llamas, and alpacas, also have distinctive traditions.

During the twentieth century, the popularity of knitting fluctuated for social, fashion, and economic reasons. Associated with the early women's suffrage movement in the United States, the image of knitting shifted, and by the 1960s, it was criticized by many feminists as an oppressive domestic pastime. Knitting, however, continued to be valued locally as an adjunct to fashion, a gesture of friendship or family connection, a charity activity, or a practical civilian contribution in wartime.

The recent development of knitting information on the Internet such as blogs, podcasts, and e-zines has supported a renaissance of knitting. Online knitting communities offer opportunities for folklorists to explore the transmission of knowledge about techniques and patterns, as well as superstitions (for example, to knit a sweater for a boyfriend is to lose him when you finish the sweater).

Folklorists Robin Hansen (2005) and Jill Breit (2005) have produced scholarly studies as well as popular instruction books on hand knitting. There is also now a growing interest in the social, therapeutic, and communitarian potential of craft knitting. These aspects of the craft have always been important, but recently many young knitters have linked their practice to an ideological position—"craftivism"—which valorizes reclaiming traditional skills as a counter to the processes of globalization and commercialization. Popular "public knitting" or "stitch 'n bitch" sessions where women gather to knit and chat together on a regular basis makes more visible what were once largely domestic craft and subsistence activities. Fashion designers interested in handcrafted and ethnic "looks" have also encouraged interest in knitting since the 1990s. Nevertheless, most craft knitters now work with commercially prepared and mass-distributed yarns.

Labor costs and the availability of mass-produced machine-knit clothing have gradually transformed the economics and meanings of knitting. While hand-knitted articles cannot compete with mass-produced machine-knitted items on cost, hand knitting has other qualities that increase its value for knitters and recipients alike. *See also:* Folk Art; Needlework; Suffrage Movement; Superstition; Women's Friendship Groups; Women's Work.

References: Breit, Jill. "Knitting it Together: The Case Study of a Sweater." *Voices: The Journal of New York Folklore,* vol. 31 (Winter 2005): 37–45; Greer, Betsy, *Taking Back the Knit: Creating Communities through Needlecraft.* Master's thesis, Goldsmith College, London, 2004; Hansen, Robin. *Favorite Mittens: Best Traditional Patterns from Fox & Geese & Fences and Flying Geese & Partridge Feet.* Portland, ME: Down East Books, 2005; MacDonald, Anne L. *No Idle Hands: The Social History of Knitting.* New York: Ballantine Books, 1988; Morgan, Gwyn. *Traditional Knitting in the British Isles.* London: Batsford Books, 1981; Rutt, Richard. *A History of Hand Knitting.* London: Batsford Books, 1987; Stoller, Debbie. *Stitch 'n Bitch: The Knitter's Handbook.* New York: Workman Publishing, 2003.

Teri Brewer

L

La Llorona

La Llorona, "The Woman Who Cries" or the "Wailing Woman," is a spirit dressed in white, often seen haunting bodies of water, or, in more modern versions of the legend, standing by the side of the road in the rain. She is usually said to be looking for her lost or murdered children. Recently, Chicana writers have reclaimed La Llorona as a figure of female empowerment.

Folklorists agree that La Llorona is descended from Aztec mythology. There one finds a primary Mother Earth goddess, Tonantzin, expressed in several personalities, including Coatlicue and Cihuacoatl. Coatlicue is the mother of the sun god and moon goddess. Cihuacoatl is the "weeping goddess" of childbirth, newborns, and women who die in childbirth. La Llorona was originally a character who simultaneously represented both of Tonantzin's aspects: life-giving power (childbirth) and life-taking power (death of children through carelessness or an evil nature). Over time, she lost her life-giving qualities and became known only for her own children's deaths. In some stories, the figure of *La Malinche* is conflated with La Llorona. La Malinche was an Aztec princess who was given to the Spanish conquistador Hernán Cortés, and who served him as translator and sexual partner; she is said to have borne the first *mestizo* (a person of mixed European and Native American ancestry) and that she cries for her "lost" children. However, the archetype of the mother/woman torn between her own needs and those of her children is universal and much older, appearing as early as Euripides' *Medea*.

Yet the story of La Llorona also includes many other universal themes, such as two lovers kept apart by race or socioeconomic class. In some Chicano stories, La Llorona is named Maria, evoking associations with the Virgin Mary's motherhood. There are two main versions of her story. In some variants, she cries because she has lost her children through her own carelessness, frequently by deserting them when she commits suicide. In another, more sinister version, she has killed her children out of vengeance by drowning them in a river, often because her upper-class lover has rejected her and married a woman of his own social standing. Other versions entail that her husband, provoked by her stretch marks, has left her for a younger and/or prettier woman, or has extramarital affairs. She kills their children, the cause of her "imperfection" as a wife. The most unusual variation on the revenge narrative casts Maria as a young woman married to an older man. She is the one having affairs; she drowns her lover's children to protect her marriage and reputation. In any case, whether the children's deaths are caused by self-hatred, carelessness, or spite, she is the spirit of a woman who has killed herself. Frequently, when she reaches heaven, she is sent back to Earth to collect the souls of her children before she can enter.

Chicana writers such as Helena Maria Viramontes ("The Cariboo Café"), Sandra Cisneros ("Woman Hollering Creek"), and Alicia Gaspar de Alba ("La Llorona on the Longfellow Bridge") have reclaimed La Llorona, rejuvenating her life-giving power and reinscribing her story to show how it is the failures and weaknesses of men that may cause women to kill their own children as acts of resistance against patriarchy's abuses of women, and especially of mothers. *See also:* Childbirth and Childrearing; Class; Death; Ethnicity; Folk Belief; Lament; Legend, Supernatural; Mothers' Folklore; Violence; Virgin, Cult of the.

References: Cisneros, Sandra. *Woman Hollering Creek and Other Stories.* New York: Vintage/Random House, 1992; Cole, SuzAnne C., and Jeff W. Lindemann. "The Legend of La Llorona: Its Origins and Purposes." *Southwestern Studies: An Interdisciplinary Journal*, vol. 2, no. 1 (1994): 3–8; Ramirez, Arturo. "La Llorona: Structure and Archetype." In *Chicano Border: Culture and Folklore*, eds. Jose Villarino and Arturo Ramirez, 19–26. San Diego, CA: Marin, 1992; Viramontes, Helena Maria. "The Cariboo Café." In *The Moths and Other Stories*. Houston: Arte Publico, 1985.

Sarah Catlin-Dupuy

Lacemaking

Lace is an ornamental network of openwork fabric formed by interwoven threads without any supporting material as a foundation. There are two main types of lace: point, also called needle lace, and bobbin lace. Though it was considered a luxury item, lace's value transcended its place in fashion—it was important on an economic level; almost every European country had a lace industry at some point. During the early centuries of its manufacture, it was primarily women and children who were involved in lace production, though sometimes men were involved in its creation and distribution.

Most scholars agree that needle lace began in Venice in the early 1500s. Intricate laces were made using just a single needle and thread. It developed from Italian *reticella* (a technique derived from embroidery) which was drawn threadwork on a support—the threads were taken or "drawn" out of the cloth, and the empty space was filled in with other thread to create a design. Unlike needle lace, the origins of bobbin lace are disputed. Though it was established in both Flanders and Venice by the mid-1500s, it is Flanders that became the preeminent center of lace production. Some think the antecedents of bobbin lace may have developed from a technique called *passamenterie*, "the weaving of braids." Passaments were ornamental braids, ribbons, and precious metals used to decorate garments. The techniques of bobbin lace and passamenterie were similar: looms or long cushion pins held the threads in place; to keep the threads from tangling, they were wound on weights or bobbins made of lead, bone, or wood.

Flanders became a major producer of bobbin lace because it was a center of the arts and had an intact infrastructure for trade, access to cheap labor from convents and poorhouses, and was a source of thread—flax was a major regional crop and of excellent quality. Since it was made by hand and very time-consuming, lace was quite expensive. The Catholic Church—which could afford it—was a principal consumer of lace, especially for the robes adorning statues of saints. Between 1600 and 1650, as many European countries grew in economic strength, lacemaking spread throughout Europe and the British Isles. During this time and into the seventeenth century, clothes with lace decoration became fashionable for both men and women of nobility. This coincided with the golden age of Queen Elizabeth I's reign, famous for its opulence and extravagance. A raised collar and large ruff, requiring yards of lace, were very stylish; Renaissance fashions helped spur the development of new lace styles and techniques. Pattern books that came into circulation after the development of the printing press were usually geared toward women and, along with new techniques, made lace production more accessible, allowing cottage industries to emerge in many places.

In 1818, the first bobbin lace net was produced by machine. Though at first machine lace was looked down upon, it was faster to produce and less expensive than handmade lace. As the Industrial Revolution expanded throughout the 1800s, it became more difficult for the handmade lace industry to thrive. By the late 1800s, with less demand for lace in clothing, both the handmade and machine-produced lace industries dwindled.

Lacemaking was first introduced to the United States during the colonial period. The colonists brought skills necessary for their new life, including lacemaking. The earliest (and only) records of large-scale U.S. lace production are from seventeenth-century Ipswich, Massachusetts, where, according to a 1797 copy of the *American Gazetteer*, women and children made lace to supplement their families' earnings. The advent of machine-made lace affected the lace-making workforce, which was periodically replenished with the arrival of new immigrants who carried the skill with them.

Other techniques for making lace-like material include crochet and tatting. Crochet, like lace, is an open fabric without a cloth ground or any other supporting material. It developed from the Asian craft of *tambour* embroidery (so-called because the work frame looked like a drum or tambourine). A hooked needle is used to make a chain of loops of thread and to link the stitches. Crochet became popular in France in the seventeenth century; by the mid-nineteenth century, it was taught throughout Ireland and became a common technique for making lace there.

Tatting originated in the mid-1800s, remained a favorite pastime through the late nineteenth century, and has recently reemerged as a popular craft. Sometimes called "knotting," it is made using a tatting shuttle, a metal or plastic oval-shaped instrument that has a hook on one end. The technique involves joining small tatted rings employing decorative loops of thread, called picots, by using the hook on the end of the shuttle to join the thread. *See also:* Embroidery; Needlework; Sewing; Women's Work.

References: Allgeier, Gretchen. "A History of American Lace and Lacemakers." *Fiberarts* 17 (January/February 1991): 11–12; Cotterell, Marta M. "Lacemaking in Colonial Ipswich, Massachusetts." *Antiques* (December 1997): 854–863; Harang, Marni. "The Flowers of Flanders: Seventeenth-Century Flemish Bobbin Tape Lace." *Piecework* (May/June 1994): 61–63; Kraatz, Anne. *Lace: History and Fashion.* New York: Rizzoli, 1998; Lauriks, Wim. "The Birthplace of Lace Making." *LACE Magazine International* 49 (Spring 1999); Levey, Santina. *Lace: A History.* London: W. S. Maney & Son Ltd., 1984.

Elena Martínez

Lament

A lament is a non-narrative poem or song expressing deep sorrow, grief, or regret; it is a dirge about loss. Goddesses wail for their lost cities in the oldest Sumerian and Asian Indian documents, and the weeping goddess emerges. The great classic female blues singers complain about their lovers' infidelities, their bosses' harassment, and other troubles. In the Baltics, such songs are called *raudas* ("weeping-songs"); in Ireland, *caoineadhs.*

In many patriarchal societies, a specialist class of mourners (moirologistres)—the weeping women—develops, whose laments offset typically male warlike, heroic, or epical songs. Like folk healers, lamenters are in an ambiguous alliance with the institutional religion which both needs and cannot totally control these channelers of dangerous expression. Their presence is tolerated, if not encouraged, at many ritual events, such as weddings and funerals.

Laments draw from the lyrical tradition often associated with women, as opposed to the more narrative or epic male musical traditions. As in other genres of music or chant, lament draws from a ritual core of formulas whose symbolism is connected with the local language. The lamenter improvises for the event and the individual. Heavy use of repetition, embellishment of the deceased's name, endearments, and diminutive names are traditional means of expressing and channeling strong emotions.

A loss occurs when a member of a group leaves on a journey into the unknown, probably never to return. Another loss happens during a rite of passage, a unidirectional change into another state. Laments may be sung when recruits leave to join the army or during weddings when a woman in a patrilocal marriage leaves her natal home. In Finnish wedding laments, the bride and her birth family are spoken of in terms of endearment. In contrast, those who come to take her away—the family into which she is marrying—are portrayed as beasts or savage, cruel strangers. These laments underscore the death of the bride's girlhood, the loss of her former self. The mother-in-law is called a stepmother—a stranger who displaces the bride's own dear mother. In matrilocal weddings, there is no need for leave-taking laments for the bride; she stays within her natal family. Nor are they needed in societies which do not put maximum value on virginity (loss of sexual innocence), nor in more egalitarian societies in which a bride does not acquire the status of servant.

The most extreme loss, as well as the final passage, is death. Funeral songs are thus most readily recognized as laments. In such, the deceased is commonly addressed directly, though often with a substitute name. Laments may also address other mourners and/or a deity. The ritual guides and strengthens the dead with praise of her/his worth as shown by the inestimable grief of those left behind. It implores those already "on the other side" to receive the dead as welcome guests and to help them in their new location.

Often a special class or caste of women specializes in the art of weeping as a way of bridging the world left behind and the world beyond. It is felt as a calling. Weeping women are usually older, and thus experienced in the suffering of life. They take up the emotions of the community by offering themselves and their own lives with projected anguish. Theirs is a shaman-like summoning and unleashing of frightening emotional powers, eliciting and channeling as "women who made the long and dangerous journeys to the domains of the dead ... explored the distant realms of the interior world ... souls traveled to frightening realms beyond the borders of common experience" (Currier 1991: 50).

Female exploration of interior hells projected as journeys to the strange and unknown can be understood in opposition to male exploration of exterior dangers consistent with physical forays in real life. The wailing woman learns to control, ride, and channel the powers unleashed and the tension felt, instead of being so overcome as to be destroyed. At funerals, the lamenters lead the departed spirit safely to the other side. The emotions in recognizing one's mortality are given expression to flow, to cleanse the grievers from being poisoned by anguish. It is also perhaps the ultimate expression of the commonality of women as a shared cycle of birth, loss, grief, suffering, and death through orphanhood, widowhood, abandonment, deaths of loved ones, and their own mortality.

Women's common roles as lamenters may result from their greater experiences of grief ensuing from stronger emotional bonds. Their expression may also be a cry for help by the weak. Further, the near-universal lower status of women tends to make acceptable their expression of extreme emotions—self-mutilation, rending clothes, and the like—which would not be tolerated in men. Professional lamenting is an occupation that affords creative expression, status, and social power in the realm of the supernatural or magical. In societies in which women's status is otherwise low and/or their social position harsh, female lamenters stand on the bridge between life and death, where even the most powerful warrior is helpless.
See also: Death; Folk Belief; Folk Custom; Folk Music and Folksong; Gender; *La Llorona*; Magic; Rites of Passage; Ritual; Wedding; Women's Work.

References: Alexiou, Margaret. *The Ritual Lament in Greek Tradition.* Second English edition revised by Dimitrios Yatromanolakis and Panagiotis Roilos. Baltimore: Rowman & Littlefield, 2002 [1974]; Bourke, Angela. "More in Anger Than In Sorrow: Irish Women's Lament Poetry." In *Feminist Messages: Coding in Women's Folk Culture,* ed. Joan Newlon Radner, 160–182. Urbana: University of Illinois Press, 1993; Currier, Alvin C. *Karelia: The Songsingers' Land and the Land of Mary's Sons (An Introduction to and Meditation on Karelian Orthodox Culture).* Madison: self-published, 1991; Feld, Steven. *Sound and Sentiment: Birds, Weeping, Poetics, and Song in Kaluli Expression.*

Philadelphia: University of Pennsylvania Press, 1982 [1978]; Jones, LeRoi [Amiri Baraka]. *Blues People.* New York: Morrow Quill Paperbacks, 1963; Kramer, Samuel. *Lamentation Over the Destruction of Ur.* Chicago: University of Chicago, 1940; Nenola-Kallio, Aili. *Studies in Ingrian Laments. Folklore Fellows Communications.* Volume C1 (No. 234). Helsinki: Academia Scientiarum Fennica, 1982; Rosenblatt, Paul, R. Patricia Walsh, and Douglas Jackson. *Grief and Mourning in Cross-Cultural Perspective.* New Haven, CT: HRAF (Human Relations Area Files) Press, 1976; Weinbaum, Batya. "Lament ritual transformed into literature: Positing women's prayer as cornerstone in western classical literature." *Journal of American Folklore,* vol. 114, no. 451 (Winter 2001): 20–39.

Aija Veldre Beldavs

Laundry

Without the aid of electricity, gas, or running water, stand-alone automatic washing machines and dryers, washing clothes was an arduous task for earlier generations of women. For those who needed to carry well water or melt ice, heat water, and then dry heavy cotton and woolen clothing, the chore could stretch out for days, especially during winter weather. Even when contained to one day, laundry helped organize the rest of the week's work. In North America, Monday was traditionally washday, in part because women could be freed from meal preparation by serving leftovers from a large weekend meal. Ironing, mending, and other household responsibilities followed for the rest of the week.

Understandably, laundry was often disliked. In 1869, Catharine Beecher called it "the American housekeeper's hardest problem" (Beecher 1869) and advocated removing laundry from the household. She had in mind forming cooperative laundries, a concept that never gained popularity. However, available evidence—how-to manuals, diaries, and household budgets—all suggest that many nineteenth-century women shared Beecher's negative view of laundry, and, whenever they had any discretionary money, would jettison the task. For women of Color and those otherwise economically disadvantaged, laundry therefore provided necessary wage-labor performed for more affluent White households. Before being eclipsed by the widespread availability of washing machines, commercial laundries were a major employer of female industrial labor.

Women continued to be burdened by laundry throughout the first half of the twentieth century, and in some neighborhoods were judged by their clotheslines; the cleanliness and brightness of the clothes, as well as the order and timeliness with which they were hung, were considered reliable marks of good housekeeping, hence good character. While today laundry is nothing like the work faced by earlier generations, and far fewer women have their self-worth assessed by a clothesline, it can be a demanding chore for contemporary women because of changing practices that, for example, might demand that a pair of jeans be worn only once before being thrown into the wash.

Despite its burdens, laundry has positive associations for some women. In the past, washday sometimes allowed women to get out of the house and socialize while hanging clothes out to dry. Enjoyment can be found in the transformation of dirty clothes to clean ones, and in the hanging out of clothes in an aesthetically pleasing pattern. Laundry can offer women an opportunity to perfect a form and to gain a sense of control rarely found in lives of domestic labor. Finally, some women consider doing laundry an expression of their ethic of care; when hanging out clothes, for example, they may feel symbolically connected to their families and even to other women across generations and cultures who have performed the same task. Roberta Canton's superb documentary film *Clothesline* (1981) uncovers both the artistry and drudgery of doing laundry. *See also:* Folklore About Women; Gender; Gossip; Housekeeping; Occupational Folklore; Region: United States; Wage Work; Women's Work.

References: Beecher, Catharine E., and Harriet Beecher Stowe. *The American Woman's Home.* New York: J. B. Ford & Co., 1869; Cantow, Roberta. *Clotheslines.* Video. Buffalo Rose Productions, 1981; Strasser, Susan. *Never Done: A History of American Housework.* New York: Pantheon Books, 1982.

Diane Tye

Legend, Local

Local legends are stories that are associated with particular locations: a striking feature of the natural landscape (a rock, hill, or swamp) or of the built environment (a house, a bridge, or a monument in a cemetery), a site of historical significance (a battle, a devastating accident, or a murder) or of an unusual and/or supernatural phenomenon (a UFO sighting, a "monster's" habitation, or an apparition of the Virgin Mary).

Local legends have an etiological function when used to explain the origin and nature of place names, striking geomorphologic features, and other local phenomena. Such stories may reinforce historical memory and/or be part of a community's larger mythological system. "Gallows Hill" in Salem, Massachusetts, for example, is designated in legends as the place where those convicted of witchcraft during the Salem witch trials were hanged in 1692. The formation known as Devil's Tower (a monolith rising 1,267 feet above the surrounding landscape in northeastern Wyoming) is explained by Kiowa legends as the product of the Great Spirit's intervention to save a group of children who were threatened by a bear. Etiological stories may also give narrative form to particular belief practices, such as the relationship between cursing and the birth of something unnatural; for example, in New Jersey, "Mother Leeds" is said to have cursed her thirteenth child and given birth to the Jersey Devil.

Local legends frequently memorialize historical events of local significance. Women often figure prominently in such legends, which, in turn, encode local norms of proper and improper gender behavior. For example, local legends foreground women's civilizing roles in saving particular towns in Georgia from the destruction of General William Tecumseh Sherman's notorious march through that area during the Civil War. Other local legends may attest to a woman's innocence or guilt in a local murder; good examples are the stories about Lizzie Borden in Fall River, Massachusetts, and Belle Gunness in La Porte, Indiana. Local legends may describe the extraordinary deeds of local personages of historical significance, such as Lady

Godiva, who rode naked on her horse through Coventry, England, in a gesture to free the town from its servitude to her husband.

Folklorists use the term "migratory legends" for stories that share traits or motifs with legends found elsewhere but have been localized through associations with local landmarks and/or the attributions of names of local personalities (a process known as "oicotypification" or "ecotypification"). These legends include stories about lover's leaps, tales of *La Llorona*, and such classic adolescent legends as "The Vanishing Hitchhiker," "The Hook," and "The Boyfriend's Death."

Sites associated with murders and other gruesome or tragic events may be said to be haunted and become the source of adolescent legend-trips, which typically involve a ritual visit. Such sites range widely from haunted statuary in cemeteries to haunted railroad crossings to university buildings and dormitory rooms said to be haunted by students who have committed suicide or who have been murdered. Often, such visits involve ostensive action, the acting out of local supernatural legends. *See also:* Borden, Lizzie; *La Llorona*; Legend, Urban/Contemporary; Local Characters; Ritual; Witchcraft, Historical.

References: Ashton, John. "Ecotypes, Etiology and Contemporary Legend: The 'Webber' Cycle in Western Newfoundland." *Contemporary Legend*, New Series 4 (2001): 48–60; Bird, S. Elizabeth. "Playing with Fear: Interpreting the Adolescent Legend Trip." *Western Folklore* 53 (1994): 191–209; Bronner, Simon J. *Piled Higher and Deeper: The Folklore of Student Life*. Little Rock, AR: August House Publishers, 1995; Brunvand, Jan Harold. *The Vanishing Hitchhiker: American Urban Legends and Their Meanings*. New York: Norton, 1981; Davidson, H. R. Ellis. "The Legend of Lady Godiva." *Folklore*, vol. 80, no. 2 (1969): 107–121; Henken, Elissa R. "Taming the Enemy: Georgian Narratives about the Civil War." *Journal of Folklore Research*, vol. 40, no. 3 (2003): 289–307; Langlois, Janet. L. "Belle Gunness, the Lady Bluebeard: Narrative Use of a Deviant Woman." In *Women's Folklore, Women's Culture*, eds. Rosan A. Jordan and Susan J. Kalčik, 109–124. Philadelphia: University of Pennsylvania Press, 1985; Lindahl, Carl. "Ostensive Healing: Pilgrimage to the San Antonio Ghost Tracts." *Journal of American Folklore* 118 (2005): 164–185; McCloy, James F., and Ray Miller. *Phantom of the Pines*. Moorestown, NJ: Middle Atlantic Press, 1998; Momaday, N. Scott. *The Way to Rainy Mountain*. Albuquerque: University of New Mexico Press, 1969.

Linda J. Lee and Cathy Lynn Preston

Legend, Religious

All legends are expressions of belief systems, but some deal specifically with religious themes, doctrines, or denominations. In the case of religious legends, the subject matter will often encompass supernatural or miraculous occurrences that correspond to and reinforce a religious belief. Both relating to and related with everyday life, religious legends represent a productive avenue for the exploration of issues of belief. They often occur on the margins of religious systems, at the cultural level, or better yet, as part of what is known as folk or vernacular religion, which has been described as "religion as it is lived" (Primiano 1995).

As such, religious legends circulate outside of the sponsorship of institutionalized denominational hierarchies, arising instead from individual needs and syncretic belief systems. For example, Lydia Fish has explored Christian legend cycles of a coming apocalypse predicted by the Vanishing Hitchhiker, a common character in secular urban legends. In the versions she collected, a motorist picks up a hitchhiker who asks a question about her or his belief in or preparation for Jesus' second coming. Soon after, the passenger disappears from the backseat of the car, and the storyteller variously identifies the passenger as Jesus, a nun, a Nephite, St. Joseph, or John the Baptist. Passed on by word of mouth and outside the official structure of any Christian denomination, such tales serve as expressions of belief about the state of the world and its eschatological future while providing dramatic narratives for their listeners.

Because they act as a widespread means of communication, legends can be found in almost all faiths and belief traditions. Michiko Iwasaka and Barre Toelken have detailed a variety of ghost legends that center on mothers and their children, and their functions within modern Japanese culture with its mixture of Buddhism, Shinto, Confucianism, and Christian elements. Catholic legend cycles are discussed in Elizabeth Mathias and Richard Raspa's study of Italian American folklore and in Deborah Anders Silverman's study of Polish American folklore. Various contemporary Jewish legends about the coming Messiah have been collected by Mordechai Staiman; Linda Dégh has discussed "testimonial miracle legends" among Pentecostals; and Bill Ellis has studied contemporary legends concerning satanism and the occult, which both oppose and are informed by mainstream American Christianity.

While legend cycles are often informed by the cultural context of specific faith traditions or denominations, legend cycles also circulate across boundaries, as the similarities of Wandering Jew legends to the Vanishing Hitchhiker stories above attest. William A. Wilson provides another example of this conflation in his discussion of a legend involving two Mormon women missionaries who, when knocking on the door of a rapist, were protected because the man saw three male figures with swords standing behind them, a reference to the Mormon legend tradition of the Three Nephites. Wilson then points to a very similar legend told within a Methodist tradition wherein a rapist declines to molest a young girl because a "huge person" (identified as the Holy Comforter) is standing beside her. From this example, it is apparent that legend motifs are dynamically shaped to fit the belief system in a new context.

Often legends involve, proclaim, or mediate gender, and the treatment of gender in religious legends can reinforce patriarchal values inscribed in traditional gender roles. However, because legends exist outside of official religious discourse, they are also an avenue of resistance and an expression of the experiences of women. For example, Margaret K. Brady has studied the narratives by Mormon women who, as a result of their visions of unborn children, decide to have another child. Brady argues that these personal-experience narratives, which become legendary as they are passed on, represent a way for women to claim power in their reproductive choices within patriarchal societies.

Depending on how broadly one defines religion—for example, Jill Dubisch has noted religious aspects related to health-food movements—religious legends are ubiquitous, but even using a more strict definition of religion, religious legends are extremely widespread within all of the various denominations and faith traditions. *See also:* Folk Belief; Legend, Supernatural; Legend, Urban/Contemporary; Personal-Experience Narrative; Pregnancy.

References: Brady, Margaret K. "Transformations of Power: Mormon Women's Visionary Narratives" *Journal of American Folklore* 100 (1987): 461–68; Dégh, Linda. *Legend and Belief: Dialectics of a Folklore Genre.* Bloomington: Indiana University Press, 2001; Dubisch, Jill. "You Are What You Eat: Religious Aspects of the Health Food Movement." In *Folk Groups and Folklore Genres: A Reader,* ed. Elliott Oring, 124–35. Logan: Utah State University Press, 1989; Ellis, Bill. *Raising the Devil: Satanism, New Religions, and the Media.* Lexington: University of Kentucky Press, 2000; Fish, Lydia. M. "Jesus on the Thruway: The Vanishing Hitchhiker Strikes Again." *Indiana Folklore,* vol. 9 no.1 (1976): 5–13; Hand, Wayland D., ed. *American Folk Legend: A Symposium.* Berkeley: University of California Press, 1971; Iwasaka, Michiko, and Barre Toelken. *Ghosts and the Japanese: Cultural Experience in Japanese Death Legends.* Logan: Utah State University Press, 1994; Mathias, Elizabeth, and Richard Raspa. *Italian Folktales in America: The Verbal Art of an Immigrant Woman.* Detroit: Wayne State University Press, 1985; Primiano, Leonard Norman. "Vernacular Religion and the Search for Method in Religious Folklife." *Western Folklore* 54 (1995): 37–56; Silverman, Deborah Anders. *Polish-American Folklore.* Urbana: University of Illinois Press, 2000; Staiman, Mordechai. *Waiting for the Messiah: Stories to Inspire Jews with Hope.* Northvale, NJ: Jason Aronson, 1997; Wilson, William A. "Mormon Folklore: Faith or Folly?" *Brigham Young Magazine,* vol. 49, no. 2 (1995): 47–54; Wojcik, Daniel. "'Polaroids from Heaven': Photography, Folk Religion, and the Miraculous Image Tradition at a Marian Apparition Site." *Journal of American Folklore* 109 (1996): 129–148.

David A. Allred

Legend, Supernatural

Supernatural legends are narratives that describe human encounters with the supernatural world, a realm that, in legend, as in experience-centered belief narratives, is "objectively real" although "qualitatively different from the everyday material world" but "that interacts with" the material world in certain ways that are inclusive of "beings that do not require a physical body in order to live" (Hufford: 11). Supernatural legends address a wide variety of topics, including witchcraft and magic, fairies and other supernatural beings, ghosts and revenants, encounters with UFOs, aliens, the "Men in Black," and religious and/or celebrity apparitions. When told as a first-hand account of a supernatural experience, the supernatural legend is called a "memorate."

Traditional witchcraft legends often present a decidedly unfavorable view of women as threatening to their community. The witch in legend is almost always devious: the child-stealing witch may indiscriminately take milk or butter from her neighbor's cow, sell her soul to the Devil to acquire knowledge of witchcraft, and/or manipulate household objects and servants to facilitate getting herself to a witches' Sabbath. Venetia Newall's *The Witch Figure* (1973) offers perspectives from a variety of cultures, while, perhaps, the oldest compilation of witchcraft beliefs and legends is *Malleus Maleficarum,* a fifteenth-century witch-hunter's guide.

Many types of supernatural beings appear in traditional legends, including fairies, household spirits, the "hidden people," trolls, jinns (or djinns), demons, and nature spirits. Such beings are often presented as ambiguous figures, alternately capable of helpful and harmful actions toward human beings. Katherine Briggs' *The Fairies in Tradition and Literature* (1967) and Diane Purkiss' *At the Bottom of the Garden* (2001) are excellent studies of supernatural beings, as is Peter Narváez's *The Good People* (1991), a collection of contemporary fairy-lore essays. Recent accounts of UFO sightings, abductions, and encounters with "Men in Black" bear a striking resemblance to traditional fairy-abduction stories, suggesting that these parallel narrative traditions address similar psychological concerns.

Ghosts that haunt various locations and objects are popular topics of both contemporary and historical supernatural legends that frequently appear in regional collections such as Ruth Ann Musick's *The Telltale Lilac Bush and Other West Virginia Ghost Tales* (1965). Craig Dominy's popular Web site, "The Moonlit Road," is a valuable textual and audio repository of ghost stories from the American South, augmented by analyses of their cultural and historical contexts. Yet other studies, like Gillian Bennett's *Alas, Poor Ghost!* (1999), address gender in relation to traditions of supernatural belief. Frightening or uncanny locations often serve as the destination for adolescent legend-trips, which typically involve a ritual visit to a supposedly haunted house, cemetery, bridge, road, or railroad crossing that has been singled out by local tradition. Such visits frequently involve ostensive action, or the literal acting out of supernatural legends, as in the legend-game "Bloody Mary" (or "Mary Whales"), performed by adolescent girls.

Similarly, religious figures such as the Virgin Mary and popular-culture celebrity figures such as Elvis Presley are said to have appeared supernaturally to people in various geographic locations and on various objects (including on a grilled-cheese sandwich in 2004), and a Martian visitation began occurring in a park in Queens, New York City, in 1968. Such sites become objects of pilgrimage for the faithful and/or the curious.

Supernatural legends became increasingly subject to commoditization in the twentieth and twenty-first centuries through sales of vanity books, on-site tourism, television shows that offer vicarious legend-trips for their viewers, and Internet auctions of haunted objects. *See also:* Bloody Mary; Cyberculture; *La Llorona*; Legend, Local; Legend, Religious; Memorate; Virgin, Cult of the; Witchcraft, Historical.

References: Bird, S. Elizabeth. "Playing with Fear: Interpreting the Adolescent Legend Trip." *Western Folklore* 53 (1994): 191–209; Bullard, Thomas E. "UFO Abduction Reports: The Supernatural Kidnap Narrative Returns in Technological Guise." *Journal of American Folklore*, vol. 102, no. 404 (1989): 147–170; Ellis, Bill. "Legend-Trips and Satanism: Adolescents' Ostensive Traditions as 'Cult' Activity." In *Contemporary Legend: A Reader*, eds. G. Bennett and P. Smith, 167–186. New York: Garland Publications, 1996; Hufford, David J. "Beings Without Bodies: An Experience-Centered Theory of the Belief in Spirits." In *Out of the Ordinary: Folklore and the Supernatural*, ed. Barbara Walker, 11–45. Logan: Utah State University Press, 1995; Langlois, Janet. "Mary Whales, I Believe in You." *Indiana Folklore, A Reader*, ed. Linda Dégh, 186–224. Bloomington: Indiana University Press, 1980; "The Moonlit Road." n.d. http://www.themoonlitroad.com/welco me001.html (accessed June 30, 2007); Tucker, Elizabeth. "Ghosts in Mirrors: Reflections of the Self." *Journal of American Folklore*, vol. 118, no. 468 (2005): 186203; Wojcik,

Daniel. "'Polaroids from Heaven': Photography, Folk Religion, and Miraculous Image Tradition at a Marian Apparition Site." *Journal of American Folklore* 109 (1996): 129–148.

Linda J. Lee and Cathy Lynn Preston

Legend, Urban/Contemporary

Urban legends are short narratives that are situated in contemporary life and that may or may not be literally true but that often "ring" true for their performers and their performers' audiences. Usually, secular in nature, set in the real world, and performed in the midst of everyday conversations, urban legends describe frightening, threatening, comic, embarrassing, or simply bizarre situations that are said to have occurred to people in the recent past, that might be happening in the present, and that could occur again in the future. Among academic folklorists, urban legends are alternatively referred to as modern legends, contemporary legends, rumor legends, and belief legends. In the popular press, urban legends are frequently identified by the misnomer "urban myths," while those who tell urban legends often refer to them simply as scary tales, watercooler stories, e-mails, and friend-of-a-friend stories (as in "A friend of a friend told me that ..." or, "I heard this from a friend of a friend").

Each of the descriptive terms associated with the urban legend suggests something about the nature of this type of story. The adjectives "urban" and "modern" are the products of initial attempts on the part of scholars to associate this kind of legend with city environments as opposed to rural areas and to differentiate it from the supernatural legends frequently associated with an agrarian lifestyle. In fact, however, urban legends circulate in both urban and rural environments, and some urban legends (such as the "blood libel" legend) predate modernity, while yet others (such as "The Vanishing Hitchhiker") have supernatural motifs; thus, many scholars' use of the term "contemporary" in relation to such legends indicates that they emerge and reemerge in different places at various times as a means of providing symbolic conduits for the negotiation of belief (hence the term "belief legend") in relation to issues that are contemporaneous with that place and time. That such stories are associated with rumor, watercoolers, e-mail, and friends of friends suggests both their ties to everyday conversation and their function as an informal conduit of information shared, for example, among adolescents at slumber parties and in school locker rooms, among adults during breaks at work or while socializing at a grocery store, in a pub, or at church. And while urban legends are frequently transmitted from one individual to another as a type of "folk news," they may also be performed purely for their entertainment value. Additionally, urban legends are frequently disseminated through e-mail and such formal channels of communication as the news (print and broadcast), informational fliers distributed by churches and schools, and television programs, movies, novels, short stories, and comic books.

The topics of urban legends range widely from the misuse of technology to mistrust of corporate culture, from food contamination to body contamination, from sex to murder, and from threatening chain letters to satanic panics. Common among adolescent and teenage girls as well as adult women are legends concerning female sexuality. Adolescent girls, for example, tell of teenage couples out on a date who find themselves at a favorite local parking place, either engaged in or presumably about to engage in some level of sexual behavior. In one legend, "The Hook," the car's radio announces that a maniac, who has a hook for a hand, has escaped from the mental hospital and is in the area. This frightens the girl, and she asks the boy to take her home. Angry, he slams his foot down on the gas pedal and quickly drives away from the parking spot. When the couple arrives at the girl's home, they discover a hook hanging from the car door on the girl's side of the car. Similarly, adult women tell stories such as "The Nude Surprise Party," a "most embarrassing moment" story in which a woman and her fiancé find themselves alone at her home and decide to have sex. Shortly after undressing, she receives a phone call requesting that she perform an errand in the basement; the two of them, still naked, run down to the basement, only to be surprised (much to the woman's embarrassment) by their extended families and friends, who have gathered to throw them an engagement party. In other versions of the legend (which displace the engagement party with a birthday party and in which there is no male sexual partner mentioned, but instead a woman who comes downstairs calling for her dog after having spread peanut butter on her crotch), the woman's embarrassment has less to do with her willingness to engage in premarital sex than with the type of sex in which she is willing to engage. Each legend and its variants situates sex as a domain of both personal pleasure and danger to the physical and/or the social self, and functions as a cautionary tale that, by foregrounding danger, seeks to curtail female sexuality.

Women are not always the victims in such stories; sometimes they are the victimizers. Furthermore, the roles of victim and victimizer may switch depending upon when the legend is told and by whom. For example, in early versions of a legend commonly known as "The Kidney Heist," a man, while out of town, drops by a bar where he is seduced by a beautiful woman and lured to her hotel room. In her room, he is drugged and passes out only to wake up the next morning in a bathtub of ice and with a freshly stitched incision on his back. The woman is gone and, as he discovers later at the hospital, so is his kidney; she removed it in the hotel room in order to sell it on the illegal organ-transplant market. Not only does the legend articulate contemporary worries concerning modern medical practices such as organ transplants, but it articulates male fears of the *femme fatale* and functions as a cautionary morality tale about casual sex. Later versions of the story, appearing around the time "roofies" (Rohypnol) and other date-rape drugs hit the formal news, switch the gender of the victim and victimizer. Interestingly, in these versions, frequently circulated among women, the woman is drugged in the bar while having a drink with friends, suggesting, as Elissa Henken (1994) argues, that women incur penalties for lesser cultural transgressions (out drinking with friends) than do men (drinking and actively seeking illicit sexual engagement).

Insomuch as heterosexual sex might lead to pregnancy, it is not surprising that another set of commonly told legends concern motherhood. "The

Babysitter and the Man Upstairs" and "The Hippie Babysitter" call into question adolescent and teenaged girls' childcare skills (and thus, by extension, their potential as mothers) through narratives in which the children in the girl's care are killed by either an intruder or accidentally by the babysitter herself. Similarly, "The Inept Mother" articulates the fears of adult women:

> A mother with three small children was giving her six-month-old baby a bath in the tub when her two-year-old cut himself very badly. She couldn't leave her baby in the water, so she told her six-year-old to run across the street to the neighbors and get help. It took so long that she left the baby to help the two-year-old, who was unconscious by now. She hears sirens, thinking help was there, but they were there because her six-year-old had been hit by a car. In the meantime, the baby in the tub drowned and the two-year-old bled to death. So she lost all three of her children in twenty minutes through no fault of her own.

Although this version of "The Inept Mother," recorded by Janet Langlois, ends with the disclaimer of "through no fault of her own," foregrounding the burdens faced by mothers who have too much to do and no help, the legend simultaneously maps society's fears of incompetent and/or "unnatural" mothers, including the possibility that encoded in the woman's incompetence is a psychological rejection of motherhood itself as a culturally required gendered performance.

While in urban legend, women are occasionally the perpetrators of violence against others, more often they are the victims of violence: female college students have their throats slit by male maniacs while alone in their dormitories ("The Roommate's Death"); women are threatened with death by men hiding in the backseats of their cars ("The Killer in the Backseat") or by men hiding under their cars that have been parked in shopping mall parking lots ("The Slasher Under the Car"). While such legends articulate the very real social problem of violence perpetrated against women and may function informationally as cautionary tales to keep women safe, such legends also work to constrict female mobility. As Lara Maynard has explained in relation to legends about violence done to women, women are told, "on the one hand, 'be liberated, be confident, be adventurous and brave' and, on the other, 'be careful, be afraid.' Both messages, in their own ways, say 'don't be a victim,' and women are left to negotiate through them by living with the attitudes of the first, but within the boundaries of the second."

In urban legends, violence may also take the form of body contamination. Fears concerning the body are encoded in narratives that speak of black widow spiders laying eggs that hatch and infest women's beehive and dreadlock hairdos, and of a woman who, while on vacation (in Africa, South America, Mexico, Spain, Portugal, or the American South), is bitten on her cheek by a spider that lays its eggs under her skin, forming a boil, which either bursts or is lanced, releasing its contents—scads of baby spiders— much to the woman's horror and frequently causing her to go insane from the shock. Or the body may be compromised by contaminated food or drink ("The Kentucky Fried Rat" and "The Mouse in the Coke"), or by disease (people are punctured by hidden HIV-contaminated needles left in the coin-return slots of public telephones or soda machines, in theater seats, or on the underside of gas pump handles). In some stories, the body's boundaries become a symbol of geographical and cultural boundaries (as in the versions of "Welcome to the World of AIDS" collected by Diane Goldstein [1992] in Newfoundland), while in others, the body's boundaries are displaced by the boundaries of the nation (as in stories collected in the United States about poisonous snakes or spiders found in imported items ranging from bananas to blankets).

A wide array of urban legends have been collected by Jan Harold Brunvand and published in a series of anthologies from *The Vanishing Hitchhiker* (1981) to *The Baby Train* (1993). Analytical and theoretical studies of urban legends (both as a broad cultural phenomenon and as the object of specific case studies) have been published as book-length collections of essays (Gillian Bennett and Paul Smith's *Perspectives on Contemporary Legend*, Volumes I–V, 1984–1990), as articles in academic Folklore journals, including *Contemporary Legend: The Journal of the International Society for Contemporary Legend Research*, as book-length studies of a particular legend (Alan Dundes, *Bloody Mary in the Mirror: Essays in Psychoanalytic Folkloristics*, 2002), and as studies of related legends (Gary Alan Fine, *Manufacturing Tales: Sex and Money in Contemporary Legends*, 1992; Bill Ellis, *Aliens, Ghosts, and Cults: Legends We Live*, 2001; and Diane E. Goldstein, *Once Upon a Virus: AIDS Legends and Vernacular Risk Perception*, 2004). Yet other studies focus on urban legends as told within specific groups (for example, Patricia A. Turner's *I Heard It Through the Grapevine: Rumor in African-American Culture*, 1993; Mariamne H. Whatley and Elissa R. Henken's *Did You Hear About the Girl Who … ?: Contemporary Legends, Folklore, & Human Sexuality*, 2000) and as related to the broad topic of folk belief (Linda Dégh, *Legend and Belief*, 2001). *See also:* Babysitting; Cyberculture; Folk Belief; Legend, Local; Legend, Religious; Legend, Supernatural; Mothers' Folklore; Pregnancy; Rumor; Sexuality; Storytelling; Violence.

References: Goldstein, Diane E. "Welcome to the Mainland, Welcome to the World of AIDS: Cultural Viability, Localization, and Contemporary Legend." *Contemporary Legend* 2 (1992): 23–40; Henken, Elissa R. "Gender Shifts in Contemporary Legend." *Western Folklore* 63 (2004): 237–256; Langlois, Janet L. "Mother's Double Talk." In *Feminist Messages: Coding in Women's Folk Culture*, ed., Joan Newlon Radner, 80–97. Urbana: University of Illinois Press, 1993; Maynard, Lara. "Locked Doors: Bearer-Centered Interpretation of 'The Roommate's Death' and Other Contemporary Legends of Special Relevance to Females." *Contemporary Legend* 4 (1998): 97–115.

Cathy Lynn Preston

Lesbian and Queer Studies

Lesbian/Queer Studies features scholarship and teaching focused on the historical and contemporary experiences of gay, lesbian, bisexual, transsexual, and transgender populations. Its inquiry documents past experiences, but also promotes diversity, dialogue, and new knowledge formation among students, teachers, librarians, researchers, independent scholars, and other interested citizens.

Lesbian/Queer Studies is a countercultural movement in the sense that it actively contests heterosexism and homophobia. It also advances a climate of rigorous teaching and research into the interdependent phenomena of society, gender, sexuality, and culture. As with other academic fields tracing their origins to social movements, Lesbian/Queer Studies does not confine its mission to the classroom. Events, services, mentoring, and academic support are all important cocurricular features of an inclusive learning environment. Further, scholars in Lesbian/Queer Studies frequently engage in advocacy beyond the campus and its immediate environs.

It is difficult to delineate Lesbian/Queer Studies as a discretely bounded set of scholarly practices or pursuits. Just as Women's Studies is not defined solely by topic, practitioner, or method, Lesbian/Queer Studies is too complex to categorize. The field involves scholars from every academic discipline. The humanities, social studies, sciences, and professions all figure within an integrated study of sexual pluralism. Far from a uniform set of questions, sources, or theories, the field nonetheless patterns itself on issue-oriented inquiry, typically pursued through interdisciplinary scholarship.

While there neither is, nor can be, a standard or official account of this field's formation, it has its origins in late-twentieth-century political movement culture. Two key influences on Lesbian/Queer Studies were the civil rights and women's movements. Both took strength from participation by college students, staff, and faculty. These academic activists directed their energy to social change, both on the campus and in the wider community. While community actions contested discriminatory practice, policy, and legislation at the local, state, and national levels, campus actions tended to target the university's silence and complicity in the face of inequality.

One lasting outcome of academic activism was the emergence of college courses, organizations, certificate programs, minors, and majors dedicated to the study of historically underrepresented and/or disenfranchised populations. Programs in African American Studies and Women's Studies, for example, became common by the 1980s. By the end of the 1990s, the same had begun to happen for Lesbian/Queer Studies.

The institutionalization of such bodies of knowledge and the agendas associated with social movements represent a mixed blessing. At the same time that progressive innovations to the curriculum prove transformative, their absorption within the conservative context of the academy carries with it a serious risk: cooptation of the movement's originating principles and the undermining of autonomy for its social and institutional critiques. At their best, such programs and centers function as agents for continued change by challenging universities to become, and remain, inclusive, equitable, and welcoming places in which people's differences are regarded as neither divisive nor definitive.

The development of Lesbian/Queer Studies is a story of generations, with each addressing the challenges and opportunities of a particular historical moment. With every decade, the perspective changes, paradigms shift, and events unfold in ways no one could forecast. Still, the movement persists.

Most timelines for the gay and lesbian movement, and along with it the emergence of Lesbian/Queer Studies, highlight the 1969 Stonewall uprising, during which gay men at the Stonewall Bar in Greenwich Village fought back for the first time *en masse* against police harassment, as a landmark in political organizing. Responses to this galvanizing incident in the United States resulted in a newly vibrant effort to uphold the human rights of sexual minorities, among whom were many increasingly committed to exercising their own civic rights and responsibilities.

In similar fashion, the late 1960s and early 1970s marked a time of grassroots action to revise university curricula to include Gay/Lesbian/Bisexual/Transsexual/Transgender (GLBT) Studies. In 1966, for instance, Columbia University in New York City hosted the nation's first documented gay student organization, the Student Homophile League.

During the 1980s, the GLBT/Queer Studies movement gained membership and momentum as the community mobilized to meet the HIV/AIDS crisis. 1983 witnessed the opening of Greenwich Village's Lesbian Gay Bisexual Transgender Community Center, which would later give rise to a number of nationally visible direct action groups working to affirm the dignity of all persons, including the Gay and Lesbian Alliance Against Defamation (GLAAD), Queer Nation, the Lesbian Avengers, and the AIDS Coalition to Unleash Power (ACT UP). These groups use tactics from lobbying to guerrilla theater to raise consciousness about, and forward resistance to, sexual oppression.

The late 1980s and 1990s witnessed emerging institutional recognition for Lesbian/Queer Studies. In 1986, the Lesbian/Gay Studies Center was established at Yale University. In 1988, the City College of San Francisco set in place America's first Gay and Lesbian Studies Department. It was also in 1990 that the City University of New York opened its Center for Lesbian and Gay Studies. Additionally, centers for sexuality studies at campuses such as Duke University and the City University of New York afford students of Lesbian/Queer Studies the opportunity to study and integrate related issues and content.

Although Lesbian/Queer Studies most often takes the form of freestanding academic courses, or units within courses, at colleges and universities in the past decade there has been a gradual shift toward formalizing courses of undergraduate study in such a way as to make possible a sustained and shared exploration of sexuality as a category of analysis. At this writing, schools offering undergraduate majors in GLBT/Queer Studies include Brown University, the University of Chicago, and Wesleyan University. Still more campuses make minors available, including University of California, Berkeley, the University of Iowa, and the University of Wisconsin, Milwaukee. Programs in gay and lesbian studies, queer studies, sexuality studies, and sexual orientation and gender identity studies all contribute to such an ongoing intellectual project.

Sexuality and gender, examined in terms of their importance to the structure of social relations, form the core enterprise of Lesbian/Queer Studies. Within the discipline, the study and advancement of the rights and conditions of sexual minorities also figure prominently. Scholars in this field contribute to new knowledge production by complicating our understanding of gender and sexual identities. Leaders in the field position themselves as public intellectuals, addressing audiences unbounded by academic politics. *See also:* Coding; Gender; Lesbian Folklore; Sexuality; Transgender Folklore.

References: Abelove, Henry, Michele Aira Barale, and David M. Halperin, eds. *The Gay and Lesbian Studies Reader.* New York: Routledge, 1993; Butler, Judith. *Gender Trouble: Feminism and the Subversion of Identity.* New York: Routledge, 1990; Cruikshank, Margaret, ed. *Lesbian Studies: Present and Future.* Old Westbury, NY: Feminist Press, 1982; Duberman, Martin, Martha Vicinus, and George Chauncey, Jr., eds. *?Hidden From History: Reclaiming the Gay and Lesbian Past.* New York: New American Library, 1989; Foster, Thomas, Carol Siegel, and Ellen E. Berry, eds. *The Gay '90s: Disciplinary and Interdisciplinary Formations in Queer Studies.* New York: NYU Press, 1997; Minton, Henry L., ed. *Gay and Lesbian Studies.* New York: Haworth Press, 1992; Ristock, Janice L., and Catherine G. Taylor, eds. *Inside the Academy and Out: Lesbian/ Gay/Queer Studies and Social Action.* Toronto: University of Toronto Press, 1998.

Linda S. Watts

Lesbian Folklore

Folklorists may mean one of two things by the term "lesbian folklore." The first is that lesbians, like any group that shares attributes, have folklore that is endemic to them as a community. But the term can also mean folklore about lesbians, shared by members of another group or other groups. The former characterization is the focus here.

Like any large group that has breadth across cultures, speaking of a coherent whole in lesbian folklore is somewhat problematic. Many scholars rely on Joseph Goodwin's (1989) notion that gay men (and, by extension, lesbians) form a subculture, in which certain beliefs, traditions, and creative processes are held in common. Goodwin's notion of subculture enables folklorists to acknowledge that there are shared forms of creative expression that are commonly known within a folk group, but also allows that some individuals may not know them or engage in them. The subcultural designation also enables folklorists to avoid the more problematic term "community," which suggests a coherent whole where none exists.

While these subcultural folkloric forms vary widely from region to region and from country to country, they do have generic coherence and continuity in respect to the experiences that many (though not all) lesbians share. Narrative (personal-experience narratives and jokes), material (personal aesthetics), and ritual and festival genres (Pride festivals, music festivals, and weddings/commitment ceremonies) are widely found across the United States and Canada and have been extensively documented by folklorists. However, folklorists have paid almost no attention to Mexican lesbian experiences, and for the rest of North America, large urban centers rather than rural locations have been their focus.

One aspect of lesbian folklore, often overemphasized in scholarship, is the coming-out experience. The process of realizing and ultimately revealing that one's sexual identity is not normatively heterosexual—the process of acknowledging both internally and externally a lesbian identity (or a gay, bisexual, queer, transgendered, or transsexual one)—is termed "coming out" (of "the closet"). The process of coming out, though arguably less hazardous in Canada and the United States now than it was in the past, often still involves shame and exclusion, if not fear of actual reprisals. In the United States in 2004, 16 percent of all hate crimes were motivated by sexual-orientation bias (*Gay Life*). However, the increasing visibility of gay men and lesbians in the public eye and the growing visibility of GLBTQ (gay, lesbian, bisexual, transgendered, queer) organization are allowing for more widespread acceptance of lesbian identity, especially in urban areas in the United States and Canada. Coming out, while not as problematic as it once was, can cause people to become alienated from friends, family, or coworkers. It often causes a backlash, especially in socially conservative contexts.

The process of coming out can be gradual and evolves over time. The basic cultural assumption of heterosexuality requires lesbians to come out as a continual process that may take many years or even an entire lifetime. Every new situation a lesbian finds herself in may require coming out. Many lesbians, as a result of this marked experience in their lives, develop a coming-out story. These are personal-experience narratives told by individuals who have undergone the experience of acknowledging their sexual identities to persons they knew or suspected may have assumed them to be heterosexual. Such stories usually involve a sequence of events: internal rehearsals of what one will say about one's sexuality, why one will say it and to whom, and descriptions of how the actual narrative was received and acted upon by others. They often focus, as do many personal-experience narratives, on both humorous situations in the coming-out process and on the more painful experiences that result from encounters with unreceptive parents or coworkers, for example.

Coming-out stories are also shared among lesbians and can serve to provide coherence among groups of women as they look for commonalities in their experiences. Because coming-out stories are so pervasive among lesbians, and because their structural narrative patterns persist through retellings and from story to story, the coming-out narrative serves as an exemplar of the personal-experience narrative as a traditional genre of folklore. It has motifs and persistence across time and space. A woman will sometimes tell parts of someone else's story because they resonate with her experience or because they otherwise carry meaning for her. In this sense, the coming-out story may function as much as legend as it does as personal-experience narrative.

Most people have multiple or differential identities from which their narratives flow. When speaking of lesbian stories, we generally mean stories that are expressly about coming out, lesbian encounters, or other issues endemic to the lesbian experience. Thus, narrative genres associated with the lesbian experience include tales of encounters with famous lesbians ("celebrity sightings") such as Ellen DeGeneres, Rosie O'Donnell, Amy Ray and Emily Saliers (of the Indigo Girls), Melissa Etheridge, or Leisha Hailey.

Other oral traditions also flourish in the lesbian context. The well-known joke cycle about how quickly romantically involved lesbians move in together persists and is often elaborated upon by lesbians in joking contexts. It is so familiar, in fact, that the *Big Gay Sketch Show*, when it premiered on the gay-and-lesbian-themed Logo cable channel in 2007, featured a sketch built around the premise. In it, two women are engaged in a speed-dating exercise. In the one minute in which they interact, they go from getting to know each other to agreeing to move in together, and then to having a fight about their feelings.

Ironically, the other persistent lesbian joke cycle focuses on the perceived lack of a sense of humor in lesbians. Joseph Goodwin writes about the phenomenon in his discussion of gay male folklore, arguing that it provides a contrast between cultural perceptions of gay men (who are thought to be funny) and lesbians (who are not). Even Emily Saliers of the Indigo Girls pokes fun at herself in a song lyric, singing, "You know me/I take everything so seriously." Lesbian comic Suzanne Westenhofer recounts on the Web site http://www.AfterEllen.com a story in which some producers were looking for a funny lesbian to cast in a television series. The producers were so sure that there aren't any funny lesbians that their casting call implied that heterosexual women who are funny and could pretend to be lesbians would be considered. Westenhofer—both very funny and a lesbian—got the job.

Personal aesthetics are critical to understanding lesbian non-narrative folklore. A lesbian's use of personal aesthetic can help communicate her sexual identity while also providing her with a means of creative expression. Lesbians use a variety of personal aesthetic choices to indicate identity and to communicate coded "lesbian messages" (see the entry on Coding). Perhaps the most clearly delineated lesbian aesthetic is that of the "butch," a term used in the past to describe a woman who dresses in a masculine style. The classic butch, as described by Elizabeth Kennedy and Madeline Davis, had a clearly defined look. Butches

> ... did not simply wear masculine clothes, but rather developed a definite style for dressing up. A distinctive part of their attire was heavily starched shirts.... They wore big cuff links in their shirts and jackets over them. ... To go with their pants, butches got the most masculine-style shoes you could find, flat shoes like oxfords. ... Their short haircuts were consciously created for the image (154–155).

If "the butch-femme aesthetic" (masculine women in men's suits with their very feminine partners dressed in the most womanly styles of the day) was all the rage in the 1940s and 1950s, it gave way to a different lesbian look in the 1970s. The women's movement was especially influential in and around New York City, where the butch-femme aesthetic changed to one that reflected the anti-heterosexist politics of the time. In one of her early novels, Rita Mae Brown describes "a large space mobbed with women. There were women in workshirts ... women in old band uniforms, and women in no shirts at all" (49). What Brown is describing is women who have rejected cultural hegemony in dress choices, and instead making clothing selections based on their own personal aesthetics and its appeal to other women. Much has been made in the media of the so-called "lipstick lesbian" of the 1990s and the various fashion choices touted on the Showtime series *The L Word*. However, since the 1940s, there has been no unifying fashion that says "lesbian."

However, it is fair to say that there are continuities across lesbian personal aesthetics beyond the stereotypes that persisted from the 1950s and 1970s. A mullet haircut, body piercings, tattoos, short hair, leather, and other clothing taken from men's fashions, from marginalized groups (like bikers), and from other countercultures can be seen as embodying a lesbian aesthetic, especially when presented in an expected context (such as at a Pride festival or lesbian bar) or as complicit coding (provided there is a high probability that others are aware of the signs).

Festival has received more attention than most of the non-narrative genres in the scholarship on lesbian folklore. The two main foci of lesbian festival scholarship have been urban Pride parades and festivals in the United States and Canada (see Hagen Smith 1997) and the Michigan Womyn's Festival, held annually since 1976. Pride festivals started in 1970 to commemorate the anniversary of the 1969 Stonewall revolt in New York City. The first such events were held in New York and Los Angeles and quickly spread to other U.S. cities with large gay and lesbian populations, including San Francisco, Chicago, and Atlanta. Most cities in the United States and Canada now hold Pride festivals and parades every summer. As with all large festivals, what happens in these contexts is multifaceted, incorporating a wide variety of folkloric genres.

On the parade or festival grounds, the visitor finds vendors from whom she can buy alcoholic drinks, kabobs, frozen lemonade, pizza, caramel apples, funnel cakes, vegetarian chili, or even the large dill pickles that come with the requisite sexual innuendo, borrowed in part from Renaissance fairs, where buying a pickle or any other phallus-shaped food will inevitably produce bawdy talk about what to do with it. Beyond food vendors, the visitor finds vendors selling consumer goods with gay and/or lesbian themes. Since the adoption of the rainbow flag and pink and black triangles as symbols of the GLBTQ community, the proliferation of items decorated with one or both symbols has increased exponentially.

Pride space usually features community groups ranging from, for example, the Protestant gay- and lesbian-oriented Metropolitan Community Church and Beth Simchat Torah in New York, to gay and lesbian square dancers and contra dancers in Boston, to labor unions in Toronto, to Zapatista movement supporters in Mexico City. Groups include social and affinal organizations, religious adherents, members of a profession (such as police officers or librarians), HIV and AIDS service organizations, and other nonprofit groups. Performers play on stages throughout the days or week that the festival is open.

Joseph Goodwin argues that gay men (and, by extension, lesbians) must operate in two cultures at once. Because in the larger cultural context, heterosexuality is assumed, lesbians know these rules as well as heterosexual women do, and therefore often hide their identity in non-queer contexts. Within the Pride festival context, however, festival rules mean that there is no need to behave in a covert or coded way. Victor Turner describes the key ingredient in festival as "communitas," a feeling of connection to the other participants. Once the threshold is established, communitas reigns, and lesbians (and gay men) do on the festival grounds what they might not otherwise do in public space. Women may go topless, often wearing just a sticker over their nipples; it is not uncommon to see explicit sexual behavior between two women in the context of Pride space.

Most large cities in North America host a parade as part of their Pride celebrations, usually on a Sunday. The modern American parade (like small-town Independence Day parades) is an official event, sanctioned by civic organizations and by the government; its meaning lies in bringing a community together to focus on shared values and experiences. Pride parades, on the other hand, hearken back to preindustrial ideas of festival while simultaneously maintaining the modern notion of the civic parade. Parts of a Pride parade look like any other such event: politicians and celebrities wave at the crowds from the backseats of convertibles, and people ride down the street on horses with fancy saddles.

But closer observation of a Pride parade reveals its differences. "Dykes on Bikes," a folk group that originated in San Francisco, generally starts it off, often having decorated their motorcycles to express lesbian pride. Lesbians parade with groups ranging from PFLAG (Parents and Friends of Lesbians and Gays), to veterans groups, to groups dressed in leather expressing their interests in alternative sex play. Drag queens, leather dykes, and floats of naked (or almost naked) people dance by, interspersed with gay and lesbian veterans' groups and human rights activists. Pride is a complicated and often subversive context.

The Michigan Womyn's Festival is one of a number of lesbian-oriented (though not exclusively so) festivals held throughout the United States annually or periodically. "Michigan" (as it is often known) is the largest of these and is a multiple-day festival with music, workshops, and time for bonding. Michigan is perhaps most notorious in recent years for excluding male-to-female and female-to-male transgender and transsexuals and others whose gender identities defy traditional categories. The festival resembles other large-scale camping festivals of the Woodstock variety where people come together to listen to music and camp for a number of days, forming a temporary space of festival and community. These events usually have consumer goods available and performances at certain times of the day. The Michigan Womyn's Festival also has a Neo-Pagan element, revealing continuities with the Burning Man Festival (an anti-consumerist participatory event usually held in Nevada) and other countercultural events. Participants often hold rituals and ceremonies, ranging from commitment ceremonies in lieu of marriage to rituals honoring the Goddess or Mother Earth.

Since the mid-1990s, the issue of weddings has been at the center of the political debate over gay men and lesbians in the media in North America. Mexico legalized civil unions, but not lesbian and gay marriages, in 2006. In Canada, gay and lesbian marriage is legal and exactly equivalent to heterosexual marriage. As of this writing, Massachusetts and California are the only states in the United States that allow same-sex marriage, though many others allow for variously described legal, same-sex domestic partnerships. Lesbian weddings and commitment ceremonies vary in form from the very traditional (that is, much like those found in heterosexual communities) to rituals that bear almost no connection to the larger tradition.

As with any multifaceted form of folklore, it is impossible to generalize, but lesbian weddings often play with notions of normative gendered behavior. For example, one wedding documented in Los Angeles in 1998 followed both normative and playful patterns in its execution. Each self-described "bride" had multiple attendants and each carried a matching bouquet. One wore a white pantsuit and the other a bridal gown. A minister administered the vows and each woman spoke briefly of her commitment to the other. They drank wine from a common cup and exchanged rings. The minister pronounced them life partners, after which they kissed passionately.

In addition to her bouquet, each woman worn a garter. At the reception, they divided their guests into four groups: lesbians, gay men, straight women, and straight men. In an inversion of the tradition of throwing a bouquet to the next woman to be married and a garter to the next groom, each group was given the opportunity to catch one of the bouquets or one of the garters. One of the brides described the garter/bouquet ritual to Elizabeth Adams as "the most subversive thing at the wedding." By dividing the guests, she was requiring each to identify (or come out) as part of one group or another, and by allowing men to catch bouquets and women to catch garters, she and her partner were marking both their compliance with heterosexual traditions and their subversion of them.

Ellen Lewin argues that lesbian weddings constitute a complicated symbolic act:

> In that ritual stands outside the routine of normal events, it can more readily dispel contradictions and embrace incongruities. Just as heterosexual weddings convey to the couples their place in the history of their families and remind them of the contribution that they will make to the continuation of tradition, so lesbian weddings claim that lesbian couples are not estranged from the value of the wider community, and that they are, in fact, part of that community. Even as they also celebrate their involvement in lesbian subculture, each of these weddings, then, makes the claim that the marrying couple are members of the wider community (128).

Lewin's point is that weddings draw a distinction to the subcultural group of lesbians but also ask that the larger culture acknowledge their partnerships.

As the debate over lesbian marriages continues, the changing nature of their forms and varieties will be interesting to track. While public argument has focused on the legal and religious ramifications of gay and lesbian marriage, folklorists would do well to watch the nature of the ceremonies themselves. As a marker of culture tradition and change, the wedding is perhaps the richest tradition for meaning and subversion in lesbian folklore in the early part of the twenty-first century. And there are undoubtedly other rich lesbian traditions still to be explored by folklorists and allied scholars. *See also:* Body Modification and Adornment; Coding; Festival; Hair; Lesbian and Queer Studies; Personal Experience Narrative; Popular Culture; Processional Performance; Ritual; Sexuality; Wedding; Wicca and Neo-Paganism; Women's Music Festivals.

References: Adams, Elizabeth T. *Folklore and the Search for Community in the Modern Urban West.* Diss., UCLA, 1999; Advocate, The. n.d. http://www.advocate.com (accessed June 26, 2007); AfterEllen.com. n.d. http://www.afterellen.com (accessed June 26, 2007); Blincoe, Deborah, and John Forrest. "The Dangers of Authenticity." Special

Issue on Prejudice and Pride: Lesbian and Gay Traditions in America, *New York Folklore*, vol. 19, nos. 1–2 (1993): 1–14; Brown, Rita Mae. *In Her Day*. New York: Bantam, 1976; Faderman, Lillian. *Odd Girls and Twilight Lovers: A History of Lesbian Life in the Twentieth Century*. New York: Penguin, 1992; Gay Life. "Gay, Lesbian, Transgender Hate Crimes Statistics." n.d. http://gaylife.about.com/od/hatecrimes/a/statistics.htm (accessed June 26, 2007); Goodwin, Joseph P. *More Man Than You'll Ever Be: Gay Folklore and Acculturation in Middle America*. Bloomington: Indiana University Press, 1989; Gross, Larry. *Up From Invisibility: Lesbians, Gay Men, and the Media in America*. New York: Columbia University Press, 2002; Hagen-Smith, Lisa. "Politics and Celebration: Manifesting the Rainbow Flag." *Canadian Folklore canadien*, vol. 19, no. 2 (1997): 113–122; Hollis, Susan Tower, Linda Pershing, and M. Jane Young, eds. *Feminist Theory and the Study of Folklore*. Urbana and Chicago: University of Illinois Press, 1993; Jolly, Margaretta. "Coming Out of the Coming Out Story: Writing Queer Lives." *Sexualities: Studies in Culture and Society* 4, no. 4 (2001): 474–496; Kennedy, Elizabeth, and Madeline Davis. *Boots of Leather, Slippers of Gold: The History of a Lesbian Community*. New York: Penguin, 1993; Kugelmass, Jack. *Masked Culture: Greenwich Village Halloween Parade*. New York: Columbia University Press, 1994; Lawless, Elaine J. "Claiming Inversion: Lesbian Constructions of Female Identity as Claims for Authority." *Journal of American Folklore*, vol. 111 (1998): 3–22; Lewin, Ellen. *Inventing Lesbian Cultures in America*. Boston: Beacon Press, 1996; Lewin, Ellen, and William Leap. *Out in the Field: Reflections of Gay and Lesbian Anthropologists*. Urbana and Chicago: University of Illinois Press, 1996; Matrix, Sidney, and Pauline Greenhill, eds. Special Issue on Wedding Realities/Les Noces en Vrai, *Ethnologies*, vol. 28, no. 2 (2006); Radner, Joan Newlon, ed. *Feminist Messages: Coding in Women's Folk Culture*. Urbana and Chicago: University of Illinois Press, 1993.

Elizabeth T. Adams

Lilith

Lilith is a she-demon or evil spirit of Hebraic tradition with origins in several Mesopotamian mythologies. In the Babylonian-Assyrian culture, Lilith is *Lil*, a storm-demon, and in Hebrew her name derives from *layil*, night. She is often associated with wild, unpeopled places and is thought to reside in the desert. The earliest written mention of a similar she-demon is in the Sumerian epic *Gilgamesh*:

> Gilgamesh struck down the serpent that could not be charmed,
> The Anzu-bird flew with his young to the mountains,
> And Lilith smashed her home and flew to the wild, uninhabited places.

The only mention of Lilith in the Hebrew Bible is found in Isaiah. God declares vengeance on the world and states that it will become a desolate place wherein Lilith will reside.

> The wild cat shall meet with the jackals,
> And the satyr shall cry to his fellow,
> Yea, Lilith shall repose there,
> And find her a place of rest (Isaiah 34:14).

Lilith's birth and life history were elaborated during the postbiblical period in the *Talmud* ("teaching," discussions by generations of rabbis, mainly the Palestinian sages) and the *Midrash* ("interpretation," ever-evolving commentaries on Jewish scriptures). There it is said that Lilith was Adam's first wife, created in similar fashion from the dust (*adama*). However, instead of using clean dust to create Lilith, God used filth and unclean sediment. Adam and Lilith were never happy. One day after an argument over who should have the dominant position during sexual intercourse (Lilith thought they were equals), Lilith flew away to the Red Sea, a place where lascivious demons lived. There she began bearing more than 100 demons a day. God sent forth three angels, named Senoy, Sansenoy, and Semangelof, to bring her back to Adam. But Lilith did not want to leave; she claimed that God had given her the right of power over newborn children (boys until their circumcision ten days after birth, and girls until their twentieth day). The angels persisted in their attempt to get her to return, so to persuade them to leave, Lilith promised that she would not harm any child with an amulet bearing the names of the angels, and that she would kill 100 of her own children each day. This is the basis for the tradition of Jewish infants wearing amulets and being protected inside a circle in which the angelic names Senoy, Sansenoy, and Semangelof have been written. Children born of unholy unions, however, were not protected; Lilith could claim their lives at any time. If a child smiled in its sleep, it was a sign that Lilith was playing with it; one should awaken the child quickly to drive her away.

Lilith was not only a child-killer, but also a succubus, a female demon who has sexual intercourse with a man while he sleeps. When Adam left Eve to fast in the desert for 130 years in penance for the sin and death they had brought into the world, Lilith visited him there in the form of a succubus, later giving birth to all the plagues of humankind. This story is the foundation for the belief that Lilith is nocturnal, and even vampiric. In the *Zohar* (a text of the mystical tradition of Kabbalah which first appeared in thirteenth-century Spain), Lilith seduces married and single men during the night by coming to them as a mature woman or as a young virgin. Men were told not to sleep in a house alone for fear that Lilith would attack them as they slept and use their semen to breed demons.

Stories regarding Lilith multiplied throughout the medieval period in Europe and have continued to do so. According to oral tradition, she was believed to be of the women who asked King Solomon to decide which of them was the true mother of a child each claimed to be hers. It was also said that she was the Queen of Sheba. Lilith is still a popular figure today. She is a vampire figure in a series of Marvel comic books in which she is represented as the daughter of Dracula. But Lilith is part of a larger mythological tradition which blends feminine strength with sexuality—and frequently with evil—in supernatural female figures. *See also:* Assault, Supernatural; Eve; Jewish Women's Folklore; Legend, Religious; Legend, Supernatural; Nature/Culture; Vampire.

References: Baring, Anne, and Jules Cashford. *The Myth of the Goddess*. New York: Penguin Books, 1991; Graves, Robert, and Raphael Patai. *Hebrew Myths: The Book of Genesis*. New York: McGraw-Hill, 1964; Melton, J. Gordon. *The Vampire Book: An Encyclopedia of the Undead*. Detroit: Visible Ink Press, 1994; Patai, Raphael. *The Hebrew Goddess*. New York: Avon Books, 1978.

Tamara Robbins-Anderson

Lilith Fair

Lilith Fair was a highly successful annual music tour developed by Canadian performer Sarah McLachlan in the late 1990s to showcase women artists in the commercial pop/rock/folk industry. McLachlan, tour promoter and lead performer, created Lilith Fair in the wake of the success of Lollapalooza (1991), whose founder Perry Farrell significantly revised the format of summer rock tours and spurred a number of emulators, including HORDE (Horizons of Rock Developing Everywhere, 1992). Like Farrell, McLachlan selected a roster of headlining artists to perform at daylong festivals stopping at venues across North America. These traveling concerts also featured side stages to showcase emerging or local artists and concession areas for food and performers' merchandise.

Lilith Fair, produced for three consecutive years (1997–1999), booked more than 100 artists at a total of 139 venues, and became one of the most successful summer tours of the 1990s. While McLachlan generally avoided calling Lilith Fair a feminist event, she maintained her commitment to promote and showcase female performers, who were significantly underrepresented at Lollapalooza and other popular traveling music festivals.

McLachlan chose an evocative name for her event. In religious and feminist scholarship, Lilith is widely represented as a transgressive mythological figure. Some versions of her story assert that Lilith chose to leave Eden rather than be subservient to Adam. In other variants, she is purely demonic, described as the wife of Satan, a threat to adult males, new mothers, and infant children. In short, McLachlan's choice juxtaposed transgressive, powerful, angry feminine with *fair*, which signifies a gentler, more bucolic event than does *festival*. Further, Lilith Fair, like the medieval and renaissance fairs of Europe and today's county fairs in the United States, is a site of commerce—of buying, selling, and economic competition.

Lilith Fair was most notable for forever shifting corporate thinking about the marketability of female performers. The event's eclectic, rotating roster of headliners included the Indigo Girls (folk-roots), Queen Latifah (rap), the Dixie Chicks (country and western), and the Pretenders (rock). While Lilith Fair was not specifically designed as a woman-only event, its producers did try to include women on the technical side as well. Through a percentage of ticket sales and corporate sponsorships, Lilith Fair raised millions of dollars for nonprofit organizations that benefit women; created a community arts project showcasing local arts in each venue; and sponsored Literary Lilith, a project that promoted reading, independent bookstores, and women writers. Three volumes of Lilith Fair live recordings chronicling the first and second tours are available on CD and video/DVD. McLachlan collaborated with director Lynne Stopkewich during the final tour in 1999 to create a documentary film, *Lilith on Top*, featured at the Toronto and Berlin International Film Festivals in 2002. *See also:* Feminisms; Festival; Film; Folklore of Subversion; Lilith; Women's Music Festivals.

References: Cantor Zuckoff, Aviva. "The Lilith Question." *Lilith: The Independent Jewish Women's Magazine*, vol. 1 (Fall 1976): 5–38; Childerhose, Buffy, and Sarah

McLachlan. *From Lilith to Lilith Fair: The Authorized Story*. New York: St. Martin's, 1998; Heck, Angela. "Behind the Scenes at *Lilith on Top*." *Horizons Magazine*, Summer 2002. http://www.herizons.ca/node/141 (accessed August 4, 2008).

Lisa L. Higgins

Local Characters

A local character is an individual whose minor nonconformity consistently challenges social norms within a particular context. A local character is regarded as nonthreatening, and often humorous, by most, if not all, other group members.

Often individuals recognize benefits, such as increased attention, that motivate them to become local characters. As part of this role, they may be tradition-bearers, such as musicians or storytellers, or may inject an element of play into routine daily interactions. Often seen in the same place and in the same way, characters may become so closely associated with a location or a group that they represent continuity for others around them.

Stories of local characters that focus on antisocial traits or behaviors help to clarify expectations for others. They offer vivid illustrations of group or community rules, and of what happens to those who break them. Women may be designated as local characters when they defy social convention or when their presence in a male-dominated space becomes a lightning rod for critical narratives. As a result, local character stories told about women often highlight group expectations of appropriate female behavior and can be powerful attempts to control women who dare to challenge social norms.

On the other hand, narrative—anecdotes and legends—can facilitate a marginal person's acceptance into a group or community. For example, a legend that explains how a haggard street person was once a beautiful and accomplished professional before tragedy hit and her entire family was killed in a fire reminds listeners that misfortune can strike anyone and encourages their generous treatment of someone less fortunate. Or, conversely, legends reassure listeners that things are not as unfair as they seem; a bag lady is not destitute but really an heiress who chooses to hoard her money.

Humorous anecdotes focusing on local characters' behaviors often hinge on status reversal: the tables are turned on an authority figure. In one example, Emma, an African Canadian who works as a cleaner for a demanding White homemaker, is asked for advice by the woman's husband. How should he deal with his wife's demands? "What would you do if you were me?" he appeals. Emma's retort is immediate: "I'd make my peace with God and take chloroform" (Tye 1987: 107). Such comic stories expose the flaws of those in authority, but admittedly any reversal is temporary. At the close of the exchange between Emma and her middle-class employer, nothing has really changed. The cleaner/character still wields little power. However, taking on a local character role or telling local character narratives may at least briefly offer voice to an individual who is positioned on a group's margins. And, importantly for the local character as well as for other community members, accounts such as this one introduce the idea of change through their suggestion of a more equitable moral order. *See also:* Borden, Lizzie; Coding; Class, Legend, Local; Tradition-Bearer.

References: Tye, Diane. "Aspects of the Local Character Phenomenon in a Nova Scotian Community." *Canadian Folklore canadien*, vol. 9, nos. 1–2 (1987): 99–111; ———. "Narrative, Gender and Marginality: The Case Study of Ella Lauchner Smith," *Canadian Folklore canadien*, vol. 13, no. 2 (1991): 25–36.

Diane Tye

Lullaby

A lullaby is a genre of song usually sung to children as they fall to sleep. However, while memories and examples of lullabies are common, explaining what distinguishes these songs as lullabies is more complex. Great differences emerge even when limiting comparison to American examples. Lullaby text may contain comforting or cautionary lyrics. A famous example of the latter is the ending of "Rock-a-Bye Baby," in which the bough breaks, causing the cradle to fall. Words of lullabies may focus on the present, or detail what the child has to look forward to upon waking, as is the case in "Hush, Little Baby" or "All the Pretty Little Horses." Some lullabies recount sad stories, such as "The Lady Bothwell's Lament" (or "Baloo, My Boy"), which tells of the babe's father being killed in battle. The striking diversity in lullabies' lyric content leads to debate about whether content or context of use actually defines the genre.

Lullabies are one of many genres that have developed to fulfill a specific purpose. Along with their counterparts the cradle song, *berceuse*, and *Wiegenlied*, lullabies are most commonly used to soothe children to sleep. Therefore, these songs are associated most closely with the activities of rocking and feeding, traditionally carried out by mothers. Thus, this genre, at least in North America, has been feminized and linked with women's culture. Lullabies also reflect the values of the background from which they emerge and give insight into the lives of the adults, by tradition primarily women, who sing them. Many lullabies, for example, tell of the father being away; perhaps he is hunting or sailing, but in any case the mother remains at home to care for the children and reassure them.

In Western tradition, lullabies are nearly always in 3/4 or 4/4 time. They may be brief or rather long and involved, but the tunes, whether in major or minor mode, are typically soothing and repetitive. The tune seems to be of paramount importance, since words often are abandoned in favor of humming. Many lullabies, particularly from countries other than the United States, feature repeated patterns of nonsense syllables, highlighting the secondary importance of the words.

Although customarily considered part of oral tradition, lullabies have long been found in classical music and have also made their way into art song repertoire, musicals, and commercial popular music. Additionally, the stated audience of lullaby lyrics has expanded beyond infants to include other groups needing assurance and rest, such as hobos and Broadway babies. Lullabies appear in operas such as Humperdinck's *Hansel and Gretel* and Alban Berg's *Wozzeck* and in vocal performance repertoire with pieces such as "American Lullaby" by Gladys Rich. Frédéric Chopin, Franz Liszt, and Igor Stravinsky all composed famous instrumental versions of *berceuses*, and examples in popular music include well-known lullabies composed and recorded by musicians such as the Beatles and Billy Joel. While typically associated with the bond between mothers and babies, these examples provide instances of male composers and performers contributing to the genre and underscore the lullaby's broad appeal. *See also:* Childbirth and Child-rearing; Folk Music and Folksong; Mothers' Folklore.

References: Boyd, Malcolm. "Wiegenlied." *Grove Music Online*, ed. L. Macy, n.d. http://www.grovemusic.com (accessed May 29, 2005); Hamilton, Kenneth L. "Berceuse." *Grove Music Online*, ed. L. Macy, n.d. http://www.grovemusic.com (accessed May 29, 2005); Hawes, Bess Lomax. "Folksongs and Function: Some Thoughts on the American Lullaby." *Journal of American Folklore*, vol. 87, no. 433 (April–June 1974): 140–148; Porter, James. "Lullaby." *Grove Music Online*, ed. L. Macy, n.d. http://www.grovemusic.com (subscribers only, accessed May 29, 2005).

Suzanne Godby Ingalsbe